POLICE CIVIL LIABILITY

Second Edition

POLICE CIVIL LIABILITY

Supreme Court Cases and Materials

Second Edition

Victor E. Kappeler
Eastern Kentucky University

WAVELAND
PRESS, INC.
Long Grove, Illinois

For information about this book, contact:
Waveland Press, Inc.
4180 IL Route 83, Suite 101
Long Grove, IL 60047-9580
(847) 634-0081
info@waveland.com
www.waveland.com

10-digit ISBN 1-57766-442-6
13-digit ISBN 978-1-57766-442-0

Printed in the United States of America

8   7   6   5

Contents

Preface

The idea of putting together a case and materials book on police civil liability came to me well over a decade ago. I wanted to create a single source that contained the essential materials students needed to understand this area of law. At that time, there simply were not enough Supreme Court decisions that addressed police civil liability to warrant the project. Instead, people teaching liability law to criminal justice students were forced to put together a wide variety of materials and to speculate about how the Supreme Court might address a particular police liability issue. In a relatively short period of time, however, the situation changed dramatically. The body of case law generated by the United States Supreme Court on municipal liability, specifically police civil liability, has grown tremendously in recent years, making the project not only viable but even more necessary.

This growth in case law changed the problem of viability into one of manageability. In essence, it was now necessary to make decisions about the scope of cases to be included in the book. This situation reflects the growing complexity and importance of case law to police civil liability. After years of copying court cases and placing them on library reserve for my students, I was driven to create a classroom resource that pulled together all the leading Supreme Court cases on police civil liability. It was my sense that this single resource should include the relevant court cases and present information about the case method and judicial reasoning. Learning the basics of judicial reasoning and how to brief cases in conjunction with mastering the content of Supreme Court cases better prepares students for the challenge of the changing nature of police civil liability law.

While the heart of this casebook is a collection of leading majority opinions of the United States Supreme Court on civil liability, the book contains materials designed to assist students in mastering these decisions. The casebook begins with a brief overview of the United States Supreme Court's history, tradition, and procedure. This information on the Court is complemented with a selected list of rules and a table of all the Justices who have served on the Court since its inception. These materials appear in the appendix and provide students with handy references. Students can quickly determine the composition of the Court during a term or refer to a rule being employed.

Following an overview of the Supreme Court, the book introduces the student to the logic of legal reasoning and the intellectual purpose of reading case law. This part of the book helps students understand the intellectual nature of reading cases. Instructors can choose to reinforce this understanding by requiring formal briefs of the opinions; to that end, a guide on how to write a case brief concludes the introduction to the book. By including these materials I hope the student will more easily master the Court opinions and begin to understand the nature of legal inquiry, analysis, and the case method.

The casebook next presents the entire texts of leading majority opinions of the United States Supreme Court addressing police civil liability issues. (Dissenting and concurring opinions have been excluded from the casebook for manageability reasons but can be assigned as part of the research and learning experience.) The opinions are grouped into seven thematic parts according to important legal issues ranging from municipal liability to the scope of individual immunity. The parts were designed both to group legal topics and to allow students to see the progression of Supreme Court decision making within a topical area; thus, the cases in each part are presented chronologically.

To assist the student in reading these opinions, a glossary of legal terms and the text of selected federal statutes are provided in the appendix. This allows the student to develop a legal vocabulary and to focus attention on the opinions rather than having to research the meaning of many of the terms and statutes used by the Court. At the conclusion of each part of the book are discussion questions and related case citations. The discussion questions are designed to focus student attention on the specifics of individual opinions as well as direct them to view all the opinions as a body of law. The related case lists give students a starting point from which to learn more about a particular area of law.

Today's police executive and tomorrow's criminal justice professional will operate in a complex environment. They will need to develop skills to manage, organize, and administer justice agencies—and the ability to do so within an increasingly complex legal environment. Mastering this environment requires an operational knowledge of criminal justice plus an understanding of the social institutions that shape the environment in which they operate. Whether this casebook is used in a course devoted solely to the law of police civil liability, as a supplement in a traditional legal aspects course, or to complement a management or administratively oriented class, it is my hope that the book will aid in integrating legal knowledge into the criminal justice curriculum.

Victor E. Kappeler
Eastern Kentucky University

Overview of the
Court and Case Law

Supreme Court of the United States[1]

CHIEF JUSTICE OF THE UNITED STATES
William H. Rehnquist

ASSOCIATE JUSTICES

John Paul Stevens	Sandra Day O'Connor
Antonin Scalia	Anthony M. Kennedy
David H. Souter	Clarence Thomas
Ruth Bader Ginsburg	Stephen G. Breyer

The Supreme Court is comprised of the chief justice of the United States and such number of associate justices as may be fixed by Congress. By the Act of June 25, 1948 (28 U.S.C. § 1), Congress established the number of associate justices as eight. Power to nominate the justices is vested in the president of the United States, and appointments are made with the advice and consent of the Senate. Article III, § 1, of the Constitution further provides that "[t]he Judges, both of the Supreme and inferior Courts, shall hold their Offices during good Behaviour, and shall, at stated Times, receive for their Services, a Compensation, which shall not be diminished during their Continuance in Office."

Article III, § 1, of the Constitution provides that "[t]he judicial Power of the United States, shall be vested in one Supreme Court, and in such inferior Courts as the Congress may from time to time ordain and

---

[1] This section of the overview was taken with modification from a booklet prepared by the Supreme Court of the United States.

1

establish." The Supreme Court of the United States was created in accordance with this provision and by authority of the Judiciary Act of September 24, 1789 (1 Stat. 73). It was organized on February 2, 1790.

According to the Constitution (Art. III, § 2):

> The judicial Power shall extend to all Cases, in Law and Equity, arising under this Constitution, the Laws of the United States, and Treaties made, or which shall be made, under their Authority;—to all Cases affecting Ambassadors, other public Ministers and Consuls;—to all Cases of admiralty and maritime Jurisdiction;—to Controversies to which the United States shall be a Party;—to Controversies between two or more States;—between a State and Citizens of another State;—between Citizens of different States;—between Citizens of the same State claiming Lands under Grants of different States, and between a State, or the Citizens thereof, and foreign States, Citizens or Subjects.
>
> In all Cases affecting Ambassadors, other public ministers and Consuls, and those in which a State shall be Party, the Supreme Court shall have original Jurisdiction. In all the other Cases before mentioned, the Supreme Court shall have appellate jurisdiction, both as to Law and Fact, with such Exceptions, and under such Regulations as the Congress shall make."
>
> Appellate jurisdiction has been conferred upon the Supreme Court by various statutes, under the authority given Congress by the Constitution. The basic statute effective at this time in conferring and controlling jurisdiction of the Supreme Court may be found in 28 U.S.C. § 1251 *et seq.*, and various special statutes. . .

The Court and Constitutional Interpretation

"Equal Justice Under Law"—these words, written above the main entrance to the Supreme Court Building, express the ultimate responsibility of the Supreme Court of the United States. The Court is the highest tribunal in the nation for all cases and controversies arising under the Constitution or the laws of the United States. As the final arbiter of the law, the Court is charged with ensuring the American people the promise of equal justice under law and, thereby, also functions as guardian and interpreter of the Constitution.

The Supreme Court is "distinctly American in concept and function," as Chief Justice Charles Evans Hughes observed. Few other courts in the world have the same authority of constitutional interpretation and none have exercised it for as long or with as much influence. A century and a half ago, the French political observer Alexis de Tocqueville noted the unique position of the Supreme Court in the history of nations and of jurisprudence. "The representative system of government has been adopted in several states of Europe," he remarked, "but I am unaware that any nation of the globe has hitherto organized a judicial power in the same manner as the Americans. . . . A more imposing judicial power was never constituted by any people."

The unique position of the Supreme Court stems, in large part, from the deep commitment of U.S. citizens to the rule of law and to constitutional government. The United States has demonstrated an unprecedented determination to preserve and protect its written Constitution, thereby providing the U.S. "experiment in democracy" with the oldest written Constitution still in force.

The Constitution of the United States is a carefully balanced document. It is designed to provide for a national government sufficiently strong and flexible to meet the needs of the republic, yet sufficiently limited and just to protect the guaranteed rights of citizens; it permits a balance between society's need for order and the individual's right to freedom.

To assure these ends, the framers of the Constitution created three independent and coequal branches of government. That this Constitution has provided continuous democratic government through the periodic stresses of more than two centuries illustrates the genius of the U.S. system of government.

The complex role of the Supreme Court in this system derives from its authority to invalidate legislation or executive actions, which, in the Court's considered judgment, conflict with the Constitution. This power of "judicial review" has given the Court a crucial responsibility in assuring individual rights, as well as in maintaining a "living Constitution" whose broad provisions are applied continually to complicated new situations.

While the function of judicial review is not explicitly provided in the Constitution, it had been anticipated before the adoption of that document. Prior to 1789, state courts had already overturned legislative acts that conflicted with state constitutions. Moreover, many of the founding fathers expected the Supreme Court to assume this role in regard to the Constitution; Alexander Hamilton and James Madison, for example, had underlined the importance of judicial review in the Federalist Papers, which urged adoption of the Constitution.

Hamilton had written that through the practice of judicial review the Court ensured that the will of the whole people, as expressed in their Constitution, would be supreme over the will of a legislature, whose statutes might express only the temporary will of part of the people. And Madison had written that constitutional interpretation must be left to the reasoned judgment of independent judges, rather than to the tumult and conflict of the political process. If every constitutional question were to be decided by public political bargaining, Madison argued, the Constitution would be reduced to a battleground of competing factions, political passion, and partisan spirit.

Despite this background, the Court's power of judicial review was not confirmed until 1803, when it was invoked by Chief Justice John Marshall in *Marbury v. Madison.* In this decision, the chief justice asserted that the

Supreme Court's responsibility to overturn unconstitutional legislation was a necessary consequence of its sworn duty to uphold the Constitution. That oath could not be fulfilled any other way. "It is emphatically the province of the judicial department to say what the law is," he declared.

In retrospect, it is evident that constitutional interpretation and application were made necessary by the very nature of the Constitution. The founding fathers had wisely worded that document in rather general terms leaving it open to future elaboration to meet changing conditions. As Chief Justice Marshall noted in *McCulloch v. Maryland*, a constitution that attempted to detail every aspect of its own application "would partake of the prolixity of a legal code, and could scarcely be embraced by the human mind. . . . Its nature, therefore, requires that only its great outlines should be marked, its important objects designated, and the minor ingredients which compose those objects be deduced from the nature of the objects themselves."

The Constitution limits the Court to dealing with "Cases" and "Controversies." John Jay, the first chief justice, clarified this restraint early in the Court's history by declining to advise President George Washington on the constitutional implications of a proposed foreign policy decision. The Court does not give advisory opinions; rather, its function is limited only to deciding specific cases.

The justices must exercise considerable discretion in deciding which cases to hear, since more than 7,000 civil and criminal cases are filed in the Supreme Court each year from the various state and federal courts. The Supreme Court also has "original jurisdiction" in a very small number of cases arising out of disputes between states or between a state and the federal government.

When the Supreme Court rules on a constitutional issue, that judgment is virtually final; its decisions can be altered only by the rarely used procedure of constitutional amendment or by a new ruling of the Court. However, when the Court interprets a statute, new legislative action can be taken.

Chief Justice Marshall expressed the challenge that the Supreme Court faces in maintaining free government by noting: "We must never forget that it is a constitution we are expounding . . . intended to endure for ages to come, and consequently, to be adapted to the various crises of human affairs."

The Court and Its Traditions

For all of the changes in its history, the Supreme Court has retained so many traditions that it is in many respects the same institution that first met in 1790, prompting one legal historian to call it "the first Court still sitting."

Recent justices have perpetuated the tradition of longevity of tenure. Justice Hugo Black served for 34 years and one month prior to his retirement in 1971. In October 1973, Justice William O. Douglas surpassed the previous longevity record of Justice Stephen J. Field, who had served for 34 years and six months from 1863 to 1897. When Justice Douglas retired on November 12, 1975, he had served a total of thirty-six years and six months.

As is customary in U.S. courts, the nine justices are seated by seniority on the Bench. The chief justice occupies the center chair; the senior associate justice sits to his/her right, the second senior to his/her left, and so on, alternating right and left by seniority.

Since at least 1800, it has been traditional for justices to wear black robes while in Court. Chief Justice Jay, and apparently his colleagues, lent a colorful air to the earlier sessions by wearing robes with a red facing, somewhat like those worn by early colonial and English judges. The Jay robe of black and salmon is now in the possession of the Smithsonian Institution.

Initially, all attorneys wore formal "morning clothes" when appearing before the Court. Senator George Wharton Pepper of Pennsylvania often told friends of the incident he provoked when, as a young lawyer in the 1890s, he arrived to argue a case in "street clothes." Justice Horace Gray was overheard whispering to a colleague, "Who is that beast who dares to come in here with a grey coat?" The young attorney was refused admission until he borrowed a "morning coat." Today, the tradition of formal dress is followed only by Department of Justice and other government lawyers, who serve as advocates for the United States government. Quill pens have remained part of the courtroom scene. White quills are placed on counsel tables each day that the Court sits, as was done at the earliest sessions of the Court. The "conference handshake" has been a tradition since the days of Chief Justice Melville W. Fuller in the late nineteenth century. When the justices assemble to go on the bench each day and at the beginning of the private conferences at which they discuss decisions, each justice shakes hands with each of the other eight. Chief Justice Fuller instituted the practice as a reminder that differences of opinion among the justices did not preclude overall harmony of purpose.

The Supreme Court has a traditional seal that displays an eagle with a single star beneath its claws—symbolizing the Constitution's creation of "one Supreme Court." The Seal of the Supreme Court of the United States is kept in the custody of the clerk of the Court and is stamped on official papers, such as certificates given to attorneys newly admitted to practice before the Supreme Court. The seal now used is the fifth in the Court's history.

The Court and Its Procedures

A term of the Supreme Court begins, by statute, on the first Monday in October. Usually Court sessions continue until late June or early July.

The term is divided between "sittings," when the justices hear cases and deliver opinions, and intervening "recesses," when they consider the business before the Court and write opinions. Sittings and recesses alternate at approximately two-week intervals.

With rare exceptions, each side is allowed 30 minutes for argument, and up to 24 cases may be argued at one sitting. Since the majority of cases involve the review of a decision of some other court, there is no jury and no witnesses are heard. For each case, the Court has before it a record of prior proceedings and printed briefs containing the arguments of each side.

During the intervening recess period, the justices study the argued and forthcoming cases and work on their opinions. Each week the justices must also evaluate more than 130 petitions seeking review of judgments of state and federal courts to determine which cases are to be granted full review with oral arguments by attorneys.

When the Court is sitting, public sessions begin promptly at 10 A.M. and continue until 3 P.M., with a one-hour lunch recess starting at noon. No public sessions are held on Thursdays or Fridays. On Fridays during and preceding argument weeks, the justices meet to discuss the argued cases and to discuss and vote on petitions for review.

When the Court is in session, the 10 A.M. entrance of the justices into the courtroom is announced by the marshal. Those present, at the sound of the gavel, rise and remain standing until the robed justices are seated following the traditional chant: "The Honorable, the Chief Justice and the Associate Justices of the Supreme Court of the United States. Oyez! Oyez! Oyez! All persons having business before the Honorable, the Supreme Court of the United States, are admonished to draw near and give their attention, for the Court is now sitting. God save the United States and this Honorable Court!" Prior to hearing oral argument, other business of the Court is transacted. On Monday mornings this includes the release of an Order List, a public report of Court actions including the acceptance and rejection of cases, and the admission of new members to the Court Bar. Opinions typically are released on Tuesday and Wednesday mornings and on the third Monday of each sitting, when the Court takes the bench but no arguments are heard.

The Court maintains this schedule each term until all cases ready for submission have been heard and decided. In May and June the Court sits only to announce orders and opinions. The Court recesses at the end of June, but the work of the justices is unceasing. During the summer they continue to analyze new petitions for review, consider motions and applications, and make preparations for cases scheduled for fall argument.

Learning Legal Reasoning and Reading Case Law

Almost all criminal justice students learn about the three major sources of law that concern judges—constitutional, statutory, and common law. In addition to learning about these sources of law, they often learn about the differences between civil and criminal law. The vast majority of criminal justice students are exposed to these sources of law by a direct examination of criminal law or by learning about the rules of criminal evidence and procedure. Learning the law from a direct examination of criminal law has the benefit of exposing students to legal authority that directly affects their future occupations. Likewise, it exposes students to a substantial body of law within a relatively short period of time. More often than not, however, a student's exposure to case law (law created when judges rule on individual cases) and legal reasoning is only superficial. This limits students' exposure to an entire body of law and the legal reasoning that underpins judicial decisions.

Most criminal justice students can describe the process by which a bill becomes a law, but far fewer can articulate the rules of logic and tradition that guide judges in deciding court cases. Given the sheer volume of judicial decisions handed down by the courts and the effects of those decisions on criminal justice practice, it is essential for students to learn how to read judicial decisions and to understand the foundations of legal reasoning. The best way to master these skills is by formally reading the law. By reading and analyzing case law, students learn both the procedural requirements of their occupation and the reasoning and authority behind those requirements. By its very nature, case law integrates constitutional, statutory, and common law; it also bridges the artificial divide between the criminal and civil law as well as theory and practice.

Mastering the Facts of a Case

When criminal justice students begin reading case law they are often captivated by the facts of a case. Perhaps their investigative curiosity is peaked or they are attracted to the sensational aspects of a court case: for example, a police officer commits an unthinkable act of brutality or a criminal assaults a police officer conducting a drug raid. Certainly the facts of many court cases are entertaining; some are even instructive for the criminal justice student or practitioner. Take the case of a police officer who suspects that a citizen is about to commit a crime and intervenes by stopping and frisking the suspect for weapons. Was the officer's intervention legally permissible? As students read more cases, however, they find there are only so many variants on a theme. Despite superficial differences, the factual patterns of many cases are strikingly similar. There are only so many ways for police officers to use force and there are only so many ways citizens can resist arrest.

Student attention might then turn to factual disputes where one party alleges that one thing occurred, but the other party claims just the opposite. The citizen subdued by a police officer was reaching for something and resisting arrest. No, the citizen stood perfectly still with his hands in the air and offered no resistance while the officer approached. Now we have the stuff of which judicial decisions are made—a controversy. When resolving controversies, a court must determine the facts of the case or at least which facts are in dispute. The court must also determine which facts are relevant to the controversy or question before it. While certainly an important aspect of case law and legal reasoning, mastering the facts of a case is only the starting point. Determining the facts of a case should not be confused with judicial decision making or the process of making case law. The student of case law will find out quickly that even the most egregious facts of a case may not determine the prevailing party. After reading a number of cases, the student learns that capturing the precedent of a case is far more important than mastering the facts.

Capturing Case Precedent

As students begin to master reading the law, they pay less attention to the facts of cases and begin to focus on the decisions judges make. In this process, students begin to detect or uncover the principle of the case or the *ratio decidendi*. Uncovering the principle of the case requires students to bracket out all the superfluous information contained in a court's opinion by isolating the rule of law. There is no single best method for isolating the principle of law established in a court case. The principle of a case can be captured by exclusion and comparison. The exclusion process involves removing from consideration: (1) the reasoning a court gives for its decision, (2) the rule of law on which the decision was predicated, and (3) *dicta* or any information that is not necessary or directly related to reaching a decision. This practice, however, does not always ensure that what remains is a clear principle of law. The principle of the case must also be determined by comparing the material facts of the case with those that were considered immaterial in conjunction with the court's decision. What remains after exclusion and comparison should be the principle of the case. The principle of the case may or may not become the rule of law for the next similar case a court faces.

Often criminal justice students are content with an ability to recite the facts of a case and to restate the principle of law decided by a court. Commanding the facts of a case and its principle of law, however, are only two stops along the path to mastering legal reasoning. It is not enough to recount the facts of *Terry v. Ohio* (1968) and proclaim that the Supreme Court decided reasonable suspicion is sufficient grounds for a police officer to stop and frisk a suspect believed to be committing or about to commit a crime. This restatement demonstrates a command of the facts of the case and the decision, but it does not capture precedent or legal reasoning.

In order to capture precedent and understand legal reasoning a student must focus on how judges select among competing rules, interpret the rules they select for application, or in some cases create the rules that they apply to disputes. Judges must not only determine the facts of cases before them and render an opinion, they must decide on the rules of law that govern the case and exactly how these rules are to be applied. Students who learn to pay less attention to both the facts of the case and the single decision of a court and begin to focus on how judges create and apply rules have begun the transformation to the process of understanding legal reasoning.

Generally, judicial decision making is an inductive process where judges search for legal precedent to apply to the controversy or questions facing them. In the common law tradition, this requires judges to look at past individual cases to determine the controlling legal rule that governs the controversy before them. Ideally, once a court has established a rule of law, it serves as a guide for future decisions. Judicial law making then involves a search for precedent from which to make a decision on a given fact pattern.

The authoritative power of precedent is captured in the doctrine of *stare decisis*. *Stare decisis* is an abbreviation of the Latin phrase "*stare decisis et non quieta mouere*," which means "to stand by precedents and not to disturb settled points." In essence the doctrine means that once a precedent has been established all later judicial decisions should follow that precedent. The doctrine of *stare decisis* is particularly binding on lower courts if a higher court established the precedent. The Supreme Court is the ultimate authority for creating and determining precedent. The doctrine in this sense provides stability and consistency in the law as well as judicial guidance for deciding cases in a predictable fashion. The doctrine of *stare decisis* forces students to think beyond a single case and look toward the body of law.

Departing from Precedent and Moving the Law Along

The student who masters case precedent soon learns, perhaps ironically, that precedent is elastic. Once a precedent has been established it inevitably raises questions of application and unanticipated issues. *Terry v. Ohio* (1968), for example, raised a host of questions and issues the Supreme Court had to address by creating or clarifying precedent. What information establishes suspicion? How long can a citizen be detained based on reasonable suspicion? When does a stop turn into an arrest? When does a frisk turn into a search? If the courts adhere to the doctrine of *stare decisis* and adhere to precedent, how is new law made and how does the law move along? The simple answer to this question is that courts create new precedent and ignore existing precedent. The more complex question is, however, how do courts depart from precedent and maintain a unified and predictable body of law.

Courts depart from precedent while adhering to the *stare decisis* in five different ways. They distinguish precedent, limit precedent, extend precedent, ignore precedent, or overrule precedent. These practices require students to understand both the precedent established in a case and how the precedent was modified.

Distinguishing a precedent involves the argument and perhaps demonstration that the case before the court can be factually distinguished from the precedent-setting case. While many cases have similar factual patterns, some contain unique facts that can distinguish them from other cases. When a court desires to deviate from a precedent or select an alternative precedent, it can argue the case it is deciding is markedly different from the precedent setting case. In the alternative the court may argue that the case before it is more akin to a different case that developed another precedent the court wishes to apply. In this fashion, the court alters precedent by making distinctions between cases and precedents.

Limiting a precedent involves application of the existing rule of law but demonstrating that the case at bar requires that the precedent be applied in a limited or restricted fashion. When limiting precedent, the court may restate the rule with a caveat or reconstruct the precedent to limit its applicability to the case at bar. This practice can restrict the scope of precedent to a narrow group of people, situations, or area of inquiry.

Extending a precedent involves two techniques. The court can expand the rule of law to cases not intended to fall within the initial precedent or it can broaden the precedent itself. A court might have established a precedent for police liability and could then extend that precedent to correctional officers, either by application or by changing the breadth of the precedent to include correctional officers. Likewise, a precedent of qualified immunity for false arrests might be extended to malicious prosecution cases.

Ignoring a precedent is simply refusing to acknowledge its existence and rendering a decision as if the precedent never existed. This technique is often employed when a precedent is poorly constructed or is in conflict with other precedents that have more authoritative force. Sometimes because of oversights or poor research, a court might not even be aware that a precedent exists.

Overruling a precedent is the most obvious and controversial form of moving the law along. This technique is a clear pronouncement that the court is departing from precedent and replacing the rule of law. While overturning precedent is not a rare event it often follows either political events, drastic changes in the composition of a court, or is done after a precedent has been eroded by other decisions that render the precedent unworkable. In part I of your casebook you will encounter the Supreme Court's use of this technique. The Court's actions created the entire body of law on municipal liability for constitutional violations.

How to Brief a Case

The historic foundation for briefing a court case is traceable to the Socratic method. Athenian philosopher Socrates was renowned for his dialectical method of teaching and inquiry. The method involved posing questions to students that led them to logical conclusions. The contemporary practice of briefing a case exhibits similar features; it is a technique for subjecting opinions to the principle of logical consistency. Students are assigned cases, which they are expected to read before coming to class. Students should be thoroughly familiar with the facts of the case, the issue presented to the court, the conclusion, and the reasons advanced for the conclusion.

Briefing a court case is useful for learning the law. The process begins with reviewing and dissecting the court opinion into its component parts. Writing the results of this process in a short paper produces a brief—an attempt to reduce the court's opinion to its most essential elements.

There are several methods or styles of briefing a case. Your professor will describe the method that matches the learning objectives of your course. From the professor's perspective, having students write case briefs insures that they have read the case and understood the important legal issues. Depending on your professor's teaching style, student case briefs may serve as the basis for classroom discussion.

The first step in briefing a case is to read the entire case from beginning to end without taking any notes. This reading allows you to become familiar with the overall nature of the case. If you begin taking notes before reading the entire case, you are likely to miss important aspects of the case or to focus on commentary that may not be relevant or important to the court's decision. Most court cases contain information (dicta) that is not essential to the court's ruling. While dicta may have argumentative value or indicate a view or perspective, they are not legally binding and should be excluded from your brief. Your goal in briefing a case is to write a clear and concise review of the court's opinion. You should exclude information not essential to the reasoning of the court. The second step in briefing a case involves rereading the case while taking notes or highlighting relevant passages.

One of the most important aspects of writing the case brief is its structure. When you begin reading the case for the second time, keep in mind that you are collecting information that will be structured into your brief. While the actual structure of the brief may vary depending on the desires of your professor, many briefs are structured in the following manner:

- **Case Citation**—This is the easiest part of the brief to write. List the full citation of the case, include the parties' names, the reporter citation, the court, and the year of the decision. Your professor may require you to list parallel citations to other reporters where the cases are published. An example of a citation to a Supreme Court case would be:

Myra Jo Collins v. City of Harker Heights, Texas, 503 U.S. 115 (1992).

The same case with parallel citations reads: *Myra Jo Collins v. City of Harker Heights, Texas*, 503 U.S. 115, 112 S.Ct. 1061, 117 L. Ed. 261 (1992).

- **Character of Action**—This part of the brief should be very short and concise. The character of action refers to the legal characteristics and procedural history of the case. Here you should identify the plaintiffs and defendants, any necessary third parties, what brings the parties to court, what the parties are asking the court to do, what court or courts have heard the case, and what they decided. It is permissible to use the language of the court if it is easily understood, but material that is quoted directly should be indicated with quotation marks. A character of action might read:

  In this 42 U.S.C. § 1983 action, petitioner Smith seeks to recover damages for injuries allegedly sustained when Respondent Jones, a police officer, used physical force against him in violation of rights secured under the Fourth Amendment to the United States Constitution. Respondent was granted a directed verdict by the district court. A divided panel of the Court of Appeals for the Fourth Circuit affirmed. The Supreme Court granted certiorari and reversed.

- **Facts of the Case**—This part of the brief involves a synopsis or restatement of the essential facts of the case. Include only the events, actions, and circumstances leading up to the litigation that directly shaped the issue before the court. Conflicts between the parties as to the facts of the case should be noted, and any facts that are not in dispute should likewise be included. Court opinions often contain facts and materials that do not directly impact the issue or ruling; this information should not be included in your facts of the case section. The facts of a case can be found in almost any part of the case. The court may present the facts in a single section, or it might disperse facts throughout the case. Some courts even put essential facts in footnotes. The facts of the case section of the brief can be written either before or after you discover the issue and holding of the court. However, it is easier to write a concise version of the facts—those that impact the decision—after the reasoning of the court has been determined.

- **Rule of Law**—This is a brief statement of the legal principle created by the court while resolving the case. It can be determined by asking what idea, concept, or principle was determined in the case that now constitutes precedent for other courts deciding similar litigation in the future. The rule of law must be written very specifically to limit its applicability to like cases or similar fact situations. The rule of law statement must not be too vague or broad to apply to factual situations that differ substantially from the facts in the case you are briefing. Conversely, the rule of law statement must be written broadly enough that it does not limit is applicability solely to the facts of the case that were presented to the court. A better understanding of how to extract the rule of law from a case can be obtained when determining the issue and decision of the court, which is the next section of your brief. An example of a rule of law might read:

> Under the provisions of 42 U.S.C. § 1983, police officers are liable for their use of deadly force that violates the Fourth Amendment.

- **Issue and Decision**—This is a statement of the legal issue addressed by the court. The issue is stated in question form and should be answerable with a simple yes or no. If you find yourself writing several sentences to express the issue, you probably have not correctly determined it. One approach to uncovering the issue of the case is to ask yourself what the parties asked for and what the court gave them. Often court cases have multiple issues and each should be presented in this format. An example of the presentation of an issue might read:

> Can police officers be held liable for their use of deadly force that violates the Fourth Amendment under the provisions of 42 U.S.C. § 1983? Yes.

- **Reasoning**—This section of the brief presents the court's reasoning and rationale for its decision. It contains a discussion of the reasoning behind the decision as it relates to the facts of the case. Additionally, it explains any political issues, justifications used by the court, or public policy considerations made by the court. Address any reasoning, circumstances, or thought patterns that influenced that court. Finally include a sentence on the disposition or resolution of the case in this section. Did the court find for the plaintiff or defendant? Was the lower court decision affirmed or reversed? Was the case remanded? This part of the section can be stated in a single sentence.

- **Significance of the Case**—Your professor may or may not require this final section of the case brief. This section places the case into a meaningful legal context. It requires that you conduct legal research and review other decisions in this area of law. After becoming informed on the state of the law in the area addressed by the court, you express an opinion on the significance of the case you just briefed. Does the decision alter the current state of the law; if so, to what extent? Did this case present a unique question not previously addressed by the courts? Was this a landmark case? Is this a case of first impression (the first time the court has decided on this issue)? Did it provide a standard or resolve a conflict among lower courts?

Students briefing cases for the first time should expect to spend a significant amount of time on the exercise. You may find that it takes several hours to read and brief your first case. As you become more proficient in briefing cases you will become faster and have better accuracy. Professors are well aware of the time it takes to brief cases, and they expect to discover mistakes in initial attempts. By the end of the semester, as you gain practice and learn the essential skills of briefing a case, you will see significant improvement in completing this intellectual exercise.

Sources

Cardozo, B. N. *The nature of the judicial process*, New Haven, CT: Yale University Press, 1921.

Carter, L. H. *Reason in law.* 2d ed. Boston: Little, Brown, 1984.

Christie, G. C. Objectivity in the law, 78 *Yale Law Journal* 1311 (1969).

Davis, K. C. The future of judge-made law in England, 61 *Columbia Law Review* 201 (1961).

Douglas, W. O. Stare decisis, 4 *The Record of the Association of the Bar of the City of New York* 152, 1949.

Friedman, L. On legalistic reasoning, *Wisconsin Law Review* 148 (1968).

Fuller, L. L. Reason and fiat in case law, 59 *Harvard Law Review* 376 (1946).

Goodhart, A. L. Determining the *ratio decidendi* of a case, 40 *Yale Law Journal* 161 (1930).

Llewellyn, K. N. *The common law tradition: Deciding appeals.* Boston: Little, Brown, 1960.

Terry v. Ohio, 392 U.S. 1 (1968).

PART I

Municipal Liability
and Immunity

The Supreme Court decisions in this part of your casebook address the scope of municipal liability and immunity for constitutional violations that are products of governmental functions. These cases provide the foundation of the case law on municipal liability. The threads of these decisions are woven throughout all subsequent decisions of the Court on municipal liability—whether they involve activities of police officers or sanitation workers. Activities of law enforcement officials have, however, played an especially important role in the development of case law on municipal liability. From law enforcement's inability to control the activities of the Ku Klux Klan in the 1970s to controversial applications of police force in the 1990s, the practices of police officers have been a springboard for the Court's decisions.

15

In the cases presented in Part I, the Supreme Court traces the history of the Ku Klux Act of 1871 and its applicability to municipalities. The Court traces the history of the Act from President Grant's letter to Congress expressing concern about the state of the justice system. At this point in history, Congress was concerned with issues of social justice as well as the activities of law enforcement officials. The concern with law enforcement was threefold. First, Congress was concerned with law enforcement's inability and unwillingness to control racially motivated crime. Second, it was concerned with the activities of state officials that supported and condoned racist and illegal activities. Third, it expressed concern about the willingness of Klan members to direct violence against law enforcement officials to accomplish their racist objectives. The Ku Klux Act of 1871 is now codified as 42 U.S.C. Section 1983 and is referred to as Section 1983. Historically the Act was referred to as the "third force bill" because it was designed to make the provisions of the legislation applicable to the states through the Due Process Clause of the Fourteenth Amendment.

In rendering its opinions on municipal liability the Court twice directly addressed the purposes of the legislation but reached two very different conclusions. In the *Monroe* decision the Court's analysis of legislative intent brought it to the conclusion that Congress never intended to expose municipalities to liability for constitutional violations. Accordingly, the Court concluded that municipalities are to be afforded immunity from liability. This result was achieved by a narrow and selective reading of the congressional debates surrounding passage of the legislation. Had this precedent remained the state of the law, all possibility of municipal liability would have been foreclosed. The Supreme Court, however, revisited the issue of municipal immunity in the *Monell* decision and once again looked at the meaning of the legislation. This time, the Court used statutory analysis to reach a different conclusion. According to the *Monell* Court, Congress never intended that municipalities be afforded the blanket immunity granted to them in the *Monroe* decision. Through a more expansive consideration of the Congressional Record and an examination of the meaning of the words used in the legislation, the Court was able to overturn its decision in *Monroe.* The *Monell* decision set the stage for the development of an entire body of case law on municipal immunity, but it left many questions unanswered as to the application and construction of Section 1983. One fundamental question left unanswered was the scope of immunity, if any, which was to be granted municipalities that violate the constitutional rights of citizen. The issue of municipal immunity was raised and settled in the Court's opinion in *Owen,* where the Court ruled that municipalities are not afforded good faith immunity for constitutional violations. These Supreme Court decisions comprise the foundation for the body of law governing municipal and police liability.

Monroe v. Pape
365 U.S. 167 (1961)

Argued November 8, 1960.
Decided February 20, 1961.
MR. JUSTICE DOUGLAS delivered the opinion of the Court.

This case presents important questions concerning the construction of R. S. 1979, 42 U.S.C. § 1983, which reads as follows:

> "Every person who, under color of any statute, ordinance, regulation, custom, or usage, of any State or Territory, subjects, or causes to be subjected, any [365 U.S. 167, 169] citizen of the United States or other person within the jurisdiction thereof to the deprivation of any rights, privileges, or immunities secured by the Constitution and laws, shall be liable to the party injured in an action at law, suit in equity, or other proper proceeding for redress."

The complaint alleges that 13 Chicago police officers broke into petitioners' home in the early morning, routed them from bed, made them stand naked in the living room, and ransacked every room, emptying drawers and ripping mattress covers. It further alleges that Mr. Monroe was then taken to the police station and detained on "open" charges for 10 hours, while he was interrogated about a two-day-old murder, that he was not taken before a magistrate, though one was accessible, that he was not permitted to call his family or attorney, that he was subsequently released without criminal charges being preferred against him. It is alleged that the officers had no search warrant and no arrest warrant and that they acted "under color of the statutes, ordinances, regulations, customs and usages" of Illinois and of the City of Chicago. Federal jurisdiction was asserted under R. S. § 1979, which we have set out above, and 28 U.S.C. § 1343[1] and 28 U.S.C. § 1331.[2] [365 U.S. 167, 170]

The City of Chicago moved to dismiss the complaint on the ground that it is not liable under the Civil Rights Acts or for acts committed in performance of its governmental functions. All defendants moved to dismiss, alleging that the complaint alleged no cause of action under those Acts or under the Federal Constitution. The District Court dismissed the complaint. The Court of Appeals affirmed, 272 F.2d 365, relying on its earlier decision, *Stift v. Lynch*, 267 F.2d 237. The case is here on a writ of certiorari, which we granted because of a seeming conflict of that ruling with our prior cases. 362 U.S. 926.

I

Petitioners claim that the invasion of their home and the subsequent search without a warrant and the arrest and detention of Mr. Monroe without a warrant and without arraignment constituted a deprivation of their "rights, privileges, or immunities secured by the Constitution" within the meaning of R. S. § 1979. It has been said that when 18 U.S.C. § 241 made criminal a conspiracy "to injure, oppress, threaten or intimidate any citizen in the free exercise or enjoyment of any right or privilege secured to him by the Constitution," it embraced only rights that an individual has by reason of his relation to the central government, not to state governments. *United States v. Williams*, 341 U.S. 70. Cf. *United States v. Cruikshank*, 92 U.S. 542; *Ex parte Yarbrough*, 110 U.S. 651; *Guinn v. United States*, 238 U.S. 347. But the history of the section of the Civil Rights Act presently involved does not permit such a narrow interpretation. [365 U.S. 167, 171]

Section 1979 came onto the books as § 1 of the Ku Klux Act of April 20, 1871. 17 Stat. 13. It was one of the means whereby Congress exercised the power vested in it by § 5 of the Fourteenth Amendment to enforce the provisions of that Amendment.[3] Senator Edmunds, Chairman of the Senate Committee on the Judiciary, said concerning this section:

> "The first section is one that I believe nobody objects to, as defining the rights secured by the Constitution of the United States when they are assailed by any State law or under color of any State law, and it is merely carrying out the principles of the civil rights bill,[4] which has since become a part of the Constitution,"[5] viz., the Fourteenth Amendment."

Its purpose is plain from the title of the legislation, "An Act to enforce the Provisions of the Fourteenth Amendment to the Constitution of the United States, and for other Purposes." 17 Stat. 13. Allegation of facts constituting a deprivation under color of state authority of a right guaranteed by the Fourteenth Amendment satisfies to that extent the requirement of R. S. § 1979. See *Douglas v. Jeannette*, 319

U.S. 157, 161-162. So far petitioners are on solid ground. For the guarantee against unreasonable searches and seizures contained in the Fourth Amendment has been made applicable to the States by reason of the Due Process Clause of the Fourteenth Amendment. *Wolf v. Colorado*, 338 U.S. 25; *Elkins v. United States*, 364 U.S. 206, 213.

II

There can be no doubt at least since *Ex parte Virginia*, 100 U.S. 339, 346-347, that Congress has the power to [365 U.S. 167, 172] enforce provisions of the Fourteenth Amendment against those who carry a badge of authority of a State and represent it in some capacity, whether they act in accordance with their authority or misuse it. See *Home Tel. & Tel. Co. v. Los Angeles*, 227 U.S. 278, 287-296. The question with which we now deal is the narrower one of whether Congress, in enacting § 1979, meant to give a remedy to parties deprived of constitutional rights, privileges and immunities by an official's abuse of his position. Cf. *Williams v. United States*, 341 U.S. 97; *Screws v. United States*, 325 U.S. 91; *United States v. Classic*, 313 U.S. 299. We conclude that it did so intend.

It is argued that "under color of" enumerated state authority excludes acts of an official or policeman who can show no authority under state law, state custom, or state usage to do what he did. In this case it is said that these policemen, in breaking into petitioners' apartment, violated the Constitution[6] and laws of Illinois. It is pointed out that under Illinois law a simple remedy is offered for that violation and that, so far as it appears, the courts of Illinois are available to give petitioners that full redress which the common law affords for violence done to a person; and it is earnestly argued that no "statute, ordinance, regulation, custom or usage" of Illinois bars that redress.

The Ku Klux Act grew out of a message sent to Congress by President Grant on March 23, 1871, reading:

> "A condition of affairs now exists in some States of the Union rendering life and property insecure and [365 U.S. 167, 173] the carrying of the mails and the collection of the revenue dangerous. The proof that such a condition of affairs exists in some localities is now before the Senate. That the power to correct these evils is beyond the control of State authorities I do not doubt; that the power of the Executive of the United States, acting within the limits of existing laws, is sufficient for present emergencies is not clear. Therefore, I urgently recommend such legislation as in the judgment of Congress shall effectually secure life, liberty, and property, and the enforcement of law in all parts of the United States. . . ."[7]

The legislation—in particular the section with which we are now concerned—had several purposes. There are threads of many thoughts running through the debates. One who reads them in their entirety sees that the present section had three main aims.

First, it might, of course, override certain kinds of state laws. Mr. Sloss of Alabama, in opposition, spoke of that object and emphasized that it was irrelevant because there were no such laws:[8]

> "The first section of this bill prohibits any invidious legislation by States against the rights or privileges of citizens of the United States. The object of this section is not very clear, as it is not pretended by its advocates on this floor that any State has passed any laws endangering the rights or privileges of the colored people."

Second, it provided a remedy where state law was inadequate. That aspect of the legislation was summed up as follows by Senator Sherman of Ohio:

> "... it is said the reason is that any offense may be committed upon a negro by a white man, and a [365 U.S. 167, 174] negro cannot testify in any case against a white man, so that the only way by which any conviction can be had in Kentucky in those cases is in the United States courts, because the United States courts enforce the United States laws by which negroes may testify."[9]

But the purposes were much broader. The *third* aim was to provide a federal remedy where the state remedy, though adequate in theory, was not available in practice. The opposition to the measure complained that "It overrides the reserved powers of the States,"[10] just as they argued that the second section of the bill "absorb[ed] the entire jurisdiction of the States over their local and domestic affairs."[11]

This Act of April 20, 1871, sometimes called "the third force bill,'" was passed by a Congress that had the Klan "particularly in mind."[12] The debates are replete with references to the lawless conditions existing in the South in 1871. There was available to the Congress during these debates a report, nearly 600 pages in length, dealing with the activities of the Klan and the inability of the state governments to cope with it.[13] This report was drawn on by many of the speakers.[14] It was not the unavailability of state remedies but the failure of certain States to enforce the laws with an equal hand that furnished [365 U.S. 167, 175] the powerful momentum behind this "force bill." Mr. Lowe of Kansas said:

> "While murder is stalking abroad in disguise, while whippings and lynchings and banishment have been visited upon unoffending American citizens, the local administrations have been found inadequate or unwilling to apply the proper corrective. Combinations, darker than the night that hides them, conspiracies, wicked as the worst of felons could devise, have gone unwhipped of justice. Immunity is given to crime, and the records of the public tribunals are searched in vain for any evidence of effective redress."[15]

Mr. Beatty of Ohio summarized in the House the case for the bill when he said:

"... certain States have denied to persons within their jurisdiction the equal protection of the laws. The proof on this point is voluminous and unquestionable. . . . [M]en were murdered, houses were burned, women were outraged, men were scourged, and officers of the law shot down; and the State made no successful effort to bring the guilty to punishment or afford protection or redress to the outraged and innocent. The State, from lack of power or inclination, practically denied the equal protection of the law to these persons."[16]

While one main scourge of the evil—perhaps the leading one— was the Ku Klux Klan,[17] the remedy created was [365 U.S. 167, 176] not a remedy against it or its members but against those who representing a State in some capacity were *unable* or *unwilling* to enforce a state law. Senator Osborn of Florida put the problem in these terms:[18]

"That the State courts in the several States have been unable to en- force the criminal laws of their respective States or to suppress the disorders existing, and in fact that the preservation of life and prop- erty in many sections of the country is beyond the power of the State government, is a sufficient reason why Congress should, so far as they have authority under the Constitution, enact the laws necessary for the protection of citizens of the United States.

The question of the constitutional authority for the requisite legislation has been sufficiently discussed."

There was, it was said, no quarrel with the state laws on the books. It was their lack of enforcement that was the nub of the difficulty. Speaking of conditions in Virginia, Mr. Porter of that State said:[19]

"The outrages committed upon loyal men there are under the forms of law."

Mr. Burchard of Illinois pointed out that the statutes of a State may show no discrimination:[20]

"If the State Legislature pass a law discriminating against any por- tion of its citizens, or if it fails to enact provisions equally applica- ble to every class for the protection of their person and property, it will be admitted that the State does not afford the equal protection. But if the statutes show no discrimination, [365 U.S. 167, 177] yet in its judicial tribunals one class is unable to secure that enforce- ment of their rights and punishment for their infraction which is ac- corded to another, or if secret combinations of men are allowed by the Executive to band together to deprive one class of citizens of their legal rights without a proper effort to discover, detect, and punish the violations of law and order, the State has not afforded to all its citizens the equal protection of the laws."

Mr. Hoar of Massachusetts stated:[21]

"Now, it is an effectual denial by a State of the equal protection of the laws when any class of officers charged under the laws with their administration permanently and as a rule refuse to extend that protection. If every sheriff in South Carolina refuses to serve a

writ for a colored man and those sheriffs are kept in office year after year by the people of South Carolina, and no verdict against
them for their failure of duty can be obtained before a South Carolina jury, the State of South Carolina, through the class of officers
who are its representatives to afford the equal protection of the
laws to that class of citizens, has denied that protection. If the jurors of South Carolina constantly and as a rule refuse to do justice
between man and man where the rights of a particular class of its
citizens are concerned, and that State affords by its legislation no
remedy, that is as much a denial to that class of citizens of the equal
protection of the laws as if the State itself put on its statute-book a
statute enacting that no verdict should be rendered in the courts of
that State in favor of this class of citizens." [365 U.S. 167, 178]

Senator Pratt of Indiana spoke of the discrimination against Union
sympathizers and Negroes in the actual enforcement of the laws:[22]

"Plausibly and sophistically it is said the laws of North Carolina do
not discriminate against them; that the provisions in favor of rights
and liberties are general; that the courts are open to all; that juries,
grand and petit, are commanded to hear and redress without distinction as to color, race, or political sentiment.
    "But it is a fact, asserted in the report, that of the hundreds of
outrages committed upon loyal people through the agency of this
Ku Klux organization not one has been punished. This defect in the
administration of the laws does not extend to other cases. Vigorously enough are the laws enforced against Union people. They only fail
in efficiency when a man of known Union sentiments, white or black,
invokes their aid. Then Justice closes the door of her temples."

It was precisely that breadth of the remedy which the opposition
emphasized. Mr. Kerr of Indiana referring to the section involved in the
present litigation said:

"This section gives to any person who may have been injured in any
of his rights, privileges, or immunities of person or property, a civil
action for damages against the wrongdoer in the Federal courts. The
offenses committed against him may be the common violations of
the municipal law of his State. It may give rise to numerous vexa-
tions and outrageous prosecutions, inspired by mere mercenary
considerations, prosecuted in a spirit of plunder, aided by the
crimes of perjury and subornation of perjury, more reckless and
dangerous to society than the alleged [365 U.S. 167, 179] offenses
out of which the cause of action may have arisen. It is a covert attempt to transfer another large portion of jurisdiction from the State
tribunals, to which it of right belongs, to those of the United States.
It is neither authorized nor expedient, and is not calculated to bring
peace, or order, or domestic content and prosperity to the disturbed
society of the South. The contrary will certainly be its effect."[23]

Mr. Voorhees of Indiana, also speaking in opposition, gave it the
same construction:[24]

"And now for a few moments let us inspect the provisions of this bill, inspired as it is by the waning and decaying fortunes of the party in power, and called for, as I have shown, by no public necessity whatever. The first and second sections are designed to transfer all criminal jurisdiction from the courts of the States to the courts of the United States. This is to be done upon the assumption that the courts of the southern States fail and refuse to do their duty in the punishment of offenders against the law."

Senator Thurman of Ohio spoke in the same vein about the section we are now considering:[25]

"It authorizes any person who is deprived of any right, privilege, or immunity secured to him by the [365 U.S. 167, 180] Constitution of the United States, to bring an action against the wrong-doer in the Federal courts, and that without any limit whatsoever as to the amount in controversy. The deprivation may be of the slightest conceivable character, the damages in the estimation of any sensible man may not be five dollars or even five cents; they may be what lawyers call merely nominal damages; and yet by this section jurisdiction of that civil action is given to the Federal courts instead of its being prosecuted as now in the courts of the States."

The debates were long and extensive. It is abundantly clear that one reason the legislation was passed was to afford a federal right in federal courts because, by reason of prejudice, passion, neglect, intolerance or otherwise, state laws might not be enforced and the claims of citizens to the enjoyment of rights, privileges, and immunities guaranteed by the Fourteenth Amendment might be denied by the state agencies.

Much is made of the history of § 2 of the proposed legislation. As introduced § 2 was very broad:

". . . if two or more persons shall, within the limits of any State, band, conspire, or combine together to do any act in violation of the rights, privileges, or immunities of any person, to which he is entitled under the Constitution and laws of the United States, which, committed within a place under the sole and exclusive jurisdiction of the United States, would, under any law of the United States then in force, constitute the crime of either murder, manslaughter, mayhem, robbery, assault and battery, perjury, subornation of perjury, criminal obstruction of legal process or resistance of officers in discharge of official duty, arson, or larceny; and if one or more of the parties to said conspiracy or combination shall do [365 U.S. 167, 181] any act to effect the object thereof, all the parties to or engaged in said conspiracy or combination, whether principals or accessories, shall be deemed guilty of a felony. . . ."

It was this provision that raised the greatest storm. It was § 2 that was rewritten so as to be in the main confined to conspiracies to interfere with a federal or state officer in the performance of his duties. 17 Stat. 13. Senator Trumbull said:[26]

"Those provisions were changed, and as the bill passed the House
of Representatives, it was understood by the members of that body
to go no further than to protect persons in the rights which were
guarantied to them by the Constitution and laws of the United
States, and it did not undertake to furnish redress for wrongs done
by one person upon another in any of the States of the Union in violation of their laws, unless he also violated some law of the United
States, nor to punish one person for an ordinary assault and battery
committed on another in a State."

But § 1—the section with which we are here concerned—was not
changed as respects any feature with which we are presently concerned.[27] The words "under [365 U.S. 167, 182] color of" law were in
the legislation from the beginning to the end. The changes hailed by the
opposition—indeed the history of the evolution of § 2 much relied
upon now—are utterly irrelevant to the problem before us, viz., the
meaning of "under color of" law. The vindication of States' rights which
was hailed in the amendments to § 2 raises no implication as to the
construction to be given to "color of any law" in § 1. The scope of § 1—
under any construction—is admittedly narrower than was the scope of
the original version of § 2. Opponents of the Act, however, did not fail
to note that by virtue of § 1 federal courts would sit in judgment on the
misdeeds of state officers.[28] Proponents of the Act, on the other hand,
were aware of the extension of federal power contemplated by every
section of the Act. They found justification, however, for this extension
in considerations such as those advanced by Mr. Hoar:[29]

"The question is not whether a majority of the people in a majority
of the States are likely to be attached to and able to secure their own
liberties. The question is not whether the majority of the people in
every State are not likely to desire to secure their own rights. It is,
whether a majority of the people in every State are sure to be so attached to the principles of civil freedom and civil justice as to be as
much desirous of preserving the liberties of others as their own, as
to insure that under no temptation of party spirit, under no political
excitement, under [365 U.S. 167, 183] no jealousy of race or caste,
will the majority either in numbers or strength in any State seek to
deprive the remainder of the population of their civil rights."

Although the legislation was enacted because of the conditions
that existed in the South at that time, it is cast in general language and
is as applicable to Illinois as it is to the States whose names were mentioned over and again in the debates. It is no answer that the State has
a law which if enforced would give relief. The federal remedy is supple-
mentary to the state remedy, and the latter need not be first sought and
refused before the federal one is invoked. Hence the fact that Illinois
by its constitution and laws outlaws unreasonable searches and seizures is no barrier to the present suit in the federal court.

We had before us in *United States v. Classic* (U.S.) *supra*, § 20 of the Criminal Code, 18 U.S.C. § 242,[30] which provides a criminal punishment for anyone who "under color of any law, statute, ordinance, regulation, or custom" subjects any inhabitant of a State to the deprivation of "any rights, privileges, or immunities secured or protected by the Constitution or laws of the United States." Section 242 first came into the law as § 2 of the Civil Rights Act, Act of April 9, 1866, 14 Stat. 27. After passage of the Fourteenth Amendment, this provision was re-enacted and amended by §§ 17, 18, Act of May 31, 1870, 16 Stat. 140, 144.[31] The right involved in the *Classic* case was the right of voters in a primary to have their votes counted. The laws of Louisiana required the defendants "to count the ballots, to record the result of the count, and [365 U.S. 167, 184] to certify the result of the election." *United States v. Classic, supra*, 325–326. But according to the indictment they did not perform their duty. In an opinion written by Mr. Justice (later Chief Justice) Stone, in which Mr. Justice Roberts, Mr. Justice Reed, and MR. JUSTICE FRANKFURTER joined, the Court ruled, "Misuse of power, possessed by virtue of state law and made possible only because the wrongdoer is clothed with the authority of state law, is action taken 'under color of' state law." *Id.* 313 U.S. 326. There was a dissenting opinion; but the ruling as to the meaning of "under color of" state law was not questioned.

That view of the meaning of the words "under color of" state law, 18 U.S.C. § 242, was reaffirmed in *Screws v. United States, supra* 325 U.S. 108-113. The acts there complained of were committed by state officers in performance of their duties, viz., making an arrest effective. It was urged there, as it is here, that "under color of" state law should not be construed to duplicate in federal law what was an offense under state law. *Id.* (dissenting opinion) 325 U.S. 138-149, 157-161. It was said there, as it is here, that the ruling in the *Classic* case as to the meaning of "under color of" state law was not in focus and was ill advised. *Id.* (dissenting opinion) 325 U.S. 146-147. It was argued there, as it is here, that "under color of" state law included only action taken by officials pursuant to state law. *Id.* (dissenting opinion) 325 U.S. 141-146. We rejected that view. *Id.* 325 U.S. 110-113 (concurring opinion) 114-117. We stated:

> "The construction given § 20 [18 U.S.C. § 242] in the *Classic* case formulated a rule of law which has become the basis of federal enforcement in this important field. The rule adopted in that case was formulated after mature consideration. It should be good for more than one day only. We do not have here a situation comparable to *Mahnich v. Southern S. S. Co.*, 321 U.S. 96, where we [365 U.S. 167, 185] overruled a decision demonstrated to be a sport in the law and inconsistent with what preceded and what followed. The *Classic* case was not the product of hasty action or inadvertence. It was not out of line with the cases that preceded. It was designed to fashion the governing rule of law in this important field. We are not dealing with constitutional interpretations which throughout the history of

the Court have wisely remained flexible and subject to frequent re-examination. The meaning which the *Classic* case gave to the phrase "under color of any law" involved only a construction of the statute. Hence if it states a rule undesirable in its consequences, Congress can change it. We add only to the instability and uncertainty of the law if we revise the meaning of 20 [18 U.S.C. § 242] to meet the exigencies of each case coming before us." *Id.*, 325 U.S. 112, 113.

We adhered to that view in *Williams v. United States, supra*, 341 U.S. 99.

Mr. Shellabarger, reporting out the bill which became the Ku Klux Act, said of the provision with which we now deal:

"The model for it will be found in the second section of the act of April 9, 1866, known as the 'civil rights act.'. . . This section of this bill, on the same state of facts, not only provides a civil remedy for persons whose former condition may have been that of slaves, but also to all people where, under color of State law, they or any of them may be deprived of rights . . . ."[32]

Thus, it is beyond doubt that this phrase should be accorded the same construction in both statutes—in § 1979 and in 18 U.S.C. § 242. [365 U.S. 167, 186]

Since the *Screws* and *Williams* decisions, Congress has had several pieces of civil rights legislation before it. In 1956 one bill reached the floor of the House. This measure had at least one provision in it penalizing actions taken "under color of law or otherwise."[33] A vigorous minority report was filed attacking, *inter alia*, the words "or otherwise."[34] But not a word of criticism of the phrase "under color of" state law as previously construed by the Court is to be found in that report.

Section 131 (c) of the Act of September 9, 1957, 71 Stat. 634, 637, amended 42 U.S.C. § 1971 by adding a new subsection which provides that no person "whether acting under color of law or otherwise" shall intimidate any other person in voting as he chooses for federal officials. A vigorous minority report was filed[35] attacking the wide scope of the new subsection by reason of the words "or otherwise." It was said in that minority report that those words went far beyond what this Court had construed "under color of law" to mean.[36] But there was not a word of criticism directed to the prior construction given by this Court to the words "under color of" law.

The Act of May 6, 1960, 74 Stat. 86, uses "under color of" law in two contexts, once when § 306 defines "officer of election" and next when § 601 (a) gives a judicial remedy on behalf of a qualified voter denied the opportunity to register. Once again there was a Committee report containing minority views.[37] Once again no one challenged the scope given by our prior decisions to the phrase "under color of" law. [365 U.S. 167, 187]

If the results of our construction of "under color of" law were as horrendous as now claimed, if they were as disruptive of our federal scheme as now urged, if they were such an unwarranted invasion of States' rights as pretended, surely the voice of the opposition would have been heard in those Committee reports. Their silence and the new uses to which "under color of" law have recently been given reinforce our conclusion that our prior decisions were correct on this matter of construction.

We conclude that the meaning given "under color of" law in the *Classic* case and in the *Screws* and *Williams* cases was the correct one; and we adhere to it.

In the *Screws* case we dealt with a statute that imposed criminal penalties for acts "wilfully" done. We construed that word in its setting to mean the doing of an act with "a specific intent to deprive a person of a federal right." 325 U.S., at 103. We do not think that gloss should be placed on § 1979 which we have here. The word "wilfully" does not appear in § 1979. Moreover, § 1979 provides a civil remedy, while in the *Screws* case we dealt with a criminal law challenged on the ground of vagueness. Section 1979 should be read against the background of tort liability that makes a man responsible for the natural consequences of his actions.

So far, then, the complaint states a cause of action. There remains to consider only a defense peculiar to the City of Chicago.

III

The City of Chicago asserts that it is not liable under § 1979. We do not stop to explore the whole range of questions tendered us on this issue at oral argument and in the briefs. For we are of the opinion that Congress did not undertake to bring municipal corporations within the ambit of § 1979. [365 U.S. 167, 188]

When the bill that became the Act of April 20, 1871, was being debated in the Senate, Senator Sherman of Ohio proposed an amendment which would have made "the inhabitants of the county, city, or parish" in which certain acts of violence occurred liable "to pay full compensation" to the person damaged or his widow or legal representative.[38] The amendment was adopted by the Senate.[39] The House, however, rejected it.[40] The Conference Committee reported another version.[41] The [365 U.S. 167, 189] House rejected the Conference report.[42] In a second conference the Sherman amendment was dropped and in its place 6 of the Act of April 20, 1871, was substituted.[43] [365 U.S. 167, 190] This new section, which is now R. S. 1981, 42 U.S.C. § 1986, dropped out all provision for municipal liability and extended liability in damages to "any person or persons, having knowledge that any" of the specified wrongs are being committed. Mr. Poland, speaking for the House Conferees about the Sherman proposal to make municipalities liable, said:

> "We informed the conferees on the part of the Senate that the House had taken a stand on that subject and would not recede from it; that that section imposing liability upon towns and counties must go out or we should fail to agree."[44]

The objection to the Sherman amendment stated by Mr. Poland was that "the House had solemnly decided that in their judgment Congress had no constitutional power to impose any obligation upon county and town organizations, the mere instrumentality for the administration of state law."[45] The question of constitutional power of Congress to impose civil liability on municipalities was vigorously debated with powerful arguments advanced in the affirmative.[46]

Much reliance is placed on the Act of February 25, 1871, 16 Stat. 431, entitled "An Act prescribing the Form of the enacting and resolving Clauses of Acts and Resolutions of Congress, and Rules for the Construction thereof." Section 2 of this Act provides that "the word 'person' may extend and be applied to bodies politic and corporate."[47] [365 U.S. 167, 191] It should be noted, however, that this definition is merely an allowable, not a mandatory, one. It is said that doubts should be resolved in favor of municipal liability because private remedies against officers for illegal searches and seizures are conspicuously ineffective,[48] and because municipal liability will not only afford plaintiffs responsible defendants but cause those defendants to eradicate abuses that exist at the police level.[49] We do not reach those policy considerations. Nor do we reach the constitutional question whether Congress has the power to make municipalities liable for acts of its officers that violate the civil rights of individuals.

The response of the Congress to the proposal to make municipalities liable for certain actions being brought within federal purview by the Act of April 20, 1871, was so antagonistic that we cannot believe that the word "person" was used in this particular Act to include them.[50] [365 U.S. 167, 192] Accordingly we hold that the motion to dismiss the complaint against the City of Chicago was properly granted. But since the complaint should not have been dismissed against the officials the judgment must be and is

Reversed.

Footnotes

[1] This section provides in material part:

"The district courts shall have original jurisdiction of any civil action authorized by law to be commenced by any person: . . .

.   .   .   .   .

(3) To redress the deprivation, under color of any State law, statute, ordinance, regulation, custom or usage, of any right, privilege or immunity secured by the Constitution of the United States or by any Act of Congress providing for equal rights of citizens or of all persons within the jurisdiction of the United States."

[2] Subsection (a) provides:

> "The district courts shall have original jurisdiction of all civil actions wherein the matter in controversy exceeds the sum or value [365 U.S. 167, 170] of $10,000, exclusive of interest and costs, and arises under the Constitution, laws, or treaties of the United States."

In their complaint, petitioners also invoked R. S. §§ 1980, 1981, 42 U.S.C. §§ 1985, 1986. Before this Court, however, petitioners have limited their claim to recovery to the liability imposed by § 1979. Accordingly, only that section is before us.

[3] See Cong. Globe, 42d Cong., 1st Sess., App. 68, 80, 83-85.

[4] Act of April 9, 1866, 14 Stat. 27.

[5] *Supra*, note 3, 568.

[6] Illinois Const., Art. II, § 6, provides:

> "The right of the people to be secure in their persons, houses, papers and effects, against unreasonable searches and seizures, shall not be violated; and no warrant shall issue without probable cause, supported by affidavit, particularly describing the place to be searched, and the persons or things to be seized." Respondents also point to Ill. Rev. Stat., c. 38, 252, 449.1; Chicago, Illinois, Municipal Code, 11-40.

[7] Cong. Globe, 42d Cong., 1st Sess., p. 244.

[8] *Id.*, App. 268.

[9] *Id.*, p. 345.

[10] *Id.*, p. 265. The speaker, Mr. Arthur of Kentucky, had no doubts as to the scope of 1: "[I]f the sheriff levy an execution, execute a writ, serve a summons, or make an arrest, all acting under a solemn, official oath, though as pure in duty as a saint and as immaculate as a seraph, *for a mere error of judgment*, [he is liable] . . . ." *Ibid.* (Italics added.)

[11] *Id.*, p. 366.

[12] Randall, The Civil War and Reconstruction (1937), p. 857.

[13] S. Rep. No. 1, 42d Cong., 1st Sess.

[14] See, *e.g.*, Cong., Globe, 42d Cong., 1st Sess., App. 166-167.

[15] *Id.*, p. 374.

[16] *Id.*, p. 428.

[17] As Randall, *op. cit.*, *supra*, note 12, p. 855, says in discussing the Ku Klux Klan: "A friendly view of the order might represent it as an agency of social control in the South. Yet it never attained the dignity of the vigilance committees of the western states nor of the committees of safety of Revolutionary times."

[18] Cong. Globe, 42d Cong., 1st Sess. 653.

[19] *Id.*, App. 277.

[20] *Id.*, App. 315.

[21] *Id.*, p. 334.

[22] *Id.*, p. 505.

[23] *Id.*, App., p. 50. Mr. Golladay of Tennessee expressed the same concern:

> "Is the great State of New York invaded every time a murder is committed within her bounds? Was the great State of Pennsylvania invaded when rioters in the city of Philadelphia burned a public building? Was the great State of Massachusetts invaded when Webster, one of her first scholars, within the walls of Harvard murdered Parkman, or later, when evil-disposed persons violated her laws in Lowell? Did they require the Army and Navy and martial law? And, sir, because a midnight murderer is sometimes found in the South it should not be regarded as an invasion." *Id.*, App. 160.

[24] *Id.*, App. 179.

[25] *Id.*, App. 216.

[26] *Id.*, p. 579.

[27] Section 1 in the bill as originally introduced read as follows:

> "That any person who, under color of any law, statute, ordinance, regula-
> tion, custom, or usage of any State, shall subject, or cause to be sub-
> jected, any person within the jurisdiction of the United States to the dep-
> rivation of any rights, privileges, or immunities secured by the Constitu-
> tion of the United States, shall, any such law, statute, ordinance,
> regulation, custom, or usage of the State to the contrary notwithstanding,
> be liable to the party injured in any action at law, suit in equity, or other
> proper proceeding for redress; such proceeding to be prosecuted in the
> several district or circuit courts of the United States, with and subject to
> the same rights of appeal, review upon error, and other remedies pro-
> vided in like cases in such [365 U.S. 167, 182] courts, under the provisions
> of the act of the ninth of April, eighteen hundred and sixty-six, entitled
> 'An act to protect all persons in the United States in their civil rights, and
> to furnish the means of their vindication,' and the other remedial laws of
> the United States which are in their nature applicable in such cases."

[28] See text at note 23, *supra*; see note 10, *supra*.

[29] Cong. Globe, 42d Cong., 1st Sess., pp. 334-335.

[30] Then 18 U.S.C. § 52.

[31] For a full history of the evolution of 18 U.S.C. 242, see *Screws v. United States*, 325 U.S. 91, 98-100; *United States v. Classic*, 313 U.S. 299, 327, n. 10; cf. *Hague v. C. I. O.*, 307 U.S. 496, 509–510.

[32] Cong. Globe, 42d Cong., 1st Sess., App. 68.

[33] H. R. Rep. No. 2187, 84th Cong., 2d Sess., p. 16.

[34] *Id.*, p. 26.

[35] H. R. Rep. No. 291, 85th Cong., 1st Sess., pp. 24-60.

[36] *Id.*, pp. 57-58.

[37] H. R. Rep. No. 956, 86th Cong., 1st Sess., pp. 32-42.

[38] Cong. Globe, 42d Cong., 1st Sess., p. 663. The proposed amendment read:

> "That if any house, tenement, cabin, shop, building, barn, or granary
> shall be unlawfully or feloniously demolished, pulled down, burned, or
> destroyed, wholly or in part, by any persons riotously and tumultuously
> assembled together; or if any person shall unlawfully and with force and
> violence be whipped, scourged, wounded, or killed by any persons riot-
> ously and tumultuously assembled together; and if such offense was
> committed to deprive any person of any right conferred upon him by
> the Constitution and laws of the United States, or to deter him or punish
> him for exercising such right, or by reason of his race, color, or previous
> condition of servitude, in every such case the inhabitants of the county,
> city, or parish in which any of the said offenses shall be committed shall
> be liable to pay full compensation to the person or persons damnified
> by such offense if living, or to his widow or legal representative if dead;
> and such compensation may be recovered by such person or his repre-
> sentative by a suit in any court of the United States of competent juris-
> diction in the district in which the offense was committed, to be in the
> name of the person injured, or his legal representative, and against said
> county, city, or parish. And execution may be issued on a judgment ren-
> dered in such suit and may be levied upon any property, real or per-
> sonal, of any person in said county, city, or parish, and the said county,
> city, or parish may recover the full amount of such judgment, costs and
> interest, from any person or persons engaged as principal or accessory
> in such riot in an action in any court of competent jurisdiction."

[39] *Id.*, 704-705.

40 *Id.,* 725.

41 "That if any house, tenement, cabin, shop, building, barn, or granary shall be unlawfully or feloniously demolished, pulled down, [365 U.S. 167, 189] burned, or
destroyed, wholly or in part, by any persons riotously and tumultuously assembled
together; or if any person shall unlawfully and with force and violence be whipped,
scourged, wounded, or killed by any persons riotously and tumultuously assembled
together, with intent to deprive any person of any right conferred upon him by the
Constitution and laws of the United States, or to deter him or punish him for exercising such right, or by reason of his race, color, or previous condition of servitude,
in every such case the county, city, or parish in which any of the said offenses shall
be committed shall be liable to pay full compensation to the person or persons dam-
nified by such offense, if living, or to his widow or legal representative if dead; and
such compensation may be recovered in an action on the case by such person or his
representative in any court of the United States of competent jurisdiction in the district in which the offense was committed, such action to be in the name of the person injured, or his legal representative, and against said county, city, or parish, and
in which action any of the parties committing such acts may be joined as defendants. And any payment of any judgment, or part thereof unsatisfied, recovered by
the plaintiff in such action, may, if not satisfied by the individual defendant therein
within two months next after the recovery of such judgment upon execution duly
issued against such individual defendant in such judgment, and returned unsatisfied, in whole or in part, be enforced against such county, city, or parish, by execution, attachment, mandamus, garnishment, or any other proceeding in aid of execution or applicable to the enforcement of judgments against municipal corporations;
and such judgment shall be a lien as well upon all moneys in the treasury of such
county, city, or parish, as upon the other property thereof. And the court in any such
action may on motion cause additional parties to be made therein prior to issue
joined, to the end that justice may be done. And the said county, city, or parish may
recover the full amount of such judgment, by it paid, with costs and interest, from
any person or persons engaged as principal or accessory in such riot, in an action in
any court of competent jurisdiction. And such county, city, or parish, so paying,
shall also be subrogated to all the plaintiff's rights under such judgment." *Id.,* 749.

42 Cong. Globe, 42d Cong., 1st Sess. 800-801.

43 *Id.,* 804.

44 *Id.,* 804.

45 *Ibid.*

46 See especially the comments of Senator Sherman. *Id.,* 820-821.

47 This Act has been described as an instance where "Congress supplies its own dictionary." Frankfurter, Some Reflections on the Reading of Statutes, 47 Col L Rev
527, 536. The present code provision defining "person" (1 U.S.C. § 1) does not in
terms apply to bodies politic. See Reviser's Note, Vol. I, Rev. U.S. Stats. 1872, p. 19.

48 See note, 100 U of Pa L Rev 1182, 1206-1212.

49 See Foote, Tort Remedies for Police Violations of Individual Rights, 39 Minn L Rev 493,
514. Cf. Fuller & Casner, Municipal Tort Liability in Operation, 54 Harv L Rev 437, 459.

50 This has been the view of the lower federal courts. *Charlton v. City of Hialeah* (CA5
Fla.), 188 F.2d 421, 423; *Hewitt v. City of Jacksonville* (CA6 Ohio), 188 F.2d 423, 424;
Cobb v. City of Malden, 202 F.2d 701, 703; *Agnew v. City of Compton* (CA9 Cal.), 239
F.2d 226, 230; *Cuiksa v. City of Mansfield* (CA6 Ohio), 250 F.2d 700, 703-704. In a few
cases in which equitable relief has been sought, a municipality has been named, along
with city officials, as defendant where violations of 42 U.S.C. § 1983 were alleged.
See, *e.g., Douglas v. City of Jeannette,* 319 U.S. 157, 87 L. Ed. 1324, 63 S. Ct. 877, 882;
Holmes v. City of Atlanta, 350 U.S. 879, 100 L. Ed. 776, 76 S. Ct. 141. The question dealt
with in our opinion was not raised in those cases, either by the parties or by the
Court. Since we hold that a municipal corporation is not a "person" within the meaning of § 1983, no inference to the contrary can any longer be drawn from those cases.

Monell v. Department of Social Services of the City of New York
436 U.S. 658 (1978)

Argued November 2, 1977
Decided June 6, 1978
MR. JUSTICE BRENNAN delivered the opinion of the Court.

Petitioners, a class of female employees of the Department of Social Services and of the Board of Education of the city of New York, commenced this action under 42 U.S.C. § 1983 in July 1971.[1] The gravamen of the complaint was that the [436 U.S. 658, 661] Board and the Department had as a matter of official policy compelled pregnant employees to take unpaid leaves of absence before such leaves were required for medical reasons.[2] Cf. *Cleveland Board of Education v. LaFleur*, 414 U.S. 632 (1974). The suit sought injunctive relief and backpay for periods of unlawful forced leave. Named as defendants in the action were the Department and its Commissioner, the Board and its Chancellor, and the city of New York and its Mayor. In each case, the individual defendants were sued solely in their official capacities.[3]

On cross-motions for summary judgment, the District Court for the Southern District of New York held moot petitioners' claims for injunctive and declaratory relief since the city of New York and the Board, after the filing of the complaint, had changed their policies relating to maternity leaves so that no pregnant employee would have to take leave unless she was medically unable to continue to perform her job. 394 F. Supp. 853, 855 (1975). No one now challenges this conclusion. [436 U.S. 658, 662] The court did conclude, however, that the acts complained of were unconstitutional under *LaFleur, supra.* 394 F. Supp., at 855. Nonetheless plaintiffs' prayers for backpay were denied because any such damages would come ultimately from the city of New York and, therefore, to hold otherwise would be to "circumven[t]" the immunity conferred on municipalities by *Monroe v. Pape,* 365 U.S. 167 (1961). See 394 F. Supp., at 855.

On appeal, petitioners renewed their arguments that the Board of Education[4] was not a "municipality" within the meaning of *Monroe v. Pape, supra,* and that, in any event, the District Court had erred in barring a damages award against the individual defendants. The Court of Appeals for the Second Circuit rejected both contentions. The court first held that the Board of Education was not a "person" under § 1983 because "it performs a vital governmental function . . ., and, significantly, while it has the right to determine how the funds appropriated to it shall be spent . . ., it has no final say in deciding what its appropriations shall be." 532 F.2d 259, 263 (1976). The individual defendants, however, were "persons" under § 1983, even when sued solely in their official capacities. 532 F.2d, at 264. Yet, because a damages award would "have to be paid by a city that was held not to be amenable to such an action in *Monroe v. Pape,*" a damages action against officials sued in their official capacities could not proceed. *Id.,* at 265.

We granted certiorari in this case, 429 U.S. 1071, to consider

> "Whether local governmental officials and/or local independent school boards are 'persons' within the meaning of 42 U.S.C. § 1983 when equitable relief in the nature of back pay is sought against them in their official capacities?" Pet. for Cert. 8. [436 U.S. 658, 663]

Although, after plenary consideration, we have decided the merits of over a score of cases brought under § 1983 in which the principal defendant was a school board[5]—and, indeed, in some of which § 1983 and its jurisdictional counterpart, 28 U.S.C. § 1343, provided the only basis for jurisdiction[6]—we indicated in *Mt. Healthy City Board of Education v. Doyle,* 429 U.S. 274, 279 (1977), last Term that the question presented here was open and would be decided "another day." That other day has come and we now overrule *Monroe v. Pape, supra,* insofar as it holds that local governments are wholly immune from suit under § 1983.[7] [436 U.S. 658, 664]

I

In *Monroe v. Pape,* we held that "Congress did not undertake to bring municipal corporations within the ambit of [§ 1983]." 365 U.S., at 187. The sole basis for this conclusion was an inference drawn from Congress' rejection of the "Sherman amendment" to the bill which became the Civil Rights Act of 1871, 17 Stat. 13, the precursor of § 1983. The amendment would have held a municipal corporation liable for damage done to the person or property of its inhabitants by *private* persons "riotously and tumultuously assembled."[8] Cong. Globe, 42d Cong., 1st Sess., 749 (1871) (hereinafter Globe). Although the Sherman amendment did not seek to amend § 1 of the Act, which is now § 1983, and although the nature of the obligation created by that amendment was vastly different from that created by § 1, the Court nonetheless concluded in *Monroe* that Congress must have meant to exclude municipal corporations from the coverage of § 1 because "'the House [in voting against the Sherman amendment] had solemnly decided that in their judgment Congress had no constitutional power to impose any *obligation* upon county and town organizations, the mere instrumentality for the administration of state law.'" 365 U.S., at 190 (emphasis added), quoting Globe 804 (Rep. Poland). This statement, we thought, showed that Congress doubted its "constitutional power . . . to impose *civil liability* on municipalities," 365 U.S., at 190 (emphasis added), and that such doubt would have extended to any type of civil liability.[9] [436 U.S. 658, 665]

A fresh analysis of the debate on the Civil Rights Act of 1871, and particularly of the case law which each side mustered in its support, shows, however, that *Monroe* incorrectly equated the "obligation" of which Representative Poland spoke with "civil liability."

A. An Overview

There are three distinct stages in the legislative consideration of the bill which became the Civil Rights Act of 1871. On March 28, 1871, Representative Shellabarger, acting for a House select committee, reported H. R. 320, a bill "to enforce the provisions of the Fourteenth Amendment to the Constitution of the United States, and for other purposes." H. R. 320 contained four sections. Section 1, now codified as 42 U.S.C. § 1983, was the subject of only limited debate and was passed without amendment.[10] Sections 2 through 4 dealt primarily with the "other purpose" of suppressing Ku Klux Klan violence in the Southern States.[11] The wisdom and constitutionality of these sections—not § 1, now § 1983—were the subject of almost all congressional debate and each of these sections was amended. The House finished its initial debates on H. R. 320 on April 7, 1871, and one week later the Senate also voted out a bill.[12] Again, debate on § 1 of the bill was limited and that section was passed as introduced. [436 U.S. 658, 666]

Immediately prior to the vote on H. R. 320 in the Senate, Senator Sherman introduced his amendment.[13] This was not an amendment to § 1 of the bill, but was to be added as § 7 at the end of the bill. Under the Senate rules, no discussion of the amendment was allowed and, although attempts were made to amend the amendment, it was passed as introduced. In this form, the amendment did not place liability on municipal corporations, but made any inhabitant of a municipality liable for damage inflicted by persons "riotously and tumultuously assembled."[14]

The House refused to acquiesce in a number of amendments made by the Senate, including the Sherman amendment, and the respective versions of H. R. 320 were therefore sent to a conference committee. Section 1 of the bill, however, was not a subject of this conference since, as noted, it was passed verbatim as introduced in both Houses of Congress.

On April 18, 1871, the first conference committee completed its work on H. R. 320. The main features of the conference committee draft of the Sherman amendment were these:[15] First, a cause of action was given to persons injured by

> "any persons riotously and tumultuously assembled together . . . with intent to deprive any person of any right conferred upon him by the Constitution and laws of the United States, or to deter him or punish him for exercising such right, or by reason of his race, color, or previous condition of servitude . . . ." [436 U.S. 658, 667]

Second, the bill provided that the action would be against the county, city, or parish in which the riot had occurred and that it could be maintained by either the person injured or his legal representative. Third, unlike the amendment as proposed, the conference substitute made the government defendant liable on the judgment if it was not satisfied against individual defendants who had committed the violence. If a municipality were liable, the judgment against it could be collected

> "by execution, attachment, mandamus, garnishment, or any other proceeding in aid of execution or applicable to the enforcement of judgments against municipal corporations; and such judgment [would become] a lien as well upon all moneys in the treasury of such county, city, or parish, as upon the other property thereof."

In the ensuing debate on the first conference report, which was the first debate of any kind on the Sherman amendment, Senator Sherman explained that the purpose of his amendment was to enlist the aid of persons of property in the enforcement of the civil rights laws by making their property "responsible" for Ku Klux Klan damage.[16] Statutes drafted on a similar theory, he stated, had long been in force in England and were in force in 1871 in a number of States.[17] [436 U.S. 658, 668] Nonetheless there were critical differences between the conference substitute and extant state and English statutes: The conference substitute, unlike most state riot statutes, lacked a short statute of limitations and imposed liability on the government defendant whether or not it had notice of the impending riot, whether or not the municipality was authorized to exercise a police power, whether or not it exerted all reasonable efforts to stop the riot, and whether or not the rioters were caught and punished.[18]

The first conference substitute passed the Senate but was rejected by the House. House opponents, within whose ranks were some who had supported § 1, thought the Federal Government could not, consistent with the Constitution, obligate municipal corporations to keep the peace if those corporations were neither so obligated nor so authorized by their state charters. And, because of this constitutional objection, opponents of the Sherman amendment were unwilling to impose damages liability for nonperformance of a duty which Congress could not require municipalities to perform. This position is reflected in Representative Poland's statement that is quoted in *Monroe*.[19]

Because the House rejected the first conference report a second conference was called and it duly issued its report. The second conference substitute for the Sherman amendment abandoned municipal liability and, instead, made "any person [436 U.S. 658, 669] or persons having knowledge [that a conspiracy to violate civil rights was afoot], and having power to prevent or aid in preventing the same," who did not attempt to stop the same, liable to any person injured by the conspiracy.[20] The amendment in this form was adopted by both Houses of Congress and is now codified as 42 U.S.C. § 1986.

The meaning of the legislative history sketched above can most readily be developed by first considering the debate on the report of the first conference committee. This debate shows conclusively that the constitutional objections raised against the Sherman amendment— on which our holding in *Monroe* was based, see *supra*, at 664—would not have prohibited congressional creation of a civil remedy against state municipal corporations that infringed federal rights. Because § 1 of the Civil Rights Act does not state expressly that municipal corporations come within its ambit, it is finally necessary to interpret § 1 to confirm that such corporations were indeed intended to be included within the "persons" to whom that section applies.

B. Debate on the First Conference Report

The style of argument adopted by both proponents and opponents of the Sherman amendment in both Houses of Congress was largely legal, with frequent references to cases decided by this Court and the Supreme Courts of the several States. Proponents of the Sherman amendment did not, however, discuss in detail the argument in favor of its constitutionality. Nonetheless, it is possible to piece together such an argument from the debates on the first conference report and those on § 2 of the civil rights bill, which, because it allowed the Federal Government to prosecute crimes "in the States," had also raised questions of federal power. The account of Representative Shellabarger, the House sponsor of H. R. 320, is the most complete. [436 U.S. 658, 670]

Shellabarger began his discussion of H. R. 320 by stating that "there is a domain of constitutional law involved in the right consideration of this measure which is wholly unexplored." Globe App. 67. There were analogies, however. With respect to the meaning of § 1 of the Fourteenth Amendment, and particularly its Privileges or Immunities Clause, Shellabarger relied on the statement of Mr. Justice Washington in *Corfield v. Coryell,* 4 Wash. C. C. 371 (CC ED Pa. 1825), which defined the privileges protected by Art. IV:

> "'What these fundamental privileges are[,] it would perhaps be more tedious than difficult to enumerate. They may, however, be all comprehended under the following general heads: protection by the Government;'"
>
> "*Mark that*"
>
> "'*protection by the Government*, the enjoyment of life and liberty, with the right to acquire and possess property of every kind, and to pursue and obtain happiness and safety . . . .'" Globe App. 69 (emphasis added), quoting 4 Wash. C. C., at 380-381.

Building on his conclusion that citizens were owed protection—a conclusion not disputed by opponents of the Sherman amendment[21]— Shellabarger then considered Congress' role in providing that protection. Here again there were precedents:

> "[Congress has always] assumed to enforce, as against [436 U.S. 658, 671] the States, and also persons, every one of the provisions of the Constitution. Most of the provisions of the Constitution which restrain and directly relate to the States, such as those in [Art. I, § 10,] relate to the divisions of the political powers of the State and General Governments. . . . These prohibitions upon political powers of the States are all of such nature that they can be, and even have been, . . . enforced by the courts of the United States declaring void all State acts of encroachment on Federal powers. Thus, and thus sufficiently, has the United States 'enforced' these provisions of the Constitution. But there are some that are not of this class. These are where the court secures the rights or the liabilities of persons within the States, as between such persons and the States.
>
> "These three are: first, that as to fugitives from justice;[22] second, that as to fugitives from service, (or slaves;)[23] third, that declaring that the 'citizens of each State shall be entitled to all the privileges and immunities of citizens in the several States.'[24] [436 U.S. 658, 672]
>
> "And, sir, every one of these—the only provisions where it was deemed that legislation was required to enforce the constitutional provisions—the only three where the rights or liabilities of persons in the States, as between these persons and the States, are directly provided for, Congress has by legislation affirmatively interfered to protect . . . such persons." Globe App. 69-70.

Of legislation mentioned by Shellabarger, the closest analog of the Sherman amendment, ironically, was the statute implementing the fugitives from justice and fugitive slave provisions of Art. IV—the Act of Feb. 12, 1793, 1 Stat. 302—the constitutionality of which had been sustained in 1842, in *Prigg v. Pennsylvania*, 16 Pet. 539. There, Mr. Justice Story, writing for the Court, held that Art. IV gave slaveowners a federal right to the unhindered possession of their slaves in whatever State such slaves might be found. 16 Pet., at 612. Because state process for recovering runaway slaves might be inadequate or even hostile to the rights of the slaveowner, the right intended to be conferred could be negated if left to state implementation. *Id.*, at 614. Thus, since the Constitution guaranteed the right and this in turn required a remedy, Story held it to be a "natural inference" that Congress had the power itself to ensure an appropriate (in the Necessary and Proper Clause sense) remedy for the right. *Id.*, at 615.

Building on *Prigg*, Shellabarger argued that a remedy against municipalities and counties was an appropriate—and hence constitutional—method for ensuring the protection which the Fourteenth Amendment made every citizen's federal right.[25] This much was clear from the adoption of such statutes by the several States as devices for suppressing riot.[26] Thus, said Shellabarger, the only serious question remaining [436 U.S. 658, 673] was "whether, since a county is an integer or part of a State, the United States can impose upon it, as such, *any obligations to keep the peace* in obedience to United States laws."[27] This he answered affirmatively, citing *Board of Comm'rs v. Aspinwall*, 24 How. 376 (1861), the first of many cases[28] upholding the power of federal courts to enforce the Contract Clause against municipalities.[29]

House opponents of the Sherman amendment—whose views are particularly important since only the House voted down the amendment—did not dispute Shellabarger's claim that the Fourteenth Amendment created a federal right to protection, see n. 21, *supra*, but they argued that the local units of government upon which the amendment fastened liability were not obligated to keep the peace at state law and further that the Federal Government could not constitutionally require local governments to create police forces, whether this requirement was levied directly, or indirectly by imposing damages for breach of the peace on municipalities. The most complete statement of this position is that of Representative Blair:[30]

> "The proposition known as the Sherman amendment [436 U.S. 658, 674] . . . is entirely new. It is altogether without a precedent in this country . . . . That amendment claims the power in the General Government to go into the States of this Union and lay such obligations as it may please upon the municipalities, which are the creations of the States alone. . . .
>
> " . . . [H]ere it is proposed, not to carry into effect an obligation which rests upon the municipality, but to [436 U.S. 658, 675] create that obligation, and that is the provision I am unable to assent to.

The parallel of the hundred does not in the least meet the case. The power that laid the obligation upon the hundred first put the duty upon the hundred that it should perform in that regard, and failing to meet the obligation which had been laid upon it, it was very proper that it should suffer damage for its neglect. . . .

". . . [T]here are certain rights and duties that belong to the States, . . . there are certain powers that inhere in the State governments. They create these municipalities, they say what their powers shall be and what their obligations shall be. If the Government of the United States can step in and add to those obligations, may it not utterly destroy the municipality? If it can say that it shall be liable for damages occurring from a riot, . . . where [will] its power . . . stop and what obligations . . . might [it] not lay upon a municipality. . . .

"Now, only the other day, the Supreme Court . . . decided [in *Collector v. Day*, 11 Wall. 113 (1871)] that there is no power in the Government of the United States, under its authority to tax, to tax the salary of a State officer. Why? Simply because the power to tax involves the power to destroy, and it was not the intent to give the Government of the United States power to destroy the government of the States in any respect. It was held also in the case of *Prigg v. Pennsylvania* [16 Pet. 539 (1842)] that it is not within the power of the Congress of the United States to lay duties upon a State officer; that we cannot command a State officer to do any duty whatever, as such; and I ask . . . the difference between that and commanding a municipality, which is equally the creature of the State, to perform a duty." Globe 795.

Any attempt to impute a unitary constitutional theory to opponents of the Sherman amendment is, of course, fraught [436 U.S. 658, 676] with difficulties, not the least of which is that most Members of Congress did not speak to the issue of the constitutionality of the amendment. Nonetheless, two considerations lead us to conclude that opponents of the Sherman amendment found it unconstitutional substantially because of the reasons stated by Representative Blair: First, Blair's analysis is precisely that of Poland, whose views were quoted as authoritative in Monroe, see *supra*, at 664, and that analysis was shared in large part by all House opponents who addressed the constitutionality of the Sherman amendment.[31] Second, Blair's exegesis of the reigning constitutional theory of his day, as we shall explain, was clearly supported by precedent—albeit precedent that has not survived, see *Ex parte Virginia*, 100 U.S. 339, 347-348 (1880); *Graves v. New York ex rel. O'Keefe*, 306 U.S. 466, 486 (1939)—and no other constitutional formula was advanced by participants in the House debates.

Collector v. Day, cited by Blair, was the clearest and, at the time of the debates, the most recent pronouncement of a doctrine of coordinate sovereignty that, as Blair stated, placed limits on even the enumerated powers of the National Government in favor of protecting state prerogatives. There, the Court held that the United States could not tax the income of Day, a Massachusetts state judge, because the independence of the States within their legitimate spheres would be imperiled if the instrumentalities through which States executed their powers were "subject to the control of another and distinct government." 11 Wall., at 127. Although the Court in Day apparently rested this holding in part on the proposition that the taxing "power acknowledges no limits but the will of the legislative body imposing the tax," *id.*, at 125-126; cf. *McCulloch v. Maryland*, 4 Wheat. 316 (1819), the Court had in other cases limited other national powers in order to avoid interference with the States.[32] [436 U.S. 658, 677]

In *Prigg v. Pennsylvania*, for example, Mr. Justice Story, in addition to confirming a broad national power to legislate under the Fugitive Slave Clause, see *supra*, at 672, held that Congress could not "insist that states . . . provide means to carry into effect the duties of the national government." 16 Pet., at 615-616.[33] And Mr. Justice McLean agreed that, "[a]s a general principle," it was true "that Congress had no power to impose duties on state officers, as provided in the [Act of Feb. 12, 1793]." Nonetheless he wondered whether Congress might not impose "positive" duties on state officers where a clause of the Constitution, like the Fugitive Slave Clause, seemed to require affirmative government assistance, rather than restraint of government, to secure federal rights. See *id.*, at 664-665.

Had Mr. Justice McLean been correct in his suggestion that, where the Constitution envisioned affirmative government assistance, the States or their officers or instrumentalities could be required to provide it, there would have been little doubt that Congress could have insisted that municipalities afford by "positive" action the protection[34] owed individuals under § 1 of the Fourteenth Amendment whether or not municipalities were obligated by state law to keep the peace. However, any such argument, largely foreclosed by *Prigg*, was made [436 U.S. 658, 678] impossible by the Court's holding in *Kentucky v. Dennison*, 24 How. 66 (1861). There, the Court was asked to require Dennison, the Governor of Ohio, to hand over Lago, a fugitive from justice wanted in Kentucky, as required by § 1 of the Act of Feb. 12, 1793,[35] which implemented Art. IV, 2, cl. 2, of the Constitution. Mr. Chief Justice Taney, writing for a unanimous Court, refused to enforce that section of the Act:

> "[W]e think it clear, that the Federal Government, under the Constitution, has no power to impose on a State officer, as such, any duty whatever, and compel him to perform it; for if it possessed this power, it might overload the officer with duties which would fill up all his time, and disable him from performing his obligations to the State, and might impose on him duties of a character incompatible with the rank and dignity to which he was elevated by the State." 24 How., at 107-108.

The rationale of *Dennison*—that the Nation could not impose duties on state officers since that might impede States in their legitimate activities—is obviously identical to that which animated the decision in *Collector v. Day.* See *supra*, at 676. And, as Blair indicated, municipalities as instrumentalities through which States executed their policies could be equally disabled from carrying out state policies if they were also obligated to carry out federally imposed duties. Although no one cited *Dennison* by name, the principle for which it [436 U.S. 658, 679] stands was well known to Members of Congress,[36] many of whom discussed *Day*[37] as well as a series of State Supreme Court cases[38] in the mid-1860s, which had invalidated a federal tax on the process of state courts on the ground that the tax threatened the independence of a vital state function.[39] Thus, there was ample support for Blair's view that the Sherman amendment, by putting municipalities to the Hobson's choice of keeping the peace or paying civil damages, attempted to impose obligations on municipalities by indirection that could not be imposed directly, thereby threatening to "destroy the government of the States." Globe 795.

If municipal liability under § 1 of the Civil Rights Act of 1871 created a similar Hobson's choice, we might conclude, as *Monroe* did, that Congress could not have intended municipalities to be among the "persons" to which that section applied. But this is not the case.

First, opponents expressly distinguished between imposing an obligation to keep the peace and merely imposing civil liability for damages on a municipality that was obligated by state law to keep the peace, but which had not in violation of the Fourteenth Amendment. Representative Poland, for example, reasoning from Contract Clause precedents, indicated that Congress could constitutionally confer jurisdiction on the federal courts to entertain suits seeking to hold municipalities [436 U.S. 658, 680] liable for using their authorized powers in violation of the Constitution—which is as far as § 1 of the Civil Rights Act went:

> "I presume . . . that where a State had imposed a duty [to keep the peace] upon [a] municipality . . . an action would be allowed to be maintained against them in the courts of the United States under the ordinary restrictions as to jurisdiction. But the enforcing a liability, existing by their own contract, or by a State law, in the courts, is a very widely different thing from devolving a new duty or liability upon them by the national Government, which has no power either to create or destroy them, and no power or control over them whatever." Globe 794.

Representative Burchard agreed:

> "[T]here is no duty imposed by the Constitution of the United States, or usually by State laws, upon a county to protect the people of that county against the commission of the offenses herein enumerated, such as the burning of buildings or any other injury to

property or injury to person. Police powers are not conferred upon counties as corporations; they are conferred upon cities that have qualified legislative power. And so far as cities are concerned, where the equal protection required to be afforded by a State is imposed upon a city by State laws, perhaps the United States courts could enforce its performance. But counties . . . do not have any control of the police. . . ." *Id.*, at 795.

See also the views of Rep. Willard, discussed at n. 30, *supra.*

Second, the doctrine of dual sovereignty apparently put no limit on the power of federal courts to enforce the Constitution against municipalities that violated it. Under the theory of dual sovereignty set out in *Prigg*, this is quite understandable. So long as federal courts were vindicating the Federal Constitution, they were providing the "positive" government action [436 U.S. 658, 681] required to protect federal constitutional rights and no question was raised of enlisting the States in "positive" action. The limits of the principles announced in *Dennison* and *Day* are not so well defined in logic, but are clear as a matter of history. It must be remembered that the same Court which rendered *Day* also vigorously enforced the Contract Clause against municipalities—an enforcement effort which included various forms of "positive" relief, such as ordering that taxes be levied and collected to discharge federal-court judgments, once a constitutional infraction was found.[40] Thus, federal judicial enforcement of the Constitution's express limits on state power, since it was done so frequently, must, notwithstanding anything said in *Dennison* or *Day*, have been permissible, at least so long as the interpretation of the Constitution was left in the hands of the judiciary. Since § 1 of the Civil Rights Act simply conferred jurisdiction on the federal courts to enforce § 1 of the Fourteenth Amendment—a situation precisely analogous to the grant of diversity jurisdiction under which the Contract Clause was enforced against municipalities [436 U.S. 658, 682]—there is no reason to suppose that opponents of the Sherman amendment would have found any constitutional barrier to § 1 suits against municipalities.

Finally, the very votes of those Members of Congress, who opposed the Sherman amendment but who had voted for § 1, confirm that the liability imposed by § 1 was something very different from that imposed by the amendment. Section 1 without question could be used to obtain a damages judgment against state or municipal *officials* who violated federal constitutional rights while acting under color of law.[41] However, for *Prigg-Dennison-Day* purposes, as Blair and others recognized,[42] there was no distinction of constitutional magnitude between officers and agents—including corporate agents—of the State: Both were state instrumentalities and the State could be impeded no matter over which sort of instrumentality the Federal Government sought to assert its power. *Dennison* and *Day*, after all, were not suits against municipalities but against *officers*, and Blair was quite conscious that he was extending these cases by applying them to municipal corporations.[43] Nonetheless, Senator Thurman, who gave the most exhaustive critique of § 1—inter alia, complaining that it would be applied to state officers, see Globe App. 217—and who opposed both. Section 1 and the Sherman amendment, the latter on *Prigg* grounds, agreed unequivocally that § 1 was constitutional.[44] [436 U.S. 658, 683] Those who voted for 1 must similarly have believed in its constitutionality despite *Prigg*, *Dennison*, and *Day*.

C. Debate on § 1 of the Civil Rights Bill

From the foregoing discussion, it is readily apparent that nothing said in debate on the Sherman amendment would have prevented holding a municipality liable under § 1 of the Civil Rights Act for its own violations of the Fourteenth Amendment. The question remains, however, whether the general language describing those to be liable under § 1— "any person"—covers more than natural persons. An examination of the debate on § 1 and application of appropriate rules of construction show unequivocally that § 1 was intended to cover legal as well as natural persons.

Representative Shellabarger was the first to explain the function of § 1:

> "[Section 1] not only provides a civil remedy for persons whose former condition may have been that of slaves, but also to all people where, under color of State law, they or any of them may be deprived of rights to which they are entitled under the Constitution by reason and virtue of their national citizenship." Globe App. 68.

By extending a remedy to all people, including whites, § 1 went beyond the mischief to which the remaining sections of the 1871 Act were addressed. Representative Shellabarger also stated without reservation that the constitutionality of § 2 of the Civil Rights Act of 1866 controlled the constitutionality of § 1 of the 1871 Act, and that the former had been [436 U.S. 658, 684] approved by "the supreme courts of at least three States of this Union" and by Mr. Justice Swayne, sitting on circuit, who had concluded: "'We have no doubt of the constitutionality of every provision of this act.'"Globe App. 68. Representative Shellabarger then went on to describe how the courts would and should interpret § 1:

> "This act is remedial, and in aid of the preservation of human liberty and human rights. All statutes and constitutional provisions authorizing such statutes are liberally and beneficently construed. It would be most strange and, in civilized law, monstrous were this not the rule of interpretation. As has been again and again decided by your own Supreme Court of the United States, and everywhere else where there is wise judicial interpretation, the largest latitude

consistent with the words employed is uniformly given in construing such statutes and constitutional provisions as are meant to protect and defend and give remedies for their wrongs to all the
people. . . . Chief Justice Jay and also Story say:

> "'Where a power is remedial in its nature there is much reason to
> contend that it ought to be construed liberally, and it is generally
> adopted in the interpretation of laws.'—1 *Story on Constitution*, sec.
> 429." Globe App., at 68.

The sentiments expressed in Representative Shellabarger's opening speech were echoed by Senator Edmunds, the manager of H. R. 320
in the Senate:

> "The first section is one that I believe nobody objects to, as defining
> the rights secured by the Constitution of the United States when
> they are assailed by any State law or under color of any State law,
> and it is merely carrying out the principles of the civil rights bill [of
> 1866], which have since become a part of the Constitution." Globe
> 568. [436 U.S. 658, 685]

> "[Section 1 is] so very simple and really reenact[s] the Constitution."
> *Id.*, at 569.

And he agreed that the bill "secure[d] the rights of white men as much
as of colored men." *Id.*, at 696.

In both Houses, statements of the supporters of § 1 corroborated
that Congress, in enacting § 1, intended to give a broad remedy for violations of federally protected civil rights.[45] Moreover, since municipalities through their official [436 U.S. 658, 686] acts could, equally with
natural persons, create the harms intended to be remedied by § 1, and,
further, since Congress intended § 1 to be broadly construed, there is
no reason to suppose that municipal corporations would have been
excluded from the sweep of § 1. Cf., *e.g.*, *Ex parte Virginia*, 100 U.S. 339,
346 -347 (1880); *Home Tel. & Tel. Co. v. Los Angeles*, 227 U.S. 278, 286
-287, 294-296 (1913). One need not rely on this inference alone, however, for the debates show that Members of Congress understood "persons" to include municipal corporations.

Representative Bingham, for example, in discussing § 1 of the bill,
explained that he had drafted § 1 of the Fourteenth Amendment with
the case of *Barron v. Mayor of Baltimore*, 7 Pet. 243 (1833), especially
in mind. "In [that] case the [436 U.S. 658, 687] *city* had taken private
property for public use, without compensation . . . , and there was no
redress for the wrong . . . ." Globe App. 84 (emphasis added). Bingham's
further remarks clearly indicate his view that such takings by cities, as
had occurred in *Barron*, would be redressable under § 1 of the bill. See
Globe App. 85. More generally, and as Bingham's remarks confirm, § 1
of the bill would logically be the vehicle by which Congress provided
redress for takings, since that section provided the only civil remedy

for Fourteenth Amendment violations and that Amendment unequivocally prohibited uncompensated takings.[46] Given this purpose, it beggars reason to suppose that Congress would have exempted municipalities from suit, insisting instead that compensation for a taking come from an officer in his individual capacity rather than from the government unit that had the benefit of the property taken.[47]

In addition, by 1871, it was well understood that corporations should be treated as natural persons for virtually all purposes of constitutional and statutory analysis. This had not always been so. When this Court first considered the question of the status of corporations, Mr. Chief Justice Marshall, writing for the Court, denied that corporations "as such" were persons as that term was used in Art. III and the Judiciary Act of 1789. See *Bank of the United States v. Deveaux*, 5 Cranch 61, 86 (1809).[48] By 1844, however, the *Deveaux* doctrine was unhesitatingly abandoned:

> "[A] corporation created by and doing business in a particular [436 U.S. 658, 688] state, is to be deemed *to all intents and purposes as a person*, although an artificial person, . . . capable of being treated as a citizen of that state, as much as a natural person." *Louisville R. Co. v. Letson*, 2 How. 497, 558 (1844) (emphasis added), discussed in Globe 752.

And only two years before the debates on the Civil Rights Act, in *Cowles v. Mercer County*, 7 Wall. 118, 121 (1869), the Letson principle was automatically and without discussion extended to municipal corporations. Under this doctrine, municipal corporations were routinely sued in the federal courts[49] and this fact was well known to Members of Congress.[50]

That the "usual" meaning of the word "person" would extend to municipal corporations is also evidenced by an Act of Congress which had been passed only months before the Civil Rights Act was passed. This Act provided that

> "in all acts hereafter passed . . . the word 'person' may extend and be applied to bodies politic and corporate . . . unless the context shows that such words were intended to be used in a more limited sense." Act of Feb. 25, 1871, § 2, 16 Stat. 431.

Municipal corporations in 1871 were included within the phrase "bodies politic and corporate"[51] and, accordingly, the [436 U.S. 658, 689] "plain meaning" of § 1 is that local government bodies were to be included within the ambit of the persons who could be sued under § 1 of the Civil Rights Act. Indeed, a Circuit Judge, writing in 1873 in what is apparently the first reported case under § 1, read the Dictionary Act in precisely this way in a case involving a corporate plaintiff and a municipal defendant.[52] See *Northwestern Fertilizing Co. v. Hyde Park*, 18 F. Cas. 393, 394 (No. 10,336) (CC ND Ill. 1873).[53] [436 U.S. 658, 690]

II

Our analysis of the legislative history of the Civil Rights Act of 1871 compels the conclusion that Congress *did* intend municipalities and other local government units to be included among those persons to whom § 1983 applies.[54] Local governing bodies,[55] therefore, can be sued directly under § 1983 for monetary, declaratory, or injunctive relief where, as here, the action that is alleged to be unconstitutional implements or executes a policy statement, ordinance, regulation, or decision officially adopted and promulgated by that body's officers. Moreover, although the touchstone of the § 1983 action against a government body is an allegation that official policy is responsible for a deprivation of rights protected by the Constitution, local governments, like every other § 1983 "person," by the very terms of the statute, may be sued for constitutional [436 U.S. 658, 691] deprivations visited pursuant to governmental "custom" even though such a custom has not received formal approval through the body's official decision making channels. As Mr. Justice Harlan, writing for the Court, said in *Adickes v. S. H. Kress & Co.*, 398 U.S. 144, 167-168 (1970): "Congress included customs and usages [in § 1983] because of the persistent and widespread discriminatory practices of state officials . . . . Although not authorized by written law, such practices of state officials could well be so permanent and well settled as to constitute a 'custom or usage' with the force of law."[56]

On the other hand, the language of § 1983, read against the background of the same legislative history, compels the conclusion that Congress did not intend municipalities to be held liable unless action pursuant to official municipal policy of some nature caused a constitutional tort. In particular, we conclude that a municipality cannot be held liable *solely* because it employs a tortfeasor—or, in other words, a municipality cannot be held liable under § 1983 on a *respondeat superior* theory.

We begin with the language of § 1983 as originally passed:

> "*[A]ny person who*, under color of any law, statute, ordinance, regulation, custom, or usage of any State, *shall subject, or cause to be subjected*, any person . . . to the deprivation of any rights, privileges, or immunities secured by the Constitution of the United States, shall, any such [436 U.S. 658, 692] law, statute, ordinance, regulation, custom, or usage of the State to the contrary notwithstanding, be liable to the party injured in any action at law, suit in equity, or other proper proceeding for redress . . . ." 17 Stat. 13 (emphasis added).

The italicized language plainly imposes liability on a government that, under color of some official policy, "causes" an employee to violate another's constitutional rights. At the same time, that language cannot be easily read to impose liability vicariously on governing bodies solely on the basis of the existence of an employer-employee relationship with a tortfeasor. Indeed, the fact that Congress did specifically provide that A's tort became B's liability if B "caused" A to subject another to a tort suggests that Congress did not intend § 1983 liability to attach where such causation was absent.[57] See *Rizzo v. Goode*, 423 U.S. 362, 370-371 (1976). [436 U.S. 658, 693]

Equally important, creation of a federal law of *respondeat superior* would have raised all the constitutional problems associated with the obligation to keep the peace, an obligation Congress chose not to impose because it thought imposition of such an obligation unconstitutional. To this day, there is disagreement about the basis for imposing liability on an employer for the torts of an employee when the sole nexus between the employer and the tort is the fact of the employer-employee relationship. See W. Prosser, Law of Torts § 69, p. 459 (4th ed. 1971). Nonetheless, two justifications tend to stand out. First is the common-sense notion that no matter how blameless an employer appears to be in an individual case, accidents might nonetheless be reduced if employers had to bear the cost of accidents. See, *e.g., ibid.*; 2 F. Harper & F. James, Law of Torts, § 26.3, pp. 1368-1369 (1956). Second is the argument that the cost of accidents should be [436 U.S. 658, 694] spread to the community as a whole on an insurance theory. See, *e.g., id.*, 26.5; Prosser, *supra*, at 459.[58]

The first justification is of the same sort that was offered for statutes like the Sherman amendment: "The obligation to make compensation for injury resulting from riot is, by arbitrary enactment of statutes, affirmatory law, and the reason of passing the statute is to secure a more perfect police regulation." Globe 777 (Sen. Frelinghuysen). This justification was obviously insufficient to sustain the amendment against perceived constitutional difficulties and there is no reason to suppose that a more general liability imposed for a similar reason would have been thought less constitutionally objectionable. The second justification was similarly put forward as a justification for the Sherman amendment: "we do not look upon [the Sherman amendment] as a punishment . . . . It is a mutual insurance." *Id.*, at 792 (Rep. Butler). Again, this justification was insufficient to sustain the amendment.

We conclude, therefore, that a local government may not be sued under § 1983 for an injury inflicted solely by its employees or agents. Instead, it is when execution of a government's policy or custom, whether made by its lawmakers or by those whose edicts or acts may fairly be said to represent official policy, inflicts the injury that the government as an entity is responsible under § 1983. Since this case unquestionably involves official policy as the moving force of the constitutional violation found by the District Court, see *supra*, at [436 U.S. 658, 695] 660-662, and n. 2, we must reverse the judgment below. In so doing, we have no occasion to address, and do not address, what the full contours of municipal liability under § 1983 may be. We have attempted only to sketch so much of the § 1983 cause of action against a local government as is apparent from the history of the 1871 Act and our prior cases, and we expressly leave further development of this action to another day.

III

Although we have stated that *stare decisis* has more force in statutory analysis than in constitutional adjudication because, in the former situation, Congress can correct our mistakes through legislation, see, *e.g., Edelman v. Jordan*, 415 U.S. 651, 671, and n. 14 (1974), we have never applied *stare decisis* mechanically to prohibit overruling our earlier decisions determining the meaning of statutes. See, *e.g., Continental T. V., Inc. v. GTE Sylvania Inc.*, 433 U.S. 36, 47-49 (1977); *Burnet v. Coronado Oil & Gas Co.*, 285 U.S. 393, 406 n. 1 (1932) (Brandeis, J., dissenting) (collecting cases). Nor is this a case where we should "place on the shoulders of Congress the burden of the Court's own error." *Girouard v. United States*, 328 U.S. 61, 70 (1946).

First, *Monroe v. Pape*, insofar as it completely immunizes municipalities from suit under § 1983, was a departure from prior practice. See, *e.g., Northwestern Fertilizing Co. v. Hyde Park*, 18 F. Cas. 393 (No. 10,336) (CC ND Ill. 1873); *City of Manchester v. Leiby*, 117 F.2d 661 (CA1 1941); *Hannan v. City of Haverhill*, 120 F.2d 87 (CA1 1941); *Douglas v. City of Jeannette*, 319 U.S. 157 (1943); *Holmes v. Atlanta*, 350 U.S. 879 (1955), in each of which municipalities were defendants in § 1983 suits.[59] Moreover, the constitutional defect [436 U.S. 658, 696] that led to the rejection of the Sherman amendment would not have distinguished between municipalities and school boards, each of which is an instrumentality of state administration. See *supra*, at 673-682. For this reason, our cases—decided both before and after *Monroe*, see n. 5, *supra*—holding school boards liable in 1983 actions are inconsistent with *Monroe*, especially as *Monroe*'s immunizing principle was extended to suits for injunctive relief in *City of Kenosha v. Bruno*, 412 U.S. 507 (1973).[60] And although in many of these cases jurisdiction was not questioned, we ought not "disregard the implications of an exercise of judicial authority assumed to be proper for 100 years." *Brown Shoe Co. v. United States*, 370 U.S. 294, 307 (1962); see *Bank of the United States v. Deveaux*, 5 Cranch, at 88 (Marshall, C. J.) ("Those decisions are not cited as authority . . . but they have much weight, as they show that this point neither occurred to the bar or the bench"). Thus, while we have reaffirmed *Monroe* without further examination on three occasions,[61] it can scarcely be said that *Monroe* is so consistent with the warp and woof of civil rights law as to be beyond question.

Second, the principle of blanket immunity established in *Monroe* cannot be cabined short of school boards. Yet such an extension would itself be inconsistent with recent expressions of congressional intent. In the wake of our decisions, Congress not only has shown no hostility to federal-court decisions against school boards, but it has indeed rejected efforts to strip the federal courts of jurisdiction over school boards.[62] Moreover, recognizing that school boards are often [436 U.S. 658, 697] defendants in school desegregation suits, which have almost without exception been § 1983 suits, Congress has twice passed legislation authorizing grants to school boards to assist them in complying with federal-court decrees.[63] Finally, in [436 U.S. 658, 698] regard to the Civil Rights Attorney's Fees Awards Act of 1976, 90 Stat. 2641, 42 U.S.C. § 1988 (1976 ed.), which allows prevailing parties (in the discretion of the court) in § 1983 suits [436 U.S. 658, 699] to obtain attorney's fees from the losing parties, the Senate stated:

> "[D]efendants in these cases are often State or local bodies or State or local officials. In such cases it is intended that the attorney's fees, like other items of costs, will be collected either directly from the official, *in his official capacity*, from funds of his agency or under his control, or *from the State or local government (whether or not the agency or government is a named party)*." S. Rep. No. 94-1011, p. 5 (1976) (emphasis added; footnotes omitted).

Far from showing that Congress has relied on *Monroe*, therefore, events since 1961 show that Congress has refused to extend the benefits of *Monroe* to school boards and has attempted to allow awards of attorney's fees against local governments even though *Monroe, City of Kenosha v. Bruno*, and *Aldinger v. Howard*, 427 U.S. 1 (1976), have made the joinder of such governments impossible.[64]

Third, municipalities can assert no reliance claim which can [436 U.S. 658, 700] support an absolute immunity. As Mr. Justice Frankfurter said in *Monroe*, "[t]his is not an area of commercial law in which, presumably, individuals may have arranged their affairs in reliance on the expected stability of decision." 365 U.S., at 221-222 (dissenting in part). Indeed, municipalities simply cannot "arrange their affairs" on an assumption that they can violate constitutional rights indefinitely since injunctive suits against local officials under § 1983 would prohibit any such arrangement. And it scarcely need be mentioned that nothing in *Monroe* encourages municipalities to violate constitutional rights or even suggests that such violations are anything other than completely wrong.

Finally, even under the most stringent test for the propriety of overruling a statutory decision proposed by Mr. Justice Harlan in *Monroe*[65]—"that it appear beyond doubt from the legislative history of the 1871 statute that [*Monroe*] misapprehended the meaning of the [section]," 365 U.S., at 192 (concurring opinion)—the overruling of *Monroe* insofar as it holds that local governments are not "persons" who may be defendants in § 1983 suits is clearly proper. It is simply beyond doubt that, under the 1871 Congress' view of the law, were § 1983 liability unconstitutional as to local governments, it would have been equally unconstitutional as to state officers. Yet everyone—proponents and opponents alike—knew § 1983 would be applied to state officers and nonetheless stated that § 1983 was constitutional. See *supra*, at 680-682. And, moreover, there can be no doubt that § 1 of the Civil Rights Act was intended to provide a remedy, to be broadly construed, against all forms of official violation of federally protected [436 U.S. 658, 701] rights. Therefore, absent a clear statement in the legislative history supporting the conclusion that § 1 was not to apply to the official acts of a municipal corporation—which simply is not present— there is no justification for excluding municipalities from the "persons" covered by § 1.

For the reasons stated above, therefore, we hold that *stare decisis* does not bar our overruling of *Monroe* insofar as it is inconsistent with Parts I and II of this opinion.[66]

IV

Since the question whether local government bodies should be afforded some form of official immunity was not presented as a question to be decided on this petition and was not briefed by the parties or addressed by the courts below, we express no views on the scope of any municipal immunity beyond holding that municipal bodies sued under § 1983 cannot be entitled to an absolute immunity, lest our decision that such bodies are subject to suit under § 1983 "be drained of meaning," *Scheuer v. Rhodes*, 416 U.S. 232, 248 (1974). Cf. *Bivens v. Six Unknown Fed. Narcotics Agents*, 403 U.S. 388, 397-398 (1971). [436 U.S. 658, 702]

V

For the reasons stated above, the judgment of the Court of Appeals is
Reversed.

Footnotes

[1] The complaint was amended on September 14, 1972, to allege a claim under Title VII of the Civil Rights Act of 1964, 78 Stat. 253, as amended, 42 U.S.C. § 2000e *et seq.* (1970 ed. and Supp. V). The District Court held that the 1972 amendments to Title VII did not apply retroactively to [436 U.S. 658, 661] discrimination suffered prior to those amendments even when an action challenging such prior discrimination was pending on the date of the amendments. 394 F. Supp. 853, 856 (SDNY 1975). This holding was affirmed on appeal. 532 F.2d 259, 261-262 (CA2 1976). Although petitioners sought certiorari on the Title VII issue as well as the § 1983 claim, we restricted our grant of certiorari to the latter issue. 429 U.S. 1071.

[2] The plaintiffs alleged that New York had a citywide policy of forcing women to take maternity leave after the fifth month of pregnancy unless a city physician and

the head of an employee's agency allowed up to an additional two months of work. Amended Complaint ¶ 28, App. 13-14. The defendants did not deny this, but stated that this policy had been changed after suit was instituted. Answer ¶ 13, App. 32-33. The plaintiffs further alleged that the Board had a policy of requiring women to take maternity leave after the seventh month of pregnancy unless that month fell in the last month of the school year, in which case the teacher could remain through the end of the school term. Amended Complaint ¶¶ 39, 42, 45, App. 18-19, 21. This allegation was denied. Answer ¶¶ 18, 22, App. 35, 37.

³ Amended Complaint ¶ 24, App. 11-12.

⁴ Petitioners conceded that the Department of Social Services enjoys the same status as New York City for *Monell* purposes. See 532 F.2d, at 263.

⁵ *Milliken v. Bradley*, 433 U.S. 267 (1977); *Dayton Board of Education v. Brinkman*, 433 U.S. 406 (1977); *Vorchheimer v. School District of Philadelphia*, 430 U.S. 703 (1977); *East Carroll Parish School Board v. Marshall*, 424 U.S. 636 (1976); *Milliken v. Bradley*, 418 U.S. 717 (1974); *Bradley v. Richmond School Board*, 416 U.S. 696 (1974); *Cleveland Board of Education v. LaFleur*, 414 U.S. 632 (1974); *Keyes v. School District No. 1, Denver, Colo.*, 413 U.S. 189 (1973); *San Antonio School District v. Rodriguez*, 411 U.S. 1 (1973); *Swann v. Charlotte-Mecklenburg Board of Education*, 402 U.S. 1 (1971); *Northcross v. Memphis Board of Education*, 397 U.S. 232 (1970); *Carter v. West Feliciana Parish School Board*, 396 U.S. 226 (1969); *Alexander v. Holmes County Board of Education*, 396 U.S. 19 (1969); *Kramer v. Union Free School District*, 395 U.S. 621 (1969); *Tinker v. Des Moines Independent School District*, 393 U.S. 503 (1969); *Monroe v. Board of Comm'rs*, 391 U.S. 450 (1968); *Raney v. Board of Education*, 391 U.S. 443 (1968); *Green v. New Kent County School Board*, 391 U.S. 430 (1968); *Abington School District v. Schempp*, 374 U.S. 203 (1963); *Goss v. Board of Education*, 373 U.S. 683 (1963); *McNeese v. Board of Education*, 373 U.S. 668 (1963); *Orleans Parish School Board v. Bush*, 365 U.S. 569 (1961); *Brown v. Board of Education*, 347 U.S. 483 (1954).

⁶ *Cleveland Board of Education v. LaFleur, supra*, at 636; App. in *Keyes v. School District No. 1, Denver, Colo.*, O. T. 1972, No. 71-507, p. 4a; App. in *Swann v. Charlotte-Mecklenburg Board of Education*, O. T. 1970, No. 281, p. 465a; Pet. for Cert. in *Northcross v. Memphis Board of Education*, O. T. 1969, No. 1136, p. 3; *Tinker v. Des Moines Independent School District, supra*, at 504; *McNeese v. Board of Education, supra*, at 671.

⁷ However, we do uphold *Monroe v. Pape* insofar as it holds that the doctrine of *respondeat superior* is not a basis for rendering municipalities [436 U.S. 658, 664] liable under § 1983 for the constitutional torts of their employees. See Part II, *infra*.

⁸ We expressly declined to consider "policy considerations" for or against municipal liability. See 365 U.S., at 191.

⁹ Mr. Justice Douglas, the author of *Monroe*, has suggested that the municipal exclusion might more properly rest on a theory that Congress sought to prevent the financial ruin that civil rights liability might impose on municipalities. See *City of Kenosha v. Bruno*, 412 U.S. 507, [436 U.S. 658, 665] 517-520 (1973). However, this view has never been shared by the Court, see *Monroe v. Pape*, 365 U.S., at 190; *Moor v. County of Alameda*, 411 U.S. 693, 708 (1973), and the debates do not support this position.

¹⁰ Globe 522.

¹¹ Briefly, § 2 created certain federal crimes in addition to those defined in § 2 of the 1866 Civil Rights Act, 14 Stat. 27, each aimed primarily at the Ku Klux Klan. Section 3 provided that the President could send the militia into any State wracked with Klan violence. Finally, § 4 provided for suspension of the writ of habeas corpus in enumerated circumstances, again primarily those thought to obtain where Klan violence was rampant. See Cong. Globe, 42d Cong., 1st Sess., App. 335-336 (1871) (hereinafter Globe App.).

¹² Globe 709.

[13] See *id.*, at 663, quoted in Appendix to this opinion, *infra*, at 702-703.

[14] *Ibid.* An action for recovery of damages was to be in the federal courts and denominated as a suit against the county, city, or parish in which the damage had occurred. *Ibid.* Execution of the judgment was not to run against the property of the government unit, however, but against the private property of any inhabitant. *Ibid.*

[15] See Globe 749 and 755, quoted in Appendix to this opinion, *infra*, at 703-704.

[16] "Let the people of property in the southern States understand that if they will not make the hue and cry and take the necessary steps to put down lawless violence in those States their property will be holden responsible, and the effect will be most wholesome." Globe 761.

Senator Sherman was apparently unconcerned that the conference committee substitute, unlike the original amendment, did not place liability for riot damage directly on the property of the well-to-do, but instead placed it on the local government. Presumably he assumed that taxes would be levied against the property of the inhabitants to make the locality whole.

[17] According to Senator Sherman, the law had originally been adopted in England immediately after the Norman Conquest and had most recently been promulgated as the law of 7 & 8 Geo. 4, ch. 31 (1827). See Globe [436 U.S. 658, 668] 760. During the course of the debates, it appeared that Kentucky, Maryland, Massachusetts, and New York had similar laws. See *id.*, at 751 (Rep. Shellabarger); *id.*, at 762 (Sen. Stevenson); *id.*, at 771 (Sen. Thurman); *id.*, at 792 (Rep. Butler). Such a municipal liability was apparently common throughout New England. See *id.*, at 761 (Sen. Sherman).

[18] In the Senate, opponents, including a number of Senators who had voted for § 1 of the bill, criticized the Sherman amendment as an imperfect and impolitic rendering of the state statutes. Moreover, as drafter, the conference substitute could be construed to protect rights that were not protected by the Constitution. A complete critique was given by Senator Thurman. See Globe 770-772.

[19] See 365 U.S., at 190, quoted *supra*, at 664.

[20] See Globe 804, quoted in Appendix to this opinion, *infra*, at 704.

[21] See Globe 758 (Sen. Trumbull); *id.*, at 772 (Sen. Thurman); *id.*, at 791 (Rep. Willard). The Supreme Court of Indiana had so held in giving effect to the Civil Rights Act of 1866. See *Smith v. Moody*, 26 Ind. 299 (1866) (following Coryell), one of three State Supreme Court cases referred to in Globe App. 68 (Rep. Shellabarger). Moreover, § 2 of the 1871 Act as passed, unlike § 1, prosecuted persons who violated federal rights whether or not that violation was under color of official authority, apparently on the theory that Ku Klux Klan violence was infringing the right of protection defined by *Coryell.* Nonetheless, opponents argued that municipalities were not generally charged by the States with keeping [436 U.S. 658, 671] the peace and hence did not have police forces, so that the duty to afford protection ought not devolve on the municipality, but on whatever agency of state government was charged by the State with keeping the peace. See *infra*, at 673, and n. 30. In addition, they argued that Congress could not constitutionally add to the duties of municipalities. See *infra*, at 673-678.

[22] U.S. Const., Art. IV, 2, cl. 2:

> "A Person charged in any State with Treason, Felony, or other Crime, who shall flee from Justice, and be found in another State, shall on Demand of the executive Authority of the State from which he fled, be delivered up, to be removed to the State having Jurisdiction of the Crime."

[23] *Id.*, cl. 3:

> "No Person held to Service or Labor in one State, under the Laws thereof, escaping into another, shall, in Consequence of any Law or Regulation therein, be discharged from such Service or Labour, but shall be delivered up on Claim of the Party to whom such Service or Labour may be due."

[24] *Id.*, cl. 1.

[25] See Globe 751. See also *id.*, at 760 (Sen. Sherman) ("If a State may . . . pass a law making a county . . . responsible for a riot in order to deter such crime, then we may pass the same remedies . . .").

[26] *Id.*, at 751; see n. 17, *supra.*

[27] Globe 751 (emphasis added). Compare this statement with Representative Poland's remark upon which our holding in *Monroe* was based. See *supra,* at 664.

[28] See, *e.g., Gelpcke v. Dubuque,* 1 Wall. 175 (1864); *Von Hoffman v. City of Quincy,* 4 Wall. 535 (1867); *Riggs v. Johnson County,* 6 Wall. 166 (1868); *Weber v. Lee County,* 6 Wall. 210 (1868); *Supervisors v. Rogers,* 7 Wall. 175 (1869); *Benbow v. Iowa City,* 7 Wall. 313 (1869); *Supervisors v. Durant,* 9 Wall. 415 (1870). See generally 6 C. Fairman, History of the Supreme Court of the United States: Reconstruction and Reunion, 1864-1888, chs. 17-18 (1971).

[29] See Globe 751-752.

[30] Others taking a view similar to Representative Blair's included: Representative Willard, see *id.*, at 791; Representative Poland, see *id.*, at 794; Representative Burchard, see *id.*, at 795; Representative Farnsworth, see *id.*, at 799. Representative Willard also took a somewhat different position: He thought that the Constitution would not allow the Federal [436 U.S. 658, 674] Government to dictate the manner in which a State fulfilled its obligation of protection. That is, he thought it a matter of state discretion whether it delegated the peacekeeping power to a municipal or county corporation, to a sheriff, etc. He did not doubt, however, that the Federal Government could impose on the States the obligation imposed by the Sherman amendment, and presumably he would have enforced the amendment against a municipal corporation to which the peacekeeping obligation had been delegated. See *id.*, at 791.

Opponents of the Sherman amendment in the Senate agreed with Blair that Congress had no power to pass the Sherman amendment because it fell outside limits on national power implicit in the federal structure of the Constitution and recognized in, *e.g., Collector v. Day,* 11 Wall. 113 (1871). However, the Senate opponents focused not on the amendment's attempt to obligate municipalities to keep the peace, but on the lien created by the amendment, which ran against all money and property of a defendant municipality, including property held for public purposes, such as jails or courthouses. Opponents argued that such a lien once entered would have the effect of making it impossible for the municipality to function, since no one would trade with it. See, *e.g.,* Globe 762 (Sen. Stevenson); *id.*, at 763 (Sen. Casserly). Moreover, everyone knew that sound policy prevented execution against public property since this, too, was needed if local government was to survive. See, *e.g., ibid.* See also *Meriwether v. Garrett,* 102 U.S. 472, 501, 513 (1880) (recognizing principle that public property of a municipality was not subject to execution); 2 J. Dillon, The Law of Municipal Corporations §§ 445-446 (1873 ed.) (same).

Although the arguments of the Senate opponents appear to be a correct analysis of then-controlling constitutional and common-law principles, their arguments are not relevant to an analysis of the constitutionality of 1 of the Civil Rights Act since any judgment under that section, as in any civil suit in the federal courts in 1871, would have been enforced pursuant to state laws under the Process Acts of 1792 and 1828. See Act of May 8, 1792, ch. 36, 1 Stat. 275; Act of May 19, 1828, 4 Stat. 278.

[31] See n. 30, *supra.*

[32] In addition to the cases discussed in the text, see *Lane County v.* [436 U.S. 658, 677] *Oregon,* 7 Wall. 71, 77, 81 (1869), in which the Court held that the federal Legal Tender Acts should not be construed to require the States to accept taxes tendered in United States notes since this might interfere with a legitimate state activity.

[33] Mr. Chief Justice Taney agreed:

"The state officers mentioned in the law [of 1793] are not bound to execute the duties imposed upon them by Congress, unless they choose to do so, or are required to do so by a law of the state; and the state legislature has the power, if it thinks proper, to prohibit them. The act of 1793, therefore, must depend altogether for its execution upon the officers of the United States named in it." 16 Pet., at 630 (concurring in part).

[34] See *supra*, at 670, and n. 21.

[35] "*Be it enacted* . . . That whenever the executive authority of any state in the Union . . . shall demand any person as a fugitive from justice . . . and shall moreover produce the copy of an indictment found . . . charging the person so demanded, with having committed treason, felony or other crime, certified as authentic by the governor or chief magistrate of the state . . . from whence the person so charged fled, it shall be the duty of the executive authority of the state or territory to which such person shall have fled, to cause him or her to be arrested and secured . . . and to cause the fugitive to be delivered to such agent [of the demanding State] when he shall appear . . . ." 1 Stat. 302.

[36] "The Supreme Court of the United States has decided repeatedly that Congress can impose no duty on a State officer." Globe 799 (Rep. Farnsworth). See also *id.*, at 788-789 (Rep. Kerr).

[37] See, *e.g.*, *id.*, at 764 (Sen. Davis); *ibid.* (Sen. Casserly); *id.*, at 772 (Sen. Thurman) (reciting logic of *Day*); *id.*, at 777 (Sen. Frelinghuysen); *id.*, at 788-789 (Rep. Kerr) (reciting logic of *Day*); *id.*, at 793 (Rep. Poland); *id.*, at 799 (Rep. Farnsworth) (also reciting logic of *Day*).

[38] *Warren v. Paul*, 22 Ind. 276 (1864); *Jones v. Estate of Keep*, 19 Wis. 369 (1865); *Fifield v. Close*, 15 Mich. 505 (1867); *Union Bank v. Hill*, 43 Tenn. 325 (1866); *Smith v. Short*, 40 Ala. 385 (1867).

[39] See Globe 764 (Sen. Davis); *ibid.* (Sen. Casserly). See also T. Cooley, Constitutional Limitations *483-*484 (1871 ed.).

[40] See cases cited in n. 28, *supra*. Since this Court granted unquestionably "positive" relief in Contract Clause cases, it appears that the distinction between the Sherman amendment and those cases was not that the former created a positive obligation whereas the latter imposed only a negative restraint. Instead, the distinction must have been that a violation of the Constitution was the predicate for "positive" relief in the Contract Clause cases, whereas the Sherman amendment imposed damages without regard to whether a local government was in any way at fault for the breach of the peace for which it was to be held for damages. See *supra*, at 668. While no one stated this distinction expressly during the debates, the inference is strong that Congressmen in 1871 would have drawn this distinction since it explains why Representatives Poland, Burchard, and Willard, see *supra*, at 680, could oppose the amendment while at the same time saying that the Federal Government might impose damages on a local government that had defaulted in a state-imposed duty to keep the peace, and it also explains why everyone agreed that a state or municipal officer could constitutionally be held liable under 1 for violations of the Constitution. See *infra*, at 682-683.

[41] See, *e.g.*, Globe 334 (Rep. Hoar); *id.*, at 365 (Rep. Arthur); *id.*, at 367-368 (Rep. Sheldon); *id.*, at 385 (Rep. Lewis); Globe App. 217 (Sen. Thurman). In addition, officers were included among those who could be sued under the second conference substitute for the Sherman amendment. See Globe 805 (exchange between Rep. Willard and Rep. Shellabarger). There were no constitutional objections to the second report.

[42] See *id.*, at 795 (Rep. Blair); *id.*, at 788 (Rep. Kerr); *id.*, at 795 (Rep. Burchard); *id.*, at 799 (Rep. Farnsworth).

[43] "[W]e cannot command a State officer to do any duty whatever, as such; and I ask . . . the difference between that and commanding a municipality . . . ." *Id.*, at 795.

[44] See Globe App. 216-217, quoted in n. 45, infra. In 1880, moreover, when the question of the limits of the Prigg principle was squarely presented in *Ex parte Virginia*, 100 U.S. 339, this Court held that *Dennison* and *Day* and the principle of federalism for which they stand did not prohibit federal enforcement of § 5 of the Fourteenth Amendment through suits directed to state officers. See 100 U.S., at 345-348.

[45] Representative Bingham, the author of § 1 of the Fourteenth Amendment, for example, declared the bill's purpose to be "the enforcement . . . of the Constitution on behalf of every individual citizen of the Republic . . . to the extent of the rights guarantied to him by the Constitution." Globe App. 81. He continued:

> "The States never had the right, though they had the power, to inflict wrongs upon free citizens by a denial of the full protection of the laws . . . . [And] the States did deny to citizens the equal protection of the laws, they did deny the rights of citizens under the Constitution, and except to the extent of the express limitations upon the States, as I have shown, the citizen had no remedy . . . . They took property without compensation, and he had no remedy. They restricted the freedom of the press, and he had no remedy. They restricted the freedom of speech, and he had no remedy. They restricted the rights of conscience, and he had no remedy. . . . Who dare say, now that the Constitution has been amended, that the nation cannot by law provide against all such abuses and denials of right as these in the States and by States, or combinations of persons?" *Id.*, at 85.

Representative Perry, commenting on Congress' action in passing the civil rights bill also stated:

> "Now, by our action on this bill we have asserted as fully as we can assert the mischief intended to be remedied. We have asserted as clearly as we can assert our belief that it is the duty of Congress to redress that mischief. We have also asserted as fully as we can assert the constitutional right of Congress to legislate." Globe 800.

See also *id.*, at 376 (Rep. Lowe); *id.*, at 428-429 (Rep. Beatty); *id.*, at 448 (Rep. Butler); *id.*, at 475-477 (Rep. Dawes); *id.*, at 578-579 (Sen. Trumbull); *id.*, at 609 (Sen. Pool); Globe App. 182 (Rep. Mercur).

Other supporters were quite clear that § 1 of the Act extended a remedy not only where a State had passed an unconstitutional statute, but also [436 U.S. 658, 686] where officers of the State were deliberately indifferent to the rights of black citizens:

> "But the chief complaint is . . . [that] by a systematic maladministration of [state law], or a neglect or refusal to enforce their provisions, a portion of the people are denied equal protection under them. Whenever such a state of facts is clearly made out, I believe [§ 5 of the Fourteenth Amendment] empowers Congress to step in and provide for doing justice to those persons who are thus denied equal protection." *Id.*, at 153 (Rep. Garfield). See also *Monroe v. Pape*, 365 U.S., at 171-187.

Importantly for our inquiry, even the opponents of § 1 agreed that it was constitutional and, further, that it swept very broadly. Thus, Senator Thurman, who gave the most exhaustive critique of § 1, said:

> "This section relates wholly to civil suits. . . . Its whole effect is to give to the Federal Judiciary that which now does not belong to it—*a jurisdiction that may be constitutionally conferred upon it, I grant*, but that has never yet been conferred upon it. It authorizes any person who is deprived of any right, privilege, or immunity secured to him by the Constitution of the United States, to bring an action against the wrong-doer in the Federal courts, and that without any limit whatsoever as to the amount in controversy. . . .

"*[T]here is no limitation whatsoever upon the terms that are employed [in the bill], and they are as comprehensive as can be used.*" Globe App. 216-217 (emphasis added).

[46] See 2 J. Story, Commentaries on the Constitution of the United States § 1956 (T. Cooley ed. 1873).

[47] Indeed the federal courts found no obstacle to awards of damages against municipalities for common-law takings. See *Sumner v. Philadelphia*, 23 F. Cas. 392 (No. 13,611) (CC ED Pa. 1873) (awarding damages of $2,273.36 and costs of $346.35 against the city of Philadelphia).

[48] Nonetheless, suits could be brought in federal court if the natural persons who were members of the corporation were of diverse citizenship from the other parties to the litigation. See 5 Cranch, at 91.

[49] See n. 28, *supra.*

[50] See, *e.g.*, Globe 777 (Sen. Sherman); *id.*, at 752 (Rep. Shellabarger) ("[C]ounties, cities, and corporations of all sorts, after years of judicial conflict, have become thoroughly established to be an individual or person or entity of the personal existence, of which, as a citizen, individual, or inhabitant, the United States Constitution does take note and endow with faculty to sue and be sued in the courts of the United States").

[51] See *Northwestern Fertilizing Co. v. Hyde Park*, 18 F. Cas. 393, 394 (No. 10,336) (CC ND Ill. 1873); 2 J. Kent, Commentaries on American Law *278-*279 (12th O. W. Holmes ed. 1873). See also *United States v. Maurice*, 2 Brock. 96, 109 (CC Va. 1823) (Marshall, C. J.) ("The United States is a government, and, consequently, a body politic and corporate"); Apps. D and E to Brief for Petitioners in *Monroe v. Pape*, O. T. 1960, [436 U.S. 658, 689] No. 39 (collecting state statutes which, in 1871, defined municipal corporations as bodies politic and corporate).

[52] The court also noted that there was no discernible reason why persons injured by municipal corporations should not be able to recover. See 18 F. Cas., at 394.

[53] In considering the effect of the Act of Feb. 25, 1871, in *Monroe*, however, Mr. Justice Douglas, apparently focusing on the word "may," stated: "[T]his definition [of person] is merely an allowable, not a mandatory, one." 365 U.S., at 191. A review of the legislative history of the Dictionary Act shows this conclusion to be incorrect. There is no express reference in the legislative history to the definition of "person," but Senator Trumbull, the Act's sponsor, discussed the phrase "words importing the masculine gender *may* be applied to females," (emphasis added), which immediately precedes the definition of "person," and stated:

"The only object [of the Act] is to get rid of a great deal of verbosity in our statutes by providing that when the word 'he' is used it *shall* include females as well as males." Cong. Globe, 41st Cong., 3d Sess., 775 (1871) (emphasis added).

Thus, in Trumbull's view the word "may" meant "shall." Such a mandatory use of the extended meanings of the words defined by the Act is also required for it to perform its intended function—to be a guide to "rules of construction" of Acts of Congress. See *ibid.* (remarks of Sen. Trumbull). Were the defined words "allowable, [but] not mandatory" constructions, as *Monroe* suggests, there would be no "rules" at all. Instead, Congress must have intended the definitions of the Act to apply across-the-board except where the Act by its terms called for a deviation from this practice—"[where] the context shows that [defined] words were to be used in a more limited sense." Certainly this is how the *Northwestern Fertilizing* court viewed the matter. Since there is nothing in the "context" of § 1 of the Civil Rights Act calling for a restricted [436 U.S. 658, 690] interpretation of the word "person," the language of that section should prima facie be construed to include "bodies politic" among the entities that could be sued.

[54] There is certainly no constitutional impediment to municipal liability. "The Tenth Amendment's reservation of nondelegated powers to the States is not implicated by a federal-court judgment enforcing the express prohibitions of unlawful state conduct enacted by the Fourteenth Amendment." *Milliken v. Bradley*, 433 U.S. 267, 291 (1977); see Ex parte Virginia, 100 U.S., at 347-348. For this reason, *National League of Cities v. Usery*, 426 U.S. 833 (1976), is irrelevant to our consideration of this case. Nor is there any basis for concluding that the Eleventh Amendment is a bar to municipal liability. See, *e.g., Fitzpatrick v. Bitzer*, 427 U.S. 445, 456 (1976); *Lincoln County v. Luning*, 133 U.S. 529, 530 (1890). Our holding today is, of course, limited to local government units, which are not considered part of the State for Eleventh Amendment purposes.

[55] Since official-capacity suits generally represent only another way of pleading an action against an entity of which an officer is an agent—at least where Eleventh Amendment considerations do not control analysis—our holding today that local governments can be sued under § 1983 necessarily decides that local government officials sued in their official capacities are "persons" under § 1983 in those cases in which, as here, a local government would be suable in its own name.

[56] See also Mr. Justice Frankfurter's statement for the *Court in Nashville, C. & St. L. R. Co. v. Browning*, 310 U.S. 362, 369 (1940):

> "It would be a narrow conception of jurisprudence to confine the notion of 'laws' to what is found written on the statute books, and to disregard the gloss which life has written upon it. Settled state practice . . . can establish what is state law. The Equal Protection Clause did not write an empty formalism into the Constitution. Deeply embedded traditional ways of carrying out state policy, such as those of which petitioner complains, are often tougher and truer law than the dead words of the written text."

[57] Support for such a conclusion can be found in the legislative history. As we have indicated, there is virtually no discussion of § 1 of the Civil Rights Act. Again, however, Congress' treatment of the Sherman amendment gives a clue to whether it would have desired to impose *respondeat superior* liability.

The primary constitutional justification for the Sherman amendment was that it was a necessary and proper remedy for the failure of localities to protect citizens as the Privileges or Immunities Clause of the Fourteenth Amendment required. See *supra*, at 670-673. And according to Sherman, Shellabarger, and Edmunds, the amendment came into play only when a locality was at fault or had knowingly neglected its duty to provide protection. See Globe 761 (Sen. Sherman); *id.*, at 756 (Sen. Edmunds); *id.*, at 751-752 (Rep. Shellabarger). But other proponents of the amendment apparently viewed it as a form of vicarious liability for the unlawful acts of the citizens of the locality. See *id.*, at 792 (Rep. Butler). And whether intended or not, the amendment as drafted did impose a species of vicarious liability on municipalities since it could be construed to impose liability even if a municipality did not know of an impending or ensuing riot or did not have the wherewithal to do anything about it. Indeed, the amendment held a municipality liable even if it had done everything in its [436 U.S. 658, 693] power to curb the riot. See *supra*, at 668; Globe 761 (Sen. Stevenson); *id.*, at 771 (Sen. Thurman); *id.*, at 788 (Rep. Kerr); *id.*, at 791 (Rep. Willard). While the first conference substitute was rejected principally on constitutional grounds, see *id.*, at 804 (Rep. Poland), it is plain from the text of the second conference substitute—which limited liability to those who, having the power to intervene against Ku Klux Klan violence, "neglect[ed] or refuse[d] so to do," see Appendix to this opinion, infra, at 704, and which was enacted as § 6 of the 1871 Act and is now codified as 42 U.S.C. § 1986— that Congress also rejected those elements of vicarious liability contained in the first conference substitute even while accepting the basic principle that the inhabitants of a community were bound to provide protection against the Ku Klux Klan. Strictly speaking, of course, the fact that Congress refused to impose vicarious liability for the wrongs of a few private citizens does not conclusively establish that it would similarly have refused to impose vicarious liability for the torts of a municipality's employees. Nonetheless, when Congress' rejection of the only form of vicarious liability presented to it is combined with the absence of any language in § 1983 which can easily be construed to create *respondeat superior* liability, the inference that Congress did not intend to impose such liability is quite strong.

[58] A third justification, often cited but which on examination is apparently insufficient to justify the doctrine of *respondeat superior*, see, *e.g.*, 2 F. Harper & F. James, § 26.3, is that liability follows the right to control the actions of a tortfeasor. By our decision in *Rizzo v. Goode*, 423 U.S. 362 (1976), we would appear to have decided that the mere right to control without any control or direction having been exercised and without any failure to supervise is not enough to support § 1983 liability. See 423 U.S., at 370-371.

[59] Each case cited by *Monroe*, see 365 U.S., at 191 n. 50, as consistent with the position that local governments were not § 1983 "persons" reached its conclusion by assuming that state-law immunities overrode the § 1983 cause of action. This has never been the law.

[60] Although many suits against school boards also include private individuals as parties, the "principal defendant is usually the local board of education or school board." *Milliken v. Bradley*, 433 U.S., at 292-293 (POWELL, J., concurring in judgment).

[61] *Moor v. County of Alameda*, 411 U.S. 693 (1973); *City of Kenosha v. Bruno*, 412 U.S. 507 (1973); *Aldinger v. Howard*, 427 U.S. 1 (1976).

[62] During the heyday of the furor over busing, both the House and the [436 U.S. 658, 697] Senate refused to adopt bills that would have removed from the federal courts jurisdiction.

> "to make any decision, enter any judgment, or issue any order requiring any *school board* to make any change in the racial composition of the student body at any public school or in any class at any public school to which students are assigned in conformity with a freedom of choice system, or requiring any *school board* to transport any students from one public school to another public school or from one place to another place or from one school district to another school district in order to effect a change in the racial composition of the student body at any school or place or in any school district, or denying to any student the right or privilege of attending any public school or class at any public school chosen by the parent of such student in conformity with a freedom of choice system, or requiring any *school board* to close any school and transfer the students from the closed school to any other school for the purpose of altering the racial composition of the student body at any public school, or precluding any *school board* from carrying into effect any provision of any contract between it and any member of the faculty of any public school it operates specifying the public school where the member of the faculty is to perform his or her duties under the contract." § 1737, 93d Cong., 1st Sess., § 1207 (1973) (emphasis added).

Other bills designed either completely to remove the federal courts from the school desegregation controversy, S. 287, 93d Cong., 1st Sess. (1973), or to limit the ability of federal courts to subject school boards to remedial orders in desegregation cases, S. 619, 93d Cong., 1st Sess. (1973); S. 179, 93d Cong., 1st Sess., § 2 (a) (1973); H. R. 13534, 92d Cong., 2d Sess., § 1 (1972), have similarly failed.

[63] In 1972, spurred by a finding "that the process of eliminating or preventing minority group isolation and improving the quality of education for all children often

involves the expenditure of additional funds to which local educational agencies do not have access," 86 Stat. 354, 20 U.S.C. § 1601 (a) (1976 ed.), Congress passed the Emergency School Aid Act. Section 706 (a) (1) (A) (i) of that Act, 20 U.S.C. § 1605 (a) (1) (A) (i) (1976 ed.), authorizes the Assistant Secretary.

> "*to make a grant to, or a contract with, a local educational agency [w]hich is implementing a plan . . . which has been undertaken pursuant to a final* [436 U.S. 658, 698] *order issued by a court of the United States* . . . which requires the desegregation of minority group segregated children or faculty in the elementary and secondary schools of such agency, or otherwise requires the elimination or reduction of minority group isolation in such schools." (Emphasis added.)

A "local educational agency" is defined by 20 U.S.C. § 1619 (8) (1976 ed.) as "a public board of education or other public authority legally constituted within a State for either administrative control or direction of, public elementary or secondary schools in a city, county, township, school district, or other political subdivision of a State, or a federally recognized Indian reservation, or such combination of school districts, or counties as are recognized in a State as an administrative agency for its public elementary or secondary schools, or a combination of local educational agencies . . . ." Congress thus clearly recognized that school boards were often parties to federal school desegregation suits. In § 718 of the Act, 86 Stat. 369, 20 U.S.C. § 1617 (1976 ed.), Congress gave its explicit approval to the institution of federal desegregation suits against school boards—presumably under § 1983. Section 718 provides:

> "Upon the entry of a final order *by a court of the United States against a local educational agency* . . . for discrimination on the basis of race, color, or national origin in violation of . . . the fourteenth amendment to the Constitution of the United States . . . the court . . . may allow the prevailing party, other than the United States, a reasonable attorney's fee as part of the costs." (Emphasis added.)

Two years later in the Equal Educational Opportunities Act of 1974, Congress found that "the implementation of desegregation plans that require extensive student transportation has, in many cases, required local educational agencies to expend large amounts of funds, thereby depleting their financial re-sources . . . ." 20 U.S.C. § 1702 (a) (3) (1976 ed.). (Emphasis added.) Congress did not respond by declaring that school boards were not subject to suit under § 1983 or any other federal statute, "but simply [legislated] revised evidentiary standards and remedial priorities to be employed by the courts in deciding such cases." Brief for National Education Assn. et al. as *Amici Curiae* 15-16. Indeed, Congress expressly reiterated that a cause of action, cognizable in the federal courts, exists for discrimination in the public school context. 20 U.S.C. §§ 1703, [436 U.S. 658, 699] 1706, 1708, 1710, 1718 (1976 ed.). The Act assumes that school boards will usually be the defendants in such suits. For example, § 211 of the Act, 88 Stat. 516, as set forth in 20 U.S.C. § 1710 (1976 ed.), provides:

> "The Attorney General shall not institute a civil action under section 1706 of this title [which allows for suit by both private parties and the Attorney General to redress discrimination in public education] before he
>
> "(a) gives to the appropriate education agency notice of the condition or conditions which, in his judgment, constitute a violation of part 2 [the prohibitions against discrimination in public education]." Section 219 of the Act, 20 U.S.C. § 1718 (1976 ed.), provides for the termination of court-ordered busing "if the court finds the defendant educational agency has satisfied the requirements of the fifth or fourteenth amend-

ments to the Constitution, whichever is applicable, and will continue to be in compliance with the requirements thereof."

[64] Whether Congress' attempt is in fact effective is the subject of *Hutto v. Finney*, O. T. 1977, No. 76-1660, cert. granted, 434 U.S. 901, and therefore we express no view on it here.

[65] We note, however, that Mr. Justice Harlan's test has not been expressly adopted by this Court. Moreover, that test is based on two factors: *stare decisis* and "indications of congressional acceptance of this Court's earlier interpretation [of the statute in question]." 365 U.S., at 192. As we have explained, the second consideration is not present in this case.

[66] No useful purpose would be served by an attempt at this late date to determine whether *Monroe* was correct on its facts. Similarly, since this case clearly involves official policy and does not involve *respondeat superior,* we do not assay a view on how our cases which have relied on that aspect of *Monroe* that is overruled today—*Moor v. County of Alameda*, 411 U.S. 693 (1973); *City of Kenosha v. Bruno*, 412 U.S. 507 (1973); and *Aldinger v. Howard*, 427 U.S. 1 (1976)—should have been decided on a correct view of § 1983. Nothing we say today affects the conclusion reached in *Moor*, see 411 U.S., at 703-704, that 42 U.S.C. § 1988 cannot be used to create a federal cause of action where § 1983 does not otherwise provide one, or the conclusion reached in *City of Kenosha*, see 412 U.S., at 513, that "nothing . . . suggest[s] that the generic word 'person' in § 1983 was intended to have a bifurcated application to municipal corporations depending on the nature of the relief sought against them."

Owen v. City of Independence, Missouri
445 U.S. 622 (1980)

Argued January 8, 1980
Decided April 16, 1980
MR. JUSTICE BRENNAN delivered the opinion of the Court.

Monell v. New York City Dept. of Social Services, 436 U.S. 658 (1978), overruled *Monroe v. Pape*, 365 U.S. 167 (1961), insofar as *Monroe* held that local governments were not among the "persons" to whom 42 U.S.C. § 1983 applies and were therefore wholly immune from suit under the statute.[1] *Monell* reserved decision, however, on the question whether local governments, although not entitled to an absolute immunity, should be afforded some form of official immunity in § 1983 suits. 436 U.S., at 701. In this action brought by petitioner in the District Court for the Western District of Missouri, the Court of Appeals for the Eighth Circuit held that respondent city of Independence, Mo., "is entitled to qualified immunity from liability" based on the good faith [445 U.S. 622, 625] of its officials: "We extend the limited immunity the district court applied to the individual defendants to cover the City as well, because its officials acted in good faith and without malice." 589 F.2d 335, 337-338 (1978). We granted certiorari. 444 U.S. 822 (1979). We reverse.

I

The events giving rise to this suit are detailed in the District Court's findings of fact, 421 F. Supp. 1110 (1976). On February 20, 1967, Robert

L. Broucek, then City Manager of respondent city of Independence, Mo., appointed petitioner George D. Owen to an indefinite term as Chief of Police.[2] In 1972, Owen and a new City Manager, Lyle W. Alberg, engaged in a dispute over petitioner's administration of the Police Department's property room. In March of that year, a handgun, which the records of the Department's property room stated had been destroyed, turned up in Kansas City in the possession of a felon. This discovery prompted Alberg to initiate an investigation of the management of the property room. Although the probe was initially directed by petitioner, Alberg soon transferred responsibility for the investigation to the city's Department of Law, instructing the City Counselor to supervise its conduct and to inform him directly of its findings.

Sometime in early April 1972, Alberg received a written report on the investigation's progress, along with copies of confidential witness statements. Although the City Auditor found that the Police Department's records were insufficient to permit an adequate accounting of the goods contained in the property room, the City Counselor concluded that there was no evidence of any criminal acts or of any violation of [445 U.S. 622, 626] state or municipal law in the administration of the property room. Alberg discussed the results of the investigation at an informal meeting with several City Council members and advised them that he would take action at an appropriate time to correct any problems in the administration of the Police Department.

On April 10, Alberg asked petitioner to resign as Chief of Police and to accept another position within the Department, citing dissatisfaction with the manner in which petitioner had managed the Department, particularly his inadequate supervision of the property room. Alberg warned that if petitioner refused to take another position in the Department his employment would be terminated, to which petitioner responded that he did not intend to resign.

On April 13, Alberg issued a public statement addressed to the Mayor and the City Council concerning the results of the investigation. After referring to "discrepancies" found in the administration, handling, and security of public property, the release concluded that "[t]here appears to be no evidence to substantiate any allegations of a criminal nature" and offered assurances that "[s]teps have been initiated on an administrative level to correct these discrepancies." Id., at 1115. Although Alberg apparently had decided by this time to replace petitioner as Police Chief, he took no formal action to that end and left for a brief vacation without informing the City Council of his decision.[3]

While Alberg was away on the weekend of April 15 and 16, two developments occurred. Petitioner, having consulted with counsel, sent Alberg a letter demanding written notice of the charges against him and a public hearing with a reasonable [445 U.S. 622, 627] opportunity to respond to those charges.[4] At approximately the same time, City

Councilman Paul L. Roberts asked for a copy of the investigative report on the Police Department property room. Although petitioner's appeal received no immediate response, the Acting City Manager complied with Roberts' request and supplied him with the audit report and witness statements.

On the evening of April 17, 1972, the City Council held its regularly scheduled meeting. After completion of the planned agenda, Councilman Roberts read a statement he had prepared on the investigation.[5] Among other allegations, [445 U.S. 622, 628] Roberts charged that petitioner had misappropriated Police Department property for his own use, that narcotics and money had "mysteriously disappeared" from his office, that traffic tickets had been manipulated, that high ranking police officials had made "inappropriate" requests affecting the police court, and that "things have occurred causing the unusual release of felons." At the close of his statement, Roberts moved that the investigative reports be released to the news media and turned over to the prosecutor for presentation to the grand jury, and that the City Manager "take all direct [445 U.S. 622, 629] and appropriate action" against those persons "involved in illegal, wrongful, or gross inefficient activities brought out in the investigative reports." After some discussion, the City Council passed Roberts' motion with no dissents and one abstention.[6]

City Manager Alberg discharged petitioner the very next day. Petitioner was not given any reason for his dismissal; he received only a written notice stating that his employment as Chief of Police was "[t]erminated under the provisions of Section 3.3 (1) of the City Charter."[7] Petitioner's earlier demand for a specification of charges and a public hearing was ignored, and a subsequent request by his attorney for an appeal of the discharge decision was denied by the city on the grounds that "there is no appellate procedure or forum provided by the Charter or ordinances of the City of Independence, Missouri, relating to the dismissal of Mr. Owen." App. 26-27.

The local press gave prominent coverage both to the City Council's action and petitioner's dismissal, linking the discharge to the investigation.[8] As instructed by the City Council, Alberg referred the investigative reports and witness statements to the Prosecuting Attorney of Jackson County, Mo., [445 U.S. 622, 630] for consideration by a grand jury. The results of the audit and investigation were never released to the public, however. The grand jury subsequently returned a "no true bill," and no further action was taken by either the City Council or City Manager Alberg.

II

Petitioner named the city of Independence, City Manager Alberg, and the present members of the City Council in their official capacities as defendants in this suit.[9] Alleging that he was discharged without notice of reasons and without a hearing in violation of his constitutional rights to procedural and substantive due process, petitioner sought declaratory and injunctive relief, including a hearing on his discharge, backpay from the date of discharge, and attorney's fees. The District Court, after a bench trial, entered judgment for respondents. 421 F. Supp. 1110 (1976).[10] [445 U.S. 622, 631]

The Court of Appeals initially reversed the District Court. 560 F.2d 925 (1977).[11] Although it agreed with the District Court that under Missouri law petitioner possessed no property interest in continued employment as Police Chief, the Court of Appeals concluded that the city's allegedly false public accusations had blackened petitioner's name and reputation, thus depriving him of liberty without due process of law. That the stigmatizing charges did not come from the City Manager and were not included in the official discharge notice was, in the court's view, immaterial. What was important, [445 U.S. 622, 632] the court explained, was that "the official actions of the city council released charges against [petitioner] contemporaneous and, in the eyes of the public, connected with that discharge." Id., at 937.[12]

Respondents petitioned for review of the Court of Appeals' decision. Certiorari was granted, and the case was remanded for further consideration in light of our supervening decision in Monell v. New York City Dept. of Social Services, 436 U.S. 658 (1978). 438 U.S. 902 (1978). The Court of Appeals [445 U.S. 622, 633] on the remand reaffirmed its original determination that the city had violated petitioner's rights under the Fourteenth Amendment, but held that all respondents, including the city, were entitled to qualified immunity from liability. 589 F.2d 335 (1978).

Monell held that "a local government may not be sued under § 1983 for an injury inflicted solely by its employees or agents. Instead, it is when execution of a government's policy or custom, whether made by its lawmakers or by those whose edicts or acts may fairly be said to represent official policy, inflicts the injury that the government as an entity is responsible under § 1983." 436 U.S., at 694. The Court of Appeals held in the instant case that the municipality's official policy was responsible for the deprivation of petitioner's constitutional rights: "[T]he stigma attached to [petitioner] in connection with his discharge was caused by the official conduct of the City's lawmakers, or by those whose acts may fairly be said to represent official policy. Such conduct amounted to official policy causing the infringement of [petitioner's] constitutional rights, in violation of Section 1983." 589 F.2d, at 337.[13] [445 U.S. 622, 634]

Nevertheless, the Court of Appeals affirmed the judgment of the District Court denying petitioner any relief against the respondent city, stating:

"The Supreme Court's decisions in Board of Regents v. Roth, 408 U.S. 564 ... (1972), and Perry v. Sindermann, 408 U.S. 593 ... (1972), crystallized the rule establishing the right to a name-clearing hearing for a government employee allegedly stigmatized in the course of his discharge. The Court decided those two cases two months after the discharge in the instant case. Thus, officials of the City of Independence could not have been aware of [petitioner's] right to a name-clearing hearing in connection with the discharge. The City of Independence should not be charged with predicting the future course of constitutional law. We extend the limited immunity the district court applied to the individual defendants to cover the City as well, because its officials acted in good faith and without malice. We hold the City not liable for actions it could not reasonably have known violated [petitioner's] constitutional rights." *Id.*, at 338 (footnote and citations omitted).[14] [445 U.S. 622, 635]

We turn now to the reasons for our disagreement with this holding.[15]

III

Because the question of the scope of a municipality's immunity from liability under § 1983 is essentially one of statutory construction, see *Wood v. Strickland*, 420 U.S. 308, 314, 316 (1975); *Tenney v. Brandhove*, 341 U.S. 367, 376 (1951), the starting point in our analysis must be the language of the statute itself. *Andrus v. Allard*, 444 U.S. 51, 56 (1979); *Blue Chip Stamps v. Manor Drug Stores*, 421 U.S. 723, 756 (1975) (POWELL, J., concurring). By its terms, § 1983 "creates a species of tort liability that on its face admits of no immunities." *Imbler v. Pachtman*, 424 U.S. 409, 417 (1976). Its language is absolute and unqualified; no mention is made of any privileges, immunities, or defenses that may be asserted. Rather, the Act imposes liability upon "*every person*" who, under color of state law or custom, "subjects, or causes to be subjected, any citizen of the United States ... to the deprivation of any rights, privileges, or immunities secured by the Constitution and laws."[16] And *Monell* held that these words were intended to encompass municipal corporations as well as natural "persons."

Moreover, the congressional debates surrounding the passage of 1 of the Civil Rights Act of 1871, 17 Stat. 13—the forerunner of § 1983—confirm the expansive sweep of the statutory [445 U.S. 622, 636] language. Representative Shellabarger, the author and manager of the bill in the House, explained in his introductory remarks the breadth of construction that the Act was to receive:

"I have a single remark to make in regard to the rule of interpretation of those provisions of the Constitution under which all the sections of the bill are framed. This act is remedial, and in aid of the preservation of human liberty and human rights. All statutes and constitutional provisions authorizing such statutes are liberally and beneficently construed. It would be most strange and, in civilized law, monstrous were this not the rule of interpretation. As has been again and again decided by your own Supreme Court of the

United States, and everywhere else where there is wise judicial interpretation, the largest latitude consistent with the words employed is uniformly given in construing such statutes and constitutional provisions as are meant to protect and defend and give remedies for their wrongs to all the people." Cong. Globe, 42d Cong., 1st Sess., App. 68 (1871) (hereinafter Globe App.).

Similar views of the Act's broad remedy for violations of federally protected rights were voiced by its supporters in both Houses of Congress. See *Monell v. New York City Dept. of Social Services*, 436 U.S., at 683-687.[17] [445 U.S. 622, 637]

However, notwithstanding § 1983's expansive language and the absence of any express incorporation of common-law immunities, we have, on several occasions, found that a tradition of immunity was so firmly rooted in the common law and was supported by such strong policy reasons that "Congress would have specifically so provided had it wished to abolish the doctrine." *Pierson v. Ray*, 386 U.S. 547, 555 (1967). Thus in *Tenney v. Brandhove, supra*, after tracing the development of an absolute legislative privilege from its source in sixteenth-century England to its inclusion in the Federal and State Constitutions, we concluded that Congress "would [not] impinge on a tradition so well grounded in history and reason by covert inclusion in the general language" of § 1983. 341 U.S., at 376.

Subsequent cases have required that we consider the personal liability of various other types of government officials. Noting that "[f]ew doctrines were more solidly established at common law than the immunity of judges from liability for damages for acts committed within their judicial jurisdiction," *Pierson v. Ray, supra*, at 553-554, held that the absolute immunity traditionally accorded judges was preserved under § 1983. In that same case, local police officers were held to enjoy a "good faith and probable cause" defense to § 1983 suits similar to that which existed in false arrest actions at common law. 386 U.S., at 555-557. Several more recent decisions have found immunities of varying scope appropriate for different state and local officials sued under § 1983. See *Procunier v. Navarette*, 434 U.S. 555 (1978) (qualified immunity [445 U.S. 622, 638] for prison officials and officers); *Imbler v. Pachtman*, 424 U.S. 409 (1976) (absolute immunity for prosecutors in initiating and presenting the State's case); *O'Connor v. Donaldson*, 422 U.S. 563 (1975) (qualified immunity for superintendent of state hospital); *Wood v. Strickland*, 420 U.S. 308 (1975) (qualified immunity for local school board members); *Scheuer v. Rhodes*, 416 U.S. 232 (1974) (qualified "good-faith" immunity for state Governor and other executive officers for discretionary acts performed in the course of official conduct).

In each of these cases, our finding of § 1983 immunity "was predicated upon a considered inquiry into the immunity historically accorded the relevant official at common law and the interests behind it." *Imbler v. Pachtman, supra,* at 421. Where the immunity claimed by the defendant was well established at common law at the time § 1983 was enacted, and where its rationale was compatible with the purposes of the Civil Rights Act, we have construed the statute to incorporate that immunity. But there is no tradition of immunity for municipal corporations, and neither history nor policy supports a construction of § 1983 that would justify the qualified immunity accorded the city of Independence by the Court of Appeals. We hold, therefore, that the municipality may not assert the good faith of its officers or agents as a defense to liability under § 1983.[18]

A

Since colonial times, a distinct feature of our Nation's system of governance has been the conferral of political power upon public and municipal corporations for the management of matters of local concern. As *Monell* recounted, by 1871, [445 U.S. 622, 639] municipalities—like private corporations—were treated as natural persons for virtually all purposes of constitutional and statutory analysis. In particular, they were routinely sued in both federal and state courts. See 436 U.S., at 687-688. Cf. *Cowles v. Mercer County,* 7 Wall. 118 (1869). Local governmental units were regularly held to answer in damages for a wide range of statutory and constitutional violations, as well as for common-law actions for breach of contract.[19] And although, as we discuss below,[20] a municipality [445 U.S. 622, 640] was not subject to suit for all manner of tortious conduct, it is clear that at the time § 1983 was enacted, local governmental bodies did not enjoy the sort of "good-faith" qualified immunity extended to them by the Court of Appeals.

As a general rule, it was understood that a municipality's tort liability in damages was identical to that of private corporations and individuals:

> "There is nothing in the character of a municipal corporation which entitles it to an immunity from liability for such malfeasances as private corporations or individuals would be liable for in a civil action. A municipal corporation is liable to the same extent as an individual for any act done by the express authority of the corporation, or of a branch of its government, empowered to act for it upon the subject to which the particular act relates, and for any act which, after it has been done, has been lawfully ratified by the corporation." T. Shearman & A. Redfield, A Treatise on the Law of Negligence 120, p. 139 (1869) (hereinafter Shearman & Redfield).

Accord, 2 Dillon 764, at 875 ("But as respects *municipal corporations proper,* . . . it is, we think, universally considered, even in the absence of statute giving the action, that they are liable for acts of *misfeasance* positively injurious to individuals, done by their authorized agents or officers, in the course of the performance of corporate powers constitutionally conferred, or in the execution of corporate duties") (emphasis in original). See 18 E. McQuillin, Municipal Corporations § 53.02 (3d rev. ed. 1977) (hereinafter McQuillin). Under this general theory of liability, a municipality was deemed responsible for any private losses generated through a wide variety of its operations and functions, from personal injuries due to its defective sewers, thoroughfares, and public utilities, to property damage caused by its trespasses and uncompensated takings.[21] [445 U.S. 622, 641]

Yet in the hundreds of cases from that era awarding damages against municipal governments for wrongs committed by them, one searches in vain for much mention of a qualified immunity based on the good faith of municipal officers. Indeed, where the issue was discussed at all, the courts had rejected the proposition that a municipality should be privileged where it reasonably believed its actions to be lawful. In the leading case of *Thayer v. Boston*, 36 Mass. 511, 515-516 (1837), for example, Chief Justice Shaw explained:

> "There is a large class of cases, in which the rights of both the public and of individuals may be deeply involved, in which it cannot be known at the time the act is done, whether it is lawful or not. The event of a legal inquiry, in a court of justice, may show that it was unlawful. Still, if it was not known and understood to be unlawful at the time, if it was an act done by the officers having competent authority, either by express vote of the city government, or by the nature of the duties and functions with which they are charged, by their offices, to act upon the general subject matter, and especially if the act was done with an honest view to obtain for the public some lawful benefit or advantage, reason and justice obviously require that the city, in its corporate capacity, should be liable to make good the damage sustained by an individual, in consequence of the acts thus done."

The *Thayer* principle was later reiterated by courts in several jurisdictions, and numerous decisions awarded damages against municipalities for violations expressly found to have been committed in good faith. See, *e.g.*, *Town Council of Akron v. McComb*, 18 Ohio 229, 230-231 (1849); *Horton v. Inhabitants of Ipswich*, 66 Mass. 488, 489, 492 (1853); *Elliot v. Concord*, 27 N. H. 204 (1853); *Hurley v. Town of Texas*, 20 Wis. 634, 637-638 (1866); *Lee v. Village of Sandy Hill*, 40 N. Y. [445 U.S. 622, 642] 442, 448-451 (1869); *Billings v. Worcester*, 102 Mass. 329, 332-333 (1869); *Squiers v. Village of Neenah*, 24 Wis. 588, 593 (1869); *Hawks v. Charlemont*, 107 Mass. 414, 417-418 (1871).[22]

That municipal corporations were commonly held liable for damages in tort was also recognized by the 42d Congress. See *Monell v. New York City Dept. of Social Services*, 436 U.S., at 688. For example, Senator Stevenson, in opposing the Sherman amendment's creation of a municipal liability for the riotous acts of its inhabitants, stated the prevailing law: "Numberless cases are to be found where a statutory liability has been created against municipal corporations for injuries resulting from a neglect of corporate duty." Cong. [445 U.S. 622, 643] Globe, 42d Cong., 1st Sess., 762 (hereinafter Globe).[23] Nowhere in the debates, however, is there a suggestion that the common law excused a city from liability on account of the good faith of its authorized agents, much less an indication of a congressional intent to incorporate such an immunity into the Civil Rights Act.[24] The absence of any allusion to a municipal immunity assumes added significance in light of the objections raised by the opponents of § 1 of the Act that its unqualified language could be interpreted to abolish the traditional good-faith immunities enjoyed by legislators, judges, governors, sheriffs, and other public officers.[25] Had [445 U.S. 622, 644] there been a similar common-law immunity for municipalities, the bill's opponents doubtless would have raised the specter of its destruction, as well.

To be sure, there were two doctrines that afforded municipal corporations some measure of protection from tort liability. The first sought to distinguish between a municipality's "governmental" and "proprietary" functions; as to the former, the city was held immune, whereas in its exercise of the latter, the city was held to the same standards of liability as any private corporation. The second doctrine immunized a municipality for its "discretionary" or "legislative" activities, but not for those which were "ministerial" in nature. A brief examination of the application and the rationale underlying each of these doctrines demonstrates that Congress could not have intended them to limit a municipality's liability under § 1983.

The governmental-proprietary distinction[26] owed its existence to the dual nature of the municipal corporation. On [445 U.S. 622, 645] the one hand, the municipality was a corporate body, capable of performing the same "proprietary" functions as any private corporation, and liable for its torts in the same manner and to the same extent, as well. On the other hand, the municipality was an arm of the State, and when acting in that "governmental" or "public" capacity, it shared the immunity traditionally accorded the sovereign.[27] But the principle of sovereign immunity—itself a somewhat arid fountainhead for municipal immunity[28]—is necessarily nullified when the [445 U.S. 622, 646] State expressly or impliedly allows itself, or its creation, to be sued. Municipalities were therefore liable not only for their "proprietary" acts, but also for those "governmental" functions as to which the State had withdrawn their immunity. And, by the end of the 19th century, courts regularly held that in imposing a specific duty on the municipality either in its charter or by statute, the State had impliedly withdrawn the city's immunity from liability for the nonperformance or misperformance of its obligation. See, e.g., *Weightman v. The Corporation of Washington*, 1 Black 39, 50-52 (1862); *Providence v. Clapp*, 17 How. 161, 167-169 (1855). See generally *Shearman & Redfield* 122-126; Note, Liability of Cities for the Negligence and Other Misconduct of their Officers and Agents, 30 Am. St. Rep. 376,

385 (1893). Thus, despite the nominal existence of an immunity for "governmental" functions, municipalities were found [445 U.S. 622, 647] liable in damages in a multitude of cases involving such activities.

That the municipality's common-law immunity for "governmental" functions derives from the principle of sovereign immunity also explains why that doctrine could not have served as the basis for the qualified privilege respondent city claims under § 1983. First, because sovereign immunity insulates the municipality from unconsented suits altogether, the presence or absence of good faith is simply irrelevant. The critical issue is whether injury occurred while the city was exercising governmental, as opposed to proprietary, powers or obligations—not whether its agents reasonably believed they were acting lawfully in so conducting themselves.[29] More fundamentally, however, the municipality's "governmental" immunity is obviously abrogated by the sovereign's enactment of a statute making it amenable to suit. Section 1983 was just such a statute. By including municipalities within the class of "persons" subject to liability for violations of the Federal Constitution and laws, Congress—the supreme sovereign on matters of federal law[30]—abolished whatever vestige [445 U.S. 622, 648] of the State's sovereign immunity the municipality possessed.

The second common-law distinction between municipal functions—that protecting the city from suits challenging "discretionary" decisions—was grounded not on the principle of sovereign immunity, but on a concern for separation of powers. A large part of the municipality's responsibilities involved broad discretionary decisions on issues of public policy—decisions that affected large numbers of persons and called for a delicate balancing of competing considerations. For a court or jury, in the guise of a tort suit, to review the reasonableness of the city's judgment on these matters would be an infringement upon the powers properly vested in a coordinate and coequal branch of government. See *Johnson v. State*, 69 Cal. 2d 782, 794, n. 8, 447 P.2d 352, 361, n. 8 (1968) (en banc) ("Immunity for 'discretionary' activities serves no purpose except to assure that courts refuse to pass judgment on policy decisions in the province of coordinate branches of government"). In order to ensure against any invasion into the legitimate sphere of the municipality's policymaking processes, courts therefore refused to entertain suits against the city "either for the non-exercise of, or for the manner in which in good faith it exercises, *discretionary powers* of a public or legislative character." 2 Dillon 753, at 862.[31]

Although many, if not all, of a municipality's activities would seem to involve at least some measure of discretion, the influence of this doctrine on the city's liability was not as significant as might be expected. For just as the courts [445 U.S. 622, 649] implied an exception to the municipality's immunity for its "governmental" functions, here, too, a distinction was made that had the effect of subjecting the city to liability for much of its tortious conduct. While the city retained its immunity for decisions as to whether the public interest required acting in one manner or another, once any particular decision was made, the city was fully liable for any injuries incurred in the execution of its judgment. See, *e.g., Hill v. Boston,* 122 Mass. 344, 358-359 (1877) (dicta) (municipality would be immune from liability for damages resulting from its decision where to construct sewers, since that involved a discretionary judgment as to the general public interest; but city would be liable for neglect in the construction or repair of any particular sewer, as such activity is ministerial in nature). See generally C. Rhyne, Municipal Law § 30.4, pp. 736-737 (1957); Williams § 7. Thus municipalities remained liable in damages for a broad range of conduct implementing their discretionary decisions.

Once again, an understanding of the rationale underlying the common-law immunity for "discretionary" functions explains why that doctrine cannot serve as the foundation for a good-faith immunity under § 1983. That common-law doctrine merely prevented courts from substituting their own judgment on matters within the lawful discretion of the municipality. But a municipality has no "discretion" to violate the Federal Constitution; its dictates are absolute and imperative. And when a court passes judgment on the municipality's conduct in a § 1983 action, it does not seek to second-guess the "reasonableness" of the city's decision nor to interfere with the local government's resolution of competing policy considerations. Rather, it looks only to whether the municipality has conformed to the requirements of the Federal Constitution and statutes. As was stated in *Sterling v. Constantin,* 287 U.S. 378, 398 (1932): "When there is a substantial showing that the exertion of state power has [445 U.S. 622, 650] overridden private rights secured by that Constitution, the subject is necessarily one for judicial inquiry in an appropriate proceeding directed against the individuals charged with the transgression."

In sum, we can discern no "tradition so well grounded in history and reason" that would warrant the conclusion that in enacting § 1 of the Civil Rights Act, the 42d Congress *sub silentio* extended to municipalities a qualified immunity based on the good faith of their officers. Absent any clearer indication that Congress intended so to limit the reach of a statute expressly designed to provide a "broad remedy for violations of federally protected civil rights," *Monell v. New York City Dept. of Social Services,* 436 U.S., at 685, we are unwilling to suppose that injuries occasioned by a municipality's unconstitutional conduct were not also meant to be fully redressable through its sweep.[32]

B

Our rejection of a construction of § 1983 that would accord municipalities a qualified immunity for their good-faith constitutional violations is compelled both by the legislative purpose in enacting the statute and by considerations of public policy. The central aim of the Civil Rights Act was to provide protection to those persons wronged by the "'[m]isuse of power, possessed by virtue of state law and made possible only because the wrongdoer is clothed with the authority of state law.'" *Monroe v. Pape*, 365 U.S., at 184 (quoting *United States v. Classic*, 313 U.S. 299, 326 (1941)). By creating an express federal remedy, Congress sought to "enforce provisions of the Fourteenth Amendment against those [445 U.S. 622, 651] who carry a badge of authority of a State and represent it in some capacity, whether they act in accordance with their authority or misuse it." *Monroe v. Pape, supra*, at 172.

How "uniquely amiss" it would be, therefore, if the government itself—"the social organ to which all in our society look for the promotion of liberty, justice, fair and equal treatment, and the setting of worthy norms and goals for social conduct"—were permitted to disavow liability for the injury it has begotten. See *Adickes v. Kress & Co.*, 398 U.S. 144, 190 (1970) (opinion of BRENNAN, J.). A damages remedy against the offending party is a vital component of any scheme for vindicating cherished constitutional guarantees, and the importance of assuring its efficacy is only accentuated when the wrongdoer is the institution that has been established to protect the very rights it has transgressed. Yet owing to the qualified immunity enjoyed by most government officials, see *Scheuer v. Rhodes*, 416 U.S. 232 (1974), many victims of municipal malfeasance would be left remediless if the city were also allowed to assert a good-faith defense. Unless countervailing considerations counsel otherwise, the injustice of such a result should not be tolerated.[33]

Moreover, § 1983 was intended not only to provide compensation to the victims of past abuses, but to serve as a deterrent against future constitutional deprivations, as well. See *Robertson v. Wegmann*, 436 U.S. 584, 590-591 (1978), *Carey v. Piphus*, 435 U.S. 247, 256-257 (1978). The knowledge that a municipality will be liable for all of its injurious conduct, whether committed in good faith or not, should create [445 U.S. 622, 652] an incentive for officials who may harbor doubts about the lawfulness of their intended actions to err on the side of protecting citizens' constitutional rights.[34] Furthermore, the threat that damages might be levied against the city may encourage those in a policymaking position to institute internal rules and programs designed to minimize the likelihood of unintentional infringements on constitutional rights.[35] Such procedures are particularly beneficial in preventing those "systemic" injuries that result not so much from the conduct of any single individual, but from the interactive behavior of several government officials, each of whom may be acting in good faith. Cf. Note, Developments in the Law: Section 1983 and Federalism, 90 Harv L Rev 1133, 1218-1219 (1977).[36]

Our previous decisions conferring qualified immunities on various government officials, see *supra*, at 637-638, are not to [445 U.S. 622,

653] be read as derogating the significance of the societal interest in compensating the innocent victims of governmental misconduct. Rather, in each case we concluded that overriding considerations of public policy nonetheless demanded that the official be given a measure of protection from personal liability. The concerns that justified those decisions, however, are less compelling, if not wholly inapplicable, when the liability of the municipal entity is at issue.[37] [445 U.S. 622, 654]

In *Scheuer v. Rhodes, supra,* at 240, THE CHIEF JUSTICE identified the two "mutually dependent rationales" on which the doctrine of official immunity rested:

> "(1) the injustice, particularly in the absence of bad faith, of subjecting to liability an officer who is required, by the legal obligations of his position, to exercise discretion; (2) the danger that the threat of such liability would deter his willingness to execute his office with the decisiveness and the judgment required by the public good."[38]

The first consideration is simply not implicated when the damages award comes not from the official's pocket, but from the public treasury. It hardly seems unjust to require a municipal defendant which has violated a citizen's constitutional rights to compensate him for the injury suffered thereby. Indeed, Congress enacted § 1983 precisely to provide a remedy for such abuses of official power. See *Monroe v. Pape,* 365 U.S., at 171-172. Elemental notions of fairness dictate that one who causes a loss should bear the loss.

It has been argued, however, that revenue raised by taxation for public use should not be diverted to the benefit of a single or discrete group of taxpayers, particularly where the municipality has at all times acted in good faith. On the contrary, the accepted view is that stated in *Thayer v. Boston*—"that the city, in its corporate capacity, should be liable to make good the damage sustained by an [unlucky] individual, [445 U.S. 622, 655] in consequence of the acts thus done." 36 Mass., at 515. After all, it is the public at large which enjoys the benefits of the government's activities, and it is the public at large which is ultimately responsible for its administration. Thus, even where some constitutional development could not have been foreseen by municipal officials, it is fairer to allocate any resulting financial loss to the inevitable costs of government borne by all the taxpayers, than to allow its impact to be felt solely by those whose rights, albeit newly recognized, have been violated. See generally 3 K. Davis, Administrative Law Treatise § 25.17 (1958 and Supp. 1970); Prosser 131, at 978; Michelman, Property, Utility, and Fairness: Some Thoughts on the Ethical Foundations of "Just Compensation" Law, 80 Harv L Rev 1165 (1967).[39]

The second rationale mentioned in *Scheuer* also loses its force when it is the municipality, in contrast to the official, whose liability is at issue. At the heart of this justification for a qualified immunity for the individual official is the concern that the threat of *personal* monetary liability will introduce an unwarranted and unconscionable consideration into the decision making process, thus paralyzing the governing official's decisiveness and distorting his judgment on matters [445 U.S. 622, 656] of public policy.[40] The inhibiting effect is significantly reduced, if not eliminated, however, when the threat of personal liability is removed. First, as an empirical matter, it is questionable whether the hazard of municipal loss will deter a public officer from the conscientious exercise of his duties; city officials routinely make decisions that either require a large expenditure of municipal funds or involve a substantial risk of depleting the public fisc. See *Kostka v. Hogg*, 560 F.2d 37, 41 (CA1 1977). More important, though, is the realization that consideration of the *municipality's* liability for constitutional violations is quite properly the concern of its elected or appointed officials. Indeed, a decision maker would be derelict in his duties if, at some point, he did not consider whether his decision comports with constitutional mandates and did not weigh the risk that a violation might result in an award of damages from the public treasury. As one commentator aptly put it: "Whatever other concerns should shape a particular official's actions, certainly one of them should be the constitutional rights of individuals who will be affected by his actions. To criticize Section 1983 liability because it leads decision makers to avoid the infringement of constitutional rights is to criticize one of the statute's *raisons d'être*."[41] [445 U.S. 622, 657]

IV

In sum, our decision holding that municipalities have no immunity from damages liability flowing from their constitutional violations harmonizes well with developments in the common law and our own pronouncements on official immunities under § 1983. Doctrines of tort law have changed significantly over the past century, and our notions of governmental responsibility should properly reflect that evolution. No longer is individual "blameworthiness" the acid test of liability; the principle of equitable loss-spreading has joined fault as a factor in distributing the costs of official misconduct.

We believe that today's decision, together with prior precedents in this area, properly allocates these costs among the three principals in the scenario of the § 1983 cause of action: the victim of the constitutional deprivation; the officer whose conduct caused the injury; and the public, as represented by the municipal entity. The innocent individual who is harmed by an abuse of governmental authority is assured that he will be compensated for his injury. The offending official, so long as he conducts himself in good faith, may go about his business secure in the knowledge that a qualified immunity will protect him from personal liability for damages that are more appropriately chargeable to the populace as a whole. And the public will be forced to bear only the costs of injury inflicted by the "execution of a government's policy or custom, whether made by its lawmakers or by those whose edicts or acts may fairly be said to represent official policy." [445 U.S. 622, 658] *Monell v. New York City Dept. of Social Services*, 436 U.S., at 694.

Reversed.

Footnotes

[1] Title 42 U.S.C. § 1983 provides:

> "Every person who, under color of any statute, ordinance, regulation, custom, or usage, of any State or Territory, subjects, or causes to be subjected, any citizen of the United States or other person within the jurisdiction thereof to the deprivation of any rights, privileges, or immunities secured by the Constitution and laws, shall be liable to the party injured in an action at law, suit in equity, or other proper proceeding for redress."

[2] Under § 3.3 (1) of the city's charter, the City Manager has sole authority to "[a]ppoint, and when deemed necessary for the good of the service, lay off, suspend, demote, or remove all directors, or heads, of administrative departments and all other administrative officers and employees of the city. . . ."

[3] Alberg returned from his vacation on the morning of April 17, and immediately met informally with four members of the City Council. Although the investigation of the Police Department was discussed, and although Alberg testified that he had found a replacement for petitioner by that time, he did not inform the Council members of his intention to discharge petitioner.

[4] The letter, dated April 15, 1972, stated in part:

> "My counsel . . . have advised me that even though the City Charter may give you authority to relieve me, they also say you cannot do so without granting me my constitutional rights of due process, which includes a written charge and specifications, together with a right to a public hearing and to be represented by counsel and to cross-examine those who may appear against me.

. . . . .

> "In spite of your recent investigation and your public statement given to the public press, your relief and discharge of me without a full public hearing upon written charges will leave in the minds of the public and those who might desire to have my services, a stigma of personal wrongdoing on my part.

> "Such action by you would be in violation of my civil rights as granted by the Constitution and Congress of the United States and you would be liable in damages to me. Further it would be in violation of the Missouri Administrative Procedure Act.

> "May I have an expression from you that you do not intend to relieve me or in the alternative give me a written charge and specifications of your basis for your grounds of intention to relieve me and to grant me a public hearing with a reasonable opportunity to respond to the charge and a right to be represented by counsel."

City Manager Alberg stated that he did not receive the letter until after petitioner's discharge.

[5] Roberts' statement, which is reproduced in full in 421 F. Supp. 1110, 1116, n. 2 (1976), in part recited:

> "On April 2, 1972, the City Council was notified of the existence of an investigative report concerning the activities of the Chief of Police of the [445 U.S. 622, 628] City of Independence, certain police officers and activities of one or more other City officials. On Saturday, April 15th for the first time I was able to see these 27 voluminous reports. The contents of these reports are astoundingly shocking and virtually unbelievable. They deal with the disappearance of 2 or more television sets from the police department and signed statement that they were taken by the Chief of Police for his own personal use.

> "The reports show that numerous firearms properly in the police department custody found their way into the hands of others including undesirables and were later found by other law enforcement agencies.

> "Reports show [sic] that narcotics held by the Independence, Missouri Chief of Police have mysteriously disappeared. Reports also indicate money has mysteriously disappeared. Reports show that traffic tickets have been manipulated. The reports show inappropriate requests affecting the police court have come from high ranking police officials. Reports indicate that things have occurred causing the unusual release of felons. The reports show gross inefficiencies on the part of a few of the high ranking officers of the police department.

> "In view of the contents of these reports, I feel that the information in the reports backed up by signed statements taken by investigation is so bad that the council should immediately make available to the news media access to copies of all of these 27 voluminous investigative reports so the public can be told what has been going on in Independence. I further believe that copies of these reports should be turned over and referred to the prosecuting attorney of Jackson Country, Missouri for consideration and presentation to the next Grand Jury. I further insist that the City Manager immediately take direct and appropriate action, permitted under the Charter, against such persons as are shown by the investigation to have been involved."

[6] Ironically, the official minutes of the City Council meeting indicate that concern was expressed by some members about possible adverse legal consequences that could flow from their release of the reports to the media. The City Counselor assured the Council that although an action might be maintained against any witnesses who made unfounded accusations, "the City does have governmental immunity in this area . . . and neither the Council nor the City as a municipal corporation can be held liable for libelous slander." App. 20-23.

[7] See n. 2, *supra*.

[8] The investigation and its culmination in petitioner's firing received front-page attention in the local press. See, *e.g.*, "Lid Off Probe, Council Seeks Action," Independence Examiner, Apr. 18, 1972, Tr. 24-25; "Independence Accusation. Police Probe Demanded," Kansas City Times, Apr. 18, 1972, Tr. 25; "Probe Culminates in Chief's Dismissal," Independence Examiner, Apr. 19, 1972, Tr. 26; "Police Probe Continues; Chief Ousted," Community Observer, Apr. 20, 1972, Tr. 26.

[9] Petitioner did not join former Councilman Roberts in the instant litigation. A separate action seeking defamation damages was brought in state court against Roberts and Alberg in their individual capacities. Petitioner dismissed the state suit against Alberg and reached a financial settlement with Roberts. See 560 F.2d 925, 930 (CA8 1977).

¹⁰ The District Court, relying on *Monroe v. Pape*, 365 U.S. 167 (1961), and *City of Kenosha v. Bruno*, 412 U.S. 507 (1973), held that § 1983 did not create a cause of action against the city, but that petitioner could base his claim for relief directly on the Fourteenth Amendment. On the merits, however, the court determined that petitioner's discharge did not deprive him of any constitutionally protected property interest because, as an untenured employee, he possessed neither a contractual nor a de facto right to continued employment as Chief of Police. Similarly, the court found that the circumstances of petitioner's dismissal did not impose a stigma of illegal or immoral conduct on his professional reputation, and hence did not deprive him of any liberty interest.

The District Court offered three reasons to support its conclusion: First, because the actual discharge notice stated only that petitioner was "[t]erminated under the provisions of Section 3.3 (1) of the City Charter," nothing in his official record imputed any stigmatizing conduct to him. Second, the court found that the City Council's actions had no causal connection to petitioner's discharge, for City Manager Alberg had apparently [445 U.S. 622, 631] made his decision to hire a new Police Chief before the Council's April 17th meeting. Lastly, the District Court determined that petitioner was "completely exonerated" from any charges of illegal or immoral conduct by the City Counselor's investigative report, Alberg's public statements, and the grand jury's return of a "no true bill." 421 F. Supp., at 1121-1122.

As an alternative ground for denying relief, the District Court ruled that the city was entitled to assert, and had in fact established, a qualified immunity against liability based on the good faith of the individual defendants who acted as its agents: "[D]efendants have clearly shown by a preponderance of the evidence that neither they, nor their predecessors, were aware in April 1972, that, under the circumstances, the Fourteenth Amendment accorded plaintiff the procedural rights of notice and a hearing at the time of his discharge. Defendants have further proven that they cannot reasonably be charged with constructive notice of such rights since plaintiff was discharged prior to the publication of the Supreme Court decisions in *Roth v. Board of Regents*, [408 U.S. 564 (1972)], and *Perry v. Sindermann*, [408 U.S. 593 (1972)]." *Id.*, at 1123.

¹¹ Both parties had appealed from the District Court's decision. On respondents' challenge to the court's assumption of subject-matter jurisdiction under 28 U.S.C. § 1331, the Court of Appeals held that the city was subject to suit for reinstatement and backpay under an implied right of action arising directly from the Fourteenth Amendment. 560 F.2d, at 932-934. See *Bivens v. Six Unknown Fed. Narcotics Agents*, 403 U.S. 388 (1971). Because the Court of Appeals concluded that petitioner's claim could rest directly on the Fourteenth Amendment, it saw no need to decide whether he could recover backpay under § 1983 from the individual defendants in their official capacities as part of general equitable relief, even though the award would be paid by the city. 560 F.2d, at 932.

¹² As compensation for the denial of his constitutional rights, the Court of Appeals awarded petitioner damages in lieu of backpay. The court explained that petitioner's termination without a hearing must be considered a nullity, and that ordinarily he ought to remain on the payroll and receive wages until a hearing is held and a proper determination on his retention is made. But because petitioner had reached the mandatory retirement age during the course of the litigation, he could not be reinstated to his former position. Thus the compensatory award was to be measured by the amount of money petitioner would likely have earned to retirement had he not been deprived of his good name by the city's actions, subject to mitigation by the amounts actually earned, as well as by the recovery from Councilman Roberts in the state defamation suit.

The Court of Appeals rejected the municipality's assertion of a good-faith defense, relying upon a footnote in *Wood v. Strickland*, 420 U.S. 308, 314-315, n. 6

(1975) ("immunity from damages does not ordinarily bar equitable relief as well"), and two of its own precedents awarding backpay in § 1983 actions against school boards. See *Wellner v. Minnesota State Jr. College Bd.*, 487 F.2d 153 (CA8 1973); *Cooley v. Board of Educ. of Forrest City School Dist.*, 453 F.2d 282 (CA8 1972). The court concluded that the primary justification for a qualified immunity—the fear that public officials might hesitate to discharge their duties if faced with the prospect of personal monetary liability—simply did not exist where the relief would be borne by a governmental unit rather than the individual officeholder. In addition, the Court of Appeals seemed to take issue with the District Court's finding of good faith on the part of the City Council: "The city officials may have acted in good faith in refusing the hearing, but lack of good faith is evidenced by the nature of the unfair attack made upon the appellant by Roberts in the official conduct of the City's business. The District Court did not address the good faith defense in light of Roberts' defamatory remarks." 560 F.2d, at 941.

¹³ Although respondents did not cross petition on this issue, they have raised a belated challenge to the Court of Appeals' ruling that petitioner was deprived of a protected "liberty" interest. See Brief for Respondents 45-46. We find no merit in their contention, however, and decline to disturb the determination of the court below.
Wisconsin v. Constantineau, 400 U.S. 433, 437 (1971), held that "[w]here a person's good name, reputation, honor, or integrity is at stake because of what the government is doing to him, notice and an opportunity to be heard are essential." In *Board of Regents v. Roth*, 408 U.S. 564, 573 (1972), we explained that the dismissal of a government employee accompanied by a "charge against him that might seriously damage his standing and associations in his community" would qualify as something "the government is doing to him," so as to trigger the due process right to a hearing at which the employee could refute the charges and publicly clear his name. In the present case, the city—through the unanimous resolution of the City Council—released to the public an allegedly false statement impugning petitioner's honesty and integrity. Petitioner was discharged [445 U.S. 622, 634] the next day. The Council's accusations received extensive coverage in the press, and even if they did not in point of fact "cause" petitioner's discharge, the defamatory and stigmatizing charges certainly "occur[red] in the course of the termination of employment." Cf. *Paul v. Davis*, 424 U.S. 693, 710 (1976). Yet the city twice refused petitioner's request that he be given written specification of the charges against him and an opportunity to clear his name. Under the circumstances, we have no doubt that the Court of Appeals correctly concluded that the city's actions deprived petitioner of liberty without due process of law.

¹⁴ Cf. *Wood v. Strickland*, 420 U.S. 308, 322 (1975) ("Therefore, in the specific context of school discipline, we hold that a school board member is not immune from liability for damages under § 1983 if he knew or reasonably should have known that the action he took within his sphere of official responsibility would violate the constitutional rights of the student affected, or if he took the action with the malicious intention to cause a deprivation of constitutional rights or other injury to the student").

¹⁵ The Courts of Appeals are divided on the question whether local governmental units are entitled to a qualified immunity based on the good faith of their officials. Compare *Bertot v. School Dist. No. 1*, 613 F.2d 245 (CA10 1979) (en banc), *Hostrop v. Board of Junior College Dist. No. 515*, 523 F.2d 569 (CA7 1975), and *Hander v. San Jacinto Jr. College*, 519 F.2d 273 (CA5), rehearing denied, 522 F.2d 204 (1975), all refusing to extend a qualified immunity to the governmental entity, with *Paxman v. Campbell*, 612 F.2d 848 (CA4 1980) (en banc), and *Sala v. County of Suffolk*, 604 F.2d 207 (CA2 1979), granting defendants a "good-faith" immunity.

¹⁶ See n. 1, *supra*.

¹⁷ As we noted in *Monell v. New York City Dept. of Social Services*, see 436 U.S., at 685-686, n. 45, even the opponents of § 1 acknowledged that its language conferred

upon the federal courts the entire power that Congress possessed to remedy constitutional violations. The remarks of Senator Thurman are illustrative:

> "[This section's] whole effect is to give to the Federal Judiciary that which now does not belong to it—a jurisdiction that may be constitutionally conferred upon it, I grant, but that has never yet been conferred upon it. It authorizes any person who is deprived of any right, privilege, or immunity secured to him by the Constitution of the United States, to bring an action [445 U.S. 622, 637] against the wrong-doer in the Federal courts, and that without any limit whatsoever as to the amount in controversy. . . .

· · · · ·

> ". . . That is the language of this bill. Whether it is the intent or not I know not, but it is the language of the bill; for there is no limitation whatsoever upon the terms that are employed, and they are as comprehensive as can be used." Globe App. 216-217.

[18] The governmental immunity at issue in the present case differs significantly from the official immunities involved in our previous decisions. In those cases, various government officers had been sued in their individual capacities, and the immunity served to insulate them from personal liability for damages. Here, in contrast, only the liability of the municipality itself is at issue, not that of its officers, and in the absence of an immunity, any recovery would come from public funds.

[19] Primary among the constitutional suits heard in federal court were those based on a municipality's violation of the Contract Clause, and the courts' enforcement efforts often included "various forms of 'positive' relief, such as ordering that taxes be levied and collected to discharge federal-court judgments, once a constitutional infraction was found." *Monell v. New York City Dept. of Social Services*, 436 U.S., at 681. Damages actions against municipalities for federal statutory violations were also entertained. See, *e.g., Levy Court v. Coroner*, 2 Wall. 501 (1865); *Corporation of New York v. Ransom*, 23 How. 487 (1860); *Bliss v. Brooklyn*, 3 F. Cas. 706 (No. 1,544) (CC EDNY 1871). In addition, state constitutions and statutes, as well as municipal charters, imposed many obligations upon the local governments, the violation of which typically gave rise to damages actions against the city. See generally Note, Streets, Change of Grade, Liability of Cities for, 30 Am. St. Rep. 835 (1893), and cases cited therein. With respect to authorized contracts— and even unauthorized contracts that are later ratified by the corporation— municipalities were liable in the same manner as individuals for their breaches. See generally 1 J. Dillon, Law of Municipal Corporations §§ 385, 394 (2d ed. 1873) (hereinafter Dillon). Of particular relevance to the instant case, included within the class of contract actions brought against a city were those for the wrongful discharge of a municipal employee, and where the claim was adjudged meritorious, damages in the nature of backpay were regularly awarded. See, *e.g., Richardson v. School Dist. No. 10*, 38 Vt. 602 (1866); *Paul v. School Dist. No. 2*, 28 Vt. 575 (1856); *Inhabitants of Searsmont v. Farwell*, 3 Me. *450 (1825); see generally F. Burke, A Treatise on the Law of Public Schools 81-85 (1880). The most frequently litigated "breach of contract" suits, however, at least in federal court, were those for failure to pay interest on municipal bonds. See, *e.g., The Supervisors v. Durant*, 9 Wall. 415 (1870); *Commissioners of Knox County v. Aspinwall*, 21 How. 539 (1859).

[20] See *infra*, at 644-650.

[21] See generally C. Rhyne, Municipal Law 729-789 (1957); Shearman & Redfield §§ 143-152; W. Williams, Liability of Municipal Corporations for Tort (1901) (hereinafter Williams).

[22] Accord, *Bunker v. City of Hudson*, 122 Wis. 43, 54, 99 N. W. 448, 452 (1904); *Oklahoma City v. Hill Bros.*, 6 Okla. 114, 137-139, 50 P. 242, 249-250 (1897); *Schussler v. Board of Comm'rs of Hennepin County*, 67 Minn. 412, 417, 70 N. W. 6, 7 (1897); *McGraw v. Town of Marion*, 98 Ky. 673, 680-683, 34 S. W. 18, 20-21 (1896). See generally Note, Liability of Cities for the Negligence and Other Misconduct of their Officers and Agents, 30 Am. St. Rep. 376, 405-411 (1893).

Even in England, where the doctrine of official immunity followed by the American courts was first established, no immunity was granted where the damages award was to come from the public treasury. As Baron Bramwell stated in *Ruck v. Williams*, 3 H. & N. 308, 320, 157 Eng. Rep. 488, 493 (Exch. 1858):

> "I can well understand if a person undertakes the office or duty of a Commissioner, and there are no means of indemnifying him against the consequences of a slip, it is reasonable to hold that he should not be responsible for it. I can also understand that, if one of several Commissioners does something not within the scope of his authority, the Commissioners as a body are not liable. But where Commissioners, who are a quasi corporate body, are not affected [i.e., personally] by the result of an action, inasmuch as they are authorized by act of parliament to raise a fund for payment of the damages, on what principle is it that, if an individual member of the public suffers from an act *bona fide* but erroneously done, he is not to be compensated? It seems to me inconsistent with actual justice, and not warranted by any principle of law."

See generally Shearman & Redfield §§ 133, 178.

[23] Senator Stevenson proceeded to read from the decision in *Prather v. Lexington*, 52 Ky. 559, 560-562 (1852):

> "Where a particular act, operating injuriously to an individual, is authorized by a municipal corporation, by a delegation of power either general or special, it will be liable for the injury in its corporate capacity, where the acts done would warrant a like action against an individual. But as a general rule a corporation is not responsible for the unauthorized and unlawful acts of its officers, although done under the color of their office; to render it liable it must appear that it expressly authorized the acts to be done by them, or that they were done in pursuance of a general authority to act for the corporation, on the subject to which they relate. (*Thayer v. Boston*, 19 Pick., 511.) It has also been held that cities are responsible to the same extent, and in the same manner, as natural persons for injuries occasioned by the negligence or unskillfulness of their agents in the construction of works for their benefit." Globe 762.

[24] At one point in the debates, Senator Stevenson did protest that the Sherman amendment would, for the first time, "create a corporate liability for personal injury which no prudence or foresight could have prevented." *Ibid.* As his later remarks made clear, however, Stevenson's objection went only to the novelty of the amendment's creation of vicarious municipal liability for the unlawful acts of private individuals, "even if a municipality did not know of an impending or ensuing riot or did not have the wherewithal to do anything about it." *Monell v. New York City Dept. of Social Services*, 436 U.S., at 692-693, n. 57.

[25] See, *e.g.*, Globe 305 (remarks of Rep. Arthur) ("But if the Legislature enacts a law, if the Governor enforces it, if the judge upon the bench renders a judgment, if the sheriff levy an execution, execute a writ, serve a summons, or make an arrest, all acting under a solemn, official oath, [445 U.S. 622, 644] though as pure in duty as a saint and as immaculate as a seraph, for a mere error in judgment, they are liable. . ."); *id.*, at 385 (remarks of Rep. Lewis); Globe App. 217 (remarks of Sen. Thurman).

[26] In actuality, the distinction between a municipality's governmental and proprietary functions is better characterized not as a line, but as a succession of points. In efforts to avoid the often-harsh results occasioned by a literal application of the test, courts frequently created highly artificial and elusive distinctions of their own. The result was that the very same activity might be considered "governmental" in one jurisdiction, and "proprietary" in another. See 18 McQuillin § 53.02, at 105. See also W. Prosser, Law of Torts § 131, p. 979 (4th ed. 1971) (hereinafter Prosser). As this Court stated, in reference to the "'nongovernmental'-'governmental' quagmire that has long plagued the law of municipal corporations":

> "A comparative study of the cases in the forty-eight States will disclose an irreconcilable conflict. More than that, the decisions in each of the States are disharmonious and disclose the inevitable chaos when courts try to apply a rule of law that is inherently unsound." *Indian Towing Co. v. United States*, 350 U.S. 61, 65 (1955) (on rehearing).

[27] "While acting in their governmental capacity, municipal corporations proper are given the benefit of that same rule which is applied to the sovereign power itself, and are afforded complete immunity from civil responsibility for acts done or omitted, unless such responsibility is expressly created by statute. When, however, they are not acting in the exercise of their purely governmental functions, but are performing duties that pertain to the exercise of those private franchises, powers, and privileges which belong to them for their own corporate benefit, or are dealing with property held by them for their own corporate gain or emolument, then a different rule of liability is applied and they are generally held responsible for injuries arising from their negligent acts or their omissions to the same extent as a private corporation under like circumstances." Williams § 4, at 9. See generally 18 McQuillin §§ 53.02, 53.04, 53.24; Prosser § 131, at 977-983; James, Tort Liability of Governmental Units and Their Officers, 22 U. Chi. L. Rev. 610, 611-612, 622-629 (1955).

[28] Although it has never been understood how the doctrine of sovereign immunity came to be adopted in the American democracy, it apparently stems from the personal immunity of the English Monarch as expressed in the maxim, "The King can do no wrong." It has been suggested, however, that the meaning traditionally ascribed to this phrase is an ironic perversion of its original intent: "The maxim merely meant that the King was not privileged to do wrong. If his acts were against the law, they were injuriae (wrongs). Bracton, while ambiguous in his several statements as to the relation between the King and the law, did not intend to convey the idea that he was incapable of committing a legal wrong." Borchard, Government Liability in Tort, 34 Yale L. J. 1, 2, n. 2 (1924). See also Kates & Kouba, Liability of Public Entities Under Section 1983 of the Civil Rights Act, 45 S. Cal. L. Rev. 131, 142 (1972).
In this country, "[t]he sovereign or governmental immunity doctrine, holding that the state, its subdivisions and municipal entities, may not be [445 U.S. 622, 646] held liable for tortious acts, was never completely accepted by the courts, its underlying principle being deemed contrary to the basic concept of the law of torts that liability follows negligence, as well as foreign to the spirit of the constitutional guarantee that every person is entitled to a legal remedy for injuries he may receive in his person or property. As a result, the trend of judicial decisions was always to restrict, rather than to expand, the doctrine of municipal immunity." 18 McQuillin § 53.02, at 104 (footnotes omitted). See also Prosser § 131, at 984 ("For well over a century the immunity of both the state and the local governments for their torts has been subjected to vigorous criticism, which at length has begun to have its effect"). The seminal opinion of the Florida Supreme Court in *Hargrove v. Town of Cocoa Beach*, 96 So.2d 130 (1957), has spawned "a minor ava-

lanche of decisions repudiating municipal immunity," Prosser § 131, at 985, which, in conjunction with legislative abrogation of sovereign immunity, has resulted in the consequence that only a handful of States still cling to the old common-law rule of immunity for governmental functions. See K. Davis, Administrative Law of the Seventies § 25.00 (1976 and Supp. 1977) (only two States adhere to the traditional common-law immunity from torts in the exercise of governmental functions); Harley & Wasinger, Government Immunity: Despotic Mantle or Creature of Necessity, 16 Washburn L. J. 12, 34-53 (1976).

[29] The common-law immunity for governmental functions is thus more comparable to an absolute immunity from liability for conduct of a certain character, which defeats a suit at the outset, than to a qualified immunity, which "depends upon the circumstances and motivations of [the official's] actions, as established by the evidence at trial." *Imbler v. Pachtman,* 424 U.S. 409, 419, n. 13 (1976).

[30] Municipal defenses—including an assertion of sovereign immunity—to a federal right of action are, of course, controlled by federal law. See *Fitzpatrick v. Bitzer,* 427 U.S. 445, 455 -456 (1976); *Hampton v. Chicago,* 484 F.2d 602, 607 (CA7 1973) (Stevens, J.) ("Conduct by persons acting under color of state law which is wrongful under 42 U.S.C. § 1983 or § 1985 (3) cannot be immunized by state law. A construction of the federal statute which permitted a state immunity defense to have controlling effect would transmute a basic guarantee into an illusory promise; and the supremacy clause of the Constitution insures that the proper construction may be enforced").

[31] See generally 18 McQuillin § 53.04a; Shearman & Redfield §§ 127-130; Williams § 6, at 15-16. Like the governmental/proprietary distinction, a clear line between the municipality's "discretionary" and "ministerial" functions was often hard to discern, a difficulty which has been mirrored in the federal courts' attempts to draw a similar distinction under the Federal Tort Claims Act, 28 U.S.C. § 2680 (a). See generally 3 K. Davis, Administrative Law Treatise § 25.08 (1958 and Supp. 1970).

[32] Cf. P. Bator, P. Mishkin, D. Shapiro, & H. Wechsler, Hart and Wechsler's The Federal Courts and the Federal System 336 (2d ed. 1973) ("[W]here constitutional rights are at stake the courts are properly astute, in construing statutes, to avoid the conclusion that Congress intended to use the privilege of immunity . . . in order to defeat them").

[33] The absence of any damages remedy for violations of all but the most "clearly established" constitutional rights, see *Wood v. Strickland,* 420 U.S., at 322, could also have the deleterious effect of freezing constitutional law in its current state of development, for without a meaningful remedy aggrieved individuals will have little incentive to seek vindication of those constitutional deprivations that have not previously been clearly defined.

[34] For example, given the discussion that preceded the Independence City Council's adoption of the allegedly slanderous resolution impugning petitioner's integrity, see n. 6, *supra,* one must wonder whether this entire litigation would have been necessary had the Council members thought that the city might be liable for their misconduct.

[35] Cf. *Albemarle Paper Co. v. Moody,* 422 U.S. 405, 417-418 (1975):

> "If employers faced only the prospect of an injunctive order, they would have little incentive to shun practices of dubious legality. It is the reasonably certain prospect of a backpay award that 'provide[s] the spur or catalyst which causes employers and unions to self-examine and to self-evaluate their employment practices and to endeavor to eliminate, so far as possible, the last vestiges of an unfortunate and ignominious page in this country's history.' *United States v. N. L. Industries, Inc.,* 479 F.2d 354, 379 (CA8 1973)."

36 In addition, the threat of liability against the city ought to increase the attentiveness with which officials at the higher levels of government supervise the conduct of their subordinates. The need to institute systemwide measures in order to increase the vigilance with which otherwise indifferent municipal officials protect citizens' constitutional rights is, of course, particularly acute where the frontline officers are judgment-proof in their individual capacities.

37 On at least two previous occasions, this Court has expressly recognized that different considerations come into play when governmental rather than personal liability is threatened. *Hutto v. Finney*, 437 U.S. 678 (1978), affirmed an award of attorney's fees out of state funds for a deprivation of constitutional rights, holding that such an assessment would not contravene the Eleventh Amendment. In response to the suggestion, adopted by the dissent, that any award should be borne by the government officials personally, the Court noted that such an allocation would not only be "manifestly unfair," but would "def[y] this Court's insistence in a related context that imposing personal liability in the absence of bad faith may cause state officers to 'exercise their discretion with undue timidity.' *Wood v. Strickland*, 420 U.S. 308, 321." *Id.*, at 699, n. 32. The Court thus acknowledged that imposing personal liability on public officials could have an undue chilling effect on the exercise of their decision-making responsibilities, but that no such pernicious consequences were likely to flow from the possibility of a recovery from public funds.

Our decision in *Lake Country Estates, Inc. v. Tahoe Regional Planning Agency*, 440 U.S. 391 (1979), also recognized that the justifications for immunizing officials from personal liability have little force when suit is brought against the governmental entity itself. Petitioners in that case had sought damages under § 1983 from a regional planning agency and the individual members of its governing agency. Relying on *Tenney v. Brandhove*, 341 U.S. 367 (1951), the Court concluded that "to the extent the evidence discloses that these individuals were acting in a capacity comparable to that of members of a state legislature, they are entitled to absolute immunity from federal damages liability." 440 U.S., at 406. At the same time, however, we cautioned: "If the respondents have enacted unconstitutional legislation, there is no reason why relief against TRPA itself should not adequately vindicate petitioners' interests. See *Monell v. New York City Dept. of Social Services*, 436 U.S. 658." *Id.*, at 405, n. 29.

38 *Wood v. Strickland*, 420 U.S. 308 (1975), mentioned a third justification for extending a qualified immunity to public officials: the fear that the threat of personal liability might deter citizens from holding public office. See *id.*, at 320 ("The most capable candidates for school board positions might be deterred from seeking office if heavy burdens upon their private resources from monetary liability were a likely prospect during their tenure"). Such fears are totally unwarranted, of course, once the threat of personal liability is eliminated.

39 *Monell v. New York City Dept. of Social Services* indicated that the principle of loss spreading was an insufficient justification for holding the municipality liable under § 1983 on a *respondeat superior* theory. 436 U.S., at 693 -694. Here, of course, quite a different situation is presented. Petitioner does not seek to hold the city responsible for the unconstitutional actions of an individual official "*solely* because it employs a tortfeasor." *Id.*, at 691. Rather, liability is predicated on a determination that "the action that is alleged to be unconstitutional implements or executes a policy statement, ordinance, regulation, or decision officially adopted and promulgated by that body's officers." *Id.*, at 690. In this circumstance—when it is the local government itself that is responsible for the constitutional deprivation—it is perfectly reasonable to distribute the loss to the public as a cost of the administration of government, rather than to let the entire burden fall on the injured individual.

[40] "The imposition of monetary costs for mistakes which were not unreasonable in the light of all the circumstances would undoubtedly deter even the most conscientious school decision maker from exercising his judgment independently, forcefully, and in a manner best serving the long-term interest of the school and the students." *Wood v. Strickland, supra,* at 319-320.

[41] Note, Developments in the Law: Section 1983 and Federalism, 90 Harv L Rev 1133, 1224 (1977). See also *Johnson v. State,* 69 Cal. 2d 782, 792-793, 447 P.2d 352, 359-360 (1968):

> "Nor do we deem an employee's concern over the potential liability of his employer, the governmental unit, a justification for an expansive definition of 'discretionary,' and hence immune, acts. As a threshold matter, we consider it unlikely that the possibility of government liability will be [445 U.S. 622, 657] a serious deterrent to the fearless exercise of judgment by the employee. In any event, however, to the extent that such a deterrent effect takes hold, it may be wholesome. An employee in a private enterprise naturally gives some consideration to the potential liability of his employer, and this attention unquestionably promotes careful work; the potential liability of a governmental entity, to the extent that it affects primary conduct at all, will similarly influence public employees." (Citation and footnote omitted.)

Leatherman v. Tarrant County Narcotics Intelligence and Coordination Unit
507 U.S. 163 (1993)

Argued January 12, 1993
Decided March 3, 1993
CHIEF JUSTICE REHNQUIST delivered the opinion of the Court.

We granted certiorari to decide whether a federal court may apply a "heightened pleading standard"—more stringent than the usual pleading requirements of Rule 8(a) of the Federal Rules of Civil Procedure—in civil rights cases alleging municipal liability under Rev. Stat. § 1979, 42 U.S.C. § 1983. We hold it may not.

We review here a decision granting a motion to dismiss, and therefore must accept as true all the factual allegations in the complaint. See *United States v. Gaubert*, 499 U.S. 315, 327 (1991). This action arose out of two separate incidents involving the execution of search warrants by local law [507 U.S. 163, 165] enforcement officers. Each involved the forcible entry into a home based on the detection of odors associated with the manufacture of narcotics. One homeowner claimed that he was assaulted by the officers after they had entered; another claimed that the police had entered her home in her absence and killed her two dogs. Plaintiffs sued several local officials in their official capacity and the county and two municipal corporations that employed the police officers involved in the incidents, asserting that the police conduct had violated the Fourth Amendment to the United

States Constitution. The stated basis for municipal liability under *Monell v. New York City Dept. of Social Services*, 436 U.S. 658 (1978), was the failure of these bodies to adequately train the police officers involved. See *Canton v. Harris*, 489 U.S. 378 (1989).

The United States District Court for the Northern District of Texas ordered the complaints dismissed because they failed to meet the "heightened pleading standard" required by the decisional law of the Court of Appeals for the Fifth Circuit. 755 F.Supp. 726 (1991). The Fifth Circuit, in turn, affirmed the judgment of dismissal, 954 F.2d 1054 (1992), and we granted certiorari, 505 U.S. 1203 (1992), to resolve a conflict among the Courts of Appeals concerning the applicability of a heightened pleading standard to § 1983 actions alleging municipal liability. Cf., *e.g.*, *Karim-Panahi v. Los Angeles Police Dept.*, 839 F.2d 621, 624 (CA9 1988) ("[A] claim of municipal liability under Section 1983 is sufficient to withstand a motion to dismiss even if the claim is based on nothing more than a bare allegation that the individual officers' conduct conformed to official policy, custom, or practice") (internal quotation marks omitted). We now reverse.

Respondents seek to defend the Fifth Circuit's application of a more rigorous pleading standard on two grounds.* [507 U.S. 163, 166] First, respondents claim that municipalities' freedom from *respondeat superior* liability, see *Monell, supra*, necessarily includes immunity from suit. In this sense, respondents assert, municipalities are no different from state or local officials sued in their individual capacity. Respondents reason that a more relaxed pleading requirement would subject municipalities to expensive and time-consuming discovery in every § 1983 case, eviscerating their immunity from suit and disrupting municipal functions.

This argument wrongly equates freedom from liability with immunity from suit. To be sure, we reaffirmed in *Monell* that "a municipality cannot be held liable under § 1983 on a *respondeat superior* theory." 436 U.S., at 691. But, contrary to respondents' assertions, this protection against liability does not encompass immunity from suit. Indeed, this argument is flatly contradicted by *Monell* and our later decisions involving municipal liability under § 1983. In *Monell*, we overruled *Monroe v. Pape*, 365 U.S. 167 (1961), insofar as it held that local governments were wholly immune from suit under § 1983, though we did reserve decision on whether municipalities are entitled to some form of limited immunity. 436 U.S., at 701. Yet, when we took that issue up again in *Owen v. City of Independence*, 445 U.S. 622, 650 (1980), we rejected a claim that municipalities should be afforded qualified immunity, much like that afforded individual officials, based on the good faith of their agents. These decisions make it quite clear that, unlike various government officials, municipalities do not enjoy immunity from suit—either absolute or qualified—under § 1983. In short, a municipality can be sued under § 1983, but it cannot be held liable unless a municipal policy or custom caused the constitutional injury. We thus have no occasion to [507 U.S. 163, 167] consider whether our qualified immunity jurisprudence would require a heightened pleading in cases involving individual government officials.

Second, respondents contend that the Fifth Circuit's heightened pleading standard is not really that at all. See Brief for Respondents Tarrant County Narcotics Intelligence and Coordination Unit et al. 9-10 ("[T]he Fifth Circuit's so-called 'heightened' pleading requirement is a misnomer"). According to respondents, the degree of factual specificity required of a complaint by the Federal Rules of Civil Procedure varies according to the complexity of the underlying substantive law. To establish municipal liability under § 1983, respondents argue, a plaintiff must do more than plead a single instance of misconduct. This requirement, respondents insist, is consistent with a plaintiff's Rule 11 obligation to make a reasonable pre-filing inquiry into the facts.

But examination of the Fifth Circuit's decision in this case makes it quite evident that the "heightened pleading standard" is just what it purports to be: a more demanding rule for pleading a complaint under § 1983 than for pleading other kinds of claims for relief. See 954 F.2d, at 1057-1058. This rule was adopted by the Fifth Circuit in *Elliott v. Perez*, 751 F.2d 1472 (1985), and described in this language:

> "In cases against governmental officials involving the likely defense of immunity, we require of trial judges that they demand that the plaintiff's complaints state with factual detail and particularity the basis for the claim, which necessarily includes why the defendant official cannot successfully maintain the defense of immunity." *Id.*, at 1473.

In later cases, the Fifth Circuit extended this rule to complaints against municipal corporations asserting liability under § 1983. See, *e.g.*, *Palmer v. San Antonio*, 810 F.2d 514 (1987). [507 U.S. 163, 168]

> We think that it is impossible to square the "heightened pleading standard" applied by the Fifth Circuit in this case with the liberal system of "notice pleading" set up by the Federal Rules. Rule 8(a)(2) requires that a complaint include only "a short and plain statement of the claim showing that the pleader is entitled to relief." In *Conley v. Gibson*, 355 U.S. 41 (1957), we said in effect that the Rule meant what it said:

> "[T]he Federal Rules of Civil Procedure do not require a claimant to set out in detail the facts upon which he bases his claim. To the contrary, all the Rules require is 'a short and plain statement of the claim' that will give the defendant fair notice of what the plaintiff's claim is and the grounds upon which it rests." *Id.*, at 47 (footnote omitted).

Rule 9(b) does impose a particularity requirement in two specific instances. It provides that, "[i]n all averments of fraud or mistake, the circumstances constituting fraud or mistake shall be stated with particularity." Thus, the Federal Rules do address in Rule 9(b) the question of the need for greater particularity in pleading certain actions, but do not include among the enumerated actions any reference to complaints alleging municipal liability under § 1983. Expressio unius est exclusio alterius.

The phenomenon of litigation against municipal corporations based on claimed constitutional violations by their employees dates from our decision in *Monell, supra,* where we for the first time construed § 1983 to allow such municipal liability. Perhaps if Rules 8 and 9 were rewritten today, claims against municipalities under § 1983 might be subjected to the added specificity requirement of Rule 9(b). But that is a result which must be obtained by the process of amending the Federal Rules, and not by judicial interpretation. In the absence of such an amendment, federal courts and litigants must rely on summary judgment and control of discovery [507 U.S. 163, 169] to weed out unmeritorious claims sooner rather than later.

The judgment of the Court of Appeals is reversed, and the case is remanded for further proceedings consistent with this opinion.

It is so ordered.

Footnote

* Respondents also argue that certain claims are barred by collateral estoppel. According-ing to respondents, petitioners brought an unsuccessful civil rights action against two of the police officers who allegedly were involved in one of the incidents. Petitioners respond that the adverse [507 U.S. 163, 166] ruling in this other litigation is currently on appeal, and thus is not final for collateral estoppel purposes. Because this issue was neither addressed by the Fifth Circuit nor included in the questions presented, we will not consider it. [507 U.S. 163, 170]

Discussion Questions

1. Why did Congress enact the Ku Klux Act of 1871 according to the *Monroe* decision? Did the behaviors of law enforcement officials affect the decision to enact the statute?

2. At the time the Ku Klux Act was passed by Congress, some contended that state laws were adequate to prevent constitutional deprivations. If this were the case, what was lacking in the criminal justice system that required passage of the legislation?

3. How did the *Monell* decision modify the Court's decision in *Monroe*? What are the consequences of this modification for police liability? Who could be held liable for a constitutional violation under *Monroe*? Who can be held liable for constitutional violations under *Monell*?

4. Does the language of the Ku Klux Act of 1871 and its contemporary counterpart (42 U.S.C. Section 1983) as well as the Court's interpretation of its provisions set the stage for a conflict between street level police officers and municipal officials?

5. What political subdivisions of government are included in the Court's construction of municipalities? Do police and sheriff's departments fall within this construction?

6. Why are the definitions of "color of law and "persons" important to police civil liability?

7. When may a municipality be held liable under Section 1983? When may an individual police officer be held liable under Section 1983? Is there any relationship between the two?

8. What is the Court's position on common-law immunities and defenses available to defendants facing Section 1983 lawsuits?

9. Does the distinction between governmental, ministerial, and discretionary functions affect litigation under Section 1983? Who is afforded the good-faith defense, and who is afforded qualified immunity? Are there any differences between the two concepts?

10. Did the Court's view of the purposes of Section 1983 change between the *Monroe* decision and the *Owen* decision? If so, how?

PART II

Individual and Official Capacity Lawsuits

One of the most challenging aspects of the law of municipal and police liability is making the distinction between municipal and individual liability. When a citizen's constitutional rights are violated, they are inevitably violated by an individual or group of individuals. Constitutional violations by individuals, however, may be the product of municipal policy, customs, or practices. In order to determine both liability and immunity for constitutional violations, courts must be able to distinguish between the constitutional violations of individual officers and those promoted by a municipality. In an attempt to distinguish Section 1983 actions from tort actions, the Supreme Court has taken the position that municipalities are not to be exposed to the common-law doctrine of *respondeat superior. Respondeat superior* literally means "a superior or master must answer" for the misdeeds of their subordinates. The doctrine holds that employers are responsible for the acts and omissions of their employees and agents, when their actions are taken within the scope of the employees' duties. The Court's position means that just because a police officer has violated a citizen's constitutional rights it does not necessary follow that the employing municipality is legally responsible. Therefore, courts must be able to distinguish between individual and municipal lawsuits.

Further clouding the issue of individual versus municipal liability are situations where governmental officials violate the constitutional rights of citizens while acting in either an official or personal capacity. Police chiefs, for example, may use the power of their office to direct officers to engage in constitutional violations. In this situation, chiefs may be said to have acted in their official capacity. Alternatively, chiefs could violate citizens' constitutional rights in manners that have little or no relationship to their official functions or power of their offices. In these cases, it might be said that they acted in their personal capacities. When Section 1983 lawsuits are brought against the police, plaintiff attorneys inevitably bring actions against all the parties involved in both their personal and official capacities. The courts must make the determination of which distinction should prevail.

The official/personal capacity distinction also impacts decisions of immunity; for example, should the municipality bear the litigation expenses? Several of the Court's decisions in this part of the casebook also deal with the issue of what political subdivisions of government fall within the meaning of the term "person." The Court takes up the issue of whether state government falls within the scope of Section 1983 actions. This issue pulls the Court back into the personal/official capacity distinction. The Court must determine whether or not state officials can be sued in either of these capacities and what immunities state officials should be afforded. Once the political subdivision argument is opened, issues of sovereign immunity and Eleventh Amendment protections creep into the Court's reasoning—forcing the Court back to a consideration of the congressional intent underlying passage of Section 1983.

Brandon v. Holt
469 U.S. 464 (1985)

Argued November 5, 1984
Decided January 21, 1985
JUSTICE STEVENS delivered the opinion of the Court.

The District Court entered a damages judgment against the Director of the Memphis (Tenn.) Police Department in his official capacity. *Brandon v. Allen*, 516 F. Supp. 1355, 1361 (WD Tenn. 1981). The Court of Appeals for the Sixth Circuit reversed, holding that he was protected by qualified immunity. *Brandon v. Allen*, 719 F.2d 151, 153 (1983). The question presented is whether the damages judgment is payable by the city of Memphis because the Director was sued in his official capacity or whether the Director is individually liable, but shielded by qualified immunity.

Petitioners brought this action under 42 U.S.C. § 1983.[1] They alleged and proved that Robert J. Allen, who was then [469 U.S. 464, 466] a Memphis police officer, viciously assaulted them on March 5, 1977.[2] They also proved that Allen had a history of violent and irregular behavior[3] that was well known within the Police Department.[4] [469 U.S. 464, 467]

E. Winslow Chapman had been the Director of the Memphis Police Department for approximately six months when Officer Allen attacked the petitioners. It is undisputed that Chapman had no actual knowledge of Allen's disciplinary record. The District Court found, however, that "Director Chapman *should have known* that Officer Allen's dangerous propensities created a threat to the rights and safety of citizens."[5] The Director's lack of actual knowledge of Allen's propensities was found to have been caused by the "policies in effect during that period

93

of Mr. Chapman's relatively new administration," which policies included "the inherently deficient nature of police administrative procedures involving the discovery of officer misconduct."[6]

Petitioners sought damages from Officer Allen and from Director Chapman. Allen did not defend the action and a default judgment was entered against him for both compensatory [469 U.S. 464, 468] and punitive damages. The award against Director Chapman was, however, limited to compensatory damages.[7] In its findings and conclusions, the District Court repeatedly and unambiguously stated that the liability of Director Chapman was "in his official capacity."[8]

The Court of Appeals reversed the judgment against Director Chapman on the ground that he had "acted in good faith and is accordingly entitled to immunity."[9] In explaining its holding, the Court of Appeals rejected the petitioners' contention that the action against Chapman was tantamount to an action against the city of Memphis. The court wrote:

> "The plaintiffs' argument that the qualified immunity is inapplicable simply because they sued Chapman in his official capacity is unavailing. Under *Owen v. City of Independence*, 445 U.S. 622 . . . (1980), a municipality is not entitled to claim the qualified immunity that the city's agents can assert. But this is a suit against an individual, not the city. In reality, plaintiffs are attempting to amend their complaint so as to treat the Police Director as though he were the City in order to avoid the qualified [469 U.S. 464, 469] immunity which shields Director Chapman. Such an argument is without support in precedent or reason."[10]

We granted certiorari to consider the validity of that argument. 467 U.S. 1204 (1984). We now reverse.

I

In *Monroe v. Pape*, 365 U.S. 167, 187-192 (1961), the Court held that a city was not "a person" within the meaning of 42 U.S.C. § 1983. That construction of § 1983 protected municipalities from liability in cases of this kind until June 6, 1978, when we decided *Monell v. New York City Dept. of Social Services*, 436 U.S. 658. The complaint in this case was filed on February 22, 1978, before *Monroe v. Pape* was overruled; this explains why the city of Memphis was not named as a defendant in this case. The timing of the complaint may also explain why petitioners did not expressly allege at the outset of the litigation that they were suing Chapman in his official capacity as Director of Police of the Memphis Police Department.[11]

The course of proceedings after *Monell* was decided did, however, make it abundantly clear that the action against Chapman was in his official capacity and only in that capacity. Thus, in petitioners' response to a defense motion for summary judgment, petitioners' counsel stated:

"Defendant Chapman is sued in his official capacity as Director of Police Services, City of Memphis, Tennessee. '[O]fficial capacity suits generally represent an action against an entity of which an officer is an agent. . . . [469 U.S. 464, 470] *Monell v. New York Department of Social Services*, 436 U.S. 658, 690 n. 55 (1978).'"[12]

The point was reiterated in counsel's opening statement,[13] in the trial court's evidentiary rulings,[14] in the findings on liability,[15] and in the proceedings relating to damages in which it was recognized that our decision in *Newport v. Facts Concert, Inc.*, 453 U.S. 247 (1981), precluded an award of punitive damages against Director Chapman.[16]

The Court of Appeals also repeatedly noted that the suit against Chapman was "in his official capacity."[17] Moreover, while the appeal was pending Director Chapman left office and was replaced by John D. Holt. Pursuant to Rule 43(c)(1) of the Federal Rules of Appellate Procedure, Holt was automatically substituted as a party.[18] It is Director Holt [469 U.S. 464, 471] who appears as a respondent in this Court, and there is not even an arguable basis for claiming that the record would support an award of damages against him individually.

Given this state of the record, even at this late stage of the proceedings, petitioners are entitled to amend their pleadings to conform to the proof and to the District Court's findings of fact.[19] Moreover, it is appropriate for us to proceed to decide the legal issues without first insisting that such a formal amendment be filed; this is because we regard the record as plainly identifying petitioners' claim for damages as one that is asserted against the office of "Director of Police, City of Memphis," rather than against the particular individual who occupied that office when the claim arose. Petitioners are claiming a right to recover damages from the city of Memphis.

II

In at least three recent cases arising under § 1983, we have plainly implied that a judgment against a public servant "in his official capacity" imposes liability on the entity that he represents provided, of course, the public entity received [469 U.S. 464, 472] notice and an opportunity to respond.[20] We now make that point explicit.

In *Monell*, the City of New York was not itself expressly named as a defendant. The suit was nominally against the city's Department of Social Services, but that Department had no greater separate identity from the city than did the Director of the Department when he was acting in his official capacity. For the purpose of evaluating the city's potential liability under § 1983, our opinion clearly equated the actions of the Director of the Department in his official capacity with the actions of the city itself.[21]

Hutto v. Finney, 437 U.S. 678 (1978), was an action against state officials rather than municipal officers. Notwithstanding our express recognition that an order requiring the Arkansas Commissioner of Corrections to pay the plaintiff's counsel fees would be satisfied with state funds, we sustained the order against an Eleventh Amendment challenge. We considered it obvious that the State would pay the award because the defendants had been sued in their "official capacities."[22]

Less than two years later, we decided *Owen v. City of Independence*, 445 U.S. 622 (1980), a § 1983 action in which the complaint named as defendants "the city of Independence, City Manager Alberg, and the present members of the City Council in their official capacities."[23] We held that the qualified immunity that protects public servants acting in good faith was not available to those defendants. In so holding, we expressly distinguished between suits against government officials "in their individual capacities" on the [469 U.S. 464, 473] one hand, and those in which "only the liability of the municipality itself was at issue," on the other.[24]

Because the Court of Appeals failed to apply that distinction in this case, it erred. Our holding in *Owen*, that a municipality is not entitled to the shield of qualified immunity from liability under § 1983, requires a reversal of the Court of Appeals' judgment. Accordingly, the judgment is reversed, and the case is remanded to that court for further proceedings consistent with this opinion.[25]

It is so ordered.

Footnotes

[1] That section provides, in pertinent part:

"Every person who, under color of any statute, ordinance, regulation, custom, or usage, of any State . . . subjects or causes to be subjected, any citizen of the United States . . . to the deprivation of any rights, privileges, or immunities secured by the Constitution and laws, shall be liable to the [469 U.S. 464, 466] party injured in an action at law, suit in equity, or other proper proceeding for redress."

[2] The following excerpt from the District Court's findings of fact adequately reflects the character of the incident:

"[Petitioners], who were seventeen years of age, drove to the Memphis Hunt and Polo Club while on a date and parked in a dark and secluded driveway area. . . . After approximately thirty minutes had elapsed, a Chevrolet pickup truck entered the driveway where [petitioners] were parked. . . . The driver of the truck identified himself to [petitioners] as a police officer and showed them an official police identification card bearing the name and photograph of Robert J. Allen. . . . Mr. Allen ordered Mr. Muse to step out of the car. After briefly questioning him, Officer Allen maliciously, and without provocation, struck Mr. Muse in the neck and head with his fist and then stabbed and cut Muse on the neck and ear with a knife. As Officer Allen tried to break into the car where [petitioner] Elizabeth A. Brandon was seated, Mr. Muse jumped into the driver's side of the car and quickly drove away. Officer Allen fired one shot at the escaping vehicle from his police revolver. The bullet shattered the front window on the driver's side of the car. Officer Allen followed plaintiffs in a high speed chase which ended at St. Joseph's Hospital East, where plaintiffs sought medical care and assistance and reported the unprovoked attack upon them by Officer Allen." *Brandon v. Allen*, 516 F. Supp. 1355, 1357 (WD Tenn. 1981).

[3] Officer Allen's police file records contained 20 complaints against him when he left the Memphis Police Department. They included complaints for "serious abuse of police authority and use of unnecessary force." *Id.*, at 1358.

[4] The District Court found that Officer Allen's "reputation for displaying maladaptive behavior was well known among Police officers in his precinct." *Ibid.* The court also found that Allen's colleagues commented thusly when the March 5 incident was reported to them: "They finally caught up with him; he's a quack; Allen has done something this time that he can't get out of." *Ibid.* Moreover, the court found that Allen's fellow officers regarded him as a "mental case"; that Allen rode in his squad car alone because of the reluctance of other officers to ride with him; and that Allen boasted of killing a man in the course of duty. *Ibid.* Additionally, the District Court wrote: [469 U.S. 464, 467]

"Officer Allen has often stated to other officers that he wished he knew the exact bullet spread in the chest of the man he killed. Officer Allen referred to a pair of gloves in his possession as his 'killing gloves,' and he would ceremoniously put those gloves on his hands when he was called to the scene of a crime." *Ibid.*

[5] *Id.*, at 1360.

[6] Regarding these policies and procedures, the District Court wrote:

"Due to a code of silence induced by peer pressure among the rank-and-file officers and among some police supervisors, few—if any—formal complaints were ever filed by police personnel. Furthermore, when complaints were filed by citizens, little disciplinary action was apparently taken against the offending officer. Instead, a standard form letter, bearing Mr. Chapman's signature, was mailed to each complainant, assuring the person that appropriate action had been taken by the Police Department, even if such action had not in fact been taken. This tended to discourage follow-up measures by the complaining citizen. Perhaps, Mr. Chapman's belief that it was better to take no disciplinary action than to act and later be reversed by a review board was responsible for this obviously inadequate solution. The end result was twofold: 1) Mr. Chapman's procedures were highly conducive to 'covering up' officer misconduct; 2) the Police Director and many of his supervisors were totally insulated from knowledge of wrongdoing by officers as a result of policies in effect during that period of Mr. Chapman's relatively new administration." *Id.*, at 1361.

[7] Petitioner Muse recovered $21,310.75 in compensatory damages and out-of-pocket expenses; petitioner Brandon recovered $5,000. App. 36a.

[8] The District Court initially summarized: "This is a civil action against the Honorable E. Winslow Chapman, *in his official capacity as director of the Memphis Police Department* and former Memphis Police Officer Robert J. Allen." *Id.*, at 1356 (emphasis added). It also later stated that "Mr. Chapman was sued in his official capacity as an agent of the Memphis Police Department," *id.*, at 1359 (emphasis added), and that "[b]ecause Mr. Chapman, *as Police Director*, should have known of Officer Allen's dangerous propensities the Court finds that he must be held liable, *in his official capacity*, to the plaintiffs." *Id.*, at 1360 (emphasis added). Finally, the court concluded: "Accordingly, Mr. Chapman *in his capacity as Director of the*

Memphis Police Department must be held liable to plaintiffs in this case." *Id.*, at 1361 (emphasis added).

[9] *Brandon v. Allen*, 719 F.2d 151, 154 (1983). The Court of Appeals also held that the award of compensatory damages against Allen was inadequate. *Id.*, at 153.

[10] *Id.*, at 154.

[11] The caption and the body of the complaint named as a defendant, "E. Winslow Chapman, Director of Police." Complaint, *Brandon v. Allen*, Civil Action No. 78-2076 (WD Tenn.). The Mayor of Memphis was also named; the District Court granted summary judgment in his favor. App. 13a-18a.

[12] Brief for Petitioners 19.

[13] Counsel stated:

> "Mr. Chapman is sued in this lawsuit in his official capacity, and as was stated in *Monell versus New York City Department of Social Services*, a 1978 Supreme Court case, official capacity suits generally represent only another way of pleading an action against an entity of which an officer is an agent." *Id.*, at 20-21.

See also Tr. 202 ("Mr. Chapman is not sued individually, but in his official capacity") (statement of petitioners' counsel during trial).

[14] The trial court held that certain out-of-court statements by police officers were admissible because the officers were employed by a party to the case, namely the city of Memphis. See *id.*, at 17-21, 45-47.

[15] See n. 8, *supra.*

[16] Chapman's attorney argued that *Newport* made it clear that no award of punitive damages could be made against Chapman "since he was found liable in his official capacity." See Brief for Defendant E. Winslow Chapman on Issue of Damages in No. C-78-2076 (WD Tenn.), p. 1.

[17] 719 F.2d, at 152, 153, 154; see also Order Denying Petition for Rehearing En Banc, *Brandon v. Allen*, Nos. 82-5321, 83-5346 (CA6) ("We do not believe that a judgment for damages against a police official in his official capacity is the same as a judgment against the city itself").

[18] Rule 43(c)(1), entitled "*Public officers; death or separation from office*," provides:

> "When a public officer is a party to an appeal or other proceeding in the court of appeals in his official capacity and during its pendency dies, resigns [469 U.S. 464, 471] or otherwise ceases to hold office, the action does not abate and his successor is automatically substituted as a party. Proceedings following the substitution shall be in the name of the substituted party, but any misnomer not affecting the substantial rights of the parties shall be disregarded. An order of substitution may be entered at any time, but the omission to enter such an order shall not affect the substitution."

See also this Court's Rule 40.3; Fed. Rule Civ. Proc. 25(d)(1).

[19] See Fed. Rule Civ. Proc. 15(b); 3 J. Moore, Federal Practice ¶ 15.132., p. 15-157 (2d ed. 1984) (amendment to conform to evidence may be made at any time); *id.*, at 15-168 (Rule 15(b) amendment allowed "so long as the opposing party has not been prejudiced in presenting his case"); 6 C. Wright & A. Miller, Federal Practice and Procedure § 1491, pp. 453, 454 (1971 ed. and Supp. 1983) (Rule 15(b) is "intended to promote the objective of deciding cases on their merits rather than in terms of the relative pleading skills of counsel"); *ibid.* ("[C]ourts should interpret [Rule 15(b)] liberally and permit an amendment whenever doing so will effectuate the underlying purpose of the rule").

[20] Here, the Police Department and the city received notice; no claim is made that the Director of Police and the city were without due notice of the proceedings.

[21] We stated that "official-capacity suits generally represent only another way of pleading an action against an entity of which an officer is an agent." 436 U.S., at 658, 690, n. 55.

[22] See 437 U.S., at 693.

[23] 445 U.S., at 630.

[24] We wrote:

> "The governmental immunity at issue in the present case differs significantly from the official immunities involved in our previous decisions. In those cases, various government officers had been sued in their individual capacities. . . . Here, in contrast, *only the liability of the municipality itself is at issue, not that of its officers. . . .*" *Id.*, at 638, n. 18 (emphasis added).

[25] As an alternative ground for affirming the judgment of the Court of Appeals, respondents argue that the record does not establish that petitioners' injury was caused by the kind of "policy or custom" that "may fairly be said to represent official policy" of the city of Memphis. See *Monell*, 436 U.S., at 694. Because the Court of Appeals did not address this argument, we do not consider it. *Monsanto v. Spray-Rite Service Corp.*, 465 U.S. 752, 759-761, n. 6 (1984); *Adickes v. S. H. Kress & Co.*, 398 U.S. 144, 147, n. 2 (1970); *Duignan v. United States*, 274 U.S. 195, 200 (1927).

Kentucky v. Graham
473 U.S. 159 (1985)

Argued April 16, 1985
Decided June 28, 1985
JUSTICE MARSHALL delivered the opinion of the Court.

The question presented is whether 42 U.S.C. § 1988 allows attorney's fees to be recovered from a governmental entity when a plaintiff sues governmental employees only in their personal capacities and prevails.

I

On November 7, 1979, a Kentucky state trooper was murdered. Suspicion quickly focused on Clyde Graham, whose stepmother's car was found near the site of the slaying and whose driver's license and billfold were discovered in nearby bushes. That evening, 30 to 40 city, county, and state police officers converged on the house of Graham's father in Elizabethtown, Kentucky. Without a warrant, the police entered the home twice and eventually arrested all the occupants, who are the six respondents here. Graham was not among them.[1] According to respondents, they were severely beaten, terrorized, illegally searched, and falsely arrested. Kenneth Brandenburgh, the Commissioner of the State Police and the highest ranking law enforcement officer in Kentucky, allegedly was directly involved in carrying out at least one of the raids. An investigation by the Kentucky Attorney General's office later concluded that the police had used excessive force and that a "complete breakdown" in police discipline had created an "uncontrolled" situation. App. to Brief for Respondents 21-22.

Alleging a deprivation of a number of federal rights, respondents filed suit in Federal District Court.[2] Their complaint [473 U.S. 159, 162]

100

sought only money damages and named as defendants various local and state law enforcement officers, the city of Elizabethtown, and Hardin County, Kentucky. Also made defendants were Commissioner Brandenburgh, "individually and as Commissioner of the Bureau of State Police," and the Commonwealth of Kentucky. The Commonwealth was sued, not for damages on the merits, but only for attorney's fees should the plaintiffs eventually prevail.[3] Shortly after the complaint was filed, the District Court, relying on the Eleventh Amendment, dismissed the Commonwealth as a party. Based on its Attorney General's report, the Commonwealth refused to defend any of the individual defendants, including Commissioner Brandenburgh, or to pay their litigation expenses.

On the second day of trial, the case was settled for $60,000.[4] The settlement agreement, embodied in a court order dismissing the case, barred respondents from seeking attorney's fees from any of the individual defendants but specifically preserved respondents' right to seek fees and court costs from the Commonwealth. Respondents then moved, pursuant to 42 U.S.C. § 1988, that the Commonwealth pay their costs and attorney's fees. At a hearing on this motion, the Commonwealth argued that the fee request had to be [473 U.S. 159, 163] denied as a matter of law, both because the Commonwealth had been dismissed as a party and because the Eleventh Amendment, in any event, barred such an award. Rejecting these arguments, the District Court ordered the Commonwealth to pay $58,521 in fees and more than $6,000 in costs and expenses.[5] In a short *per curiam* opinion relying solely on this Court's decision in *Hutto v. Finney*, 437 U.S. 678 (1978), the Court of Appeals for the Sixth Circuit affirmed. *Graham v. Wilson*, 742 F.2d 1455 (1984).

We granted certiorari to address the proposition, rejected by at least two Courts of Appeals,[6] that fees can be recovered from a governmental entity when a plaintiff prevails in a suit against government employees in their personal capacities. 469 U.S. 1156 (1985). We now reverse.

II

This case requires us to unravel once again the distinctions between personal- and official-capacity suits, see *Brandon v. Holt*, 469 U.S. 464 (1985), this time in the context of fee awards under 42 U.S.C. § 1988. The relevant portion of § 1988, enacted as the Civil Rights Attorney's Fees Awards Act of 1976, 90 Stat. 2641, provides:

> "In any action or proceeding to enforce a provision of Sections 1981, 1982, 1983, 1985, and 1986 of this title, title IX of Public Law 92-318, or title VI of the Civil Rights Act of 1964, the court, in its discretion, may allow *the prevailing party*, other than the United States, a reasonable attorney's fee as part of the costs" (emphasis added). [473 U.S. 159, 164]

If a plaintiff prevails in a suit covered by § 1988, fees should be awarded as costs "unless special circumstances would render such an award unjust." S. Rep. No. 94-1011, p. 4 (1976); see *Supreme Court of Virginia v. Consumers Union of United States, Inc.*, 446 U.S. 719, 737 (1980). Section 1988 does not in so many words define the parties who must bear these costs. Nonetheless, it is clear that the logical place to look for recovery of fees is to the losing party—the party legally responsible for relief on the merits. That is the party who must pay the costs of the litigation, see generally Fed. Rule Civ. Proc. 54(d),[7] and it is clearly the party who should also bear fee liability under § 1988.

We recognized as much in *Supreme Court of Virginia, supra.* There a three-judge District Court had found the Virginia Supreme Court and its chief justice in his official capacity liable for promulgating, and refusing to amend, a State Bar Code that violated the First Amendment. The District Court also awarded fees against these defendants pursuant to § 1988. We held that absolute legislative immunity shielded these defendants for acts taken in their legislative capacity. We then vacated the fee award, stating that we found nothing "in the legislative history of the Act to suggest that Congress intended to permit an award of attorney's fees to be premised on acts for which defendants would enjoy absolute legislative immunity." 446 U.S., at 738.[8] [473 U.S. 159, 165] Thus, liability on the merits and responsibility for fees go hand in hand; where a defendant has not been prevailed against, either because of legal immunity or on the merits, § 1988 does not authorize a fee award against that defendant.[9] Cf. *Pulliam v. Allen*, 466 U.S. 522, 543-544 (1984) (state judge liable for injunctive and declaratory relief under § 1983 also liable for fees under § 1988).

A

Proper application of this principle in damages actions against public officials requires careful adherence to the distinction between personal- and official-capacity suits.[10] Because this distinction apparently continues to confuse lawyers and confound lower courts, we attempt to define it more clearly through concrete examples of the practical and doctrinal differences between personal- and official-capacity actions.

Personal-capacity suits seek to impose personal liability upon a government official for actions he takes under color of state law. See, *e.g., Scheuer v. Rhodes*, 416 U.S. 232, 237-238 (1974). Official-capacity suits, in contrast, "generally represent only another way of pleading an action against an entity of which an officer is an agent." *Monell v. New York City Dept. of Social Services*, 436 U.S. 658, 690, n. 55 [473 U.S. 159, 166] (1978). As long as the government entity receives notice and an opportunity to respond, an official-capacity suit is, in all respects other than name, to be treated as a suit against the entity. *Brandon*, 469 U.S., at 471-472. It is not a suit against the official personally, for the real party in interest is the entity. Thus, while an award of damages against an official in his personal capacity can be executed only against the official's personal assets, a plaintiff seeking to recover on a damages judgment in an official-capacity suit must look to the government entity itself.[11]

On the merits, to establish *personal* liability in a § 1983 action, it is enough to show that the official, acting under color of state law, caused the deprivation of a federal right. See, *e.g., Monroe v. Pape*, 365 U.S. 167 (1961). More is required in an official-capacity action, however, for a governmental entity is liable under § 1983 only when the entity itself is a "'moving force'" behind the deprivation, *Polk County v. Dodson*, 454 U.S. 312, 326 (1981) (quoting *Monell, supra,* at 694); thus, in an official-capacity suit the entity's "policy or custom" must have played a part in the violation of federal law. *Monell, supra; Oklahoma City v. Tuttle*, 471 U.S. 808, 817-818 (1985); *id.*, at 827-828 (BRENNAN, J., concurring in judgment).[12] When it comes to defenses to liability, an official in a personal-capacity action may, depending on his position, be able to assert personal immunity defenses, such [473 U.S. 159, 167] as objectively reasonable reliance on existing law. See *Imbler v. Pachtman*, 424 U.S. 409 (1976) (absolute immunity); *Pierson v. Ray*, 386 U.S. 547 (1967) (same); *Harlow v. Fitzgerald*, 457 U.S. 800 (1982) (qualified immunity); *Wood v. Strickland*, 420 U.S. 308 (1975) (same). In an official-capacity action, these defenses are unavailable. *Owen v. City of Independence*, 445 U.S. 622 (1980); see also *Brandon v. Holt*, 469 U.S. 464 (1985).[13] The only immunities that can be claimed in an official-capacity action are forms of sovereign immunity that the entity, *qua* entity, may possess, such as the Eleventh Amendment. While not exhaustive, this list illustrates the basic distinction between personal- and official-capacity actions.[14]

With this distinction in mind, it is clear that a suit against a government official in his or her personal capacity cannot lead to imposition of fee liability upon the governmental entity. A victory in a personal-capacity action is a victory against the individual defendant, rather than against the [473 U.S. 159, 168] entity that employs him. Indeed, unless a distinct cause of action is asserted against the entity itself, the entity is not even a party to a personal-capacity lawsuit and has no opportunity to present a defense. That a plaintiff has prevailed against one party does not entitle him to fees from another party, let alone from a nonparty. Cf. *Hensley v. Eckerhart*, 461 U.S. 424 (1983). Yet that would be the result were we to hold that fees can be recovered from a governmental entity following victory in a personal-capacity action against government officials.

B

Such a result also would be inconsistent with the statement in *Monell, supra*, that a municipality cannot be made liable under 42 U.S.C. § 1983 on a *respondeat superior* basis. Nothing in the history of § 1988, a statute designed to make effective the remedies created in § 1983 and similar statutes, suggests that fee liability, unlike merits liability, *was* intended to be imposed on a *respondeat superior* basis. On the contrary, just as Congress rejected making § 1983 a "mutual insurance" scheme, 436 U.S., at 694, Congress sought to avoid making § 1988 a "'relief fund for lawyers.'" *Hensley, supra,* at 446 (opinion of BRENNAN, J.) (quoting 122 Cong. Rec. 33314 (1976) (remarks of Sen. Kennedy)). Section 1988 does not guarantee that lawyers will recover fees anytime their clients sue a government official in his personal capacity, with the governmental entity as ultimate insurer. Instead, fee liability runs with merits liability; if federal law does not make the government substantively liable on a *respondeat superior* basis, the government similarly is not liable for fees on that basis under § 1988. Section 1988 simply does not create fee liability where merits liability is nonexistent.

III

We conclude that this case was necessarily litigated as a personal-capacity action and that the Court of Appeals therefore erred in awarding fees against the Commonwealth of [473 U.S. 159, 169] Kentucky.[15] In asserting the contrary, respondents point out that the complaint expressly named Commissioner Brandenburgh in both his "individual" and "official" capacities and that the Commonwealth of Kentucky was named as a defendant for the limited purposes of a fee award. Nonetheless, given Eleventh Amendment doctrine, there can be no doubt that this damages action did not seek to impose monetary liability on the Commonwealth.[16]

The Court has held that, absent waiver by the State or valid congressional override, the Eleventh Amendment bars a damages action against a State in federal court.[17] See, *e.g., Ford Motor Co. v. Department of Treasury of Indiana,* 323 U.S. 459, 464 (1945). This bar remains in effect when state officials are sued for damages in their official capacity. *Cory v. White,* 457 U.S. 85, 90 (1982); *Edelman v. Jordan,* 415 U.S. 651, 663 (1974). That is so because, as discussed above, "a judgment against a public servant 'in his official capacity' imposes liability on the entity that he represents . . . ." *Brandon, supra,* at 471.[18] [473 U.S. 159, 170]

Given this understanding of the law, an official-capacity action for damages could not have been maintained against Commissioner Brandenburgh in federal court.[19] Although respondents fail to acknowledge this point, they freely concede that money damages were never sought from the Commonwealth and could not have been awarded against it;[20] respondents cannot reach this same end simply by suing state officials in their official capacity. Nor did respondents' action on the merits become a suit against Kentucky when the Commonwealth was named a defendant on the limited issue of fee liability. There is no cause of action against a defendant for fees absent that defendant's liability for relief on the merits. See *supra,* at 167-168. Naming the Commonwealth for fees did not create, out of whole cloth, the cause of action on the merits necessary to support this fee request. Thus, no claim for merits relief capable of being asserted in federal court was asserted against the Commonwealth of Kentucky. In the absence of such a claim, the fee award against the Commonwealth must be reversed.

IV

Despite the Court of Appeals' contrary view, the result we reach today is fully consistent with *Hutto v. Finney*, 437 U.S. 678 (1978). *Hutto* holds only that, when a State in a § 1983 action has been prevailed against for relief on the merits, either because the State was a proper party defendant or because state officials properly were sued in their official capacity, fees may also be available from the State under § 1988. *Hutto* does not alter the basic philosophy of [473 U.S. 159, 171] § 1988, namely, that fee and merits liability run together. As a result, Hutto neither holds nor suggests that fees are available from a governmental entity simply because a government official has been prevailed against in his or her personal capacity.

Respondents vigorously protest that this holding will "effectively destro[y]" § 1988 in cases such as this one. Brief for Respondents 19. This fear is overstated. Fees are unavailable only where a governmental entity cannot be held liable on the merits; today we simply apply the fee-shifting provisions of § 1988 against a pre-existing background of substantive liability rules.

V

Only in an official-capacity action is a plaintiff who prevails entitled to look for relief, both on the merits and for fees, to the governmental entity. Because the Court's Eleventh Amendment decisions required this case to be litigated as a personal-capacity action, the award of fees against the Commonwealth of Kentucky must be reversed.

It is so ordered.

Footnotes

[1] Clyde Graham was killed by a Kentucky state trooper a month later at a motel in Illinois.

[2] Respondents asserted causes of action under 42 U.S.C. §§ 1983, 1985, 1986, and 1988, as well as the Fourth, Fifth, Sixth, Eleventh, and Fourteenth Amendments. Complaint ¶ 13. Because the case was settled, there has been no need below to separate out or distinguish any of these purported causes of action. Before this Court, the parties briefed and argued the case as if it had been brought simply as a § 1983 action and we, accordingly, [473 U.S. 159, 162] analyze it the same way. Our discussion throughout is therefore not meant to express any view on suits brought under any provision of federal law other than § 1983.

[3] The complaint states:

"Pursuant to the provisions of 42 U.S.C. § 1988, the Commonwealth of Kentucky, d/b/a Bureau of State Police is liable for the payment of reasonable attorney fees incurred in this action." Complaint ¶ 4(D). According to respondents, "[p]aragraph 4(D) . . . states the sole basis for including the Commonwealth as a named party." Brief for Respondents 14.

[4] Five thousand dollars came from the city and $10,000 from the county. The remaining $45,000 was to be paid by Commissioner Brandenburgh, both personally and as agent for the "Kentucky State Police Legal Fund." The latter was not a named defendant but presumably represented the interests of the individual officers sued.

[5] Petitioner did not appeal from the award of costs and expenses, and we therefore have no occasion to consider the appropriateness of these portions of the award.

[6] *Berry v. McLemore*, 670 F.2d 30 (CA5 1982) (municipal officials); *Morrison v. Fox*, 660 F.2d 87 (CA3 1981) (same). At least one Court of Appeals appears to have reached the same result as that of the lower court in this case. See *Glover v. Alabama Department of Corrections*, 753 F.2d 1569 (CA11 1985).

[7] See 6 J. Moore, W. Taggart, & J. Wicker, Moore's Federal Practice § 54.701., p. 1301 (1985) ("Costs" are awarded "against the losing party and as an incident of the judgment"); 10 C. Wright, A. Miller, & M. Kane, Federal Practice and Procedure § 2666, p. 173 (1983) ("'Costs' refers to those charges that one party has incurred and is permitted to have reimbursed by his opponent as part of the judgment in the action").

[8] We did hold that the court and its chief justice in his official capacity could be enjoined from *enforcing* the State Bar Code and suggested that fees could be recovered from these defendants in their enforcement roles. Because the fee award had clearly been made against the defendants in their legislative roles, however, the award had to be vacated and the case remanded for further proceedings. That fees could be awarded against [473 U.S. 159, 165] the Virginia Supreme Court and its chief justice pursuant to an injunction against enforcement of the Code further illustrates that fee liability is tied to liability on the merits.

[9] The rules are somewhat different with respect to prevailing defendants. Prevailing defendants generally are entitled to costs, see Fed. Rule Civ. Proc. 54(d), but are entitled to fees only where the suit was vexatious, frivolous, or brought to harass or embarrass the defendant. See *Hensley v. Eckerhart*, 461 U.S. 424, 429, n. 2 (1983). We express no view as to the nature or degree of success necessary to make a plaintiff a prevailing party. See *Maher v. Gagne*, 448 U.S. 122 (1980).

[10] Personal-capacity actions are sometimes referred to as individual-capacity actions.

[11] Should the official die pending final resolution of a personal-capacity action, the plaintiff would have to pursue his action against the decedent's estate. In an official-capacity action in federal court, death or replacement of the named official will result in automatic substitution of the official's successor in office. See Fed. Rule Civ. Proc. 25(d)(1); Fed. Rule App. Proc. 43(c)(1); this Court's Rule 40.3.

[12] See *Monell*, 436 U.S., at 694 ("[A] local government may not be sued under § 1983 for an injury inflicted solely by its employees or agents. Instead, it is when execution of a government's policy or custom, whether made by its lawmakers or by those whose edicts or acts may fairly be said to represent official policy, inflicts the injury that the government as an entity is responsible under § 1983").

[13] In addition, punitive damages are not available under § 1983 from a municipality, *Newport v. Fact Concerts, Inc.*, 453 U.S. 247 (1981), but are available in a suit against an official personally, see *Smith v. Wade*, 461 U.S. 30 (1983).

[14] There is no longer a need to bring official-capacity actions against local government officials, for under *Monell, supra*, local government units can be sued directly for damages and injunctive or declaratory relief. See, *e.g.*, *Memphis Police*

Dept. v. Garner, 471 U.S. 1 (1985) (decided with *Tennessee v. Garner*) (damages action against municipality). Unless a State has waived its Eleventh Amendment immunity or Congress has overridden it, however, a State cannot be sued directly in its own name regardless of the relief sought. *Alabama v. Pugh,* 438 U.S. 781 (1978) (*per curiam*). Thus, implementation of state policy or custom may be reached in federal court only because official-capacity actions for prospective relief are not treated as actions against the State. See *Ex parte Young,* 209 U.S. 123 (1908). In many cases, the complaint will not clearly specify whether officials are sued personally, in their official capacity, or both. "The course of proceedings" in such cases typically will indicate the nature of the liability sought to be imposed. *Brandon v. Holt,* 469 U.S. 464, 469 (1985).

[15] The city and county were sued directly as entities, but that aspect of the case is not before us.

[16] See also n. 3, *supra.*

[17] The Court has held that § 1983 was not intended to abrogate a State's Eleventh Amendment immunity. *Quern v. Jordan,* 440 U.S. 332 (1979); *Edelman v. Jordan,* 415 U.S. 651 (1974). Because this action comes to us as if it arose solely under § 1983, see n. 2, *supra,* we cannot conclude that federal law authorized an official-capacity action for damages against Commissioner Brandenburgh to be brought in federal court. As to legislative waiver of immunity, petitioners assert that the Commonwealth of Kentucky has not waived its Eleventh Amendment immunity. This contention is not disputed, and we therefore accept it for purposes of this case.

[18] In an injunctive or declaratory action grounded on federal law, the State's immunity can be overcome by naming state officials as defendants. See *Penn-hurst State School & Hospital v. Halderman,* 465 U.S. 89 (1984); see also *Ex parte Young, supra.* Monetary relief that is "ancillary" to injunctive relief also is not barred by the Eleventh Amendment. *Edelman v. Jordan, supra,* at 667-668.

[19] No argument has been made that the Commonwealth waived its Eleventh Amendment immunity by failing specifically to seek dismissal of that portion of the damages action that named Commissioner Brandenburgh in his official capacity. Nor is the Commonwealth alleged to have done so by allowing him to enter the settlement agreement; the Commonwealth did not even have notice of the settlement negotiations.

[20] Brief for Respondents 17; Tr. of Oral Arg. 18. [473 U.S. 159, 172]

Will v. Michigan
Department of State Police
491 U.S. 58 (1989)

Argued December 5, 1988
Decided June 15, 1989
JUSTICE WHITE delivered the opinion of the Court.

This case presents the question whether a State, or an official of the State while acting in his or her official capacity, is a "person" within the meaning of Rev. Stat. 1979, 42 U.S.C. § 1983.

Petitioner Ray Will filed suit in Michigan Circuit Court alleging various violations of the United States and Michigan Constitutions as grounds for a claim under § 1983.[1] He alleged that he had been denied a promotion to a data systems analyst position with the Department of State Police for an improper reason, that is, because his brother had been a student activist and the subject of a "red squad" file maintained by respondent. Named as defendants were the Department of State Police and the Director of State Police in his official capacity, also a respondent here.[2]

The Circuit Court remanded the case to the Michigan Civil Service Commission for a grievance hearing. While the grievance was pending, petitioner filed suit in the Michigan [491 U.S. 58, 61] Court of Claims raising an essentially identical § 1983 claim. The Civil Service Commission ultimately found in petitioner's favor, ruling that respondents had refused to promote petitioner because of "partisan considerations." App. 46. On the basis of that finding, the state-court judge, acting in both the Circuit Court and the Court of Claims cases, concluded that petitioner had established a violation of the United States Constitution. The judge held that the Circuit Court action was barred under state law

108

but that the Claims Court action could go forward. The judge also ruled that respondents were persons for purposes of § 1983.

The Michigan Court of Appeals vacated the judgment against the Department of State Police, holding that a State is not a person under § 1983, but remanded the case for determination of the possible immunity of the Director of State Police from liability for damages. The Michigan Supreme Court granted discretionary review and affirmed the Court of Appeals in part and reversed in part. *Smith v. Department of Pub. Health*, 428 Mich. 540, 410 N. W. 2d 749 (1987). The Supreme Court agreed that the State itself is not a person under § 1983, but held that a state official acting in his or her official capacity also is not such a person.

The Michigan Supreme Court's holding that a State is not a person under § 1983 conflicts with a number of state- and federal-court decisions to the contrary.[3] We granted certiorari to resolve the conflict. 485 U.S. 1005 (1988). [491 U.S. 58, 62]

Prior to *Monell v. New York City Dept. of Social Services*, 436 U.S. 658 (1978), the question whether a State is a person within the meaning of § 1983 had been answered by this Court in the negative. In *Monroe v. Pape*, 365 U.S. 167, 187-191 (1961), the Court had held that a municipality was not a person under § 1983. "[T]hat being the case," we reasoned, § 1983 "could not have been intended to include States as parties defendant." *Fitzpatrick v. Bitzer*, 427 U.S. 445, 452 (1976).

But in *Monell*, the Court overruled *Monroe*, holding that a municipality was a person under § 1983. 436 U.S., at 690. Since then, various members of the Court have debated whether a State is a person within the meaning of § 1983, see *Hutto v. Finney*, 437 U.S. 678, 700-704 (1978) (BRENNAN, J., concurring); *id.*, at 708, n. 6 (Powell, J., concurring in [491 U.S. 58, 63] part and dissenting in part), but this Court has never expressly dealt with that issue.[4]

Some courts, including the Michigan Supreme Court here, have construed our decision in *Quern v. Jordan*, 440 U.S. 332 (1979), as holding by implication that a State is not a person under § 1983. See *Smith v. Department of Pub. Health, supra*, at 581, 410 N. W. 2d, at 767. See also, *e.g., State v. Green*, 633 P.2d 1381, 1382 (Alaska 1981); *Woodbridge v. Worcester State Hospital*, 384 Mass. 38, 44-45, n. 7, 423 N. E. 2d 782, 786, n. 7 (1981); *Edgar v. State*, 92 Wash. 2d 217, 221, 595 P.2d 534, 537 (1979), cert. denied, 444 U.S. 1077 (1980). *Quern* held that § 1983 does not override a State's Eleventh Amendment immunity, a holding that the concurrence suggested was "patently dicta" to the effect that a State is not a person, 440 U.S., at 350 (BRENNAN, J., concurring in judgment).

Petitioner filed the present § 1983 actions in Michigan state court, which places the question whether a State is a person under § 1983 squarely before us since the Eleventh Amendment [491 U.S. 58, 64] does not apply in state courts. *Maine v. Thiboutot*, 448 U.S. 1, 9, n. 7 (1980). For the reasons that follow, we reaffirm today what we had concluded prior to *Monell* and what some have considered implicit in *Quern*: that a State is not a person within the meaning of § 1983.

We observe initially that if a State is a "person" within the meaning of § 1983, the section is to be read as saying that "every person, including a State, who, under color of any statute, ordinance, regulation, custom, or usage, of any State or Territory or the District of Columbia, subjects . . . ." That would be a decidedly awkward way of expressing an intent to subject the States to liability. At the very least, reading the statute in this way is not so clearly indicated that it provides reason to depart from the often-expressed understanding that "'in common usage, the term 'person' does not include the sovereign, [and] statutes employing the [word] are ordinarily construed to exclude it.'" *Wilson v. Omaha Tribe*, 442 U.S. 653, 667 (1979) (quoting *United States v. Cooper Corp.*, 312 U.S. 600, 604 (1941)). See also *United States v. Mine Workers*, 330 U.S. 258, 275 (1947).

This approach is particularly applicable where it is claimed that Congress has subjected the States to liability to which they had not been subject before. In *Wilson v. Omaha Tribe, supra*, we followed this rule in construing the phrase "white person" contained in 25 U.S.C. § 194, enacted as Act of June 30, 1834, 4 Stat. 729, as not including the "sovereign States of the Union." 442 U.S., at 667. This common usage of the term "person" provides a strong indication that "person" as used in § 1983 likewise does not include a State.[5] [491 U.S. 58, 65]

The language of § 1983 also falls far short of satisfying the ordinary rule of statutory construction that if Congress intends to alter the "usual constitutional balance between the States and the Federal Government," it must make its intention to do so "unmistakably clear in the language of the statute." *Atascadero State Hospital v. Scanlon*, 473 U.S. 234, 242 (1985); see also *Pennhurst State School and Hospital v. Halderman*, 465 U.S. 89, 99 (1984). Atascadero was an Eleventh Amendment case, but a similar approach is applied in other contexts. Congress should make its intention "clear and manifest" if it intends to pre-empt the historic powers of the States, *Rice v. Santa Fe Elevator Corp.*, 331 U.S. 218, 230 (1947), or if it intends to impose a condition on the grant of federal moneys, *Pennhurst State School and Hospital v. Halderman*, 451 U.S. 1, 16 (1981); *South Dakota v. Dole*, 483 U.S. 203, 207 (1987). "In traditionally sensitive areas, such as legislation affecting the federal balance, the requirement of clear statement assures that the legislature has in fact faced, and intended to bring into issue, the critical matters involved in the judicial decision." *United States v. Bass*, 404 U.S. 336, 349 (1971).

Our conclusion that a State is not a "person" within the meaning of § 1983 is reinforced by Congress' purpose in enacting [491 U.S. 58, 66] the statute. Congress enacted § 1 of the Civil Rights Act of 1871, 17 Stat. 13, the precursor to § 1983, shortly after the end of the Civil War "in response to the widespread deprivations of civil rights in the Southern States and the inability or unwillingness of authorities in those States to protect those rights or punish wrongdoers." *Felder v. Casey*, 487 U.S. 131, 147 (1988). Although Congress did not establish federal courts as the exclusive forum to remedy these deprivations, *ibid.*, it is plain that "Congress assigned to the federal courts a paramount role" in this endeavor, *Patsy v. Board of Regents of Florida*, 457 U.S. 496, 503 (1982).

Section 1983 provides a federal forum to remedy many deprivations of civil liberties, but it does not provide a federal forum for litigants who seek a remedy against a State for alleged deprivations of civil liberties. The Eleventh Amendment bars such suits unless the State has waived its immunity, *Welch v. Texas Dept. of Highways and Public Transportation*, 483 U.S. 468, 472-473 (1987) (plurality opinion), or unless Congress has exercised its undoubted power under § 5 of the Fourteenth Amendment to override that immunity. That Congress, in passing § 1983, had no intention to disturb the States' Eleventh Amendment immunity and so to alter the federal-state balance in that respect was made clear in our decision in *Quern.* Given that a principal purpose behind the enactment of § 1983 was to provide a federal forum for civil rights claims, and that Congress did not provide such a federal forum for civil rights claims against States, we cannot accept petitioner's argument that Congress intended nevertheless to create a cause of action against States to be brought in state courts, which are precisely the courts Congress sought to allow civil rights claimants to avoid through § 1983.

This does not mean, as petitioner suggests, that we think that the scope of the Eleventh Amendment and the scope of § 1983 are not separate issues. Certainly they are. But in deciphering congressional intent as to the scope of § 1983, the [491 U.S. 58, 67] scope of the Eleventh Amendment is a consideration, and we decline to adopt a reading of § 1983 that disregards it.[6]

Our conclusion is further supported by our holdings that in enacting § 1983, Congress did not intend to override well-established immunities or defenses under the common law. "One important assumption underlying the Court's decisions in this area is that members of the 42d Congress were familiar with common-law principles, including defenses previously recognized in ordinary tort litigation, and that they likely intended these common-law principles to obtain, absent specific provisions to the contrary." *Newport v. Fact Concerts, Inc.*, 453 U.S. 247, 258 (1981). *Stump v. Sparkman*, 435 U.S. 349, 356 (1978); *Scheuer v. Rhodes*, 416 U.S. 232, 247 (1974); *Pierson v. Ray*, 386 U.S. 547, 554 (1967); and *Tenney v. Brandhove*, 341 U.S. 367, 376 (1951), are also to this effect. The doctrine of sovereign immunity was a familiar doctrine at common law. "The principle is elementary that a State cannot be sued in its own courts without its consent." *Railroad Co. v. Tennessee*, 101 U.S. 337, 339 (1880). It is an "established principle of jurisprudence" that the sovereign cannot be sued in its own courts without its consent. *Beers v. Arkansas*, 20 How. 527, 529 (1858). We cannot conclude that § 1983 was intended to disregard the well-established immunity of a State from being sued without its consent.[7] [491 U.S. 58, 68]

The legislative history of § 1983 does not suggest a different conclusion. Petitioner contends that the congressional debates on § 1 of the 1871 Act indicate that § 1983 was intended to extend to the full reach of the Fourteenth Amendment and thereby to provide a remedy "'against all forms of official violation of federally protected rights.'" Brief for Petitioner 16 (quoting *Monell*, 436 U.S., at 700-701). He refers us to various parts of the vigorous debates accompanying the passage of § 1983 and revealing that it was the failure of the States to take appropriate action that was undoubtedly the motivating force behind § 1983. The inference must be drawn, it is urged, that Congress must have intended to subject the States themselves to liability. But the intent of Congress to provide a remedy for unconstitutional state action does not without more include the sovereign States among those persons against whom § 1983 actions would lie. Construing § 1983 as a remedy for "official violation of federally protected rights" does no more than confirm that the section is directed against state action— action "under color of" state law. It does not suggest that the State itself was a person that Congress intended to be subject to liability.

Although there were sharp and heated debates, the discussion of § 1 of the bill, which contained the present § 1983, was not extended. And although in other respects the impact on state sovereignty was much talked about, no one suggested that § 1 would subject the States themselves to a damages suit under federal law. *Quern*, 440 U.S., at 343. There was complaint that § 1 would subject state officers to damages liability, but no suggestion that it would also expose the States themselves. Cong. Globe, 42d Cong., 1st Sess., [491 U.S. 58, 69] 366, 385 (1871). We find nothing substantial in the legislative history that leads us to believe that Congress intended that the word "person" in § 1983 included the States of the Union. And surely nothing in the debates rises to the clearly expressed legislative intent necessary to permit that construction.

Likewise, the Act of Feb. 25, 1871, § 2, 16 Stat. 431 (the "Dictionary Act"),[8] on which we relied in *Monell, supra*, at 688-689, does not counsel a contrary conclusion here. As we noted in *Quern*, that Act, while adopted prior to § 1 of the Civil Rights Act of 1871, was adopted after § 2 of the Civil Rights Act of 1866, from which § 1 of the 1871 Act was derived. 440 U.S., at 341, n. 11. Moreover, we disagree with JUSTICE BRENNAN that at the time the Dictionary Act was passed "the phrase 'bodies politic and corporate' was understood to include the States." *Post*, at 78. Rather, an examination of authorities of the era suggests that the phrase was used to mean corporations, both private and public (municipal), and not to include the States.[9] In our view, the [491 U.S. 58,

70] Dictionary Act, like § 1983 itself and its legislative history, fails to evidence a clear congressional intent that States be held liable.

Finally, *Monell* itself is not to the contrary. True, prior to *Monell* the Court had reasoned that if municipalities were not persons then surely States also were not. *Fitzpatrick v. Bitzer*, 427 U.S., at 452. And *Monell* overruled *Monroe*, undercutting that logic. But it does not follow that if municipalities are persons then so are States. States are protected by the Eleventh Amendment while municipalities are not, *Monell*, 436 U.S., at 690, n. 54, and we consequently limited our holding in *Monell* "to local government units which are not considered part of the State for Eleventh Amendment purposes," *ibid.* Conversely, our holding here does not cast any doubt on *Monell*, and applies only to States or governmental entities that are considered "arms of the State" for Eleventh Amendment purposes. See, *e.g.*, *Mt. Healthy Bd. of Ed. v. Doyle*, 429 U.S. 274, 280 (1977).

Petitioner asserts, alternatively, that state officials should be considered "persons" under § 1983 even though acting in their official capacities. In this case, petitioner named as defendant not only the Michigan Department of State Police but also the Director of State Police in his official capacity. [491 U.S. 58, 71]

Obviously, state officials literally are persons. But a suit against a state official in his or her official capacity is not a suit against the official but rather is a suit against the official's office. *Brandon v. Holt*, 469 U.S. 464, 471 (1985). As such, it is no different from a suit against the State itself. See, *e.g.*, *Kentucky v. Graham*, 473 U.S. 159, 165-166 (1985); *Monell, supra*, at 690, n. 55. We see no reason to adopt a different rule in the present context, particularly when such a rule would allow petitioner to circumvent congressional intent by a mere pleading device.[10]

We hold that neither a State nor its officials acting in their official capacities are "persons" under § 1983. The judgment of the Michigan Supreme Court is affirmed.

It is so ordered.

Footnotes

[1] Section 1983 provides as follows:

"Every person who, under color of any statute, ordinance, regulation, custom, or usage, of any State or Territory or the District of Columbia, subjects, or causes to be subjected, any citizen of the United States or other person within the jurisdiction thereof to the deprivation of any rights, privileges, or immunities secured by the Constitution and laws, shall be liable to the party injured in an action at law, suit in equity, or other proper proceeding for redress. For the purposes of this section, any Act of Congress applicable exclusively to the District of Columbia shall be considered to be a statute of the District of Columbia." 42 U.S.C. § 1983.

[2] Also named as defendants were the Michigan Department of Civil Service and the State Personnel Director, but those parties were subsequently dismissed by the state courts.

114

³ The courts in the following cases have taken the position that a State is a person under § 1983. See *Della Grotta v. Rhode Island*, 781 F.2d 343, 349 (CA1 1986); *Gay Student Services v. Texas A&M University*, 612 F.2d 160, 163-164 (CA5), cert. denied, 449 U.S. 1034 (1980); *Uberoi v. University of Colorado*, 713 P.2d 894, 900-901 (Colo. 1986); *Stanton v. Godfrey*, 415 N. E. 2d 103, 107 (Ind. App. 1981); *Gumbhir v. Kansas State Bd. of Pharmacy*, 231 Kan. 507, 512-513, 646 P.2d 1078, 1084 (1982), cert. denied, 459 U.S. 1103 (1983); *Rahmah Navajo School Bd., Inc. v. Bureau of Revenue*, 104 N. M. 302, 310, 720 P.2d 1243, 1251 (App.), cert. denied, 479 U.S. 940 (1986).

A large number of courts have agreed with the Michigan Supreme Court that a State is not a person under § 1983. See *Ruiz v. Estelle*, [491 U.S. 58, 62] 679 F.2d 1115, 1137 (CA5), modified on other grounds, 688 F.2d 266 (1982), cert. denied, 460 U.S. 1042 (1983); *Toledo, P. & W. R. Co. v. Illinois*, 744 F.2d 1296, 1298-1299, and n. 1 (CA7 1984), cert. denied, 470 U.S. 1051 (1985); *Harris v. Missouri Court of Appeals*, 787 F.2d 427, 429 (CA8), cert. denied, 479 U.S. 851 (1986); *Aubuchon v. Missouri*, 631 F.2d 581, 582 (CA8 1980) (*per curiam*), cert. denied, 450 U.S. 915 (1981); *State v. Green*, 633 P.2d 1381, 1382 (Alaska 1981); *St. Mary's Hospital and Health Center v. State*, 150 Ariz. 8, 11, 721 P.2d 666, 669 (App. 1986); *Mezey v. State*, 161 Cal. App. 3d 1060, 1065, 208 Cal. Rptr. 40, 43 (1984); *Hill v. Florida Dept. of Corrections*, 513 So.2d 129, 132 (Fla. 1987), cert. denied, 484 U.S. 1064 (1988); *Merritt ex rel. Merritt v. State*, 108 Idaho 20, 26, 696 P.2d 871, 877 (1985); *Woodbridge v. Worcester State Hospital*, 384 Mass. 38, 44-45, n. 7, 423 N. E. 2d 782, 786, n. 7 (1981); *Bird v. State Dept. of Public Safety*, 375 N. W. 2d 36, 43 (Minn. App. 1985); *Shaw v. St. Louis*, 664 S. W. 2d 572, 576 (Mo. App. 1983), cert. denied, 469 U.S. 849 (1984); *Fuchilla v. Layman*, 109 N. J. 319, 323-324, 537 A. 2d 652, 654, cert. denied, 488 U.S. 826 (1988); *Burkey v. Southern Ohio Correctional Facility*, 38 Ohio App. 3d 170, 170-171, 528 N. E. 2d 607, 608 (1988); *Gay v. State*, 730 S. W. 2d 154, 157-158 (Tex. App. 1987); *Edgar v. State*, 92 Wash. 2d 217, 221, 595 P.2d 534, 537 (1979), cert. denied, 444 U.S. 1077 (1980); *Boldt v. State*, 101 Wis. 2d 566, 584, 305 N. W. 2d 133, 143-144, cert. denied, 454 U.S. 973 (1981).

⁴ Petitioner cites a number of cases from this Court that he asserts have "assumed" that a State is a person. Those cases include ones in which a State has been sued by name under § 1983, see, *e.g.*, *Maine v. Thiboutot*, 448 U.S. 1 (1980); *Martinez v. California*, 444 U.S. 277 (1980), various cases awarding attorney's fees against a State or a state agency, *Maine v. Thiboutot, supra*; *Hutto v. Finney*, 437 U.S. 678 (1978), and various cases discussing the waiver of Eleventh Amendment immunity by States, see, *e.g.*, *Kentucky v. Graham*, 473 U.S. 159, 167, n. 14 (1985); *Edelman v. Jordan*, 415 U.S. 651 (1974). But the Court did not address the meaning of person in any of those cases, and in none of the cases was resolution of that issue necessary to the decision. Petitioner's argument evidently rests on the proposition that whether a State is a person under § 1983 is "jurisdictional" and "thus could have been raised by the Court on its own motion" in those cases. Brief for Petitioner 25, n. 15. Even assuming that petitioner's premise and characterization of the cases is correct, "this Court has never considered itself bound [by prior sub silentio holdings] when a subsequent case finally brings the jurisdictional issue before us." *Hagans v. Lavine*, 415 U.S. 528, 535, n. 5 (1974).

⁵ *Jefferson County Pharmaceutical Assn. v. Abbott Laboratories*, 460 U.S. 150 (1983), on which petitioner relies, is fully reconcilable with our holding in the present case. In Jefferson County, the Court held that States were persons that could be sued under the Robinson-Patman Act, 15 U.S.C. §§ 13(a) and 13(f). 460 U.S., at 155 -157. But the plaintiff there was seeking only injunctive relief and not damages against the State [491 U.S. 58, 65] defendant, the Board of Trustees of the University of Alabama; the District Court had dismissed the plaintiff's damages claim as barred by the Eleventh Amendment. *Id.*, at 153, n. 5. Had the present § 1983 action been

brought in federal court, a similar disposition would have resulted. Of course, the Court would never be faced with a case such as Jefferson County that had been brought in a state court because the federal courts have exclusive jurisdiction over claims under the federal antitrust laws. 15 U.S.C. §§ 15 and 26. Moreover, the Court in Jefferson County was careful to limit its holding to "state purchases for the purpose of competing against private enterprise . . . in the retail market." 460 U.S., at 154. It assumed without deciding "that Congress did not intend the Act to apply to state purchases for consumption in traditional governmental functions," *ibid.*, which presents a more difficult question because it may well "affec[t] the federal balance." See *United States v. Bass*, 404 U.S. 336, 349 (1971).

[6] Petitioner argues that Congress would not have considered the Eleventh Amendment in enacting § 1983 because in 1871 this Court had not yet held that the Eleventh Amendment barred federal-question cases against States in federal court. This argument is no more than an attempt to have this Court reconsider *Quern v. Jordan*, 440 U.S. 332 (1979), which we decline to do.

[7] Our recognition in *Monell v. New York City Dept. of Social Services*, 436 U.S. 658 (1978), that a municipality is a person under § 1983, is fully consistent with this reasoning. In *Owen v. City of Independence*, 445 U.S. 622 (1980), we noted that by the time of the enactment of § 1983, municipalities no longer retained the sovereign immunity they had previously shared with the States. "[B]y the end of the 19th century, courts [491 U.S. 58, 68] regularly held that in imposing a specific duty on the municipality either in its charter or by statute, the State had impliedly withdrawn the city's immunity from liability for the nonperformance or misperformance of its obligation," *id.*, at 646, and, as a result, municipalities had been held liable for damages "in a multitude of cases" involving previously immune activities, *id.*, at 646-647.

[8] The Dictionary Act provided that

> "in all acts hereafter passed . . . the word 'person' may extend and be applied to bodies politic and corporate . . . unless the context shows that such words were intended to be used in a more limited sense." Act of Feb. 25, 1871, 2, 16 Stat. 431.

[9] See *United States v. Fox*, 94 U.S. 315, 321 (1877); 1 B. Abbott, Dictionary of Terms and Phrases Used in American or English Jurisprudence 155 (1879) ("most exact expression" for "public corporation"); W. Anderson, A Dictionary of Law 127 (1893) ("most exact expression for a public corporation or corporation having powers of government"); Black's Law Dictionary 143 (1891) ("body politic" is "term applied to a corporation, which is usually designated as a 'body corporate and politic'" and "is particularly appropriate to a public corporation invested with powers and duties of government"); 1 A. Burrill, A Law Dictionary and Glossary 212 (2d ed. 1871) ("body politic" is "term applied to a corporation, which is usually designated as a *body corporate and politic*"). A public corporation, in ordinary usage, was another term for a municipal corporation, and included towns, cities, and counties, but not States. See 2 Abbott, *supra*, [491 U.S. 58, 70] at 347; Anderson, *supra*, at 264-265; Black, *supra*, at 278; 2 Burrill, *supra*, at 352.

JUSTICE BRENNAN appears to confuse this precise definition of the phrase with its use "in a rather loose way," see Black, *supra*, at 143, to refer to the state (as opposed to a State). This confusion is revealed most clearly in JUSTICE BRENNAN's reliance on the 1979 edition of Black's Law Dictionary, which defines "body politic or corporate" as "[a] social compact by which the whole people covenants with each citizen, and each citizen with the whole people, that all shall be governed by certain laws for the common good." *Post*, at 79. To the extent JUSTICE BRENNAN's citation of other authorities does not suffer from the same confusion, those authorities at best suggest that the phrase is ambiguous, which still renders the Dictionary Act incapable of supplying the necessary clear intent.

[10] Of course a state official in his or her official capacity, when sued for injunctive relief, would be a person under § 1983 because "official-capacity actions for prospective relief are not treated as actions against the State." *Kentucky v. Graham*, 473 U.S., at 167, n. 14; *Ex parte Young*, 209 U.S. 123, 159-160 (1908). This distinction is "commonplace in sovereign immunity doctrine," L. Tribe, American Constitutional Law 3-27, p. 190, n. 3 (2d ed. 1988), and would not have been foreign to the nineteenth-century Congress that enacted § 1983, see, *e.g.*, *In re Ayers*, 123 U.S. 443, 506-507 (1887); *United States v. Lee*, 106 U.S. 196, 219 -222 (1882); *Board of Liquidation v. McComb*, 92 U.S. 531, 541 (1876); *Osborn v. Bank of United States*, 9 Wheat. 738 (1824). *City of Kenosha v. Bruno*, 412 U.S. 507, 513 (1973), on which JUSTICE STEVENS relies, see *post*, at 93, n. 8, is not to the contrary. That case involved municipal liability under § 1983, and the fact that nothing in § 1983 suggests its "bifurcated application to municipal corporations depending on the nature of the relief sought against them," 412 U.S., at 513, is not surprising, since by the time of the enactment of § 1983 municipalities were no longer protected by sovereign immunity. *Supra*, at 67-68, n. 7.

Hafer v. Melo
502 U.S. 21 (1991)

Argued October 15, 1991
Decided November 5, 1991
JUSTICE O'CONNOR delivered the opinion of the Court.

In *Will v. Michigan Dept. of State Police*, 491 U.S. 58 (1989), we held that state officials "acting in their official capacities" are outside the class of "persons" subject to liability [502 U.S. 21, 23] under 42 U.S.C. § 1983. 491 U.S., at 71. Petitioner takes this language to mean that § 1988 does not authorize suits against state officers for damages arising from official acts. We reject this reading of *Will*, and hold that state officials sued in their individual capacities are "persons" for purposes of § 1983.

I

In 1988, petitioner Barbara Hafer sought election to the *post* of Auditor General of Pennsylvania. Respondents allege that, during the campaign, United States Attorney James West gave Hafer a list of 21 employees in the Auditor General's Office who secured their jobs through payments to a former employee of the office. App. 10. They further allege that Hafer publicly promised to fire all employees on the list if elected. *Ibid*

Hafer won the election. Shortly after becoming Auditor General, she dismissed 18 employees, including named respondent James Melo, Jr., on the basis that they "bought" their jobs. Melo and seven other terminated employees sued Hafer and West in Federal District Court. They asserted state and federal claims, including a claim under § 1983, and sought monetary damages. Carl Gurley and the remaining respondents in this

117

case also lost their jobs with the Auditor General soon after Hafer took office. These respondents allege that Hafer discharged them because of their Democratic political affiliation and support for her opponent in the 1988 election. *Id.,* at 28, 35, 40. They too filed suit against Hafer, seeking monetary damages and reinstatement under § 1983.

After consolidating the *Melo* and *Gurley* actions, the District Court dismissed all claims. In relevant part, the court held that the § 1983 claims against Hafer were barred because, under *Will,* she could not be held liable for employment decisions made in her official capacity as Auditor General. [502 U.S. 21, 24]

The Court of Appeals for the Third Circuit reversed this portion of the District Court's decision. 912 F.2d 628 (1990). As to claims for reinstatement brought against Hafer in her official capacity, the court rested on our statement in *Will* that state officials sued for injunctive relief in their official capacities are "persons" subject to liability under § 1983. See *Will, supra,* at 71, n. 10. Turning to respondents' monetary claims, the court found that six members of the Gurley group had expressly sought damages from Hafer in her personal capacity. The remaining plaintiffs "although not as explicit, signified a similar intent." 912 F.2d, at 636.* The court found this critical. While Hafer's power to hire and fire derived from her position as Auditor General, it said, a suit for damages based on the exercise of this authority could be brought against Hafer in her personal capacity. Because Hafer acted under color of state law, respondents could maintain a § 1983 individual-capacity suit against her.

We granted certiorari, 498 U.S. 1118 (1991), to address the question whether state officers may be held personally liable for damages under § 1983 based upon actions taken in their official capacities. [502 U.S. 21, 25]

II

In *Kentucky v. Graham,* 473 U.S. 159 (1985), the Court sought to eliminate lingering confusion about the distinction between personal- and official-capacity suits. We emphasized that official-capacity suits "'generally represent only another way of pleading an action against an entity of which an officer is an agent.'" *Id.,* at 165 (quoting *Monell v. New York City Dept. of Social Servs.,* 436 U.S. 658, 690, n. 55 (1978)). A suit against a state official in her official capacity therefore should be treated as a suit against the State. 473 U.S., at 166. Indeed, when an official sued in this capacity in federal court dies or leaves office, her successor automatically assumes her role in the litigation. See Fed. Rule Civ. Proc. 25(d)(1); Fed. Rule App. Proc. 43(c)(1); this Court's Rule 35.3. Because the real party in interest in an official-capacity suit is the governmental entity, and not the named official, "the entity's 'policy or custom' must have played a part in the violation of federal law." *Graham, supra,* at 166 (quoting *Monell, supra,* at 694). For the same reason, the only immunities available to the defendant in an official-capacity action are those that the governmental entity possesses. 473 U.S., at 167.

Personal-capacity suits, on the other hand, seek to impose individual liability upon a government officer for actions taken under color of state law. Thus, "[o]n the merits, to establish *personal* liability in a § 1983 action, it is enough to show that the official, acting under color of state law, caused the deprivation of a federal right." *Id.*, at 166. While the plaintiff in a personal-capacity suit need not establish a connection to governmental "policy or custom," officials sued in their personal capacities, unlike those sued in their official capacities, may assert personal immunity defenses such as objectively reasonable reliance on existing law. *Id.*, at 166-167.

Our decision in *Will v. Michigan Dept. of State Police*, 491 U.S. 58 (1989), turned in part on these differences between [502 U.S. 21, 26] personal- and official-capacity actions. The principal issue in *Will* was whether States are "persons" subject to suit under § 1983. Section 1983 provides, in relevant part:

> "Every person who, under color of any statute, ordinance, regulation, custom, or usage, of any State . . . subjects, or causes to be subjected, any citizen of the United States or other person within the jurisdiction thereof to the deprivation of any rights, privileges, or immunities secured by the Constitution and laws, shall be liable to the party injured. . . ."

The Court held that interpreting the words "[e]very person" to exclude the States accorded with the most natural reading of the law, with its legislative history, and with the rule that Congress must clearly state its intention to alter "'the federal balance'" when it seeks to do so. *Will, supra,* at 65 (quoting *United States v. Bass*, 404 U.S. 336, 349 (1971)).

The Court then addressed the related question whether state officials, sued for monetary relief in their official capacities, are persons under § 1983. We held that they are not. Although "state officials literally are persons," an official-capacity suit against a state officer "is not a suit against the official, but rather is a suit against the official's office. As such, it is no different from a suit against the State itself." 491 U.S., at 71 (citation omitted).

Summarizing our holding, we said: "[N]either a State nor its officials acting in their official capacities are 'persons' under § 1983." *Ibid.* Hafer relies on this recapitulation for the proposition that she may not be held personally liable under § 1983 for discharging respondents, because she "act[ed]" in her official capacity as Auditor General of Pennsylvania. Of course, the claims considered in *Will* were official-capacity claims; the phrase "acting in their official capacities" is best understood as a reference to the capacity in which the state officer is sued, not the capacity in which the officer inflicts the alleged injury. To the extent that *Will* [502 U.S. 21, 27] allows the construction Hafer suggests, however, we now eliminate that ambiguity.

A

Will itself make clear that the distinction between official-capacity suits and personal-capacity suits is more than "a mere pleading device." *Ibid.* State officers sued for damages in their official capacity are not "persons" for purposes of the suit, because they assume the identity of the government that employs them. *Ibid.* By contrast, officers sued in their personal capacity come to court as individuals. A government official in the role of personal-capacity defendant thus fits comfortably within the statutory term "person." Cf. *id.*, at 71, n. 10 ("[A] state official in his or her official capacity, when sued for injunctive relief, would be a person under § 1983 because 'official-capacity actions for prospective relief are not treated as actions against the State'") (quoting *Graham*, 473 U.S., at 167, n. 14).

Hafer seeks to overcome the distinction between official- and personal-capacity suits by arguing that § 1983 liability turns not on the capacity in which state officials are sued, but on the capacity in which they acted when injuring the plaintiff. Under *Will*, she asserts, state officials may not be held liable in their personal capacity for actions they take in their official capacity. Although one Court of Appeals has endorsed this view, see *Cowan v. University of Louisville School of Medicine*, 900 F.2d 936, 942-943 (CA6 1990), we find it both unpersuasive as an interpretation of § 1983 and foreclosed by our prior decisions.

Through § 1983, Congress sought "to give a remedy to parties deprived of constitutional rights, privileges and immunities by an official's abuse of his position." *Monroe v. Pape*, 365 U.S. 167, 172 (1961). Accordingly, it authorized suits to redress deprivations of civil rights by persons acting "under color of any [state] statute, ordinance, regulation, custom, or usage." 42 U.S.C. § 1983. The requirement of action under color of state law means that Hafer may be liable for [502 U.S. 21, 28] discharging respondents precisely because of her authority as Auditor General. We cannot accept the novel proposition that this same official authority insulates Hafer from suit.

In an effort to limit the scope of her argument, Hafer distinguishes between two categories of acts taken under color of state law: those outside the official's authority or not essential to the operation of state government, and those both within the official's authority and necessary to the performance of governmental functions. Only the former group, she asserts, can subject state officials to personal liability under § 1983; the latter group (including the employment decisions at issue in this case) should be considered acts of the State that cannot give rise to a personal-capacity action.

The distinction Hafer urges finds no support in the broad language of § 1983. To the contrary, it ignores our holding that Congress enacted § 1983 "to enforce provisions of the Fourteenth Amendment against those who carry a badge of authority of a State and represent it in some capacity, whether they act in accordance with their authority or misuse it." *Scheuer v. Rhodes*, 416 U.S. 232, 243 (1974) (quoting *Monroe v. Pape, supra*, at 171-172). Because of that intent, we have held that, in § 1983 actions, the statutory requirement of action "under color of" state law is just as broad as the Fourteenth Amendment's "state action" requirement. *Lugar v. Edmondson Oil Co.*, 457 U.S. 922, 929 (1982).

Furthermore, Hafer's distinction cannot be reconciled with our decisions regarding immunity of government officers otherwise personally liable for acts done in the course of their official duties. Her theory would absolutely immunize state officials from personal liability for acts within their authority and necessary to fulfilling governmental responsibilities. Yet our cases do not extend absolute immunity to all officers who engage in necessary official acts. Rather, immunity from suit under § 1983 is "predicated upon a considered inquiry into the immunity historically accorded the relevant [502 U.S. 21, 29] official at common law and the interests behind it," *Imbler v. Pachtman*, 424 U.S. 409, 421 (1976), and officials seeking absolute immunity must show that such immunity is justified for the governmental function at issue, *Burns v. Reed*, 500 U.S. 478, 486-487 (1991).

This Court has refused to extend absolute immunity beyond a very limited class of officials, including the President of the United States, legislators carrying out their legislative functions, and judges carrying out their judicial functions, "whose special functions or constitutional status requires complete protection from suit." *Harlow v. Fitzgerald*, 457 U.S. 800, 807 (1982). State executive officials are not entitled to absolute immunity for their official actions. *Scheuer v. Rhodes, supra.* In several instances, moreover, we have concluded that no more than a qualified immunity attaches to administrative employment decisions, even if the same official has absolute immunity when performing other functions. See *Forrester v. White*, 484 U.S. 219 (1988) (dismissal of court employee by state judge); *Harlow v. Fitzgerald, supra*, (discharge of Air Force employee, allegedly orchestrated by senior White House aides) (*Bivens* action); *Davis v. Passman*, 442 U.S. 228 (1979) (dismissal of congressional aide) (*Bivens* action). That Hafer may assert personal immunity within the framework of these cases in no way supports her argument here.

B

Hafer further asks us to read *Will's* language concerning suits against state officials as establishing the limits of liability under the Eleventh Amendment. She asserts that imposing personal liability on officeholders may infringe on state sovereignty by rendering government less effective; thus, she argues, the Eleventh Amendment forbids personal-capacity suits against state officials in federal court. [502 U.S. 21, 30]

Most certainly, *Will*'s holding does not rest directly on the Eleventh Amendment. Whereas the Eleventh Amendment bars suits in federal court "by private parties seeking to impose a liability which must be paid from public funds in the state treasury," *Edelman v. Jordan*, 415 U.S. 651, 663 (1974), *Will* arose from a suit in state court. We considered the Eleventh Amendment in *Will* only because the fact that Congress did not intend to override state immunity when it enacted § 1983 was relevant to statutory construction: "Given that a principal purpose behind the enactment of § 1983 was to provide a federal forum for civil rights claims," Congress' failure to authorize suits against States in federal courts suggested that it also did not intend to authorize such claims in state courts. 491 U.S., at 66.

To the extent that Hafer argues from the Eleventh Amendment itself, she makes a claim that failed in *Scheuer v. Rhodes, supra*. In *Scheuer*, personal representatives of the estates of three students who died at Kent State University in May, 1970, sought damages from the Governor of Ohio and other state officials. The District Court dismissed their complaints on the theory that the suits, although brought against state officials in their personal capacities, were in substance actions against the State of Ohio, and therefore barred by the Eleventh Amendment.

We rejected this view. "[S]ince *Ex parte Young*, 209 U.S. 123 (1908)," we said, "it has been settled that the Eleventh Amendment provides no shield for a state official confronted by a claim that he had deprived another of a federal right under the color of state law." *Scheuer, supra*, at 237. While the doctrine of *Ex parte Young* does not apply where a plaintiff seeks damages from the public treasury, damages awards against individual defendants in federal courts "are a permissible remedy in some circumstances notwithstanding the fact that they hold public office." 416 U.S., at 238. That is, the Eleventh Amendment does not erect a barrier [502 U.S. 21, 31] against suits to impose "individual and personal liability" on state officials under § 1983. *Ibid.*

To be sure, imposing personal liability on state officers may hamper their performance of public duties. But such concerns are properly addressed within the framework of our personal immunity jurisprudence. See *Forrester v. White, supra*, at 223. Insofar as respondents seek damages against Hafer personally, the Eleventh Amendment does not restrict their ability to sue in federal court.

We hold that state officials, sued in their individual capacities, are "persons" within the meaning of § 1983. The Eleventh Amendment does not bar such suits, nor are state officers absolutely immune from personal liability under § 1983 solely by virtue of the "official" nature of their acts.

The judgment of the Court of Appeals is

Affirmed.

Footnote

* The Third Circuit looked to the proceedings below to determine whether certain respondents brought their claims for damages against Hafer in her official capacity or her personal capacity. 912 F.2d 628, 635-636 (1990). Several other Courts of Appeals adhere to this practice. See *Conner v. Reinhard*, 847 F.2d 384, 394, n. 8 (CA7), cert. denied, 488 U.S. 856 (1988); *Houston v. Reich*, 932 F.2d 883, 885 (CA10 1991); *Lundgren v. McDaniel*, 814 F.2d 600, 603-604 (CA11 1987). Still others impose a more rigid pleading requirement. See *Wells v. Brown*, 891 F.2d 591, 592 (CA6 1989) (Section 1983 plaintiff must specifically plead that suit for damages is brought against state official in individual capacity); *Nix v. Norman*, 879 F.2d 429, 431 (CA8 1989) (same). Because this issue is not properly before us, we simply reiterate the Third Circuit's view that "[i]t is obviously preferable for the plaintiff to be specific in the first instance to avoid any ambiguity." 912 F.2d, at 636, n. 7. See this Court's Rule 14.1(a) ("Only the questions set forth in the petition, or fairly included therein, will be considered by the Court"). [502 U.S. 21, 32]

Inyo County, California, et al. v. Paiute-Shoshone Indians of the Bishop Community of the Bishop Colony et al. 538 U. S. __ (2003)

Argued March 31, 2003
Decided May 19, 2003
JUSTICE GINSBURG delivered the opinion of the Court.

This case stems from a California county's investigation of Native American tribe members for alleged off-reservation crimes. Pursuing the investigation, county law-enforcement officers executed a state court warrant for casino employment records kept by the Tribe on its reservation. The Tribe sued the County, the District Attorney, and the Sheriff in federal court, asserting sovereign immunity from state court processes and seeking declaratory, injunctive, and monetary relief.

The parties and, as *amicus curiae*, the United States agree that a Native American Tribe, like a State of the United States, is not a "person" subject to suit under 42 U. S. C. §1983. We hold that, in the situation here presented, the Tribe does not qualify as a "person" who may sue under §1983. Whether the Tribe's suit qualifies for federal-court jurisdiction because it arises under some federal law other than §1983 is an issue the parties have not precisely addressed, and the trial and appellate courts have not clearly decided. We therefore remand the case for close consideration and specific resolution of that threshold question.

I

The Bishop Paiute Tribe is a federally recognized tribe located on the Bishop Paiute Reservation in California. The Bishop Paiute Gaming Corporation, chartered and wholly owned by the Tribe, operates and manages the Paiute Palace Casino, a tribal gaming operation run under the Indian Gaming Regulatory Act, 102 Stat. 2467, 25 U. S. C. §2701 *et seq.*

In March 1999, the Inyo County Department of Health and Human Services received information from the State Department of Social Services indicating that three Casino employees had failed to report Casino earnings on their applications for state welfare benefits. Brief for Petitioners 4–5. According to the County, the employees failed to respond when the Department requested that they reconcile the apparent discrepancies between their Casino earnings and their welfare application forms. *Id.*, at 5. The Department then forwarded the matter to the Inyo County District Attorney's Office, which, in turn, asked the employees to reconcile the apparent discrepancies. *Id.*, at 6. That request, the County asserts, was also ignored. *Ibid.*

In February 2000, the District Attorney's Office asked the Casino for the three employees' employment records, explaining that it was investigating "alleged welfare fraud." 291 F. 3d 549, 554 (CA9 2002). The Tribe responded that its privacy policy precluded release of the records without the employees' consent.

The District Attorney then sought and, on showing probable cause, obtained a search warrant from the Inyo County Superior Court. The warrant authorized a search of the Casino for payroll records of the three employees. On March 23, 2000, the Inyo County Sheriff and the District Attorney executed the warrant. They did so over the objection of tribal officials. Those officials urged that the state court lacked jurisdiction to authorize a search of premises and seizure of records belonging to a sovereign tribe.[1] The Sheriff and the District Attorney, lacking cooperation from the Tribe, cut the locks off the storage facility containing the Casino's personnel records. The county officials seized timecard entries, payroll registers, and payroll check registers relating to the three employees; the seizure also garnered information contained in quarterly wage and withholding reports the Corporation had submitted to the State. Each item seized contained at least one reference to an employee under investigation.

In July 2000, the District Attorney's Office asked the Tribe for the personnel records of six other Casino employees. The Tribe reiterated its privacy policy, but offered to accept as evidence of consent a redacted copy of the last page of each employee's signed welfare application. That page contained a statement that employment records of individuals applying for public assistance were subject to review by county officials. The District Attorney refused the offer.[2]

To ward off any additional searches, the Tribe and the Corporation filed suit in Federal District Court naming as defendants the District Attorney and the Sheriff in their individual and official capacities, and the County. Asserting federal question jurisdiction under 28 U. S. C. §§1331, 1337, 1343(i)(3)(4), and the "federal common law of Indian affairs," the Tribe sought injunctive and declaratory relief to vindicate its status as a sovereign immune from state processes under federal law, and to establish that state law was preempted to the extent that it purported to authorize seizure of tribal records. App. 97, ¶1, 105–114, ¶¶26–53. The Tribe's complaint also sought relief under 42 U. S. C. §1983, including compensatory damages. In this regard, the Tribe alleged that by acting beyond the scope of their jurisdiction and "without authorization of law" in executing the warrant,[3] the defendants violated the Tribe's and Corporation's Fourth and Fourteenth Amendments rights, and the Tribe's right to self-government. App. 109, ¶38; see *id.*, at 108–110, ¶¶133–39.

On November 22, 2000, the District Court, on defendants' motion, dismissed the Tribe's complaint. Tribal sovereign immunity, the court held, did not categorically preclude the search and seizure of the Casino's personnel records. Taking into account the competing interests of the State and the Tribe, the court concluded that, "[i]n the interest of a fair and uniform application of California's criminal law, state officials should be able to execute search warrant[s] against the tribe and tribal property." App. to Pet. for Cert. 62a. The court also held that the District Attorney and the Sheriff had qualified immunity from suit in their individual capacities. *Id.*, at 57a–58a.

The Court of Appeals for the Ninth Circuit reversed the District Court's judgment dismissing the action. "[E]xecution of a search warrant against the Tribe," the Court of Appeals said, "interferes with 'the right of reservation Indians to make their own laws and be ruled by them.'" 291 F. 3d, at 558 (quoting *Williams v. Lee*, 358 U. S. 217, 220 (1959)). In the appellate court's view, the District Court should not have "balanced the interests at stake" to determine whether the warrant was enforceable. 291 F. 3d, at 559. This Court's precedent, the Ninth Circuit said, advanced "a more categorical approach denying state jurisdiction . . . over a tribe absent a waiver by the tribe or a clear grant of authority by Congress." *Ibid.* (citing *Oklahoma Tax Comm'n v. Chickasaw Nation*, 515 U. S. 450, 458 (1995)).

"[E]ven if a balancing test is the appropriate legal framework," the Court of Appeals added, "the balance of interests favors a ruling for the Tribe." 291 F. 3d, at 559. The Tribe's privacy policies regarding employee records "promote tribal [self-government] interests," the Ninth Circuit reasoned; notably, those policies fostered "a trusting relationship with tribal members," and "affect[ed] the Casino, the Tribe's predominant source of economic development revenue." *Ibid.* The appeals court recognized the State's countervailing "interest in investigating potential welfare fraud," but thought it incumbent upon the State to further that interest "through far less intrusive means." *Ibid.*

The Court of Appeals also ruled that the District Attorney and the Sheriff were not shielded by qualified immunity. "[A] reasonable county officer," it held, "would have known . . . that seizing tribal property held on tribal land violated the Fourth Amendment because the property and land were outside the officer's jurisdiction." *Id.*, at 568. The appeals court acknowledged prior Ninth Circuit precedent holding that the right to tribal self-government is not protected by §1983. *Id.*, at 568, n. 7 (citing *Hoopa Valley Tribe v. Nevins*, 881 F. 2d 657 (1989)); see Brief for United States as *Amicus Curiae* 29, n. 15. But in this case, the Court of Appeals concluded, a §1983 claim could be maintained because the Tribe sought "protection from an unlawful search and seizure," a right secured by the Fourth Amendment and therefore within §1983's compass. 291 F. 3d, at 568, and n. 7. On December 2, 2002, we granted certiorari. 537 U. S. 1043 (2002).

II

Central to our review is the question whether the Tribe's complaint is actionable under §1983. That provision permits "citizen[s]" and "other person[s] within the jurisdiction" of the United States to seek legal and equitable relief from "person[s]" who, under color of state law, deprive them of federally protected rights.[4] In *Will v. Michigan Dept. of State Police*, 491 U. S. 58 (1989), this Court held that a State is not a "person" amenable to suit under §1983. "[I]n enacting §1983," the Court said, "Congress did not intend to override well-established immunities or defenses under the common law," including "[t]he doctrine of sovereign immunity." *Id.*, at 67. Although this case does not squarely present the question, the parties agree, and we will assume for purposes of this opinion, that Native American tribes, like States of the Union, are not subject to suit under § 1983. See Brief for Petitioners 35–38; Tr. of Oral Arg. 49; *Kiowa Tribe of Okla. v. Manufacturing Technologies, Inc.*, 523 U. S. 751, 754 (1998) ("an Indian tribe is subject to suit only where Congress has authorized the suit or the tribe has waived its immunity").

The issue pivotal here is whether a tribe qualifies *as a claimant*— a "person within the jurisdiction" of the United States—under §1983.[5] The United States maintains it does not, invoking the Court's "longstanding interpretive presumption that 'person' does not include the sovereign," a presumption that "may be disregarded only upon some affirmative showing of statutory intent to the contrary." Brief for United States as *Amicus Curiae* 7–8 (quoting *Vermont Agency of Natural Resources v. United States ex rel. Stevens*, 529 U. S. 765, 780–781 (2000)); see *Will*, 491 U. S., at 64. Nothing in the text, purpose, or history of §1983, the Government contends, overcomes the interpretive pre-

sumption that "'person' does not include the sovereign." Brief for
United States as *Amicus Curiae* 7-8 (some internal quotation marks
omitted). Furthermore, the Government urges, given the Court's decision that "person" excludes sovereigns as defendants under §1983, it
would be anomalous for the Court to give the same word a different
meaning when it appears later in the same sentence. *Id.,* at 8; see *Brown
v. Gardner,* 513 U. S. 115, 118 (1994) (the "presumption that a given
term is used to mean the same thing throughout a statute" is "surely at
its most vigorous when a term is repeated within a given sentence"); cf.
Lafayette v. Louisiana Power & Light Co., 435 U. S. 389, 397 (1978)
(because municipalities are "persons" entitled to sue under the antitrust laws, they are also, in principle, "persons" capable of being sued
under those laws).

The Tribe responds that Congress intended §1983 "to provide a
powerful civil remedy 'against all forms of official violation of federally
protected rights.'" Brief for Respondents 45 (quoting *Monell v. New
York City Dept. of Social Servs.,* 436 U. S. 658, 700-701 (1978)). To
achieve that remedial purpose, the Tribe maintains, § 1983 should be
"broadly construed." Brief for Respondents 45 (citing *Monell,* 436 U. S.,
at 684-685) (internal quotation marks omitted). Indian tribes, the Tribe
here asserts, "have been especially vulnerable to infringement of their
federally protected rights by states." Brief for Respondents 42 (citing,
inter alia, The Kansas Indians, 5 Wall. 737 (1867) (state taxation of tribal
lands); *Minnesota v. Mille Lacs Band of Chippewa Indians,* 526 U. S. 172
(1999) (state infringement on tribal rights to hunt, fish, and gather on
ceded lands); *Mississippi Band of Choctaw Indians v. Holyfield,* 490 U. S.
30 (1989) (tribal jurisdiction over Indian child custody proceedings);
California v. Cabazon Band of Mission Indians, 480 U. S. 202 (1987)
(state attempt to regulate gambling on tribal land)). To guard against
such infringements, the Tribe contends, the Court should read §1983
to encompass suits brought by Indian tribes.

As we have recognized in other contexts, qualification of a sovereign as a "person" who may maintain a particular claim for relief
depends not "upon a bare analysis of the word 'person,'" *Pfizer Inc. v.
Government of India,* 434 U. S. 308, 317 (1978), but on the "legislative
environment" in which the word appears, *Georgia v. Evans,* 316 U. S.
159, 161 (1942). Thus, in *Georgia,* the Court held that a State, as purchaser of asphalt shipped in interstate commerce, qualified as a "person" entitled to seek redress under the Sherman Act for restraint of
trade. *Id.,* at 160-163. Similarly, in *Pfizer,* the Court held that a foreign
nation, as purchaser of antibiotics, ranked as a "person" qualified to
sue pharmaceuticals manufacturers under our antitrust laws. *Pfizer,*
434 U. S., at 309-320; cf. *Stevens,* 529 U. S., at 787, and n. 18 (deciding
States are not "person[s]" subject to *qui tam* liability under the False
Claims Act, but leaving open the question whether they "can be 'per-

sons' for purposes of commencing an FCA *qui tam* action" (emphasis deleted)); *United States v. Cleveland Indians Baseball Co.*, 532 U. S. 200, 213 (2001) ("Although we generally presume that identical words used in different parts of the same act are intended to have the same meaning, the presumption is not rigid, and the meaning of the same words well may vary to meet the purposes of the law." (internal quotation marks, brackets, and citations omitted)).

There is in this case no allegation that the County lacked probable cause or that the warrant was otherwise defective. It is only by virtue of the Tribe's asserted "sovereign" status that it claims immunity from the County's processes. See App. 97–105, ¶¶1–25, 108–110, ¶¶33–39; 291 F. 3d, at 554 (Court of Appeals "find[s] that the County and its agents *violated the Tribe's sovereign immunity* when they obtained and executed a search warrant against the Tribe and tribal property." (emphasis added)). Section 1983 was designed to secure private rights against government encroachment, see *Will*, 491 U. S., at 66, not to advance a sovereign's prerogative to withhold evidence relevant to a criminal investigation. For example, as the County acknowledges, a tribal member complaining of a Fourth Amendment violation would be a "person" qualified to sue under §1983. See Brief for Petitioners 20, n. 7. But, like other private persons, that member would have no right to immunity from an appropriately executed search warrant based on probable cause. Accordingly, we hold that the Tribe may not sue under §1983 to vindicate the sovereign right it here claims.[6]

III

In addition to §1983, the Tribe asserted as law under which its claims arise the "federal common law of Indian affairs." *Supra*, at 4 (quoting App. 97, ¶1). But the Tribe has not explained, and neither the District Court nor the Court of Appeals appears to have carefully considered, what prescription of federal common law enables a tribe to maintain an action for declaratory and injunctive relief establishing its sovereign right to be free from state criminal processes. In short, absent §1983 as a foundation for the Tribe's action, it is unclear what federal law, if any, the Tribe's case "aris[es] under." 28 U. S. C. §1331. We therefore remand for focused consideration and resolution of that jurisdictional question.

The judgment of the United States Court of Appeals for the Ninth Circuit is vacated, and the case is remanded for further proceedings consistent with this opinion.

It is so ordered.

Footnotes

[1] The United States maintains, and the County does not dispute, that the Corporation is an "arm" of the Tribe for sovereign immunity purposes. See Brief for United States as Amicus Curiae 11–14.

2 At oral argument, the County defended this refusal by asserting that federal law prohibited it from releasing the relevant pages of the employees' welfare applications. See Tr. of Oral Arg. 4-5. But the United States assured the Court that "[t]here is no Federal regulation or other Federal requirement" that would have prevented the County from sharing the relevant information with the Tribe. *Id.*, at 21. This entire controversy, it thus appears, might have been avoided had the county officials understood that federal law allowed the accommodation sought by the Tribe.

3 The Tribe did not dispute the State's authority over the crimes under investigation. See Brief for United States as *Amicus Curiae* 29.

4 The relevant portion of 42 U. S. C. §1983 reads: "Every person who, under color of any statute, ordinance, regulation, custom, or usage, of any State or Territory or the District of Columbia, subjects, or causes to be subjected, any citizen of the United States or other person within the jurisdiction thereof to the deprivation of any rights, privileges, or immunities secured by the Constitution and laws, shall be liable to the party injured in an action at law, suit in equity, or other proper proceeding for redress."

5 Courts of Appeals have expressed divergent views on this question. See *Native Village of Venetie IRA Council v. Alaska*, 155 F. 3d 1150, 1152, n. 1 (CA9 1998) (concluding that Tribes are persons entitled to sue under §1983); *American Vantage Co. v. Table Mountain Rancheria*, 292 F. 3d 1091, 1097, n. 4 (CA9 2002) ("[I]t is doubtful whether [a] Tribe qua sovereign would qualify as a 'citizen of the United States or other person' eligible to bring an action under §1983." (quoting *White Mountain Apache Tribe v. Williams*, 810 F. 2d 844, 865, n. 16 (CA9 1987) (Fletcher, J., dissenting))); cf. *Illinois v. Chicago*, 137 F. 3d 474, 477 (CA7 1998) (stating in dictum that "a state is not a 'person' under [§1983]"); *Pennsylvania v. Porter*, 659 F. 2d 306, 314-318 (CA3 1981) (en banc) (holding that a State may bring a §1983 action in a *parens patriae* capacity).

6 It hardly "demean[s] . . . Native American Tribes," see *post*, at 1 (STEVENS, J., concurring in judgment), in our view, to bracket them with States of the Union in this regard.

Discussion Questions

1. Why is it important to be able to distinguish between a municipal entity and a municipal official acting in an official capacity? Does the distinction affect immunity?

2. What is the distinction between a law enforcement official acting in a personal as opposed to an official capacity? What impact does this distinction have on litigation under Section 1983?

3. What are the differences between an individual, personal, and official capacity lawsuit? Do the practices of law enforcement personnel impact these distinctions?

4. Does the distinction between individual, personal, and official capacity lawsuits set the stage for conflict between street enforcement officers and law enforcement officials?

5. Who can act in an official capacity? Can a street enforcement officer, not a police chief or supervisor, act in an official capacity? What law enforcement practices would be considered official as opposed to personal?

6. Would a municipal official acting outside the scope of legal behavior be acting in an official capacity?

7. How has the Court's interpretation of the purposes of Section 1983 changed in these cases as compared to the decisions in Part I of your casebook?

8. Did the Court redefine "persons" in the decisions presented in Part II of your casebook? If so, how and what is the affect on policing?

9. Did the Court change its position on common-law immunities and defense available to governmental entities to render its decisions in this part of your casebook?

PART III

Policy, Custom, and Policymakers

In this section of your casebook, the Court considers the issues of what constitutes municipal policy and custom as well as who is considered a policymaker. To determine municipal liability, it is necessary for courts to be able to define with clarity the difference between the actions of individual police officers that are the product of their own decisions and those that are the product of a municipal policy or custom promulgated by a policymaker. In constructing what constitutes municipal policy or custom, it is necessary for the courts to determine whether a single, isolated incident of police behavior can be a product of a municipal policy or custom so as to render the municipality liable for the constitutional violation. Additionally, it is necessary for the

Court to distinguish between the creation of a municipal policy that results in a constitutional violation and the decision of a policymaker that may result in a constitutional violation but does not constitute official policy or custom. Thus what constitutes policy and whether a single incident of constitutional violation can become the basis for municipal liability are considered by the Court in great detail.

Making these matters more complex, courts must also determine who is and who is not a policymaker for purposes of municipal liability. The Court addresses not only how this determination is to be made, but also the level of culpability required to render a municipality liable for a constitutional violation attributable to a policymaker. The Court then turns its attention to the causal requirements of municipal liability. Just because there is a constitutional violation that is related to a policy or decision of a policymaker does not in itself render a municipality liable for the resulting damage or injury. In this section of the casebook, the Court struggles with developing standards for determining the required level of causation for municipal liability. This issue requires the Court to disentangle the behavior of individual officers, policymakers, and the circumstances that lead to constitutional violations. The Court, therefore, attempts to develop a legal standard to determine the nexus between an individual officer's constitutional violation and the contribution of the policymaker.

City of Oklahoma City
v. Tuttle
471 U.S. 808 (1985)

Argued January 8, 1985
Decided June 3, 1985
JUSTICE REHNQUIST announced the judgment of the Court, and delivered the opinion of the Court with respect to Part II, and an opinion
with respect to Part III, in which THE CHIEF JUSTICE, JUSTICE WHITE,
and JUSTICE O'CONNOR joined.

In *Monell v. New York City Dept. of Social Services*, 436 U.S. 658 (1978),
this Court held that municipalities are "persons" subject to damages
liability under § 1 of the Ku Klux Act of 1871, 42 U.S.C. § 1983, for violations of that Act visited by municipal officials. The Court noted, however, that municipal liability could not be premised on the mere fact
that the municipality employed the offending official. Instead, we held
that municipal liability could only be imposed for injuries inflicted pursuant to government "policy or custom." *Id.*, at 694. We noted at that
time that we had "no occasion to address . . . the full contours of municipal immunity under § 1983 . . .," *id.*, at 695, and expressly left such
development "to another day." Today we take a small but necessary
step toward defining those contours.

I

On October 4, 1980, Officer Julian Rotramel, a member of the Oklahoma City police force, shot and killed Albert Tuttle outside the We'll
Do Club, a bar in Oklahoma City. Officer Rotramel, who had been on

135

the force for 10 months, had [471 U.S. 808, 811] responded to an all points bulletin indicating that there was a robbery in progress at the Club. The bulletin, in turn, was the product of an anonymous telephone call. The caller had reported the robbery in progress, and had described the robber and reported that the robber had a gun. The parties stipulated at trial that Tuttle had placed the call.

Rotramel was the first officer to reach the bar, and the testimony concerning what happened thereafter is sharply conflicting. Rotramel's version was that when he entered the bar Tuttle walked toward him, and Rotramel grabbed Tuttle's arm and requested that he stay within the bar. Tuttle matched the description contained in the bulletin. Rotramel proceeded to question the barmaid concerning the reported robbery, but while doing so he once again had to restrain Tuttle from leaving, this time by grabbing Tuttle's arm and holding it. The barmaid testified that she told Rotramel that no robbery had occurred. Rotramel testified that while he was questioning the barmaid Tuttle kept bending towards his boots, and attempting to squirm from the officer's grip. Tuttle finally broke away from Rotramel, and, ignoring the officer's commands to "halt," went outside. When Rotramel cleared the threshold to the outside door, he saw Tuttle crouched down on the sidewalk, with his hands in or near his boot. Rotramel again ordered Tuttle to halt, but when Tuttle started to come out of his crouch Rotramel discharged his weapon. Rotramel testified at trial that he believed Tuttle had removed a gun from his boot, and that his life was in danger. Tuttle died from the gunshot wound. When his boot was removed at the hospital prior to surgery, a toy pistol fell out.

Respondent Rose Marie Tuttle is Albert Tuttle's widow, and the administratrix of his estate. She brought suit under § 1983 in the United States District Court, Western District of Oklahoma, against Rotramel and the city, alleging that their actions had deprived Tuttle of certain of his constitutional rights. At trial respondent introduced evidence concerning the facts surrounding the incident, and also adduced [471 U.S. 808, 812] testimony from an expert in police training practices. The expert testified that, based upon Rotramel's conduct during the incident in question and the expert's review of the Oklahoma City police training curriculum, it was his opinion that Rotramel's training was grossly inadequate. Respondent introduced no evidence that Rotramel or any other member of the Oklahoma City police force had been involved in a similar incident.

The case was presented to the jury on the theory that Rotramel's act had deprived Tuttle of life without due process of law, or that he had violated Tuttle's rights by using "excessive force in his apprehension." App. 38. With respect to respondent's suit against Rotramel individually, the jury was charged that Rotramel was entitled to qualified immunity to the extent that he had acted in good faith and with a reasonable belief that his actions were lawful.[1] Respondent also sought to hold the city liable under *Monell*, presumably on the theory that a municipal "custom or policy" had led to the constitutional violations. With respect to municipal liability the trial judge instructed the jury:

> "If a police officer denies a person his constitutional rights, the city that employs that officer is not liable for such a denial of the right simply because of the employment relationship. . . . But there are circumstances under which a city is liable for a deprivation of a constitutional right. Where the official policy of the city causes an employee of the city to deprive a person of such rights in the execution of that policy, the city may be liable. . . . .

> "It is the plaintiff's contention that such a policy existed and she relies upon allegations that the city is [471 U.S. 808, 813] grossly negligent in training of police officers, in its failure to supervise police officers, and in its failure to review and discipline its officers. The plaintiff has alleged that the failure of the city to adequately supervise, train, review, and discipline the police officers constitutes deliberate indifference to the constitutional rights of the decedent and acquiescence in the probability of serious police misconduct. . . . .

> "Absent more evidence of supervisory indifference, such as acquiescence in a prior matter of conduct, official policy such as to impose liability . . . under the federal Civil Rights Act cannot ordinarily be inferred from a single incident of illegality such as a first excessive use of force to stop a suspect; *but a single, unusually excessive use of force may be sufficiently out of the ordinary to warrant an inference that it was attributable to inadequate training or supervision amounting to 'deliberate indifference' or 'gross negligence' on the part of the officials in charge.* The city cannot be held liable for simple negligence. Furthermore, the plaintiff must show a causal link between the police misconduct and the adoption of a policy or plan by the defendant municipality." *Id.*, at 42-44. (Emphasis supplied.)

The jury returned a verdict in favor of Rotramel but against the city, and awarded respondent $1,500,000 in damages. The city appealed to the Court of Appeals for the Tenth Circuit, arguing, inter alia, that the trial court had improperly instructed the jury on the standard for municipal liability. In particular, petitioner claimed it was error to instruct the jury that a municipality could be held liable for a "policy" of "inadequate training" based merely upon evidence of a single incident of unconstitutional activity. The Court of Appeals rejected petitioner's claims. 728 F.2d 456 (1984).

Viewing the instructions "as a whole," that court first determined that the trial court properly had instructed the [471 U.S. 808, 814] jury that proof of "gross negligence" was required to hold the city liable for inadequate training. The court then addressed petitioner's contention that the trial court nevertheless had erred in instructing the jury that petitioner could be held liable based on proof of a single unconstitutional act. It distinguished cases indicating that proof of more than a single incident is required, and decided that where, as here, the act "was so plainly and grossly negligent that it spoke out very positively on the issue of lack of training . . .," the "single incident rule is not to be considered as an absolute . . . ." *Id.*, at 461. The instruction at issue was therefore "proper." *Id.*, at 459. The court also referred to "independent evidence" of inadequate training, and concluded that the "action, coupled with the clearly inadequate training," was sufficient to justify municipal liability. *Id.*, at 461. We granted certiorari because the Court of Appeals' holding that proof of a single incident of unconstitutional activity by a police officer could suffice to establish municipal liability seemed to conflict with the decisions of other Courts of Appeals. 469 U.S. 814 (1984). See, *e.g.*, *Languirand v. Hayden*, 717 F.2d 220, 228-230 (CA5 1983); *Wellington v. Daniels*, 717 F.2d 932, 936-937 (CA4 1983). But cf. *Owens v. Haas*, 601 F.2d 1242, 1246-1247 (CA2 1979).[2] We reverse. [471 U.S. 808, 815]

II

Before proceeding to the merits, we must address respondent's procedural argument that petitioner failed to object at trial to the "single incident" instruction with sufficient specificity to satisfy Federal Rule of Civil Procedure 51, and that therefore the question is not preserved for our review. We disagree. Respondent first referred to the requirements of Rule 51 in one sentence of her brief on the merits in this Court, at which time respondent did not even suggest that the "single incident" question was not preserved. The issue was raised again at oral argument, and respondent has filed a supplemental postargument brief on the question. But respondent's present protests cannot obscure her prior failures. In the Court of Appeals petitioner argued that proof of a single incident of the use of unreasonable force was insufficient to justify municipal liability, and specifically referred to the trial court's single-incident instruction highlighted above. The claim was rejected on the merits, and the Court of Appeals' opinion does not even mention the requirements of Rule 51, so it seems clear that respondent did not refer to the Rule below. The petition for certiorari again centered on the single-incident issue, but respondent's brief in opposition did not hint that the "questions presented" might not be properly preserved. Respondent's attempt to avoid the question now comes far too late.

We do not mean to give short shrift to the provisions of Rule 51. Indeed, respondent's argument might have prevailed had it been made to the Court of Appeals.[3] But we do not think that judicial economy is served by invoking the [471 U.S. 808, 816] Rule at this point, after we have granted certiorari and the case has received plenary consideration on the merits. Our decision to grant certiorari represents a commitment of scarce judicial resources with a view to deciding the merits of one or more of the questions presented in the petition. Nonjurisdictional defects of this sort should be brought to our attention no later than in respondent's brief in opposition to the petition for certiorari; if not, we consider it within our discretion to deem the defect waived. Here we granted certiorari to review an issue squarely presented to and decided by the Court of Appeals, and we will proceed to decide it. Cf. *On Lee v. United States*, 343 U.S. 747, 749-750, n. 3 (1952).

III

Respondent's lawsuit is brought pursuant to 42 U.S.C. § 1983. Although this Court has decided a host of cases under this statute in recent years, it can never hurt to embark on statutory construction with the Act's precise language in mind. The statute states:

> "Every person who, under color of any statute, ordinance, regulation, custom, or usage, of any State . . ., subjects, or causes to be subjected, any citizen of the United States or other person within the jurisdiction thereof to the deprivation of any rights, privileges, or immunities secured by the Constitution and laws, shall be liable to the party injured in an action at law, suit in equity, or other proper proceeding for redress. . . ."

By its terms, of course, the statute creates no substantive rights; it merely provides remedies for deprivations of rights established elsewhere. See *Baker v. McCollan*, 443 U.S. 137, 140, 144, n. 3 (1979). Here respondent's claim is that her husband was deprived of his life "without due process of law," in violation of the Fourteenth Amendment, or that he was deprived of his right to be free from the use of "excessive force in his apprehension"—presumably a right secured by [471 U.S. 808, 817] the Fourth and Fourteenth Amendments.[4] Having established a deprivation of a constitutional right, however, respondent still must establish that the city was the "person" who "cause[d] [Tuttle] to be subjected" to the deprivation. *Monell* teaches that the city may only be held accountable if the deprivation was the result of municipal "custom or policy."

In *Monell*, the plaintiffs challenged the defendant's policy of compelling pregnant employees to take unpaid sick leave before such leave was necessary for medical reasons, on the ground that the policy violated the Due Process or Equal Protection Clauses of the Fourteenth Amendment. Since the defendant was a municipal entity, this Court first addressed whether such an entity was a suable "person" as that term is used in § 1983. The Court's analysis focused on § 1983's legislative history, and in particular on the debate surrounding the proposed "Sherman amendment" to the 1871 Ku Klux Act, from which § 1983 is derived. The Sherman amendment would have held municipalities responsible for damage to person or property caused by private persons "riotously and tumultuously assembled." Cong. Globe, 42d Cong., 1st Sess., 749 (1871). Congress' refusal to adopt this [471 U.S. 808, 818] amendment, and the reasons given, were the basis for this Court's holding in *Monroe v. Pape*, 365 U.S. 167, 187-192 (1961), that municipalities were not suable "persons" under § 1983; a more extensive analysis of the Act's legislative history led this Court in *Monell* to overrule that part of *Monroe*. The principal objections to the Sherman amendment voiced in the 42nd Congress were that the section appeared to impose a federal obligation to keep the peace—a requirement the Congressmen thought was of doubtful constitutionality, but which in any event seemed to place the municipalities in the position of insurers for harms suffered within their borders. The *Monell* Court found that these concerns, although fatal to the Sherman amendment, were nevertheless consistent with holding a municipality liable "for *its own* violations of the Fourteenth Amendment." *Monell*, 436 U.S., at 683 (emphasis supplied).

Having determined that municipalities were suable "persons," the *Monell* Court went on to discuss the circumstances under which municipal liability could be imposed. The Court's holding that a city could not be held liable under § 1983 based upon theories akin to *respondeat superior* was based in part upon the language of the statute, and in part upon the rejection of the proposed Sherman amendment mentioned above. The Court noted that § 1983 only imposes liability for deprivations "cause[d]" by a particular defendant, and that it was hard to find such causation where liability is imposed merely because of an employment relationship. It also considered Congress' rejection of the Sherman amendment to be telling evidence that municipal liability should not be imposed when the municipality was not itself at fault. Given this legislative history, the *Monell* Court held that only deprivations visited pursuant to municipal "custom" or "policy" could lead to municipal liability. This language tracks the language of the statute; it also provides a fault-based analysis for imposing municipal liability.[5] [471 U.S. 808, 819]

The *Monell* Court went on to hold that the sick-leave policy at issue was "unquestionably" "the moving force of the constitutional violation found by the District Court," and that it therefore had "no occasion to address . . . what the full contours [471 U.S. 808, 820] of municipal liability may be." *Id.*, at 694-695. Subsequent decisions of this Court have added little to the *Monell* Court's formulation, beyond reaffirming that the municipal policy must be "the moving force of the constitutional violation." *Polk County v. Dodson*, 454 U.S. 312, 326 (1981). Cases construing *Monell* in the Courts of Appeals, however, have served to highlight the full range of questions, and subtle factual distinctions, that arise in administering the "policy" or "custom" standard. See, *e.g.*, *Bennett v. City of Slidell*, 728 F.2d 762 (CA5 1984); *Gilmere v. City of Atlanta*, 737 F.2d 894 (CA11 1984), rehear en banc, January 1985; *Languirand*, 717 F.2d, at 220.

With the development of municipal liability under § 1983 in this somewhat sketchy state, we turn to examine the basis upon which respondent seeks to have liability imposed upon the city. Respondent did not claim in the District Court that Oklahoma City had a "custom" or "policy" of authorizing its police force to use excessive force in the apprehension of suspected criminals, and the jury was not instructed on that theory of municipal liability. Rather, respondent's theory of liability was that the "policy" in question was the city's policy of training and supervising police officers, and that this "policy" resulted in inadequate training, and the constitutional violations alleged. Respondent in her brief says:

> "Respondent offered direct evidence that the shooting was caused by municipal policies. The officer who shot Tuttle testified that city training policies were inadequate and had led to Tuttle's death. The official who was Chief of Police when Tuttle was shot insisted that the shooting was entirely consistent with city policy." Brief for Respondent 13-14.

The District Court apparently accepted this theory of liability, though it charged the jury that the city's "policymakers" could not merely have been "negligent" in establishing training policies, but that they must have been guilty of [471 U.S. 808, 821] "gross negligence" or "deliberate indifference" to the "police misconduct" that they could thus engender.

Respondent then proceeds to argue that the question presented by petitioner—whether a single isolated incident of the use of excessive force by a police officer establishes an official custom or policy of a municipality—is in truth not presented by this record because there was more evidence of an official "policy" of "inadequate training" than might be inferred from the incident giving rise to Tuttle's death. But unfortunately for respondent, the instruction given by the District Court allowed the jury to impose liability on the basis of such a single incident without the benefit of the additional evidence. The trial court stated that the jury could "infer," from "a single, unusually excessive use of force . . . that it was attributable to inadequate training or supervision amounting to 'deliberate indifference' or 'gross negligence' on the part of the officials in charge." App. 44.

We think this inference unwarranted; first, in its assumption that the act at issue arose from inadequate training, and second, in its further assumption concerning the state of mind of the municipal policymakers. But more importantly, the inference allows a § 1983 plaintiff to establish municipal liability without submitting proof of a single action taken by a municipal policymaker. The foregoing discussion of the origins of *Monell's* "policy or custom" requirement should make clear that, at the least, that requirement was intended to prevent the imposition of municipal liability under circumstances where no wrong could be ascribed to municipal decision makers. Presumably, here the jury could draw the stated inference even in the face of uncontradicted evidence that the municipality scrutinized each police applicant and met the highest training standards imaginable. To impose liability under those circumstances would be to impose it simply because the municipality hired one "bad apple."

The fact that in this case respondent introduced independent evidence of inadequate training makes no difference, because [471 U.S. 808, 822] the instruction allowed the jury to impose liability even if it did not believe respondent's expert at all. Nor can we read this charge "as a whole" to avoid the difficulty. There is nothing elsewhere in this charge that would detract from the jury's perception that it could impose liability based solely on this single incident. Indeed, that was the intent of the charge, and that is what the Court of Appeals held in upholding it. The Court of Appeals' references to "independent evidence" in portions of its opinion are thus irrelevant; the general verdict yields no opportunity for determining whether liability was premised on the independent evidence, or solely on the inference sanctioned by the instruction. Cf. *Stromberg v. California*, 283 U.S. 359, 367-368 (1931).

Respondent contends that *Monell* suggests the contrary result, because it "expressly provided that an official 'decision' would suffice to establish liability, although a single decision will often have only a single victim." App. 14. But this very contention illustrates the wide difference between the municipal "policy" at issue in *Monell* and the "policy" alleged here. The "policy" of the New York City Department of Social Services that was challenged in *Monell* was a policy that by its terms compelled pregnant employees to take mandatory leaves of absence before such leaves were required for medical reasons; this policy in and of itself violated the constitutional rights of pregnant employees by reason of our decision in *Cleveland Board of Education v. LaFleur*, 414 U.S. 632 (1974). Obviously, it requires only one application of a policy such as this to satisfy fully *Monell's* requirement that a municipal corporation be held liable only for constitutional violations resulting from the municipality's official policy.

Here, however, the "policy" that respondent seeks to rely upon is far more nebulous, and a good deal further removed from the constitutional violation, than was the policy in *Monell*. To establish the constitutional violation in *Monell* no evidence was needed other than a statement of the policy [471 U.S. 808, 823] by the municipal corporation, and its exercise; but the type of "policy" upon which respondent relies, and its causal relation to the alleged constitutional violation, are not susceptible to such easy proof. In the first place, the word "policy" generally implies a course of action consciously chosen from among various alternatives;[6] it is therefore difficult in one sense even to accept the submission that someone pursues a "policy" of "inadequate training," unless evidence be adduced which proves that the inadequacies resulted from conscious choice—that is, proof that the policymakers deliberately chose a training program that would prove inadequate. And in the second place, some limitation must be placed on establishing municipal liability through policies that are not themselves unconstitutional, or the test set out in *Monell* will become a dead letter. Obviously, if one retreats far enough from a constitutional violation some municipal "policy" can be identified behind almost any such harm inflicted by a municipal official; for example, Rotramel would never have killed Tuttle if Oklahoma City did not have a "policy" of establishing a police force. But *Monell* must be taken to require proof of a city policy different in kind from this latter example before a claim can be sent to a jury on the theory that a particular violation was "caused" by the municipal "policy." At the very least there must be an affirmative link between the policy and the particular constitutional violation alleged.

Here the instructions allowed the jury to infer a thoroughly nebulous "policy" of "inadequate training" on the part of the municipal corporation from the single incident described earlier in this opinion, and at the same time sanctioned the inference that the "policy" was the cause of the incident. Such an approach provides a means for circumventing *Monell's* limitations altogether. Proof of a single [471 U.S. 808, 824] incident of unconstitutional activity is not sufficient to impose liability under *Monell*, unless proof of the incident includes proof that it was caused by an existing, unconstitutional municipal policy, which policy can be attributed to a municipal policymaker. Otherwise the existence of the unconstitutional policy, and its origin, must be separately proved. But where the policy relied upon is not itself unconstitutional, considerably more proof than the single incident will be necessary in every case to establish both the requisite fault on the part of the municipality,[7] and the causal connection between the "policy" and the constitutional deprivation.[8] Under the charge upheld by the Court of Appeals the jury could properly have imposed liability on the city based solely upon proof that it employed a nonpolicymaking officer who violated the Constitution. The decision of the Court of Appeals is accordingly

Reversed.

JUSTICE POWELL took no part in the decision of this case.

Footnotes

[1] This case was tried some three weeks prior to our decision in *Harlow v. Fitzgerald*, 457 U.S. 800 (1982), which modified the standard for qualified executive immunity. An executive official is now entitled to immunity unless he violated "clearly established statutory or constitutional rights of which a reasonable person would have known." *Id.*, at 818.

[2] The actual "question presented" in the petition for certiorari is:

"Whether a single isolated incident of the use of excessive force by a police officer establishes an official policy or practice of a municipality sufficient to render the municipality liable for damages under 42 U.S.C. § 1983." Pet. for Cert. i.

Although much of the petition for certiorari was directed to pointing out the general uncertainties concerning municipal liability for "inadequate training" of its police force, and although respondent's brief in opposition said nothing to dispel the notion that this general question was presented, we confine our holding to the above question. In reaching our conclusion, however, we find it necessary to discuss the many unanswered questions concerning municipal liability that we must assume have an answer in order to properly address this question.

[3] Federal Rule of Civil Procedure 51 requires counsel objecting to a jury instruction to "stat[e] distinctly the matter to which he objects and the grounds of his objection." Apparently, the only objection to the single-incident instruction contained in the record consists of the statement: "we make a second objection, your honor, particularly to the one, the Oklahoma City language, the language in the light of the City of Oklahoma City, which is single occurrence language." Tr. 693.

[4] The trial court correctly charged the jury that a federal right—here a constitutional right—had to be violated to establish liability under § 1983. Petitioner did not object to the trial court's description of the rights at issue, and we do not pass on whether the jury was correctly charged on this aspect of the case. The facts of this case are, of course, very similar to the facts of *Tennessee v. Garner*, *ante*, p. 1, in which we recently held that "[w]here the officer has probable cause to believe that the suspect poses a threat of serious physical harm, either to the officer or to others, it is not constitutionally unreasonable to prevent escape by using deadly force." *Ante*, at 11. Here the jury's verdict in favor of Rotramel must have been based upon a finding that he acted in "good faith and with a reasonable belief in the legality of his actions." We note that this Court has never held that every instance of use of "unreasonable force" in affecting an arrest constitutes a violation of the Fourth Amendment; nor has this Court held under circumstances such as these that there has been a deprivation of life "without due process of law."

[5] Although apparently agreeing with the result we reach in light of *Monell*, see *post*, at 842, JUSTICE STEVENS' dissent would have us overrule [471 U.S. 808, 819] *Monell's* limitation on municipal liability altogether. We see no reason here to depart from the important and established principle of *stare decisis*. The question we address involves only statutory construction, so any error we may commit is subject to reversal by Congress. Cf. *Burnet v. Coronado Oil & Gas Co.*, 285 U.S. 393, 406-407 (1932) (Brandeis, J., dissenting). In addition, the law in this area has taken enough 90-degree turns in recent years. *Monell* was decided only seven years ago. That decision, of course, overruled *Monroe v. Pape's* 17-year-old holding that municipalities were never subject to suit under § 1983. One reason why courts render decisions and written opinions is so that parties can order their conduct accordingly, and we may assume that decisions on issues such as this are appropriately considered by municipalities in ordering their financial affairs. The principle of *stare decisis* gives rise to and supports these legitimate expectations, and, where our decision is subject to correction by Congress, we do a great disservice when we subvert these concerns and maintain the law in a state of flux.

We note in addition that JUSTICE STEVENS' position, which is based substantially on his perception of the common law of municipal liability at the time § 1983 was enacted, is by no means representative of all the contemporary authorities. Both the majority and dissenting opinions in *Owen v. City of Independence*, 445 U.S. 622 (1980), recognized that certain rather complicated municipal tort immunities existed at the time § 1983 was enacted, see *id.*, at 644-650; *id.*, at 676-679 (POW-

ELL, J., dissenting); we are therefore somewhat surprised to learn that the "common law" at the time applied the doctrine of *respondeat superior* "to municipal corporations, and to the wrongful acts of police officers." *Post*, at 836-837. Even those cases known to allow municipal liability at the time hardly support the broad vicarious liability suggested by the dissent; the famous case of *Thayer v. Boston*, 36 Mass. 511, 516-517 (1837), for example, spoke in guarded language that seems in harmony with the limitations on municipal liability expressed in *Monell*. That court stated:

> "As a general rule, the corporation is not responsible for the unauthorized and unlawful acts of its officers, though done *colore officii*; it must further appear, that they were expressly authorized to do the acts, by the city government, or that they were done *bona fide* in pursuance of a general authority to act for the city, on the subject to which they relate; or that, in either case, the act was adopted and ratified by the corporation." 36 Mass., at 316-317.

[6] One well-known dictionary, for example, defines "policy" as "a definite course or method of action selected from among alternatives and in light of given conditions to guide and determine present and future decisions." Webster's Ninth New Collegiate Dictionary 910 (1983).

[7] We express no opinion on whether a policy that itself is not unconstitutional, such as the general "inadequate training" alleged here, can ever meet the "policy" requirement of *Monell*. In addition, even assuming that such a "policy" would suffice, it is open to question whether a policymaker's "gross negligence" in establishing police training practice could establish a "policy" that constitutes a "moving force" behind subsequent unconstitutional conduct, or whether a more conscious decision on the part of the policymaker would be required.

[8] In this regard, we cannot condone the loose language in the charge leaving it to the jury to determine whether the alleged inadequate training would likely lead to "police misconduct." The fact that a municipal "policy" might lead to "police misconduct" is hardly sufficient to satisfy *Monell's* requirement that the particular policy be the "moving force" behind a constitutional violation. There must at least be an affirmative [471 U.S. 808, 825] link between the training inadequacies alleged, and the particular constitutional violation at issue.

Pembaur v.
City of Cincinnati
475 U.S. 469 (1986)

Argued December 2, 1985
Decided March 25, 1986
JUSTICE BRENNAN delivered the opinion of the Court,
except as to Part II-B.

In *Monell v. New York City Dept. of Social Services*, 436 U.S. 658 (1978), the Court concluded that municipal liability under 42 U.S.C. § 1983 is limited to deprivations of federally protected rights caused by action taken "pursuant to official municipal policy of some nature . . . ." *Id.*, at 691. The question presented is whether, and in what circumstances, a decision by municipal policymakers on a single occasion may satisfy this requirement.

I

Bertold Pembaur is a licensed Ohio physician and the sole proprietor of the Rockdale Medical Center, located in the city of Cincinnati in Hamilton County. Most of Pembaur's patients are welfare recipients who rely on government assistance to pay for medical care. During the spring of 1977, Simon Leis, the Hamilton County Prosecutor, began investigating charges that Pembaur fraudulently had accepted payments from state welfare agencies for services not actually provided to patients. A grand jury was convened, and the case was assigned to Assistant Prosecutor William Whalen. [475 U.S. 469, 472] In April, the grand jury charged Pembaur in a six-count indictment.

146

During the investigation, the grand jury issued subpoenas for the appearance of two of Pembaur's employees. When these employees failed to appear as directed, the Prosecutor obtained capiases for their arrest and detention from the Court of Common Pleas of Hamilton County.[1]

On May 19, 1977, two Hamilton County Deputy Sheriffs attempted to serve the capiases at Pembaur's clinic. Although the reception area is open to the public, the rest of the clinic may be entered only through a door next to the receptionist's window. Upon arriving, the Deputy Sheriffs identified themselves to the receptionist and sought to pass through this door, which was apparently open. The receptionist blocked their way and asked them to wait for the doctor. When Pembaur appeared a moment later, he and the receptionist closed the door, which automatically locked from the inside, and wedged a piece of wood between it and the wall. Returning to the receptionist's window, the Deputy Sheriffs identified themselves to Pembaur, showed him the capiases and explained why they were there. Pembaur refused to let them enter, claiming that the police had no legal authority to be there and requesting that they leave. He told them that he had called the Cincinnati police, the local media, and his lawyer. The Deputy Sheriffs decided not to take further action until the Cincinnati police arrived.

Shortly thereafter, several Cincinnati police officers appeared. The Deputy Sheriffs explained the situation to them and asked that they speak to Pembaur. The Cincinnati police told Pembaur that the papers were lawful and that he should allow the Deputy Sheriffs to enter. When Pembaur refused, the Cincinnati police called for a superior officer. When he too failed to persuade Pembaur to open the door, [475 U.S. 469, 473] the Deputy Sheriffs decided to call their supervisor for further instructions. Their supervisor told them to call Assistant Prosecutor Whalen and to follow his instructions. The Deputy Sheriffs then telephoned Whalen and informed him of the situation. Whalen conferred with County Prosecutor Leis, who told Whalen to instruct the Deputy Sheriffs to "go in and get [the witnesses]." Whalen in turn passed these instructions along to the Deputy Sheriffs.

After a final attempt to persuade Pembaur voluntarily to allow them to enter, the Deputy Sheriffs tried unsuccessfully to force the door. City police officers, who had been advised of the County Prosecutor's instructions to "go in and get" the witnesses, obtained an axe and chopped down the door. The Deputy Sheriffs then entered and searched the clinic. Two individuals who fit descriptions of the witnesses sought were detained, but turned out not to be the right persons.

After this incident, the Prosecutor obtained an additional indictment against Pembaur for obstructing police in the performance of an authorized act. Although acquitted of all other charges, Pembaur was convicted for this offense. The Ohio Court of Appeals reversed, reasoning that Pembaur was privileged under state law to exclude the deputies because the search of his office violated the Fourth Amendment. *State v. Pembaur*, No. C-790380 (Hamilton County Court of Appeals, Nov. 3, 1982). The Ohio Supreme Court reversed and reinstated the conviction. *State v. Pembaur*, 9 Ohio St. 3d 136, 459 N. E. 2d 217, cert. denied, 467 U.S. 1219 (1984). The Supreme Court held that the state-law privilege applied only to bad-faith conduct by law enforcement officials, and that, under the circumstances of this case, Pembaur was obliged to acquiesce to the search and seek redress later in a civil action for damages. 9 Ohio St. 3d, at 138, 459 N. E. 2d, at 219.

On April 20, 1981, Pembaur filed the present action in the United States District Court for the Southern District of Ohio against the city of Cincinnati, the County of Hamilton, [475 U.S. 469, 474] the Cincinnati Police Chief, the Hamilton County Sheriff, the members of the Hamilton Board of County Commissioners (in their official capacities only), Assistant Prosecutor Whalen, and nine city and county police officers.[2] Pembaur sought damages under 42 U.S.C. § 1983, alleging that the county and city police had violated his rights under the Fourth and Fourteenth Amendments. His theory was that, absent exigent circumstances, the Fourth Amendment prohibits police from searching an individual's home or business without a search warrant even to execute an arrest warrant for a third person. We agreed with that proposition in *Steagald v. United States*, 451 U.S. 204 (1981), decided the day after Pembaur filed this lawsuit. Pembaur sought $10 million in actual and $10 million in punitive damages, plus costs and attorney's fees.

Much of the testimony at the 4-day trial concerned the practices of the Hamilton County Police in serving capiases. Frank Webb, one of the Deputy Sheriffs present at the clinic on May 19, testified that he had previously served capiases on the property of third persons without a search warrant, but had never been required to use force to gain access. Assistant Prosecutor Whalen was also unaware of a prior instance in which police had been denied access to a third person's property in serving a capias and had used force to gain entry. Lincoln Stokes, the County Sheriff, testified that the Department had no written policy respecting the serving of capiases on the property of third persons and that the proper response in any given situation would depend upon the circumstances. He too could not recall a specific instance in [475 U.S. 469, 475] which entrance had been denied and forcibly gained. Sheriff Stokes did testify, however, that it was the practice in his Department to refer questions to the County Prosecutor for instructions under appropriate circumstances and that "it was the proper thing to do" in this case.

The District Court awarded judgment to the defendants and dismissed the complaint in its entirety. The court agreed that the entry and search of Pembaur's clinic violated the Fourth Amendment under

Steagald, supra, but held Steagald inapplicable since it was decided nearly four years after the incident occurred. Because it construed the law in the Sixth Circuit in 1977 to permit law enforcement officials to enter the premises of a third person to serve a capias, the District Court held that the individual municipal officials were all immune under *Harlow v. Fitzgerald,* 457 U.S. 800 (1982).

The claims against the county and the city were dismissed on the ground that the individual officers were not acting pursuant to the kind of "official policy" that is the predicate for municipal liability under *Monell.* With respect to Hamilton County, the court explained that, even assuming that the entry and search were pursuant to a governmental policy, "it was not a policy of Hamilton County per se" because "[t]he Hamilton County Board of County Commissioners, acting on behalf of the county, simply does not establish or control the policies of the Hamilton County Sheriff." With respect to the city of Cincinnati, the court found that "the only policy or custom followed . . . was that of aiding County Sheriff's Deputies in the performance of their duties." The court found that any participation by city police in the entry and search of the clinic resulted from decisions by individual officers as to the permissible scope of assistance they could provide, and not from a city policy to provide this particular kind of assistance.

On appeal, Pembaur challenged only the dismissal of his claims against Whalen, Hamilton County, and the city of Cincinnati. [475 U.S. 469, 476] The Court of Appeals for the Sixth Circuit upheld the dismissal of Pembaur's claims against Whalen and Hamilton County, but reversed the dismissal of his claim against the city of Cincinnati on the ground that the District Court's findings concerning the policies followed by the Cincinnati police were clearly erroneous. 746 F.2d 337 (1984).[3]

The Court of Appeals affirmed the District Court's dismissal of Pembaur's claim against Hamilton County, but on different grounds. The court held that the County Board's lack of control over the Sheriff would not preclude county liability if "the nature and duties of the Sheriff are such that his acts may fairly be said to represent the county's official policy with respect to the specific subject matter." *Id.,* at 340-341. Based upon its examination of Ohio law, the Court of Appeals found it "clea[r]" that the Sheriff and the Prosecutor were both county officials authorized to establish "the official policy of Hamilton County" with respect to matters of law enforcement. *Id.,* at 341. Notwithstanding these conclusions, however, the court found that Pembaur's claim against the county had been properly dismissed:

> "We believe that Pembaur failed to prove the existence of a county policy in this case. Pembaur claims that the deputy sheriffs acted pursuant to the policies of the Sheriff and Prosecutor by forcing entry into the medical center. Pembaur has failed to establish, however, anything more than that, on this *one occasion,* the Prosecutor and

the Sheriff decided to force entry into his office. . . . That single, discrete decision is insufficient, [475 U.S. 469, 477] by itself, to establish that the Prosecutor, the Sheriff, or both were implementing a governmental policy." *Ibid.* (footnote omitted) (emphasis in original).

Pembaur petitioned for certiorari to review only the dismissal of his claim against Hamilton County. The decision of the Court of Appeals conflicts with holdings in several other Courts of Appeals,[4] and we granted the petition to resolve the conflict. 472 U.S. 1016 (1985). We reverse.

II

A

Our analysis must begin with the proposition that "Congress did not intend municipalities to be held liable unless action pursuant to official municipal policy of some nature caused a constitutional tort." *Monell v. New York City Dept. of Social Services*, 436 U.S., at 691.[5] As we read its opinion, the Court of Appeals held that a single decision to [475 U.S. 469, 478] take particular action, although made by municipal policymakers, cannot establish the kind of "official policy" required by *Monell* as a predicate to municipal liability under § 1983.[6] The Court of Appeals reached this conclusion without referring to *Monell*—indeed, without any explanation at all. However, examination of the opinion in *Monell* clearly demonstrates that the Court of Appeals misinterpreted its holding.

Monell is a case about responsibility. In the first part of the opinion, we held that local government units could be made liable under § 1983 for deprivations of federal rights, overruling a contrary holding in *Monroe v. Pape*, 365 U.S. 167 (1961). In the second part of the opinion, we recognized a limitation on this liability and concluded that a municipality cannot be made liable by application of the doctrine of *respondeat superior*. See *Monell*, 436 U.S., at 691. In part, this conclusion rested upon the language of § 1983, which imposes liability only on a person who "subjects, or causes to be subjected," any individual to a deprivation of federal rights; we noted that this language "cannot easily be read to impose liability vicariously on government bodies solely on the basis of the existence of an employer-employee relationship with a tortfeasor." *Id.*, at 692. Primarily, [475 U.S. 469, 479] however, our conclusion rested upon the legislative history, which disclosed that, while Congress never questioned its power to impose civil liability on municipalities for their own illegal acts, Congress did doubt its constitutional power to impose such liability in order to oblige municipalities to control the conduct of others. *Id.*, at 665-683.[7] We found that, because of these doubts, Congress chose not to create such obligations in § 1983.

Recognizing that this would be the effect of a federal law of *respondeat superior*, we concluded that § 1983 could not be interpreted to incorporate doctrines of vicarious liability. *Id.*, at 692-694, and n. 57.

The conclusion that tortious conduct, to be the basis for municipal liability under § 1983, must be pursuant to a municipality's "official policy" is contained in this discussion. The "official policy" requirement was intended to distinguish acts of the municipality from acts of employees of the municipality, and thereby make clear that municipal liability is limited to action for which the municipality is actually responsible.[8] [475 U.S. 469, 480] *Monell* reasoned that recovery from a municipality is limited to acts that are, properly speaking, acts "of the municipality"—that is, acts which the municipality has officially sanctioned or ordered.

With this understanding, it is plain that municipal liability may be imposed for a single decision by municipal policymakers under appropriate circumstances. No one has ever doubted, for instance, that a municipality may be liable under § 1983 for a single decision by its properly constituted legislative body—whether or not that body had taken similar action in the past or intended to do so in the future—because even a single decision by such a body unquestionably constitutes an act of official government policy. See, *e.g.*, *Owen v. City of Independence*, 445 U.S. 622 (1980) (City Council passed resolution firing plaintiff without a pretermination hearing); *Newport v. Fact Concerts, Inc.*, 453 U.S. 247 (1981) (City Council canceled license permitting concert because of dispute over content of performance). But the power to establish policy is no more the exclusive province of the legislature at the local level than at the state or national level. *Monell's* language makes clear that it expressly envisioned other officials "whose acts or edicts may fairly be said to represent official policy," *Monell, supra*, at 694, and whose decisions therefore may give rise to municipal liability under § 1983.

Indeed, any other conclusion would be inconsistent with the principles underlying § 1983. To be sure, "official policy" often refers to formal rules or understandings—often but not always committed to writing—that are intended to, and do, establish fixed plans of action to be followed under similar circumstances [475 U.S. 469, 481] consistently and over time. That was the case in *Monell* itself, which involved a written rule requiring pregnant employees to take unpaid leaves of absence before such leaves were medically necessary. However, as in *Owen* and *Newport*, a government frequently chooses a course of action tailored to a particular situation and not intended to control decisions in later situations. If the decision to adopt that particular course of action is properly made by that government's authorized decision makers, it surely represents an act of official government "policy" as that term is commonly understood.[9] More importantly, where action is directed by those who establish governmental policy, the municipality is equally responsible whether that action is to be taken only once or to be taken repeatedly. To deny compensation to the victim would therefore be contrary to the fundamental purpose of § 1983.

B

Having said this much, we hasten to emphasize that not every decision by municipal officers automatically subjects the municipality to § 1983 liability. Municipal liability attaches only where the decision maker possesses final authority to establish municipal policy with respect to the action ordered.[10] The fact that a particular official—even a policy-making [475 U.S. 469, 482] official—has discretion in the exercise of particular functions does not, without more, give rise to municipal liability based on an exercise of that discretion. See, *e.g., Oklahoma City v. Tuttle*, 471 U.S., at 822-824.[11] The official [475 U.S. 469, 483] must also be responsible for establishing final government policy respecting such activity before the municipality can be held liable.[12] Authority to make municipal policy may be granted directly by a legislative enactment or may be delegated by an official who possesses such authority, and of course, whether an official had final policymaking authority is a question of state law. However, like other governmental entities, municipalities often spread policymaking authority among various officers and official bodies. As a result, particular officers may have authority to establish binding county policy respecting particular matters and to adjust that policy for the county in changing circumstances. To hold a municipality liable for actions ordered by such officers exercising their policymaking authority is no more an application of the theory of *respondeat superior* than was holding the municipalities liable for the decisions of the City Councils in *Owen* and *Newport.* In each case municipal liability attached to a single decision to take unlawful action made by municipal policymakers. We hold that municipal liability under § 1983 attaches where—and only where—a deliberate choice to follow a course of action is made from among various alternatives by the official or officials responsible for establishing final policy with respect to the subject matter in question. [475 U.S. 469, 484] See *Tuttle, supra*, at 823 ("'policy' generally implies a course of action consciously chosen from among various alternatives").

C

Applying this standard to the case before us, we have little difficulty concluding that the Court of Appeals erred in dismissing petitioner's claim against the county. The Deputy Sheriffs who attempted to serve the capiases at petitioner's clinic found themselves in a difficult situation. Unsure of the proper course of action to follow, they sought instructions from their supervisors. The instructions they received were to follow the orders of the County Prosecutor. The Prosecutor made a considered decision based on his understanding of the law and commanded the officers forcibly to enter petitioner's clinic. That decision directly caused the violation of petitioner's Fourth Amendment rights.

Respondent argues that the County Prosecutor lacked authority to establish municipal policy respecting law enforcement practices because only the County Sheriff may establish policy respecting such practices. Respondent suggests that the County Prosecutor was merely rendering "legal advice" when he ordered the Deputy Sheriffs to "go in and get" the witnesses. Consequently, the argument concludes, the action of the individual Deputy Sheriffs in following this advice and forcibly entering petitioner's clinic was not pursuant to a properly established municipal policy.

We might be inclined to agree with respondent if we thought that the Prosecutor had only rendered "legal advice." However, the Court of Appeals concluded, based upon its examination of Ohio law, that both the County Sheriff and the County Prosecutor could establish county policy under appropriate circumstances, a conclusion that we do not question here.[13] Ohio Rev. Code Ann. 309.09(A) (1979) [475 U.S. 469, 485] provides that county officers may "require . . . instructions from [the County Prosecutor] in matters connected with their official duties." Pursuant to standard office procedure, the Sheriff's Office referred this matter to the Prosecutor and then followed his instructions. The Sheriff testified that his Department followed this practice under appropriate circumstances and that it was "the proper thing to do" in this case. We decline to accept respondent's invitation to overlook this delegation of authority by disingenuously labeling the Prosecutor's clear command mere "legal advice." In ordering the Deputy Sheriffs to enter petitioner's clinic the County Prosecutor was acting as the final decision maker for the County, and the county may therefore be held liable under § 1983.

The decision of the Court of Appeals is reversed, and the case is remanded for further proceedings consistent with this opinion.

It is so ordered.

Footnotes

[1] A capias is a writ of attachment commanding a county official to bring a subpoenaed witness who has failed to appear before the court to testify and to answer for civil contempt. See Ohio Rev. Code Ann. § 2317.21 (1981).

[2] Hamilton County Prosecutor Leis was not made a defendant because counsel for petitioner believed that Leis was absolutely immune. Tr., Mar. 14-Mar. 17, p. 267. We express no view as to the correctness of this evaluation. Cf. *Imbler v. Pachtman,* 424 U.S. 409, 430-431 (1976) (leaving open the question of a prosecutor's immunity when he acts "in the role of an administrator or investigative officer rather than that of an advocate").

³ The court found that there was a city policy respecting the use of force in serving capiases as well as a policy of aiding county police. It based this conclusion on the testimony of Cincinnati Chief of Police Myron Leistler, who stated that it was the policy of his Department to take whatever steps were necessary, including the forcing of doors, to serve an arrest document. 746 F.2d, at 341-342; see also, Tr., Mar. 14-Mar. 17, pp. 43-45, 46-47. The court remanded the case for a determination whether Pembaur's injury was incurred as a result of the execution of this policy. 746 F.2d, at 342.

⁴ See, e.g., McKinley v. City of Eloy, 705 F.2d 1110, 1116-1117 (CA9 1983); Berdin v. Duggan, 701 F.2d 909, 913-914 (CA11), cert. denied, 464 U.S. 893 (1983); Van Ooteghem v. Gray, 628 F.2d 488, 494-495 (CA5 1980), cert. denied, 455 U.S. 909 (1982); Quinn v. Syracuse Model Neighborhood Corp., 613 F.2d 438, 448 (CA2 1980). See also Sanders v. St. Louis County, 724 F.2d 665, 668 (CA8 1983) (per curiam) ("It may be that one act of a senior county official is enough to establish the liability of the county, if that official was in a position to establish policy and if that official himself directly violated another's constitutional rights"). But see Losch v. Borough of Parkesburg, Pa., 736 F.2d 903, 910-911 (CA3 1984) ("[E]ven if [the Police Chief] were the final authority with regard to police activities, . . . there is no regulation or evidence of any repeated action by [the chief] . . . that can transmute his actions in the Losch incident into a general Borough policy").

⁵ There is no question in this case that petitioner suffered a constitutional deprivation. The Court of Appeals found, and respondent concedes, that the entry and search of petitioner's clinic violated the Fourth Amendment under Steagald v. United States, 451 U.S. 204 (1981). See 746 F.2d, at 340, n. 1; Brief for Respondents 11. Respondent never challenged and has in fact also conceded that Steagald applies retroactively to this case. See Tr. of Oral Arg. 26-27. We decide this case in light of respondent's concessions.

⁶ The opinion below also can be read as holding that municipal liability cannot be imposed for a single incident of unconstitutional conduct by municipal employees whether or not that conduct is pursuant to municipal policy. Such a conclusion is unsupported by either the language or reasoning of Monell, or by any of our subsequent decisions. As we explained last Term in Oklahoma City v. Tuttle, 471 U.S. 808 (1985), once a municipal policy is established, "it requires only one application . . . to satisfy fully Monell's requirement that a municipal corporation be held liable only for constitutional violations resulting from the municipality's official policy." Id., at 822 (plurality opinion); see also, id., at 831-832 (BRENNAN, J., concurring in part and concurring in judgment.). The only issue before us, then, is whether petitioner satisfied Monell's requirement that the tortious conduct be pursuant to "official municipal policy."

⁷ This legislative history is discussed at length in Monell and need only be summarized here. The distinction between imposing liability on municipalities for their own violations and imposing liability to force municipalities to prevent violations by others was made by Members of the House of Representatives who successfully opposed the "Sherman amendment" to the Civil Rights Act of 1871, 17 Stat. 13, the precursor of § 1983. The Sherman amendment sought to impose civil liability on municipalities for damage done to the person or property of its inhabitants by private persons "riotously and tumultuously assembled." Cong. Globe, 42d Cong., 1st Sess., 749 (1871) (quoted in Monell, 436 U.S., at 664). Opponents of the amendment argued that, in effect, it imposed an obligation on local governments to keep the peace, and that the Federal Government could not constitutionally require local governments to keep the peace if state law did not. This argument succeeded in blocking passage of the amendment. However, even the opponents of the Sherman amendment recognized Congress' power to impose civil liability on a local government already obligated to keep the peace by state law if

that government failed to do so and thereby violated the Fourteenth Amendment. See *id.*, at 665-683.

[8] Thus, our statement of the conclusion juxtaposes the policy requirement with imposing liability on the basis of *respondeat superior.*

> "We conclude, therefore, that a local government may not be sued under § 1983 for an injury inflicted solely by its employees or agents. Instead, it is when execution of a government's policy . . ., whether made by its lawmakers or by those whose edicts or acts may fairly be said to represent official policy, inflicts the injury that the government as an entity is responsible under § 1983." *Id.*, at 694.

[9] While the dictionary is not the source definitively to resolve legal questions, we note that this description of "policy" is consistent with the word's ordinary definition. For example, Webster's defines the word as "a specific decision or set of decisions designed to carry out such a chosen course of action." Webster's Third New International Dictionary 1754 (1981). Similarly, the Oxford English Dictionary defines "policy" as "[a] course of action adopted and pursued by a government, party, ruler, statesman, etc.; any course of action adopted as advantageous or expedient." VII Oxford English Dictionary 1071 (1933). See also, Webster's New Twentieth Century Dictionary 1392 (2d ed. 1979) ("any governing principle, plan, or course of action"); Random House Dictionary 1113 (1966) ("a course of action adopted and pursued by a government, ruler, political party, etc.").

[10] Section 1983 also refers to deprivations under color of a state "custom or usage," and the Court in *Monell* noted accordingly that "local governments, [475 U.S. 469, 482] like every other § 1983 'person,' . . . may be sued for constitutional deprivations visited pursuant to governmental 'custom' even though such a custom has not received formal approval through the body's official decisionmaking channels." 436 U.S., at 690-691. A § 1983 plaintiff thus may be able to recover from a municipality without adducing evidence of an affirmative decision by policymakers if able to prove that the challenged action was pursuant to a state "custom or usage." Because there is no allegation that the action challenged here was pursuant to a local "custom," this aspect of *Monell* is not at issue in this case.

[11] Respondent argues that the holding in *Tuttle* is far broader than this. It relies on the statement near the end of JUSTICE REHNQUIST's plurality opinion that "[p]roof of a single incident of unconstitutional activity is not sufficient to impose liability under *Monell* unless proof of the incident includes proof that it was caused by an *existing*, unconstitutional municipal policy, which policy can be attributed to a municipal policymaker." 471 U.S., at 823 -824 (emphasis added). Respondent contends that a policy cannot be said to be "existing" unless similar action has been taken in the past.

This reading of the *Tuttle* plurality is strained, and places far too much weight on a single word. The plaintiff in *Tuttle* alleged that a police officer's use of excessive force deprived her decedent of life without due process of law. The plaintiff proved only a single instance of unconstitutional action by a nonpolicymaking employee of the city. She argued that the city had "caused" the constitutional deprivation by adopting a "policy" of inadequate training. The trial judge instructed the jury that a single, unusually excessive use of force may warrant an inference that it was attributable to grossly inadequate training, and that the municipality could be held liable on this basis. We reversed the judgment against the city. Although there was no opinion for the Court on this question, both the plurality and the opinion concurring in the judgment found plaintiff's submission inadequate because she failed to establish that the unconstitutional act was taken *pursuant* to a municipal policy rather than simply resulting from such a policy in a "but for" sense. *Id.*, at 822-824 (plurality opinion), 829-830 (BRENNAN, J., concurring in part and concurring in judgment). That conclusion is entirely consistent with our holding today that the policy which ordered or authorized an unconstitutional act can be established by a single decision by proper municipal policymakers.

[12] Thus, for example, the County Sheriff may have discretion to hire and fire employees without also being the county official responsible for establishing county employment policy. If this were the case, the Sheriff's decisions respecting employment would not give rise to municipal liability, although similar decisions with respect to law enforcement practices, over which the Sheriff is the official policymaker, would give rise to municipal liability. Instead, if county employment policy was set by the Board of County Commissioners, only that body's decisions would provide a basis for county liability. This would be true even if the Board left the Sheriff discretion to hire and fire employees and the Sheriff exercised that discretion in an unconstitutional manner; the decision to act unlawfully would not be a decision of the Board. However, if the Board delegated its power to establish final employment policy to the Sheriff, the Sheriff's decisions would represent county policy and could give rise to municipal liability.

[13] We generally accord great deference to the interpretation and application of state law by the courts of appeals. *United States v. S.A. Empresa de Viacao Aerea Rio Grandense*, 467 U.S. 797, 815, n. 12 (1984); *Brockett* [475 U.S. 469, 485] v. *Spokane Arcades, Inc.*, 472 U.S. 491, 499-500 (1985) (citing cases); see also *Bishop v. Wood*, 426 U.S. 341, 345-347 (1976).

City of St. Louis
v. Praprotnik
485 U.S. 112 (1988)

Argued October 7, 1987
Decided March 2, 1988
JUSTICE O'CONNOR announced the judgment of the Court and
delivered an opinion, in which THE CHIEF JUSTICE, JUSTICE WHITE,
and JUSTICE SCALIA join.

This case calls upon us to define the proper legal standard for determining when isolated decisions by municipal officials or employees
may expose the municipality itself to liability under 42 U.S.C. § 1983.

I

The principal facts are not in dispute. Respondent James H. Praprotnik is
an architect who began working for petitioner city of St. Louis in 1968.
For several years, respondent consistently received favorable evaluations
of his job performance, uncommonly quick promotions, and significant
increases in salary. By 1980, he was serving in a management-level city
planning position at petitioner's Community Development Agency (CDA).

The Director of CDA, Donald Spaid, had instituted a requirement
that the agency's professional employees, including architects, obtain
advance approval before taking on private clients. Respondent and
other CDA employees objected [485 U.S. 112, 115] to the requirement.
In April 1980, respondent was suspended for 15 days by CDA's Director of Urban Design, Charles Kindleberger, for having accepted outside
employment without prior approval. Respondent appealed to the city's

Civil Service Commission, a body charged with reviewing employee grievances. Finding the penalty too harsh, the Commission reversed the suspension, awarded respondent backpay, and directed that he be reprimanded for having failed to secure a clear understanding of the rule.

The Commission's decision was not well received by respondent's supervisors at CDA. Kindleberger later testified that he believed respondent had lied to the Commission, and that Spaid was angry with respondent.

Respondent's next two annual job performance evaluations were markedly less favorable than those in previous years. In discussing one of these evaluations with respondent, Kindleberger apparently mentioned his displeasure with respondent's 1980 appeal to the Civil Service Commission. Respondent appealed both evaluations to the Department of Personnel. In each case, the Department ordered partial relief and was upheld by the city's Director of Personnel or the Civil Service Commission.

In April 1981, a new Mayor came into office, and Donald Spaid was replaced as Director of CDA by Frank Hamsher. As a result of budget cuts, a number of layoffs and transfers significantly reduced the size of CDA and of the planning section in which respondent worked. Respondent, however, was retained.

In the spring of 1982, a second round of layoffs and transfers occurred at CDA. At that time, the city's Heritage and Urban Design Commission (Heritage) was seeking approval to hire someone who was qualified in architecture and urban planning. Hamsher arranged with the Director of Heritage, Henry Jackson, for certain functions to be transferred from CDA to Heritage. This arrangement, which made it possible for Heritage to employ a relatively high-level "city planning [485 U.S. 112, 116] manager," was approved by Jackson's supervisor, Thomas Nash. Hamsher then transferred respondent to Heritage to fill this position.

Respondent objected to the transfer, and appealed to the Civil Service Commission. The Commission declined to hear the appeal because respondent had not suffered a reduction in his pay or grade. Respondent then filed suit in Federal District Court, alleging that the transfer was unconstitutional. The city was named as a defendant, along with Kindleberger, Hamsher, Jackson (whom respondent deleted from the list before trial), and Deborah Patterson, who had succeeded Hamsher at CDA.

At Heritage, respondent became embroiled in a series of disputes with Jackson and Jackson's successor, Robert Killen. Respondent was dissatisfied with the work he was assigned, which consisted of unchallenging clerical functions far below the level of responsibilities that he had previously enjoyed. At least one adverse personnel decision was taken against respondent, and he obtained partial relief after appealing that decision.

In December 1983, respondent was laid off from Heritage. The layoff was attributed to a lack of funds, and this apparently meant that respondent's supervisors had concluded that they could create two lower level positions with the funds that were being used to pay respondent's salary. Respondent then amended the complaint in his lawsuit to include a challenge to the layoff. He also appealed to the Civil Service Commission, but proceedings in that forum were postponed because of the pending lawsuit and have never been completed. Tr. Oral Arg. 31-32.

The case went to trial on two theories: (1) that respondent's First Amendment rights had been violated through retaliatory actions taken in response to his appeal of his 1980 suspension; and (2) that respondent's layoff from Heritage was carried out for pretextual reasons in violation of due process. The jury returned special verdicts exonerating [485 U.S. 112, 117] each of the three individual defendants, but finding the city liable under both theories. Judgment was entered on the verdicts, and the city appealed.

A panel of the Court of Appeals for the Eighth Circuit found that the due process claim had been submitted to the jury on an erroneous legal theory and vacated that portion of the judgment. With one judge dissenting, however, the panel affirmed the verdict holding the city liable for violating respondent's First Amendment rights. 798 F.2d 1168 (1986). Only the second of these holdings is challenged here.

The Court of Appeals found that the jury had implicitly determined that respondent's layoff from Heritage was brought about by an unconstitutional city policy. *Id.*, at 1173. Applying a test under which a "policymaker" is one whose employment decisions are "final" in the sense that they are not subjected to de novo review by higher ranking officials, the Court of Appeals concluded that the city could be held liable for adverse personnel decisions taken by respondent's supervisors. *Id.*, at 1173-1175. In response to petitioner's contention that the city's personnel policies are actually set by the Civil Service Commission, the Court of Appeals concluded that the scope of review before that body was too "highly circumscribed" to allow it fairly to be said that the Commission, rather than the officials who initiated the actions leading to respondent's injury, were the "final authority" responsible for setting city policy. *Id.*, at 1175.

Turning to the question whether a rational jury could have concluded that respondent had been injured by an unconstitutional policy, the Court of Appeals found that respondent's transfer from CDA to Heritage had been "orchestrated" by Hamsher, that the transfer had amounted to a "constructive discharge," and that the injury had reached fruition when respondent was eventually laid off by Nash and Killen. *Id.*, at 1175-1176, and n. 8. The court held that the jury's verdict exonerating Hamsher and the other individual defendants could be reconciled with a finding of liability [485 U.S. 112, 118] against the city because "the named defendants were not the supervisors directly causing the lay off, when the actual damages arose." *Id.*, at 1173, n. 3. Cf. *Los Angeles v. Heller*, 475 U.S. 796 (1986).

The dissenting judge relied on our decision in *Pembaur v. Cincinnati*, 475 U.S. 469 (1986). He found that the power to set employment policy for petitioner city of St. Louis lay with the Mayor and Aldermen, who were authorized to enact ordinances, and with the Civil Service Commission, whose function was to hear appeals from city employees who believed that their rights under the city's Charter, or under applicable rules and ordinances, had not been properly respected. 798 F.2d, at 1180. The dissent concluded that respondent had submitted no evidence proving that the Mayor and Aldermen, or the Commission, had established a policy of retaliating against employees for appealing from adverse personnel decisions. *Id.*, at 1179-1181. The dissenting judge also concluded that, even if there were such a policy, the record evidence would not support a finding that respondent was in fact transferred or laid off in retaliation for the 1980 appeal from his suspension. *Id.*, at 1181-1182.

We granted certiorari, 479 U.S. 1029 (1987), and we now reverse.

II

We begin by addressing a threshold procedural issue. The second question presented in the petition for certiorari reads as follows:

> "Whether the failure of a local government to establish an appellate procedure for the review of officials' decisions which does not defer in substantial part to the original decisionmaker's decision constitutes a delegation of authority to establish final government policy such that liability may be imposed on the local government on the basis of the decisionmaker's act alone, when the act is neither taken pursuant to a rule of general applicability [485 U.S. 112, 119] nor is a decision of specific application adopted as the result of a formal process?" Pet. for Cert. i.

Although this question was manifestly framed in light of the holding of the Court of Appeals, respondent argues that petitioner failed to preserve the question through a timely objection to the jury instructions under Federal Rule of Civil Procedure 51. Arguing that both parties treated the identification of municipal "policymakers" as a question of fact at trial, respondent emphasizes that the jury was given the following instruction, which was offered by the city itself:

> "As a general principle, a municipality is not liable under 42 U.S.C. § 1983 for the actions of its employees. However, a municipality may be held liable under 42 U.S.C. § 1983 if the allegedly unconstitutional act was committed by an official high enough in the government so that his or her actions can be said to represent a government decision." App. 113.

Relying on *Oklahoma City v. Tuttle*, 471 U.S. 808 (1985), and *Springfield v. Kibbe*, 480 U.S. 257 (1987), respondent contends that the jury instructions should be reviewed only for plain error, and that the jury's verdict should be tested only for sufficiency of the evidence.

Declining to defend the legal standard adopted by the Court of Appeals, respondent vigorously insists that the judgment should be affirmed on the basis of the jury's verdict and petitioner's alleged failure to comply with Rule 51.

Petitioner argues that it preserved the legal issues presented by its petition for certiorari in at least two ways. First, it filed a pretrial motion for summary judgment, or alternatively for judgment on the pleadings. In support of that motion, petitioner argued that respondent had failed to allege the existence of any impermissible municipal policy or of any facts that would indicate that such a policy existed. Second, petitioner filed a motion for directed verdict at the close of respondent's case, renewed that motion at the close [485 U.S. 112, 120] of all the evidence, and eventually filed a motion for judgment notwithstanding the verdict.

Respondent's arguments do not bring our jurisdiction into question, and we must not lose sight of the fact, stressed in *Tuttle*, that the "decision to grant certiorari represents a commitment of scarce judicial resources with a view to deciding the merits of one or more of the questions presented in the petition." 471 U.S., at 816. In *Kibbe*, it is true, the writ was dismissed in part because the petitioner sought to challenge a jury instruction to which it had not objected at trial. In the case before us, the focus of petitioner's challenge is not on the jury instruction itself, but on the denial of its motions for summary judgment and a directed verdict. Although the same legal issue was raised both by those motions and by the jury instruction, "the failure to object to an instruction does not render the instruction the 'law of the case' for purposes of appellate review of the denial of a directed verdict or judgment notwithstanding the verdict." *Kibbe, supra*, at 264 (dissenting opinion) (citations omitted). Petitioner's legal position in the District Court—that respondent had failed to establish an unconstitutional municipal policy—was consistent with the legal standard that it now advocates. It should not be surprising if petitioner's arguments in the District Court were much less detailed than the arguments it now makes in response to the decision of the Court of Appeals. That, however, does not imply that petitioner failed to preserve the issue raised in its petition for certiorari. Cf. *post*, at 165-167 (STEVENS, J., dissenting). Accordingly, we find no obstacle to reviewing the question presented in the petition for certiorari, a question that was very clearly considered, and decided, by the Court of Appeals.

We note, too, that petitioner has throughout this litigation been confronted with a legal landscape whose contours are "in a state of evolving definition and uncertainty." *Newport v. Fact Concerts, Inc.*, 453 U.S. 247, 256 (1981). We therefore do not believe that our review of the decision of the [485 U.S. 112, 121] Court of Appeals, a decision raising a question that "is important and appears likely to recur in § 1983 litigation against municipalities," *id.,* at 257, will undermine the policy of judicial efficiency that underlies Rule 51. The definition of municipal liability manifestly needs clarification, at least in part to give lower courts and litigants a fairer chance to craft jury instructions that will not require scrutiny on appellate review.

III

A

Section 1 of the Ku Klux Act of 1871, Rev. Stat. 1979, as amended, 42 U.S.C. § 1983, provides:

> "Every person who, under color of any statute, ordinance, regulation, custom, or usage, of any State . . ., subjects, or causes to be subjected, any citizen of the United States or other person within the jurisdiction thereof to the deprivation of any rights, privileges, or immunities secured by the Constitution and laws, shall be liable to the party injured in an action at law, suit in equity, or other proper proceeding for redress. . . ."

Ten years ago, this Court held that municipalities and other bodies of local government are "persons" within the meaning of this statute. Such a body may therefore be sued directly if it is alleged to have caused a constitutional tort through "a policy statement, ordinance, regulation, or decision officially adopted and promulgated by that body's officers." *Monell v. New York City Dept. of Social Services,* 436 U.S. 658, 690 (1978). The Court pointed out that § 1983 also authorizes suit "for constitutional deprivations visited pursuant to governmental 'custom' even though such a custom has not received formal approval through the body's official decisionmaking channels." *Id.,* at 690-691. At the same time, the Court rejected the use of the doctrine of *respondeat superior* and concluded that municipalities could be held liable only when an injury was inflicted by a government's [485 U.S. 112, 122] "lawmakers or by those whose edicts or acts may fairly be said to represent official policy." *Id.,* at 694.

Monell's rejection of *respondeat superior,* and its insistence that local governments could be held liable only for the results of unconstitutional governmental "policies," arose from the language and history of § 1983. For our purposes here, the crucial terms of the statute are those that provide for liability when a government "subjects [a person], or causes [that person] to be subjected," to a deprivation of constitutional rights. Aware that governmental bodies can act only through natural persons, the Court concluded that these governments should be held responsible when, and only when, their official policies cause their employees to violate another person's constitutional rights. Reading the statute's language in the light of its legislative history, the Court found that vicarious liability would be incompatible with the causation requirement set out on the face of § 1983. See *id.*, at 691. That conclusion, like decisions that have widened the scope of § 1983 by recognizing constitutional rights that were unheard of in 1871, has been repeatedly reaffirmed. See, *e.g.*, *Owen v. City of Independence*, 445 U.S. 622, 633, 655, n. 39 (1980); *Polk County v. Dodson*, 454 U.S. 312, 325 (1981); *Tuttle*, 471 U.S., at 818, and n. 5 (plurality opinion); *id.*, at 828 (BRENNAN, J., concurring in part and concurring in judgment); *Pembaur v. Cincinnati*, 475 U.S., at 478-480, and nn. 7-8. Cf. *Newport v. Fact Concerts, Inc., supra*, at 259 ("[B]ecause the 1871 Act was designed to expose state and local officials to a new form of liability, it would defeat the promise of the statute to recognize any pre-existing immunity without determining both the policies that it serves and its compatibility with the purposes of § 1983").

In *Monell* itself, it was undisputed that there had been an official policy requiring city employees to take actions that were unconstitutional under this Court's decisions. Without attempting to draw the line between actions taken pursuant to official policy and the independent actions of employees [485 U.S. 112, 123] and agents, the *Monell* Court left the "full contours" of municipal liability under § 1983 to be developed further on "another day." 436 U.S., at 695.

In the years since *Monell* was decided, the Court has considered several cases involving isolated acts by government officials and employees. We have assumed that an unconstitutional governmental policy could be inferred from a single decision taken by the highest officials responsible for setting policy in that area of the government's business. See, *e.g.*, *Owen v. City of Independence, supra; Newport v. Fact Concerts, Inc.*, 453 U.S. 247 (1981). Cf. *Pembaur, supra*, at 480. At the other end of the spectrum, we have held that an unjustified shooting by a police officer cannot, without more, be thought to result from official policy. *Tuttle*, 471 U.S., at 821 (plurality opinion); *id.*, at 830-831, and n. 5 (BRENNAN, J., concurring in part and concurring in judgment). Cf. *Kibbe*, 480 U.S., at 260 (dissenting opinion).

Two Terms ago, in *Pembaur, supra*, we undertook to define more precisely when a decision on a single occasion may be enough to establish an unconstitutional municipal policy. Although the Court was unable to settle on a general formulation, JUSTICE BRENNAN's opinion articulated several guiding principles. First, a majority of the Court agreed that municipalities may be held liable under § 1983 only for acts for which the municipality itself is actually responsible, "that is, acts which the municipality has officially sanctioned or ordered." *Id.*, at 480. Second, only those municipal officials who have "final policymaking authority" may by their actions subject the government to § 1983 liability. *Id.*, at 483 plurality opinion). Third, whether a particular official has "final policymaking authority" is a question of state law. *Ibid.* (plurality opinion). Fourth, the challenged action must have been taken pursuant to a policy adopted by the official or officials responsible under state law for making policy in that area of the city's business. *Id.*, at 482-483, and n. 12 (plurality opinion). [485 U.S. 112, 124]

The Courts of Appeals have already diverged in their interpretations of these principles. Compare, for example, *Williams v. Butler*, 802 F.2d 296, 299-302 (CA8 1986) (en banc), cert. pending sub nom. Little *Rock v. Williams*, No. 86-1049, with *Jett v. Dallas Independent School Dist.*, 798 F.2d 748, 759-760 (CA5 1986) (dictum). Today, we set out again to clarify the issue that we last addressed in Pembaur.

B

We begin by reiterating that the identification of policymaking officials is a question of state law. "Authority to make municipal policy may be granted directly by a legislative enactment or may be delegated by an official who possesses such authority, and of course, whether an official had final policymaking authority is a question of state law." *Pembaur v. Cincinnati, supra*, at 483 (plurality opinion).[1] Thus the identification of policymaking officials is not a question of federal law, and it is not a question of fact in the usual sense. The States have extremely wide latitude in determining the form that local government takes, and local preferences have led to a profusion of distinct forms. Among the many kinds of municipal corporations, political subdivisions, and special districts of all sorts, one may expect to find a rich variety of ways in which the power of government [485 U.S. 112, 125] is distributed among a host of different officials and official bodies. See generally C. Rhyne, The Law of Local Government Operations §§ 1.3-1.7 (1980). Without attempting to canvass the numberless factual scenarios that may come to light in litigation, we can be confident that state law (which may include valid local ordinances and regulations) will always direct a court to some official or body that has the responsibility for making law or setting policy in any given area of a local government's business.[2]

We are not, of course, predicting that state law will always speak with perfect clarity. We have no reason to suppose, [485 U.S. 112, 126] however, that federal courts will face greater difficulties here than those that they routinely address in other contexts. We are also aware that there will be cases in which policymaking responsibility is shared among more than one official or body. In the case before us, for example, it appears that the Mayor and Aldermen are authorized to adopt such ordinances relating to personnel administration as are compatible with the City Charter. See *St. Louis City Charter*, Art. XVIII, 7(b), App. 62-63. The Civil Service Commission, for its part, is required to "prescribe . . . rules for the administration and enforcement of the provisions of this article, and of any ordinance adopted in pursuance thereof, and not inconsistent therewith." 7(a), App. 62. Assuming that applicable law does not make the decisions of the Commission reviewable by the Mayor and Aldermen, or vice versa, one would have to conclude that policy decisions made either by the Mayor and Aldermen or by the Commission would be attributable to the city itself. In any event, however, a federal court would not be justified in assuming that municipal policymaking authority lies somewhere other than where the applicable law purports to put it. And certainly there can be no justification for giving a jury the discretion to determine which officials are high enough in the government that their actions can be said to represent a decision of the government itself.

As the plurality in *Pembaur* recognized, special difficulties can arise when it is contended that a municipal policymaker has delegated his policymaking authority to another official. 475 U.S., at 482-483, and n. 12. If the mere exercise of discretion by an employee could give rise to a constitutional violation, the result would be indistinguishable from *respondeat superior* liability. If, however, a city's lawful policymakers could insulate the government from liability simply by delegating their policymaking authority to others, § 1983 could not serve its intended purpose. It may not be possible to draw an [485 U.S. 112, 127] elegant line that will resolve this conundrum, but certain principles should provide useful guidance.

First, whatever analysis is used to identify municipal policymakers, egregious attempts by local governments to insulate themselves from liability for unconstitutional policies are precluded by a separate doctrine. Relying on the language of § 1983, the Court has long recognized that a plaintiff may be able to prove the existence of a widespread practice that, although not authorized by written law or express municipal policy, is "so permanent and well settled as to constitute a 'custom or usage' with the force of law." *Adickes v. S. H. Kress & Co.*, 398 U.S. 144, 167-168 (1970). That principle, which has not been affected by *Monell* or subsequent cases, ensures that most deliberate municipal evasions of the Constitution will be sharply limited.

Second, as the *Pembaur* plurality recognized, the authority to make municipal policy is necessarily the authority to make *final* policy. 475 U.S., at 481-484. When an official's discretionary decisions are constrained by policies not of that official's making, those policies, rather than the subordinate's departures from them, are the act of the municipality. Similarly, when a subordinate's decision is subject to review by the municipality's authorized policymakers, they have retained the authority to measure the official's conduct for conformance with *their* policies. If the authorized policymakers approve a subordinate's decision and the basis for it, their ratification would be chargeable to the municipality because their decision is final.

C

Whatever refinements of these principles may be suggested in the future, we have little difficulty concluding that the Court of Appeals applied an incorrect legal standard in this case. In reaching this conclusion, we do not decide whether the First Amendment forbade the city to retaliate against respondent for having taken advantage of the grievance mechanism in 1980. Nor do we decide whether there [485 U.S. 112, 128] was evidence in this record from which a rational jury could conclude either that such retaliation actually occurred or that respondent suffered any compensable injury from whatever retaliatory action may have been taken. Finally, we do not address petitioner's contention that the jury verdict exonerating the individual defendants cannot be reconciled with the verdict against the city. Even assuming that all these issues were properly resolved in respondent's favor, we would not be able to affirm the decision of the Court of Appeals.

The city cannot be held liable under § 1983 unless respondent proved the existence of an unconstitutional municipal policy. Respondent does not contend that anyone in city government ever promulgated, or even articulated, such a policy. Nor did he attempt to prove that such retaliation was ever directed against anyone other than himself. Respondent contends that the record can be read to establish that his supervisors were angered by his 1980 appeal to the Civil Service Commission; that new supervisors in a new administration chose, for reasons passed on through some informal means, to retaliate against respondent two years later by transferring him to another agency; and that this transfer was part of a scheme that led, another year and a half later, to his layoff. Even if one assumes that all this was true, it says nothing about the actions of those whom the law established as the makers of municipal policy in matters of personnel administration. The Mayor and Aldermen enacted no ordinance designed to retaliate against respondent or against similarly situated employees. On the contrary, the city established an independent Civil Service Commission and empowered it to review and correct improper personnel actions. Respondent does not deny that his repeated appeals from adverse personnel decisions repeatedly brought him at least partial relief, and the Civil Service Commission never so much as hinted that retaliatory transfers or layoffs were permissible. Respondent points to no evidence indicating that the Commission delegated to anyone its final authority to [485 U.S. 112, 129] interpret and enforce the following policy set out in Article XVIII of the city's Charter, § 2(a), App. 49:

"Merit and fitness. All appointments and promotions to positions in the service of the city and all measures for the control and regulation of employment in such positions, and separation therefrom, shall be on the sole basis of merit and fitness . . . ."

The Court of Appeals concluded that "appointing authorities," like Hamsher and Killen, who had the authority to initiate transfers and layoffs, were municipal "policymakers." The court based this conclusion on its findings (1) that the decisions of these employees were not individually reviewed for "substantive propriety" by higher supervisory officials; and (2) that the Civil Service Commission decided appeals from such decisions, if at all, in a circumscribed manner that gave substantial deference to the original decision maker. 798 F.2d, at 1174-1175. We find these propositions insufficient to support the conclusion that Hamsher and Killen were authorized to establish employment policy for the city with respect to transfers and layoffs. To the contrary, the City Charter expressly states that the Civil Service Commission has the power and the duty:

"To consider and determine any matter involved in the administration and enforcement of this [Civil Service] article and the rules and ordinances adopted in accordance therewith that may be referred to it for decision by the director [of personnel], or on appeal by any appointing authority, employee, or taxpayer of the city, from any act of the director or of any appointing authority. The decision of the commission in all such matters shall be final, subject, however, to any right of action under any law of the state or of the United States." St. Louis City Charter, Art. XVIII, § 7(d), App. 63.

This case therefore resembles the hypothetical example in Pembaur: "[I]f [city] employment policy was set by the [485 U.S. 112, 130] [Mayor and Aldermen and by the Civil Service Commission], only [those] bod[ies'] decisions would provide a basis for [city] liability. This would be true even if the [Mayor and Aldermen and the Commission] left the [appointing authorities] discretion to hire and fire employees and [they] exercised that discretion in an unconstitutional manner . . . ." 47 U.S., at 483, n. 12. A majority of the Court of Appeals panel determined that the Civil Service Commission's review of individual employment actions gave too much deference to the decisions of appointing authorities like Hamsher and Killen. Simply going along with discretionary decisions made by one's subordinates, however, is not a delegation to them of the authority to make policy. It is equally consistent with a presumption that the subordinates are faithfully attempting to comply with the policies that are supposed to guide them. It would be a different matter if a particular decision by a subordinate was cast in the form of a policy statement and expressly approved by the supervising policymaker. It would also be a different matter if a series of decisions by a subordinate official manifested a "custom or usage" of which the supervisor must have been aware. See *supra,* at 127. In both those cases, the supervisor could realistically be deemed to have adopted a policy that happened to have been formulated or initiated by a lower ranking official. But the mere failure to investigate the basis of a subordinate's discretionary decisions does not amount to a delegation of policymaking authority, especially where (as here) the wrongfulness of the subordinate's decision arises from a retaliatory motive or other unstated rationale. In such circumstances, the purposes of § 1983 would not be served by treating a subordinate employee's decision as if it were a reflection of municipal policy.

JUSTICE BRENNAN'S opinion, concurring in the judgment, finds implications in our discussion that we do not think necessary or correct. See *post,* at 142-147. We nowhere say or imply, for example, that "a municipal charter's precatory [485 U.S. 112, 131] admonition against discrimination or any other employment practice not based on merit and fitness effectively insulates the municipality from any liability based on acts inconsistent with that policy." *Post,* at 145, n. 7. Rather, we would respect the decisions, embodied in state and local law, that allocate policymaking authority among particular individuals and bodies. Refusals to carry out stated policies could obviously help to show that a municipality's actual policies were different from the ones that had been announced. If such a showing were made, we would be confronted with a different case than the one we decide today.

Nor do we believe that we have left a "gaping hole" in § 1983 that needs to be filled with the vague concept of "de facto final policymaking authority." *Post,* at 144. Except perhaps as a step towards overruling *Monell* and adopting the doctrine of *respondeat superior,* ad hoc searches for officials possessing such "de facto" authority would serve primarily to foster needless unpredictability in the application of § 1983.

IV

We cannot accept either the Court of Appeals' broad definition of municipal policymakers or respondent's suggestion that a jury should be entitled to define for itself which officials' decisions should expose a municipality to liability. Respondent has suggested that the record will support an inference that policymaking authority was in fact delegated to individuals who took retaliatory action against him and who were not exonerated by the jury. Respondent's arguments appear to depend on a legal standard similar to the one suggested in JUSTICE STEVENS' dissenting opinion, *post,* at 171, which we do not accept. Our examination of the record and state law, however, suggests that further review of this case may be warranted in light of the principles we have discussed. That task is best left to the Court of Appeals, which will be free to invite additional briefing and argument if necessary. Accordingly, the decision of the Court of Appeals is [485 U.S. 112, 132] reversed, and the case is remanded for further proceedings consistent with this opinion.

It is so ordered.

Footnotes

[1] Unlike JUSTICE BRENNAN, we would not replace this standard with a new approach in which state law becomes merely an "appropriate starting point" for an "assessment of a municipality's actual power structure." *Post,* at 143, 145. Municipalities cannot be expected to predict how courts or juries will assess their "actual power structures," and this uncertainty could easily lead to results that would be hard in practice to distinguish from the results of a regime governed by the doctrine of *respondeat superior.* It is one thing to charge a municipality with responsibility for the decisions of officials invested by law, or by a "custom or usage" having the force of law, with policymaking authority. It would be something else, and something inevitably more capricious, to hold a municipality responsible for every decision that is perceived as "final" through the lens of a particular fact finder's evaluation of the city's "actual power structure."

[2] JUSTICE STEVENS, who believes that *Monell* incorrectly rejected the doctrine of *respondeat superior,* suggests a new theory that reflects his perceptions of the congressional purposes underlying § 1983. See *post,* at 148, n. 1. This theory would apparently ignore state law, and distinguish between "high" officials and "low" officials on the basis of an independent evaluation of the extent to which a particular official's actions have "the potential of controlling governmental decisionmaking," or are "perceived as the actions of the city itself." *Post,* at 171. Whether this evaluation would be conducted by judges or juries, we think the legal test is too imprecise to hold much promise of consistent adjudication or principled analysis. We can see no reason, except perhaps a desire to come as close as possible to *respondeat superior* without expressly adopting that doctrine, that could justify introducing such unpredictability into a body of law that is already so difficult.

As JUSTICE STEVENS acknowledges, see *post,* at 148, n. 1, this Court has repeatedly rejected his interpretation of Congress' intent. We have held that Congress intended to hold municipalities responsible under § 1983 only for the execution of official policies and customs, and not for injuries inflicted solely by employees or agents. See, *e.g., Monell v. New York City Dept. of Social Services,* 436 U.S. 658, 694 (1978); *Pembaur v. Cincinnati,* 475 U.S. 469, 478-480 (1986). Like the Pembaur plurality, we think it is self-evident that official policies can only be adopted by those legally charged with doing so. See *supra,* at 124, and n. 1. We are aware of nothing in § 1983 or its legislative history, and JUSTICE STEVENS points to nothing, that would support the notion that unauthorized acts of subordinate employees are official policies because they may have the "potential" to become official policies or may be "perceived as" official policies. Accordingly, we conclude that JUSTICE STEVENS' proposal is without a basis in the law.

Board of the County Commissioners of Bryan County, Oklahoma v. Brown, et al.
520 U.S. 397 (1997)

Argued November 5, 1996
Decided April 28, 1997
JUSTICE O'CONNOR delivered the opinion of the Court.

Respondent Jill Brown brought a claim for damages against petitioner Bryan County under Rev. Stat. § 1979, 42 U.S.C. § 1983. She alleged that a county police officer used excessive force in arresting her, and that the county itself was liable for her injuries based on its sheriff's hiring and training decisions. She prevailed on her claims against the county following a jury trial, and the Court of Appeals for the Fifth Circuit affirmed the judgment against the county on the basis of the hiring claim alone. 67 F. 3d 1174 (1995). We granted certiorari. We conclude that the Court of Appeals' decision cannot be squared with our recognition that, in enacting § 1983, Congress did not intend to impose liability on a municipality unless *deliberate* action attributable to the municipality itself is the "moving force" behind the plaintiff's deprivation of federal rights. *Monell v. New York City Dept. of Social Servs.*, 436 U.S. 658, 694 (1978).

I

In the early morning hours of May 12, 1991, respondent Jill Brown and her husband were driving from Grayson County, Texas, to their

170

home in Bryan County, Oklahoma. After crossing into Oklahoma, they approached a police checkpoint. Mr. Brown, who was driving, decided to avoid the checkpoint and return to Texas. After seeing the Browns' truck turn away from the checkpoint, Bryan County Deputy Sheriff Robert Morrison and Reserve Deputy Stacy Burns pursued the vehicle. Although the parties' versions of events differ, at trial both deputies claimed that their patrol car reached speeds in excess of 100 miles per hour. Mr. Brown testified that he was unaware of the deputies' attempts to overtake him. The chase finally ended four miles south of the police checkpoint.

After he got out of the squad car, Deputy Sheriff Morrison pointed his gun toward the Browns' vehicle and ordered the Browns to raise their hands. Reserve Deputy Burns, who was unarmed, rounded the corner of the vehicle on the passenger's side. Burns twice ordered respondent Jill Brown from the vehicle. When she did not exit, he used an "arm bar" technique, grabbing respondent's arm at the wrist and elbow, pulling her from the vehicle, and spinning her to the ground. Respondent's knees were severely injured, and she later underwent corrective surgery. Ultimately, she may need knee replacements.

Respondent sought compensation for her injuries under 42 U.S.C. § 1983 and state law from Burns, Bryan County Sheriff B. J. Moore, and the county itself. Respondent claimed, among other things, that Bryan County was liable for Burns' alleged use of excessive force based on Sheriff Moore's decision to hire Burns, the son of his nephew. Specifically, respondent claimed that Sheriff Moore had failed to adequately review Burns' background. Burns had a record of driving infractions and had pleaded guilty to various driving related and other misdemeanors, including assault and battery, resisting arrest, and public drunkenness. Oklahoma law does not preclude the hiring of an individual who has committed a misdemeanor to serve as a peace officer. See Okla. Stat., Tit. 70, § 3311(D)(2)(a) (1991) (requiring that the hiring agency certify that the prospective officer's records do not reflect a felony conviction). At trial, Sheriff Moore testified that he had obtained Burns' driving record and a report on Burns from the National Crime Information Center, but had not closely reviewed either. Sheriff Moore authorized Burns to make arrests, but not to carry a weapon or to operate a patrol car.

In a ruling not at issue here, the District Court dismissed respondent's § 1983 claim against Sheriff Moore prior to trial. App. 28. Counsel for Bryan County stipulated that Sheriff Moore "was the policy maker for Bryan County regarding the Sheriff's Department." *Id.*, at 30. At the close of respondent's case and again at the close of all of the evidence, Bryan County moved for judgment as a matter of law. As to respondent's claim that Sheriff Moore's decision to hire Burns triggered municipal liability, the county argued that a single hiring decision by a municipal policymaker could not give rise to municipal liability under § 1983. *Id.*, at 59-60. The District Court denied the county's motions.

The court also overruled the county's objections to jury instructions on the § 1983 claim against the county. *Id.*, at 125-126, 132.

To resolve respondent's claims, the jury was asked to answer several interrogatories. The jury concluded that Stacy Burns had arrested respondent without probable cause and had used excessive force, and therefore found him liable for respondent's injuries. It also found that the "hiring policy" and the "training policy" of Bryan County "in the case of Stacy Burns as instituted by its policymaker, B. J. Moore," were each "so inadequate as to amount to deliberate indifference to the constitutional needs of the Plaintiff." *Id.*, at 135. The District Court entered judgment for respondent on the issue of Bryan County's § 1983 liability. The county appealed on several grounds, and the Court of Appeals for the Fifth Circuit affirmed. 67 F. 3d 1174 (1995). The court held, among other things, that Bryan County was properly found liable under § 1983 based on Sheriff Moore's decision to hire Burns. *Id.*, at 1185. The court addressed only those points that it thought merited review; it did not address the jury's determination of county liability based on inadequate training of Burns, *id.*, at 1178, nor do we. We granted certiorari, 517 U. S.___ (1996), to decide whether the county was properly held liable for respondent's injuries based on Sheriff Moore's single decision to hire Burns. We now reverse.

II

Title 42 U.S.C. § 1983 provides in relevant part:

> "Every person who, under color of any statute, ordinance, regulation, custom, or usage, of any State or Territory or the District of Columbia, subjects, or causes to be subjected, any citizen of the United States or other person within the jurisdiction thereof to the deprivation of any rights, privileges, or immunities secured by the Constitution and laws, shall be liable to the party injured in an action at law, suit in equity, or other proper proceeding for redress."

We held in *Monell v. New York City Dept. of Social Servs.*, 436 U.S., at 689, that municipalities and other local governmental bodies are "persons" within the meaning of § 1983. We also recognized that a municipality may not be held liable under § 1983 solely because it employs a tortfeasor. Our conclusion rested partly on the language of § 1983 itself. In light of the statute's imposition of liability on one who "subjects [a person], or causes [that person] to be subjected," to a deprivation of federal rights, we concluded that it "cannot be easily read to impose liability vicariously on governing bodies solely on the basis of the existence of an employer employee relationship with a tortfeasor." *Id.*, at 692. Our conclusion also rested upon the statute's legislative history. As stated in *Pembaur v. Cincinnati*, 475 U.S. 469, 479 (1986), "while Congress never questioned its power to impose civil liability on municipalities for their own illegal acts, Congress did doubt its constitutional power to impose such liability in order to oblige municipalities to control the conduct of *others*" (citing *Monell, supra*, at 665-683). We have consistently refused to hold municipalities liable under a theory of *respondeat superior.* See *Oklahoma City v. Tuttle*, 471 U.S. 808, 818 (1985) (plurality opinion); *id.*, at 828 (opinion of Brennan, J.); *Pembaur, supra*, at 478-479; *St. Louis v. Praprotnik*, 485 U.S. 112, 122 (1988) (plurality opinion); *id.*, at 137 (opinion of Brennan, J.); *Canton v. Harris*, 489 U.S. 378, 392 (1989).

Instead, in *Monell* and subsequent cases, we have required a plaintiff seeking to impose liability on a municipality under § 1983 to identify a municipal "policy" or "custom" that caused the plaintiff's injury. See *Monell, supra*, at 694; *Pembaur, supra*, at 480-481; *Canton, supra*, at 389. Locating a "policy" ensures that a municipality is held liable only for those deprivations resulting from the decisions of its duly constituted legislative body or of those officials whose acts may fairly be said to be those of the municipality. *Monell, supra*, at 694. Similarly, an act performed pursuant to a "custom" that has not been formally approved by an appropriate decision maker may fairly subject a municipality to liability on the theory that the relevant practice is so widespread as to have the force of law. 436 U.S., at 690-691 (citing *Adickes v. S. H. Kress & Co.*, 398 U.S. 144, 167-168 (1970)).

The parties join issue on whether, under *Monell* and subsequent cases, a single hiring decision by a county sheriff can be a "policy" that triggers municipal liability. Relying on our decision in *Pembaur*, respondent claims that a single act by a decision maker with final authority in the relevant area constitutes a "policy" attributable to the municipality itself. So long as a § 1983 plaintiff identifies a decision properly attributable to the municipality, respondent argues, there is no risk of imposing *respondeat superior* liability. Whether that decision was intended to govern only the situation at hand or to serve as a rule to be applied over time is immaterial. Rather, under respondent's theory, identification of an act of a proper municipal decision maker is all that is required to ensure that the municipality is held liable only for its own conduct. The Court of Appeals accepted respondent's approach.

As our § 1983 municipal liability jurisprudence illustrates, however, it is not enough for a § 1983 plaintiff merely to identify conduct properly attributable to the municipality. The plaintiff must also demonstrate that, through its *deliberate* conduct, the municipality was the "moving force" behind the injury alleged. That is, a plaintiff must show that the municipal action was taken with the requisite degree of culpability and must demonstrate a direct causal link between the municipal action and the deprivation of federal rights.

Where a plaintiff claims that a particular municipal action *itself* violates federal law, or directs an employee to do so, resolving these issues of fault and causation is straightforward. Section 1983 itself "contains no state of mind requirement independent of that necessary to state a violation" of the underlying federal right. *Daniels v. Williams*, 474 U.S. 327, 330 (1986). In any § 1983 suit, however, the plaintiff must establish the state of mind required to prove the underlying violation. Accordingly, proof that a municipality's legislative body or authorized decisionmaker has intentionally deprived a plaintiff of a federally protected right necessarily establishes that the municipality acted culpably. Similarly, the conclusion that the action taken or directed by the municipality or its authorized decisionmaker itself violates federal law will also determine that the municipal action was the moving force behind the injury of which the plaintiff complains.

Sheriff Moore's hiring decision was itself legal, and Sheriff Moore did not authorize Burns to use excessive force. Respondent's claim, rather, is that a single facially lawful hiring decision can launch a series of events that ultimately cause a violation of federal rights. Where a plaintiff claims that the municipality has not directly inflicted an injury, but nonetheless has caused an employee to do so, rigorous standards of culpability and causation must be applied to ensure that the municipality is not held liable solely for the actions of its employee. See *Canton*, 489 U.S., at 391-392; *Tuttle, supra,* at 824 (plurality opinion). See also *Springfield v. Kibbe*, 480 U.S. 257, 270-271 (1987) (dissent from dismissal of writ as improvidently granted).

In relying heavily on *Pembaur*, respondent blurs the distinction between § 1983 cases that present no difficult questions of fault and causation and those that do. To the extent that we have recognized a cause of action under § 1983 based on a single decision attributable to a municipality, we have done so only where the evidence that the municipality had acted and that the plaintiff had suffered a deprivation of federal rights also proved fault and causation. For example, *Owen v. Independence*, 445 U.S. 622 (1980), and *Newport v. Fact Concerts, Inc.*, 453 U.S. 247 (1981), involved formal decisions of municipal legislative bodies. In *Owen*, the city council allegedly censured and discharged an employee without a hearing. 445 U.S., at 627-629, 633, and n. 13. In *Fact Concerts*, the city council canceled a license permitting a concert following a dispute over the performance's content. 453 U.S., at 252. Neither decision reflected implementation of a generally applicable rule. But we did not question that each decision, duly promulgated by city lawmakers, could trigger municipal liability if the decision itself were found to be unconstitutional. Because fault and causation were obvious in each case, proof that the municipality's decision was unconstitutional would suffice to establish that the municipality itself was liable for the plaintiff's constitutional injury.

Similarly, *Pembaur v. Cincinnati* concerned a decision by a county prosecutor, acting as the county's final decisionmaker, 475 U.S., at 485, to direct county deputies to forcibly enter petitioner's place of business to serve *capiases* upon third parties. Relying on *Owen* and *Newport*, we concluded that a final decision maker's adoption of a course of action "tailored to a particular situation and not intended to control decisions in later situations" may, in some circumstances, give rise to municipal liability under § 1983. 475 U.S., at 481. In *Pembaur*, it was not disputed that the prosecutor had specifically directed the action resulting in the deprivation of petitioner's rights. The conclusion that the decision was that of a final municipal decision maker and was therefore properly attributable to the municipality established municipal liability. No questions of fault or causation arose.

Claims not involving an allegation that the municipal action itself violated federal law, or directed or authorized the deprivation of federal rights, present much more difficult problems of proof. That a plaintiff has suffered a deprivation of federal rights at the hands of a municipal employee will not alone permit an inference of municipal culpability and causation; the plaintiff will simply have shown that the *employee* acted culpably. We recognized these difficulties in *Canton v. Harris, supra*, where we considered a claim that inadequate training of shift supervisors at a city jail led to a deprivation of a detainee's constitutional rights. We held that, quite apart from the state of mind required to establish the underlying constitutional violation—in that case, a violation of due process, 489 U.S., at 388-389, n. 8—a plaintiff seeking to establish municipal liability on the theory that a facially lawful municipal action has led an employee to violate a plaintiff's rights must demonstrate that the municipal action was taken with "deliberate indifference" as to its known or obvious consequences. *Id.*, at 388. A showing of simple or even heightened negligence will not suffice.

We concluded in *Canton* that an "inadequate training" claim could be the basis for § 1983 liability in "limited circumstances." *Id.*, at 387. We spoke, however, of a deficient training "program," necessarily intended to apply over time to multiple employees. *Id.*, at 390. Existence of a "program" makes proof of fault and causation at least possible in an inadequate training case. If a program does not prevent constitutional violations, municipal decision makers may eventually be put on notice that a new program is called for. Their continued adherence to an approach that they know or should know has failed to prevent tortious conduct by employees may establish the conscious disregard for the consequences of their action—the "deliberate indifference"— necessary to trigger municipal liability. *Id.*, at 390, n. 10 ("It could . . . be that the police, in exercising their discretion, so often violate constitutional rights that the need for further training must have been plainly obvious to the city policymakers, who, nevertheless, are 'deliberately indifferent' to the need"); *id.*, at 397 (O'Connor, J., concurring in part and dissenting in part) ("[M]unicipal liability for failure to train may be proper where it can be shown that policymakers were aware of, and acquiesced in, a pattern of constitutional violations . . ."). In addition, the existence of a pattern of tortious conduct by inadequately trained employees may tend to show that the lack of proper training, rather than a one time negligent administration of the program or factors peculiar to the officer involved in a particular incident, is the "moving force" behind the plaintiff's injury. See *id.*, at 390-391.

Before trial, counsel for Bryan County stipulated that Sheriff Moore "was the policy maker for Bryan County regarding the Sheriff's Department." App. 30. Indeed, the county sought to avoid liability by claiming that its Board of Commissioners participated in no policy decisions regarding the conduct and operation of the office of the Bryan County Sheriff. *Id.*, at 32. Accepting the county's representations below, then, this case presents no difficult questions concerning whether Sheriff Moore has final authority to act for the municipality in hiring matters. Cf. *Jett v. Dallas Independent School Dist.*, 491 U.S. 701 (1989); *St. Louis v. Praprotnik*, 485 U.S. 112 (1988). Respondent does not claim that she can identify any pattern of injuries linked to Sheriff Moore's hiring practices. Indeed, respondent does not contend that Sheriff Moore's hiring practices are generally defective. The only evidence on this point at trial suggested that Sheriff Moore had adequately screened the backgrounds of all prior deputies he hired. App. 106-110. Respondent instead seeks to trace liability to what can only be described as a deviation from Sheriff Moore's ordinary hiring practices. Where a claim of municipal liability rests on a single decision, not itself representing a violation of federal law and not directing such a violation, the danger that a municipality will be held liable without fault is high. Because the decision necessarily governs a single case, there can be no notice to the municipal decision maker, based on previous violations of federally protected rights, that his approach is inadequate. Nor will it be readily apparent that the municipality's action caused the injury in question, because the plaintiff can point to no other incident tending to make it more likely that the plaintiff's own injury flows from the municipality's action, rather than from some other intervening cause.

In *Canton*, we did not foreclose the possibility that evidence of a single violation of federal rights, accompanied by a showing that a municipality has failed to train its employees to handle recurring situations presenting an obvious potential for such a violation, could trigger municipal liability. 489 U.S., at 390, and n. 10 ("[I]t may happen that in light of the duties assigned to specific officers or employees the need for more or different training is so obvious . . . that the policymakers of the city can reasonably be said to have been deliberately indifferent to the need"). Respondent purports to rely on *Canton*, arguing that Burns' use of excessive force was the plainly obvious consequence of Sheriff Moore's failure to screen Burns' record. In essence, respondent claims that this showing of "obviousness" would demonstrate both that Sheriff Moore acted with conscious disregard for the consequences of his action and that the Sheriff's action directly caused her injuries, and would thus substitute for the pattern of injuries ordinarily necessary to establish municipal culpability and causation.

The proffered analogy between failure to train cases and inadequate screening cases is not persuasive. In leaving open in *Canton* the possibility that a plaintiff might succeed in carrying a failure to train claim without showing a pattern of constitutional violations, we simply hypothesized that, in a narrow range of circumstances, a violation of federal rights may be a highly predictable consequence of a failure to equip law enforcement officers with specific tools to handle recurring situations. The likelihood that the situation will recur and the predictability that an officer lacking specific tools to handle that situation will violate citizens' rights could justify a finding that policymakers' decision not to train the officer reflected "deliberate indifference" to the obvious consequence of the policymakers' choice—namely, a violation of a specific constitutional or statutory right. The high degree of predictability may also support an inference of causation—that the municipality's indifference led directly to the very consequence that was so predictable.

Where a plaintiff presents a § 1983 claim premised upon the inadequacy of an official's review of a prospective applicant's record, however, there is a particular danger that a municipality will be held liable for an injury not directly caused by a deliberate action attributable to the municipality itself. Every injury suffered at the hands of a municipal employee can be traced to a hiring decision in a "but for" sense: But for the municipality's decision to hire the employee, the plaintiff would not have suffered the injury. To prevent municipal liability for a hiring decision from collapsing into *respondeat superior* liability, a court must carefully test the link between the policymaker's inadequate decision and the particular injury alleged.

In attempting to import the reasoning of *Canton* into the hiring context, respondent ignores the fact that predicting the consequence of a single hiring decision, even one based on an inadequate assessment of a record, is far more difficult than predicting what might flow from the failure to train a single law enforcement officer as to a specific skill necessary to the discharge of his duties. As our decision in Canton makes clear, "deliberate indifference" is a stringent standard of fault, requiring proof that a municipal actor disregarded a known or obvious consequence of his action. Unlike the risk from a particular glaring omission in a training regimen, the risk from a single instance of inadequate screening of an applicant's background is not "obvious" in the abstract; rather, it depends upon the background of the applicant. A lack of scrutiny may increase the likelihood that an unfit officer will be hired, and that the unfit officer will, when placed in a particular position to affect the rights of citizens, act improperly. But that is only a generalized showing of risk. The fact that inadequate scrutiny of an applicant's background would make a violation of rights more *likely* cannot alone give rise to an inference that a policymaker's failure to scrutinize the record of a particular applicant produced a specific constitutional violation. After all, a full screening of an applicant's background might reveal no cause for concern at all; if so, a hiring official who failed to scrutinize the applicant's background cannot be said to have consciously disregarded an obvious risk that the officer would subsequently inflict a particular constitutional injury.

We assume that a jury could properly find in this case that Sheriff Moore's assessment of Burns' background was inadequate. Sheriff Moore's own testimony indicated that he did not inquire into the underlying conduct or the disposition of any of the misdemeanor charges reflected on Burns' record before hiring him. But this showing of an instance of inadequate screening is not enough to establish "deliberate indifference." In layman's terms, inadequate screening of an applicant's record may reflect "indifference" to the applicant's background. For purposes of a legal inquiry into municipal liability under § 1983, however, that is not the *relevant* "indifference." A plaintiff must demonstrate that a municipal decision reflects deliberate indifference to the risk that a violation of a particular constitutional or statutory right will follow the decision. Only where adequate scrutiny of an applicant's background would lead a reasonable policymaker to conclude that the plainly obvious consequence of the decision to hire the applicant would be the deprivation of a third party's federally protected right can the official's failure to adequately scrutinize the applicant's background constitute "deliberate indifference."

Neither the District Court nor the Court of Appeals directly tested the link between Burns' actual background and the risk that, if hired, he would use excessive force. The District Court instructed the jury on a theory analogous to that reserved in *Canton.* The court required respondent to prove that Sheriff Moore's inadequate screening of Burns' background was "so likely to result in *violations of constitutional rights*" that the Sheriff could "reasonably [be] said to have been deliberately indifferent to the constitutional needs of the Plaintiff." App. 123 (emphasis added). The court also instructed the jury, without elaboration, that respondent was required to prove that the "inadequate hiring . . . policy directly caused the Plaintiff's injury." *Ibid.*

As discussed above, a finding of culpability simply cannot depend on the mere probability that any officer inadequately screened will inflict any constitutional injury. Rather, it must depend on a finding that *this* officer was highly likely to inflict the *particular* injury suffered by the plaintiff. The connection between the background of the particular applicant and the specific constitutional violation alleged must be strong. What the District Court's instructions on culpability, and therefore the jury's finding of municipal liability, failed to capture is whether Burns' background made his use of excessive force in making an arrest a plainly obvious consequence of the hiring decision. The Court of Appeals' affirmance of the jury's finding of municipal liability depended on its view that the jury could have found that "inadequate screening of a *deputy* could likely result in the violation of *citizens' constitutional rights.*" 67 F. 3d, at 1185 (emphasis added). Beyond relying on a risk of violations of unspecified constitutional rights, the Court of Appeals also posited that Sheriff Moore's decision reflected indifference to "the public's welfare." *Id.*, at 1184.

Even assuming without deciding that proof of a single instance of inadequate screening could ever trigger municipal liability, the evidence in this case was insufficient to support a finding that, in hiring Burns, Sheriff Moore disregarded a known or obvious risk of injury. To test the link between Sheriff Moore's hiring decision and respondent's injury, we must ask whether a full review of Burns' record reveals that Sheriff Moore should have concluded that Burns' use of excessive force would be a plainly obvious consequence of the hiring decision.[1] On this point, respondent's showing was inadequate. To be sure, Burns' record reflected various misdemeanor infractions. Respondent claims that the record demonstrated such a strong propensity for violence that Burns' application of excessive force was highly likely. The primary charges on which respondent relies, however, are those arising from a fight on a college campus where Burns was a student. In connection with this single incident, Burns was charged with assault and battery, resisting arrest, and public drunkenness.[2] In January 1990, when he pleaded guilty to those charges, Burns also pleaded guilty to various driving related offenses, including nine moving violations and a charge of driving with a suspended license. In addition, Burns had previously pleaded guilty to being in actual physical control of a vehicle while intoxicated.

The fact that Burns had pleaded guilty to traffic offenses and other misdemeanors may well have made him an extremely poor candidate for reserve deputy. Had Sheriff Moore fully reviewed Burns' record, he might have come to precisely that conclusion. But unless he would necessarily have reached that decision because Burns' use of excessive force would have been a plainly obvious consequence of the hiring decision, Sheriff Moore's inadequate scrutiny of Burns' record cannot constitute "deliberate indifference" to respondent's federally protected right to be free from a use of excessive force.

Justice Souter's reading of the case is that the jury believed that Sheriff Moore in fact read Burns' entire record. *Post*, at 12-13. That is plausible, but it is also irrelevant. It is not sufficient for respondent to show that Sheriff Moore read Burns' *record* and therefore hired Burns with knowledge of his background. Such a decision may reflect indifference to Burns' record, but what is required is deliberate indifference to a plaintiff's constitutional right. That is, whether Sheriff Moore failed to examine Burns' record, partially examined it, or fully examined it, Sheriff Moore's hiring decision could not have been "deliberately indifferent" unless in light of that record Burns' use of excessive force would have been a plainly obvious consequence of the hiring decision. Because there was insufficient evidence on which a jury could base a finding that Sheriff Moore's decision to hire Burns reflected conscious disregard of an obvious risk that a use of excessive force would follow, the District Court erred in submitting respondent's inadequate screening claim to the jury.

III

Cases involving constitutional injuries allegedly traceable to an ill considered hiring decision pose the greatest risk that a municipality will be held liable for an injury that it did not cause. In the broadest sense, every injury is traceable to a hiring decision. Where a court fails to adhere to rigorous requirements of culpability and causation, municipal liability collapses into *respondeat superior* liability. As we recognized in *Monell* and have repeatedly reaffirmed, Congress did not intend municipalities to be held liable unless *deliberate* action attributable to the municipality directly caused a deprivation of federal rights. A failure to apply stringent culpability and causation requirements raises serious federalism concerns, in that it risks constitutionalizing particular hiring requirements that States have themselves elected not to impose. Cf. *Canton v. Harris*, 489 U.S., at 392. *Bryan County* is not liable for Sheriff Moore's isolated decision to hire Burns without adequate screening, because respondent has not demonstrated that his decision reflected a conscious disregard for a high risk that Burns would use excessive force in violation of respondent's federally protected right. We therefore vacate the judgment of the Court of Appeals and remand this case for further proceedings consistent with this opinion.

It is so ordered.

Footnotes

[1] In suggesting that our decision complicates this Court's § 1983 municipal liability jurisprudence by altering the understanding of culpability, Justice Souter and Justice Breyer misunderstand our approach. *Post*, at 8; *post*, at 1, 5. We do not suggest that a plaintiff in an inadequate screening case must show a higher degree of culpability than the "deliberate indifference" required in *Canton v. Harris*, 489 U.S. 378 (1989); we need not do so, because, as discussed below, respondent has not made a showing of deliberate indifference here. *See infra*, at 15-16. Furthermore, in assessing the risks of a decision to hire a particular individual, we draw no distinction between what is "so obvious" or "so likely to occur" and what is "plainly obvious." The difficulty with the lower courts' approach is that it fails to connect the background of the particular officer hired in this case to the particular consti-

tutional violation the respondent suffered. *Supra*, at 13-14. Ensuring that lower courts link the background of the officer to the constitutional violation alleged does not complicate our municipal liability jurisprudence with degrees of "obviousness," but seeks to ensure that a plaintiff in an inadequate screening case establishes a policymaker's deliberate indifference—that is, conscious disregard for the known and obvious consequences of his actions.

[2] Justice Souter implies that Burns' record reflected assault and battery charges arising from more than one incident. *Post*, at 14. There has never been a serious dispute that a single misdemeanor assault and battery conviction arose out of a single campus fight. Nor did petitioner's expert testify that the record reflected any assault charge without a disposition, see 9 Record 535-536, although Justice Souter appears to suggest otherwise, *post*, at 15, n. 6.

In fact, respondent's own expert witness testified that Burns' record reflected a single assault conviction. 7 Record 318; see also *id.*, at 320. Petitioner has repeatedly so claimed. See, *e.g.*, Suggestion for Rehearing En Banc in No. 93-5376 (CA5), p. 12 ("Burns had one misdemeanor assault conviction stemming from a campus fight"); Pet. for Rehearing of Substituted Opinion in No. 93-5376 (CA5), p. 11 (same); 3 Record 927 (Brief in Support of Defendants' Motion for Judgment Notwithstanding the Verdict 10); Pet. for Cert. 16 ("Burns pled guilty to assault and battery" as a result of "one campus fight").

Respondent has not once contested this characterization. See, *e.g.*, 3 Record 961 (Brief in Support of Plaintiff's Response to Defendants' Motion for Judgment Notwithstanding the Jury Verdict 4); Brief for Appellee/Cross Appellant Brown et al. in No. 93-5376 (CA5), pp. 3-4; Brief in Opposition 1. Indeed, since the characterization is reflected in the County's petition for certiorari, under this Court's Rule 15(2) respondent would have had an obligation in her brief in opposition to correct "any perceived misstatement" in the petition. She did not. Involvement in a single fraternity fracas does not demonstrate "a proclivity to violence against the person." *Post*, at 15, n. 6.

McMillian v. Monroe County, Alabama
520 U.S. 781 (1997)

Argued March 18, 1997
Decided June 2, 1997
CHIEF JUSTICE REHNQUIST delivered the opinion of the Court.

Petitioner sued Monroe County, Alabama under 42 U.S.C. § 1983 for allegedly unconstitutional actions taken by Monroe County Sheriff Tom Tate. If the sheriff's actions constitute county "policy," then the county is liable for them. *Monell v. New York City Dept. of Social Servs.*, 436 U.S. 658, 694 (1978). The parties agree that the sheriff is a "policymaker" for § 1983 purposes, but they disagree about whether he is a policymaker for Monroe County or for the State of Alabama. We hold that, as to the actions at issue here, Sheriff Tate represents the State of Alabama and is therefore not a county policymaker. We thus affirm the Court of Appeals' dismissal of petitioner's § 1983 claims against Monroe County.

I

In November 1986, Ronda Morrison was murdered in Monroe County, a sparsely populated county located in southwest Alabama. Petitioner and one Ralph Myers were indicted for this crime. Myers then pleaded guilty to a lesser offense and testified against petitioner at his trial. A jury convicted petitioner of capital murder, and the trial court sentenced him to death. After two remands, the Alabama Court of Criminal Appeals reversed petitioner's conviction, holding that the State had violated *Brady v. Maryland*, 373 U.S. 83 (1963), by suppressing statements from Myers that contradicted his trial testimony and other exculpatory evidence. *McMillian v. State*, 616 So. 2d 933, 942-948 (1993). Thus, after spending six years in prison, petitioner was released.

He then brought this § 1983 lawsuit in the District Court for the Middle District of Alabama against respondent Monroe County and numerous officials, including the three men in charge of investigating the Morrison murder—Tom Tate, the Sheriff of Monroe County; Larry Ikner, an investigator with the District Attorney's office in Monroe County; and Simon Benson, an investigator with the Alabama Bureau of Investigation. Only two of the officials were sued in their official capacities—Sheriff Tate and investigator Ikner—and it is only these official capacity suits that concern us here.[1] Petitioner principally alleged that Tate and Ikner, in their capacities as officials of Monroe County, not as officers of the State of Alabama, intimidated Myers into making false statements and suppressed exculpatory evidence. App. to Pet. for Cert. 26a-33a; *McMillian v. Johnson*, 878 F. Supp. 1473, 1486-1488 (MD Ala. 1995).

The District Court dismissed the claims against Monroe County and the claims against Tate and Ikner in their official capacities. The court held that "any unlawful acts of Defendants Tate and Ikner cannot be said to represent [Monroe] County's policy," because "an Alabama county has [no] authority to make policy in the area of law enforcement." App to Pet. for Cert. 55a. Petitioner appealed the District Court's decision as to Sheriff Tate. The Court of Appeals for the Eleventh Circuit affirmed, agreeing with the District Court that "Sheriff Tate is not a final policymaker for Monroe County in the area of law enforcement, because Monroe County has no law enforcement authority." *McMillian v. Johnson*, 88 F. 3d 1573, 1583 (1996). We granted certiorari, 519 U. S. ___ (1996), and now affirm.

II

A

We held in *Monell*, 436 U.S., at 694, that a local government is liable under § 1983 for its policies that cause constitutional torts. These policies may be set by the government's lawmakers, "or by those whose edicts or acts may fairly be said to represent official policy." *Ibid.* A court's task is to "identify those officials or governmental bodies who speak with final policymaking authority for the local governmental actor concerning the action alleged to have caused the particular constitutional or statutory violation at issue." *Jett v. Dallas Independent School Dist.*, 491 U.S. 701, 737 (1989). Here, the parties agree that Sheriff Tate has "final policymaking authority" in the area of law enforcement. They sharply disagree, however, about whether Alabama sheriffs are policymakers for the State or for the county when they act in a law enforcement capacity.[2]

In deciding this dispute, our inquiry is guided by two principles. First, the question is not whether Sheriff Tate acts for Alabama or Monroe County in some categorical, "all or nothing" manner. Our cases on the liability of local governments under § 1983 instruct us to ask whether governmental officials are final policymakers for the local government in a particular area, or on a particular issue. See *Jett*, 491 U.S., at 737 (court must identify "those officials who have the power to make official policy *on a particular issue*" (emphasis added)); *id.*, at 738 (question is whether school district superintendent "possessed final policymaking authority *in the area of* employee transfers" (emphasis added)); *St. Louis v. Praprotnik*, 485 U.S. 112, 123 (1988) (plurality opinion) ("[T]he challenged action must have been taken pursuant to a policy adopted by the official or officials responsible under state law for making policy in *that* area of the city's business" (emphasis added)). Thus, we are not seeking to make a characterization of Alabama sheriffs that will hold true for every type of official action they engage in. We simply ask whether Sheriff Tate represents the State or the county when he acts in a law enforcement capacity.

Second, our inquiry is dependent on an analysis of state law. Cf. *Jett, supra*, at 737 ("'[W]hether a particular official has "final policymaking authority" is a question of *state law*'" (quoting, with original emphasis, *Praprotnik, supra*, at 123 (plurality opinion)); *Pembaur v. Cincinnati*, 475 U.S. 469, 483 (1986) (plurality opinion) (same). This is not to say that state law can answer the question for us by, for example, simply labeling as a state official an official who clearly makes county policy. But our understanding of the actual function of a governmental official, in a particular area, will necessarily be dependent on the definition of the official's functions under relevant state law. Cf. *Regents of University of California v. Doe*, 519 U. S. ___ , ___ (*slip. op.*, at 5, n. 5) ("[The] federal question can be answered only after considering the provisions of state law that define the agency's character").

B

The Court of Appeals for the Eleventh Circuit determined that under Alabama law, a sheriff acting in his law enforcement capacity is not a policymaker for the county. Since the jurisdiction of the Court of Appeals includes Alabama, we defer considerably to that court's expertise in interpreting Alabama law.[3] See *Jett, supra*, at 738 ("We think the Court of Appeals [for the Fifth Circuit], whose expertise in interpreting Texas law is greater than our own, is in a better position to determine whether [the school district superintendent] possessed final policymaking authority in the area of employee transfers"); *Pembaur, supra*, at 484, n. 13 ("We generally accord great deference to the interpretation and application of state law by the courts of appeals").

We begin with the Alabama Constitution, "the supreme law of the state." *Alexander v. State ex rel. Carver*, 150 So. 2d 204, 208 (1963). We agree with the Court of Appeals that the constitutional provisions concerning sheriffs, the historical development of those provisions, and the interpretation given them by the Alabama Supreme Court strongly support Monroe County's contention that sheriffs represent the State, at least for some purposes. Alabama's Constitution, adopted in 1901, states that "[t]he executive department shall consist of a governor, lieutenant governor, attorney general, state auditor, secretary of state, state treasurer, superintendent of education, commissioner of agriculture and industries, and a sheriff for each county." Ala. Const. of 1901, Art. V, § 112. This designation is especially important for our purposes, because although every Alabama Constitution has included sheriffs as constitutional officers and has provided for their election by county voters, see Ala. Const. of 1819, Art. IV, § 24; Ala. Const. of 1861, Art. IV, § 24; Ala. Const. of 1865, Art. VII, § 3; Ala. Const. of 1867, Art. V, § 21; Ala. Const. of 1875, Art. V, § 26; Ala. Const. of 1901, Art. V, § 138, sheriffs have not always been explicitly listed as members of the state "executive department." Thus, the 1867 Constitution listed only the "governor, lieutenant governor, secretary of state, auditor, treasurer, and attorney general" as constituting "the executive department." Ala. Const. of 1867, Art. V, § 1. This changed with the 1875 Constitution, when sheriffs and the Superintendent of Education were added to the list. Ala. Const. of 1875, Art. V, § 1.[4]

The framers of the 1901 Constitution took two significant steps in an attempt to solidify the place of sheriffs in the executive department, and to clarify that sheriffs were acting for the State when exercising their law enforcement functions. First, faced with reports that sheriffs were allowing mobs to abduct prisoners and lynch them, the framers made such "neglect" by sheriffs an impeachable offense. See Ala. Const. of 1901, Art. V, § 138 ("Whenever any prisoner is taken from jail, or from the custody of any sheriff or his deputy, and put to death, or suffers grievous bodily harm, owing to the neglect, connivance, cowardice, or other grave fault of the sheriff, such sheriff may be impeached"); *State ex rel. Garber v. Cazalas*, 162 Ala. 210, 50 So. 296 (1909) (sheriff's failure to close jail doors, resulting in lynching of prisoner, constitutes impeachable offense); M. McMillan, Constitutional Development in Alabama, 1789-1901, p. 338, n. 186 (1955) (impeachment provision resulted in "much progress made against lynching").

Second, authority to impeach sheriffs was moved from the county courts to the State Supreme Court, because of "[t]he failure of county courts to punish sheriffs for neglect of duty." *Parker v. Amerson*, 519 So. 2d 442, 443 (Ala. 1987). One of the primary purposes of this change, proposed by ex Governor Thomas Goode Jones at the 1901 Convention, was "to augment the power of the Governor." *Id.*, at 444. After this change, the governor could order the State Supreme Court, rather than the county court, to begin impeachment proceedings against a wayward sheriff, and would not have to worry that local support for the sheriff would annul his effort at centralized control. See *ibid.*; Strengthening the Power of the Executive, Address of Emmet O'Neal, Governor of Alabama, 9-10 (Sept. 12, 1911) (new impeachment provision increases Governor's control of sheriffs and "gives the Executive real power which is respected and feared"). Thus, sheriffs now share the same impeachment procedures as state legal officers and lower state court judges, Ala. Const. of 1901, Art. VII, § 174, rather than county and municipal officers, Ala. Const. of 1875, Art. VII, § 3.

Critically for our case, the Alabama Supreme Court has interpreted these provisions and their historical background as evidence of "the framers' intent to ensure that sheriffs be considered executive officers of the state." *Parker*, 519 So. 2d, at 444. Based primarily on this understanding of the State Constitution, the court has held unequivocally that sheriffs are state officers, and that tort claims brought against sheriffs based on their officials acts therefore constitute suits against the State, not suits against the sheriff's county. *Id.*, at 443-445.[5] Thus, Alabama counties are not liable under a theory of *respondeat superior* for a sheriff's official acts that are tortious. *Id.*, at 442. The issues in *Parker* are strikingly similar to the ones in the present case, and that decision is therefore strong evidence in favor of the Court of Appeals' conclusion that sheriffs act on behalf of the State, rather than the county, when acting in their law enforcement capacity.

Turning from the Alabama Constitution to the Alabama Code, the relevant provisions are less compelling, but still support the conclusion of the Court of Appeals to some extent. Section 36-22-3 of the Code sets out a sheriff's duties. First, a sheriff must "attend upon" the state courts in his county, must "obey the lawful orders and directions" of those courts, and must "execute and return the process and orders" of any state court, even those outside his county. Ala. Code §§ 36-22-3(1), (2) (1991). Thus, judges (who are state officers, see Ala. Const. of 1901, Amdt. 328, § 6.01) may order the sheriff to take certain actions, even if the judge sits in a distant county. And under Ala. Code § 12-17-24 (1995), the presiding circuit judge "exercise[s] a general supervision" over the county sheriffs in his circuit,[6] just as if the sheriffs are normal "court [i.e., state] employees" (see § 12-17-1).

Second, the sheriff must give to the county treasurer a sworn written statement detailing the funds he has received for the county since his last statement, and must pay these funds to the treasurer. § 36-22-3(3). In contrast to the state judges, however, the county treasurer does not appear to have any statutory authority to direct the sheriff to take specific actions.

Third and most importantly, "[i]t shall be the duty of sheriffs in their respective counties, by themselves or deputies, to ferret out crime, to apprehend and arrest criminals and, insofar as within their power, to secure evidence of crimes in their counties and to present a report of the evidence so secured to the district attorney or assistant district attorney for the county." § 36-22-3(4). By this mandate, sheriffs are given complete authority to enforce the state criminal law in their counties. In contrast, the "powers and duties" of the counties themselves—creatures of the State who have only the powers granted to them by the *State, Alexander,* 150 So. 2d, at 206—do not include any provision in the area of law enforcement. Ala. Code § 11-3-11 (1989). Thus, the "governing body" of the counties—which in every Alabama county is the county commission, see *Calvert v. Cullman County Comm'n,* 669 So. 2d 119 (Ala. 1995) (citing § 11-1-5)—cannot instruct the sheriff how to ferret out crime, how to arrest a criminal, or how to secure evidence of a crime. And when the sheriff does secure such evidence, he has an obligation to share this information not with the county commission, but with the district attorney (a state official, see *Hooks v. Hitt,* 539 So. 2d 157, 159 (Ala. 1988)).

While the county commission thus has no direct control over how the sheriff fulfills his law enforcement duty, the governor and the attorney general do have this kind of control. Pursuant to § 36-22-5, they can direct the sheriff to investigate "any alleged violation of law in their counties." And after "proceed[ing] promptly" to complete this investigation, the sheriff must "promptly" write a report to the state official in charge of the investigation, stating his findings, listing the witnesses he has secured, and summarizing what the witnesses can prove. *Ibid.* In addition, the salaries of all sheriffs are set by the state legislature, not by the county commissions. § 36-22-16.

To all of this, petitioner counters with four important provisions that cut in favor of the conclusion that sheriffs are county officials. First, the sheriff's salary is paid "out of the county treasury." *Ibid.* Second, the county provides the sheriff with equipment (including cruisers), supplies, lodging, and reimbursement for expenses, to the extent "reasonably needed for the proper and efficient conduct of the affairs of the sheriff's office." § 36-22-18. Third, the sheriff's jurisdiction is limited to the borders of his county. See, *e.g.,* § 36-22-3(4) ("It shall be the duty of sheriffs in *their respective counties* . . . to ferret out crime" (emphasis added)). Fourth, the sheriff is elected locally by the voters in his county (as he has been since Alabama's 1819 Constitution). See Ala. Const. of 1901, Art. V, § 138; Ala. Const. of 1819, Art. IV, § 24.

We do not find these provisions sufficient to tip the balance in favor of petitioner. The county's payment of the sheriff's salary does not translate into control over him, since the county neither has the authority to change his salary nor the discretion to refuse payment completely. The county commissions do appear to have the discretion to deny funds to the sheriffs for their operations beyond what is "reasonably necessary." See *Etowah County Comm'n v. Hayes,* 569 So. 2d 397, 399 (Ala. 1990) (*per curiam*). But at most, this discretion would allow the commission to exert an attenuated and indirect influence over the sheriff's operations.

   Petitioner's contention that sheriffs are county officials because "state policymakers" typically make policy for the entire State (without limits on their jurisdiction) and are typically elected on a statewide (not local) basis, surely has some force. But district attorneys and state judges are often considered (and in Alabama are considered) state officials, even though they too have limited jurisdictions and are elected locally. These characteristics are therefore consistent with an understanding of the 67 Alabama sheriffs as state officials who have been locally placed throughout the State, with an element of control granted to the officials and residents of the county that receives the sheriff's services.[7]

   In sum, although there is some evidence in Alabama law that supports petitioner's argument, we think the weight of the evidence is strongly on the side of the conclusion reached by the Court of Appeals: Alabama sheriffs, when executing their law enforcement duties, represent the State of Alabama, not their counties. Cf. *Praprotnik*, 485 U.S., at 125 ("We are not, of course, predicting that state law will always speak with perfect clarity"); *id.*, at 126-127 ("It may not be possible to draw an elegant line that will resolve this conundrum").

C

   Petitioner argues that this conclusion will create a lack of uniformity in Alabama and throughout the country. First, he argues that it is anomalous to have 67 different "state policymakers" in the person of Alabama's 67 county sheriffs, all of whom may have different "state law enforcement policies" in their counties. Second, he points out that most Federal Courts of Appeals have found county sheriffs to be county, not state, officials, and he implies that our affirmance of the Court of Appeals will either call those decisions into question or create an unacceptable patchwork of rulings as to § 1983 liability of counties for the acts of their sheriffs. We reject both arguments: the first ignores the history of sheriffs, and the second ignores our Nation's federal nature.

   English sheriffs (or "shire reeves") were the King's "reeves" (officers or agents) in the "shires" (counties), at least after the Norman Conquest in 1066. See C. Wigan & D. Meston, Mather on Sheriff and Execution Law 1-2 (1935). Although chosen locally by the shire's inhabitants, the sheriff did "all the king's business in the county," 1 W. Blackstone, Commentaries on the Laws of England 328 (1765), and was "the keeper of the king's peace," *id.*, at 332. See also Wigan & Meston, *supra*, at 2 ("It is this position of the Sheriff as the executive officer of the Crown which has all along been the outstanding characteristic of the office").

   As the basic forms of English government were transplanted in our country, it also became the common understanding here that the sheriff, though limited in jurisdiction to his county and generally elected by county voters,[8] was in reality an officer of the State, and ultimately represented the State in fulfilling his duty to keep the peace.

See, *e.g.*, Wager, Introduction, in County Government Across the Nation 5 (P. Wager ed. 1950) ("The office of sheriff has an unbroken lineage from the Anglo Saxon shire-reeve"); 1 W. Anderson, A Treatise on the Law of Sheriffs, Coroners and Constables 5 (1941) ("In the exercise of executive and administrative functions, in conserving the public peace, in vindicating the law, and in preserving the rights of the government, he (the sheriff) represents the sovereignty of the State and he has no superior in his county"); R. Cooley, Handbook on the Law of Municipal Corporations 512 (1914) ("Sheriffs, coroners, clerks and other so called county officers are properly state officers for the county. Their functions and duties pertain chiefly to the affairs of state in the county"); 3 J. Bouvier, Bouvier's Law Dictionary 3058 (8th ed. 1914) (defining sheriff as "[a] county officer representing the executive or administrative power of the state within his county").

This historical sketch indicates that the common law itself envisioned the possibility that state law enforcement "policies" might vary locally, as particular sheriffs adopted varying practices for arresting criminals or securing evidence.[9] Thus, petitioner's disagreement with the concept that "county sheriffs" may actually be state officials is simply a disagreement with the ancient understanding of what it has meant to be a sheriff.

Petitioner's second concern is that under our holding here, sheriffs will be characterized differently in different States. But while it might be easier to decide cases arising under § 1983 and *Monell* if we insisted on a uniform, national characterization for all sheriffs, such a blunderbuss approach would ignore a crucial axiom of our government: the States have wide authority to set up their state and local governments as they wish. Understandably, then, the importance of counties and the nature of county government have varied historically from region to region, and from State to State. See, *e.g.*, Wager, *supra*, at 5-8 (describing different systems of rural government that developed in the Massachusetts, New York, Pennsylvania, and Virginia colonies, which later resulted in counties having widely varying roles in the four regions); Martin, American County Government, in County Governments in an Era of Change 3-5 (P. Berman ed. 1993) (same); DeSantis & Renner, Governing the County, *id.*, at 16-25 (describing varying levels of power currently exercised by counties in different States, and explaining how regional influences have resulted in different forms of county government in different States); Sokolow, Legislatures and Legislating in County Government, *id.*, at 37 (listing Alabama as 37th among the 50 States in amount of discretionary authority granted to its counties). Thus, since it is entirely natural that both the role of sheriffs and the importance of counties vary from State to State, there is no inconsistency created by court decisions that declare sheriffs to be county officers in one State, and not in another.[10]

The final concern of petitioner and his amici is that state and local governments will manipulate the titles of local officials in a blatant effort to shield the local governments from liability. But such efforts are already foreclosed by our decision in Praprotnik. See 485 U.S., at 127 (plurality opinion) ("[E]gregious attempts by local governments to insulate themselves from liability for unconstitutional policies are precluded" by allowing plaintiffs to prove that "a widespread practice" has been established by "'custom or usage' with the force of law"). And there is certainly no evidence of such manipulation here; indeed, the Alabama provisions that cut most strongly against petitioner's position predate our decision in *Monell* by some time.

The judgment of the Court of Appeals is therefore

Affirmed.

Footnotes

[1] The claims against the defendants in their individual capacities have proceeded independently in the lower courts, with some of petitioner's claims surviving motions for summary judgment. See *McMillian v. Johnson*, 878 F. Supp. 1473, 1544-1545 (MD Ala. 1995).

[2] We have explained that a suit against a governmental officer "in his official capacity" is the same as a suit "'against [the] entity of which [the] officer is an agent,'" *Kentucky v. Graham*, 473 U.S. 159, 165 (1985) (quoting *Monell v. New York City Dept. of Social Servs.*, 436 U.S. 658, 690, n. 55 (1978)), and that victory in such an "official capacity" suit "imposes liability on the entity that [the officer] represents," *Brandon v. Holt*, 469 U.S. 464, 471 (1985).

[3] We note that two of the three judges on the Eleventh Circuit's panel are based in Alabama. In addition, this is the second Eleventh Circuit panel to have reached this conclusion. See *Swint v. Wadley*, 5 F. 3d 1435, 1450-1451 (1993), vacated for lack of appellate jurisdiction, 514 U.S. 35 (1995).

[4] Executive department officers have to take the constitutional oath of office, Ala. Const of 1901, Art. XVII, § 279; Ala. Const. of 1875, Art. XV, § 1, and are required to submit written reports to the governor on demand. Submitting a false report was originally a crime, Ala. Const. of 1875, Art. V, § 9, and is now an impeachable offense, Ala. Const. of 1901, Art. V, § 121.

[5] As a result of this holding and the State Constitution's sovereign immunity provision, see Ala. Const. of 1901, Art. I, § 14 ("[T]he State of Alabama shall never be made a defendant in any court of law or equity"), the Alabama Supreme Court has held that a sheriff is absolutely immune from all suits for damages based on his official acts. *Parker v. Amerson*, 519 So. 2d, 442, 446 (Ala. 1987). See also *King v. Colbert County*, 620 So. 2d 623, 626 (Ala. 1993); *Boshell v. Walker County Sheriff*, 598 So. 2d 843, 844 (Ala. 1992); *Hereford v. Jefferson County*, 586 So. 2d 209, 210 (Ala. 1991).

[6] Seventeen of the forty judicial circuits in Alabama contain more than one county, including the circuit in which Monroe County sits. Ala. Code § 12-11-2 (1995).

[7] Petitioner also makes three other points that we believe have little merit. First, he points out that when the sheriff's office is vacant or when the sheriff is incapacitated, it is the county coroner that fills in for the sheriff. Ala. Code § 11-5-5 (1989). We note that this temporary assignment only lasts until the Governor appoints a replacement for the sheriff, who then serves out the remainder of the sheriff's

term. Ala. Code § 36-9-17 (1991). Thus, even assuming that the county coroner is a county official, we place little weight on this assignment of temporary responsibility, which by its nature must fall to an official who is already in the county and available to step in for the sheriff at any time. Second, petitioner cites several instances in the Code where a group of officials that includes the sheriff is designated a group of "county officials" or "county employees." See, e.g., §§ 36-3-4, 36-15-1, 36-22-16. But in light of the Alabama Supreme Court's conclusion that (i) sheriffs are state officials according to the State Constitution, see *Parker*, 519 So. 2d, at 443, and (ii) contrary statements in that court's prior decisions had ignored the Constitution and therefore should not be followed, *id.*, at 445 (citing, among other cases, *In re Opinions of Justices*, 225 Ala. 359, 143 So. 345 (1932)), we think that any contrary implication in the Code is entitled to little weight. Finally, petitioner relies on the Monroe County Commission's insurance policy—which, according to the District Court, "may cover . . . some, but not all, of the claims made against" Monroe County and Sheriff Tate in this suit, App. to Cert. Pet. 77a—to establish that the commission will pay any judgment rendered against Sheriff Tate. But this policy shows, at the most, that there was uncertainty as to whether the courts would consider Sheriff Tate a county policymaker in these circumstances, not that the county would pay any judgment against him.

[8] See W. Murfree, A Treatise on the Law of Sheriffs and Other Ministerial Officers 6 (1890) (sheriffs elected by county voters in all States but two).

[9] Cf. *McMillian v. Johnson*, 88 F. 3d, 1573, 1579 (CA11 1996) ("[W]e see no anomaly in having different state policymakers in different counties. Such a situation would be no different than if each of a city's police precinct commanders had unreviewable authority over how arrestees were processed. Each commander might have a different processing policy, but that does not render a commander's policy that of her precinct as opposed to that of the city when the city is sued under § 1983").

[10] Compare, *e.g.*, *Strickler v. Waters*, 989 F. 2d 1375, 1390 (CA4 1993) (Virginia "city sheriff" does not set city policy in area of jail conditions); *Thompson v. Duke*, 882 F. 2d 1180, 1187 (CA7 1989) (Illinois sheriff does not set county policy in area of training jail employees, because county board of commissioners has no authority to set policy in this area), with *Dotson v. Chester*, 937 F. 2d 920, 926-928 (CA4 1991) (Maryland sheriff sets county policy in area of jail conditions, based on exhaustive survey of Maryland law; citing no constitutional provision to the contrary); *Davis v. Mason County*, 927 F. 2d 1473, 1480 (CA9 1991) (Washington sheriff sets county policy in area of training deputy sheriffs, based on statutory provision labeling sheriff "chief executive officer . . . of the county"; citing no constitutional provision to the contrary (internal quotation marks omitted)); *Turner v. Upton County*, 915 F. 2d 133, 136-137 (CA5 1990) (Texas sheriff sets county policy in area of law enforcement, based on "unique structure of county government in Texas"; citing no constitutional provision to the contrary (internal quotation marks omitted)); *Crowder v. Sinyard*, 884 F. 2d 804, 828 (CA5 1989) (Arkansas sheriff sets county policy in area of law enforcement; citing no constitutional provision to the contrary).

Discussion Questions

1. What is official policy? How does official policy differ from custom?

2. What standard is needed to establish the existence of either an official policy or a custom in a police agency?

3. Can a single violation of the constitution by a police officer or a policymaker establish municipal liability? If not, what is required to establish liability?

4. Is Section 1983 a source of substantive rights? Why is the answer to this question important?

5. Is there a standard of culpability required to establish municipal liability? What is the standard of proof required to establish municipal liability? Do these standards conflict with the Court's position that municipalities are not afforded the good-faith defense?

6. Is there a difference between a single incident by a police officer that violates the Constitution and a single decision of a policymaker that violates the Constitution? What are the requirements for establishing municipal liability based on a single decision of a policymaker?

7. How does the Court determine who is and who is not a policymaker? Is a police chief or sheriff a policymaker?

8. When making a decision about who is a policymaker, what roles do the delegation of authority and the actual practices of an officeholder have on the decision?

9. Does the Court's decision in *McMillian* blur or clarify which political subdivision of government can be held liable under Section 1983? What effect does this decision have on making determinations of who is a policymaker?

PART IV

Police Use
of Force

Police use of force is perhaps one of the most controversial aspects of
policing. The use of force by police officers crosses many aspects of the
police social function as well as constitutional boundaries. In this section of your casebook, the Court considers several of the issues surrounding the police use of force. The Court distinguishes between
deadly and nonlethal force and develops a legal standard for determining liability in excessive force cases. In these decisions, the Court outlines the contexts in which police officers can constitutionally use both
deadly and nonlethal force. While liability for the use of force has been
historically analyzed under various constitutional amendments, the
Court adopts a single standard for the analysis of excessive force

against free citizens by the police. In doing so, the Court distinguishes between the various amendments that apply to claims of unconstitutional force and outlines the balance of interests that lower courts are to consider when making decisions about whether an officer's use of force is a constitutional violation. In the balancing act, courts are to weigh the governmental interest in law enforcement with that of individuals' interest in protecting their rights from infringements. In addressing these issues, the Court revisits the common-law doctrines on use of force and once again addresses the applicability of a good-faith defense. In delineating the standards for constitutional uses of force, the Court addresses the level of culpability required for an application of police force to be considered a constitutional violation. In the decisions, the Court further builds on the foundation it has constructed in other police liability decisions and further refines the law of municipal liability, making it even more distinguishable from both common-law doctrines and tort liability.

Tennessee v. Garner
471 U.S. 1 (1985)

Argued October 30, 1984
Decided March 27, 1985
JUSTICE WHITE delivered the opinion of the Court.

This case requires us to determine the constitutionality of the use of deadly force to prevent the escape of an apparently unarmed suspected felon. We conclude that such force may not be used unless it is necessary to prevent the escape and the officer has probable cause to believe that the suspect poses a significant threat of death or serious physical injury to the officer or others.

I

At about 10:45 p.m. on October 3, 1974, Memphis Police Officers Elton Hymon and Leslie Wright were dispatched to answer a "prowler inside call." Upon arriving at the scene they saw a woman standing on her porch and gesturing toward the adjacent house.[1] She told them she had heard glass breaking and that "they" or "someone" was breaking in next door. While Wright radioed the dispatcher to say that they were on the scene, Hymon went behind the house. He heard a door slam and saw someone run across the backyard. The fleeing suspect, who was appellee-respondent's decedent, Edward Garner, stopped at a 6-feet-high chain link fence at the edge of the yard. With the aid of a flashlight, Hymon was able to see Garner's face and hands. He saw no sign of a weapon, and, though not certain, was "reasonably sure" and "figured" that Garner was unarmed. App. 41, 56; Record 219. He thought Garner was 17 or 18 years old and [471 U.S. 1, 4] about 5' 5" or 5' 7" tall.[2] While Garner was crouched at the base of the fence, Hymon called out "police, halt" and took a few steps toward him. Garner then began to climb over the fence. Convinced that if Garner made it over the fence he would elude capture,[3] Hymon shot him. The bullet hit Garner in the back of the head. Garner was taken by ambulance to a hospital, where he died on the operating table. Ten dollars and a purse taken from the house were found on his body.[4]

In using deadly force to prevent the escape, Hymon was acting under the authority of a Tennessee statute and pursuant to Police Department policy. The statute provides that "[i]f, after notice of the intention to arrest the defendant, he either flee or forcibly resist, the officer may use all the necessary means to effect the arrest." Tenn. Code Ann. [471 U.S. 1, 5] 40-7-108 (1982).[5] The Department policy was slightly more restrictive than the statute, but still allowed the use of deadly force in cases of burglary. App. 140-144. The incident was reviewed by the Memphis Police Firearm's Review Board and presented to a grand jury. Neither took any action. *Id.*, at 57.

Garner's father then brought this action in the Federal District Court for the Western District of Tennessee, seeking damages under 42 U.S.C. § 1983 for asserted violations of Garner's constitutional rights. The complaint alleged that the shooting violated the Fourth, Fifth, Sixth, Eighth, and Fourteenth Amendments of the United States Constitution. It named as defendants Officer Hymon, the Police Department, its Director, and the Mayor and city of Memphis. After a 3-day bench trial, the District Court entered judgment for all defendants. It dismissed the claims against the Mayor and the Director for lack of evidence. It then concluded that Hymon's actions were authorized by the Tennessee statute, which in turn was constitutional. Hymon had employed the only reasonable and practicable means of preventing Garner's escape. Garner had "recklessly and heedlessly attempted to vault over the fence to escape, thereby assuming the risk of being fired upon." App. To Pet. for Cert. A10.

The Court of Appeals for the Sixth Circuit affirmed with regard to Hymon, finding that he had acted in good-faith reliance on the Tennessee statute and was therefore within the scope of his qualified immunity. 600 F.2d 52 (1979). It remanded for reconsideration of the possible liability of the city, however, in light of *Monell v. New York City Dept. of Social Services*, 436 U.S. 658 (1978), which had come down after the District Court's decision. The District Court was [471 U.S. 1, 6] directed to consider whether a city enjoyed a qualified immunity, whether the use of deadly force and hollow point bullets in these circumstances was constitutional, and whether any unconstitutional municipal conduct flowed from a "policy or custom" as required for liability under *Monell*. 600 F.2d, at 54-55.

The District Court concluded that *Monell* did not affect its decision. While acknowledging some doubt as to the possible immunity of the city, it found that the statute, and Hymon's actions, were constitutional. Given this conclusion, it declined to consider the "policy or custom" question. App. To Pet. for Cert. A37-A39.

The Court of Appeals reversed and remanded. 710 F.2d 240 (1983). It reasoned that the killing of a fleeing suspect is a "seizure" under the Fourth Amendment,[6] and is therefore constitutional only if "reasonable." The Tennessee statute failed as applied to this case because it did not adequately limit the use of deadly force by distinguishing between felonies of different magnitudes—"the facts, as found, did not justify the use of deadly force under the Fourth Amendment." *Id.*, at 246. Officers cannot resort to deadly force unless they "have probable cause . . . to believe that the suspect [has committed a felony and] poses a threat to the safety of the officers or a danger to the community if left at large." *Ibid.*[7] [471 U.S. 1, 7]

The State of Tennessee, which had intervened to defend the statute, see 28 U.S.C. § 2403(b), appealed to this Court. The city filed a petition for certiorari. We noted probable jurisdiction in the appeal and granted the petition. 465 U.S. 1098 (1984).

II

Whenever an officer restrains the freedom of a person to walk away, he has seized that person. *United States v. Brignoni-Ponce*, 422 U.S. 873, 878 (1975). While it is not always clear just when minimal police interference becomes a seizure, see *United States v. Mendenhall*, 446 U.S. 544 (1980), there can be no question that apprehension by the use of deadly force is a seizure subject to the reasonableness requirement of the Fourth Amendment.

A

A police officer may arrest a person if he has probable cause to believe that person committed a crime. *E.g., United States v. Watson*, 423 U.S. 411 (1976). Petitioners and appellant argue that if this requirement is satisfied the Fourth Amendment has nothing to say about how that seizure is made. This submission ignores the many cases in which this Court, by balancing the extent of the intrusion against the need for it, has examined the reasonableness of [471 U.S. 1, 8] the manner in which a search or seizure is conducted. To determine the constitutionality of a seizure "[w]e must balance the nature and quality of the intrusion on the individual's Fourth Amendment interests against the importance of the governmental interests alleged to justify the intrusion." *United States v. Place*, 462 U.S. 696, 703 (1983); see *Delaware v. Prouse*, 440 U.S. 648, 654 (1979); *United States v. Martinez-Fuerte*, 428 U.S. 543, 555 (1976). We have described "the balancing of competing interests" as "the key principle of the Fourth Amendment." *Michigan v. Summers*, 452 U.S. 692, 700, n. 12 (1981). See also *Camara v. Municipal Court*, 387

U.S. 523, 536-537 (1967). Because one of the factors is the extent of the intrusion, it is plain that reasonableness depends on not only when a seizure is made, but also how it is carried out. *United States v. Ortiz,* 422 U.S. 891, 895 (1975); *Terry v. Ohio,* 392 U.S. 1, 28-29 (1968).

Applying these principles to particular facts, the Court has held that governmental interests did not support a lengthy detention of luggage, *United States v. Place, supra,* an airport seizure not "carefully tailored to its underlying justification," *Florida v. Royer,* 460 U.S. 491, 500 (1983) (plurality opinion), surgery under general anesthesia to obtain evidence, *Winston v. Lee,* 470 U.S. 753 (1985), or detention for fingerprinting without probable cause, *Davis v. Mississippi,* 394 U.S. 721 (1969); *Hayes v. Florida,* 470 U.S. 811 (1985). On the other hand, under the same approach it has upheld the taking of fingernail scrapings from a suspect, *Cupp v. Murphy,* 412 U.S. 291 (1973), an unannounced entry into a home to prevent the destruction of evidence, *Ker v. California,* 374 U.S. 23 (1963), administrative housing inspections without probable cause to believe that a code violation will be found, *Camara v. Municipal Court, supra,* and a blood test of a drunken-driving suspect, *Schmerber v. California,* 384 U.S. 757 (1966). In each of these cases, the question was whether [471 U.S. 1, 9] the totality of the circumstances justified a particular sort of search or seizure.

B

The same balancing process applied in the cases cited above demonstrates that, notwithstanding probable cause to seize a suspect, an officer may not always do so by killing him. The intrusiveness of a seizure by means of deadly force is unmatched. The suspect's fundamental interest in his own life need not be elaborated upon. The use of deadly force also frustrates the interest of the individual, and of society, in judicial determination of guilt and punishment. Against these interests are ranged governmental interests in effective law enforcement.[8] It is argued that overall violence will be reduced by encouraging the peaceful submission of suspects who know that they may be shot if they flee. Effectiveness in making arrests requires the resort to deadly [471 U.S. 1, 10] force, or at least the meaningful threat thereof. "Being able to arrest such individuals is a condition precedent to the state's entire system of law enforcement." Brief for Petitioners 14.

Without in any way disparaging the importance of these goals, we are not convinced that the use of deadly force is a sufficiently productive means of accomplishing them to justify the killing of nonviolent suspects. Cf. *Delaware v. Prouse, supra,* at 659. The use of deadly force is a self-defeating way of apprehending a suspect and so setting the criminal justice mechanism in motion. If successful, it guarantees that that mechanism will not be set in motion. And while the meaningful threat of deadly force might be thought to lead to the arrest of more live suspects by discouraging escape attempts,[9] the presently available evidence does not support this thesis.[10] The fact is that a majority of police departments [471 U.S. 1, 11] in this country have forbidden the use of deadly force against nonviolent suspects. See *infra*, at 18-19. If those charged with the enforcement of the criminal law have abjured the use of deadly force in arresting nondangerous felons, there is a substantial basis for doubting that the use of such force is an essential attribute of the arrest power in all felony cases. See *Schumann v. McGinn*, 307 Minn. 446, 472, 240 N. W. 2d 525, 540 (1976) (Rogosheske, J., dissenting in part). Petitioners and appellant have not persuaded us that shooting nondangerous fleeing suspects is so vital as to outweigh the suspect's interest in his own life.

The use of deadly force to prevent the escape of all felony suspects, whatever the circumstances, is constitutionally unreasonable. It is not better that all felony suspects die than that they escape. Where the suspect poses no immediate threat to the officer and no threat to others, the harm resulting from failing to apprehend him does not justify the use of deadly force to do so. It is no doubt unfortunate when a suspect who is in sight escapes, but the fact that the police arrive a little late or are a little slower afoot does not always justify killing the suspect. A police officer may not seize an unarmed, nondangerous suspect by shooting him dead. The Tennessee statute is unconstitutional insofar as it authorizes the use of deadly force against such fleeing suspects.

It is not, however, unconstitutional on its face. Where the officer has probable cause to believe that the suspect poses a threat of serious physical harm, either to the officer or to others, it is not constitutionally unreasonable to prevent escape by using deadly force. Thus, if the suspect threatens the officer with a weapon or there is probable cause to believe that he has committed a crime involving the infliction or threatened infliction of serious physical harm, deadly force may be used if necessary to prevent escape, and if, where [471 U.S. 1, 12] feasible, some warning has been given. As applied in such circumstances, the Tennessee statute would pass constitutional muster.

III

A

It is insisted that the Fourth Amendment must be construed in light of the common-law rule, which allowed the use of whatever force was necessary to effect the arrest of a fleeing felon, though not a misdemeanant. As stated in Hale's posthumously published Pleas of the Crown:

> "[I]f persons that are pursued by these officers for felony or the just suspicion thereof . . . shall not yield themselves to these officers, but shall either resist or fly before they are apprehended or being

apprehended shall rescue themselves and resist or fly, so that they cannot be otherwise apprehended, and are upon necessity slain therein, because they cannot be otherwise taken, it is no felony." 2 M. Hale, Historia Placitorum Coronae 85 (1736).

See also 4 W. Blackstone, Commentaries *289. Most American jurisdictions also imposed a flat prohibition against the use of deadly force to stop a fleeing misdemeanant, coupled with a general privilege to use such force to stop a fleeing felon. *E.g., Holloway v. Moser*, 193 N.C. 185, 136 S. E. 375 (1927); *State v. Smith*, 127 Iowa 534, 535, 103 N. W. 944, 945 (1905); *Reneau v. State*, 70 Tenn. 720 (1879); *Brooks v. Commonwealth*, 61 Pa. 352 (1869); *Roberts v. State*, 14 Mo. 138 (1851); see generally *R. Perkins & R. Boyce*, Criminal Law 1098-1102 (3d ed. 1982); Day, Shooting the Fleeing Felon: State of the Law, 14 Crim. L. Bull. 285, 286-287 (1978); Wilgus, Arrest Without a Warrant, 22 Mich. L. Rev. 798, 807-816 (1924). But see *Storey v. State*, 71 Ala. 329 (1882); *State v. Bryant*, 65 N.C. 327, 328 (1871); *Caldwell v. State*, 41 Tex. 86 (1874). [471 U.S. 1, 13]

The State and city argue that because this was the prevailing rule at the time of the adoption of the Fourth Amendment and for some time thereafter, and is still in force in some States, use of deadly force against a fleeing felon must be "reasonable." It is true that this Court has often looked to the common law in evaluating the reasonableness, for Fourth Amendment purposes, of police activity. See, *e.g., United States v. Watson*, 423 U.S. 411, 418-419 (1976); *Gerstein v. Pugh*, 420 U.S. 103, 111, 114 (1975); *Carroll v. United States*, 267 U.S. 132, 149-153 (1925). On the other hand, it "has not simply frozen into constitutional law those law enforcement practices that existed at the time of the Fourth Amendment's passage." *Payton v. New York*, 445 U.S. 573, 591, n. 33 (1980). Because of sweeping change in the legal and technological context, reliance on the common-law rule in this case would be a mistaken literalism that ignores the purposes of a historical inquiry.

B

It has been pointed out many times that the common-law rule is best understood in light of the fact that it arose at a time when virtually all felonies were punishable by death.[11] "Though effected without the protections and formalities of an orderly trial and conviction, the killing of a resisting or [471 U.S. 1, 14] fleeing felon resulted in no greater consequences than those authorized for punishment of the felony of which the individual was charged or suspected." American Law Institute, Model Penal Code 3.07, Comment 3, p. 56 (Tentative Draft No. 8, 1958) (hereinafter Model Penal Code Comment). Courts have also justified the common-law rule by emphasizing the relative dangerousness of felons. See, *e.g., Schumann v. McGinn*, 307 Minn., at 458, 240 N. W. 2d, at 533; *Holloway v. Moser, supra*, at 187, 136 S. E., at 376 (1927).

Neither of these justifications makes sense today. Almost all crimes formerly punishable by death no longer are or can be. See, *e.g., Enmund v. Florida,* 458 U.S. 782 (1982); *Coker v. Georgia,* 433 U.S. 584 (1977). And while in earlier times "the gulf between the felonies and the minor offences was broad and deep," 2 Pollock & Maitland 467, n. 3; *Carroll v. United States, supra,* at 158, today the distinction is minor and often arbitrary. Many crimes classified as misdemeanors, or non-existent, at common law are now felonies. Wilgus, 22 Mich. L. Rev., at 572-573. These changes have undermined the concept, which was questionable to begin with, that use of deadly force against a fleeing felon is merely a speedier execution of someone who has already forfeited his life. They have also made the assumption that a "felon" is more dangerous than a misdemeanant untenable. Indeed, numerous misdemeanors involve conduct more dangerous than many felonies.[12]

There is an additional reason why the common-law rule cannot be directly translated to the present day. The common-law rule developed at a time when weapons were rudimentary. Deadly force could be inflicted almost solely in a hand-to-hand struggle during which, necessarily, the safety [471 U.S. 1, 15] of the arresting officer was at risk. Handguns were not carried by police officers until the latter half of the last century. L. Kennett & J. Anderson, The Gun in America 150-151 (1975). Only then did it become possible to use deadly force from a distance as a means of apprehension. As a practical matter, the use of deadly force under the standard articulation of the common-law rule has an altogether different meaning—and harsher consequences—now than in past centuries. See Wechsler & Michael, A Rationale for the Law of Homicide: I, 37 Colum. L. Rev. 701, 741 (1937).[13]

One other aspect of the common-law rule bears emphasis. It forbids the use of deadly force to apprehend a misdemeanant, condemning such action as disproportionately severe. See *Holloway v. Moser,* 193 N.C., at 187, 136 S. E., at 376; *State v. Smith,* 127 Iowa, at 535, 103 N. W., at 945. See generally Annot., 83 A. L. R. 3d 238 (1978).

In short, though the common-law pedigree of Tennessee's rule is pure on its face, changes in the legal and technological context mean the rule is distorted almost beyond recognition when literally applied.

C

In evaluating the reasonableness of police procedures under the Fourth Amendment, we have also looked to prevailing [471 U.S. 1, 16] rules in individual jurisdictions. See, *e.g., United States v. Watson,* 423 U.S., at § 421-422. The rules in the States are varied. See generally Comment, 18 Ga. L. Rev. 137, 140-144 (1983). Some 19 States have codified the common-law rule,[14] though in two of these the courts have significantly limited the statute.[15] Four States, though without a relevant statute, apparently retain the common-law rule.[16] Two States have adopted the Model Penal Code's [471 U.S. 1, 17] provision verbatim.[17] Eighteen others allow, in slightly varying language, the use of deadly force only if the suspect has committed a felony involving the use or threat of physical or deadly force, or is escaping with a deadly weapon, or is likely to endanger life or inflict serious physical injury if not arrested.[18] Louisiana and Vermont, though without statutes or case law on point, do forbid the use of deadly force to prevent any but violent felonies.[19] The remaining States either have no relevant statute or case law, or have positions that are unclear.[20] [471 U.S. 1, 18]

It cannot be said that there is a constant or overwhelming trend away from the common-law rule. In recent years, some States have reviewed their laws and expressly rejected abandonment of the common-law rule.[21] Nonetheless, the long-term movement has been away from the rule that deadly force may be used against any fleeing felon, and that remains the rule in less than half the States.

This trend is more evident and impressive when viewed in light of the policies adopted by the police departments themselves. Overwhelmingly, these are more restrictive than the common-law rule. C. Milton, J. Halleck, J. Lardner, & G. Abrecht, Police Use of Deadly Force 45-46 (1977). The Federal Bureau of Investigation and the New York City Police Department, for example, both forbid the use of firearms except when necessary to prevent death or grievous bodily harm. *Id.*, at 40-41; App. 83. For accreditation by the Commission on Accreditation for Law Enforcement Agencies, a department must restrict the use of deadly force to situations where "the officer reasonably believes that the action is in defense of human life ... or in defense of any person in immediate danger of serious physical injury." Commission on Accreditation for Law Enforcement Agencies, Inc., Standards for Law Enforcement Agencies 1-2 (1983) (italics deleted). A 1974 study reported that the police department regulations in a majority of the large cities of the United States allowed the firing of a weapon only when a [471 U.S. 1, 19] felon presented a threat of death or serious bodily harm. Boston Police Department, Planning & Research Division, The Use of Deadly Force by Boston Police Personnel (1974), cited in *Mattis v. Schnarr*, 547 F.2d 1007, 1016, n. 19 (CA8 1976), vacated as moot sub nom. *Ashcroft v. Mattis*, 431 U.S. 171 (1977). Overall, only 7.5% of departmental and municipal policies explicitly permit the use of deadly force against any felon; 86.8% explicitly do not. K. Matulia, A Balance of Forces: A Report of the International Association of Chiefs of Police 161 (1982) (table). See also Record 1108-1368 (written policies of 44 departments). See generally W. Geller & K. Karales, Split-Second Decisions 33-42 (1981); Brief for Police Foundation et al. as *Amici Curiae*. In light of the rules adopted by those who must actually administer them, the older and fading common-law view is a dubious indicium of the constitutionality of the Tennessee statute now before us.

D

Actual departmental policies are important for an additional reason. We would hesitate to declare a police practice of long standing "unreasonable" if doing so would severely hamper effective law enforcement. But the indications are to the contrary. There has been no suggestion that crime has worsened in any way in jurisdictions that have adopted, by legislation or departmental policy, rules similar to that announced today. Amici note that "[a]fter extensive research and consideration, [they] have concluded that laws permitting police officers to use deadly force to apprehend unarmed, non-violent fleeing felony suspects actually do not protect citizens or law enforcement officers, do not deter crime or alleviate problems caused by crime, and do not improve the crime-fighting ability of law enforcement agencies." *Id.*, at 11. The submission is that the obvious state interests in apprehension are not sufficiently served to warrant the use of lethal weapons against all fleeing felons. See *supra*, at 10-11, and n. 10. [471 U.S. 1, 20]

Nor do we agree with petitioners and appellant that the rule we have adopted requires the police to make impossible, split-second evaluations of unknowable facts. See Brief for Petitioners 25; Brief for Appellant 11. We do not deny the practical difficulties of attempting to assess the suspect's dangerousness. However, similarly difficult judgments must be made by the police in equally uncertain circumstances. See, *e.g.*, *Terry v. Ohio*, 392 U.S., at 20, 27. Nor is there any indication that in States that allow the use of deadly force only against dangerous suspects, see nn. 15, 17-19, *supra*, the standard has been difficult to apply or has led to a rash of litigation involving inappropriate second-guessing of police officers' split-second decisions. Moreover, the highly technical felony/misdemeanor distinction is equally, if not more, difficult to apply in the field. An officer is in no position to know, for example, the precise value of property stolen, or whether the crime was a first or second offense. Finally, as noted above, this claim must be viewed with suspicion in light of the similar self-imposed limitations of so many police departments.

IV

The District Court concluded that Hymon was justified in shooting Garner because state law allows, and the Federal Constitution does not forbid, the use of deadly force to prevent the escape of a fleeing felony suspect if no alternative means of apprehension is available. See App. to Pet. for Cert. A9-A11, A38. This conclusion made a determination of Garner's apparent dangerousness unnecessary. The court did find, however, that Garner appeared to be unarmed, though Hymon could not be certain that was the case. *Id.*, at A4, A23. See also App. 41, 56; Record 219. Restated in Fourth Amendment terms, this means Hymon had no articulable basis to think Garner was armed.

In reversing, the Court of Appeals accepted the District Court's factual conclusions and held that "the facts, as found, did not justify the use of deadly force." 710 F.2d, at 246. [471 U.S. 1, 21] We agree. Officer Hymon could not reasonably have believed that Garner—young, slight, and unarmed—posed any threat. Indeed, Hymon never attempted to justify his actions on any basis other than the need to prevent an escape. The District Court stated in passing that "[t]he facts of this case did not indicate to Officer Hymon that Garner was 'nondangerous.'" App. to Pet. for Cert. A34. This conclusion is not explained, and seems to be based solely on the fact that Garner had broken into a house at night. However, the fact that Garner was a suspected burglar could not, without regard to the other circumstances, automatically justify the use of deadly force. Hymon did not have probable cause to believe that Garner, whom he correctly believed to be unarmed, posed any physical danger to himself or others.

The dissent argues that the shooting was justified by the fact that Officer Hymon had probable cause to believe that Garner had committed a nighttime burglary. *Post*, at 29, 32. While we agree that burglary is a serious crime, we cannot agree that it is so dangerous as automatically to justify the use of deadly force. The FBI classifies burglary as a "property" rather than a "violent" crime. See Federal Bureau of Investigation, Uniform Crime Reports, Crime in the United States 1 (1984).[22] Although the armed burglar would present a different situation, the fact that an unarmed suspect has broken into a dwelling at night does not automatically mean he is physically dangerous. This case demonstrates as much. See also *Solem v. Helm*, 463 U.S. 277, 296-297, and nn. 22-23 (1983). In fact, the available statistics demonstrate that burglaries only rarely involve physical violence. During the 10-year period from 1973-1982, only 3.8% of all burglaries involved violent crime. Bureau of Justice Statistics, Household [471 U.S. 1, 22] Burglary 4 (1985).[23] See also T. Reppetto, Residential Crime 17, 105 (1974); Conklin & Bittner, Burglary in a Suburb, 11 Criminology 208, 214 (1973).

V

We wish to make clear what our holding means in the context of this case. The complaint has been dismissed as to all the individual defendants. The State is a party only by virtue of 28 U.S.C. § 2403(b) and is not subject to liability. The possible liability of the remaining defendants—the Police Department and the city of Memphis—hinges on *Monell v. New York City Dept. of Social Services*, 436 U.S. 658 (1978), and is left for remand. We hold that the statute is invalid insofar as it purported to give Hymon the authority to act as he did. As for the policy of the Police Department, the absence of any discussion of this issue by the courts below, and the uncertain state of the record, precludes any consideration of its validity.

The judgment of the Court of Appeals is affirmed, and the case is remanded for further proceedings consistent with this opinion.

So ordered.

Footnotes

[1] The owner of the house testified that no lights were on in the house, but that a back door light was on. Record 160. Officer Hymon, though uncertain, stated in his deposition that there were lights on in the house. *Id.*, at 209.

[2] In fact, Garner, an eighth-grader, was 15. He was 5' 4" tall and weighed somewhere around 100 or 110 pounds. App. to Pet. for Cert. A5.

[3] When asked at trial why he fired, Hymon stated:

> "Well, first of all it was apparent to me from the little bit that I knew about the area at the time that he was going to get away because, number 1, I couldn't get to him. My partner then couldn't find where he was because, you know, he was late coming around. He didn't know where I was talking about. I couldn't get to him because of the fence here, I couldn't have jumped this fence and come up, consequently jumped this fence and caught him before he got away because he was already up on the fence, just one leap and he was already over the fence, and so there is no way that I could have caught him." App. 52.

He also stated that the area beyond the fence was dark, that he could not have gotten over the fence easily because he was carrying a lot of equipment and wearing heavy boots, and that Garner, being younger and more energetic, could have outrun him. *Id.*, at 53-54.

[4] Garner had rummaged through one room in the house, in which, in the words of the owner, "[a]ll the stuff was out on the floors, all the drawers was pulled out, and stuff was scattered all over." *Id.*, at 34. The owner testified that his valuables were untouched but that, in addition to the purse and the 10 dollars, one of his wife's rings was missing. The ring was not recovered. *Id.*, at 34-35.

[5] Although the statute does not say so explicitly, Tennessee law forbids the use of deadly force in the arrest of a misdemeanant. See *Johnson v. State*, 173 Tenn. 134, 114 S. W. 2d 819 (1938).

[6] "The right of the people to be secure in their persons . . . against unreasonable searches and seizures, shall not be violated . . . ." U.S. Const., Amdt. 4.

[7] The Court of Appeals concluded that the rule set out in the Model Penal Code "accurately states Fourth Amendment limitations on the use of deadly force against fleeing felons." 710 F.2d, at 247. The relevant portion of the Model Penal Code provides:

> "The use of deadly force is not justifiable . . . unless (i) the arrest is for a felony; and (ii) the person effecting the arrest is authorized to act as a peace officer or is assisting a person whom he believes to be authorized to act as a peace officer; and (iii) the actor believes that the force employed creates no substantial risk of injury to innocent persons; and (iv) the actor believes [471 U.S. 1, 7] that (1) the crime for which the arrest is made involved conduct including the use or threatened use of deadly force; or (2) there is a substantial risk that the person to be arrested will cause death or serious bodily harm if his apprehension is delayed." American Law Institute, Model Penal Code § 3.07(2)(b) (Proposed Official Draft 1962).

The court also found that "[a]n analysis of the facts of this case under the Due Process Clause" required the same result, because the statute was not narrowly drawn to further a compelling state interest. 710 F.2d, at 246-247. The court considered the generalized interest in effective law enforcement sufficiently compelling only when the suspect is dangerous. Finally, the court held, relying on *Owen v. City of Independence*, 445 U.S. 622 (1980), that the city was not immune.

[8] The dissent emphasizes that subsequent investigation cannot replace immediate apprehension. We recognize that this is so, see n. 13, infra; indeed, that is the reason why there is any dispute. If subsequent arrest were assured, no one would argue that use of deadly force was justified. Thus, we proceed on the assumption that subsequent arrest is not likely. Nonetheless, it should be remembered that failure to apprehend at the scene does not necessarily mean that the suspect will never be caught.

In lamenting the inadequacy of later investigation, the dissent relies on the report of the President's Commission on Law Enforcement and Administration of Justice. It is worth noting that, notwithstanding its awareness of this problem, the Commission itself proposed a policy for use of deadly force arguably even more stringent than the formulation we adopt today. See President's Commission on Law Enforcement and Administration of Justice, Task Force Report: The Police 189 (1967). The Commission proposed that deadly force be used only to apprehend "perpetrators who, in the course of their crime threatened the use of deadly force, or if the officer believes there is a substantial risk that the person whose arrest is sought will cause death or serious bodily harm if his apprehension is delayed." In addition, the officer would have "to know, as a virtual certainty, that the suspect committed an offense for which the use of deadly force is permissible." *Ibid.*

[9] We note that the usual manner of deterring illegal conduct—through punishment—has been largely ignored in connection with flight from arrest. Arkansas, for example, specifically excepts flight from arrest from the offense of "obstruction of governmental operations." The commentary notes that this "reflects the basic policy judgment that, absent the use of force or violence, a mere attempt to avoid apprehension by a law enforcement officer does not give rise to an independent offense." Ark. Stat. Ann. § 41-2802(3)(a) (1977) and commentary. In the few States that do outlaw flight from an arresting officer, the crime is only a misdemeanor. See, *e.g.,* Ind. Code § 35-44-3-3 (1982). Even forceful resistance, though generally a separate offense, is classified as a misdemeanor. *E.g.,* Ill. Rev. Stat., ch. 38, ¶ 31-1 (1984); Mont. Code Ann. § 45-7-301 (1984); N. H. Rev. Stat. Ann. § 642:2 (Supp. 1983); Ore. Rev. Stat. § 162.315 (1983).

This lenient approach does avoid the anomaly of automatically transforming every fleeing misdemeanant into a fleeing felon—subject, under the common-law rule, to apprehension by deadly force—solely by virtue of his flight. However, it is in real tension with the harsh consequences of flight in cases where deadly force is employed. For example, Tennessee does not outlaw fleeing from arrest. The Memphis City Code does, § 22-34.1 (Supp. 17, 1971), subjecting the offender to a maximum fine of $50, § 1-8 (1967). Thus, Garner's attempted escape subjected him to (a) a $50 fine, and (b) being shot.

[10] See Sherman, Reducing Police Gun use, in Control in the Police Organization 98, 120-123 (M. Punch ed. 1983); Fyfe, Observations on Police [471 U.S. 1, 11] Deadly Force, 27 Crime & Delinquency 376, 378-381 (1981); W. Geller & K. Karales, Split-Second Decisions 67 (1981); App. 84 (affidavit of William Bracey, Chief of Patrol, New York City Police Department). See generally Brief for Police Foundation et al. as Amici Curiae.

[11] The roots of the concept of a "felony" lie not in capital punishment but in forfeiture. 2 F. Pollock & F. Maitland, The History of English Law 465 (2d ed. 1909) (hereinafter Pollock & Maitland). Not all felonies were always punishable by death. See *id.,* at 466-467, n. 3. Nonetheless, the link was profound. Blackstone was able to write: "The idea of felony is indeed so generally connected with that of capital

punishment, that we find it hard to separate them; and to this usage the interpretations of the law do now conform. And therefore if a statute makes any new offence felony, the law implies that is shall be punished with death, viz. by hanging, as well as with forfeiture . . . ." 4 W. Blackstone, Commentaries *98. See also R. Perkins & R. Boyce, Criminal Law 14-15 (3d ed. 1982); 2 Pollock & Maitland 511.

[12] White-collar crime, for example, poses a less significant physical threat than, say, drunken driving. See *Welsh v. Wisconsin*, 466 U.S. 740 (1984); *id.*, at 755 (BLACKMUN, J., concurring). See Model Penal Code Comment, at 57.

[13] It has been argued that sophisticated techniques of apprehension and increased communication between the police in different jurisdictions have made it more likely that an escapee will be caught than was once the case, and that this change has also reduced the "reasonableness" of the use of deadly force to prevent escape. *E.g.*, Sherman, Execution Without Trial: Police Homicide and the Constitution, 33 Vand. L. Rev. 71, 76 (1980). We are unaware of any data that would permit sensible evaluation of this claim. Current arrest rates are sufficiently low, however, that we have some doubt whether in past centuries the failure to arrest at the scene meant that the police had missed their only chance in a way that is not presently the case. In 1983, 21% of the offenses in the Federal Bureau of Investigation crime index were cleared by arrest. Federal Bureau of Investigation, Uniform Crime Reports, Crime in the United States 159 (1984). The clearance rate for burglary was 15%. *Ibid.*

[14] Ala. Code § 13A-3-27 (1982); Ark. Stat. Ann. § 41-510 (1977); Cal. Penal Code Ann. § 196 (West 1970); Conn. Gen. Stat. § 53a-22 (1972); Fla. Stat. § 776.05 (1983); Idaho Code § 19-610 (1979); Ind. Code § 35-41-3-3 (1982); Kan. Stat. Ann. § 21-3215 (1981); Miss. Code Ann. § 97-3-15(d) (Supp. 1984); Mo. Rev. Stat. § 563.046 (1979); Nev. Rev. Stat. § 200.140 (1983); N. M. Stat. Ann. § 30-2-6 (1984); Okla. Stat., Tit. 21, § 732 (1981); R. I. Gen. Laws § 12-7-9 (1981); S. D. Codified Laws § 22-16-32, 22-16-33 (1979); Tenn. Code Ann. § 40-7-108 (1982); Wash. Rev. Code § 9A.16.040(3) (1977). Oregon limits use of deadly force to violent felons, but also allows its use against any felon if "necessary." Ore. Rev. Stat. § 161.239 (1983). Wisconsin's statute is ambiguous, but should probably be added to this list. Wis. Stat. § 939.45(4) (1981-1982) (officer may use force necessary for "a reasonable accomplishment of a lawful arrest"). But see *Clark v. Ziedonis*, 368 F. Supp. 544 (ED Wis. 1973), aff'd on other grounds, 513 F.2d 79 (CA7 1975).

[15] In California, the police may use deadly force to arrest only if the crime for which the arrest is sought was "a forcible and atrocious one which threatens death or serious bodily harm," or there is a substantial risk that the person whose arrest is sought will cause death or serious bodily harm if apprehension is delayed. *Kortum v. Alkire*, 69 Cal. App. 3d 325, 333, 138 Cal. Rptr. 26, 30-31 (1977). See also *People v. Ceballos*, 12 Cal. 3d 470, 476-484, 526 P.2d 241, 245-250 (1974); *Long Beach Police Officers Assn. v. Long Beach*, 61 Cal. App. 3d 364, 373-374, 132 Cal. Rptr. 348, 353-354 (1976). In Indiana, deadly force may be used only to prevent injury, the imminent danger of injury or force, or the threat of force. It is not permitted simply to prevent escape. *Rose v. State*, 431 N. E. 2d 521 (Ind. App. 1982).

[16] These are Michigan, Ohio, Virginia, and West Virginia. *Werner v. Hartfelder*, 113 Mich. App. 747, 318 N. W. 2d 825 (1982); *State v. Foster*, 60 Ohio Misc. 46, 59-66, 396 N. E. 2d 246, 255-258 (Com. Pl. 1979) (citing cases); *Berry v. Hamman*, 203 Va. 596, 125 S. E. 2d 851 (1962); *Thompson v. Norfolk & W. R. Co.*, 116 W. Va. 705, 711-712, 182 S. E. 880, 883-884 (1935).

[17] Haw. Rev. Stat. § 703-307 (1976); Neb. Rev. Stat. § 28-1412 (1979). Massachusetts probably belongs in this category. Though it once rejected distinctions between felonies, *Uraneck v. Lima*, 359 Mass. 749, 750, 269 N. E. 2d 670, 671 (1971), it has since adopted the Model Penal Code limitations with regard to private citizens, *Commonwealth v. Klein*, 372 Mass. 823, 363 N. E. 2d 1313 (1977), and seems to

have extended that decision to police officers, *Julian v. Randazzo*, 380 Mass. 391, 403 N. E. 2d 931 (1980).

[18] Alaska Stat. Ann. § 11.81.370(a) (1983); Ariz. Rev. Stat. Ann. § 13-410 (1978); Colo. Rev. Stat. § 18-1-707 (1978); Del. Code Ann., Tit. 11, 467 (1979) (felony involving physical force and a substantial risk that the suspect will cause death or serious bodily injury or will never be recaptured); Ga. Code § 16-3-21(a) (1984); Ill. Rev. Stat., ch. 38, ¶ 7-5 (1984); Iowa Code § 804.8 (1983) (suspect has used or threatened deadly force in commission of a felony, or would use deadly force if not caught); Ky. Rev. Stat. § 503.090 (1984) (suspect committed felony involving use or threat of physical force likely to cause death or serious injury, and is likely to endanger life unless apprehended without delay); Me. Rev. Stat. Ann., Tit. 17-A, 107 (1983) (commentary notes that deadly force may be used only "where the person to be arrested poses a threat to human life"); Minn. Stat. § 609.066 (1984); N. H. Rev. Stat. Ann. § 627:5(II) (Supp. 1983); N. J. Stat. Ann. § 2C-3-7 (West 1982); N. Y. Penal Law 35.30 (McKinney Supp. 1984-1985); N.C. Gen. Stat. § 15A-401 (1983); N. D. Cent. Code § 12.1-05-07.2.d (1976); 18 Pa. Cons. Stat. § 508 (1982); Tex. Penal Code Ann. § 9.51(c) (1974); Utah Code Ann. § 76-2-404 (1978).

[19] See La. Rev. Stat. Ann. § 14:20(2) (West 1974); Vt. Stat. Ann., Tit. 13, § 2305 (1974 and Supp. 1984). A Federal District Court has interpreted the Louisiana statute to limit the use of deadly force against fleeing suspects to situations where "life itself is endangered or great bodily harm is threatened." *Sauls v. Hutto*, 304 F. Supp. 124, 132 (ED La. 1969).

[20] These are Maryland, Montana, South Carolina, and Wyoming. A Maryland appellate court has indicated, however, that deadly force may not be used against a felon who "was in the process of fleeing and, at the [471 U.S. 1, 18] time, presented no immediate danger to . . . anyone . . . ." *Giant Food, Inc. v. Scherry*, 51 Md. App. 586, 589, 596, 444 A. 2d 483, 486, 489 (1982).

[21] In adopting its current statute in 1979, for example, Alabama expressly chose the common-law rule over more restrictive provisions. Ala. Code §§ 13A-3-27, Commentary, pp. 67-63 (1982). Missouri likewise considered but rejected a proposal akin to the Model Penal Code rule. See *Mattis v. Schnarr*, 547 F.2d 1007, 1022 (CA8 1976) (Gibson, C. J., dissenting), vacated as moot sub nom. *Ashcroft v. Mattis*, 431 U.S. 171 (1977). Idaho, whose current statute codifies the common-law rule, adopted the Model Penal Code in 1971, but abandoned it in 1972.

[22] In a recent report, the Department of Corrections of the District of Columbia also noted that "there is nothing inherently dangerous or violent about the offense," which is a crime against property. D.C. Department of Corrections, Prisoner Screening Project 2 (1985).

[23] The dissent points out that three-fifths of all rapes in the home, three-fifths of all home robberies, and about a third of home assaults are committed by burglars. *Post*, at 26-27. These figures mean only that if one knows that a suspect committed a rape in the home, there is a good chance that the suspect is also a burglar. That has nothing to do with the question here, which is whether the fact that someone has committed a burglary indicates that he has committed, or might commit, a violent crime.

The dissent also points out that this 3.8% adds up to 2.8 million violent crimes over a 10-year period, as if to imply that today's holding will let loose 2.8 million violent burglars. The relevant universe is, of course, far smaller. At issue is only that tiny fraction of cases where violence has [471 U.S. 1, 23] taken place and an officer who has no other means of apprehending the suspect is unaware of its occurrence.

Graham v. Connor
490 U.S. 386 (1989)

Argued February 21, 1989
Decided May 15, 1989
CHIEF JUSTICE REHNQUIST delivered the opinion of the Court.

This case requires us to decide what constitutional standard governs a free citizen's claim that law enforcement officials used excessive force in the course of making an arrest, investigatory stop, or other "seizure" of his person. We hold that such claims are properly analyzed under the Fourth Amendment's "objective reasonableness" standard, rather than under a substantive due process standard.

In this action under 42 U.S.C. § 1983, petitioner Dethorne Graham seeks to recover damages for injuries allegedly sustained when law enforcement officers used physical force against him during the course of an investigatory stop. Because the case comes to us from a decision of the Court of Appeals affirming the entry of a directed verdict for respondents, we take the evidence hereafter noted in the light most favorable to petitioner. On November 12, 1984, Graham, a diabetic, felt the onset of an insulin reaction. He asked a friend, William Berry, to drive him to a nearby convenience store so he could purchase some orange juice to counteract the reaction. Berry agreed, but when Graham entered the store, he saw a number of people ahead of him in the checkout [490 U.S. 386, 389] line. Concerned about the delay, he hurried out of the store and asked Berry to drive him to a friend's house instead.

Respondent Connor, an officer of the Charlotte, North Carolina, Police Department, saw Graham hastily enter and leave the store. The officer became suspicious that something was amiss and followed Berry's car. About one-half mile from the store, he made an investiga-

tive stop. Although Berry told Connor that Graham was simply suffering from a "sugar reaction," the officer ordered Berry and Graham to
wait while he found out what, if anything, had happened at the convenience store. When Officer Connor returned to his patrol car to call for
backup assistance, Graham got out of the car, ran around it twice, and
finally sat down on the curb, where he passed out briefly.

In the ensuing confusion, a number of other Charlotte police
officers arrived on the scene in response to Officer Connor's request
for backup. One of the officers rolled Graham over on the sidewalk and
cuffed his hands tightly behind his back, ignoring Berry's pleas to get
him some sugar. Another officer said: "I've seen a lot of people with
sugar diabetes that never acted like this. Ain't nothing wrong with the
M. F. but drunk. Lock the S. B. up." App. 42. Several officers then lifted
Graham up from behind, carried him over to Berry's car, and placed
him face down on its hood. Regaining consciousness, Graham asked
the officers to check in his wallet for a diabetic decal that he carried. In
response, one of the officers told him to "shut up" and shoved his face
down against the hood of the car. Four officers grabbed Graham and
threw him headfirst into the police car. A friend of Graham's brought
some orange juice to the car, but the officers refused to let him have it.
Finally, Officer Connor received a report that Graham had done nothing wrong at the convenience store, and the officers drove him home
and released him. [490 U.S. 386, 390]

At some point during his encounter with the police, Graham sustained a broken foot, cuts on his wrists, a bruised forehead, and an
injured shoulder; he also claims to have developed a loud ringing in his
right ear that continues to this day. He commenced this action under
42 U.S.C. § 1983 against the individual officers involved in the incident,
all of whom are respondents here,[1] alleging that they had used excessive force in making the investigatory stop, in violation of "rights
secured to him under the Fourteenth Amendment to the United States
Constitution and 42 U.S.C. 1983." Complaint ¶ 10, App. 5.[2] The case
was tried before a jury. At the close of petitioner's evidence, respondents moved for a directed verdict. In ruling on that motion, the District Court considered the following four factors, which it identified as
"[t]he factors to be considered in determining when the excessive use
of force gives rise to a cause of action under § 1983": (1) the need for
the application of force; (2) the relationship between that need and the
amount of force that was used; (3) the extent of the injury inflicted; and
(4) "[w]hether the force was applied in a good faith effort to maintain
and restore discipline or maliciously and sadistically for the very purpose of causing harm." 644 F. Supp. 246, 248 (WDNC 1986). Finding
that the amount of force used by the officers was "appropriate under
the circumstances," that "[t]here was no discernable injury inflicted,"
and that the force used "was not applied maliciously or sadistically for

the very purpose of causing harm," but in "a good faith effort to maintain or restore order in the face of a potentially explosive [490 U.S. 386, 391] situation." *id.*, at 248-249, the District Court granted respondents' motion for a directed verdict.

A divided panel of the Court of Appeals for the Fourth Circuit affirmed. 827 F.2d 945 (1987). The majority ruled first that the District Court had applied the correct legal standard in assessing petitioner's excessive force claim. *Id.*, at 948-949. Without attempting to identify the specific constitutional provision under which that claim arose,[3] the majority endorsed the four-factor test applied by the District Court as generally applicable to all claims of "constitutionally excessive force" brought against governmental officials. *Id.*, at 948. The majority rejected petitioner's argument, based on Circuit precedent,[4] that it was error to require him to prove that the allegedly excessive force used against him was applied "maliciously and sadistically for the very purpose of causing harm."[5] *Ibid.* Finally, the majority held that a reasonable jury applying the four-part test it had just endorsed [490 U.S. 386, 392] to petitioner's evidence "could not find that the force applied was constitutionally excessive." *Id.*, at 949-950. The dissenting judge argued that this Court's decisions in *Terry v. Ohio*, 392 U.S. 1 (1968), and *Tennessee v. Garner*, 471 U.S. 1 (1985), required that excessive force claims arising out of investigatory stops be analyzed under the Fourth Amendment's "objective reasonableness" standard. 827 F.2d, at 950-952. We granted certiorari, 488 U.S. 816 (1988), and now reverse.

Fifteen years ago, in *Johnson v. Glick*, 481 F.2d 1028, cert. denied, 414 U.S. 1033 (1973), the Court of Appeals for the Second Circuit addressed a § 1983 damages claim filed by a pretrial detainee who claimed that a guard had assaulted him without justification. In evaluating the detainee's claim, Judge Friendly applied neither the Fourth Amendment nor the Eighth, the two most textually obvious sources of constitutional protection against physically abusive governmental conduct.[6] Instead, he looked to "substantive due process," holding that "quite apart from any 'specific' of the Bill of Rights, application of undue force by [490 U.S. 386, 393] law enforcement officers deprives a suspect of liberty without due process of law." 481 F.2d, at 1032. As support for this proposition, he relied upon our decision in *Rochin v. California*, 342 U.S. 165 (1952), which used the Due Process Clause to void a state criminal conviction based on evidence obtained by pumping the defendant's stomach. 481 F.2d, at 1032-1033. If a police officer's use of force which "shocks the conscience" could justify setting aside a criminal conviction, Judge Friendly reasoned, a correctional officer's use of similarly excessive force must give rise to a due process violation actionable under § 1983. *Ibid.* Judge Friendly went on to set forth four factors to guide courts in determining "whether the constitutional line has been crossed" by a particular use of force—the same four factors relied upon by the courts below in this case. *Id.*, at 1033.

In the years following *Johnson v. Glick*, the vast majority of lower federal courts have applied its four-part "substantive due process" test indiscriminately to all excessive force claims lodged against law enforcement and prison officials under § 1983, without considering whether the particular application of force might implicate a more specific constitutional right governed by a different standard.[7] Indeed, many courts have seemed to assume, as did the courts below in this case, that there is a generic "right" to be free from excessive force, grounded not in any particular constitutional provision but rather in "basic principles of § 1983 jurisprudence."[8]

We reject this notion that all excessive force claims brought under § 1983 are governed by a single generic standard. As we have said many times, § 1983 "is not itself a [490 U.S. 386, 394] source of substantive rights," but merely provides "a method for vindicating federal rights elsewhere conferred." *Baker v. McCollan*, 443 U.S. 137, 144, n. 3 (1979). In addressing an excessive force claim brought under § 1983, analysis begins by identifying the specific constitutional right allegedly infringed by the challenged application of force. See *id.*, at 140 ("The first inquiry in any § 1983 suit" is "to isolate the precise constitutional violation with which [the defendant] is charged").[9] In most instances, that will be either the Fourth Amendment's prohibition against unreasonable seizures of the person, or the Eighth Amendment's ban on cruel and unusual punishments, which are the two primary sources of constitutional protection against physically abusive governmental conduct. The validity of the claim must then be judged by reference to the specific constitutional standard that governs that right, rather than to some generalized "excessive force" standard. See *Tennessee v. Garner, supra*, at 7-22 (claim of excessive force to effect arrest analyzed under a Fourth Amendment standard); *Whitley v. Albers*, 475 U.S. 312, 318-326 (1986) (claim of excessive force to subdue convicted prisoner analyzed under an Eighth Amendment standard).

Where, as here, the excessive force claim arises in the context of an arrest or investigatory stop of a free citizen, it is most properly characterized as one invoking the protections of the Fourth Amendment, which guarantees citizens the right "to be secure in their persons . . . against unreasonable . . . seizures" of the person. This much is clear from our decision in *Tennessee v. Garner, supra*. In *Garner*, we addressed a claim that the use of deadly force to apprehend a fleeing suspect who did not appear to be armed or otherwise dangerous violated the suspect's constitutional rights, notwithstanding the existence of probable cause to arrest. [490 U.S. 386, 395] Though the complaint alleged violations of both the Fourth Amendment and the Due Process Clause, see 471 U.S., at 5, we analyzed the constitutionality of the challenged application of force solely by reference to the Fourth Amendment's prohibition against unreasonable seizures of the person, holding that the "reasonableness" of a particular seizure depends not only on when it is made, but also on how it is carried out. *Id.*, at 7-8. Today we make explicit what was implicit in *Garner's* analysis, and hold that *all* claims that law enforcement officers have used excessive force—deadly or not—in the course of an arrest, investigatory stop, or other "seizure" of a free citizen should be analyzed under the Fourth Amendment and its "reasonableness" standard, rather than under a "substantive due process" approach. Because the Fourth Amendment provides an explicit textual source of constitutional protection against this sort of physically intrusive governmental conduct, that Amendment, not the more generalized notion of "substantive due process," must be the guide for analyzing these claims.[10] [490 U.S. 386, 396]

Determining whether the force used to effect a particular seizure is "reasonable" under the Fourth Amendment requires a careful balancing of "'the nature and quality of the intrusion on the individual's Fourth Amendment interests'" against the countervailing governmental interests at stake. *Id.*, at 8, quoting *United States v. Place*, 462 U.S. 696, 703 (1983). Our Fourth Amendment jurisprudence has long recognized that the right to make an arrest or investigatory stop necessarily carries with it the right to use some degree of physical coercion or threat thereof to effect it. See *Terry v. Ohio*, 392 U.S., at 22-27. Because "[t]he test of reasonableness under the Fourth Amendment is not capable of precise definition or mechanical application," *Bell v. Wolfish*, 441 U.S. 520, 559 (1979), however, its proper application requires careful attention to the facts and circumstances of each particular case, including the severity of the crime at issue, whether the suspect poses an immediate threat to the safety of the officers or others, and whether he is actively resisting arrest or attempting to evade arrest by flight. See *Tennessee v. Garner*, 471 U.S., at 8-9 (the question is "whether the totality of the circumstances justifie[s] a particular sort of . . . seizure").

The "reasonableness" of a particular use of force must be judged from the perspective of a reasonable officer on the scene, rather than with the 20/20 vision of hindsight. See *Terry v. Ohio, supra*, at 20-22. The Fourth Amendment is not violated by an arrest based on probable cause, even though the wrong person is arrested, *Hill v. California*, 401 U.S. 797 (1971), nor by the mistaken execution of a valid search warrant on the wrong premises, *Maryland v. Garrison*, 480 U.S. 79 (1987). With respect to a claim of excessive force, the same standard of reasonableness at the moment applies: "Not every push or shove, even if it may later seem unnecessary in the peace of a judge's chambers," *Johnson v. Glick*, 481 F.2d, at 1033, violates the Fourth Amendment. The calculus of reasonableness must embody [490 U.S. 386, 397] allowance for the fact that police officers are often forced to make split-second judgments—in circumstances that are tense, uncertain, and rapidly evolving—about the amount of force that is necessary in a particular situation.

As in other Fourth Amendment contexts, however, the "reasonableness" inquiry in an excessive force case is an objective one: the question is whether the officers' actions are "objectively reasonable" in light of the facts and circumstances confronting them, without regard to their underlying intent or motivation. See *Scott v. United States*, 436 U.S. 128, 137-139 (1978); see also *Terry v. Ohio, supra*, at 21 (in analyzing the reasonableness of a particular search or seizure, "it is imperative that the facts be judged against an objective standard"). An officer's evil intentions will not make a Fourth Amendment violation out of an objectively reasonable use of force; nor will an officer's good intentions make an objectively unreasonable use of force constitutional. See *Scott v. United States, supra*, at 138, citing *United States v. Robinson*, 414 U.S. 218 (1973).

Because petitioner's excessive force claim is one arising under the Fourth Amendment, the Court of Appeals erred in analyzing it under the four-part *Johnson v. Glick* test. That test, which requires consideration of whether the individual officers acted in "good faith" or "maliciously and sadistically for the very purpose of causing harm," is incompatible with a proper Fourth Amendment analysis. We do not agree with the Court of Appeals' suggestion, see 827 F.2d, at 948, that the "malicious and sadistic" inquiry is merely another way of describing conduct that is objectively unreasonable under the circumstances. Whatever the empirical correlations between "malicious and sadistic" behavior and objective unreasonableness may be, the fact remains that the "malicious and sadistic" factor puts in issue the subjective motivations of the individual officers, which our prior cases make clear has no bearing on whether a particular seizure is "unreasonable" under the Fourth Amendment. Nor do we agree with the [490 U.S. 386, 398] Court of Appeals' conclusion, see *id.*, at 948, n. 3, that because the subjective motivations of the individual officers are of central importance in deciding whether force used against a convicted prisoner violates the Eighth Amendment, see *Whitley v. Albers*, 475 U.S., at 320-321,[11] it cannot be reversible error to inquire into them in deciding whether force used against a suspect or arrestee violates the Fourth Amendment. Differing standards under the Fourth and Eighth Amendments are hardly surprising: the terms "cruel" and "punishments" clearly suggest some inquiry into subjective state of mind, whereas the term "unreasonable" does not. Moreover, the less protective Eighth Amendment standard applies "only after the State has complied with the constitutional guarantees traditionally associated with criminal prosecutions." *Ingraham v. Wright*, 430 U.S. 651, 671, [490 U.S. 386, 399] n. 40 (1977). The Fourth Amendment inquiry is one of "objective reasonableness" under the circumstances, and subjective concepts like "malice" and "sadism" have no proper place in that inquiry.[12]

Because the Court of Appeals reviewed the District Court's ruling on the motion for directed verdict under an erroneous view of the governing substantive law, its judgment must be vacated and the case remanded to that court for reconsideration of that issue under the proper Fourth Amendment standard.

It is so ordered.

Footnotes

[1] Also named as a defendant was the city of Charlotte, which employed the individual respondents. The District Court granted a directed verdict for the city, and petitioner did not challenge that ruling before the Court of Appeals. Accordingly, the city is not a party to the proceedings before this Court.

[2] Petitioner also asserted pendent state-law claims of assault, false imprisonment, and intentional infliction of emotional distress. Those claims have been dismissed from the case and are not before this Court.

[3] The majority did note that because Graham was not an incarcerated prisoner, "his complaint of excessive force did not, therefore, arise under the eighth amendment." 827 F.2d, at 948, n. 3. However, it made no further effort to identify the constitutional basis for his claim.

[4] Petitioner's argument was based primarily on *Kidd v. O'Neil*, 774 F.2d 1252 (CA4 1985), which read this Court's decision in *Tennessee v. Garner*, 471 U.S. 1 (1985), as mandating application of a Fourth Amendment "objective reasonableness" standard to claims of excessive force during arrest. See 774 F.2d, at 1254-1257. The reasoning of *Kidd* was subsequently rejected by the en banc Fourth Circuit in *Justice v. Dennis*, 834 F.2d 380, 383 (1987), cert. pending, No. 87-1422.

[5] The majority noted that in *Whitley v. Albers*, 475 U.S. 312 (1986), we held that the question whether physical force used against convicted prisoners in the course of quelling a prison riot violates the Eighth Amendment "ultimately turns on 'whether force was applied in a good faith effort to maintain or restore discipline or maliciously and sadistically for the very purpose of causing harm.'" 827 F.2d, at 948, n. 3, quoting *Whitley v. Albers, supra*, at 320-321. Though the Court of Appeals acknowledged that petitioner was not a convicted prisoner, it thought it "unreasonable . . . to suggest that a conceptual factor could be central to one type of excessive force claim but reversible error when merely considered by the court in another context." *ibid.*

[6] Judge Friendly did not apply the Eighth Amendment's Cruel and Unusual Punishments Clause to the detainee's claim for two reasons. First, he thought that the Eighth Amendment's protections did not attach until after conviction and sentence. 481 F.2d, at 1032. This view was confirmed by *Ingraham v. Wright*, 430 U.S. 651, 671, n. 40 (1977) ("Eighth Amendment scrutiny is appropriate only after the State has complied with the constitutional guarantees traditionally associated with criminal prosecutions"). Second, he expressed doubt whether a "spontaneous attack" by a prison guard, done without the authorization of prison officials, fell within the traditional Eighth Amendment definition of "punishments." 481 F.2d, at 1032. Although Judge Friendly gave no reason for not analyzing the detainee's claim under the Fourth Amendment's prohibition against "unreasonable . . . seizures" of the person, his refusal to do so was apparently based on a belief that the protections of the Fourth Amendment did not extend to pretrial detainees. See *id.*, at 1033 (noting that "most of the courts faced with challenges to the conditions of pretrial detention have primarily based their analysis directly on the due process clause"). See n. 10, *infra*.

[7] See Freyermuth, Rethinking Excessive Force, 1987 Duke L. J. 692, 694-696, and nn. 16-23 (1987) (collecting cases).

[8] See *Justice v. Dennis, supra,* at 382 ("There are . . . certain basic principles in section 1983 jurisprudence as it relates to claims of excessive force that are beyond question [,] [w]hether the factual circumstances involve an arrestee, a pretrial detainee or a prisoner").

[9] The same analysis applies to excessive force claims brought against federal law enforcement and correctional officials under *Bivens v. Six Unknown Fed. Narcotics Agents,* 403 U.S. 388 (1971).

[10] A "seizure" triggering the Fourth Amendment's protections occurs only when government actors have, "by means of physical force or show of authority, . . . in some way restrained the liberty of a citizen," *Terry v. Ohio,* 392 U.S. 1, 19, n. 16 (1968); see *Brower v. County of Inyo,* 489 U.S. 593, 596 (1989). Our cases have not resolved the question whether the Fourth Amendment continues to provide individuals with protection against the deliberate use of excessive physical force beyond the point at which arrest ends and pretrial detention begins, and we do not attempt to answer that question today. It is clear, however, that the Due Process Clause protects a pretrial detainee from the use of excessive force that amounts to punishment. See *Bell v. Wolfish,* 441 U.S. 520, 535-539 (1979). After conviction, the Eighth Amendment "serves as the primary source of substantive protection . . . in cases . . . where the deliberate use of force is challenged as excessive and unjustified." *Whitley v. Albers,* 475 U.S., at 327. Any protection that "substantive due process" affords convicted prisoners against excessive force is, we have held, at best redundant of that provided by the Eighth Amendment. *Ibid.*

[11] In *Whitley,* we addressed a § 1983 claim brought by a convicted prisoner, who claimed that prison officials had violated his Eighth Amendment rights by shooting him in the knee during a prison riot. We began our Eighth Amendment analysis by reiterating the long-established maxim that an Eighth Amendment violation requires proof of the ""'unnecessary and wanton infliction of pain.'"" 475 U.S., at 319, quoting *Ingraham v. Wright,* 430 U.S., at 670, in turn quoting *Estelle v. Gamble,* 429 U.S. 97, 103 (1976). We went on to say that when prison officials use physical force against an inmate "to restore order in the face of a prison disturbance, . . . the question whether the measure taken inflicted unnecessary and wanton pain . . . *ultimately turns* on 'whether the force was applied in a good faith effort to maintain or restore discipline or maliciously and sadistically for the very purpose of causing harm.'" 475 U.S., at 320 –321 (emphasis added), quoting *Johnson v. Glick,* 481 F.2d, at 1033. We also suggested that the other prongs of the *Johnson v. Glick* test might be useful in analyzing excessive force claims brought under the Eighth Amendment. 475 U.S., at 321. But we made clear that this was so not because Judge Friendly's four-part test is some talismanic formula generally applicable to all excessive force claims, but because its four factors help to focus the central inquiry in the Eighth Amendment context, which is whether the particular use of force amounts to the "unnecessary and wanton infliction of pain." See *id.,* at 320-321. Our endorsement of the *Johnson v. Glick* test in Whitley thus had no implications beyond the Eighth Amendment context.

[12] Of course, in assessing the credibility of an officer's account of the circumstances that prompted the use of force, a fact finder may consider, along with other factors, evidence that the officer may have harbored ill will toward the citizen. See *Scott v. United States,* 436 U.S. 128, 139, n. 13 (1978). Similarly, the officer's objective "good faith"—that is, whether he could reasonably have believed that the force used did not violate the Fourth Amendment—may be relevant to the availability of the qualified immunity defense to monetary liability under § 1983. See *Anderson v. Creighton,* 483 U.S. 635 (1987). Since no claim of qualified immunity has been raised in this case, however, we express no view on its proper application in excessive force cases that arise under the Fourth Amendment.

City of Los Angeles
v. Heller
475 U.S. 796 (1986)

Decided April 21, 1986
PER CURIAM.

Respondent Ronald Heller sued petitioners, city of Los Angeles and individual members of the Los Angeles Police Commission, and two Los Angeles police officers in the United States District Court for the Central District of California under the provisions of 42 U.S.C. § 1983. He claimed damages by reason of having been arrested without probable cause and having been the victim of excessive force in the making of the arrest. The incident arose as a result of the two Los Angeles police officers stopping him because of a suspicion that he was driving while intoxicated. In the words of the Court of Appeals for the Ninth Circuit:

> "The officers administered a series of field sobriety tests. Apparently dissatisfied with the results, the officers decided to take Heller to the station to undergo a breath test. When notified that he was under arrest, however, Heller became belligerent. One of the defendants, Officer Bushey, attempted to handcuff him. An altercation ensued. In the course of the struggle, Heller fell through a plate glass window." *Heller v. Bushey,* 759 F.2d 1371, 1372-1373 (1985).

The District Court held a bifurcated trial, and first heard respondent's claims against one of the individual police officers.* The jury was instructed that Heller would make out his constitutional claim if he were arrested without reasonable cause, or if he were arrested with "unreasonable force" that exceeded the force necessary under the circumstances to effect arrest. *Id.,* at 1374. The jury was not instructed on

217

any affirmative defenses that might have been asserted by [475 U.S. 796, 798] the individual police officer. Tr. in No. 80-2643 (CD Cal.), pp. 803-822, 843. The jury returned a verdict for the defendant police officer and against respondent. The District Court then dismissed the action against petitioners, concluding that if the police officer had been exonerated by the jury there could be no basis for assertion of liability against the city or the persons constituting its Police Commission.

Respondent appealed to the Court of Appeals for the Ninth Circuit, and that court reversed the judgment of the District Court dismissing respondent's case against petitioners even though it did not disturb the verdict for the defendant police officer. Respondent urged, and the Court of Appeals apparently agreed, that "the jury could have believed that Bushey, having followed Police Department regulations, was entitled in substance to a defense of good faith. Such a belief would not negate the existence of a constitutional injury" (footnote omitted). 759 F.2d, at 1373-1374.

The difficulty with this position is that the jury was not charged on any affirmative defense such as good faith which might have been availed of by the individual police officer. Respondent contends in his brief in opposition to certiorari that even though no issue of qualified immunity was presented to the jury, the jury might nonetheless have considered evidence which would have supported a finding of such immunity. But the theory under which jury instructions are given by trial courts and reviewed on appeal is that juries act in accordance with the instructions given them, see *Aspen Skiing Co. v. Aspen Highlands Skiing Corp.*, 472 U.S. 585, 604 (1985), and that they do not consider and base their decisions on legal questions with respect to which they are not charged. We think that the Court of Appeals' search for ambiguity in the verdict was unavailing; as that court itself noted later in its opinion, "[b]ecause the instructions required a verdict for [respondent] if either the due process or the excessive force claim was found, the jury's [475 U.S. 796, 799] verdict for the defendant required a negative finding on both claims." 759 F.2d, at 1374, n. 3. This negative, it seems to us, was conclusive not only as to Officer Bushey, but also as to the city and its Police Commission. They were sued only because they were thought legally responsible for Bushey's actions; if the latter inflicted no constitutional injury on respondent, it is inconceivable that petitioners could be liable to respondent.

The Court of Appeals also stated:

"We must conclude that the general verdict does not foreclose a finding that Heller suffered a constitutional deprivation. Heller's *Monell* claim survived the general verdict. . . . The jury verdict, of course, conclusively determined that there was probable cause to arrest Heller. On the other hand, it is equally clear that whether the application of force in accordance with Police Department regulations in this case exceeded constitutional limits has not been determined." *Id.*, at 1374-1375.

But this was an action for damages, and neither *Monell v. New York City Dept. of Social Services*, 436 U.S. 658 (1978), nor any other of our cases authorizes the award of damages against a municipal corporation based on the actions of one of its officers when in fact the jury has concluded that the officer inflicted no constitutional harm. If a person has suffered no constitutional injury at the hands of the individual police officer, the fact that the departmental regulations might have authorized the use of constitutionally excessive force is quite beside the point.

The petition for certiorari is granted, the judgment of the Court of Appeals is reversed, and the case is remanded for further proceedings consistent with this opinion.

It is so ordered.

Saucier v. Katz, et al.
533 U.S. _____ (2001)

Argued March 20, 2001
Decided June 18, 2001
JUSTICE KENNEDY delivered the opinion of the Court.

In this case a citizen alleged excessive force was used to arrest him. The arresting officer asserted the defense of qualified immunity. The matter we address is whether the requisite analysis to determine qualified immunity is so intertwined with the question whether the officer used excessive force in making the arrest that qualified immunity and constitutional violation issues should be treated as one question, to be decided by the trier of fact. The Court of Appeals held the inquiries do merge into a single question. We now reverse and hold that the ruling on qualified immunity requires an analysis not susceptible of fusion with the question whether unreasonable force was used in making the arrest.

I

In autumn of 1994, the Presidio Army Base in San Francisco was the site of an event to celebrate conversion of the base to a national park. Among the speakers was Vice President Albert Gore, Jr., who attracted several hundred observers from the military and the general public. Some in attendance were not on hand to celebrate, however. Respondent Elliot Katz was concerned that the Army's Letterman Hospital would be used for conducting experiments on animals. (Katz was president of a group called In Defense of Animals. Although both he and the group are respondents here, the issues we discuss center upon Katz, and we refer to him as "respondent.") To voice opposition to the possibility that the hospital might be used for experiments, respondent brought with him a cloth banner, approximately 4 by 3 feet, that read "Please Keep Animal Torture Out of Our National Parks." In the past, as respondent was aware, members of the public had been asked to leave the military base when they engaged in certain activities, such as distributing handbills; and he kept the banner concealed under his jacket as he walked through the base.

The area designated for the speakers contained seating for the general public, separated from the stage by a waist-high fence. Respondent sat in the front row of the public seating area. At about the time Vice President Gore began speaking, respondent removed the banner from his jacket, started to unfold it, and walked toward the fence and speakers' platform.

Petitioner Donald Saucier is a military police officer who was on duty that day. He had been warned by his superiors of the possibility of demonstrations, and respondent had been identified as a potential protestor. Petitioner and Sergeant Steven Parker also a military police officer, but not a party to the suit—recognized respondent and moved to intercept him as he walked toward the fence. As he reached the barrier and began placing the banner on the other side, the officers grabbed respondent from behind, took the banner, and rushed him out of the area. Each officer had one of respondent's arms, half-walking, half-dragging him, with his feet "barely touching the ground." App. 24. Respondent was wearing a visible, [533 U.S. _____ , 3] knee-high leg brace, although petitioner later testified he did not remember noticing it at the time. Saucier and Parker took respondent to a nearby military van, where, respondent claims, he was shoved or thrown inside. *Id.,* at 25. The reason for the shove remains unclear. It seems agreed that respondent placed his feet somewhere on the outside of the van, perhaps the bumper, but there is a dispute whether he did so to resist. As a result of the shove, respondent claims, he fell to the floor of the van, where he caught himself just in time to avoid any injury. The officers drove respondent to a military police station, held him for a brief time, and then released him. Though the details are not clear, it appears that at least one other protestor was also placed into the van and detained for a brief time. *Id.,* at 27.

Respondent brought this action in the United States District Court for the Northern District of California against petitioner and other officials pursuant to *Bivens v. Six Unknown Fed. Narcotics Agents,* 403 U.S. 388 (1971), alleging, *inter alia*, that defendants had violated respondent's Fourth Amendment rights by using excessive force to arrest him. The District Court granted the defendants' motions for summary judgment on the grounds of qualified immunity on all claims other than the excessive force claim against Saucier. It held a dispute on a material fact existed concerning whether excessive force was used to remove respondent from the crowd and place him into the van. App. to Pet. for Cert. 27a. The District Court held that the law governing excessive force claims was clearly established at the time of the arrest, and that "[i]n the Fourth Amendment context, the qualified immunity inquiry is the same as the inquiry made on the merits." *Id.,* at 29a-30a. As a result, it ruled, petitioner was not entitled to summary judgment. *Id.,* at 30a.

In the United States Court of Appeals for the Ninth Circuit petitioner filed an interlocutory appeal from the denial of qualified immunity. 194 F. 3d 962 (1999). The Court of Appeals affirmed, noting at the outset its two-part analysis for qualified immunity questions. First, the Court of Appeals considers "whether the law governing the official's conduct was clearly established." *Id.,* at 967. If it was not, that ends the matter, and the official is entitled to immunity. If, however, the law was clearly established when the conduct occurred, the Court of Appeals' second step is to determine if a reasonable officer could have believed, in light of the clearly established law, that his conduct was lawful. *Ibid.* As to the first step of its analysis, the court observed that *Graham v. Connor,* 490 U.S. 386 (1989), sets forth the objective reasonableness test for evaluating excessive force claims, a principle the Court of Appeals concluded was clearly established for qualified immunity purposes. The court then concluded that the second step of the qualified immunity inquiry and the merits of the Fourth Amendment excessive force claim are identical, since both concern the objective reasonableness of the officer's conduct in light of the circumstances the officer faced on the scene. 194 F. 3d, at 968. On this reasoning, summary judgment based on qualified immunity was held inappropriate. *Id.,* at 968-969. Saucier, represented by the Government of the United States, sought review here, arguing the Court of Appeals erred in its view that the qualified immunity inquiry is the same as the constitutional inquiry and so becomes superfluous or duplicative when excessive force is alleged. We granted certiorari, 531 U.S. 991 (2000).

II

The Court of Appeals ruled first that the right was clearly established; and second that the reasonableness inquiry into excessive force meant that it need not consider aspects of qualified immunity, leaving the whole matter to the jury. 194 F. 3d, at 967. This approach [533 U.S. —— , 5] cannot be reconciled with *Anderson v. Creighton,* 483 U.S. 635 (1987), however, and was in error in two respects. As we shall explain, the first inquiry must be whether a constitutional right would have been violated on the facts alleged; second, assuming the violation is established, the question whether the right was clearly established must be considered on a more specific level than recognized by the Court of Appeals.

In a suit against an officer for an alleged violation of a constitutional right, the requisites of a qualified immunity defense must be considered in proper sequence. Where the defendant seeks qualified immunity, a ruling on that issue should be made early in the proceedings so that the costs and expenses of trial are avoided where the defense is dispositive. Qualified immunity is "an entitlement not to stand trial or face the other burdens of litigation."

Mitchell v. Forsyth, 472 U.S. 511, 526 (1985). The privilege is "an *immunity from suit* rather than a mere defense to liability; and like an absolute immunity, it is effectively lost if a case is erroneously permitted to go to trial." *Ibid.* As a result, "we repeatedly have stressed the importance of resolving immunity questions at the earliest possible stage in litigation." *Hunter v. Bryant,* 502 U.S. 224, 227 (1991) *(per curiam).*

A court required to rule upon the qualified immunity issue must consider, then, this threshold question: Taken in the light most favorable to the party asserting the injury, do the facts alleged show the officer's conduct violated a constitutional right? This must be the initial inquiry. *Siegert v. Gilley,* 500 U.S. 226, 232 (1991). In the course of determining whether a constitutional right was violated on the premises alleged, a court might find it necessary to set forth principles which will become the basis for a holding that a right is clearly established. This is the process for the law's elaboration from case to case, and it is one reason for our insisting upon turning to the existence or nonexistence of a constitutional right as the first inquiry. The law might be deprived of this explanation were a court simply to skip ahead to the question whether the law clearly established that the officer's conduct was unlawful in the circumstances of the case. If no constitutional right would have been violated were the allegations established, there is no necessity for further inquiries concerning qualified immunity. On the other hand, if a violation could be made out on a favorable view of the parties' submissions, the next, sequential step is to ask whether the right was clearly established. This inquiry, it is vital to note, must be undertaken in light of the specific context of the case, not as a broad general proposition; and it too serves to advance understanding of the law and to allow officers to avoid the burden of trial if qualified immunity is applicable.

In this litigation, for instance, there is no doubt that *Graham v. Connor, supra,* clearly establishes the general proposition that use of force is contrary to the Fourth Amendment if it is excessive under objective standards of reasonableness. Yet that is not enough. Rather, we emphasized in *Anderson* "that the right the official is alleged to have violated must have been 'clearly established' in a more particularized, and hence more relevant, sense: The contours of the right must be sufficiently clear that a reasonable official would understand that what he is doing violates that right." 483 U.S., at 640. The relevant, dispositive inquiry in determining whether a right is clearly established is whether it would be clear to a reasonable officer that his conduct was unlawful in the situation he confronted. See *Wilson v. Layne,* 526 U.S. 603, 615 (1999) ("[A]s we explained in *Anderson,* the right allegedly violated must be defined at the appropriate level of specificity before a court can determine if it was clearly established"). The approach the Court of Appeals adopted—to deny [533 U.S. _____ , 7] summary judgment any time a material issue of fact remains on the excessive force claim—could undermine the goal of qualified immunity to "avoid excessive disruption of government and permit the resolution of many insubstantial claims on summary judgment." *Harlow v. Fitzgerald,* 457 U.S. 800, 818 (1982). If the law did not put the officer on notice that his conduct would be clearly unlawful, summary judgment based on qualified immunity is appropriate. See *Malley v. Briggs,* 475 U.S. 335, 341 (1986) (qualified immunity protects "all but the plainly incompetent or those who knowingly violate the law").

This is not to say that the formulation of a general rule is beside the point, nor is it to insist the courts must have agreed upon the precise formulation of the standard. Assuming, for instance, that various courts have agreed that certain conduct is a constitutional violation under facts not distinguishable in a fair way from the facts presented in the case at hand, the officer would not be entitled to qualified immunity based simply on the argument that courts had not agreed on one verbal formulation of the controlling standard.

The Court of Appeals concluded that qualified immunity is merely duplicative in an excessive force case, eliminating the need for the second step where a constitutional violation could be found based on the allegations. In *Anderson,* a warrantless search case, we rejected the argument that there is no distinction between the reasonableness standard for warrantless searches and the qualified immunity inquiry. We acknowledged there was some "surface appeal" to the argument that, because the Fourth Amendment's guarantee was a right to be free from "unreasonable" searches and seizures, it would be inconsistent to conclude that an officer who acted unreasonably under the constitutional standard nevertheless was entitled to immunity because he "'reasonably' acted unreasonably." 483 U.S., at 643. This superficial similarity, however, could not overcome either our history of applying qualified immunity analysis to Fourth Amendment claims against officers or the justifications for applying the doctrine in an area where officers perform their duties with considerable uncertainty as to "whether particular searches or seizures comport with the Fourth Amendment." *Id.,* at 644. With respect, moreover, to the argument made in *Anderson* that an exception should be made for Fourth Amendment cases, we observed "the heavy burden this argument must sustain to be successful," since "the doctrine of qualified immunity reflects a balance that has been struck 'across the board.'" *Id.,* at 642 (quoting *Harlow v. Fitzgerald, supra,* at 821). We held that qualified immunity applied in the Fourth Amendment context just as it would for any other claim of official misconduct. 483 U.S., at 644.

Faced, then, with the heavy burden of distinguishing *Anderson* and of carving out an exception to the typical qualified immunity analysis applied in other Fourth Amendment contexts, the primary submission by respondent in defense of the Court of Appeals' decision is that our decision in *Graham v. Connor,* 490 U.S. 386 (1989), somehow changes matters. *Graham,* in respondent's view, sets forth an excessive force analysis indistinguishable from qualified immunity, rendering the separate immunity inquiry superfluous and inappropriate. Respondent asserts that, like the qualified immunity analysis applicable in other contexts, the excessive force test already affords officers latitude for mistaken beliefs as to the amount of force necessary, so that *"Graham* has addressed for the excessive force area most of the concerns expressed in *Anderson."* Brief for Respondents 7. Respondent points out that *Graham* did not address the interaction of excessive force claims and qualified immunity, since the issue was not raised, see 490 U.S., at 399, n. 12; and respondent [533 U.S. _____ , 9] seeks to distinguish *Anderson* on the theory that the issue of probable cause implicates evolving legal standards and resulting legal uncertainty, a subject raising recurrent questions of qualified immunity. By contrast, respondent says, excessive force is governed by the standard established in *Graham,* a standard providing ample guidance for particular situations. Finally, respondent adopts the suggestion made by one Court of Appeals that the relevant distinction is that probable cause is an *ex post* inquiry, whereas excessive force, like qualified immunity, should be evaluated from an *ex ante* perspective. See *Finnegan v. Fountain,* 915 F. 2d 817, 824, n. 11 (CA2 1990).

These arguments or attempted distinctions cannot bear the weight respondent seeks to place upon them. *Graham* did not change the qualified immunity framework explained in *Anderson.* The inquiries for qualified immunity and excessive force remain distinct, even after *Graham.* In *Graham,* we held that claims of excessive force in the context of arrests or investigatory stops should be analyzed under the Fourth Amendment's "objective reasonableness standard," not under substantive due process principles. 490 U.S., at 388, 394. Because "police officers are often forced to make split-second judgments—in circumstances that are tense, uncertain, and rapidly evolving—about the amount of force that is necessary in a particular situation," *id.,* at 397, the reasonableness of the officer's belief as to the appropriate level of force should be judged from that on-scene perspective. *Id.,* at 396. We set out a test that cautioned against the "20/20 vision of hindsight" in favor of deference to the judgment of reasonable officers on the scene. *Id.,* at 393, 396. *Graham* sets forth a list of factors relevant to the merits of the constitutional excessive force claim, "requir[ing] careful attention to the facts and circumstances of each particular case, including the severity of the crime at issue, whether the suspect poses an immediate threat to the safety of the officers or others, and whether he is actively resisting arrest or attempting to evade arrest by flight." *Id.,* at 396. If an officer reasonably, but mistakenly, believed that a suspect was likely to fight back, for instance, the officer would be justified in using more force than in fact was needed.

The qualified immunity inquiry, on the other hand, has a further dimension. The concern of the immunity inquiry is to acknowledge that reasonable mistakes can be made as to the legal constraints on particular police conduct. It is sometimes difficult for an officer to determine how the relevant legal doctrine, here excessive force, will apply to the factual situation the officer confronts. An officer might correctly perceive all of the relevant facts but have a mistaken understanding as to whether a particular amount of force is legal in those circumstances. If the officer's mistake as to what the law requires is reasonable, however, the officer is entitled to the immunity defense. *Graham* does not always give a clear answer as to whether a particular application of force will be deemed excessive by the courts. This is the nature of a test which must accommodate limitless factual circumstances. This reality serves to refute respondent's claimed distinction between excessive force and other Fourth Amendment contexts; in both spheres the law must be elaborated from case to case. Qualified immunity operates in this case, then, just as it does in others, to protect officers from the sometimes "hazy border between excessive and acceptable force," *Priester v. Riviera Beach,* 208 F. 3d 919, 926-927 (CA11 2000), and to ensure that before they are subjected to suit, officers are on notice their conduct is unlawful.

Graham and *Anderson* refute the excessive force/probable cause distinction on which much of respondent' s position seems to depend. The deference owed officers facing suits for alleged excessive force is not different in some qualitative respect from the probable cause inquiry in *Anderson.* Officers can have reasonable, but [533 U.S. _____, 11] mistaken, beliefs as to the facts establishing the existence of probable cause or exigent circumstances, for example, and in those situations courts will not hold that they have violated the Constitution. Yet, cvcn if a court wcrc to hold that the officer violated the Fourth Amendment by conducting an unreasonable, warrantless search, *Anderson* still operates to grant officers immunity for reasonable mistakes as to the legality of their actions. The same analysis is applicable in excessive force cases, where in addition to the deference officers receive on the underlying constitutional claim, qualified immunity can apply in the event the mistaken belief was reasonable.

The temporal perspective of the inquiry, whether labeled as *ex ante* or *ex post,* offers no meaningful distinction between excessive force and other Fourth Amendment suits. *Graham* recognized as much, reviewing several of our probable cause and search warrant cases, then stating that "[w]ith respect to a claim of excessive force, the same standard of reasonableness at the moment applies." 490 U.S., at 396 (discussing use of force under *Terry v. Ohio,* 392 U.S. 1 (1968); probable cause to arrest under *Hill v. California,* 401 U.S. 797 (1971); and search warrant requirements under *Maryland v. Garrison,* 480 U.S. 79 (1987)); see also *Hunter v. Bryant,* 502 U.S., at 228 ("Probable cause existed if 'at the moment the arrest was made . . . the facts and circumstances within their knowledge and of which they had reasonably trustworthy information were sufficient to warrant a prudent man in believing'" a crime had been committed (quoting *Beck v. Ohio,* 379 U.S. 89, 91 (1964).) Excessive force claims, like most other Fourth Amendment issues, are evaluated for objective reasonableness based upon the information the officers had when the conduct occurred.

III

The case was presented to the Court of Appeals on the assumption that respondent's seizure and brief detention did not violate clearly established First Amendment privileges and did not violate the Fourth Amendment right to be free from arrest without probable cause, as distinct from the force used to detain. The sole question, then, is whether the force used violated a clearly established Fourth Amendment protection so that petitioner was not entitled to immunity.

Our instruction to the district courts and courts of appeal to concentrate at the outset on the definition of the constitutional right and to determine whether, on the facts alleged, a constitutional violation could be found is important. As we have said, the procedure permits courts in appropriate cases to elaborate the constitutional right with greater degrees of specificity. Because we granted certiorari only to determine whether qualified immunity was appropriate, however, and because of the limits imposed upon us by the questions on which we granted review, we will assume a constitutional violation could have occurred under the facts alleged based simply on the general rule prohibiting excessive force, then proceed to the question whether this general prohibition against excessive force was the source for clearly established law that was contravened in the circumstances this officer faced. There was no contravention under this standard. Though it is doubtful that the force used was excessive, we need not rest our conclusion on that determination. The question is what the officer reasonably understood his powers and responsibilities to be, when he acted, under clearly established standards.

Respondent's excessive force claim for the most part depends upon the "gratuitously violent shove" allegedly received when he was placed into the van, although respondent notes as well that the alleged violation resulted from the "totality of the circumstances," including the way he was removed from the speaking area. See Brief for [533 U.S. _____, 13] Respondents 3, n. 2.

These circumstances, however, disclose substantial grounds for the officer to have concluded he had legitimate justification under the law for acting as he did. In *Graham* we noted that "[o]ur Fourth Amendment jurisprudence has long recognized that the right to make an arrest or investigatory stop necessarily carries with it the right to use some degree of physical coercion or threat thereof to effect it." 490 U.S., at 396. A reasonable officer in petitioner's position could have believed that hurrying respondent away from the scene, where the Vice President was speaking and respondent had just approached the fence designed to separate the public from the speakers, was within the bounds of appropriate police responses. Petitioner did not know the full extent of the threat respondent posed or how many other persons there might be who, in concert with respondent, posed a threat to the security of the Vice President. There were other potential protestors in the crowd, and at least one other individual was arrested and placed into the van with respondent. In carrying out the detention, as it has been assumed the officers had the right to do, petitioner was required to recognize the necessity to protect the Vice President by securing respondent and restoring order to the scene. It cannot be said there was a clearly established rule that would prohibit using the force petitioner did to place respondent into the van to accomplish these objectives. As for the shove respondent received when he was placed into the van, those same circumstances show some degree of urgency. We have approved the observation that "[n]ot every push or shove, even if it may later seem unnecessary in the peace of a judge's chambers, violates the Fourth Amendment." *Ibid.* (citations omitted). Pushes and shoves, like other police conduct, must be judged under the Fourth Amendment standard of reasonableness. In the circumstances presented to this officer, which included the duty to protect the safety and security of the Vice President of the United States from persons unknown in number, neither respondent nor the Court of Appeals has identified any case demonstrating a clearly established rule prohibiting the officer from acting as he did, nor are we aware of any such rule. Our conclusion is confirmed by the uncontested fact that the force was not so excessive that respondent suffered hurt or injury. On these premises, petitioner was entitled to qualified immunity, and the suit should have been dismissed at an early stage in the proceedings.

The judgment of the Court of Appeals is reversed, and the case is remanded for further proceedings consistent with this opinion.

It is so ordered.

Discussion Questions

1. What constitutional amendment governs the police use of deadly force? Is there any possibility that other constitutional amendments could be applied?

2. What is the standard the Court uses to determine whether a police officer's use of force was excessive? What factors are considered in making this decision?

3. When the Court considers a police officer's use of force, it uses a balancing test. What factors are considered in the application of the balancing test?

4. What is the relationship between the constitutional amendment that governs police use of force and qualified immunity? What role does probable cause play in the analysis?

5. Does the Court's rejection of the common-law rules governing police use of force conflict with its use of common law in the context of municipal liability as presented in Parts I, II, and III of your casebook?

6. How did the Court's decision in *Graham* extend or modify its decision in *Garner*?

7. What is the legal standard governing police use of nondeadly force? What factors does the Court consider important in making a decision as to the reasonableness of a police use of nondeadly force? How do these factors differ from the use of deadly force?

8. What role does the culpability or mental state of a police officer play in making a determination of whether a use of force was reasonable?

9. What are the implications of the Court's decisions on the development of agency policy? If a police department develops an unconstitutional use of force policy, can it be the sole basis for municipal liability?

PART V

Inadequate Training
and Due Process

In the course of their law enforcement activities, police officers routinely conduct searches and seizures of property and persons. The police may search and seize property to uncover evidence of criminal activity, or they may seize persons suspected of committing crimes. The Court considers several of the issues surrounding police liability for searches, seizures, and violation of liberty interests.

In this part of your casebook the Court considers whether a constitutional policy generated by a municipality that results in the deprivation of a citizen's constitutional rights can form the basis of a Section 1983 action. On first impression it seems that the Court is charting new legal territory by allowing actions to be brought against municipalities where the policies themselves are constitutional but result in constitutional deprivations. On closer inspection, however, the Court is refining the basic legal standard of municipal liability first articulated in the *Monell* decision. The Court takes up these issues in the context of failure to provide officers with adequate training to carry out their social function. Concluding that a constitutional policy can indeed form the basis of a Section 1983 action, the Court develops the standards necessary for making determinations of municipal liability.

The Court outlines the standard for culpability of a municipality in a fashion that distinguishes Section 1983 actions from *respondeat superior* claims. In doing so, the Court refines the deliberate indifference standard and articulates under what conditions a municipality's policies can render it liable for a citizen injury. Additionally, the Court carves out a requirement for causation. In doing so, the Court distinguishes the forms of causation normally associated with common-law torts from those of Section 1983 actions that require a municipality's policy to be closely related to the constitutional deprivation, so as to be "obvious" that it is the moving force behind the deprivation. Finally, the Court considers the difference between liability for failure to adequately train police officers in situations that result in a citizen injury or constitutional deprivation and liability for inadequate training that results in an employee's injury.

The Court also sets the standard for determining whether a police search or seizure is actionable under the provisions of Section 1983. In constructing this standard, the Court determines whether property interests are protected only by the Due Process clauses of the Fifth and Fourteenth Amendments or whether the provisions of the Fourth Amendment also protect them. In distinguishing between the applicability of these amendments to cases of police civil liability for unlawful search and seizure, the Court considers whether a search or seizure requires interference with a citizen's liberty interest for liability to attach. The Court considers the extent to which property, privacy, and liberty are protected by the Constitution. In taking up these issues, the Court distinguishes the boundaries of both the Fourth and Fourteenth Amendments and determines their applicability to both the circumstance surrounding a lawful search and the continued restraint of a citizen following a lawful detention.

City of Canton, Ohio v. Harris

489 U.S. 378 (1989)

Argued November 8, 1988
Decided February 28, 1989
JUSTICE WHITE delivered the opinion of the Court.

In this case, we are asked to determine if a municipality can ever be liable under 42 U.S.C. § 1983[1] for constitutional violations resulting from its failure to train municipal employees. We hold that, under certain circumstances, such liability is permitted by the statute. [489 U.S. 378, 381]

I

In April 1978, respondent Geraldine Harris was arrested by officers of the Canton Police Department. Mrs. Harris was brought to the police station in a patrol wagon.

When she arrived at the station, Mrs. Harris was found sitting on the floor of the wagon. She was asked if she needed medical attention, and responded with an incoherent remark. After she was brought inside the station for processing, Mrs. Harris slumped to the floor on two occasions. Eventually, the police officers left Mrs. Harris lying on the floor to prevent her from falling again. No medical attention was ever summoned for Mrs. Harris. After about an hour, Mrs. Harris was released from custody, and taken by an ambulance (provided by her family) to a nearby hospital. There, Mrs. Harris was diagnosed as suffering from several emotional ailments; she was hospitalized for one week and received subsequent outpatient treatment for an additional year.

Some time later, Mrs. Harris commenced this action alleging many state-law and constitutional claims against the city of Canton and its officials. Among these claims was one seeking to hold the city liable under 42 U.S.C. § 1983 for its violation of Mrs. Harris' right, under the Due Process Clause of the Fourteenth Amendment, to receive necessary medical attention while in police custody.

A jury trial was held on Mrs. Harris' claims. Evidence was presented that indicated that, pursuant to a municipal regulation,[2] shift commanders were authorized to determine, in their sole discretion, whether a detainee required medical [489 U.S. 378, 382] care. Tr. 2-139-2-143. In addition, testimony also suggested that Canton shift commanders were not provided with any special training (beyond first-aid training) to make a determination as to when to summon medical care for an injured detainee. *Ibid.*; App. to Pet. for Cert. 4a.

At the close of the evidence, the District Court submitted the case to the jury, which rejected all of Mrs. Harris' claims except one: her § 1983 claim against the city resulting from its failure to provide her with medical treatment while in custody. In rejecting the city's subsequent motion for judgment notwithstanding the verdict, the District Court explained the theory of liability as follows:

> "The evidence construed in a manner most favorable to Mrs. Harris could be found by a jury to demonstrate that the City of Canton had a custom or policy of vesting complete authority with the police supervisor of when medical treatment would be administered to prisoners. Further, the jury could find from the evidence that the vesting of such carte blanche authority with the police supervisor without adequate training to recognize when medical treatment is needed was grossly negligent or so reckless that future police misconduct was almost inevitable or substantially certain to result." *Id.*, at 16a.

On appeal, the Sixth Circuit affirmed this aspect of the District Court's analysis, holding that "a municipality is liable for failure to train its police force, [where] the plaintiff . . . prove[s] that the municipality acted recklessly, intentionally, or with gross negligence." *Id.*, at 5a.[3] The Court of Appeals also stated that an additional prerequisite of this theory [489 U.S. 378, 383] of liability was that the plaintiff must prove "that the lack of training was so reckless or grossly negligent that deprivations of persons' constitutional rights were substantially certain to result." *Ibid.* Thus, the Court of Appeals found that there had been no error in submitting Mrs. Harris' "failure to train" claim to the jury. However, the Court of Appeals reversed the judgment for respondent, and remanded this case for a new trial, because it found that certain aspects of the District Court's jury instructions might have led the jury to believe that it could find against the city on a mere *respondeat superior* theory. Because the jury's verdict did not state the basis on which it had ruled for Mrs. Harris on her § 1983 claim, a new trial was ordered.

The city petitioned for certiorari, arguing that the Sixth Circuit's holding represented an impermissible broadening of municipal liability under § 1983. We granted the petition. 485 U.S. 933 (1988).

II

We first address respondent's contention that the writ of certiorari should be dismissed as improvidently granted, because "petitioner failed to preserve for review the principal issues it now argues in this Court." Brief for Respondent 5.

We think it clear enough that petitioner's three "Questions Presented" in its petition for certiorari encompass the critical question before us in this case: Under what circumstances can inadequate training be found to be a "policy" that is actionable under § 1983? See Pet. for Cert. i. The petition itself addressed this issue directly, attacking the Sixth Circuit's "failure to train" theory as inconsistent with this Court's precedents. See *id.*, at 8-12. It is also clear—as respondent conceded at argument, Tr. of Oral Arg. 34, 54—that her brief in opposition to our granting of certiorari did not raise the objection that petitioner had failed to press its claims on the courts below.

As to respondent's contention that the claims made by petitioner here were not made in the same fashion below, that [489 U.S. 378, 384] failure, if it occurred, does not affect our jurisdiction; and because respondent did not oppose our grant of review at that time based on her contention that these claims were not pressed below, we will not dismiss the writ as improvidently granted. "[T]he 'decision to grant certiorari represents a commitment of scarce judicial resources with a view to deciding the merits . . . of the questions presented in the petition.'" *St. Louis v. Praprotnik*, 485 U.S. 112, 120 (1988) (quoting *Oklahoma City v. Tuttle*, 471 U.S. 808, 816 (1985)). As we have expressly admonished litigants in respondent's position: "Nonjurisdictional defects of this sort should be brought to our attention no later than in respondent's brief in opposition to the petition for certiorari; if not, we consider it within our discretion to deem the defect waived." *Tuttle, supra*, at 816.

It is true that petitioner's litigation posture with respect to the questions presented here has not been consistent; most importantly, petitioner conceded below that "'inadequate training' [is] a means of establishing municipal liability under Section 1983." Reply Brief for Petitioner 4, n. 3; see also Petition for Rehearing in No. 85-3314 (CA6), p. 1. However, at each stage in the proceedings below, petitioner contested any finding of liability on this ground, with objections of varying specificity. It opposed the District Court's jury instructions on this issue, Tr. 4-369; claimed in its judgment notwithstanding verdict motion that there was "no evidence of a . . . policy or practice on the part of the City . . . [of] den[ying] medical treatment to prisoners,"

Motion for Judgment Notwithstanding Verdict in No. C80-18-A (ND Ohio), p. 1; and argued to the Court of Appeals that there was no basis for finding a policy of denying medical treatment to prisoners in this case. See Brief for Appellant in No. 85-3314 (CA6), pp. 26-29. Indeed, petitioner specifically contended that the Sixth Circuit precedents that permitted inadequate training to be a basis for municipal liability on facts similar to these, see n. 3, *supra*, were in conflict with [489 U.S. 378, 385] our decision in *Tuttle*. Brief for Appellant *supra* at 29. These various presentations of the issues below might have been so inexact that we would have denied certiorari had this matter been brought to our attention at the appropriate stage in the proceedings. But they were at least adequate to yield a decision by the Sixth Circuit on the questions presented for our review now.

Here the Sixth Circuit held that where a plaintiff proves that a municipality, acting recklessly, intentionally, or with gross negligence, has failed to train its police force—resulting in a deprivation of constitutional rights that was "substantially certain to result"—§ 1983 permits that municipality to be held liable for its actions. Petitioner's petition for certiorari challenged the soundness of that conclusion, and respondent did not inform us prior to the time that review was granted that petitioner had arguably conceded this point below. Consequently, we will not abstain from addressing the question before us.

III

In *Monell v. New York City Dept. of Social Services*, 436 U.S. 658 (1978), we decided that a municipality can be found liable under § 1983 only where the municipality itself causes the constitutional violation at issue. *Respondeat superior* or vicarious liability will not attach under § 1983. *Id.*, at 694-695. "It is only when the 'execution of the government's policy or custom . . . inflicts the injury' that the municipality may be held liable under § 1983." *Springfield, Mass. v. Kibbe*, 480 U.S. 257, 267 (1987) (O'CONNOR, J., dissenting) (quoting *Monell, supra*, at 694).

Thus, our first inquiry in any case alleging municipal liability under § 1983 is the question whether there is a direct causal link between a municipal policy or custom and the alleged constitutional deprivation. The inquiry is a difficult one; one that has left this Court deeply divided in a series of [489 U.S. 378, 386] cases that have followed *Monell*;[4] one that is the principal focus of our decision again today.

A

Based on the difficulty that this Court has had defining the contours of municipal liability in these circumstances, petitioner urges us to adopt the rule that a municipality can be found liable under § 1983 only where "the policy in question [is] itself unconstitutional." Brief for Petitioner 15. Whether such a rule is a valid construction of § 1983 is a question the Court has left unresolved. See, *e.g., St. Louis v. Praprotnik, supra,* at 147 (BRENNAN, J., concurring in judgment); *Oklahoma City v. Tuttle, supra,* at 824, n. 7. Under such an approach, the outcome here would be rather clear: we would have to reverse and remand the case with instructions that judgment be entered for petitioner.[5] There can be little doubt that on its face the city's policy regarding medical treatment for detainees is constitutional. The policy states that the city jailer "shall . . . have [a person needing medical care] taken to a hospital for medical treatment, with [489 U.S. 378, 387] permission of his supervisor . . . ." App. 33. It is difficult to see what constitutional guarantees are violated by such a policy.

Nor, without more, would a city automatically be liable under § 1983 if one of its employees happened to apply the policy in an unconstitutional manner, for liability would then rest on *respondeat superior.* The claim in this case, however, is that if a concededly valid policy is unconstitutionally applied by a municipal employee, the city is liable if the employee has not been adequately trained and the constitutional wrong has been caused by that failure to train. For reasons explained below, we conclude, as have all the Courts of Appeals that have addressed this issue,[6] that there are limited circumstances in which an allegation of a "failure to train" can be the basis for liability under § 1983. Thus, we reject petitioner's contention that only unconstitutional policies are actionable under the statute. [489 U.S. 378, 388]

B

Though we agree with the court below that a city can be liable under § 1983 for inadequate training of its employees, we cannot agree that the District Court's jury instructions on this issue were proper, for we conclude that the Court of Appeals provided an overly broad rule for when a municipality can be held liable under the "failure to train" theory. Unlike the question whether a municipality's failure to train employees can ever be a basis for § 1983 liability—on which the Courts of Appeals have all agreed, see n. 6, *supra*—there is substantial division among the lower courts as to what *degree of fault* must be evidenced by the municipality's inaction before liability will be permitted.[7] We hold today that the inadequacy of police training may serve as the basis for § 1983 liability only where the failure to train amounts to deliberate indifference to the rights of persons with whom the police come into contact.[8] This rule is most consistent with our admonition [489 U.S. 378, 389] in *Monell,* 436 U.S., at 694, and *Polk County v. Dodson,* 454 U.S. 312, 326 (1981), that a municipality can be liable under § 1983 only where its policies are the "moving force [behind] the constitutional violation." Only where a municipality's failure to train its employees in a relevant respect evidences a "deliberate indifference" to the rights of its inhabitants can such a shortcoming be properly thought of as a city

"policy or custom" that is actionable under § 1983. As JUSTICE BREN-
NAN's opinion in *Pembaur v. Cincinnati*, 475 U.S. 469, 483-484 (1986)
(plurality) put it: "[M]unicipal liability under § 1983 attaches where—
and only where—a deliberate choice to follow a course of action is
made from among various alternatives" by city policymakers. See also
Oklahoma City v. Tuttle, 471 U.S., at 823 (opinion of REHNQUIST, J.).
Only where a failure to train reflects a "deliberate" or "conscious"
choice by a municipality—a "policy" as defined by our prior cases—can
a city be liable for such a failure under § 1983.

    Monell's rule that a city is not liable under § 1983 unless a munic-
ipal policy causes a constitutional deprivation will not be satisfied by
merely alleging that the existing training program for a class of
employees, such as police officers, represents a policy for which the
city is responsible.[9] That much [489 U.S. 378, 390] may be true. The
issue in a case like this one, however, is whether that training program
is adequate; and if it is not, the question becomes whether such inadequate training can justifiably be said to represent "city policy." It may
seem contrary to common sense to assert that a municipality will actually have a policy of not taking reasonable steps to train its employees.
But it may happen that in light of the duties assigned to specific officers or employees the need for more or different training is so obvious,
and the inadequacy so likely to result in the violation of constitutional
rights, that the policymakers of the city can reasonably be said to have
been deliberately indifferent to the need.[10] In that event, the failure to
provide proper training may fairly be said to represent a policy for
which the city is responsible, and for which the city may be held liable
if it actually causes injury.[11]

    In resolving the issue of a city's liability, the focus must be on ade-
quacy of the training program in relation to the tasks the particular
officers must perform. That a particular officer may be unsatisfactorily
trained will not alone suffice to fasten liability on the city, for the
officer's shortcomings may [489 U.S. 378, 391] have resulted from factors other than a faulty training program. See *Springfield v. Kibbe*, 480
U.S., at 268 (O'CONNOR, J., dissenting); *Oklahoma City v. Tuttle, supra*,
at 821 (opinion of REHNQUIST, J.). It may be, for example, that an otherwise sound program has occasionally been negligently administered.
Neither will it suffice to prove that an injury or accident could have
been avoided if an officer had had better or more training, sufficient to
equip him to avoid the particular injury-causing conduct. Such a claim
could be made about almost any encounter resulting in injury, yet not
condemn the adequacy of the program to enable officers to respond
properly to the usual and recurring situations with which they must
deal. And plainly, adequately trained officers occasionally make mistakes; the fact that they do says little about the training program or the
legal basis for holding the city liable.

Moreover, for liability to attach in this circumstance the identified deficiency in a city's training program must be closely related to the ultimate injury. Thus in the case at hand, respondent must still prove that the deficiency in training actually caused the police officers' indifference to her medical needs.[12] Would the injury have been avoided had the employee been trained under a program that was not deficient in the identified respect? Predicting how a hypothetically well-trained officer would have acted under the circumstances may not be an easy task for the fact finder, particularly since matters of judgment may be involved, and since officers who are well trained are not free from error and perhaps might react very much like the untrained officer in similar circumstances. But judge and jury, doing their respective jobs, will be adequate to the task.

To adopt lesser standards of fault and causation would open municipalities to unprecedented liability under § 1983. [489 U.S. 378, 392] In virtually every instance where a person has had his or her constitutional rights violated by a city employee, a § 1983 plaintiff will be able to point to something the city "could have done" to prevent the unfortunate incident. See *Oklahoma City v. Tuttle*, 471 U.S., at 823 (opinion of REHNQUIST, J.). Thus, permitting cases against cities for their "failure to train" employees to go forward under § 1983 on a lesser standard of fault would result in *de facto respondeat superior* liability on municipalities—a result we rejected in *Monell*, 436 U.S., at 693-694. It would also engage the federal courts in an endless exercise of second-guessing municipal employee-training programs. This is an exercise we believe the federal courts are ill suited to undertake, as well as one that would implicate serious questions of federalism. Cf. *Rizzo v. Goode*, 423 U.S. 362, 378-380 (1976).

Consequently, while claims such as respondent's—alleging that the city's failure to provide training to municipal employees resulted in the constitutional deprivation she suffered—are cognizable under § 1983, they can only yield liability against a municipality where that city's failure to train reflects deliberate indifference to the constitutional rights of its inhabitants.

IV

The final question here is whether this case should be remanded for a new trial, or whether, as petitioner suggests, we should conclude that there are no possible grounds on which respondent can prevail. See Tr. of Oral Arg. 57-58. It is true that the evidence in the record now does not meet the standard of § 1983 liability we have set forth above. But, the standard of proof the District Court ultimately imposed on respondent (which was consistent with Sixth Circuit precedent) was a lesser one than the one we adopt today, see Tr. 4-389 - 4-390. Whether respondent should have an opportunity to prove her case under the "deliberate indifference" rule we have adopted is a matter for the Court of Appeals to deal with on remand. [489 U.S. 378, 393]

V

Consequently, for the reasons given above, we vacate the judgment of the Court of Appeals and remand this case for further proceedings consistent with this opinion.

It is so ordered.

Footnotes

[1] Title 42 U.S.C. § 1983 provides, in relevant part, that:

"Every person who, under color of any statute, ordinance, regulation, custom, or usage . . . subjects, or causes to be subjected, any citizen of the United States or other person within the jurisdiction thereof to the deprivation of any rights, privileges, or immunities secured by the Constitution and laws, shall be liable to the party injured in an action at law, suit in equity, or other proper proceeding for redress. . . ."

[2] The city regulation in question provides that a police officer assigned to act as "jailer" at the city police station

"shall, when a prisoner is found to be unconscious or semi-unconscious, or when he or she is unable to explain his or her condition, or who complains of being ill, have such person taken to a hospital for medical treatment, with permission of his supervisor before admitting the person to City Jail." App. 33.

[3] In upholding Mrs. Harris' "failure to train" claim, the Sixth Circuit relied on two of its previous decisions which had approved such a theory of municipal liability under § 1983. See *Rymer v. Davis*, 754 F.2d 198, vacated and remanded sub nom. *Shepherdsville v. Rhymer*, 473 U.S. 901, reinstated, 775 F.2d 756, 757 (1985); *Hays v. Jefferson County*, 668 F.2d 869, 874 (1982).

[4] See, *e.g.*, *St. Louis v. Praprotnik*, 485 U.S. 112 (1988); *Springfield v. Kibbe*, 480 U.S. 257 (1987); *Los Angeles v. Heller*, 475 U.S. 796 (1986); *Oklahoma City v. Tuttle*, 471 U.S. 808 (1985).

[5] In this Court, in addition to suggesting that the city's failure to train its officers amounted to a "policy" that resulted in the denial of medical care to detainees, respondent also contended the city had a "custom" of denying medical care to those detainees suffering from emotional or mental ailments. See Brief for Respondent 31-32; Tr. of Oral Arg. 38-39. As respondent described it in her brief, and at argument, this claim of an unconstitutional "custom" appears to be little more than a restatement of her "failure-to-train as policy" claim. See *ibid.* However, to the extent that this claim poses a distinct basis for the city's liability under § 1983, we decline to determine whether respondent's contention that such a "custom" existed is an alternative ground for affirmance. The "custom" claim was not passed on by the Court of Appeals—nor does it appear to have been presented to that court as a distinct ground for its decision. See Brief of Appellee in No. 85-3314 (CA6), pp. 4-9, 11. Thus, we will not consider it here.

[6] In addition to the Sixth Circuit decisions discussed in n. 3, *supra*, most of the other Courts of Appeals have held that a failure to train can create liability under § 1983. See, *e.g.*, *Spell v. McDaniel*, 824 F.2d 1380, 1389-1391 (CA4 1987); *Haynesworth v. Miller*, 261 U.S. App. D.C. 66, 80-83, 820 F.2d 1245, 1259-1262 (1987); *Warren v. Lincoln*, 816 F.2d 1254, 1262-1263 (CA8 1987); *Bergquist v. County of*

Cochise, 806 F.2d 1364, 1369-1370 (CA9 1986); *Wierstak v. Heffernan*, 789 F.2d 968, 974 (CA1 1986); *Fiacco v. Rensselaer*, 783 F.2d 319, 326-327 (CA2 1986); *Gilmere v. Atlanta*, 774 F.2d 1495, 1503-1504 (CA11 1985) (*en banc*); *Rock v. McCoy*, 763 F.2d 394, 397-398 (CA10 1985); *Languirand v. Hayden*, 717 F.2d 220, 227-228 (CA5 1983). Two other Courts of Appeals have stopped short of expressly embracing this rule, and have instead only implicitly endorsed it. See, *e.g.*, *Colburn v. Upper Darby Township*, 838 F.2d 663, 672-673 (CA3 1988); *Lenard v. Argento*, 699 F.2d 874, 885-887 (CA7 1983).

In addition, six current Members of this Court have joined opinions in the past that have (at least implicitly) endorsed this theory of liability under § 1983. See *Oklahoma City v. Tuttle, supra*, at 829-831 (BRENNAN, J., joined by MARSHALL and BLACKMUN, JJ., concurring in part and concurring in judgment); *Springfield v. Kibbe, supra*, at 268-270 (O'CONNOR, J., joined by REHNQUIST, C. J., and Powell and WHITE, JJ., dissenting).

[7] Some courts have held that a showing of "gross negligence" in a city's failure to train its employees is adequate to make out a claim under § 1983. See, *e.g.*, *Bergquist v. County of Cochise, supra*, at 1370; *Herrera v. Valentine*, 653 F.2d 1220, 1224 (CA8 1981). But the more common rule is that a city must exhibit "deliberate indifference" towards the constitutional rights of persons in its domain before a § 1983 action for "failure to train" is permissible. See, *e.g.*, *Fiacco v. Rensselaer, supra*, at 326; *Patzner v. Burkett*, 779 F.2d 1363, 1367 (CA8 1985); *Wellington v. Daniels*, 717 F.2d 932, 936 (CA4 1983); *Languirand v. Hayden, supra*, at 227.

[8] The "deliberate indifference" standard we adopt for § 1983 "failure to train" claims does not turn upon the degree of fault (if any) that a plaintiff must show to make out an underlying claim of a constitutional violation. For example, this Court has never determined what degree of culpability must be shown before the particular constitutional deprivation asserted in this case - a denial of the due process right to medical care while in detention - is established. Indeed, in *Revere v. Massachusetts General Hospital*, 463 U.S. 239, 243 -245 (1983), we reserved decision on the question whether something less than the Eighth Amendment's "deliberate indifference" test may be applicable in claims by detainees asserting violations of their due process right to medical care while in custody.

We need not resolve here the question left open in Revere for two reasons. First, petitioner has conceded that, as the case comes to us, we [489 U.S. 378, 389] must assume that respondent's constitutional right to receive medical care was denied by city employees—whatever the nature of that right might be. See Tr. of Oral Arg. 8-9. Second, the proper standard for determining when a municipality will be liable under § 1983 for constitutional wrongs does not turn on any underlying culpability test that determines when such wrongs have occurred. Cf. Brief for Respondent 27.

[9] The plurality opinion in *Tuttle* explained why this must be so:

> "Obviously, if one retreats far enough from a constitutional violation some municipal 'policy' can be identified behind almost any . . . harm inflicted by a municipal official; for example, [a police officer] would never have killed Tuttle if Oklahoma City did not have a 'policy' of establishing a police force. But *Monell* must be taken to require proof of a city policy different in kind from this latter example before a claim can be sent to a jury on the theory [489 U.S. 378, 390] that a particular violation was 'caused' by the municipal 'policy.'" 471 U.S., at 823. Cf. also *id.*, at 833, n. 9 (opinion of BRENNAN, J.).

[10] For example, city policymakers know to a moral certainty that their police officers will be required to arrest fleeing felons. The city has armed its officers with firearms, in part to allow them to accomplish this task. Thus, the need to train officers

in the constitutional limitations on the use of deadly force, see *Tennessee v. Garner*, 471 U.S. 1 (1985), can be said to be "so obvious," that failure to do so could properly be characterized as "deliberate indifference" to constitutional rights.

It could also be that the police, in exercising their discretion, so often violate constitutional rights that the need for further training must have been plainly obvious to the city policymakers, who, nevertheless, are "deliberately indifferent" to the need.

[11] The record indicates that city did train its officers and that its training included first-aid instruction. See App. to Pet. for Cert. 4a. Petitioner argues that it could not have been obvious to the city that such training was insufficient to administer the written policy, which was itself constitutional. This is a question to be resolved on remand. See Part IV, *infra*.

[12] Respondent conceded as much at argument. See Tr. of Oral Arg. 50-51; cf. also *Oklahoma City v. Tuttle, supra*, at 831 (opinion of BRENNAN, J.).

Collins v. City of Harker Heights, Texas
503 U.S. 115 (1992)

Argued November 5, 1991
Decided February 26, 1992
JUSTICE STEVENS delivered the opinion of the Court.

The question presented is whether § 1 of the Civil Rights Act of 1871, 42 U.S.C. § 1983, provides a remedy for a municipal employee who is fatally injured in the course of his employment because the city customarily failed to train or warn its employees about known hazards in the workplace. Even though the city's conduct may be actionable under state law, we hold that § 1983 does not apply, because such conduct does not violate the Due Process Clause.

On October 21, 1988, Larry Michael Collins, an employee in the sanitation department of the city of Harker Heights, Texas, died of asphyxia after entering a manhole to unstop a sewer line. Petitioner, his widow, brought this action alleging that Collins "had a constitutional right to be free from unreasonable risks of harm to his body, mind and emotions and a constitutional right to be protected from the city of Harker Heights' custom and policy of deliberate indifference toward the safety of its employees." App. 7. Her complaint alleged that the city violated that right by following a custom and policy of not training its employees about the dangers of working in sewer lines and manholes, not providing safety equipment at job sites, and not providing safety warnings. The complaint also alleged that a prior incident [503 U.S. 115, 118] had given the city notice of the risks of entering the sewer lines,[1] and that the city had systematically and intentionally failed to provide the equipment and training required by a Texas statute. *Ibid.* The District Court dismissed the complaint on the ground that a constitutional violation had not been alleged. No. W-89-CA-168 (W.D.Tex., Oct. 30, 1988), App. 20. The Court of Appeals for the Fifth Circuit affirmed on a different theory. 916 F.2d 284 (CA5 1990). It did not reach the question whether the city had violated Collins' constitutional rights, because it denied recovery on the ground that there had been no "abuse of governmental power," which the Fifth Circuit had found to be a necessary element of a § 1983 action.[2] *Id.*, at 287-288, and n. 3. [503 U.S. 115, 119]

The contrary decision in *Ruge v. City of Bellevue*, 892 F.2d 738 (CA8 1989), together with our concern about the Court of Appeals' interpretation of the statute, prompted our grant of certiorari, 499 U.S. 958 (1991).

I

Our cases do not support the Court of Appeals' reading of § 1983 as requiring proof of an abuse of governmental power separate and apart from the proof of a constitutional violation. Although the statute provides the citizen with an effective remedy against those abuses of state power that violate federal law, it does not provide a remedy for abuses that do not violate federal law, see, *e.g.*, *Martinez v. California*, 444 U.S. 277 (1980); *DeShaney v. Winnebago County Department of Social Services*, 489 U.S. 189 (1989). More importantly, the statute does not draw any distinction between abusive and nonabusive federal violations.

The Court of Appeals' analysis rests largely on the fact that the city had, through allegedly tortious conduct, harmed one of its employees, rather than an ordinary citizen over whom it exercised governmental power. The employment relationship, however, is not of controlling significance. On the one hand, if the city had pursued a policy of equally deliberate indifference to the safety of pedestrians that resulted in a fatal injury to one who inadvertently stepped into an open manhole, the Court of Appeals' holding would not speak to this situation at all, although it would seem that a claim by such a pedestrian should be analyzed in a similar manner as the claim by this petitioner. On the other hand, a logical application of the holding might also bar potentially meritorious claims by employees if, for example, the city had given an employee a particularly dangerous assignment in retaliation for a political speech, cf. *St. Louis v. Praprotnik*, 485 U.S. 112 (1988), or because of his or her gender, cf. *Monell v. New York City Dept. of Social Services*, 436 U.S. 658 (1978). The First Amendment, the Equal Protection and [503 U.S. 115, 120] Due Process Clauses of the Fourteenth Amendment, and other provisions of the Federal Constitution afford protection to employees who serve the government as well as to those who are served by them, and § 1983 provides a cause of action for all citizens injured by an abridgement of those protections. Neither the fact that petitioner's decedent was a government employee nor the characterization of the city's deliberate indifference to his safety as something other than an "abuse of governmental power" is a sufficient reason for refusing to entertain petitioner's federal claim under § 1983.

Nevertheless, proper analysis requires us to separate two different issues when a § 1983 claim is asserted against a municipality: (1) whether plaintiff's harm was caused by a constitutional violation, and (2) if so, whether the city is responsible for that violation. See *Oklahoma City v. Tuttle*, 471 U.S. 808, 817 (1985) (opinion of REHNQUIST, J.); *id.*, at 828-829 (opinion of Brennan, J., concurring in part and concurring in judgment). Because most of our opinions discussing municipal policy have involved the latter issue, it is appropriate to discuss it before considering the question whether petitioner's complaint has alleged a constitutional violation.

II

Section 1983 provides a remedy against "any person" who, under color of state law, deprives another of rights protected by the Constitution.[3] In *Monell*, the Court held that Congress intended municipalities and other local government entities to be included among those persons to whom § 1983 applies. 436 U.S., at 690. At the same time, the Court [503 U.S. 115, 121] made it clear that municipalities may not be held liable "unless action pursuant to official municipal policy of some nature caused a constitutional tort." *Id.*, at 691.[4] The Court emphasized that

> "a municipality cannot be held liable solely because it employs a tortfeasor—or, in other words, a municipality cannot be held liable under § 1983 on a *respondeat superior* theory."

> .   .   .   .   .

> "[T]herefore, . . . a local government may not be sued under § 1983 for an injury inflicted *solely* by its employees or agents. Instead, it is when execution of a government's policy or custom, whether made by its lawmakers or by those whose edicts or acts may fairly be said to represent official policy, inflicts the injury that the government as an entity is responsible under § 1983." *Id.*, at 691 (emphasis in original).

In a series of later cases, the Court has considered whether an alleged injury caused by municipal employees acting under color of state law provided a proper basis for imposing liability on a city. In each of those cases, the Court assumed that a constitutional violation had been adequately alleged or proved, and focused its attention on the separate issue of municipal liability. Thus, for example, in *Oklahoma City v. Tuttle, supra*, it was assumed that the police officer had violated the decedent's constitutional rights, but we held that the wrongful conduct of a single officer without any policymaking authority did not establish municipal policy. And in *St. Louis v. Praprotnik*, 485 U.S. 112 (1988), without reaching [503 U.S. 115, 122] the question whether the adverse employment action taken against the plaintiff violated his First Amendment rights, the Court concluded that decisions by subordinate employees did not necessarily reflect official policy. On the other hand, in *Pembaur v. Cincinnati*, 475 U.S. 469 (1986), the Court held that the County was responsible for unconstitutional actions taken pursuant to decisions made by the County Prosecutor and the County Sheriff because they were the "officials responsible for establishing final policy with respect to the subject matter in question," *id.*, at 483-484.

Our purpose in citing these cases is to emphasize the separate character of the inquiry into the question of municipal responsibility and the question whether a constitutional violation occurred. It was necessary to analyze whether execution of a municipal policy inflicted the injury in these cases because, unlike ordinary tort litigation, the doctrine of *respondeat superior* was inapplicable. The city is not vicariously liable under § 1983 for the constitutional torts of its agents: it is only liable when it can be fairly said that the city itself is the wrongdoer. Because petitioner in this case relies so heavily on our reasoning in *Canton v. Harris*, 489 U.S. 378 (1989)—and in doing so, seems to assume that the case dealt with the constitutional issue—it is appropriate to comment specifically on that case.

In *Canton*, we held that a municipality can, in some circumstances, be held liable under § 1983 "for constitutional violations resulting from its failure to train municipal employees." *Id.*, at 380. Among the claims advanced by the plaintiff in that case was a violation of the "right, under the Due Process Clause of the Fourteenth Amendment, to receive necessary medical attention while in police custody." *Id.*, at 381.[5] Because we assumed arguendo that the plaintiff's [503 U.S. 115, 123] constitutional right to receive medical care had been denied, *id.*, at 388-389, n. 8, our opinion addressed only the question whether the constitutional deprivation was attributable to a municipal policy or custom.

We began our analysis by plainly indicating that we were not deciding the constitutional issue.

> "In *Monell v. New York City Dept. of Social Services*, 436 U.S. 658 (1978), we decided that a municipality can be found liable under § 1983 only where the municipality *itself* causes the constitutional violation at issue. *Respondeat superior* or vicarious liability will not attach under § 1983. *Id.* at 694-695. 'It is only when the "execution of the government's policy or custom . . . inflicts the injury" that the municipality may be held liable under § 1983.' *Springfield v. Kibbe*, 480 U.S. 257, 267 (1987) (O'CONNOR, J., dissenting) (quoting *Monell, supra*, [436 U.S.] at 694).

> "Thus, our first inquiry in any case alleging municipal liability under § 1983 is the question whether there is a direct causal link between a municipal policy or custom and the alleged constitutional deprivation." *Id.* at 385.

We did not suggest that all harm-causing municipal policies are actionable under § 1983 or that all such policies are unconstitutional. Moreover, we rejected the city's argument that only unconstitutional policies can create municipal liability under the statute. *Id.* at 387. Instead, we concluded that, if a city employee violates another's constitutional rights, the city may be liable if it had a policy or custom of failing to train its employees, and that failure to train caused the constitutional violation. In particular, we held that the inadequate training of police officers could be characterized as the cause of the constitutional tort if—and only if—the [503 U.S. 115, 124] failure to train amounted to "deliberate indifference" to the rights of persons with whom the police come into contact. *Id.*, at 388.[6]

Although the term "deliberate indifference" has been used in other contexts to define the threshold for finding a violation of the Eighth Amendment, see *Estelle v. Gamble*, 429 U.S. 97, 104 (1976), as we have explained, that term was used in the *Canton* case for the quite different purpose of identifying the threshold for holding a city responsible for the constitutional torts committed by its inadequately trained agents.[7] In this case, petitioner has used that term to characterize the city's failure to train the employees in its sanitation department. We assume for the purpose of decision that the allegations in the complaint are sufficient to provide a substitute for the doctrine of *respondeat superior* as a basis for imposing liability on the city for the tortious conduct of its agents, but that assumption does not confront the question whether the complaint has alleged a constitutional violation. To that question we now turn. [503 U.S. 115, 125]

III

Petitioner's constitutional claim rests entirely on the Due Process Clause of the Fourteenth Amendment.[8] The most familiar office of that Clause is to provide a guarantee of fair procedure in connection with any deprivation of life, liberty, or property by a State. Petitioner, however, does not advance a procedural due process claim in this case. Instead, she relies on the substantive component of the Clause that protects individual liberty against "certain government actions regardless of the fairness of the procedures used to implement them." *Daniels v. Williams*, 474 U.S. 327, 331 (1986).

As a general matter, the Court has always been reluctant to expand the concept of substantive due process, because guideposts for responsible decision making in this unchartered area are scarce and open-ended. *Regents of University of Michigan v. Ewing*, 474 U.S. 214,

225-226 (1985). The doctrine of judicial self-restraint requires us to exercise the utmost care whenever we are asked to break new ground in this field. It is important, therefore, to focus on the allegations in the complaint to determine how petitioner describes the constitutional right at stake and what the city allegedly did to deprive her husband of that right.

A fair reading of petitioner's complaint does not charge the city with a willful violation of Collins' rights. Petitioner does not claim that the city or any of its agents deliberately harmed her husband. In fact, she does not even allege that his supervisor instructed him to go into the sewer when the supervisor knew or should have known that there was a significant risk that he would be injured. Instead, she makes the more general allegation that the city deprived him of [503 U.S. 115, 126] life and liberty by failing to provide a reasonably safe work environment.[9] Fairly analyzed, her claim advances two theories: that the Federal Constitution imposes a duty on the city to provide its employees with minimal levels of safety and security in the workplace, or that the city's "deliberate indifference" to Collins' safety was arbitrary government action that must "shock the conscience" of federal judges. Cf. *Rochin v. California*, 342 U.S. 165, 172 (1952).

Neither the text nor the history of the Due Process Clause supports petitioner's claim that the governmental employer's duty to provide its employees with a safe working environment is a substantive component of the Due Process Clause. "[T]he Due Process Clause of the Fourteenth Amendment was intended to prevent government "'from abusing [its] power, or employing it as an instrument of oppression.'" *DeShaney v. Winnebago County Department of Social Services*, 489 U.S., at 196 (quoting *Davidson v. Cannon*, 474 U.S. 344, 348 (1986)). As we recognized in *DeShaney*,

> "The Clause is phrased as a limitation on the State's power to act, not as a guarantee of certain minimal levels of safety and security. It forbids the State itself to deprive individuals of life, liberty, or property without "due process of law," but its language cannot fairly be extended to impose an affirmative obligation on the State to ensure that those interests do not come to harm through other means. Nor does history support such [503 U.S. 115, 127] an expansive reading of the constitutional text. 489 U.S., at 195.[10]

Petitioner's submission that the city violated a federal constitutional obligation to provide its employees with certain minimal levels of safety and security is unprecedented. It is quite different from the constitutional claim advanced by plaintiffs in several of our prior cases who argued that the State owes a duty to take care of those who have already been deprived of their liberty. We have held, for example, that, apart from the protection against cruel and unusual punishment provided by the Eighth Amendment, cf. *Hutto v. Finney*, 437 U.S. 678

(1978), the Due Process Clause of its own force requires that conditions of confinement satisfy certain minimal standards for pretrial detainees, see *Bell v. Wolfish*, 441 U.S. 520, 535, n. 16, 545 (1979), for persons in mental institutions, *Youngberg v. Romeo*, 457 U.S. 307, 315-316 (1982), for convicted felons, *Turner v. Safley*, 482 U.S. 78, 94-99 (1987), and for persons under arrest, see *Revere v. Massachusetts General Hospital*, 463 U.S. 239, 244-245 (1983). The "process" that the Constitution guarantees in [503 U.S. 115, 128] connection with any deprivation of liberty thus includes a continuing obligation to satisfy certain minimal custodial standards. See *DeShaney*, 489 U.S., at 200. Petitioner cannot maintain, however, that the city deprived Collins of his liberty when it made, and he voluntarily accepted, an offer of employment.

We also are not persuaded that the city's alleged failure to train its employees, or to warn them about known risks of harm, was an omission that can properly be characterized as arbitrary, or conscience-shocking, in a constitutional sense. Petitioner's claim is analogous to a fairly typical state law tort claim: the city breached its duty of care to her husband by failing to provide a safe work environment. Because the Due Process Clause "does not purport to supplant traditional tort law in laying down rules of conduct to regulate liability for injuries that attend living together in society," *Daniels v. Williams*, 474 U.S., at 332, we have previously rejected claims that the Due Process Clause should be interpreted to impose federal duties that are analogous to those traditionally imposed by state tort law, see, *e.g., id.*, at 332-333; *Baker v. McCollan*, 443 U.S. 137, 146 (1979); *Paul v. Davis*, 424 U.S. 693, 701 (1976). The reasoning in those cases applies with special force to claims asserted against public employers, because state law, rather than the Federal Constitution, generally governs the substance of the employment relationship. See, *e.g., Bishop v. Wood*, 426 U.S. 341, 350 (1976); *Board of Regents of State Colleges v. Roth*, 408 U.S. 564, 577-578 (1972).

Our refusal to characterize the city's alleged omission in this case as arbitrary in a constitutional sense rests on the presumption that the administration of Government programs is based on a rational decision making process that takes account of competing social, political, and economic forces. Cf. *Walker v. Rowe*, 791 F.2d 507, 510 (CA7 1986). Decisions concerning the allocation of resources to individual programs, such as sewer maintenance, and to particular aspects [503 U.S. 115, 129] of those programs, such as the training and compensation of employees, involve a host of policy choices that must be made by locally elected representatives, rather than by federal judges interpreting the basic charter of Government for the entire country. The Due Process Clause "is not a guarantee against incorrect or ill-advised personnel decisions." *Bishop v. Wood*, 426 U.S., at 350. Nor does it guarantee municipal employees a workplace that is free of unreasonable risks of harm.

Finally, we reject petitioner's suggestion that the Texas Hazard Communication Act[11] supports her substantive due process claim. We assume that the Act imposed a duty on the city to warn its sanitation employees about the dangers of noxious gases in the sewers and to provide safety training and protective equipment to minimize those dangers.[12] We also assume, as petitioner argues, that the Act created an entitlement that qualifies as a "liberty interest" protected by the Due Process Clause. But even with these assumptions, petitioner's claim must fail, for she has not alleged that the deprivation of this liberty interest was arbitrary in the constitutional sense. Cf. *Harrah Independent School Dist. v.* [503 U.S. 115, 130] *Martin,* 440 U.S. 194, 198-199 (1979). The reasons why the city's alleged failure to train and warn did not constitute a constitutionally arbitrary deprivation of Collins' life, see *supra,* at 128-129, apply a fortiori to the less significant liberty interest created by the Texas statute.

In sum, we conclude that the Due Process Clause does not impose an independent federal obligation upon municipalities to provide certain minimal levels of safety and security in the workplace and the city's alleged failure to train or to warn its sanitation department employees was not arbitrary in a constitutional sense. The judgment of the Court of Appeals is therefore affirmed.

It is so ordered.

Footnotes

[1] In particular, the complaint alleged that, ""[p]rior to October, 1988, the City of Harker Heights was on notice of the dangers to which the employees were exposed because Larry Michael Collins' supervisor had been rendered unconscious in a manhole several months prior to October, 1988, in fact, several months before Larry Michael Collins began work at the City of Harker Heights." App. 7.

[2] The Court of Appeals explained:

"The question presented in this case is whether a plaintiff seeking recovery under § 1983 for injury to a governmental employee must demonstrate, inter alia, that the conduct in issue was an abuse of *governmental* power. More particularly, does alleged wrongful conduct by government—in its capacity as employer rather than as a governing authority—that deprives its employee of an alleged constitutional right give rise to a § 1983 action? We base our holding on the abuse of government power standard, separate from the constitutional deprivation element or standard. The district court appears to have merged those two standards, which are among those necessary for bringing § 1983 into play here. In reviewing this Rule 12(b)(6) dismissal, we will keep them separate.

.   .   .   .   .

"In this Circuit, there is a separate standard that must also be satisfied—an abuse of government power. While this element is in many ways similar to, and often blends with, other necessary elements for a § 1983 action, such as deprivation of a constitutional right, and springs from the same sources as the deprivation element, it is separate none-theless." 916 F.2d, at 286-287.

[3] The section states, in relevant part:

"Every person who, under color of any statute, ordinance, regulation, custom, or usage, of any State . . . subjects, or causes to be subjected, any citizen of the United States . . . to the deprivation of any rights, priv-ileges, or immunities secured by the Constitution and laws, shall be lia-ble to the party injured in an action at law, suit in equity, or other proper proceeding for redress. . . ." 42 U.S.C. § 1983.

[4] Petitioners in *Monell*, a class of female employees of the New York City Depart-ment of Social Services and Board of Education, alleged that the Board and Depart-ment violated their due process rights by implementing an official policy that compelled pregnant employees to take unpaid leaves of absences before such leaves were required for medical reasons. 436 U.S., at 660 -661.

[5] "At the close of the evidence, the District Court submitted the case to the jury, which rejected all of Mrs. Harris' claims except one: her § 1983 claim against the city resulting *from its failure to provide her with medical* [503 U.S. 115, 123] *treat-ment while in custody*." *Canton v. Harris*, 489 U.S., at 382 (emphasis added).

[6] We added:

"Only where a municipality's failure to train its employees in a relevant respect evidences a 'deliberate indifference' to the rights of its inhabit-ants can such a shortcoming be properly thought of as a city 'policy or custom' that is actionable under § 1983.

.   .   .   .

"Consequently, while claims such as respondent's—alleging that the city's failure to provide training to municipal employees resulted in the constitutional deprivation she suffered—are cognizable under § 1983, they can only yield liability against a municipality where that city's fail-ure to train reflects deliberate indifference to the constitutional rights of its inhabitants." *Id.*, at 389, 392.

[7] Indeed, we expressly stated: "The 'deliberate indifference' standard we adopt for § 1983 'failure to train' claims does not turn upon the degree of fault (if any) that a plaintiff must show to make out an underlying claim of a constitutional viola-tion." *Id.*, at 388, n. 8.

[8] The Due Process Clause of the Fourteenth Amendment states: "nor shall any State deprive any person of life, liberty, or property, without due process of law."

[9] Petitioner alleges that her husband had "a constitutional right to be free from unreasonable risks of harm to his body, mind and emotions and a constitutional right to be protected from the City of Harker Heights' custom and policy of delib-erate indifference toward the safety of its employees." App. 7. The city's policy and custom of not training its employees and not warning them of the danger allegedly caused Collins' death, and thus deprived him of those rights. *Id.*, at 8.

[10] "Historically, this guarantee of due process has been applied to *deliberate* deci-sions of government officials to deprive a person of life, liberty, or property. *E.g.*, *Davidson v. New Orleans*, 96 U.S. 97 (1878) (assessment of real estate); *Rochin v. California*, 342 U.S. 165 (1952) (stomach pumping); *Bell v. Burson*, 402 U.S. 535 (1971) (suspension of driver's license); *Ingraham v. Wright*, 430 U.S. 651 (1977) (paddling student); *Hudson v. Palmer*, 468 U.S. 517 (1984) (intentional destruction of inmate's property). No decision of this Court before *Parratt v. Taylor*, 451 U.S. 527 (1981), supported the view that negligent conduct by a state official, even

though causing injury, constitutes a deprivation under the Due Process Clause. This history reflects the traditional and common-sense notion that the Due Process Clause, like its forebear in the Magna Carta, see Corwin, The Doctrine of Due Process of Law Before the Civil War, 24Harv L Rev 366, 368 (1911), was "intended to secure the individual from the arbitrary exercise of the powers of government," Hurtado v. California, 110 U.S. 516, 527 (1884). *Daniels v. Williams*, 474 U.S. 327, 331 (1986).

[11] Tex.Rev.Civ.Stat.Ann., Art. 5182b (Vernon 1987).

[12] Section 10(a) of the Act states, for example:

"Every employer shall provide, at least annually, an education and training program for employees using or handling hazardous chemicals. . . . Additional instruction shall be provided when the potential for exposure to hazardous chemicals is altered or when new and significant information is received by the employer concerning the hazards of a chemical. New or newly assigned employees shall be provided training before working with or in a work area containing hazardous chemicals."

And § 15(a) states:

"Employees who may be exposed to hazardous chemicals shall be informed of the exposure and shall have access to the workplace chemical list and [material safety data sheets] for the hazardous chemicals. . . . In addition, employees shall receive training on the hazards of the chemicals and on measures they can take to protect themselves from those hazards and shall be provided with appropriate personal protective equipment. These rights are guaranteed on the effective date of this Act." [503 U.S. 115, 131]

Soldal v.
Cook County, Illinois
506 U.S. 56 (1992)

Argued October 5, 1992
Decided December 8, 1992
JUSTICE WHITE delivered the opinion of the Court.

I

Edward Soldal and his family resided in their trailer home, which was located on a rented lot in the Willoway Terrace mobile [506 U.S. 56, 58] home park in Elk Grove, Illinois. In May 1987, Terrace Properties, the owner of the park, and Margaret Hale, its manager, filed an eviction proceeding against the Soldals in an Illinois state court. Under the Illinois Forcible Entry and Detainer Act, Ill.Rev.Stat., ch. 110, ¶ 9-101 *et seq.* (1991), a tenant cannot be dispossessed absent a judgment of eviction. The suit was dismissed on June 2, 1987. A few months later, in August 1987, the owner brought a second proceeding of eviction, claiming nonpayment of rent. The case was set for trial on September 22, 1987.

Rather than await judgment in their favor, Terrace Properties and Hale, contrary to Illinois law, chose to evict the Soldals forcibly two weeks prior to the scheduled hearing. On September 4, Hale notified the Cook County's Sheriff's Department that she was going to remove the trailer home from the park, and requested the presence of sheriff deputies to forestall any possible resistance. Later that day, two Terrace Properties employees arrived at the Soldals' home accompanied by Cook County Deputy Sheriff O'Neil. The employees proceeded to wrench the sewer and water connections off the side of the trailer

253

home, disconnect the phone, tear off the trailer's canopy and skirting, and hook the home to a tractor. Meanwhile, O'Neil explained to Edward Soldal that "'he was there to see that [Soldal] didn't interfere with [Willoway's] work.'" Brief for Petitioner 6.

By this time, two more deputy sheriffs had arrived at the scene, and Soldal told them that he wished to file a complaint for criminal trespass. They referred him to deputy Lieutenant Jones, who was in Hale's office. Jones asked Soldal to wait outside while he remained closeted with Hale and other Terrace Properties employees for over 20 minutes. After talking to a district attorney and making Soldal wait another half hour, Jones told Soldal that he would not accept a complaint because "'it was between the landlord and the tenant . . . [and] they were going to go ahead and continue to move [506 U.S. 56, 59] out the trailer.'" *Id.*, at 8.[1] Throughout this period, the deputy sheriffs knew that Terrace Properties did not have an eviction order and that its actions were unlawful. Eventually, and in the presence of an additional two deputy sheriffs, the Willoway workers pulled the trailer free of its moorings and towed it onto the street. Later, it was hauled to a neighboring property.

On September 9, the state judge assigned to the pending eviction proceedings ruled that the eviction had been unauthorized, and ordered Terrace Properties to return the Soldals' home to the lot. The home, however, was badly damaged.[2] The Soldals brought this action under 42 U.S.C. § 1983, alleging a violation of their rights under the Fourth and Fourteenth Amendments. They claimed that Terrace Properties and Hale had conspired with Cook County deputy sheriffs to unreasonably seize and remove the Soldals' trailer home. The District Judge granted defendants' motion for summary judgment on the grounds that the Soldals had failed to adduce any evidence to support their conspiracy theory and, therefore, the existence of state action necessary under § 1983.[3]

The Court of Appeals for the Seventh Circuit, construing the facts in petitioners' favor, accepted their contention that there was state action. However, it went on to hold that [506 U.S. 56, 60] the removal of the Soldals' trailer did not constitute a seizure for purposes of the Fourth Amendment or a deprivation of due process for purposes of the Fourteenth.

On rehearing, a majority of the Seventh Circuit, sitting en banc, reaffirmed the panel decision.[4] Acknowledging that what had occurred was a "seizure" in the literal sense of the word, the court reasoned that, because it was not made in the course of public law enforcement, and because it did not invade the Soldals' privacy, it was not a seizure as contemplated by the Fourth Amendment. 942 F.2d 1073, 1076 (1991). Interpreting prior cases of this Court, the Seventh Circuit concluded that, absent interference with privacy or liberty, a "pure deprivation of property" is not cognizable under the Fourth Amendment. *Id.*, at 1078-

1079. Rather, petitioners' property interests were protected only by the Due Process Clauses of the Fifth and Fourteenth Amendments.[5]

We granted certiorari to consider whether the seizure and removal of the Soldals' trailer home implicated their Fourth Amendment rights, 503 U.S. 918 (1992), and now reverse.[6] [506 U.S. 56, 61]

II

The Fourth Amendment, made applicable to the States by the Fourteenth, *Ker v. California*, 374 U.S. 23, 30 (1963), provides in pertinent part that the "right of the people to be secure in their persons, houses, papers, and effects, against unreasonable searches and seizures, shall not be violated. . . ."

A "seizure" of property, we have explained, occurs when "there is some meaningful interference with an individual's possessory interests in that property." *United States v. Jacobsen*, 466 U.S. 109, 113 (1984). In addition, we have emphasized that "at the very core" of the Fourth Amendment "stands the right of a man to retreat into his own home." *Silverman v. United States*, 365 U.S. 505, 511 (1961). See also *Oliver v. United States*, 466 U.S. 170, 178-179 (1984); *Wyman v. James*, 400 U.S. 309, 316 (1971); *Payton v. New York*, 445 U.S. 573, 601 (1980).

As a result of the state action in this case, the Soldals' domicile was not only seized, it literally was carried away, giving new meaning to the term "mobile home." We fail to see how being unceremoniously dispossessed of one's home in the manner alleged to have occurred here can be viewed as anything but a seizure invoking the protection of the Fourth Amendment. Whether the Amendment was in fact [506 U.S. 56, 62] violated is, of course, a different question that requires determining if the seizure was reasonable. That inquiry entails the weighing of various factors, and is not before us.

The Court of Appeals recognized that there had been a seizure, but concluded that it was a seizure only in a "technical" sense, not within the meaning of the Fourth Amendment. This conclusion followed from a narrow reading of the Amendment, which the court construed to safeguard only privacy and liberty interests, while leaving unprotected possessory interests where neither privacy nor liberty was at stake. Otherwise, the court said,

> "a constitutional provision enacted two centuries ago [would] make every repossession and eviction with police assistance actionable under—of all things—the Fourth Amendment[, which] would both trivialize the amendment and gratuitously shift a large body of routine commercial litigation from the state courts to the federal courts. That trivializing, this shift, can be prevented by recognizing the difference between possessory and privacy interests." 942 F.2d, at 1077.

Because the officers had not entered Soldal's house, rummaged through his possessions, or, in the Court of Appeals' view, interfered with his liberty in the course of the eviction, the Fourth Amendment offered no protection against the "grave deprivation" of property that had occurred. *Ibid.*

We do not agree with this interpretation of the Fourth Amendment. The Amendment protects the people from unreasonable searches and seizures of "their persons, houses, papers, and effects." This language surely cuts against the novel holding below, and our cases unmistakably hold that the Amendment protects property as well as privacy.[7] This much [506 U.S. 56, 63] was made clear in *Jacobsen, supra,* where we explained that the first Clause of the Fourth Amendment

> "protects two types of expectations, one involving "searches," the other "seizures." A "search" occurs when an expectation of privacy that society is prepared to consider reasonable is infringed. A "seizure" of property occurs where there is some meaningful interference with an individual's possessory interests in that property." 466 U.S., at 113 (footnote omitted).

See also *id.*, at 120; *Horton v. California*, 496 U.S. 128, 133 (1990); *Arizona v. Hicks*, 480 U.S. 321, 328 (1987); *Maryland v. Macon*, 472 U.S. 463, 469 (1985); *Texas v. Brown*, 460 U.S. 730, 747-748 (1983) (STEVENS, J., concurring in judgment); *United States v. Salvucci*, 448 U.S. 83, 91, n. 6 (1980). Thus, having concluded that chemical testing of powder found in a package did not compromise its owner's privacy, the Court in *Jacobsen* did not put an end to its inquiry, as would be required under the view adopted by the Court of Appeals and advocated by respondents. Instead, adhering to the teachings of *United States v. Place*, 462 U.S. 696 (1983), it went on to determine whether the invasion of the owners' "possessory interests" occasioned by the destruction of the powder was reasonable under the Fourth Amendment. *Jacobsen, supra,* at 124-125. In *Place*, although we found that subjecting luggage to a "dog sniff" did not constitute a search for Fourth Amendment purposes because it did not compromise any privacy interest, taking custody of Place's suitcase was deemed an unlawful seizure, for it unreasonably infringed "the suspect's possessory interest in his luggage." 462 U.S., at 708.[8] Although lacking a privacy component, the property rights in both instances nonetheless were not [506 U.S. 56, 64] disregarded, but rather were afforded Fourth Amendment protection.

Respondents rely principally on precedents such as *Katz v. United States*, 389 U.S. 347 (1967), *Warden, Maryland Penitentiary v. Hayden*, 387 U.S. 294 (1967), and *Cardwell v. Lewis*, 417 U.S. 583 (1974), to demonstrate that the Fourth Amendment is only marginally concerned with property rights. But the message of those cases is that property rights are not the sole measure of Fourth Amendment violations. The *Warden* opinion thus observed, citing *Jones v. United States*, 362 U.S. 257 (1960), and *Silverman v. United States*, 365 U.S. 505 (1961), that the "principal" object of the Amendment is the protection of privacy, rather than property, and that "this shift in emphasis from property to privacy has come about through a subtle interplay of substantive and procedural reform." 387 U.S., at 304. There was no suggestion that this shift in emphasis had snuffed out the previously recognized protection for property under the Fourth Amendment. *Katz*, in declaring violative of the Fourth Amendment the unwarranted overhearing of a telephone booth conversation, effectively ended any lingering notions that the protection of privacy depended on trespass into a protected area. In the course of its decision, the *Katz* Court stated that the Fourth Amendment can neither be translated into a provision dealing with constitutionally protected areas nor into a general constitutional right to privacy. The Amendment, the Court said, protects individual privacy against certain kinds of governmental intrusion, "but its protections go further, and often have nothing to do with privacy at all." 389 U.S., at 350.

As for *Cardwell*, a plurality of this Court held in that case that the Fourth Amendment did not bar the use in evidence of paint scrapings taken from and tire treads observed on the defendant's automobile, which had been seized in a parking lot and towed to a police lockup. Gathering this evidence was not deemed to be a search, for nothing from the [506 U.S. 56, 65] interior of the car and "no personal effects, which the Fourth Amendment traditionally has been deemed to protect" were searched or seized. *Cardwell*, 417 U.S., at 591 (opinion of BLACKMUN, J.). No meaningful privacy rights were invaded. But this left the argument, pressed by the dissent, that the evidence gathered was the product of a warrantless, and hence illegal, seizure of the car from the parking lot where the defendant had left it. However, the plurality was of the view that, because, under the circumstances of the case, there was probable cause to seize the car as an instrumentality of the crime, Fourth Amendment precedent permitted the seizure without a warrant. *Id.*, at 593. Thus, both the plurality and dissenting Justices considered the defendant's auto deserving of Fourth Amendment protection even though privacy interests were not at stake. They differed only in the degree of protection that the Amendment demanded.

The Court of Appeals appeared to find more specific support for confining the protection of the Fourth Amendment to privacy interests in our decision in *Hudson v. Palmer*, 468 U.S. 517 (1984). There, a state prison inmate sued, claiming that prison guards had entered his cell without consent and had seized and destroyed some of his personal effects. We ruled that an inmate, because of his status, enjoyed neither a right to privacy in his cell nor protection against unreasonable seizures of his personal effects. *Id.*, at 526-528, and n. 8; *id.*, at 538 (O'CONNOR, J., concurring). Whatever else the case held, it is of limited usefulness outside the prison context with respect to the coverage of the Fourth Amendment.

We thus are unconvinced that any of the Court's prior cases supports the view that the Fourth Amendment protects against unreasonable seizures of property only where privacy or liberty is also implicated. What is more, our "plain view" decisions make untenable such a construction of the Amendment. Suppose, for example, that police officers lawfully enter a house, by either complying with the warrant requirement or satisfying one of its recognized exceptions—[506 U.S. 56, 66] *e.g.*, through a valid consent or a showing of exigent circumstances. If they come across some item in plain view and seize it, no invasion of personal privacy has occurred. *Horton*, 496 U.S., at 133-134; *Brown, supra*, at 739 (opinion of REHNQUIST, J.). If the boundaries of the Fourth Amendment were defined exclusively by rights of privacy, "plain view" seizures would not implicate that constitutional provision at all. Yet, far from being automatically upheld, "plain view" seizures have been scrupulously subjected to Fourth Amendment inquiry. Thus, in the absence of consent or a warrant permitting the seizure of the items in question, such seizures can be justified only if they meet the probable-cause standard, *Arizona v. Hicks*, 480 U.S. 321, 326-327 (1987),[9] and if they are unaccompanied by unlawful trespass, *Horton*, 496 U.S., at 136-137.[10] That is because, the absence of a privacy interest notwithstanding, "[a] seizure of the article . . . would obviously invade the owner's possessory interest." *Id.*, at 134; see also *Brown, supra*, 460 U.S., at 739 (opinion of REHNQUIST, J.). The plain-view doctrine "merely reflects an application of the Fourth Amendment's central requirement of reasonableness to the law governing seizures of property." *Ibid.*; *Coolidge v. New Hampshire*, 403 U.S. 443, 468 (1971); *id.*, at 516 (WHITE, J., concurring and dissenting).

The Court of Appeals understandably found it necessary to reconcile its holding with our recognition in the plain-view cases that the Fourth Amendment protects property as such. In so doing, the court did not distinguish this case on the ground that the seizure of the Soldals' home took place in a [506 U.S. 56, 67] noncriminal context. Indeed, it acknowledged what is evident from our precedents—that the Amendment's protection applies in the civil context as well. See *O'Connor v. Ortega*, 480 U.S. 709 (1987); *New Jersey v. T.L.O.*, 469 U.S. 325, 334-335 (1985); *Michigan v. Tyler*, 436 U.S. 499, 504-506 (1978); *Marshall v. Barlow's, Inc.*, 436 U.S. 307, 312-313 (1978); *Camara v. Municipal Court of San Francisco*, 387 U.S. 523, 528 (1967).[11]

Nor did the Court of Appeals suggest that the Fourth Amendment applied exclusively to law enforcement activities. It observed, for example, that the Amendment's protection would be triggered "by a search or other entry into the home incident to an eviction or repossession," 942 F.2d, at 1077.[12] Instead, the court sought to explain why the Fourth Amendment protects against seizures of property in the plain-view context, but not in this case, as follows:

"[S]eizures made in the course of investigations by police or other law enforcement officers are almost always, as in the plain view cases, the culmination of searches. The police search in order to seize, and it is the search [506 U.S. 56, 68] and *ensuing seizure* that the Fourth Amendment, by its reference to "searches and seizures," seeks to regulate. Seizure means one thing when it is the outcome of a search; it may mean something else when it stands apart from a search or any other investigative activity. The Fourth Amendment may still nominally apply, but, precisely because there is no invasion of privacy, the usual rules do not apply." *Id.,* at 1079 (emphasis in original).

We have difficulty with this passage. The court seemingly construes the Amendment to protect only against seizures that are the outcome of a search. But our cases are to the contrary, and hold that seizures of property are subject to Fourth Amendment scrutiny even though no search within the meaning of the Amendment has taken place. See, *e.g., Jacobsen,* 466 U.S., at 120-125; *Place,* 462 U.S., at 706 - 707; *Cardwell,* 417 U.S., at 588-589.[13] More generally, an officer who happens to come across an individual's property in a public area could seize it only if Fourth Amendment standards are satisfied—for example, if the items are evidence of a crime or contraband. Cf. *Payton v. New York,* [506 U.S. 56, 69] 445 U.S., at 587. We are also puzzled by the last sentence of the excerpt, where the court announces that the "usual rules" of the Fourth Amendment are inapplicable if the seizure is not the result of a search or any other investigative activity "precisely because there is no invasion of privacy." For the plain-view cases clearly state that, notwithstanding the absence of any interference with privacy, seizures of effects that are not authorized by a warrant are reasonable only because there is probable cause to associate the property with criminal activity. The seizure of the weapons in *Horton,* for example, occurred in the midst of a search, yet we emphasized that it did not "involve any invasion of privacy." 496 U.S., at 133. In short, our statement that such seizures must satisfy the Fourth Amendment and will be deemed reasonable only if the item's incriminating character is "immediately apparent," *id.,* at 136-137, is at odds with the Court of Appeals' approach.

The Court of Appeals' effort is both interesting and creative, but, at bottom, it simply reasserts the earlier thesis that the Fourth Amendment protects privacy, but not property. We remain unconvinced, and see no justification for departing from our prior cases. In our view, the reason why an officer might enter a house or effectuate a seizure is wholly irrelevant to the threshold question whether the Amendment applies. What matters is the intrusion on the people's security from governmental interference. Therefore, the right against unreasonable seizures would be no less transgressed if the seizure of the house was undertaken to collect evidence, verify compliance with a housing regulation, effect an eviction by the police, or on a whim, for no reason at all. As we have observed on more than one occasion, it would be "anomalous to say that the individual and his private property are fully protected by the Fourth Amendment only when the individual is suspected of criminal behavior." *Camara* 387 U.S., at 530; see also *O'Connor*, 480 U.S., at 715; *T.L.O.*, 469 U.S., at 335. [506 U.S. 56, 70]

The Court of Appeals also stated that, even if, contrary to its previous rulings, "there is some element or tincture of a Fourth Amendment seizure, it cannot carry the day for the Soldals." 942 F.2d, at 1080. Relying on our decision in *Graham v. Connor*, 490 U.S. 386 (1989), the court reasoned that it should look at the "dominant character of the conduct challenged in a section 1983 case [to] determine the constitutional standard under which it is evaluated." 942 F.2d, at 1080. Believing that the Soldals' claim was more akin to a challenge against the deprivation of property without due process of law than against an unreasonable seizure, the court concluded that they should not be allowed to bring their suit under the guise of the Fourth Amendment.

But we see no basis for doling out constitutional protections in such fashion. Certain wrongs affect more than a single right, and, accordingly, can implicate more than one of the Constitution's commands. Where such multiple violations are alleged, we are not in the habit of identifying, as a preliminary matter, the claim's "dominant" character. Rather, we examine each constitutional provision in turn. See, *e.g., Hudson v. Palmer*, 468 U.S. 517 (1984) (Fourth Amendment and Fourteenth Amendment Due Process Clause); *Ingraham v. Wright*, 430 U.S. 651 (1977) (Eighth Amendment and Fourteenth Amendment Due Process Clause). *Graham* is not to the contrary. Its holding was that claims of excessive use of force should be analyzed under the Fourth Amendment's reasonableness standard, rather than the Fourteenth Amendment's substantive due process test. We were guided by the fact that, in that case, both provisions targeted the same sort of governmental conduct and, as a result, we chose the more "explicit textual source of constitutional protection" over the "more generalized notion of 'substantive due process.'" 490 U.S., at 394-395. Surely, *Graham* does not bar resort in this case to the Fourth Amendment's specific protection for "houses, papers, [506 U.S. 56, 71] and effects," rather than the general protection of property in the Due Process Clause.

III

Respondents are fearful, as was the Court of Appeals, that applying the Fourth Amendment in this context inevitably will carry it into territory unknown and unforeseen: routine repossessions, negligent actions of public employees that interfere with individuals' right to enjoy their homes, and the like, thereby federalizing areas of law traditionally the concern of the States. For several reasons, we think the risk is exaggerated. To begin, our decision will have no impact on activities such as repossessions or attachments if they involve entry into the home, intrusion on individuals' privacy, or interference with their liberty, because they would implicate the Fourth Amendment even on the Court of Appeals' own terms. This was true of the Tenth Circuit's decision in *Specht*, with which, as we previously noted, the Court of Appeals expressed agreement.

More significantly, "reasonableness is still the ultimate standard" under the Fourth Amendment, *Camara, supra*, at 539, which means that numerous seizures of this type will survive constitutional scrutiny. As is true in other circumstances, the reasonableness determination will reflect a "careful balancing of governmental and private interests." *T.L.O., supra*, at 341. Assuming, for example, that the officers were acting pursuant to a court order, as in *Specht v. Jensen*, 832 F.2d 1516 (CA10 1987), or *Fuentes v. Shevin*, 407 U.S. 67, (1972), and, as often would be the case, a showing of unreasonableness on these facts would be a laborious task indeed. Cf. *Simms and Wise v. Slacum*, 3 Cranch 300, 301 (1806). Hence, while there is no guarantee against the filing of frivolous suits, had the ejection in this case properly awaited the state court's judgment, it is quite unlikely that the federal court would have been bothered with a 1983 action alleging a Fourth Amendment violation. [506 U.S. 56, 72]

Moreover, we doubt that the police will often choose to further an enterprise knowing that it is contrary to the law, or proceed to seize property in the absence of objectively reasonable grounds for doing so. In short, our reaffirmance of Fourth Amendment principles today should not foment a wave of new litigation in the federal courts.

IV

The complaint here alleges that respondents, acting under color of state law, dispossessed the Soldals of their trailer home by physically tearing it from its foundation and towing it to another lot. Taking these allegations as true, this was no "garden variety" landlord-tenant or commercial dispute. The facts alleged suffice to constitute a "seizure" within the meaning of the Fourth Amendment, for they plainly implicate the interests protected by that provision. The judgment of the Court of Appeals is, accordingly, reversed, and the case is remanded for further proceedings consistent with this opinion.

So ordered.

Footnotes

[1] Jones' statement was prompted by a district attorney's advice that no criminal charges could be brought because, under Illinois law, a criminal action cannot be used to determine the right of possession. See Ill.Rev.Stat. ch. 110, ¶ 9-101 *et seq.* (1991); *People v. Evans*, 163 Ill.App. 3d 561, 114 Ill.Dec. 662, 516 N.E.2d 817 (1st Dist. 1987).

[2] The Soldals ultimately were evicted per court order in December 1987.

[3] Title 42 U.S.C. § 1983 provides that:

> "Every person who, under color of any statute, ordinance, regulation, custom or usage, of any State . . . subjects, or causes to be subjected, any citizen of the United States . . . to the deprivation of any rights, privileges, or immunities secured by the Constitution and laws, shall be liable to the party injured in an action at law, suit in equity, or other proper proceeding for redress."

[4] The court reiterated the panel's conclusion that a conspiracy must be assumed on the state of the record and, therefore, that the case must be treated in its current posture "as if the deputy sheriffs themselves seized the trailer, disconnected it from the utilities, and towed it away." 942 F.2d 1073, 1075 (CA7 1991) (en banc).

[5] The court noted that, in light of the existence of adequate judicial remedies under state law, a claim for deprivation of property without due process of law was unlikely to succeed. *Id.*, at 1075-1076. See *Parratt v. Taylor*, 451 U.S. 527 (1981). In any event, the Soldals did not claim a violation of their procedural rights. As noted, the Seventh Circuit also held that respondents had not violated the Soldals' substantive due process rights under the Fourteenth Amendment. Petitioners assert that this was error, but, in view of our disposition of the case, we need not address the question at this time.

[6] Under 42 U.S.C. § 1983, the Soldals were required to establish that the respondents, acting under color of state law, deprived them of a constitutional right, in this instance, their Fourth and Fourteenth Amendment freedom from unreasonable seizures by the State. See *Monroe v. Pape*, [506 U.S. 56, 61] 365 U.S. 167, 184 (1961). Respondents request that we affirm on the ground that the Court of Appeals erred in holding that there was sufficient state action to support a 1983 action. The alleged injury to the Soldals, it is urged, was inflicted by private parties for whom the county is not responsible. Although respondents did not cross-petition, they are entitled to ask us to affirm on that ground if such action would not enlarge the judgment of the Court of Appeals in their favor. The Court of Appeals found that, because the police prevented Soldal from using reasonable force to protect his home from private action that the officers knew was illegal, there was sufficient evidence of conspiracy between the private parties and the officers to foreclose summary judgment for respondents. We are not inclined to review that holding. See *Adickes v. S.H. Kress & Co.*, 398 U.S. 144, 152-161 (1970).

[7] In holding that the Fourth Amendment's reach extends to property as such, we are mindful that the Amendment does not protect possessory interests in all kinds of property. See, *e.g., Oliver v. United States*, 466 U.S. 170, 176-177 (1984). This case, however, concerns a house, which the Amendment's language explicitly includes, as it does a person's effects.

[8] *Place* also found that to detain luggage for 90 minutes was an unreasonable deprivation of the individual's "liberty interest in proceeding with his itinerary," which also is protected by the Fourth Amendment. 462 U.S., at 708-710.

[9] When "operational necessities" exist, seizures can be justified on less than probable cause. 480 U.S., at 327. That in no way affects our analysis, for even then it is clear that the Fourth Amendment applies. *Ibid*; see also *United States v. Place*, 462 U.S. 696, at 703 (1983).

[10] Of course, if the police officers' presence in the home itself entailed a violation of the Fourth Amendment, no amount of probable cause to believe that an item in plain view constitutes incriminating evidence will justify its seizure. *Horton*, 496 U.S., at 136-137.

[11] It is true that *Murray's Lessee v. Hoboken Land & Improvement Co.*, 18 How. 272 (1856), cast some doubt on the applicability of the Amendment to noncriminal encounters such as this. *Id.*, 18 How. at 285. But cases since that time have shed a

different light, making clear that Fourth Amendment guarantees are triggered by governmental searches and seizures "without regard to the use to which [houses, papers, and effects] are applied." *Warden, Maryland Penitentiary v. Hayden,* 387 U.S. 294, 301 (1967). Murray's Lessee's broad statement that the Fourth Amendment "has no reference to civil proceedings for the recovery of debt" arguably only meant that the warrant requirement did not apply, as was suggested in *G.M. Leasing Corp. v. United States,* 429 U.S. 338, 352 (1977). Whatever its proper reading, we reaffirm today our basic understanding that the protection against unreasonable searches and seizures fully applies in the civil context.

[12] This was the view expressed by the Court of Appeals for the Tenth Circuit in *Specht v. Jensen,* 832 F.2d 1516 (1987), remanded on unrelated grounds, 853 F.2d 805 (1988) (en banc), with which the Seventh Circuit expressly agreed. 942 F.2d, at 1076.

[13] The officers in these cases were engaged in law enforcement, and were looking for something that was found and seized. In this broad sense, the seizures were the result of "searches," but not in the Fourth Amendment sense. That the Court of Appeals might have been suggesting that the plain-view cases are explainable because they almost always occur in the course of law enforcement activities receives some support from the penultimate sentence of the quoted passage, where the court states that the word "seizure" might lose its usual meaning "when it stands apart from a search *or any other investigative activity.*" *Id.,* at 1079 (emphasis added). And, in the following paragraph, it observes that, "[o]utside of the law enforcement area, the Fourth Amendment retains its force as a protection against searches, because they invade privacy. That is why we decline to confine the amendment to the law enforcement setting." *Id.,* at 1079-1080. Even if the court meant that seizures of property in the course of law enforcement activities, whether civil or criminal, implicate interests safeguarded by the Fourth Amendment, but that pure property interests are unprotected in the non-law-enforcement setting, we are not in accord, as indicated in the body of this opinion. [506 U.S. 56, 73]

Albright v. Oliver
510 U.S. 266 (1994)

Argued October 12, 1993
Decided January 24, 1994
CHIEF JUSTICE REHNQUIST announced the judgment of the Court
and delivered an opinion, in which JUSTICE O'CONNOR,
JUSTICE SCALIA, and JUSTICE GINSBURG joined.

A warrant was issued for petitioner's arrest by Illinois authorities, and, upon learning of it, he surrendered and was released on bail. The prosecution was later dismissed on the ground that the charge did not state an offense under Illinois law. Petitioner asks us to recognize a substantive right under the Due Process Clause of the Fourteenth Amendment to be free from criminal prosecution except upon probable cause. We decline to do so.

This case comes to us from a decision of the Court of Appeals for the Seventh Circuit affirming the grant of a motion to dismiss the complaint pursuant to Federal Rule of Civil Procedure 12(b)(6), and we must therefore accept the well-pleaded allegations of the complaint as true. Illinois authorities issued an arrest warrant for petitioner Kevin Albright, charging him on the basis of a previously filed criminal information with the sale of a substance which looked like an illegal drug. When he learned of the outstanding warrant, petitioner surrendered to respondent, Roger Oliver, a police detective employed by the city of Macomb, but denied his guilt of such an offense. He was released after posting bond, one of the conditions of which was that he not leave the State without permission of the court[1] [510 U.S. 268].

At a preliminary hearing, respondent Oliver testified that petitioner sold the look-alike substance to Moore, and the court found

264

probable cause to bind petitioner over for trial. At a later pretrial hearing, the court dismissed the criminal action against petitioner on the ground that the charge did not state an offense under Illinois law.

Albright then instituted this action under Rev. Stat. § 1979, 42 U.S.C. § 1983, against Detective Oliver in his individual and official capacity, alleging that Oliver deprived him of substantive due process under the Fourteenth Amendment—his "liberty interest"—to be free from criminal prosecution except upon probable cause.[2] The District Court granted respondent's motion to dismiss under Rule 12(b)(6) on the ground that the complaint did not state a claim under § 1983.[3] The Court of Appeals for the Seventh Circuit affirmed, 975 F.2d 343 (1992), relying on our decision in *Paul v. Davis,* 424 U.S. 693 (1976). The Court of Appeals held that prosecution without probable cause is a constitutional tort actionable under § 1983 only if accompanied by incarceration or loss of employment or some other "palpable [510 U.S. 269] consequenc[e]." 975 F.2d, at 346-347. The panel of the Seventh Circuit reasoned that, "just as in the garden variety public officer defamation case that does not result in exclusion from an occupation, state tort remedies should be adequate, and the heavy weaponry of constitutional litigation can be left at rest. *Id.,* at 347.[4] We granted certiorari, 507 U.S. [510 U.S. 270] ___ (1993), and while we affirm the judgment below, we do so on different grounds. We hold that it is the Fourth Amendment, and not substantive due process, under which petitioner Albright's claims must be judged.

Section 1983 "is not itself a source of substantive rights," but merely provides "a method for vindicating federal rights elsewhere conferred." *Baker v. McCollan,* 443 U.S. 137, 144, n. 3 (1979). The first step in any such claim is to identify the specific constitutional right allegedly infringed. *Graham v. Connor,* 490 U.S. 386, 394 (1989); and *Baker v. McCollan, supra,* at 140.

Petitioner's claim before this Court is a very limited one. He claims that the action of respondents infringed his substantive due process right to be free of prosecution without probable cause. He does not claim that Illinois denied him the procedural due process guaranteed by the Fourteenth Amendment. Nor does he claim a violation of his Fourth Amendment rights, notwithstanding the fact that his surrender to the State's show of authority constituted a seizure for purposes of the Fourth Amendment. *Terry v. Ohio,* 392 U.S. 1, 19 (1968); *Brower v. County of Inyo,* 489 U.S. 593, 596 (1989).[5]

We begin analysis of petitioner's claim by repeating our observation in *Collins v. Harker Heights,* 503 U.S. ___, ___ (1992) (*slip op.,* at 9). "As a general matter, the Court has always been reluctant to expand the concept of substantive due process [510 U.S. 271], because the guideposts for responsible decisionmaking in this unchartered area are scarce and open-ended." The protections of substantive due process have, for the most part, been accorded to matters relating to marriage, family, procreation, and the right to bodily integrity. See, *e.g.*, *Planned Parenthood of Southeastern Pa. v. Casey*, 505 U.S. 833, 847-849 (1992) (describing cases in which substantive due process rights have been recognized). Petitioner's claim to be free from prosecution except on the basis of probable cause is markedly different from those recognized in this group of cases.

Petitioner relies on our observations in cases such as *United States v. Salerno*, 481 U.S. 739, 746 (1987), and *Daniels v. Williams*, 474 U.S. 327, 331 (1986), that the Due Process Clause of the Fourteenth Amendment confers both substantive and procedural rights. This is undoubtedly true, but it sheds little light on the scope of substantive due process. Petitioner points in particular to language from *Hurtado v. California*, 110 U.S. 516, 527 (1884), later quoted in *Daniels*, *supra*, stating that the words "by the law of the land" from the Magna Carta were "'intended to secure the individual from the arbitrary exercise of the powers of government.'" This, too, may be freely conceded, but it does not follow that, in all of the various aspects of a criminal prosecution, the only inquiry mandated by the Constitution is whether, in, the view of the Court, the governmental action in question was "arbitrary."

Hurtado held that the Due Process Clause did not make applicable to the States the Fifth Amendment's requirement that all prosecutions for an infamous crime be instituted by the indictment of a grand jury. In the more than 100 years which have elapsed since *Hurtado* was decided, the Court has concluded that a number of the procedural protections contained in the Bill of Rights were made applicable to the States by the Fourteenth Amendment. See *Mapp v. Ohio*, 367 U.S. 643 (1961), overruling *Wolf v. Colorado*, 338 U.S. 25 [510 U.S. 272] (1949), and holding the Fourth Amendment's exclusionary rule applicable to the States; *Malloy v. Hogan*, 378 U.S. 1 (1964), overruling *Twining v. New Jersey*, 211 U.S. 78 (1908), and holding the Fifth Amendment's privilege against self-incrimination applicable to the States; *Benton v. Maryland*, 395 U.S. 784 (1969), overruling *Palko v. Connecticut*, 302 U.S. 319 (1937), and holding the Double Jeopardy Clause of the Fifth Amendment applicable to the States; *Gideon v. Wainwright*, 372 U.S. 335 (1963), overruling *Betts v. Brady*, 316 U.S. 455 (1942), and holding that the Sixth Amendment's right to counsel was applicable to the States. See also *Klopfer v. North Carolina*, 386 U.S. 213 (1967) (Sixth Amendment speedy trial right applicable to the States); *Washington v. Texas*, 388 U.S. 14 (1967) (Sixth Amendment right to compulsory process applicable to the States); *Duncan v. Louisiana*, 391 U.S. 145 (1968) (Sixth Amendment right to jury trial applicable to the States).

This course of decision has substituted, in these areas of criminal procedure, the specific guarantees of the various provisions of the Bill of Rights embodied in the first 10 Amendments to the Constitution for the more generalized language contained in the earlier cases construing the Fourteenth Amendment. It was through these provisions of the Bill of Rights that their Framers sought to restrict the exercise of arbitrary authority by the Government in particular situations. Where a particular amendment "provides an explicit textual source of constitutional protection" against a particular sort of government behavior, "that Amendment, not the more generalized notion of 'substantive due process,' must be the guide for analyzing these claims." *Graham v. Connor, supra*, at 395[6] [510 U.S. 273].

We think this principle is likewise applicable here. The Framers considered the matter of pretrial deprivations of liberty, and drafted the Fourth Amendment to address it. The Fourth Amendment provides:

> "The right of the people to be secure in their persons, houses, papers, and effects, against unreasonable searches and seizures, shall not be violated, and no Warrants shall issue, but upon probable cause, supported by Oath or affirmation, and particularly describing the place to be searched, and the persons or things to be seized."

We have in the past noted the Fourth Amendment's relevance to the deprivations of liberty that go hand in hand with criminal prosecutions. See *Gerstein v. Pugh*, 420 U.S. 103, 114 (1975) (holding that the Fourth Amendment requires a judicial determination of probable cause as a prerequisite to any extended restraint on liberty following an arrest). We have said that the accused is not "entitled to judicial oversight or review of the decision to prosecute." *Id.*, at 118-119. See also *Beck v. Washington*, 369 U.S. 541, 545 (1962); *Lem Woon v. Oregon*, 229 U.S. 586 (1913). But here petitioner was not merely charged; he submitted himself to arrest [510 U.S. 274].

We express no view as to whether petitioner's claim would succeed under the Fourth Amendment, since he has not presented that question in his petition for certiorari. We do hold that substantive due process, with its "scarce and open-ended" "guideposts," *Collins v. Harker Heights*, 503 U.S., at ___ (*slip op.*, at 9), can afford him no relief.[7]

The judgment of the Court of Appeals is therefore

Affirmed.

Footnotes

[1] Before the criminal information was filed, one Veda Moore, an undercover informant, had told Oliver that she bought cocaine from one John Albright, Jr., at a student hotel in Macomb. The "cocaine" turned out to be baking powder, however, and the grand jury indicted John Albright, Jr., for selling a "look-alike" substance. When Detective Oliver went to serve the arrest warrant, he discovered that John Albright, Jr., was a retired pharmacist in his sixties, and apparently realized he was on a false scent. After discovering that it could not have been the elderly Albright's son, John David, who was involved in the incident, Detective Oliver contacted Moore to see if the sale was actually made to petitioner Kevin Albright, a second son of John Albright, Jr. Moore confirmed that petitioner Kevin Albright made the sale.

[2] The complaint also named the City of Macomb as a defendant to the 1983 action, and charged a common law malicious prosecution claim against Detective Oliver.

[3] The District Court also held that Detective Oliver was entitled to a defense of qualified immunity, and that the complaint failed to allege facts sufficient to support municipal liability against the city of Macomb. The District Court also dismissed without prejudice the common law claim of malicious prosecution against Detective Oliver. These issues are not before this Court.

[4] As noted by the Court of Appeals below, the extent to which a claim of malicious prosecution is actionable under § 1983 is one "on which there is an embarrassing diversity of judicial opinion." 975 F.2d, at 345, citing *Brummett v. Camble*, 946 F.2d 1178, 1180, n. 2 (CA5 1991) (cataloging divergence of approaches by the Courts of Appeals). Most of the lower courts recognize some form of malicious prosecution action under § 1983. The disagreement among the courts concerns whether malicious prosecutions, standing alone, can violate the Constitution. The most expansive approach is exemplified by the Third Circuit, which holds that the elements of a malicious prosecution action under § 1983 are the same as the common law tort of malicious prosecution. See, *e.g.*, *Lee v. Mihalich*, 847 F.2d 66, 70 (CA3 1988) ("[T]he elements of liability for the constitutional tort of malicious prosecution under § 1983 coincide with those of the common law tort"). See also, *Sanders v. English*, 950 F.2d 1152, 1159 (CA5 1992) ("[O]ur circuit recognizes causes of action under § 1983 for false arrest, illegal detention . . . and malicious prosecution" because these causes of action "implicate the constitutional 'guarantees of the fourth and fourteenth amendments' . . ."); *Robinson v. Maruffi*, 895 F.2d 649 (CA10 1990); *Strength v. Hubert*, 854 F.2d 421, 426, and n. 5 (CA11 1988) (recognizing that "freedom from malicious prosecution is a federal right protected by § 1983"). Other Circuits, however, require a showing of some injury or deprivation of a constitutional magnitude in addition to the traditional elements of common law malicious prosecution. The exact standards announced by the courts escape easy classification. See *e.g.*, *Torres v. Superintendent of Police of Puerto Rico*, 893 F.2d 404, 409 (CA1 1990) (the challenged conduct must be "so egregious that it violated substantive or procedural due process rights under the Fourteenth Amendment"); *Usher v. Los Angeles*, 828 F.2d 556, 561-562 (CA9 1987) ("[T]he general rule is that a claim of malicious prosecution is not cognizable under 42 U.S.C. § 1983 if process is available within the state judicial system to provide a remedy . . . [h]owever, 'an exception exists to the general rule when a malicious prosecution is conducted with the intent to deprive a person of equal protection of the laws or is otherwise intended to subject a person to a denial of constitutional rights'"); *Coogan v. Wixom*, 820 F.2d 170, 175 (CA6 1987) (in addition to elements of malicious prosecution under state law, plaintiff must show an egregious misuse of a legal proceeding resulting in a constitutional deprivation). In holding that malicious prosecution is not actionable under § 1983 unless it is accompanied by incarceration, loss of protected status, or some other palpable consequence, the Seventh Circuit's decision below places it in this latter camp. In view of our disposition of this case, it is evident that substantive due process may not furnish the constitutional peg on which to hang such a "tort."

[5] Thus, Albright may have missed the statute of limitations for any claim he had based on an unconstitutional arrest or seizure. 975 F.2d 343, 345 (CA7 1992). We express no opinion as to the timeliness of any such claim he might have.

[6] JUSTICE STEVENS' dissent faults us for ignoring, inter alia, our decision in *In re Winship*, 397 U.S. 358 (1970). *Winship* undoubtedly rejected the notion that all of the required incidents of a fundamentally fair trial were to be found in the provisions of the Bill of Rights, but it did so as a matter of procedural due process: "'This notion [that the government must prove the elements of a criminal case beyond a reasonable doubt]—basic in our law and rightly one of the boasts of a

free society—is a requirement and a safeguard of due process of law in the historic, procedural content of "due process."'" *Id.*, at 362, quoting *Leland v. Oregon,* 343 U.S. 790, 802-803 (1952) (Frankfurter, J., dissenting).

Similarly, other cases relied on by the dissent, including *Mooney v. Holohan,* 294 U.S. 103 (1935), *Napue v. Illinois,* 360 U.S. 264 (1959), *Brady v. Maryland,* 373 U.S. 83 (1963), *Giglio v. United States,* 405 U.S. 150 (1972), and *United States v. Agurs,* 427 U.S. 97 (1976), were accurately described in the latter opinion as "dealing with the defendant's right to a fair trial mandated by the Due Process Clause of the Fifth Amendment to the Constitution." *Id.*, at 107.

[7] Petitioner appears to have argued in the Court of Appeals some variant of a violation of his constitutional right to interstate travel because of the condition imposed upon him pursuant to his release on bond. But he has not presented any such question in his petition for certiorari, and has not briefed the issue here. We therefore do not consider it.

Wilson v. Layne
526 U.S. 603 (1999)

Argued March 24, 1999
Decided May 24, 1999
Chief Justice Rehnquist delivered the opinion of the Court.

While executing an arrest warrant in a private home, police officers invited representatives of the media to accompany them. We hold that such a "media ride along" does violate the Fourth Amendment, but that because the state of the law was not clearly established at the time the search in this case took place, the officers are entitled to the defense of qualified immunity.

I

In early 1992, the Attorney General of the United States approved "Operation Gunsmoke," a special national fugitive apprehension program in which United States Marshals worked with state and local police to apprehend dangerous criminals. The "Operation Gunsmoke" policy statement explained that the operation was to concentrate on "armed individuals wanted on federal and/or state and local warrants for serious drug and other violent felonies." App. 15. This effective program ultimately resulted in over 3,000 arrests in 40 metropolitan areas. Brief for Federal Respondents Layne et al. 2.

    One of the dangerous fugitives identified as a target of "Operation Gunsmoke" was Dominic Wilson, the son of petitioners Charles and Geraldine Wilson. Dominic Wilson had violated his probation on previous felony charges of robbery, theft, and assault with intent to rob, and the police computer listed "caution indicators" that he was likely to be armed, to resist arrest, and to "assaul[t] police." App. 40. The computer also listed his address as 909 North StoneStreet Avenue in Rockville, Maryland. Unknown to the police, this was actually the home of petitioners, Dominic Wilson's parents. Thus, in April 1992, the Circuit Court for Montgomery County issued three arrest warrants for Dominic Wilson, one for each of his probation violations. The warrants were each addressed to "any duly authorized peace officer," and commanded such officers to arrest him and bring him "immediately" before the Circuit Court to answer an indictment as to his probation violation. The warrants made no mention of media presence or assistance.[1]

In the early morning hours of April 16, 1992, a Gunsmoke team of Deputy United States Marshals and Montgomery County Police officers assembled to execute the Dominic Wilson warrants. The team was accompanied by a reporter and a photographer from the *Washington Post*, who had been invited by the Marshals to accompany them on their mission as part of a Marshal's Service ride-along policy.

At around 6:45 a.m., the officers, with media representatives in tow, entered the dwelling at 909 North StoneStreet Avenue in the Lincoln Park neighborhood of Rockville. Petitioners Charles and Geraldine Wilson were still in bed when they heard the officers enter the home. Petitioner Charles Wilson, dressed only in a pair of briefs, ran into the living room to investigate. Discovering at least five men in street clothes with guns in his living room, he angrily demanded that they state their business, and repeatedly cursed the officers. Believing him to be an angry Dominic Wilson, the officers quickly subdued him on the floor. Geraldine Wilson next entered the living room to investigate, wearing only a nightgown. She observed her husband being restrained by the armed officers.

When their protective sweep was completed, the officers learned that Dominic Wilson was not in the house, and they departed. During the time that the officers were in the home, the *Washington Post* photographer took numerous pictures. The print reporter was also apparently in the living room observing the confrontation between the police and Charles Wilson. At no time, however, were the reporters involved in the execution of the arrest warrant. Brief for Federal Respondents Layne et al. 4. The *Washington Post* never published its photographs of the incident.

Petitioners sued the law enforcement officials in their personal capacities for money damages under *Bivens v. Six Unknown Fed. Narcotics Agents*, 403 U. S. 388 (1971) (the U. S. Marshals Service respondents) and, Rev. Stat. § 1979, 42 U. S. C. § 1983 (the Montgomery County Sheriff's Department respondents). They contended that the officers' actions in bringing members of the media to observe and record the attempted execution of the arrest warrant violated their Fourth Amendment rights. The District Court denied respondents' motion for summary judgment on the basis of qualified immunity.

On interlocutory appeal to the Court of Appeals, a divided panel reversed and held that respondents were entitled to qualified immunity. The case was twice reheard en banc, where a divided Court of Appeals again upheld the defense of qualified immunity. The Court of Appeals declined to decide whether the actions of the police violated the Fourth Amendment. It concluded instead that because no court had held (at the time of the search) that media presence during a police entry into a residence violated the Fourth Amendment, the right allegedly violated by petitioners was not "clearly established" and thus qualified immunity was proper. 141 F. 3d 111 (CA4 1998). Five judges dissented, arguing that the officers' actions did violate the Fourth Amendment, and that the clearly established protections of the Fourth Amendment were violated in this case. *Id.*, at 119 (opinion of Murnaghan, J.)

Recognizing a split among the Circuits on this issue, we granted certiorari in this case and another raising the same question, *Hanlon v. Berger*, 525 U. S. ___ (1998), and now affirm the Court of Appeals, although by different reasoning.

II

The petitioners sued the federal officials under *Bivens* and the state officials under § 1983. Both *Bivens* and § 1983 allow a plaintiff to seek money damages from government officials who have violated his Fourth Amendment rights. See § 1983; *Bivens, supra*, at 397. But government officials performing discretionary functions generally are granted a qualified immunity and are "shielded from liability for civil damages insofar as their conduct does not violate clearly established statutory or constitutional rights of which a reasonable person would have known." *Harlow v. Fitzgerald*, 457 U. S. 800, 818 (1982).

Although this case involves suits under both § 1983 and *Bivens*, the qualified immunity analysis is identical under either cause of action. See, *e.g.*, *Graham v. Connor*, 490 U. S. 386, 394, n. 9 (1989); *Malley v. Briggs*, 475 U. S. 335, 340, n. 2 (1986). A court evaluating a claim of qualified immunity "must first determine whether the plaintiff has alleged the deprivation of an actual constitutional right at all, and if so, proceed to determine whether that right was clearly established at the time of the alleged violation." *Conn v. Gabbert*, 526 U. S. ___, ___ (1999) (*slip op.*, at 4). This order of procedure is designed to "spare a defendant not only unwarranted liability, but unwarranted demands customarily imposed upon those defending a long drawn-out lawsuit." *Siegert v. Gilley*, 500 U. S. 226, 232 (1991). Deciding the constitutional question before addressing the qualified immunity question also promotes clarity in the legal standards for official conduct, to the benefit of both the officers and the general public. See *County of Sacramento v. Lewis*, 523 U. S. 833, 840-842, n. 5 (1998). We now turn to the Fourth Amendment question.

In 1604, an English court made the now-famous observation that "the house of every one is to him as his castle and fortress, as well for his defence against injury and violence, as for his repose." *Semayne's Case*, 77 Eng. Rep. 194, 5 Co. Rep. 91a, 91b, 195 (K. B.). In his *Commentaries on the Laws of England*, William Blackstone noted that

> "the law of England has so particular and tender a regard to the immunity of a man's house, that it stiles it his castle, and will never suffer it to be violated with impunity: agreeing herein with the sentiments of antient Rome. . . . For this reason no doors can in general be broken open to execute any civil process; though, in criminal causes, the public safety supersedes the private." William Blackstone, 4 Commentaries on the Laws of England 223 (1765-1769).

The Fourth Amendment embodies this centuries-old principle of respect for the privacy of the home: "The right of the people to be secure in their persons, *houses*, papers, and effects, against unreasonable searches and seizures, shall not be violated, and no Warrants shall issue, but upon probable cause, supported by Oath or affirmation, and particularly describing the place to be searched, and the persons or things to be seized." U. S. Const. Amd. IV (Emphasis added.) See also *United States v. United States District Court* 407 U. S. 297, 313 (1972) ("[P]hysical entry of the home is the chief evil against which the wording of the Fourth Amendment is directed").

Our decisions have applied these basic principles of the Fourth Amendment to situations, like those in this case, in which police enter a home under the authority of an arrest warrant in order to take into custody the suspect named in the warrant. In *Payton v. New York*, 445 U. S. 573, 602 (1980), we noted that although clear in its protection of the home, the common-law tradition at the time of the drafting of the Fourth Amendment was ambivalent on the question of whether police could enter a home without a warrant. We were ultimately persuaded that the "overriding respect for the sanctity of the home that has been embedded in our traditions since the origins of the Republic" meant that absent a warrant or exigent circumstances, police could not enter a home to make an arrest. *Id.*, at 603-604. We decided that "an arrest warrant founded on probable cause implicitly carries with it the limited authority to enter a dwelling in which the suspect lives when there is reason to believe the suspect is within." *Ibid.*

Here, of course, the officers had such a warrant, and they were undoubtedly entitled to enter the Wilson home in order to execute the arrest warrant for Dominic Wilson. But it does not necessarily follow that they were entitled to bring a newspaper reporter and a photographer with them. In *Horton v. California*, 496 U. S. 128, 140 (1990), we held "[i]f the scope of the search exceeds that permitted by the terms of a validly issued warrant or the character of the relevant exception from the warrant requirement, the subsequent seizure is unconstitutional without more." While this does not mean that every police action while inside a home must be explicitly authorized by the text of the warrant, see *Michigan v. Summers*, 452 U. S. 692, 705 (1981) (Fourth Amendment allows temporary detainer of homeowner while police search the home pursuant to warrant), the Fourth Amendment does require that police actions in execution of a warrant be related to the objectives of the authorized intrusion, see *Arizona v. Hicks*, 480 U. S. 321, 325 (1987). See also *Maryland v. Garrison*, 480 U. S. 79, 87 (1987) ("[T]he purposes justifying a police search strictly limit the permissible extent of the search").

Certainly the presence of reporters inside the home was not related to the objectives of the authorized intrusion. Respondents concede that the reporters did not engage in the execution of the warrant, and did not assist the police in their task. The reporters therefore were not present for any reason related to the justification for police entry into the home—the apprehension of Dominic Wilson.

This is not a case in which the presence of the third parties directly aided in the execution of the warrant. Where the police enter a home under the authority of a warrant to search for stolen property, the presence of third parties for the purpose of identifying the stolen property has long been approved by this Court and our common-law tradition. See, *e.g.*, *Entick v. Carrington*, 19 How. St. Tr. 1029, 1067 (K. B. 1765) (in search for stolen goods case, "'[t]he owner must swear that the goods are lodged in such a place. He must attend at the execution of the warrant to shew them to the officer, who must see that they answer the description") (quoted with approval in *Boyd v. United States*, 116 U. S. 616, 628 (1886)).

Respondents argue that the presence of the Washington Post reporters in the Wilsons' home nonetheless served a number of legitimate law enforcement purposes. They first assert that officers should be able to exercise reasonable discretion about when it would "further their law enforcement mission to permit members of the news media to accompany them in executing a warrant." Brief for Respondents Layne et al. 15. But this claim ignores the importance of the right of residential privacy at the core of the Fourth Amendment. It may well be that media ride-alongs further the law enforcement objectives of the police in a general sense, but that is not the same as furthering the purposes of the search. Were such generalized "law enforcement objectives" themselves sufficient to trump the Fourth Amendment, the protections guaranteed by that Amendment's text would be significantly watered down.

Respondents next argue that the presence of third parties could serve the law enforcement purpose of publicizing the government's efforts to combat crime, and facilitate accurate reporting on law enforcement activities. There is certainly language in our opinions interpreting the First Amendment which points to the importance of "the press" in informing the general public about the administration of criminal justice.

In *Cox Broadcasting Corp. v. Cohn*, 420 U. S. 469, 491-492 (1975), for example, we said "in a society in which each individual has but limited time and resources with which to observe at first hand the operations of his government, he relies necessarily upon the press to bring to him in convenient form the facts of those operations." See also *Richmond Newspapers, Inc. v. Virginia*, 448 U. S. 555, 572-573 (1980). No one could gainsay the truth of these observations, or the importance of the First Amendment in protecting press freedom from abridgement by the government. But the Fourth Amendment also protects a very important right, and in the present case it is in terms of that right that the media ride-alongs must be judged.

Surely the possibility of good public relations for the police is simply not enough, standing alone, to justify the ride-along intrusion into a private home. And even the need for accurate reporting on police issues in general bears no direct relation to the constitutional justification for the police intrusion into a home in order to execute a felony arrest warrant.

Finally, respondents argue that the presence of third parties could serve in some situations to minimize police abuses and protect suspects, and also to protect the safety of the officers. While it might be reasonable for police officers to themselves videotape home entries as part of a "quality control" effort to ensure that the rights of homeowners are being respected, or even to preserve evidence, cf. *Ohio v. Robinette*, 519 U. S. 33, 35 (1996) (noting the use of a "mounted video camera" to record the details of a routine traffic stop), such a situation is significantly different from the media presence in this case. The Washington *Post* reporters in the Wilsons' home were working on a story for their own purposes. They were not present for the purpose of protecting the officers, much less the Wilsons. A private photographer was acting for private purposes, as evidenced in part by the fact that the newspaper and not the police retained the photographs. Thus, although the presence of third parties during the execution of a warrant may in some circumstances be constitutionally permissible, see *supra* at 7-8, the presence of these third parties was not.

The reasons advanced by respondents, taken in their entirety, fall short of justifying the presence of media inside a home. We hold that it is a violation of the Fourth Amendment for police to bring members of the media or other third parties into a home during the execution of a warrant when the presence of the third parties in the home was not in aid of the execution of the warrant.[2]

III

Since the police action in this case violated the petitioners' Fourth Amendment right, we now must decide whether this right was clearly established at the time of the search. See *Siegert*, 500 U. S., at 232-233. As noted above, Part-II *supra*, government officials performing discretionary functions generally are granted a qualified immunity and are "shielded from liability for civil damages insofar as their conduct does not violate clearly established statutory or constitutional rights of which a reasonable person would have known." *Harlow v. Fitzgerald*, 457 U. S., at 818. What this means in practice is that "whether an official protected by qualified immunity may be held personally liable for an allegedly unlawful official action generally turns on the 'objective legal reasonableness' of the action, assessed in light of the legal rules that were 'clearly established' at the time it was taken." *Anderson v. Creighton*, 483 U. S. 635, 639 (1987) (citing *Harlow, supra*, at 819); see also *Graham v. Connor*, 490 U. S., at 397.

In *Anderson*, we explained that what "clearly established" means in this context depends largely "upon the level of generality at which the relevant 'legal rule' is to be established." 483 U. S., at 639. "Clearly established" for purposes of qualified immunity means that "[t]he contours of the right must be sufficiently clear that a reasonable official would understand that what he is doing violates that right. This is not to say that an official action is protected by qualified immunity unless the very action in question has previously been held unlawful, but it is to say that in the light of pre-existing law the unlawfulness must be apparent." *Id.*, at 640 (internal citations omitted); see also *United States v. Lanier*, 520 U. S. 259, 270 (1997).

It could plausibly be asserted that any violation of the Fourth Amendment is "clearly established," since it is clearly established that the protections of the Fourth Amendment apply to the actions of police. Some variation of this theory of qualified immunity is urged upon us by the petitioners, Brief for Petitioner 37, and seems to have been at the core of the dissenting opinion in the Court of Appeals, see 141 F. 3d, at 123. However, as we explained in *Anderson*, the right allegedly violated must be defined at the appropriate level of specificity before a court can determine if it was clearly established. *Anderson*, 483 U. S., at 641. In this case, the appropriate question is the objective inquiry of whether a reasonable officer could have believed that bringing members of the media into a home during the execution of an arrest warrant was lawful, in light of clearly, established law and the information the officers possessed. Cf. *ibid.*

We hold that it was not unreasonable for a police officer in April 1992 to have believed that bringing media observers along during the execution of an arrest warrant (even in a home) was lawful. First, the constitutional question presented by this case is by no means open and shut. The Fourth Amendment protects the rights of homeowners from entry without a warrant, but there was a warrant here. The question is whether the invitation to the media exceeded the scope of the search authorized by the warrant. Accurate media coverage of police activities serves an important public purpose, and it is not obvious from the general principles of the Fourth Amendment that the conduct of the officers in this case violated the Amendment.

Second, although media ride-alongs of one sort or another had apparently become a common police practice,[3] in 1992 there were no judicial opinions holding that this practice became unlawful when it entered a home. The only published decision directly on point was a state intermediate court decision which, though it did not engage in an extensive Fourth Amendment analysis, nonetheless held that such conduct was not unreasonable. *Prahl v. Brosamle*, 98 Wis. 2d 130, 154-155, 295 N. W. 2d 768, 782 (App. 1980). From the federal courts, the parties have only identified two unpublished District Court decisions dealing with media entry into homes, each of which upheld the search on unorthodox non-Fourth Amendment right to privacy theories. *Moncrief v. Hanton*, 10 Media L. Rptr. 1620 (ND Ohio 1984); *Higbee v. Times-Advocate*, 5 Media L. Rptr. 2372 (SD Cal. 1980). These cases, of course, cannot "clearly establish" that media entry into homes during a police ride-along violates the Fourth Amendment.

At a slightly higher level of generality, petitioners point to *Bills v. Aseltine*, 958 F. 2d 697 (CA6 1992), in which the Court of Appeals for the Sixth Circuit held that there were material issues of fact precluding summary judgment on the question of whether police exceeded the scope of a search warrant by allowing a private security guard to participate in the search to identify stolen property other than that described in the warrant. *Id.*, at 709. *Bills*, which was decided a mere five weeks before the events of this case, did anticipate today's holding that police may not bring along third parties during an entry into a private home pursuant to a warrant for purposes unrelated to those justifying the warrant. *Id.*, at 706. However, we cannot say that even in light of *Bills*, the law on third-party entry into homes was clearly established in April 1992. Petitioners have not brought to our attention any cases of controlling authority in their jurisdiction at the time of the incident, which clearly established the rule on which they seek to rely, nor have they identified a consensus of cases of persuasive authority such that a reasonable officer could not have believed that his actions were lawful.

Finally, important to our conclusion was the reliance by the United States marshals in this case on a Marshal's Service ride-along policy which explicitly contemplated that media who engaged in ride-alongs might enter private homes with their cameras as part of fugitive apprehension arrests.[4] The Montgomery County Sheriff's Department also at this time had a ride-along program that did not expressly prohibit media entry into private homes. Deposition of Sheriff Raymond M. Kight, in No. PJM-94-1718, p. 8. Such a policy, of course, could not make reasonable a belief that was contrary to a decided body of case law. But here the state of the law as to third parties accompanying police on home entries was at best undeveloped, and it was not unreasonable for law enforcement officers to look and rely on their formal ride-along policies.

Given such an undeveloped state of the law, the officers in this case cannot have been "expected to predict the future course of constitutional law." *Procunier v. Navarette*, 434 U. S. 555, 562 (1978). See also *Wood v. Strickland*, 420 U. S. 308, 321 (1975); *Pierson v. Ray*, 386 U. S. 547, 557 (1967). Between the time of the events of this case and today's decision, a split among the Federal Circuits in fact developed on the question whether media ride-alongs that enter homes subject the police to money damages. See 141 F. 3d, at 118-119; *Ayeni v. Mottola*, 35 F. 3d 680 (CA2 1994), cert. denied, 514 U. S. 1062 (1995); *Parker v. Boyer*, 93 F. 3d 445 (CA8 1996), cert. denied, 519 U. S. 1148 (1997); *Berger v. Hanlon*, 129 F. 3d 505 (CA9 1997), cert. granted, 525 U. S. ___ (1998). If judges thus disagree on a constitutional question, it is unfair to subject police to money damages for picking the losing side of the controversy.

For the foregoing reasons, the judgment of the Court of Appeals is affirmed.

It is so ordered.

Footnotes

[1] The warrants were identical in all relevant respects. By way of example, one of them read as follows:

"The State of Maryland, to any duly authorized peace officer, greeting: you are hereby commanded to take Dominic Jerome Wilson if he/she shall be found in your bailiwick, and have him immediately before the Circuit Court for Montgomery County, now in session, at the Judicial Center, in Rockville, to answer an indictment, or information, or criminal appeals unto the State of Maryland, of and concerning a certain charge of Robbery [Violation of Probation] by him committed, as hath been presented, and so forth. Hereof fail not at your peril, and have you then and there this writ. Witness." App. 36-37.

[2] Even though such actions might violate the Fourth Amendment, if the police are lawfully present, the violation of the Fourth Amendment is the presence of the media and not the presence of the police in the home. We have no occasion here to decide whether the exclusionary rule would apply to any evidence discovered or developed by the media representatives.

[3] See, *e.g.*, *Florida Publishing Co. v. Fletcher*, 340 So. 2d 914, 918 (1976) (it "'is a widespread practice of long-standing'" for media to accompany officers into homes), cert. denied, 431 U. S. 930 (1977); Zoglin, Live on the Vice Beat, *Time*, Dec. 22, 1986, p. 60 (noting "the increasingly common practice of letting TV crews tag along on drug raids").

[4] A booklet distributed to Marshals recommended that "fugitive apprehension cases . . . normally offer the best possibilities for ride-alongs." App. 4-5. In its discussion of the best way to make ride-alongs useful to the media and portray the Marshal's Service in a favorable light, the booklet noted that reporters were likely to want to be able to shoot "good action footage, not just a mop-up scene." It advised agents that "[i]f the arrest is planned to take place inside a house or building, agree ahead of time on when the camera can enter and who will give the signal." *Id.*, at 7.

Groh v. Ramirez et al.
540 U. S. ___ (2004)

Argued November 4, 2003
Decided February 24, 2004
JUSTICE STEVENS delivered the opinion of the Court.

Petitioner conducted a search of respondents' home pursuant to a warrant that failed to describe the "persons or things to be seized." U. S. Const., Amdt. 4. The questions presented are (1) whether the search violated the Fourth Amendment, and (2) if so, whether petitioner nevertheless is entitled to qualified immunity, given that a Magistrate Judge (Magistrate), relying on an affidavit that particularly described the items in question, found probable cause to conduct the search.

I

Respondents, Joseph Ramirez and members of his family, live on a large ranch in Butte-Silver Bow County, Montana. Petitioner, Jeff Groh, has been a Special Agent for the Bureau of Alcohol, Tobacco and Firearms (ATF) since 1989. In February 1997, a concerned citizen informed petitioner that on a number of visits to respondents' ranch the visitor had seen a large stock of weaponry, including an automatic rifle, grenades, a grenade launcher, and a rocket launcher.[1] Based on that information, petitioner prepared and signed an application for a warrant to search the ranch. The application stated that the search was for "any automatic firearms or parts to automatic weapons, destructive devices to include but not limited to grenades, grenade launchers, rocket launchers, and any and all receipts pertaining to the purchase or manufacture of automatic weapons or explosive devices or launchers."

App. to Pet. for Cert. 28a. Petitioner supported the application with a detailed affidavit, which he also prepared and executed, that set forth the basis for his belief that the listed items were concealed on the ranch. Petitioner then presented these documents to a Magistrate, along with a warrant form that petitioner also had completed. The Magistrate signed the warrant form.

Although the application particularly described the place to be searched and the contraband petitioner expected to find, the warrant itself was less specific; it failed to identify any of the items that petitioner intended to seize. In the portion of the form that called for a description of the "person or property" to be seized, petitioner typed a description of respondents' two-story blue house rather than the alleged stockpile of firearms.[2] The warrant did not incorporate by reference the itemized list contained in the application. It did, however, recite that the Magistrate was satisfied the affidavit established probable cause to believe that contraband was concealed on the premises, and that sufficient grounds existed for the warrant's issuance.[3]

The day after the Magistrate issued the warrant, petitioner led a team of law enforcement officers, including both federal agents and members of the local sheriff's department, in the search of respondents' premises. Although respondent Joseph Ramirez was not home, his wife and children were. Petitioner states that he orally described the objects of the search to Mrs. Ramirez in person and to Mr. Ramirez by telephone. According to Mrs. Ramirez, however, petitioner explained only that he was searching for "'an explosive device in a box.'" *Ramirez v. Butte-Silver Bow County*, 298 F. 3d 1022, 1026 (CA9 2002). At any rate, the officers' search uncovered no illegal weapons or explosives. When the officers left, petitioner gave Mrs. Ramirez a copy of the search warrant, but not a copy of the application, which had been sealed. The following day, in response to a request from respondents' attorney, petitioner faxed the attorney a copy of the page of the application that listed the items to be seized. No charges were filed against the Ramirezes.

Respondents sued petitioner and the other officers under *Bivens v. Six Unknown Fed. Narcotics Agents*, 403 U. S. 388 (1971), and Rev. Stat. §1979, 42 U. S. C. §1983, raising eight claims, including violation of the Fourth Amendment. App. 17-27. The District Court entered summary judgment for all defendants. The court found no Fourth Amendment violation, because it considered the case comparable to one in which the warrant contained an inaccurate address, and in such a case, the court reasoned, the warrant is sufficiently detailed if the executing officers can locate the correct house. App. to Pet. for Cert. 20a-22a. The court added that even if a constitutional violation occurred, the defendants were entitled to qualified immunity because the failure of the warrant to describe the objects of the search amounted to a mere "typographical error." *Id.*, at 22a-24a.

The Court of Appeals affirmed the judgment with respect to all defendants and all claims, with the exception of respondents' Fourth Amendment claim against petitioner. 298 F. 3d, at 1029-1030. On that claim, the court held that the warrant was invalid because it did not "describe with particularity the place to be searched and the items to be seized," and that oral statements by petitioner during or after the search could not cure the omission. *Id.*, at 1025-1026. The court observed that the warrant's facial defect "increased the likelihood and degree of confrontation between the Ramirezes and the police" and deprived respondents of the means "to challenge officers who might have exceeded the limits imposed by the magistrate." *Id.*, at 1027. The court also expressed concern that "permitting officers to expand the scope of the warrant by oral statements would broaden the area of dispute between the parties in subsequent litigation." *Ibid.* The court nevertheless concluded that all of the officers except petitioner were protected by qualified immunity. With respect to petitioner, the court read our opinion in *United States v. Leon*, 468 U. S. 897 (1984), as precluding qualified immunity for the leader of a search who fails to "read the warrant and satisfy [himself] that [he] understand[s] its scope and limitations, and that it is not defective in some obvious way." 298 F. 3d, at 1027. The court added that "[t]he leaders of the search team must also make sure that a copy of the warrant is available to give to the person whose property is being searched at the commencement of the search, and that such copy has no missing pages or other obvious defects." *Ibid.* (footnote omitted). We granted certiorari. 537 U. S. 1231 (2003).

II

The warrant was plainly invalid. The Fourth Amendment states unambiguously that "no Warrants shall issue, but upon probable cause, supported by Oath or affirmation, and *particularly describing* the place to be searched, and *the persons or things to be seized.*" (Emphasis added.) The warrant in this case complied with the first three of these requirements: It was based on probable cause and supported by a sworn affidavit, and it described particularly the place of the search. On the fourth requirement, however, the warrant failed altogether. Indeed, petitioner concedes that "the warrant . . . was deficient in particularity because it provided no description of the type of evidence sought." Brief for Petitioner 10.

The fact that the *application* adequately described the "things to be seized" does not save the *warrant* from its facial invalidity. The Fourth Amendment by its terms requires particularity in the warrant, not in the supporting documents. See *Massachusetts v. Sheppard*, 468 U. S. 981, 988, n. 5 (1984) ("[A] warrant that fails to conform to the particularity requirement of the Fourth Amendment is unconstitutional"); see also *United States v. Stefonek*, 179 F. 3d 1030, 1033 (CA7 1999)

("The Fourth Amendment requires that the *warrant* particularly describe the things to be seized, not the papers presented to the judicial officer . . . asked to issue the warrant"). And for good reason: "The presence of a search warrant serves a high function," *McDonald v. United States,* 335 U. S. 451, 455 (1948), and that high function is not necessarily vindicated when some other document, somewhere, says something about the objects of the search, but the contents of that document are neither known to the person whose home is being searched nor available for her inspection. We do not say that the Fourth Amendment forbids a warrant from cross-referencing other documents. Indeed, most Courts of Appeals have held that a court may construe a warrant with reference to a supporting application or affidavit if the warrant uses appropriate words of incorporation, and if the supporting document accompanies the warrant. See, *e.g., United States v. McGrew,* 122 F. 3d 847, 849–850 (CA9 1997); *United States v. Williamson,* 1 F. 3d 1134, 1136, n. 1 (CA10 1993); *United States v. Blakeney,* 942 F. 2d 1001, 1025–1026 (CA6 1991); *United States v. Maxwell,* 920 F. 2d 1028, 1031 (CADC 1990); *United States v. Curry,* 911 F. 2d 72, 76–77 (CA8 1990); *United States v. Roche,* 614 F. 2d 6, 8 (CA1 1980). But in this case the warrant did not incorporate other documents by reference, nor did either the affidavit or the application (which had been placed under seal) accompany the warrant. Hence, we need not further explore the matter of incorporation.

Petitioner argues that even though the warrant was invalid, the search nevertheless was "reasonable" within the meaning of the Fourth Amendment. He notes that a Magistrate authorized the search on the basis of adequate evidence of probable cause, that petitioner orally described to respondents the items to be seized, and that the search did not exceed the limits intended by the Magistrate and described by petitioner. Thus, petitioner maintains, his search of respondents' ranch was functionally equivalent to a search authorized by a valid warrant.

We disagree. This warrant did not simply omit a few items from a list of many to be seized, or misdescribe a few of several items. Nor did it make what fairly could be characterized as a mere technical mistake or typographical error. Rather, in the space set aside for a description of the items to be seized, the warrant stated that the items consisted of a "single dwelling residence . . . blue in color." In other words, the warrant did not describe the items to be seized *at all.* In this respect the warrant was so obviously deficient that we must regard the search as "warrantless" within the meaning of our case law. See *Leon,* 468 U. S., at 923; cf. *Maryland v. Garrison,* 480 U. S. 79, 85 (1987); *Steele v. United States,* 267 U. S. 498, 503–504 (1925). "We are not dealing with formalities." *McDonald,* 335 U. S., at 455. Because "'the right of a man to retreat into his own home and there be free from unreasonable governmental intrusion'" stands "'[a]t the very core' of the Fourth Amendment," *Kyllo v. United States,* 533 U. S. 27, 31 (2001) (quoting *Silverman v. United States,* 365 U. S. 505, 511 (1961)), our cases have firmly established the "'basic principle of Fourth Amendment law' that searches and seizures inside a home without a warrant are presumptively unreasonable," *Payton v. New York,* 445 U. S. 573, 586 (1980) (footnote omitted). Thus, "absent exigent circumstances, a warrantless entry to search for weapons or contraband is unconstitutional even when a felony has been committed and there is probable cause to believe that incriminating evidence will be found within." *Id.,* at 587–588 (footnote omitted). See *Kyllo,* 533 U. S., at 29; *Illinois v. Rodriguez,* 497 U. S. 177, 181 (1990); *Chimel v. California,* 395 U. S. 752, 761–763 (1969); *McDonald,* 335 U. S., at 454; *Johnson v. United States,* 333 U. S. 10 (1948).

We have clearly stated that the presumptive rule against warrantless searches applies with equal force to searches whose only defect is a lack of particularity in the warrant. In *Sheppard,* for instance, the petitioner argued that even though the warrant was invalid for lack of particularity, "the search was constitutional because it was reasonable within the meaning of the Fourth Amendment." 468 U. S., at 988, n. 5. In squarely rejecting that position, we explained:

> "The uniformly applied rule is that a search conducted pursuant to a warrant that fails to conform to the particularity requirement of the Fourth Amendment is unconstitutional. *Stanford v. Texas,* 379 U. S. 476 (1965); *United States v. Cardwell,* 680 F. 2d 75, 77–78 (CA9 1982); *United States v. Crozier,* 674 F. 2d 1293, 1299 (CA9 1982); *United States v. Klein,* 565 F. 2d 183, 185 (CA1 1977); *United States v. Gardner,* 537 F. 2d 861, 862 (CA6 1976); *United States v. Marti,* 421 F. 2d 1263, 1268–1269 (CA2 1970). That rule is in keeping with the well-established principle that 'except in certain carefully defined classes of cases, a search of private property without proper consent is "unreasonable" unless it has been authorized by a valid search warrant.' *Camara v. Municipal Court,* 387 U. S. 523, 528–529 (1967). See *Steagald v. United States,* 451 U. S. 204, 211–212 (1981); *Jones v. United States,* 357 U. S. 493, 499 (1958)." *Ibid.*

Petitioner asks us to hold that a search conducted pursuant to a warrant lacking particularity should be exempt from the presumption of unreasonableness if the goals served by the particularity requirement are otherwise satisfied. He maintains that the search in this case satisfied those goals—which he says are "to prevent general searches, to prevent the seizure of one thing under a warrant describing another, and to prevent warrants from being issued on vague or dubious information," Brief for Petitioner 16—because the scope of the search did not exceed the limits set forth in the application. But unless the particular items described in the affidavit are also set forth in the warrant itself (or at least incorporated by reference, and the affidavit present at the search), there can be no written assurance that the Magistrate actually found probable cause to search for, and to seize, every item mentioned in the affidavit. See McDonald, 335 U. S., at 455 ("Absent some grave emergency, the Fourth Amendment has interposed a magistrate between the citizen and the police. This was done . . . so that an objective mind might weigh the need to invade [the citizen's] privacy in order to enforce the law"). In this case, for example, it is at least theoretically possible that the Magistrate was satisfied that the search for weapons and explosives was justified by the showing in the affidavit, but not convinced that any evidentiary basis existed for rummaging through respondents' files and papers for receipts pertaining to the purchase or manufacture of such items. Cf. *Stanford v. Texas*, 379 U. S. 476, 485–486 (1965). Or, conceivably, the Magistrate might have believed that some of the weapons mentioned in the affidavit could have been lawfully possessed and therefore should not be seized. See 26 U. S. C. §5861 (requiring registration, but not banning possession of, certain firearms). The mere fact that the Magistrate issued a warrant does not necessarily establish that he agreed that the scope of the search should be as broad as the affiant's request. Even though petitioner acted with restraint in conducting the search, "the inescapable fact is that this restraint was imposed by the agents themselves, not by a judicial officer." *Katz v. United States*, 389 U. S. 347, 356 (1967).[4]

We have long held, moreover, that the purpose of the particularity requirement is not limited to the prevention of general searches. See *Garrison*, 480 U. S., at 84. A particular warrant also "assures the individual whose property is searched or seized of the lawful authority of the executing officer, his need to search, and the limits of his power to search." *United States v. Chadwick*, 433 U. S. 1, 9 (1977) (citing *Camara v. Municipal Court of City and County of San Francisco*, 387 U. S. 523, 532 (1967)), abrogated on other grounds, *California v. Acevedo*, 500 U. S. 565 (1991). See also *Illinois v. Gates*, 462 U. S. 213, 236 (1983) ("[P]ossession of a warrant by officers conducting an arrest or search greatly reduces the perception of unlawful or intrusive police conduct").[5]

Petitioner argues that even if the goals of the particularity requirement are broader than he acknowledges, those goals nevertheless were served because he orally described to respondents the items for which he was searching. Thus, he submits, respondents had all of the notice that a proper warrant would have accorded. But this case presents no occasion even to reach this argument, since respondents, as noted above, dispute petitioner's account. According to Mrs. Ramirez, petitioner stated only that he was looking for an "'explosive device in a box.'" 298 F. 3d, at 1026. Because this dispute is before us on petitioner's motion for summary judgment, App. to Pet. for Cert. 13a, "[t]he evidence of the nonmovant is to be believed, and all justifiable inferences are to be drawn in [her] favor," *Anderson v. Liberty Lobby, Inc.*, 477 U. S. 242, 255 (1986) (citation omitted). The posture of the case therefore obliges us to credit Mrs. Ramirez's account, and we find that petitioner's description of "'an explosive device in a box'" was little better than no guidance at all. See *Stefonek*, 179 F. 3d, at 1032–1033 (holding that a search warrant for "'evidence of crime'" was "[s]o open-ended" in its description that it could "only be described as a general warrant").

It is incumbent on the officer executing a search warrant to ensure the search is lawfully authorized and lawfully conducted.[6] Because petitioner did not have in his possession a warrant particularly describing the things he intended to seize, proceeding with the search was clearly "unreasonable" under the Fourth Amendment. The Court of Appeals correctly held that the search was unconstitutional.

III

Having concluded that a constitutional violation occurred, we turn to the question whether petitioner is entitled to qualified immunity despite that violation. See *Wilson v. Layne*, 526 U. S. 603, 609 (1999). The answer depends on whether the right that was transgressed was "'clearly established'"—that is, "whether it would be clear to a reasonable officer that his conduct was unlawful in the situation he confronted." *Saucier v. Katz*, 533 U. S. 194, 202 (2001).

Given that the particularity requirement is set forth in the text of the Constitution, no reasonable officer could believe that a warrant that plainly did not comply with that requirement was valid. See *Harlow v. Fitzgerald*, 457 U. S. 800, 818–819 (1982) ("If the law was clearly established, the immunity defense ordinarily should fail, since a reasonably competent public official should know the law governing his conduct"). Moreover, because petitioner himself prepared the invalid warrant, he may not argue that he reasonably relied on the Magistrate's assurance that the warrant contained an adequate description of the things to be seized and was therefore valid. Cf. *Sheppard*, 468 U. S., at 989–990. In fact, the guidelines of petitioner's own department placed him on notice that he might be liable for executing a manifestly invalid warrant. An ATF directive in force at the time of this search warned: "Special agents are liable if they exceed their authority while executing a search warrant and must be sure that a search warrant is sufficient on its face even when issued by a magistrate." Searches and Examinations, ATF Order O 3220.1(7)(d) (Feb. 13, 1997). See also *id.*, at 3220.1(23)(b) ("If any error or deficiency is discovered and there is a reasonable probability that it will invalidate the warrant, such warrant shall not be executed. The search shall be postponed until a satisfactory warrant has been obtained").[7] And even a cursory reading of the warrant in this case—perhaps just a simple glance—would have revealed a glaring deficiency that any reasonable police officer would have known was constitutionally fatal.

No reasonable officer could claim to be unaware of the basic rule, well established by our cases, that, absent consent or exigency, a warrantless search of the home is presumptively unconstitutional. See *Payton*, 445 U. S., at 586–588. Indeed, as we noted nearly 20 years ago in *Sheppard*: "The uniformly applied rule is that a search conducted pursuant to a warrant that fails to conform to the particularity requirement of the Fourth Amendment is unconstitutional." 468 U. S., at 988, n. 5.[8] Because not a word in any of our cases would suggest to a reasonable officer that this case fits within any exception to that fundamental tenet, petitioner is asking us, in effect, to craft a new exception. Absent any support for such an exception in our cases, he cannot reasonably have relied on an expectation that we would do so.

Petitioner contends that the search in this case was the product, at worst, of a lack of due care, and that our case law requires more than negligent behavior before depriving an official of qualified immunity. See *Malley v. Briggs*, 475 U. S. 335, 341 (1986). But as we observed in the companion case to *Sheppard*, "a warrant may be so facially deficient—*i.e.*, in failing to particularize the place to be searched or the things to be seized—that the executing officers cannot reasonably presume it to be valid." *Leon*, 468 U. S., at 923. This is such a case.[9]

Accordingly, the judgment of the Court of Appeals is affirmed.

It is so ordered.

Footnotes

[1] Possession of these items, if unregistered, would violate 18 U. S. C. §922(o)(1) and 26 U. S. C. §5861.

[2] The warrant stated: "[T]here is now concealed [on the specified premises] a certain person or property, namely [a] single dwelling residence two story in height which is blue in color and has two additions attached to the east. The front entrance to the residence faces in a southerly direction." App. to Pet. for Cert. 26a.

[3] The affidavit was sealed. Its sufficiency is not disputed.

[4] For this reason petitioner's argument that any constitutional error was committed by the Magistrate, not petitioner, is misplaced. In *Massachusetts v. Sheppard*, 468 U. S. 981 (1984), we suggested that "the judge, not the police officers," may have committed "[a]n error of constitutional dimension," *id.*, at 990, because the judge had assured the officers requesting the warrant that he would take the steps necessary to conform the warrant to constitutional requirements, *id.*, at 986. Thus, "it was not unreasonable for the police in [that] case to rely on the judge's assurances that the warrant authorized the search they had requested." *Id.*, at 990, n. 6. In this case, by contrast, petitioner did not alert the Magistrate to the defect in the warrant that petitioner had drafted, and we therefore cannot know whether the Magistrate was aware of the scope of the search he was authorizing. Nor would it have been reasonable for petitioner to rely on a warrant that was so patently defective, even if the Magistrate was aware of the deficiency. See *United States v. Leon*, 468 U. S. 897, 915, 922, n. 23 (1984).

[5] It is true, as petitioner points out, that neither the Fourth Amendment nor Rule 41 of the Federal Rules of Criminal Procedure requires the executing officer to serve the warrant on the owner before commencing the search. Rule 41(f)(3) provides that "[t]he officer executing the warrant must: (A) give a copy of the warrant and a receipt for the property taken to the person from whom, or from whose pre-

mises, the property was taken; or (B) leave a copy of the warrant and receipt at the place where the officer took the property." Quite obviously, in some circumstances—a surreptitious search by means of a wiretap, for example, or the search of empty or abandoned premises—it will be impracticable or imprudent for the officers to show the warrant in advance. See *Katz v. United States*, 389 U. S. 347, 355, n. 16 (1967); *Ker v. California*, 374 U. S. 23, 37–41 (1963). Whether it would be unreasonable to refuse a request to furnish the warrant at the outset of the search when, as in this case, an occupant of the premises is present and poses no threat to the officers' safe and effective performance of their mission, is a question that this case does not present.

[6] The Court of Appeals' decision is consistent with this principle. Petitioner mischaracterizes the court's decision when he contends that it imposed a novel proofreading requirement on officers executing warrants. The court held that officers leading a search team must "mak[e] sure that they have a proper warrant that in fact authorizes the search and seizure they are about to conduct." 298 F. 3d 1022, 1027 (CA9 2002). That is not a duty to proofread; it is, rather, a duty to ensure that the warrant conforms to constitutional requirements.

[7] We do not suggest that an official is deprived of qualified immunity whenever he violates an internal guideline. We refer to the ATF Order only to underscore that petitioner should have known that he should not execute a patently defective warrant.

[8] Although both *Sheppard* and *Leon* involved the application of the "good faith" exception to the Fourth Amendment's general exclusionary rule, we have explained that "the same standard of objective reasonableness that we applied in the context of a suppression hearing in *Leon* defines the qualified immunity accorded an officer." *Malley v. Briggs*, 475 U. S. 335, 344 (1986) (citation omitted).

[9] JUSTICE KENNEDY argues in dissent that we have not allowed "'ample room for mistaken judgments,'" *post*, at 6 (quoting *Malley*, 475 U. S., at 343), because "difficult and important tasks demand the officer's full attention in the heat of an ongoing and often dangerous criminal investigation," *post*, at 3. In this case, however, petitioner does not contend that any sort of exigency existed when he drafted the affidavit, the warrant application, and the warrant, or when he conducted the search. This is not the situation, therefore, in which we have recognized that "officers in the dangerous and difficult process of making arrests and executing search warrants" require "some latitude." *Maryland v. Garrison*, 480 U. S. 79, 87 (1987).

Nor are we according "the correctness of paper forms" a higher status than "substantive rights." *Post*, at 6. As we have explained, the Fourth Amendment's particularity requirement assures the subject of the search that a magistrate has duly authorized the officer to conduct a search of limited scope. This substantive right is not protected when the officer fails to take the time to glance at the authorizing document and detect a glaring defect that JUSTICE KENNEDY agrees is of constitutional magnitude, *post*, at 1.

Muehler et al. v. Mena
544 U. S. ___ (2005)

Argued December 8, 2004
Decided March 22, 2005
CHIEF JUSTICE REHNQUIST delivered the opinion of the Court.

Respondent Iris Mena was detained in handcuffs during a search of the premises that she and several others occupied. Petitioners were lead members of a police detachment executing a search warrant of these premises. She sued the officers under Rev. Stat. §1979, 42 U. S. C. §1983, and the District Court found in her favor. The Court of Appeals affirmed the judgment, holding that the use of handcuffs to detain Mena during the search violated the Fourth Amendment and that the officers' questioning of Mena about her immigration status during the detention constituted an independent Fourth Amendment violation. *Mena v. Simi Valley*, 332 F. 3d 1255 (CA9 2003). We hold that Mena's detention in handcuffs for the length of the search was consistent with our opinion in *Michigan v. Summers*, 452 U. S. 692 (1981), and that the officers' questioning during that detention did not violate her Fourth Amendment rights.

* * *

Based on information gleaned from the investigation of a gang-related, driveby shooting, petitioners Muehler and Brill had reason to believe at least one member of a gang—the West Side Locos—lived at 1363 Patricia Avenue. They also suspected that the individual was armed and dangerous, since he had recently been involved in the driveby shooting. As a result, Muehler obtained a search warrant for 1363 Patricia Avenue that authorized a broad search of the house and premises for, among other things, deadly weapons and evidence of gang membership. In light of the high degree of risk involved in searching a house suspected of housing at least one, and perhaps multiple, armed gang members, a Special Weapons and Tactics (SWAT) team was used to secure the residence and grounds before the search.

At 7 a.m. on February 3, 1998, petitioners, along with the SWAT team and other officers, executed the warrant. Mena was asleep in her bed when the SWAT team, clad in helmets and black vests adorned with badges and the word "POLICE," entered her bedroom and placed her in handcuffs at gunpoint. The SWAT team also handcuffed three other individuals found on the property. The SWAT team then took those individuals and Mena into a converted garage, which contained several beds and some other bedroom furniture. While the search proceeded, one or two officers guarded the four detainees, who were allowed to move around the garage but remained in handcuffs.

Aware that the West Side Locos gang was composed primarily of illegal immigrants, the officers had notified the Immigration and Naturalization Service (INS) that they would be conducting the search, and an INS officer accompanied the officers executing the warrant. During their detention in the garage, an officer asked for each detainee's name, date of birth, place of birth, and immigration status. The INS officer later asked the detainees for their immigration documentation. Mena's status as a permanent resident was confirmed by her papers.

The search of the premises yielded a .22 caliber handgun with .22 caliber ammunition, a box of .25 caliber ammunition, several baseball bats with gang writing, various additional gang paraphernalia, and a bag of marijuana. Before the officers left the area, Mena was released.

In her §1983 suit against the officers she alleged that she was detained "for an unreasonable time and in an unreasonable manner" in violation of the Fourth Amendment. App. 19. In addition, she claimed that the warrant and its execution were overbroad, that the officers failed to comply with the "knock and announce" rule, and that the officers had needlessly destroyed property during the search. The officers moved for summary judgment, asserting that they were entitled to qualified immunity, but the District Court denied their motion. The Court of Appeals affirmed that denial, *except* for Mena's claim that the warrant was overbroad; on this claim the Court of Appeals held that the officers were entitled to qualified immunity. *Mena v. Simi Valley*, 226 F. 3d 1031 (CA9 2000). After a trial, a jury, pursuant to a special verdict form, found that Officers Muehler and Brill violated Mena's Fourth Amendment right to be free from unreasonable seizures by detaining her both with force greater than that which was reasonable and for a longer period than that which was reasonable. The jury awarded Mena $10,000 in actual damages and $20,000 in punitive damages against each petitioner for a total of $60,000.

The Court of Appeals affirmed the judgment on two grounds. 332 F. 3d 1255 (CA9 2003). Reviewing the denial of qualified immunity *de novo, id.,* at 1261, n. 2, it first held that the officers' detention of Mena violated the Fourth Amendment because it was objectively unreasonable to confine her in the converted garage and keep her in handcuffs during the search, *id.,* at 1263-1264. In the Court of Appeals' view, the officers should have released Mena as soon as it became clear that she posed no immediate threat. *Id.,* at 1263. The court additionally held that the questioning of Mena about her immigration status constituted an independent Fourth Amendment violation. *Id.,* at 1264-1266. The Court of Appeals went on to hold that those rights were clearly established at the time of Mena's questioning, and thus the officers were not entitled to qualified immunity. *Id.,* at 1266-1267. We granted certiorari, 542 U. S. ___ (2004), and now vacate and remand.

* * *

In *Michigan v. Summers,* 452 U. S. 692 (1981), we held that officers executing a search warrant for contraband have the authority "to detain the occupants of the premises while a proper search is conducted." *Id.,* at 705. Such detentions are appropriate, we explained, because the character of the additional intrusion caused by detention is slight and because the justifications for detention are substantial. *Id.,* at 701-705. We made clear that the detention of an occupant is "surely less intrusive than the search itself," and the presence of a warrant assures that a neutral magistrate has determined that probable cause exists to search the home. *Id.,* at 701. Against this incremental intrusion, we posited three legitimate law enforcement interests that provide substantial justification for detaining an occupant: "preventing flight in the event that incriminating evidence is found"; "minimizing the risk of harm to the officers"; and facilitating "the orderly completion of the search," as detainees' "self-interest may induce them to open locked doors or locked containers to avoid the use of force." *Id.,* at 702-703.

Mena's detention was, under *Summers,* plainly permissible.[1] An officer's authority to detain incident to a search is categorical; it does not depend on the "quantum of proof justifying detention or the extent of the intrusion to be imposed by the seizure." *Id.,* at 705, n. 19. Thus, Mena's detention for the duration of the search was reasonable under *Summers* because a warrant existed to search 1363 Patricia Avenue and she was an occupant of that address at the time of the search.

Inherent in *Summers'* authorization to detain an occupant of the place to be searched is the authority to use reasonable force to effectuate the detention. See *Graham v. Connor,* 490 U. S. 386, 396 (1989) ("Fourth Amendment jurisprudence has long recognized that the right to make an arrest or investigatory stop necessarily carries with it the right to use some degree of physical coercion or threat thereof to effect it"). Indeed, *Summers* itself stressed that the risk of harm to officers and occupants is minimized "if the officers routinely exercise unquestioned command of the situation." 452 U. S., at 703.

The officers' use of force in the form of handcuffs to effectuate Mena's detention in the garage, as well as the detention of the three other occupants, was reasonable because the governmental interests outweigh the marginal intrusion. See *Graham, supra,* at 396-397. The imposition of correctly applied handcuffs on Mena, who was already being lawfully detained during a search of the house, was undoubtedly a separate intrusion in addition to detention in the converted garage.[2] The detention was thus more intrusive than that which we upheld in *Summers.* See 452 U. S., at 701-702 (concluding that the additional intrusion in the form of a detention was less than that of the warrant-sanctioned search); *Maryland v. Wilson,* 519 U. S. 408, 413-414 (1997) (concluding that the additional intrusion from ordering passengers out of a car, which was already stopped, was minimal).

But this was no ordinary search. The governmental interests in not only detaining, but using handcuffs, are at their maximum when, as here, a warrant authorizes a search for weapons and a wanted gang member resides on the premises. In such inherently dangerous situations, the use of handcuffs minimizes the risk of harm to both officers and occupants. Cf. *Summers, supra,* at 702-703 (recognizing the execution of a warrant to search for drugs "may give rise to sudden violence or frantic efforts to conceal or destroy evidence"). Though this safety risk inherent in executing a search warrant for weapons was sufficient to justify the use of handcuffs, the need to detain multiple occupants made the use of handcuffs all the more reasonable. Cf. *Maryland v. Wilson, supra,* at 414 (noting that "danger to an officer from a traffic stop is likely to be greater when there are passengers in addition to the driver in the stopped car").

Mena argues that, even if the use of handcuffs to detain her in the garage was reasonable as an initial matter, the duration of the use of handcuffs made the detention unreasonable. The duration of a detention can, of course, affect the balance of interests under *Graham.* However, the 2- to 3-hour detention in handcuffs in this case does not outweigh the government's continuing safety interests. As we have noted, this case involved the detention of four detainees by two officers during a search of a gang house for dangerous weapons. We conclude that the detention of Mena in handcuffs during the search was reasonable.

The Court of Appeals also determined that the officers violated Mena's Fourth Amendment rights by questioning her about her immigration status during the detention. 332 F. 3d, at 1264-1266. This holding, it appears, was premised on the assumption that the officers were required to have independent reasonable suspicion in order to question Mena concerning her immigration status because the questioning constituted a discrete Fourth Amendment event. But the premise is faulty. We have "held repeatedly that mere police questioning does not constitute a seizure." *Florida v. Bostick*, 501 U. S. 429, 434 (1991); see also *INS v. Delgado*, 466 U. S. 210, 212 (1984). "[E]ven when officers have no basis for suspecting a particular individual, they may generally ask questions of that individual; ask to examine the individual's identification; and request consent to search his or her luggage." *Bostick*, *supra*, at 434–435 (citations omitted). As the Court of Appeals did not hold that the detention was prolonged by the questioning, there was no additional seizure within the meaning of the Fourth Amendment. Hence, the officers did not need reasonable suspicion to ask Mena for her name, date and place of birth, or immigration status.

Our recent opinion in *Illinois v. Caballes*, 543 U. S. __ (2005), is instructive. There, we held that a dog sniff performed during a traffic stop does not violate the Fourth Amendment. We noted that a lawful seizure "can become unlawful if it is prolonged beyond the time reasonably required to complete that mission," but accepted the state court's determination that the duration of the stop was not extended by the dog sniff. *Id.*, at __ (slip op., at 2–3). Because we held that a dog sniff was not a search subject to the Fourth Amendment, we rejected the notion that "the shift in purpose" "from a lawful traffic stop into a drug investigation" was unlawful because it "was not supported by any reasonable suspicion." *Id.*, at __ (slip op., at 3–4). Likewise here, the initial *Summers* detention was lawful; the Court of Appeals did not find that the questioning extended the time Mena was detained. Thus no additional Fourth Amendment justification for inquiring about Mena's immigration status was required.[3]

In summary, the officers' detention of Mena in handcuffs during the execution of the search warrant was reasonable and did not violate the Fourth Amendment. Additionally, the officers' questioning of Mena did not constitute an independent Fourth Amendment violation. Mena has advanced in this Court, as she did before the Court of Appeals, an alternative argument for affirming the judgment below. She asserts that her detention extended beyond the time the police completed the tasks incident to the search. Because the Court of Appeals did not address this contention, we too decline to address it. See *Pierce County v. Guillen*, 537 U. S. 129, 148, n. 10 (2003); *National Collegiate Athletic Assn. v. Smith*, 525 U. S. 459, 469–470 (1999).

The judgment of the Court of Appeals is therefore vacated, and the case is remanded for further proceedings consistent with this opinion.

It is so ordered.

Footnotes

[1] In determining whether a Fourth Amendment violation occurred we draw all reasonable factual inferences in favor of the jury verdict, but as we made clear in

Ornelas v. United States, 517 U. S. 690, 697-699 (1996), we do not defer to the jury's legal conclusion that those facts violate the Constitution.

[2] In finding the officers should have released Mena from the handcuffs, the Court of Appeals improperly relied upon the fact that the warrant did not include Mena as a suspect. See *Mena v. Simi Valley*, 332 F. 3d 1255, 1263, n. 5 (CA9 2003). The warrant was concerned not with individuals but with locations and property. In particular, the warrant in this case authorized the search of 1363 Patricia Avenue and its surrounding grounds for, among other things, deadly weapons and evidence of street gang membership. In this respect, the warrant here resembles that at issue in *Michigan v. Summers*, 452 U. S. 692 (1981), which allowed the search of a residence for drugs without mentioning any individual, including the owner of the home whom police ultimately arrested. See *People v. Summers*, 407 Mich. 432, 440-443, 286 N. W. 2d 226, 226-227 (1979), rev'd, *Michigan v. Summers, supra.* *Summers* makes clear that when a neutral magistrate has determined police have probable cause to believe contraband exists, "[t]he connection of an occupant to [a] home" alone "justifies a detention of that occupant." 452 U. S., at 703-704.

[3] The Court of Appeals' reliance on *United States v. Brignoni-Ponce*, 422 U. S. 873 (1975), is misplaced. *Brignoni-Ponce* held that stops by roving patrols near the border "may be justified on facts that do not amount to the probable cause require[ment] for an arrest." *Id.*, at 880. We considered only whether the patrols had the "authority to *stop* automobiles in areas near the Mexican border," *id.*, at 874 (emphasis added), and expressed no opinion as to the appropriateness of questioning when an individual was already seized. See *United States v. Martinez-Fuerte*, 428 U. S. 543, 556-562 (1976). We certainly did not, as the Court of Appeals suggested, create a "requirement of particularized reasonable suspicion for purposes of inquiry into citizenship status." 332 F. 3d, at 1267.

Discussion Questions

1. What constitutional amendment governs searches and seizures by police officers? Is it possible for a search or seizure to violate other constitutional amendments?

2. In police use of force cases, the Court adopted the "objective reasonableness" standard. Did the Court apply this standard to police searches? What are the implications of this position?

3. How does the Court make decisions about which constitutional amendment should be used to analyze a search or seizure?

4. Can searches and seizures be effected without the actual taking of property or control of an individual? What police actions constitute a deprivation of liberty?

5. What is the role of probable cause in determining both liability and immunity for a claim of an illegal search or seizure?

6. Was the *Wilson* case a search and seizure or a liberty interest case?

7. Can the actions of a nonpolice third party render the police liable for an illegal search and seizure?

8. What are the implications of the *Wilson* decision for police/citizen and police/community relations?

9. How did agency policy influence the Court in making its decision in the *Wilson* case? What does this mean for the creation of future law enforcement policy?

10. Can the Court's decision in *Wilson* be applied to excessive force cases or other police activities?

11. What is required to establish municipal liability for failure to train police officers?

12. Is there a degree of culpability or fault required to establish municipal liability for failure to train? If so, what is the standard and how is it met?

13. Must there be a causal link between a municipality's failure to train and constitutional violation caused by an officer to establish liability?

14. If Section 1983 is not a source of substantive rights, what constitutional amendment governs police failure to train?

15. According to the Court what areas of police practice require adequate training? How is this determination made? What are the implications of this decision-making process for the future of police training?

16. Does the *Collins* decision overturn or modify the *Canton* decision?

17. Does the *Collins* decision close the door on all claims of workplace injury based on inadequate training?

18. If a police officer were shot and killed by a fellow police officer during a drug raid because of inadequate training, would the officer's family have a viable cause of action under Section 1983? Would this situation be analyzed under the provisions of the Fourth Amendment or as a failure to train?

PART VI

Police Use
of Vehicles

In this part of your casebook, the Court continues to define the boundaries of the Fourth and Fourteenth Amendments as they apply to the liability of law enforcement officers for the violation of citizens' constitutional rights. The Court takes up the issue of police use of motor vehicles and under what circumstances their use can result in violation of constitutional rights that lead to liability. Central to the issues addressed by the Court in these opinions are the applicability of the Fourth Amendment's reasonableness standard and the Fourteenth Amendment's due process clause.

The Court distinguishes between seizures that are brought about by means of motor vehicles, as in the case of police roadblocks, and injuries sustained as a result of police vehicular pursuits. In drawing a line between the applicability of these two amendments, the Court articulates a standard for determining whether a police action constitutes a seizure that brings litigation under the provisions of the Fourth Amendment and behaviors that "shock the conscience" so as to violate the due process clause of the Fourteenth Amendment. In making this distinction, the Court must revisit the differences between the objective reasonableness standard and the subjective aspects of culpability. The Court then turns its attention to the level of culpability required for a law enforcement officer to violate the provisions of the Fourteenth Amendment and distinguishes this level of culpability from its earlier articulated deliberate indifference standard. In these opinions, the Court refines the decision-making process for determining police civil liability.

Brower v. County of Inyo
489 U.S. 593 (1989)

Argued January 11, 1989
Decided March 21, 1989
JUSTICE SCALIA delivered the opinion of the Court.

On the night of October 23, 1984, William James Caldwell (Brower) was killed when the stolen car that he had been driving at high speeds for approximately 20 miles in an effort to elude pursuing police crashed into a police roadblock. His heirs, petitioners here, brought this action in Federal District Court under 42 U.S.C. § 1983, claiming, *inter alia*, that respondents used "brutal, excessive, unreasonable and unnecessary physical force" in establishing the roadblock, and thus effected an unreasonable seizure of Brower, in violation of the Fourth Amendment. Petitioners alleged that "under color of statutes, regulations, customs and usages," respondents (1) caused an 18-wheel tractor-trailer to be placed across both lanes of a two-lane highway in the path of Brower's flight, (2) "effectively concealed" this roadblock by placing it behind a curve and leaving it unilluminated, and (3) positioned a police car, with its headlights on, between Brower's oncoming vehicle and the truck, so that Brower would be "blinded" on his approach. App. 8-9. Petitioners further alleged that Brower's fatal collision with the truck was "a proximate result" of this official conduct. *Id.*, at 9. The District Court granted respondents' motion to dismiss the complaint for failure to state a claim on the ground (insofar as the Fourth Amendment claim was concerned) that "establishing a roadblock [was] not unreasonable under the circumstances." App. to Pet. for Cert. A-21. A divided panel of the Court of Appeals for the Ninth Circuit affirmed the dismissal of the Fourth Amendment claim on the basis that no "seizure" had occurred. 817 F.2d 540, 545-546 (1987). We granted certiorari, 487 U.S. 1217 (1988), to resolve a conflict between that decision and the contrary holding [489 U.S. 593, 595] of the Court of Appeals for the Fifth Circuit in *Jamieson v. Shaw*, 772 F.2d 1205 (1985).

The Fourth Amendment to the Constitution provides:

> "The right of the people to be secure in their persons, houses, papers, and effects, against unreasonable searches and seizures, shall not be violated, and no Warrants shall issue, but upon probable cause, supported by Oath or affirmation, and particularly describing the place to be searched, and the person or things to be seized."

In *Tennessee v. Garner*, 471 U.S. 1 (1985), all Members of the Court agreed that a police officer's fatal shooting of a fleeing suspect constituted a Fourth Amendment "seizure." See *id.*, at 7; *id.*, at 25 (O'CONNOR, J., dissenting). We reasoned that "[w]henever an officer restrains the freedom of a person to walk away, he has seized that person." *Id.*, at 7. While acknowledging *Garner*, the Court of Appeals here concluded that no "seizure" occurred when Brower collided with the police roadblock because "[p]rior to his failure to stop voluntarily, his freedom of movement was never arrested or restrained" and because "[h]e had a number of opportunities to stop his automobile prior to the impact." 817 F.2d, at 546. Essentially the same thing, however, could have been said in *Garner*. Brower's independent decision to continue the chase can no more eliminate respondents' responsibility for the termination of his movement effected by the roadblock than Garner's independent decision to flee eliminated the Memphis police officer's responsibility for the termination of his movement effected by the bullet.

The Court of Appeals was impelled to its result by consideration of what it described as the "analogous situation" of a police chase in which the suspect unexpectedly loses control of his car and crashes. See *Galas v. McKee*, 801 F.2d 200, 202-203 (CA6 1986) (no seizure in such circumstances). We agree that no unconstitutional seizure occurs there, but not for a reason that has any application to the present case. [489 U.S. 593, 596] Violation of the Fourth Amendment requires an intentional acquisition of physical control. A seizure occurs even when an unintended person or thing is the object of the detention or taking, see *Hill v. California*, 401 U.S. 797, 802-805 (1971); cf. *Maryland v. Garrison*, 480 U.S. 79, 85-89 (1987), but the detention or taking itself must be willful. This is implicit in the word "seizure," which can hardly be applied to an unknowing act. The writs of assistance that were the principal grievance against which the Fourth Amendment was directed, see *Boyd v. United States*, 116 U.S. 616, 624-625 (1886); T. Cooley, Constitutional Limitations *301-*302, did not involve unintended consequences of government action. Nor did the general warrants issued by Lord Halifax in the 1760's, which produced "the first and only major litigation in the English courts in the field of search and seizure," T.

Taylor, Two Studies in Constitutional Interpretation 26 (1969), including the case we have described as a "monument of English freedom" "undoubtedly familiar" to "every American statesman" at the time the Constitution was adopted, and considered to be "the true and ultimate expression of constitutional law," *Boyd, supra,* at 626 (discussing *Entick v. Carrington,* 19 How. St. Tr. 1029, 95 Eng. Rep. 807 (K. B. 1765)). In sum, the Fourth Amendment addresses "misuse of power," *Byars v. United States,* 273 U.S. 28, 33 (1927), not the accidental effects of otherwise lawful government conduct.

Thus, if a parked and unoccupied police car slips its brake and pins a passerby against a wall, it is likely that a tort has occurred, but not a violation of the Fourth Amendment. And the situation would not change if the passerby happened, by lucky chance, to be a serial murderer for whom there was an outstanding arrest warrant—even if, at the time he was thus pinned, he was in the process of running away from two pursuing constables. It is clear, in other words, that a Fourth Amendment seizure does not occur whenever there is a governmentally caused termination of an [489 U.S. 593, 597] individual's freedom of movement (the innocent passerby), nor even whenever there is a governmentally caused and governmentally *desired* termination of an individual's freedom of movement (the fleeing felon), but only when there is a governmental termination of freedom of movement *through means intentionally applied.* That is the reason there was no seizure in the hypothetical situation that concerned the Court of Appeals. The pursuing police car sought to stop the suspect only by the show of authority represented by flashing lights and continuing pursuit; and though he was in fact stopped, he was stopped by a different means—his loss of control of his vehicle and the subsequent crash. If, instead of that, the police cruiser had pulled alongside the fleeing car and sideswiped it, producing the crash, then the termination of the suspect's freedom of movement would have been a seizure.

This analysis is reflected by our decision in *Hester v. United States,* 265 U.S. 57 (1924), where an armed revenue agent had pursued the defendant and his accomplice after seeing them obtain containers thought to be filled with "moonshine whisky." During their flight they dropped the containers, which the agent recovered. The defendant sought to suppress testimony concerning the containers' contents as the product of an unlawful seizure. Justice Holmes, speaking for a unanimous Court, concluded: "The defendant's own acts, and those of his associates, disclosed the jug, the jar and the bottle—and there was no seizure in the sense of the law when the officers examined the contents of each after they had been abandoned." *Id.,* at 58. Thus, even though the incriminating containers were unquestionably taken into possession as a result (in the broad sense) of action by the police, the Court held that no seizure had taken place. It would have been quite different, of course, if the revenue agent had shouted, "Stop and give us those bottles, in the name of the law!" and the defendant and his accomplice had complied. Then the taking of possession would have been [489 U.S. 593, 598] not merely the result of government action but the result of the very means (the show of authority) that the government selected, and a Fourth Amendment seizure would have occurred.

In applying these principles to the dismissal of petitioners' Fourth Amendment complaint for failure to state a claim, we can sustain the District Court's action only if, taking the allegations of the complaint in the light most favorable to petitioners, see *Scheuer v. Rhodes*, 416 U.S. 232, 236 (1974), we nonetheless conclude that they could prove no set of facts entitling them to relief for a "seizure." See *Conley v. Gibson*, 355 U.S. 41, 45-46 (1957). Petitioners have alleged the establishment of a roadblock crossing both lanes of the highway. In marked contrast to a police car pursuing with flashing lights, or to a policeman in the road signaling an oncoming car to halt, see *Kibbe v. Springfield*, 777 F.2d 801, 802-803 (CA1 1985), cert. dism'd, 480 U.S. 257 (1987), a roadblock is not just a significant show of authority to induce a voluntary stop, but is designed to produce a stop by physical impact if voluntary compliance does not occur. It may well be that respondents here preferred, and indeed earnestly hoped, that Brower would stop on his own, without striking the barrier, but we do not think it practicable to conduct such an inquiry into subjective intent. See *United States v. Leon*, 468 U.S. 897, 922, n. 23 (1984); see also *Anderson v. Creighton*, 483 U.S. 635, 641 (1987); *Harlow v. Fitzgerald*, 457 U.S. 800, 815-819 (1982). Nor do we think it possible, in determining whether there has been a seizure in a case such as this, to distinguish between a roadblock that is designed to give the oncoming driver the option of a voluntary stop (*e.g.*, one at the end of a long straightaway), and a roadblock that is designed precisely to produce a collision (*e.g.*, one located just around a bend). In determining whether the means that terminates the freedom of movement is the very means that the government intended we cannot draw too fine a line, or we will be driven to saying that one is not seized who has been [489 U.S. 593, 599] stopped by the accidental discharge of a gun with which he was meant only to be bludgeoned, or by a bullet in the heart that was meant only for the leg. We think it enough for a seizure that a person be stopped by the very instrumentality set in motion or put in place in order to achieve that result. It was enough here, therefore, that, according to the allegations of the complaint, Brower was meant to be stopped by the physical obstacle of the roadblock—and that he was so stopped.

This is not to say that the precise character of the roadblock is irrelevant to further issues in this case. "Seizure" alone is not enough for § 1983 liability; the seizure must be "unreasonable." Petitioners can claim the right to recover for Brower's death only because the unreasonableness they allege consists precisely of setting up the roadblock in such manner as to be likely to kill him. This should be contrasted with the situation that would obtain if the sole claim of unreasonableness were that there was no probable cause for the stop. In that case, if Brower had had the opportunity to stop voluntarily at the roadblock, but had negligently or intentionally driven into it, then, because of lack of proximate causality, respondents, though responsible for depriving him of his freedom of movement, would not be liable for his death. See *Martinez v. California*, 444 U.S. 277, 285 (1980); *Cameron v. Pontiac*, 813 F.2d 782, 786 (CA6 1987). Thus, the circumstances of this roadblock, including the allegation that headlights were used to blind the oncoming driver, may yet determine the outcome of this case.

The complaint here sufficiently alleges that respondents, under color of law, sought to stop Brower by means of a roadblock and succeeded in doing so. That is enough to constitute a "seizure" within the meaning of the Fourth Amendment. Accordingly, we reverse the judgment of the Court of Appeals and remand for consideration of whether the District Court properly dismissed the Fourth Amendment claim [489 U.S. 593, 600] on the basis that the alleged roadblock did not effect a seizure that was "unreasonable."

It is so ordered.

County of Sacramento
v. Lewis
523 U.S. 833 (1998)

Argued December 9, 1997
Decided May 26, 1998
JUSTICE SOUTER delivered the opinion of the Court.

The issue in this case is whether a police officer violates the Fourteenth Amendment's guarantee of substantive due process by causing death through deliberate or reckless indifference to life in a high-speed automobile chase aimed at apprehending a suspected offender. We answer no, and hold that in such circumstances only a purpose to cause harm unrelated to the legitimate object of arrest will satisfy the element of arbitrary conduct shocking to the conscience, necessary for a due process violation.

I

On May 22, 1990, at approximately 8:30 p.m., petitioner James Everett Smith, a Sacramento County sheriff's deputy, along with another officer, Murray Stapp, responded to a call to break up a fight. Upon returning to his patrol car, Stapp saw a motorcycle approaching at high speed. It was operated by 18-year-old Brian Willard and carried Philip Lewis, respondents' 16-year-old decedent, as a passenger. Neither boy had anything to do with the fight that prompted the call to the police.

Stapp turned on his overhead rotating lights, yelled to the boys to stop, and pulled his patrol car closer to Smith's, attempting to pen the motorcycle in. Instead of pulling over in response to Stapp's warning lights and commands, Willard slowly maneuvered the cycle between the two police cars and sped off. Smith immediately switched on his own emergency lights and siren, made a quick turn, and began pursuit at high speed. For 75 seconds over a course of 1.3 miles in a residential neighborhood, the motorcycle wove in and out of oncoming traffic, forcing two cars and a bicycle to swerve off of the road. The motorcycle and patrol car reached speeds up to 100 miles an hour, with Smith following at a distance as short as 100 feet; at that speed, his car would have required 650 feet to stop.

The chase ended after the motorcycle tipped over as Willard tried a sharp left turn. By the time Smith slammed on his brakes, Willard was out of the way, but Lewis was not. The patrol car skidded into him at 40 miles an hour, propelling him some 70 feet down the road and inflicting massive injuries. Lewis was pronounced dead at the scene.

Respondents, Philip Lewis's parents and the representatives of his estate, brought this action under Rev. Stat. § 1979, 42 U.S.C. § 1983 against petitioners Sacramento County, the Sacramento County Sheriff's Department and Deputy Smith, alleging a deprivation of Philip Lewis's Fourteenth Amendment substantive due process right to life.[1]

The District Court granted summary judgment for Smith, reasoning that even if he violated the Constitution, he was entitled to qualified immunity, because respondents could point to no "state or federal opinion published before May, 1990, when the alleged misconduct took place, that supports [their] view that [the decedent had] a Fourteenth Amendment substantive due process right in the context of high speed police pursuits." App. to Pet. for Cert. 52.[2]

The Court of Appeals for the Ninth Circuit reversed, holding that "the appropriate degree of fault to be applied to high-speed police pursuits is deliberate indifference to, or reckless disregard for, a person's right to life and personal security," 98 F. 3d 434, 441 (1996), and concluding that "the law regarding police liability for death or injury caused by an officer during the course of a high-speed chase was clearly established" at the time of Philip Lewis's death, id., at 445. Since Smith apparently disregarded the Sacramento County Sheriff's Department's General Order on police pursuits, the Ninth Circuit found a genuine issue of material fact that might be resolved by a finding that Smith's conduct amounted to deliberate indifference:

> "The General Order requires an officer to communicate his intention to pursue a vehicle to the sheriff's department dispatch center. But defendants concede that Smith did not contact the dispatch center. The General Order requires an officer to consider whether the seriousness of the offense warrants a chase at speeds in excess of the posted limit. But here, the only apparent 'offense' was the boys' refusal to stop when another officer told them to do so. The General Order requires an officer to consider whether the need for

> apprehension justifies the pursuit under existing conditions. Yet Smith apparently only 'needed' to apprehend the boys because they refused to stop. The General Order requires an officer to consider whether the pursuit presents unreasonable hazards to life and property. But taking the facts here in the light most favorable to plaintiffs, there existed an unreasonable hazard to Lewis's and Willard's lives. The General Order also directs an officer to discontinue a pursuit when the hazards of continuing outweigh the benefits of immediate apprehension. But here, there was no apparent danger involved in permitting the boys to escape. There certainly was risk of harm to others in continuing the pursuit." *Id.*, at 442.

Accordingly, the Court of Appeals reversed the summary judgment in favor of Smith and remanded for trial.

We granted certiorari, 520 U. S. ___ (1997), to resolve a conflict among the Circuits over the standard of culpability on the part of a law enforcement officer for violating substantive due process in a pursuit case. Compare 98 F. 3d, at 441 ("deliberate indifference" or "reckless disregard"),[3] with *Evans v. Avery*, 100 F. 3d 1033, 1038 (CA1 1996) ("shocks the conscience"), cert. denied, 520 U. S. ___ (1997), *Williams v. Denver*, 99 F. 3d 1009, 10141015 (CA10 1996) (same), *Fagan v. Vineland*, 22 F. 3d 1296, 1306-1307 (CA3 1994) (en banc) (same), *Temkin v. Frederick County Commissioners*, 945 F. 2d 716, 720 (CA4 1991) (same), cert. denied, 502 U.S. 1095 (1992), and *Checki v. Webb*, 785 F. 2d 534, 538 (CA5 1986) (same). We now reverse.

II

Our prior cases have held the provision that "[n]o State shall ... deprive any person of life, liberty, or property, without due process of law," U. S. Const., Amdt. 14, § 1, to "guarante[e] more than fair process," *Washington v. Glucksberg*, 521 U. S. ___, ___ (1997) (*slip op.*, at 15), and to cover a substantive sphere as well, "barring certain government actions regardless of the fairness of the procedures used to implement them," *Daniels v. Williams*, 474 U.S. 327, 331 (1986); see also *Zinermon v. Burch*, 494 U.S. 113, 125 (1990) (noting that substantive due process violations are actionable under § 1983). The allegation here that Lewis was deprived of his right to life in violation of substantive due process amounts to a such claim, that under the circumstances described earlier, Smith's actions in causing Lewis's death were an abuse of executive power so clearly unjustified by any legitimate objective of law enforcement as to be barred by the Fourteenth Amendment. Cf. *Collins v. Harker Heights*, 503 U.S. 115, 126 (1992) (noting that the Due Process Clause was intended to prevent government officials "'from abusing [their] power, or employing it as an instrument of oppression'") (quoting *DeShaney v. Winnebago County Dept. of Social Servs.*, 489 U.S. 189, 196 (1989) (quoting *Davidson v. Cannon*, 474 U.S. 344, 348 (1986)).[4]

Leaving aside the question of qualified immunity, which formed the basis for the District Court's dismissal of their case,[5] respondents face two principal objections to their claim. The first is that its subject is necessarily governed by a more definite provision of the Constitution (to the exclusion of any possible application of substantive due process); the second, that in any event the allegations are insufficient to state a substantive due process violation through executive abuse of power. Respondents can meet the first objection, but not the second.

A

Because we have "always been reluctant to expand the concept of substantive due process," *Collins v. Harker Heights, supra,* at 125, we held in *Graham v. Connor* that "[w]here a particular amendment provides an explicit textual source of constitutional protection against a particular sort of government behavior, that Amendment, not the more generalized notion of substantive due process, must be the guide for analyzing these claims." *Albright v. Oliver,* 510 U.S. 266, 273 (1994) (plurality opinion of REHNQUIST, C. J.) (quoting *Graham v. Connor,* 490 U.S. 386, 395 (1989)) (internal quotation marks omitted). Given the rule in *Graham,* we were presented at oral argument with the threshold issue raised in several *amicus* briefs,[6] whether facts involving a police chase aimed at apprehending suspects can ever support a due process claim. The argument runs that in chasing the motorcycle, Smith was attempting to make a seizure within the meaning of the Fourth Amendment, and, perhaps, even that he succeeded when Lewis was stopped by the fatal collision. Hence, any liability must turn on an application of the reasonableness standard governing searches and seizures, not the due process standard of liability for constitutionally arbitrary executive action. See *Graham v. Connor, supra,* at 395 ("all claims that law enforcement officers have used excessive force—deadly or not—in the course of an arrest, investigatory stop, or other 'seizure' of a free citizen should be analyzed under the Fourth Amendment and its 'reasonableness' standard, rather than under a 'substantive due process' approach"); *Albright v. Oliver,* 510 U.S., at 276 (GINSBURG, J., concurring); *id.,* at 288, n. 2 (SOUTER, J., concurring in judgment). One Court of Appeals has indeed applied the rule of *Graham* to preclude the application of principles of generalized substantive due process to a motor vehicle passenger's claims for injury resulting from reckless police pursuit. See *Mays v. East St. Louis,* 123 F. 3d 999, 10021003 (CA7 1997).

The argument is unsound. Just last Term, we explained that *Graham*

"does not hold that all constitutional claims relating to physically abusive government conduct must arise under either the Fourth or Eighth Amendments; rather, *Graham* simply requires that if a constitutional claim is covered by a specific constitutional provision, such as the Fourth or Eighth Amendment, the claim must be analyzed under the standard appropriate to that specific provision, not under the rubric of substantive due process." *United States v. Lanier*, 520 U. S. ____, ____, n. 7, (1997) (*slip op.*, at 13). Substantive due process analysis is therefore inappropriate in this case only if respondents' claim is "covered by" the Fourth Amendment. It is not.

The Fourth Amendment covers only "searches and seizures," U. S. Const., Amdt. 4, neither of which took place here. No one suggests that there was a search, and our cases foreclose finding a seizure. We held in *California v. Hodari D.*, 499 U.S. 621, 626 (1991), that a police pursuit in attempting to seize a person does not amount to a "seizure" within the meaning of the Fourth Amendment. And in *Brower v. County of Inyo*, 489 U.S. 593, 596–597 (1989), we explained "that a Fourth Amendment seizure does not occur whenever there is a governmentally caused termination of an individual's freedom of movement (the innocent passerby), nor even whenever there is a governmentally caused and governmentally *desired* termination of an individual's freedom of movement (the fleeing felon), but only when there is a governmental termination of freedom of movement *through means intentionally applied.*" We illustrated the point by saying that no Fourth Amendment seizure would take place where a "pursuing police car sought to stop the suspect only by the show of authority represented by flashing lights and continuing pursuit," but accidentally stopped the suspect by crashing into him. *Id.*, at 597. That is exactly this case. See, *e.g.*, *Campbell v. White*, 916 F. 2d 421, 423 (CA7 1990) (following *Brower* and finding no seizure where a police officer accidentally struck and killed a fleeing motorcyclist during a high-speed pursuit), cert. denied, 499 U.S. 922 (1991). *Graham's* more-specific provision rule is therefore no bar to respondents' suit. See, *e.g.*, *Frye v. Akron*, 759 F. Supp. 1320, 1324 (ND Ind. 1991) (parents of a motorcyclist who was struck and killed by a police car during a high-speed pursuit could sue under substantive due process because no Fourth Amendment seizure took place); *Evans v. Avery*, 100 F. 3d, at 1036 (noting that "outside the context of a seizure, . . . a person injured as a result of police misconduct may prosecute a substantive due process claim under section § 1983"); *Pleasant v. Zamieski*, 895 F. 2d 272, 276, n. 2 (CA6) (noting that *Graham* "preserve[s] Fourteenth Amendment substantive due process analysis for those instances in which a free citizen is denied his or her constitutional right to life through means other than a law enforcement official's arrest, investigatory stop or other seizure"), cert. denied, 498 U.S. 851 (1990).[7]

B

Since the time of our early explanations of due process, we have understood the core of the concept to be protection against arbitrary action:

"The principal and true meaning of the phrase has never been more tersely or accurately stated than by Mr. Justice Johnson, in *Bank of Columbia v. Okely*, 4 Wheat. 235-244 [(1819)]: 'As to the words from Magna Charta, incorporated into the Constitution of Maryland, after volumes spoken and written with a view to their exposition, the good sense of mankind has at last settled down to this: that they were intended to secure the individual from the arbitrary exercise of the powers of government, unrestrained by the established principles of private right and distributive justice.'" *Hurtado v. California*, 110 U.S. 516, 527 (1884).

We have emphasized time and again that "[t]he touchstone of due process is protection of the individual against arbitrary action of government," *Wolff v. McDonnell*, 418 U.S. 539, 558 (1974), whether the fault lies in a denial of fundamental procedural fairness, see, *e.g.*, *Fuentes v. Shevin*, 407 U.S. 67, 82 (1972) (the procedural due process guarantee protects against "arbitrary takings"), or in the exercise of power without any reasonable justification in the service of a legitimate governmental objective, see, *e.g.*, *Daniels v. Williams*, 474 U.S., at 331 (the substantive due process guarantee protects against government power arbitrarily and oppressively exercised). While due process protection in the substantive sense limits what the government may do in both its legislative, see, *e.g.*, *Griswold v. Connecticut*, 381 U.S. 479 (1965), and its executive capacities, see, *e.g.*, *Rochin v. California*, 342 U.S. 165 (1952), criteria to identify what is fatally arbitrary differ depending on whether it is legislation or a specific act of a governmental officer that is at issue.

Our cases dealing with abusive executive action have repeatedly emphasized that only the most egregious official conduct can be said to be "arbitrary in the constitutional sense," *Collins v. Harker Heights*, 503 U.S., at 129, thereby recognizing the point made in different circumstances by Chief Justice Marshall, "'that it is *a constitution* we are expounding,'" *Daniels v. Williams, supra*, at 332 (quoting *McCulloch v. Maryland*, 4 Wheat. 316, 407 (1819) (emphasis in original)). Thus, in *Collins v. Harker Heights*, for example, we said that the Due Process Clause was intended to prevent government officials "'from abusing [their] power, or employing it as an instrument of oppression.'" 503 U.S., at 126 (quoting *DeShaney v. Winnebago County Dept. of Social Servs.*, 489 U.S., at 196 (quoting *Davidson v. Cannon*, 474 U.S., at 348)).

To this end, for half a century now we have spoken of the cognizable level of executive abuse of power as that which shocks the conscience. We first put the test this way in *Rochin v. California, supra*, at 172-173, where we found the forced pumping of a suspect's stomach enough to offend due process as conduct "that shocks the conscience" and violates the "decencies of civilized conduct." In the intervening years we have repeatedly adhered to *Rochin's* benchmark. See, *e.g.*, *Breithaupt v. Abram*, 352 U.S. 432, 435 (1957) (reiterating that conduct that "'shocked the conscience' and was so 'brutal' and 'offensive' that it did not comport with traditional ideas of fair play and decency" would violate substantive due process); *Whitley v. Albers*, 475 U.S. 312, 327 (1986) (same); *United States v. Salerno*, 481 U.S. 739, 746 (1987) ("So-called 'substantive due process' prevents the government from engaging in conduct that 'shocks the conscience,' . . . or interferes with rights 'implicit in the concept of ordered liberty'") (quoting *Rochin v. California, supra*, at 172, and *Palko v. Connecticut*, 302 U.S. 319, 325-326 (1937)). Most recently, in *Collins v. Harker Heights, supra*, at 128, we said again that the substantive component of the Due Process Clause is violated by executive action only when it "can properly be characterized as arbitrary, or conscience shocking, in a constitutional sense." While the measure of what is conscience shocking is no calibrated yardstick, it does, as Judge Friendly put it, "poin[t] the way." *Johnson v. Glick*, 481 F. 2d 1028, 1033 (CA2), cert. denied, 414 U.S. 1033 (1973).[8] It should not be surprising that the constitutional concept of conscience-shocking duplicates no traditional category of common-law fault, but rather points clearly away from liability, or clearly toward it, only at the ends of the tort law's spectrum of culpability. Thus, we have made it clear that the due process guarantee does not entail a body of constitutional law imposing liability whenever someone cloaked with state authority causes harm. In *Paul v. Davis*, 424 U.S. 693, 701 (1976), for example, we explained that the Fourteenth Amendment is not a "font of tort law to be superimposed upon whatever systems may already be administered by the States," and in *Daniels v. Williams*, 474 U.S., at 332, we reaffirmed the point that "[o]ur Constitution deals with the large concerns of the governors and the governed, but it does not purport to supplant traditional tort law in laying down rules of conduct to regulate liability for injuries that attend living together in society." We have accordingly rejected the lowest common denominator of customary tort liability as any mark of sufficiently shocking conduct, and have held that the Constitution does not guarantee due care on the part of state officials; liability for negligently inflicted harm is categorically beneath the threshold of constitutional due process. See *Daniels v. Williams, supra*, at 328; see also *Davidson v. Cannon*, 474 U.S. 344, 348 (1986) (clarifying that Daniels applies to substantive, as well as procedural, due process). It is, on the contrary, behavior at the other end of the culpability spectrum that would most probably support a substantive due process claim; conduct intended to injure in some way unjustifiable by any government interest is the sort of official action most likely to rise to the conscience-shocking level. See *Daniels v. Williams*, 474 U.S., at 331 ("Historically, this guarantee of due process has been applied to *deliberate* decisions of government officials to deprive a person of life, liberty, or property") (emphasis in original).

Whether the point of the conscience-shocking is reached when injuries are produced with culpability falling within the middle range, following from something more than negligence but "less than intentional conduct, such as recklessness or 'gross negligence,'" *id.*, at 334, n. 3, is a matter for closer calls.[9] To be sure, we have expressly recognized the possibility that some official acts in this range may be actionable under the Fourteenth Amendment, *ibid.*, and our cases have compelled recognition that such conduct is egregious enough to state a substantive due process claim in at least one instance. We held in *City of Revere v. Massachusetts Gen. Hospital*, 463 U.S. 239 (1983), that "the due process rights of a [pretrial detainee] are at least as great as the Eighth Amendment protections available to a convicted prisoner." *Id.*, at 244 (citing *Bell v. Wolfish*, 441 U.S. 520, 535, n. 16, 545 (1979)). Since it may suffice for Eighth Amendment liability that prison officials were deliberately indifferent to the medical needs of their prisoners, see *Estelle v. Gamble*, 429 U.S. 97, 104 (1976), it follows that such deliberately indifferent conduct must also be enough to satisfy the fault requirement for due process claims based on the medical needs of someone jailed while awaiting trial, see, *e.g.*, *Barrie v. Grand County, Utah*, 119 F. 3d 862, 867 (CA10 1997); *Weyant v. Okst*, 101 F. 3d 845, 856 (CA2 1996).[10]

Rules of due process are not, however, subject to mechanical application in unfamiliar territory. Deliberate indifference that shocks in one environment may not be so patently egregious in another, and our concern with preserving the constitutional proportions of substantive due process demands an exact analysis of circumstances before any abuse of power is condemned as conscience-shocking. What we have said of due process in the procedural sense is just as true here:

> "The phrase [due process of law] formulates a concept less rigid and more fluid than those envisaged in other specific and particular provisions of the Bill of Rights. Its application is less a matter of rule. Asserted denial is to be tested by an appraisal of the totality of facts in a given case. That which may, in one setting, constitute a denial of fundamental fairness, shocking to the universal sense of justice, may, in other circumstances, and in the light of other considerations, fall short of such denial." *Betts v. Brady*, 316 U.S. 455, 462 (1942).

Thus, attention to the markedly different circumstances of normal pretrial custody and high-speed law enforcement chases shows why the deliberate indifference that shocks in the one case is less egregious in the other (even assuming that it makes sense to speak of indifference as deliberate in the case of sudden pursuit). As the very term "deliberate indifference" implies, the standard is sensibly employed only when actual deliberation is practical, see *Whitley v. Albers*, 475 U.S., at 320,[11] and in the custodial situation of a prison, forethought about an inmate's welfare is not only feasible but obligatory under a regime that incapacitates a prisoner to exercise ordinary responsibility for his own welfare.

> "[W]hen the State takes a person into its custody and holds him
> there against his will, the Constitution imposes upon it a corre-
> sponding duty to assume some responsibility for his safety and
> general well-being. The rationale for this principle is simple enough:
> when the State by the affirmative exercise of its power so restrains
> an individual's liberty that it renders him unable to care for himself,
> and at the same time fails to provide for his basic human needs—
> *e.g.*, food, clothing, shelter, medical care, and reasonable safety—it
> transgresses the substantive limits on state action set by the . . . Due
> Process Clause." *DeShaney v. Winnebago County Dept. of Social
> Servs.*, 489 U.S., at 199 –200 (citation and footnote omitted).

Nor does any substantial countervailing interest excuse the State
from making provision for the decent care and protection of those it
locks up; "the State's responsibility to attend to the medical needs of prisoners [or detainees] does not ordinarily clash with other equally important governmental responsibilities." *Whitley v. Albers, supra*, at 320.[12]

But just as the description of the custodial prison situation shows
how deliberate indifference can rise to a constitutionally shocking level,
so too does it suggest why indifference may well not be enough for liability in the different circumstances of a case like this one. We have,
indeed, found that deliberate indifference does not suffice for constitutional liability (albeit under the Eighth Amendment) even in prison circumstances when a prisoner's claim arises not from normal custody but
from response to a violent disturbance. Our analysis is instructive here:

> "[I]n making and carrying out decisions involving the use of force
> to restore order in the face of a prison disturbance, prison officials
> undoubtedly must take into account the very real threats the unrest
> presents to inmates and prison officials alike, in addition to the
> possible harms to inmates against whom force might be used. . . .
> In this setting, a deliberate indifference standard does not ade-
> quately capture the importance of such competing obligations, or
> convey the appropriate hesitancy to critique in hindsight decisions
> necessarily made in haste, under pressure, and frequently without
> the luxury of a second chance." *Whitley v. Albers*, 475 U.S., at 320.

We accordingly held that a much higher standard of fault than
deliberate indifference has to be shown for officer liability in a prison
riot. In those circumstances, liability should turn on "whether force
was applied in a good faith effort to maintain or restore discipline or
maliciously and sadistically for the very purpose of causing harm." *Id.*,
at 320-321 (internal quotation marks omitted). The analogy to sudden
police chases (under the Due Process Clause) would be hard to avoid.

Like prison officials facing a riot, the police on an occasion calling
for fast action have obligations that tend to tug against each other. Their
duty is to restore and maintain lawful order, while not exacerbating disorder more than necessary to do their jobs. They are supposed to act
decisively and to show restraint at the same moment, and their decisions

have to be made "in haste, under pressure, and frequently without the luxury of a second chance." *Id.*, at 320; cf. *Graham v. Connor*, 490 U.S., at 397 ("police officers are often forced to make split-second judgments in circumstances that are tense, uncertain, and rapidly evolving"). A police officer deciding whether to give chase must balance on one hand the need to stop a suspect and show that flight from the law is no way to freedom, and, on the other, the high-speed threat to everyone within stopping range, be they suspects, their passengers, other drivers, or bystanders.

To recognize a substantive due process violation in these circumstances when only mid-level fault has been shown would be to forget that liability for deliberate indifference to inmate welfare rests upon the luxury enjoyed by prison officials of having time to make unhurried judgments, upon the chance for repeated reflection, largely uncomplicated by the pulls of competing obligations. When such extended opportunities to do better are teamed with protracted failure even to care, indifference is truly shocking. But when unforeseen circumstances demand an officer's instant judgment, even precipitate recklessness fails to inch close enough to harmful purpose to spark the shock that implicates "the large concerns of the governors and the governed." *Daniels v. Williams*, 474 U.S., at 332. Just as a purpose to cause harm is needed for Eighth Amendment liability in a riot case, so it ought to be needed for Due Process liability in a pursuit case. Accordingly, we hold that high-speed chases with no intent to harm suspects physically or to worsen their legal plight do not give rise to liability under the Fourteenth Amendment, redressible by an action under § 1983.[13]

The fault claimed on Smith's part in this case accordingly fails to meet the shocks-the-conscience test. In the count charging him with liability under § 1983, respondents' complaint alleges a variety of culpable states of mind: "negligently responsible in some manner," (App. 11, Count one, ¶ 2668), "reckless and careless" (*id.*, at 12, ¶ 26615), "recklessness, gross negligence and conscious disregard for [Lewis's] safety" (*id.*, at 13, ¶ 26618), and "oppression, fraud and malice" (*Ibid.*) The subsequent summary judgment proceedings revealed that the height of the fault actually claimed was "conscious disregard," the malice allegation having been made in aid of a request for punitive damages, but unsupported either in allegations of specific conduct or in any affidavit of fact offered on the motions for summary judgment. The Court of Appeals understood the claim to be one of deliberate indifference to Lewis's survival, which it treated as equivalent to one of reckless disregard for life. We agree with this reading of respondents' allegations, but consequently part company from the Court of Appeals, which found them sufficient to state a substantive due process claim, and from the District Court, which made the same assumption *arguendo*.[14]

Smith was faced with a course of lawless behavior for which the police were not to blame. They had done nothing to cause Willard's high-speed driving in the first place, nothing to excuse his flouting of the commonly understood law enforcement authority to control traffic, and nothing (beyond a refusal to call off the chase) to encourage him to race through traffic at breakneck speed forcing other drivers out of their travel lanes. Willard's outrageous behavior was practically instantaneous, and so was Smith's instinctive response. While prudence would have repressed the reaction, the officer's instinct was to do his job as a law enforcement officer, not to induce Willard's lawlessness, or to terrorize, cause harm, or kill. Prudence, that is, was subject to countervailing enforcement considerations, and while Smith exaggerated their demands, there is no reason to believe that they were tainted by an improper or malicious motive on his part.

Regardless whether Smith's behavior offended the reasonableness held up by tort law or the balance struck in law enforcement's own codes of sound practice, it does not shock the conscience, and petitioners are not called upon to answer for it under § 1983. The judgment below is accordingly reversed.

It is so ordered.

Footnotes

[1] Respondents also brought claims under state law. The District Court found that Smith was immune from state tort liability by operation of California Vehicle Code § 17004, which provides that "[a] public employee is not liable for civil damages on account of personal injury to or death of any person or damage to property resulting from the operation, in the line of duty, of an authorized emergency vehicle . . . when in the immediate pursuit of an actual or suspected violator of the law." Cal. Veh. Code Ann. § 17004 (West 1971). The court declined to rule on the potential liability of the County under state law, instead dismissing the tort claims against the County without prejudice to refiling in state court.

[2] The District Court also granted summary judgment in favor of the County and the Sheriff's Department on the § 1983 claim, concluding that municipal liability would not lie under *Monell v. New York City Dept. of Social Servs.*, 436 U.S. 658 (1978), after finding no genuine factual dispute as to whether the County adequately trains its officers in the conduct of vehicular pursuits or whether the pursuit policy of the Sheriff's Department evinces deliberate indifference to the constitutional rights of the public. The Ninth Circuit affirmed the District Court on these points, 98 F. 3d 434, 446-447 (1996) and the issue of municipal liability is not before us.

[3] In *Jones v. Sherrill*, 827 F. 2d 1102, 1106 (1987), the Sixth Circuit adopted a "gross negligence" standard for imposing liability for harm caused by police pursuit. Subsequently, in *Foy v. Berea*, 58 F. 3d 227, 230 (1995), the Sixth Circuit, without specifically mentioning Jones, disavowed the notion that "gross negligence is sufficient to support a substantive due process claim." Although Foy involved police inaction, rather than police pursuit, it seems likely that the Sixth Circuit would now apply the "deliberate indifference" standard utilized in that case, see 58 F. 3d, at 232-233, rather than the "gross negligence" standard adopted in Jones, in a police pursuit situation.

[4] Respondents do not argue that they were denied due process of law by virtue of the fact that California's post-deprivation procedures and rules of immunity have

effectively denied them an adequate opportunity to seek compensation for the state-occasioned deprivation of their son's life. We express no opinion here on the merits of such a claim, cf. *Albright v. Oliver*, 510 U.S. 266, 281-286 (1994) (KENNEDY, J., concurring in judgment); *Parratt v. Taylor*, 451 U.S. 527 (1981), or on the adequacy of California's post-deprivation compensation scheme.

[5] As in any action under § 1983, the first step is to identify the exact contours of the underlying right said to have been violated. See *Graham v. Connor*, 490 U.S. 386, 394 (1989). The District Court granted summary judgment to Smith on the basis of qualified immunity, assuming without deciding that a substantive due process violation took place but holding that the law was not clearly established in 1990 so as to justify imposition of § 1983 liability. We do not analyze this case in a similar fashion because, as we have held, the better approach to resolving cases in which the defense of qualified immunity is raised is to determine first whether the plaintiff has alleged a deprivation of a constitutional right at all. Normally, it is only then that a court should ask whether the right allegedly implicated was clearly established at the time of the events in question. See *Siegert v. Gilley*, 500 U.S. 226, 232 (1991) ("A necessary concomitant to the determination of whether the constitutional right asserted by a plaintiff is 'clearly established' at the time the defendant acted is the determination of whether the plaintiff has asserted a violation of a constitutional right at all," and courts should not "assum[e], without deciding, this preliminary issue"). JUSTICE STEVENS suggests that the rule of Siegert should not apply where, as here, the constitutional question presented "is both difficult and unresolved." *Post*, at 1. But the generally sound rule of avoiding determination of constitutional issues does not readily fit the situation presented here; when liability is claimed on the basis of a constitutional violation, even a finding of qualified immunity requires some determination about the state of constitutional law at the time the officer acted. What is more significant is that if the policy of avoidance were always followed in favor of ruling on qualified immunity whenever there was no clearly settled constitutional rule of primary conduct, standards of official conduct would tend to remain uncertain, to the detriment both of officials and individuals. An immunity determination, with nothing more, provides no clear standard, constitutional or non-constitutional. In practical terms, escape from uncertainty would require the issue to arise in a suit to enjoin future conduct, in an action against a municipality, or in litigating a suppression motion in a criminal proceeding; in none of these instances would qualified immunity be available to block a determination of law. See Shapiro, Public Officials' Qualified Immunity in Section 1983 Actions Under *Harlow v. Fitzgerald* and its Progeny, 22 U. Mich. J. L. Ref. 249, 265, n. 109 (1989). But these avenues would not necessarily be open, and therefore the better approach is to determine the right before determining whether it was previously established with clarity.

[6] See Brief for National Association of Counties et al. as *Amici Curiae* 8-13; Brief for Grand Lodge of the Fraternal Order of Police as *Amicus Curiae* 4-9; Brief for City and County of Denver, Colorado as *Amici Curiae* 2-7; Brief for County of Riverside et al. as *Amici Curiae* 6-18; Brief for Gabriel Torres et al. as *Amici Curiae* 3-11.

[7] Several amici suggest that, for the purposes of Graham, the Fourth Amendment should cover not only seizures, but also failed attempts to make a seizure. See, *e.g.*, Brief for National Association of Counties et al. as *Amici Curiae* 10-11. This argument is foreclosed by *California v. Hodari D.*, in which we explained that "neither usage nor common-law tradition makes an attempted seizure a seizure. The common law may have made an attempted seizure unlawful in certain circumstances; but it made many things unlawful, very few of which were elevated to constitutional proscriptions." 499 U.S. 621, 626, n. 2, (1991). Attempted seizures of a person are beyond the scope of the Fourth Amendment. See *id.*, at 646 (STEVENS, J., dissenting) (disagreeing with the Court's position that "an attempt to make [a] . . . seizure is beyond the coverage of the Fourth Amendment").

⁸ As JUSTICE SCALIA has explained before, he fails to see "the usefulness of 'conscience shocking' as a legal test," *Herrera v. Collins*, 506 U.S. 390, 428 (1993), and his independent analysis of this case is therefore understandable. He is, however, simply mistaken in seeing our insistence on the shocks-the-conscience standard as an atavistic return to a scheme of due process analysis rejected by the Court in *Washington v. Glucksberg* S. ___ (1997). Glucksberg presented a disagreement about the significance of historical examples of protected liberty in determining whether a given statute could be judged to contravene the Fourteenth Amendment. The differences of opinion turned on the issues of how much history indicating recognition of the asserted right, viewed at what level of specificity, is necessary to support the finding of a substantive due process right entitled to prevail over state legislation. As we explain in the text, a case challenging executive action on substantive due process grounds, like this one, presents an issue antecedent to any question about the need for historical examples of enforcing a liberty interest of the sort claimed. For executive action challenges raise a particular need to preserve the constitutional proportions of constitutional claims, lest the Constitution be demoted to what we have called a font of tort law. Thus, in a due process challenge to executive action, the threshold question is whether the behavior of the governmental officer is so egregious, so outrageous, that it may fairly be said to shock the contemporary conscience. That judgment may be informed by a history of liberty protection, but it necessarily reflects an understanding of traditional executive behavior, of contemporary practice, and of the standards of blame generally applied to them. Only if the necessary condition of egregious behavior were satisfied would there be a possibility of recognizing a substantive due process right to be free of such executive action, and only then might there be a debate about the sufficiency of historical examples of enforcement of the right claimed, or its recognition in other ways. In none of our prior cases have we considered the necessity for such examples, and no such question is raised in this case. In sum, the difference of opinion in Glucksberg was about the need for historical examples of recognition of the claimed liberty protection at some appropriate level of specificity. In an executive action case, no such issue can arise if the conduct does not reach the degree of the egregious.

⁹ In *Rochin v. California*, 342 U.S. 165 (1952), the case in which we formulated and first applied the shocks-the-conscience test, it was not the ultimate purpose of the government actors to harm the plaintiff, but they apparently acted with full appreciation of what the Court described as the brutality of their acts. Rochin, of course, was decided long before *Graham v. Connor* (and *Mapp v. Ohio*, 367 U.S. 643 (1961)), and today would be treated under the Fourth Amendment, albeit with the same result.

¹⁰ We have also employed deliberate indifference as a standard of culpability sufficient to identify a dereliction as reflective of municipal policy and to sustain a claim of municipal liability for failure to train an employee who causes harm by unconstitutional conduct for which he would be individually liable. See *Canton v. Harris*, 489 U.S. 378, 388-389 (1989).

¹¹ By "actual deliberation," we do not mean "deliberation" in the narrow, technical sense in which it has sometimes been used in traditional homicide law. See, *e.g. Caldwell v. State*, 84 So. 272, 276 (Ala. 1919) (noting that "'delibera-tion here does not mean that the man slayer must ponder over the killing for a long time'"; rather, "it may exist and may be entertained while the man slayer is pressing the trigger of the pistol that fired the fatal shot[,] even if it be only for a moment or instant of time").

¹² *Youngberg v. Romeo*, 457 U.S. 307 (1982), can be categorized on much the same terms. There, we held that a severely retarded person could state a claim under § 1983 for a violation of substantive due process if the personnel at the mental

institution where he was confined failed to exercise professional judgment when denying him training and habilitation. *Id.,* at 319-325. The combination of a patient's involuntary commitment and his total dependence on his custodians obliges the government to take thought and make reasonable provision for the patient's welfare.

[13] Cf. *Checki v. Webb,* 785 F. 2d 534, 538 (CA5 1986) ("Where a citizen suffers physical injury due to a police officer's negligent use of his vehicle, no section § 1983 claim is stated. It is a different story when a citizen suffers or is seriously threatened with physical injury due to a police officer's intentional misuse of his vehicle") (citation omitted).

[14] To say that due process is not offended by the police conduct described here is not, of course, to imply anything about its appropriate treatment under state law. See *Collins v. Harker Heights,* 503 U.S. 115, 128-129 (1992) (decisions about civil liability standards that "involve a host of policy choices . . . must be made by locally elected representatives [or by courts enforcing the common law of torts], rather than by federal judges interpreting the basic charter of Government for the entire country"). Cf. *Thomas v. City of Richmond,* 9 Cal. 4th 1154, 892 F.2d 1185 (1995) (*en banc*) (discussing municipal liability under California law for injuries caused by police pursuits).

Chavez v. Martinez
538 U. S. ___ (2003)

Argued December 4, 2002
Decided May 27, 2003
JUSTICE THOMAS announced the judgment of the Court
and delivered an opinion.*

This case involves a §1983 suit arising out of petitioner Ben Chavez's allegedly coercive interrogation of respondent Oliverio Martinez. The United States Court of Appeals for the Ninth Circuit held that Chavez was not entitled to a defense of qualified immunity because he violated Martinez's clearly established constitutional rights. We conclude that Chavez did not deprive Martinez of a constitutional right.

I

On November 28, 1997, police officers Maria Peña and Andrew Salinas were near a vacant lot in a residential area of Oxnard, California, investigating suspected narcotics activity. While Peña and Salinas were questioning an individual, they heard a bicycle approaching on a darkened path that crossed the lot. They ordered the rider, respondent Martinez, to dismount, spread his legs, and place his hands behind his head. Martinez complied. Salinas then conducted a patdown frisk and discovered a knife in Martinez's waistband. An altercation ensued.[1]

There is some dispute about what occurred during the altercation. The officers claim that Martinez drew Salinas' gun from its holster and pointed it at them; Martinez denies this. Both sides agree, however, that

---

* THE CHIEF JUSTICE joins this opinion in its entirety. JUSTICE O'CONNOR joins Parts I and II-A of this opinion. JUSTICE SCALIA joins Parts I and II of this opinion.

Salinas yelled, "'He's got my gun!'" App. to Pet. for Cert. 3a. Peña then drew her gun and shot Martinez several times, causing severe injuries that left Martinez permanently blinded and paralyzed from the waist down. The officers then placed Martinez under arrest.

Petitioner Chavez, a patrol supervisor, arrived on the scene minutes later with paramedics. Chavez accompanied Martinez to the hospital and then questioned Martinez there while he was receiving treatment from medical personnel. The interview lasted a total of about 10 minutes, over a 45-minute period, with Chavez leaving the emergency room for periods of time to permit medical personnel to attend to Martinez.

At first, most of Martinez's answers consisted of "I don't know," "I am dying," and "I am choking." App. 14, 17, 18. Later in the interview, Martinez admitted that he took the gun from the officer's holster and pointed it at the police. *Id.*, at 16. He also admitted that he used heroin regularly. *Id.*, at 18. At one point, Martinez said "I am not telling you anything until they treat me," yet Chavez continued the interview. *Id.*, at 14. At no point during the interview was Martinez given Miranda warnings under *Miranda v. Arizona*, 384 U. S. 436 (1966). App. 4.

Martinez was never charged with a crime, and his answers were never used against him in any criminal prosecution. Nevertheless, Martinez filed suit under Rev. Stat. §1979, 42 U. S. C. §1983, maintaining that Chavez's actions violated his Fifth Amendment right not to be "compelled in any criminal case to be a witness against himself," as well as his Fourteenth Amendment substantive due process right to be free from coercive questioning. The District Court granted summary judgment to Martinez as to Chavez's qualified immunity defense on both the Fifth and Fourteenth Amendment claims. Chavez took an interlocutory appeal to the Ninth Circuit, which affirmed the District Court's denial of qualified immunity. *Martinez v. Oxnard*, 270 F. 3d 852 (2001). Applying *Saucier v. Katz*, 533 U. S. 194 (2001), the Ninth Circuit first concluded that Chavez's actions, as alleged by Martinez, deprived Martinez of his rights under the Fifth and Fourteenth Amendments. The Ninth Circuit did not attempt to explain how Martinez had been "compelled in any criminal case to be a witness against himself." Instead, the Ninth Circuit reiterated the holding of an earlier Ninth Circuit case, *Cooper v. Dupnik*, 963 F. 2d 1220, 1229 (1992) (en banc), that "the Fifth Amendment's purpose is to prevent coercive interrogation practices that are destructive of human dignity," 270 F. 3d, at 857 (internal quotation marks omitted), and found that Chavez's "coercive questioning" of Martinez violated his Fifth Amendment rights, "[e]ven though Martinez's statements were not used against him in a criminal proceeding," *ibid.* As to Martinez's due process claim, the Ninth Circuit held that "a police officer violates the Fourteenth Amendment when he obtains a confession by coercive conduct, regardless of whether the confession is subsequently used at trial." *Ibid.*

The Ninth Circuit then concluded that the Fifth and Fourteenth Amendment rights asserted by Martinez were clearly established by federal law, explaining that a reasonable officer "would have known that persistent interrogation of the suspect despite repeated requests to stop violated the suspect's Fifth and Fourteenth Amendment right to be free from coercive interrogation." *Id.,* at 858.

We granted certiorari. 535 U. S. 1111 (2002).

II

In deciding whether an officer is entitled to qualified immunity, we must first determine whether the officer's alleged conduct violated a constitutional right. See *Katz,* 533 U. S., at 201. If not, the officer is entitled to qualified immunity, and we need not consider whether the asserted right was "clearly established." *Ibid.* We conclude that Martinez's allegations fail to state a violation of his constitutional rights.

A

1

The Fifth Amendment, made applicable to the States by the Fourteenth Amendment, *Malloy v. Hogan,* 378 U. S. 1 (1964), requires that "[n]o person . . . shall be compelled *in any criminal case* to be a *witness* against himself." U. S. Const., Amdt. 5 (emphases added). We fail to see how, based on the text of the Fifth Amendment, Martinez can allege a violation of this right, since Martinez was never prosecuted for a crime, let alone compelled to be a witness against himself in a criminal case.

Although Martinez contends that the meaning of "criminal case" should encompass the entire criminal investigatory process, including police interrogations, Brief for Respondent 23, we disagree. In our view, a "criminal case" at the very least requires the initiation of legal proceedings. See *Blyew v. United States,* 13 Wall. 581, 595 (1872) ("The words 'case' and 'cause' are constantly used as synonyms in statutes and judicial decisions, each meaning *a proceeding in court, a suit, or action*" (emphasis added)); Black's Law Dictionary 215 (6th ed. 1990) (defining "[c]ase" as "[a] general term for an action, cause, suit, or controversy at law . . . a question *contested before a court of justice*" (emphasis added)). We need not decide today the precise moment when a "criminal case" commences; it is enough to say that police questioning does not constitute a "case" any more than a private investigator's precomplaint activities constitute a "civil case." Statements compelled by police interrogations of course may not be used against a defendant at trial, see *Brown v. Mississippi,* 297 U. S. 278, 286 (1936), but it is not until their use in a criminal case that a violation of the Self-Incrimination Clause occurs, see *United States v. Verdugo-Urquidez,* 494 U. S. 259, 264 (1990) ("The privilege against self-incrimination guaranteed by the

Fifth Amendment is a *fundamental trial right* of criminal defendants. Although conduct by law enforcement officials prior to trial may ultimately impair that right, a *constitutional violation occurs only at trial*" (emphases added; citations omitted)); *Withrow v. Williams*, 507 U. S. 680, 692 (1993) (describing the Fifth Amendment as a "'trial right'"); *id.*, at 705 (O'CONNOR, J., concurring in part and dissenting in part) (describing "true Fifth Amendment claims" as "the extraction *and use* of compelled testimony" (emphasis altered)).

Here, Martinez was never made to be a "witness" against himself in violation of the Fifth Amendment's Self-Incrimination Clause because his statements were never admitted as testimony against him in a criminal case. Nor was he ever placed under oath and exposed to "'the cruel trilemma of self-accusation, perjury or contempt.'" *Michigan v. Tucker*, 417 U. S. 433, 445 (1974) (quoting *Murphy v. Waterfront Comm'n of N. Y. Harbor*, 378 U. S. 52, 55 (1964)). The text of the Self-Incrimination Clause simply cannot support the Ninth Circuit's view that the mere use of compulsive questioning, without more, violates the Constitution.

2

Nor can the Ninth Circuit's approach be reconciled with our case law. It is well established that the government may compel witnesses to testify at trial or before a grand jury, on pain of contempt, so long as the witness is not the target of the criminal case in which he testifies. See *Minnesota v. Murphy*, 465 U. S. 420, 427 (1984); *Kastigar v. United States*, 406 U. S. 441, 443 (1972). Even for persons who have a legitimate fear that their statements may subject them to criminal prosecution, we have long permitted the compulsion of incriminating testimony so long as those statements (or evidence derived from those statements) cannot be used against the speaker in any criminal case. See *Brown v. Walker*, 161 U. S. 591, 602–604 (1896); *Kastigar, supra,* at 458; *United States v. Balsys*, 524 U. S. 666, 671–672 (1998). We have also recognized that governments may penalize public employees and government contractors (with the loss of their jobs or government contracts) to induce them to respond to inquiries, so long as the answers elicited (and their fruits) are immunized from use in any criminal case against the speaker. See *Lefkowitz v. Turley*, 414 U. S. 70, 84–85 (1973) ("[T]he State may insist that [contractors] . . . either respond to relevant inquiries about the performance of their contracts or suffer cancellation"); *Lefkowitz v. Cunningham*, 431 U. S. 801, 806 (1977) ("Public employees may constitutionally be discharged for refusing to answer potentially incriminating questions concerning their official duties if they have not been required to surrender their constitutional immunity" against later use of statements in criminal proceedings).[2] By contrast, no "penalty" may ever be imposed on someone who exercises his core Fifth Amendment right not to be a "witness" against himself in a "criminal case." See *Griffin v. California*, 380 U. S. 609, 614 (1965) (the trial court's and the prosecutor's comments on the defendant's failure to testify violates the Self-Incrimination Clause of the Fifth Amendment). Our holdings in these cases demonstrate that, contrary to the Ninth Circuit's view, mere coercion does not violate the text of the Self-Incrimination Clause absent use of the compelled statements in a criminal case against the witness.

We fail to see how Martinez was any more "compelled in any criminal case to be a witness against himself" than an immunized witness forced to testify on pain of contempt. One difference, perhaps, is that the immunized witness *knows* that his statements will not, and may not, be used against him, whereas Martinez likely did not. But this does not make the statements of the immunized witness any less "compelled" and lends no support to the Ninth Circuit's conclusion that coercive police interrogations, absent the use of the involuntary statements in a criminal case, violate the Fifth Amendment's Self-Incrimination Clause. Moreover, our cases provide that those subjected to coercive police interrogations have an *automatic* protection from the use of their involuntary statements (or evidence derived from their statements) in any subsequent criminal trial. *Oregon v. Elstad*, 470 U. S. 298, 307–308 (1985); *United States v. Blue*, 384 U. S. 251, 255 (1966); *Leyra v. Denno*, 347 U. S. 556, 558 (1954); *Ashcraft v. Tennessee*, 322 U. S. 143, 155 (1944). See also *Pillsbury Co. v. Conboy*, 459 U. S. 248, 278 (1983) (Blackmun, J., concurring in judgment); *Williams v. United States*, 401 U. S. 646, 662 (1971) (Brennan, J., concurring in result). This protection is, in fact, coextensive with the use and derivative use immunity mandated by *Kastigar* when the government compels testimony from a reluctant witness. See 406 U. S., at 453. Accordingly, the fact that Martinez did not *know* his statements could not be used against him does not change our view that no violation of Fifth Amendment's Self-Incrimination Clause occurred here.

3

Although our cases have permitted the Fifth Amendment's self-incrimination privilege to be asserted in noncriminal cases, see *id.*, at 444–445 (recognizing that the "Fifth Amendment privilege against compulsory self incrimination . . . *can be asserted in any proceeding,* civil or criminal, administrative or judicial, investigatory or adjudicatory . . ."); *Lefkowitz v. Turley, supra,* at 77 (stating that the Fifth Amendment privilege allows one "not to answer official questions put to him in any other proceeding, civil or criminal, formal or informal, where the answers might incriminate him in future criminal proceedings"), that does not alter our conclusion that a violation of the constitutional *right* against self-incrimination occurs only if one has been compelled to be a witness against himself in a criminal case.

In the Fifth Amendment context, we have created prophylactic rules designed to safeguard the core constitutional right protected by the Self-Incrimination Clause. See, *e.g., Tucker*, 417 U. S., at 444 (describing the "procedural safeguards" required by *Miranda* as "not themselves rights protected by the Constitution but . . . measures to insure that the right against compulsory self-incrimination was protected" to "provide practical reinforcement for the right"); *Elstad, supra*, at 306 (stating that "[t]he *Miranda* exclusionary rule . . . serves the Fifth Amendment and sweeps more broadly than the Fifth Amendment itself"). Among these rules is an evidentiary privilege that protects witnesses from being forced to give incriminating testimony, even in noncriminal cases, unless that testimony has been immunized from use and derivative use in a future criminal proceeding before it is compelled. See *Kastigar, supra*, at 453; *Maness v. Meyers*, 419 U. S. 449, 461–462 (1975) (noting that the Fifth Amendment privilege may be asserted if one is "compelled to produce evidence which later *may* be used against him as an accused in a criminal action" (emphasis added)).

By allowing a witness to insist on an immunity agreement *before* being compelled to give incriminating testimony in a noncriminal case, the privilege preserves the core Fifth Amendment right from invasion by the use of that compelled testimony in a subsequent criminal case. See *Tucker, supra*, at 440–441 ("Testimony obtained in civil suits, or before administrative or legislative committees, could [absent a grant of immunity] prove so incriminating that a person compelled to give such testimony might readily be convicted on the basis of those disclosures in a subsequent criminal proceeding"). Because the failure to assert the privilege will often forfeit the right to exclude the evidence in a subsequent "criminal case," see *Murphy*, 465 U. S., at 440; *Garner v. United States*, 424 U. S. 648, 650 (1976) (failure to claim privilege against self-incrimination before disclosing incriminating information on tax returns forfeited the right to exclude that information in a criminal prosecution); *United States v. Kordel*, 397 U. S. 1, 7 (1970) (criminal defendant forfeited his right to assert Fifth Amendment privilege with regard to answers he gave to interrogatories in a prior civil proceeding), it is necessary to allow assertion of the privilege prior to the commencement of a "criminal case" to safeguard the core Fifth Amendment trial right. If the privilege could not be asserted in such situations, testimony given in those judicial proceedings would be deemed "voluntary," see *Rogers v. United States*, 340 U. S. 367, 371 (1951); *United States v. Monia*, 317 U. S. 424, 427 (1943); hence, insistence on a prior grant of immunity is essential to memorialize the fact that the testimony had indeed been compelled and therefore protected from use against the speaker in any "criminal case."

Rules designed to safeguard a constitutional right, however, do not extend the scope of the constitutional right itself, just as violations of judicially crafted prophylactic rules do not violate the constitutional rights of any person. As we explained, we have allowed the Fifth Amendment privilege to be asserted by witnesses in noncriminal cases in order to safeguard the core constitutional right defined by the Self-Incrimination Clause—the right not to be compelled in any criminal case to be a witness against oneself.[3] We have likewise established the *Miranda* exclusionary rule as a prophylactic measure to prevent violations of the right protected by the text of the Self-Incrimination Clause—the admission into evidence in criminal case of confessions obtained through coercive custodial questioning. See *Warren v. Lincoln,* 864 F. 2d 1436, 1442 (CA8 1989) (alleged *Miranda* violation not actionable under §1983); *Giuffre v. Bissell,* 31 F. 3d 1241, 1256 (CA3 1994) (same); *Bennett v. Passic,* 545 F. 2d 1260, 1263 (CA10 1976) (same); see also *New York v. Quarles,* 467 U. S. 649, 686 (1984) (Marshall, J., dissenting) ("All the Fifth Amendment forbids is the introduction of coerced statements at trial"). Accordingly, Chavez's failure to read Miranda warnings to Martinez did not violate Martinez's constitutional rights and cannot be grounds for a §1983 action. See *Connecticut v. Barrett,* 479 U. S. 523, 528 (1987) (*Miranda's* warning requirement is "not itself required by the Fifth Amendmen[t] . . . but is instead justified only by reference to its prophylactic purpose"); *Tucker,* 417 U. S., at 444 (*Miranda's* safeguards "were not themselves rights protected by the Constitution but were instead measures to insure that the right against compulsory self-incrimination was protected"). And the absence of a "criminal case" in which Martinez was compelled to be a "witness" against himself defeats his core Fifth Amendment claim. The Ninth Circuit's view that mere compulsion violates the Self-Incrimination Clause, see 270 F. 3d, at 857; *California Attorneys for Criminal Justice v. Butts,* 195 F. 3d 1039, 1045-1046 (1999); *Cooper,* 963 F. 2d, at 1243-1244, finds no support in the text of the Fifth Amendment and is irreconcilable with our case law.[4] Because we find that Chavez's alleged conduct did not violate the Self-Incrimination Clause, we reverse the Ninth Circuit's denial of qualified immunity as to Martinez's Fifth Amendment claim.

Our views on the proper scope of the Fifth Amendment's Self-Incrimination Clause do not mean that police torture or other abuse that results in a confession is constitutionally permissible so long as the statements are not used at trial; it simply means that the Fourteenth Amendment's Due Process Clause, rather than the Fifth Amendment's Self-Incrimination Clause, would govern the inquiry in those cases and provide relief in appropriate circumstances.[5]

B

The Fourteenth Amendment provides that no person shall be deprived "of life, liberty, or property, without due process of law." Convictions based on evidence obtained by methods that are "so brutal and so offensive to human dignity" that they "shoc[k] the conscience" violate the Due Process Clause. *Rochin v. California*, 342 U. S. 165, 172, 174 (1952) (overturning conviction based on evidence obtained by involuntary stomach pumping). See also *Breithaupt v. Abram*, 352 U. S. 432, 435 (1957) (reiterating that evidence obtained through conduct that "'shock[s] the conscience'" may not be used to support a criminal conviction). Although *Rochin* did not establish a civil remedy for abusive police behavior, we recognized in *County of Sacramento v. Lewis*, 523 U. S. 833, 846 (1998), that deprivations of liberty caused by "the most egregious official conduct," *id.*, at 846, 847–848, n. 8, may violate the Due Process Clause. While we rejected, in *Lewis*, a §1983 plaintiff's contention that a police officer's deliberate indifference during a high-speed chase that caused the death of a motorcyclist violated due process, *id.*, at 854, we left open the possibility that unauthorized police behavior in other contexts might "shock the conscience" and give rise to §1983 liability. *Id.*, at 850.

We are satisfied that Chavez's questioning did not violate Martinez's due process rights. Even assuming, *arguendo*, that the persistent questioning of Martinez somehow deprived him of a liberty interest, we cannot agree with Martinez's characterization of Chavez's behavior as "egregious" or "conscience shocking." As we noted in *Lewis*, the official conduct "most likely to rise to the conscience-shocking level," is the "conduct intended to injure in some way unjustifiable by any government interest." *Id.*, at 849. Here, there is no evidence that Chavez acted with a purpose to harm Martinez by intentionally interfering with his medical treatment. Medical personnel were able to treat Martinez throughout the interview, App. to Pet. for Cert. 4a, 18a, and Chavez ceased his questioning to allow tests and other procedures to be performed. *Id.*, at 4a. Nor is there evidence that Chavez's conduct exacerbated Martinez's injuries or prolonged his stay in the hospital. Moreover, the need to investigate whether there had been police misconduct constituted a justifiable government interest given the risk that key evidence would have been lost if Martinez had died without the authorities ever hearing his side of the story.

The Court has held that the Due Process Clause also protects certain "fundamental liberty interest[s]" from deprivation by the government, regardless of the procedures provided, unless the infringement is narrowly tailored to serve a compelling state interest. *Washington v. Glucksberg*, 521 U. S. 702, 721 (1997). Only fundamental rights and liberties which are "'deeply rooted in this Nation's history and tradition'" and "'implicit in the concept of ordered liberty'" qualify for such protection. *Ibid.* Many times, however, we have expressed our reluctance to expand the doctrine of substantive due process, see *Lewis, supra*, at 842; *Glucksberg, supra*, at 720; *Albright v. Oliver*, 510 U. S. 266, 271

(1994); *Reno v. Flores*, 507 U. S. 292, 302 (1993); in large part "because guideposts for responsible decisionmaking in this unchartered area are scarce and open-ended," *Collins v. Harker Heights*, 503 U. S. 115, 125 (1992). See also *Regents of Univ. of Mich. v. Ewing*, 474 U. S. 214, 225–226 (1985).

Glucksberg requires a "'careful description'" of the asserted fundamental liberty interest for the purposes of substantive due process analysis; vague generalities, such as "the right not to be talked to," will not suffice. 521 U. S., at 721. We therefore must take into account the fact that Martinez was hospitalized and in severe pain during the interview, but also that Martinez was a critical nonpolice witness to an altercation resulting in a shooting by a police officer, and that the situation was urgent given the perceived risk that Martinez might die and crucial evidence might be lost. In these circumstances, we can find no basis in our prior jurisprudence, see, *e.g., Miranda*, 384 U. S., at 477–478 ("It is an act of responsible citizenship for individuals to give whatever information they may have to aid in law enforcement"), or in our Nation's history and traditions to suppose that freedom from unwanted police questioning is a right so fundamental that it cannot be abridged absent a "compelling state interest." *Flores, supra*, at 302. We have never required such a justification for a police interrogation, and we decline to do so here. The lack of any "guideposts for responsible decisionmaking" in this area, and our oft-stated reluctance to expand the doctrine of substantive due process, further counsel against recognizing a new "fundamental liberty interest" in this case.

We conclude that Martinez has failed to allege a violation of the Fourteenth Amendment, and it is therefore unnecessary to inquire whether the right asserted by Martinez was clearly established.

III

Because Chavez did not violate Martinez's Fifth and Fourteenth Amendment rights, he was entitled to qualified immunity. The judgment of the Court of Appeals for the Ninth Circuit is therefore reversed and the case is remanded for further proceedings.

It is so ordered.

Footnotes

[1] The parties disagree over what triggered the altercation. The officers maintain that Martinez ran away from them and that they tackled him while in pursuit; Martinez asserts that he never attempted to flee and Salinas tackled him without warning.

[2] The government may not, however, penalize public employees and government contractors to induce them to waive their *immunity* from the use of their compelled statements in subsequent criminal proceedings. See *Uniformed Sanitation Men Assn., Inc. v. Commissioner of Sanitation of City of New York*, 392 U. S. 280 (1968); *Lefkowitz v. Turley*, 414 U. S. 70 (1973), and this is true even though immu-

nity is not itself a right secured by the text of the Self-Incrimination Clause, but rather a prophylactic rule we have constructed to protect the Fifth Amendment's right from invasion. See Part II–A–3, *infra.* Once an immunity waiver is signed, the signatory is unable to assert a Fifth Amendment objection to the subsequent use of his statements in a criminal case, even if his statements were in fact compelled. A waiver of immunity is therefore a prospective waiver of the core self-incrimination right in any subsequent criminal proceeding, and States cannot condition public employment on the waiver of constitutional rights, *Lefkowitz, supra,* at 85.

[3] That the privilege is a prophylactic one does not alter our penalty cases jurisprudence, which allows such privilege to be asserted prior to, and outside of, criminal proceedings.

[4] It is JUSTICE KENNEDY's indifference to the text of the Self-Incrimination Clause, as well as a conspicuous absence of a single citation to the actual text of the Fifth Amendment, that permits him to adopt the Ninth Circuit's interpretation.

Mincey v. Arizona, 437 U. S. 385 (1978), on which JUSTICE KENNEDY and JUSTICE GINSBURG rely in support of their reading of the Fifth Amendment, was a case addressing the *admissibility* of a coerced confession under the *Due Process* Clause. *Mincey* did not even mention the Fifth Amendment or the Self-Incrimination Clause, and refutes JUSTICE KENNEDY's and JUSTICE GINSBURG's assertions that their interpretation of that Clause would have been known to any reasonable officer at the time Chavez conducted his interrogation.

[5] We also do not see how, in light of *Graham v. Connor,* 490 U. S. 386 (1989), JUSTICE KENNEDY can insist that "the Self-Incrimination Clause is applicable at the time and place police use compulsion to extract a statement from a suspect" while at the same time maintaining that the use of "torture or its equivalent in an attempt to induce a statement" violates the Due Process Clause. *Post,* at 8. *Graham* foreclosed the use of substantive due process analysis in claims involving the use of excessive force in effecting an arrest and held that such claims are governed *solely* by the Fourth Amendment's prohibitions against "unreasonable" seizures, because the Fourth Amendment provided the explicit source of constitutional protection against such conduct. 490 U. S., at 394–395. If, as JUSTICE KENNEDY believes, the Fifth Amendment's Self-Incrimination Clause governs coercive police interrogation even absent use of compelled statements in a criminal case, then *Graham* suggests that the Due Process Clause would not.

Town of Castle Rock, Colorado v. Gonzales, Individually and as Next Best Friend of Her Deceased Minor Children, Gonzales et al.

545 U. S. ___ (2005)

Argued March 21, 2005
Decided June 27, 2005
JUSTICE SCALIA delivered the opinion of the Court.

We decide in this case whether an individual who has obtained a state-law restraining order has a constitutionally protected property interest in having the police enforce the restraining order when they have probable cause to believe it has been violated.

I

The horrible facts of this case are contained in the complaint that respondent Jessica Gonzales filed in Federal District Court. (Because the case comes to us on appeal from a dismissal of the complaint, we assume its allegations are true. See *Swierkiewicz v. Sorema N. A.*, 534 U. S. 506, 508, n. 1 (2002).) Respondent alleges that petitioner, the town of Castle Rock, Colorado, violated the Due Process Clause of the Fourteenth Amendment to the United States Constitution when its police officers, acting pursuant to official policy or custom, failed to respond properly to her repeated reports that her estranged husband was violating the terms of a restraining order.[1]

The restraining order had been issued by a state trial court several weeks earlier in conjunction with respondent's divorce proceedings. The original form order, issued on May 21, 1999, and served on respondent's husband on June 4, 1999, commanded him not to "molest or disturb the peace of [respondent] or of any child," and to remain at least 100 yards from the family home at all times. 366 F. 3d 1093, 1143 (CA10 2004) (en banc) (appendix to dissenting opinion of O'Brien, J.). The bottom of the preprinted form noted that the reverse side contained "IMPORTANT NOTICES FOR RESTRAINED PARTIES AND LAW ENFORCEMENT OFFICIALS." *Ibid.* (emphasis deleted). The preprinted text on the back of the form included the following "**WARNING**":

> "**A KNOWING VIOLATION OF A RESTRAINING ORDER IS A CRIME** . . . . A VIOLATION WILL ALSO CONSTITUTE CONTEMPT OF COURT. **YOU MAY BE ARRESTED** WITHOUT NOTICE IF A LAW ENFORCEMENT OFFICER HAS PROBABLE CAUSE TO BELIEVE THAT YOU HAVE KNOWINGLY VIOLATED THIS ORDER." *Id.,* at 1144.

The preprinted text on the back of the form also included a "**NOTICE TO LAW ENFORCEMENT OFFICIALS**," which read in part:

> "YOU SHALL USE EVERY REASONABLE MEANS TO ENFORCE THIS RESTRAINING ORDER. YOU SHALL ARREST, OR, IF AN ARREST WOULD BE IMPRACTICAL UNDER THE CIRCUMSTANCES, SEEK A WARRANT FOR THE ARREST OF THE RESTRAINED PERSON WHEN YOU HAVE INFORMATION AMOUNTING TO PROBABLE CAUSE THAT THE RESTRAINED PERSON HAS VIOLATED OR ATTEMPTED TO VIOLATE ANY PROVISION OF THIS ORDER AND THE RESTRAINED PERSON HAS BEEN PROPERLY SERVED WITH A COPY OF THIS ORDER OR HAS RECEIVED ACTUAL NOTICE OF THE EXISTENCE OF THIS ORDER." *Ibid.*

On June 4, 1999, the state trial court modified the terms of the restraining order and made it permanent. The modified order gave respondent's husband the right to spend time with his three daughters (ages 10, 9, and 7) on alternate weekends, for two weeks during the summer, and, "'upon reasonable notice,'" for a mid-week dinner visit "'arranged by the parties'"; the modified order also allowed him to visit the home to collect the children for such "parenting time." *Id.,* at 1097 (majority opinion).

According to the complaint, at about 5 or 5:30 p.m. on Tuesday, June 22, 1999, respondent's husband took the three daughters while they were playing outside the family home. No advance arrangements had been made for him to see the daughters that evening. When respondent noticed the children were missing, she suspected her husband had taken them. At about 7:30 p.m., she called the Castle Rock Police Department, which dispatched two officers. The complaint continues: "When [the officers] arrived . . . , she showed them a copy of the TRO and requested that it be enforced and the three children be returned to her immediately. [The officers] stated that there was nothing they could do about the TRO and suggested that [respondent] call the Police Department again if the three children did not return home by 10:00 p.m." App. to Pet. for Cert. 126a.[2]

At approximately 8:30 p.m., respondent talked to her husband on his cellular telephone. He told her "he had the three children [at an] amusement park in Denver." *Ibid.* She called the police again and asked them to "have someone check for" her husband or his vehicle at the amusement park and "put out an [all points bulletin]" for her husband, but the officer with whom she spoke "refused to do so," again telling her to "wait until 10:00 p.m. and see if" her husband returned the girls. *Id.*, at 126a–127a.

At approximately 10:10 p.m., respondent called the police and said her children were still missing, but she was now told to wait until midnight. She called at midnight and told the dispatcher her children were still missing. She went to her husband's apartment and, finding nobody there, called the police at 12:10 a.m.; she was told to wait for an officer to arrive. When none came, she went to the police station at 12:50 a.m. and submitted an incident report. The officer who took the report "made no reasonable effort to enforce the TRO or locate the three children. Instead, he went to dinner." *Id.*, at 127a.

At approximately 3:20 a.m., respondent's husband arrived at the police station and opened fire with a semiautomatic handgun he had purchased earlier that evening. Police shot back, killing him. Inside the cab of his pickup truck, they found the bodies of all three daughters, whom he had already murdered. *Ibid.*

On the basis of the foregoing factual allegations, respondent brought an action under Rev. Stat. §1979, 42 U. S. C. §1983, claiming that the town violated the Due Process Clause because its police department had "an official policy or custom of failing to respond properly to complaints of restraining order violations" and "tolerate[d] the non-enforcement of restraining orders by its police officers." App. to Pet. for Cert. 129a.[3] The complaint also alleged that the town's actions "were taken either willfully, recklessly or with such gross negligence as to indicate wanton disregard and deliberate indifference to" respondent's civil rights. *Ibid.*

Before answering the complaint, the defendants filed a motion to dismiss under Federal Rule of Civil Procedure 12(b)(6). The District Court granted the motion, concluding that, whether construed as making a substantive due process or procedural due process claim, respondent's complaint failed to state a claim upon which relief could be granted.

A panel of the Court of Appeals affirmed the rejection of a substantive due process claim, but found that respondent had alleged a cognizable procedural due process claim. 307 F. 3d 1258 (CA10 2002). On rehearing en banc, a divided court reached the same disposition, concluding that respondent had a "protected property interest in the enforcement of the terms of her restraining order" and that the town had deprived her of due process because "the police never 'heard' nor seriously entertained her request to enforce and protect her interests in the restraining order." 366 F. 3d, at 1101, 1117. We granted certiorari. 543 U. S. ___ (2004).

II

The Fourteenth Amendment to the United States Constitution provides that a State shall not "deprive any person of life, liberty, or property, without due process of law." Amdt. 14, §1. In 42 U. S. C. §1983, Congress has created a federal cause of action for "the deprivation of any rights, privileges, or immunities secured by the Constitution and laws." Respondent claims the benefit of this provision on the ground that she had a property interest in police enforcement of the restraining order against her husband; and that the town deprived her of this property without due process by having a policy that tolerated nonenforcement of restraining orders.

As the Court of Appeals recognized, we left a similar question unanswered in *DeShaney v. Winnebago County Dept. of Social Servs.*, 489 U. S. 189 (1989), another case with "undeniably tragic" facts: Local child-protection officials had failed to protect a young boy from beatings by his father that left him severely brain damaged. *Id.*, at 191–193. We held that the so-called "substantive" component of the Due Process Clause does not "requir[e] the State to protect the life, liberty, and property of its citizens against invasion by private actors." *Id.*, at 195. We noted, however, that the petitioner had not properly preserved the argument that—and we thus "decline[d] to consider" whether—state "child protection statutes gave [him] an 'entitlement' to receive protective services in accordance with the terms of the statute, an entitlement which would enjoy due process protection." *Id.*, at 195, n. 2.

The procedural component of the Due Process Clause does not protect everything that might be described as a "benefit": "To have a property interest in a benefit, a person clearly must have more than an abstract need or desire" and "more than a unilateral expectation of it. He must, instead, have a legitimate claim of entitlement to it." *Board of Regents of State Colleges v. Roth*, 408 U. S. 564, 577 (1972). Such entitlements are "'of course, . . . not created by the Constitution. Rather, they are created and their dimensions are defined by existing rules or understandings that stem from an independent source such as state law.'" *Paul v. Davis*, 424 U. S. 693, 709 (1976) (quoting *Roth, supra*, at 577); see also *Phillips v. Washington Legal Foundation*, 524 U. S. 156, 164 (1998).

A

Our cases recognize that a benefit is not a protected entitlement if government officials may grant or deny it in their discretion. See, *e.g., Kentucky Dept. of Corrections v. Thompson*, 490 U. S. 454, 462–463 (1989). The Court of Appeals in this case determined that Colorado law created an entitlement to enforcement of the restraining order because the "court-issued restraining order . . . specifically dictated that its terms must be enforced" and a "state statute command[ed]" enforcement of the order when certain objective conditions were met (probable cause to believe that the order had been violated and that the object of the order had received notice of its existence). 366 F. 3d, at 1101, n. 5; see also *id.*, at 1100, n. 4; *id.*, at 1104–1105, and n. 9. Respondent contends that we are obliged "to give deference to the Tenth Circuit's analysis of Colorado law on" whether she had an entitlement to enforcement of the restraining order. Tr. of Oral Arg. 52.

We will not, of course, defer to the Tenth Circuit on the ultimate issue: whether what Colorado law has given respondent constitutes a property interest for purposes of the Fourteenth Amendment. That determination, despite its state-law underpinnings, is ultimately one of federal constitutional law. "Although the underlying substantive interest is created by 'an independent source such as state law,' *federal constitutional law* determines whether that interest rises to the level of a 'legitimate claim of entitlement' protected by the Due Process Clause." *Memphis Light, Gas & Water Div. v. Craft*, 436 U. S. 1, 9 (1978) (emphasis added) (quoting *Roth, supra*, at 577); cf. *United States ex rel. TVA v. Powelson*, 319 U. S. 266, 279 (1943). Resolution of the federal issue begins, however, with a determination of what it is that state law provides. In the context of the present case, the central state-law question is whether Colorado law gave respondent a right to police enforcement of the restraining order. It is on this point that respondent's call for deference to the Tenth Circuit is relevant.

We have said that a "presumption of deference [is] given the views of a federal court as to the law of a State within its jurisdiction." *Phillips, supra*, at 167. That presumption can be overcome, however, see *Leavitt v. Jane L.*, 518 U. S. 137, 145 (1996) (*per curiam*), and we think deference inappropriate here. The Tenth Circuit's opinion, which reversed the Colorado District Judge, did not draw upon a deep well of state-specific expertise, but consisted primarily of quoting language from the restraining order, the statutory text, and a state-legislative-hearing transcript. See 366 F. 3d, at 1103–1109. These texts, moreover, say nothing distinctive to Colorado, but use mandatory language that (as we shall discuss) appears in many state and federal statutes. As for case law: the only state-law cases about restraining orders that the Court of Appeals relied upon were decisions of Federal District Courts in Ohio and Pennsylvania and state courts in New Jersey, Oregon, and Tennessee. *Id.*, at 1104–1105, n. 9, 1109.[4] Moreover, if we were simply to accept the Court of Appeals' conclusion, we would necessarily have to decide conclusively a federal constitutional question (*i.e.*, whether such an entitlement constituted property under the Due Process Clause and, if so, whether petitioner's customs or policies provided too little process to protect it). We proceed, then, to our own analysis of whether Colorado law gave respondent a right to enforcement of the restraining order.[5]

B

The critical language in the restraining order came not from any part of the order itself (which was signed by the state-court trial judge and directed to the restrained party, respondent's husband), but from the preprinted notice to law-enforcement personnel that appeared on the back of the order. See *supra*, at 2–3. That notice effectively restated the statutory provision describing "peace officers' duties" related to the crime of violation of a restraining order. At the time of the conduct at issue in this case, that provision read as follows:

> "(a) Whenever a restraining order is issued, the protected person shall be provided with a copy of such order. *A peace officer shall use every reasonable means to enforce a restraining order.*

> "(b) *A peace officer shall arrest, or, if an arrest would be impractical under the circumstances, seek a warrant for the arrest of a restrained person* when the peace officer has information amounting to probable cause that:

> "(I) The restrained person has violated or attempted to violate any provision of a restraining order; and

> "(II) The restrained person has been properly served with a copy of the restraining order or the restrained person has received actual notice of the existence and substance of such order.

> "(c) In making the probable cause determination described in paragraph (b) of this subsection (3), a peace officer shall assume that the information received from the registry is accurate. *A peace officer shall enforce a valid restraining order whether or not there is a record of the restraining order in the registry.*" Colo. Rev. Stat. §18-6-803.5(3) (Lexis 1999) (emphases added).

The Court of Appeals concluded that this statutory provision—especially taken in conjunction with a statement from its legislative history,[6] and with another statute restricting criminal and civil liability for officers making arrests[7]—established the Colorado Legislature's clear intent "to alter the fact that the police were not enforcing domestic abuse retraining orders," and thus its intent "that the recipient of a domestic abuse restraining order have an entitlement to its enforcement." 366 F. 3d, at 1108. Any other result, it said, "would render domestic abuse restraining orders utterly valueless." *Id.*, at 1109.

This last statement is sheer hyperbole. Whether or not respondent had a right to enforce the restraining order, it rendered certain otherwise lawful conduct by her husband both criminal and in contempt of court. See §§18-6-803.5(2)(a), (7). The creation of grounds on which he could be arrested, criminally prosecuted, and held in contempt was hardly "valueless"—even if the prospect of those sanctions ultimately failed to prevent him from committing three murders and a suicide.

We do not believe that these provisions of Colorado law truly made enforcement of restraining orders *mandatory.* A well established tradition of police discretion has long coexisted with apparently mandatory arrest statutes.

> "In each and every state there are long-standing statutes that, by their terms, seem to preclude nonenforcement by the police. . . . However, for a number of reasons, including their legislative history, insufficient resources, and sheer physical impossibility, it has been recognized that such statutes cannot be interpreted literally. . . . [T]hey clearly do not mean that a police officer may not lawfully decline to make an arrest. As to third parties in these states, the full-enforcement statutes simply have no effect, and their significance is further diminished." 1 ABA Standards for Criminal Justice 1-4.5, commentary, pp. 1-124 to 1-125 (2d ed. 1980) (footnotes omitted).

The deep-rooted nature of law-enforcement discretion, even in the presence of seemingly mandatory legislative commands, is illustrated by *Chicago v. Morales*, 527 U. S. 41 (1999), which involved an ordinance that said a police officer "'shall order'" persons to disperse in certain circumstances, *id.*, at 47, n. 2. This Court rejected out of hand the possibility that "the mandatory language of the ordinance . . . afford[ed] the police *no* discretion." *Id.*, at 62, n. 32. It is, the Court proclaimed, simply "common sense that *all* police officers must use some discretion in deciding when and where to enforce city ordinances." *Ibid.* (emphasis added).

Against that backdrop, a true mandate of police action would require some stronger indication from the Colorado Legislature than "shall use every reasonable means to enforce a restraining order" (or even "shall arrest . . . or . . . seek a warrant"), §§18-6-803.5(3)(a), (b). That language is not perceptibly more mandatory than the Colorado statute which has long told municipal chiefs of police that they "shall pursue and arrest any person fleeing from justice in any part of the state" and that they "shall apprehend any person in the act of committing any offense . . . and, forthwith and without any warrant, bring such person before a . . . competent authority for examination and trial." Colo. Rev. Stat. §31-4-112 (Lexis 2004). It is hard to imagine that a Colorado peace officer would not have some discretion to determine that—despite probable cause to believe a restraining order has been violated—the circumstances of the violation or the competing duties of that officer or his agency counsel decisively against enforcement in a particular instance.[8] The practical necessity for discretion is particularly apparent in a case such as this one, where the suspected violator is not actually present and his whereabouts are unknown. Cf. *Donaldson v. Seattle*, 65 Wash. App. 661, 671–672, 831 P. 2d 1098, 1104 (1992) ("There is a vast difference between a mandatory duty to arrest [a violator who is on the scene] and a mandatory duty to conduct a follow up investigation [to locate an absent violator]. . . . A mandatory duty to investigate would be completely open-ended as to priority, duration and intensity").

The dissent correctly points out that, in the specific context of domestic violence, mandatory-arrest statutes have been found in some States to be more mandatory than traditional mandatory-arrest statutes. *Post*, at 7–13 (opinion of STEVENS, J.). The Colorado statute mandating arrest for a domestic-violence offense is different from but related to the one at issue here, and it includes similar though not identical phrasing. See Colo. Rev. Stat. §18–6–803.6(l) (Lexis 1999) ("When a peace officer determines that there is probable cause to believe that a crime or offense involving domestic violence . . . has been committed, the officer shall, without undue delay, arrest the person suspected of its commission . . ."). Even in the domestic-violence context, however, it is unclear how the mandatory-arrest paradigm applies to cases in which the offender is not present to be arrested. As the dissent explains, *post*, at 9–10, and n. 8, much of the impetus for mandatory-arrest statutes and policies derived from the idea that it is better for police officers to arrest the aggressor in a domestic-violence incident than to attempt to mediate the dispute or merely to ask the offender to leave the scene. Those other options are only available, of course, when the offender is present at the scene. See Hanna, No Right to Choose: Mandated Victim Participation in Domestic Violence Prosecutions, 109 Harv. L. Rev. 1849, 1860 (1996) ("[T]he clear trend in police practice is to arrest the batterer *at the scene* . . ." (emphasis added)).

As one of the cases cited by the dissent, *post*, at 12, recognized, "there will be situations when no arrest is possible, *such as when the alleged abuser is not in the home.*" *Donaldson*, 65 Wash. App., at 674, 831 P. 2d, at 1105 (emphasis added). That case held that Washington's mandatory-arrest statute required an arrest only in "cases where the offender is on the scene," and that it "d[id] not create an on-going mandatory duty to conduct an investigation" to locate the offender. *Id.*, at 675, 831 P. 2d, at 1105. Colorado's restraining-order statute appears to contemplate a similar distinction, providing that when arrest is "impractical"—which was likely the case when the whereabouts of respondent's husband were unknown—the officers' statutory duty is to "seek a warrant" rather than "arrest." §18-6-803.5(3)(b).

Respondent does not specify the precise means of enforcement that the Colorado restraining-order statute assertedly mandated—whether her interest lay in having police arrest her husband, having them seek a warrant for his arrest, or having them "use every reasonable means, up to and including arrest, to enforce the order's terms," Brief for Respondent 29-30.[9] Such indeterminacy is not the hallmark of a duty that is mandatory. Nor can someone be safely deemed "entitled" to something when the identity of the alleged entitlement is vague. See *Roth*, 408 U. S., at 577 (considering whether "certain benefits" were "secure[d]" by rule or understandings); cf. *Natale v. Ridgefield*, 170 F. 3d 258, 263 (CA2 1999) ("There is no reason . . . to restrict the 'uncertainty' that will preclude existence of a federally protectable property interest to the uncertainty that inheres in the exercise of discretion"). The dissent, after suggesting various formulations of the entitlement in question,[10] ultimately contends that the obligations under the statute were quite precise: either make an arrest or (if that is impractical) seek an arrest warrant, *post*, at 14. The problem with this is that the seeking of an arrest warrant would be an entitlement to nothing but procedure—which we have held inadequate even to support standing, see *Lujan v. Defenders of Wildlife*, 504 U. S. 555 (1992); much less can it be the basis for a property interest. See *post*, at 3-4 (SOUTER, J., concurring). After the warrant is sought, it remains within the discretion of a judge whether to grant it, and after it is granted, it remains within the discretion of the police whether and when to execute it.[11] Respondent would have been assured nothing but the seeking of a warrant. This is not the sort of "entitlement" out of which a property interest is created.

Even if the statute could be said to have made enforcement of restraining orders "mandatory" because of the domestic-violence context of the underlying statute, that would not necessarily mean that state law gave *respondent* an entitlement to *enforcement* of the mandate. Making the actions of government employees obligatory can serve various legitimate ends other than the conferral of a benefit on a specific class of people. See, *e.g., Sandin v. Conner*, 515 U. S. 472, 482 (1995) (finding no constitutionally protected liberty interest in prison regulations phrased in mandatory terms, in part because "[s]uch guidelines are not set forth solely to benefit the prisoner"). The serving of public rather than private ends is the normal course of the criminal law because criminal acts, "besides the injury [they do] to individuals, . . . strike at the very being of society; which cannot possibly subsist, where actions of this sort are suffered to escape with impunity." 4 W. Blackstone, Commentaries on the Laws of England 5 (1769); see also *Huntington v. Attrill*, 146 U. S. 657, 668 (1892). This principle underlies, for example, a Colorado district attorney's discretion to prosecute a domestic assault, even though the victim withdraws her charge. See *People v. Cunefare*, 102 P. 3d 302, 311–312 (Colo. 2004) (Bender, J., concurring in part, dissenting in part, and dissenting in part to the judgment).

Respondent's alleged interest stems only from a State's *statutory* scheme—from a restraining order that was authorized by and tracked precisely the statute on which the Court of Appeals relied. She does not assert that she has any common-law or contractual entitlement to enforcement. If she was given a statutory entitlement, we would expect to see some indication of that in the statute itself. Although Colorado's statute spoke of "protected person[s]" such as respondent, it did so in connection with matters other than a right to enforcement. It said that a "protected person shall be provided with a copy of [a restraining] order" when it is issued, §18-6-803.5(3)(a); that a law enforcement agency "shall make all reasonable efforts to contact the protected party upon the arrest of the restrained person," §18-6-803.5(3)(d); and that the agency "shall give [to the protected person] a copy" of the report it submits to the court that issued the order, §18-6803.5(3)(e). Perhaps most importantly, the statute spoke directly to the protected person's power to "initiate contempt proceedings against the restrained person if the order [was] issued in a civil action or request the prosecuting attorney to initiate contempt proceedings if the order [was] issued in a criminal action." §18-6-803.5(7). The protected person's express power to "initiate" civil contempt proceedings contrasts tellingly with the mere ability to "request" initiation of criminal contempt proceedings—and even more dramatically with the complete silence about any power to "request" (much less demand) that an arrest be made.

The creation of a personal entitlement to something as vague and novel as enforcement of restraining orders cannot "simply g[o] without saying." *Post*, at 17, n. 16 (STEVENS, J., dissenting). We conclude that Colorado has not created such an entitlement.

C

Even if we were to think otherwise concerning the creation of an entitlement by Colorado, it is by no means clear that an individual entitlement to enforcement of a restraining order could constitute a "property" interest for purposes of the Due Process Clause. Such a right would not, of course, resemble any traditional conception of property. Although that alone does not disqualify it from due process protection, as *Roth* and its progeny show, the right to have a restraining order enforced does not "have some ascertainable monetary value," as even our "*Roth*-type property-as-entitlement" cases have implicitly required. Merrill, The Landscape of Constitutional Property, 86 Va. L. Rev. 885, 964 (2000).[12] Perhaps most radically, the alleged property interest here arises *incidentally*, not out of some new species of government benefit or service, but out of a function that government actors have always performed—to wit, arresting people who they have probable cause to believe have committed a criminal offense.[13]

The indirect nature of a benefit was fatal to the due process claim of the nursing-home residents in *O'Bannon v. Town Court Nursing Center*, 447 U. S. 773 (1980). We held that, while the withdrawal of "direct benefits" (financial payments under Medicaid for certain medical services) triggered due process protections, *id.*, at 786–787, the same was not true for the "indirect benefit[s]" conferred on Medicaid patients when the Government enforced "minimum standards of care" for nursing-home facilities, *id.*, at 787. "[A]n indirect and incidental result of the Government's enforcement action . . . does not amount to a deprivation of any interest in life, liberty, or property." *Ibid.* In this case, as in *O'Bannon*, "[t]he simple distinction between government action that directly affects a citizen's legal rights . . . and action that is directed against a third party and affects the citizen only indirectly or incidentally, provides a sufficient answer to" respondent's reliance on cases that found government-provided services to be entitlements. *Id.*, at 788. The *O'Bannon* Court expressly noted, *ibid.*, that the distinction between direct and indirect benefits distinguished *Memphis Light, Gas & Water Div. v. Craft*, 436 U. S. 1 (1978), one of the government-services cases on which the dissent relies, *post*, at 19.

III

We conclude, therefore, that respondent did not, for purposes of the Due Process Clause, have a property interest in police enforcement of the restraining order against her husband. It is accordingly unnecessary to address the Court of Appeals' determination (366 F. 3d, at 1110–1117) that the town's custom or policy prevented the police from giving her due process when they deprived her of that alleged interest. See *American Mfrs. Mut. Ins. Co. v. Sullivan*, 526 U. S. 40, 61 (1999).[14]

In light of today's decision and that in *DeShaney*, the benefit that a third party may receive from having someone else arrested for a crime generally does not trigger protections under the Due Process Clause, neither in its procedural nor in its "substantive" manifestations. This result reflects our continuing reluctance to treat the Fourteenth Amendment as "'a font of tort law,'" *Parratt v. Taylor*, 451 U. S. 527, 544 (1981) (quoting *Paul v. Davis*, 424 U. S., at 701), but it does not mean States are powerless to provide victims with personally enforceable remedies. Although the framers of the Fourteenth Amendment and the Civil Rights Act of 1871, 17 Stat. 13 (the original source of §1983), did not create a system by which police departments are generally held financially accountable for crimes that better policing might have prevented, the people of Colorado are free to craft such a system under state law. Cf. *DeShaney*, 489 U. S., at 203.[15]

The judgment of the Court of Appeals is

Reversed.

Footnotes

[1] Petitioner claims that respondent's complaint "did not allege ... that she ever notified the police of her contention that [her husband] was actually in violation of the restraining order." Brief for Petitioner 7, n. 2. The complaint does allege, however, that respondent "showed [the police] a copy of the [temporary restraining order (TRO)] and requested that it be enforced." App. to Pet. for Cert. 126a. At this stage in the litigation, we may assume that this reasonably implied the order was being violated. See *Steel Co. v. Citizens for Better Environment*, 523 U. S. 83, 104 (1998).

[2] It is unclear from the complaint, but immaterial to our decision, whether respondent showed the police only the original "TRO" or also the permanent, modified restraining order that had superseded it on June 4.

[3] Three police officers were also named as defendants in the complaint, but the Court of Appeals concluded that they were entitled to qualified immunity, 366 F. 3d 1093, 1118 (CA10 2004) (en banc). Respondent did not file a cross-petition challenging that aspect of the judgment.

[4] Most of the Colorado-law cases cited by the Court of Appeals appeared in footnotes declaring them to be irrelevant because they involved only substantive due process (366 F. 3d, at 1100-1101, nn. 4-5), only statutes without restraining orders (*id.*, at 1101, n. 5), or Colorado's Government Immunity Act, which the Court of Appeals concluded applies "only to ... state tort law claims" (*id.*, at 1108-1109, n. 12). Our analysis is likewise unaffected by the Immunity Act or by the way that Colorado has dealt with substantive due process or cases that do not involve restraining orders.

[5] In something of an anyone-but-us approach, the dissent simultaneously (and thus unpersuasively) contends not only that this Court should certify a question to the Colorado Supreme Court, *post*, at 5-7 (opinion of STEVENS, J.), but also that it should defer to the Tenth Circuit (which itself did not certify any such question), *post*, at 3-4. No party in this case has requested certification, even as an alternative disposition. See Tr. of Oral Arg. 56 (petitioner's counsel "disfavor[ing]" certification); *id.*, at 25-26 (counsel for the United States arguing against certification). At oral argument, in fact, respondent's counsel declined JUSTICE STEVENS' invitation to request it. *Id.*, at 53.

[6] The Court of Appeals quoted one lawmaker's description of how the bill "'would really attack the domestic violence problems'":

> "'[T]he entire criminal justice system must act in a consistent manner, which does not now occur. The police must make probable cause arrests. The prosecutors must prosecute every case. Judges must apply appropriate sentences, and probation officers must monitor their probationers closely. And the offender needs to be sentenced to offender-specific therapy.

> "'[T]he entire system must send the same message ... [that] violence is criminal. And so we hope that House Bill 1253 starts us down this road.'" 366 F. 3d, at 1107 (quoting Tr. of Colorado House Judiciary Hearings on House Bill 1253, Feb. 15, 1994) (emphases omitted).

[7] Under Colo. Rev. Stat. §18-6-803.5(5) (Lexis 1999), "[a] peace officer arresting a person for violating a restraining order or otherwise enforcing a restraining order" was not to be held civilly or criminally liable unless he acted "in bad faith and with malice" or violated "rules adopted by the Colorado supreme court."

[8] Respondent in fact concedes that an officer may "properly" decide not to enforce a restraining order when the officer deems "a technical violation" too "immaterial" to justify arrest. Respondent explains this as a determination that there is no

probable cause. Brief for Respondent 28. We think, however, that a determination of no probable cause to believe a violation has occurred is quite different from a determination that the violation is too insignificant to pursue.

[9] Respondent characterizes her entitlement in various ways. See Brief for Respondent 12 ("'entitlement' to receive protective services"); *id.*, at 13 ("interest in police enforcement action"); *id.*, at 14 ("specific government benefit" consisting of "the government service of enforcing the objective terms of the court order protecting her and her children against her abusive husband"); *id.*, at 32 ("[T]he restraining order here mandated the arrest of Mr. Gonzales under specified circumstances, or at a minimum required the use of reasonable means to enforce the order").

[10] See *post*, at 1 ("entitlement to police protection"); *post*, at 2 ("entitlement to mandatory individual protection by the local police force"); *ibid.* ("a right to police assistance"); *post*, at 8 ("a citizen's interest in the government's commitment to provide police enforcement in certain defined circumstances"); *post*, at 18 ("respondent's property interest in the enforcement of her restraining order"); *post*, at 20 (the "service" of "protection from her husband"); *post*, at 21-22 ("interest in the enforcement of the restraining order").

[11] The dissent asserts that the police would lack discretion in the execution of this warrant, *post*, at 13-14, n. 12, but cites no statute mandating immediate execution. The general Colorado statute governing arrest provides that police "may arrest" when they possess a warrant "commanding" arrest. Colo. Rev. Stat. §16-3-102(1) (Lexis 1999).

[12] The dissent suggests that the interest in having a restraining order enforced does have an ascertainable monetary value, because one may "contract with a private security firm . . . to provide protection" for one's family. *Post*, at 2, 20, and n. 18. That is, of course, not as precise as the analogy between public and private schooling that the dissent invokes. *Post*, at 20, n. 18. Respondent probably could have hired a private firm to guard her house, to prevent her husband from coming onto the property, and perhaps even to search for her husband after she discovered that her children were missing. Her alleged entitlement here, however, does not consist in an abstract right to "protection," but (according to the dissent) in enforcement of her restraining order through the arrest of her husband, or the seeking of a warrant for his arrest, after she gave the police probable cause to believe the restraining order had been violated. A private person would not have the power to arrest under those circumstances because the crime would not have occurred in his presence. Colo. Rev. Stat. §16-3-201 (Lexis 1999). And, needless to say, a private person would not have the power to obtain an arrest warrant.

[13] In other contexts, we have explained that "a private citizen lacks a judicially cognizable interest in the prosecution or nonprosecution of another." *Linda R. S. v. Richard D.*, 410 U. S. 614, 619 (1973).

[14] Because we simply do not address whether the process would have been adequate if respondent had had a property interest, the dissent is correct to note that we do not "contest" the point, *post*, at 2. Of course we do not *accept* it either.

[15] In Colorado, the general statutory immunity for government employees does not apply when "the act or omission causing . . . injury was willful and wanton." Colo. Rev. Stat. §24-10-118(2)(a) (Lexis 1999). Respondent's complaint does allege that the police officers' actions "were taken either willfully, recklessly or with such gross negligence as to indicate wanton disregard and deliberate indifference to" her civil rights. App. to Pet. for Cert. 128a.

The state cases cited by the dissent that afford a cause of action for police failure to enforce restraining orders, *post*, at 11-12, 14-15, n. 13, vindicate state common-law or statutory tort claims—not procedural due process claims under the Federal Constitution. See *Donaldson v. Seattle*, 65 Wash. App. 661, 881 P. 2d 1098 (1992) (city could be liable under some circumstances for *per se* negligence in failing to meet statutory duty to arrest); *Matthews v. Pickett County*, 996 S. W. 2d 162 (Tenn. 1999) (county could be liable under Tennessee's Governmental Tort Liability Act where restraining order created a special duty); *Campbell v. Campbell*, 294 N. J. Super. 18, 682 A. 2d 272 (1996) (rejecting four specific defenses under the New Jersey Tort Claims Act in negligence action against individual officers); *Sorichetti v. New York*, 65 N. Y. 2d 461, 482 N. E. 2d 70 (1985) (city breached duty of care arising from special relationship between police and victim); *Nearing v. Weaver*, 295 Ore. 702, 670 P. 2d 137 (1983) (statutory duty to individual plaintiffs arising independently of tort-law duty of care).

Discussion Questions

1. Does the Court distinguish between a seizure brought about by a direct police use of force and a seizure brought about indirectly by the use of a motor vehicle? If so, how is this distinction made?

2. Under what conditions are roadblocks considered seizures?

3. How does the Court determine what constitutional amendment governs a police roadblock or a police pursuit? How does this decision affect the proof necessary to establish police liability?

4. If all seizures are to be analyzed under the Fourth Amendment and the "objective reasonableness" standard, how will the Court distinguish between an intentional seizure using a motor vehicle and an accident?

5. What constitutional amendment governs police vehicular pursuits? Can a police vehicular pursuit be considered a seizure? How does this decision affect the proof necessary to establish police liability?

6. Did the Court change its position on culpability in the *Sacramento* decision? If so, how? If not, does its position conflict with earlier decisions?

7. What is the standard required to establish liability for violation of the Fourteenth Amendment? Are there any police behaviors that would rise to the level of a Fourteenth Amendment violation?

8. What are the implications of the Court's decisions in Part VII of your casebook for the development of police policy on the use of motor vehicles?

PART VII

The Scope of
Individual Immunity

In this part of your casebook, the Court considers the scope of individual immunities extended to law enforcement officers. The Court addresses the immunity of executive officials for their official actions that result in constitutional violations. The Court discusses the concept of absolute immunity and determines which public officials enjoy this form of immunity and under what circumstances absolute immunity is granted. The Court limits the application of absolute immunity to a narrow range of official activities. In doing so, the Court constructs a decision-making process for determining absolute immunity. In developing this decision-making process, the Court outlines the rationale and purpose of absolute immunity and addresses the reasons why witnesses are granted this form of immunity in civil cases. In these cases, the Court distinguishes between special functions, discretionary functions, and derivative immunity.

The Court then turns its attention to developing and articulating the legal principles of qualified immunity and distinguishing this form of immunity from absolute immunity. In these opinions, the Court addresses the applicability of qualified immunity to an array of law enforcement activities from illegal search and seizures to the service of warrants not based on probable cause. The Court addresses both the subjective and objective aspects of qualified immunity. In doing so the Court articulates a requisite knowledge on the part of a law enforcement officer for a finding of qualified immunity and describes the necessary state of the law before qualified immunity can be granted. The Court also takes up the issue of whether it is appropriate to extend qualified immunity to law enforcement officers when they are sued in their personal capacities.

Harlow v. Fitzgerald
457 U.S. 800 (1982)

Argued November 30, 1981
Decided June 24, 1982
JUSTICE POWELL delivered the opinion of the Court.

The issue in this case is the scope of the immunity available to the senior aides and advisers of the President of the United States in a suit for damages based upon their official acts.

I

In this suit for civil damages petitioners Bryce Harlow and Alexander Butterfield are alleged to have participated in a conspiracy to violate the constitutional and statutory rights of the respondent A. Ernest Fitzgerald. Respondent avers that petitioners entered the conspiracy in their capacities as senior White House aides to former President Richard M. Nixon. As the alleged conspiracy is the same as that involved in *Nixon v. Fitzgerald, ante,* p. 731, the facts need not be repeated in detail.

Respondent claims that Harlow joined the conspiracy in his role as the Presidential aide principally responsible for congressional relations.[1] At the conclusion of discovery the [457 U.S. 800, 803] supporting evidence remained inferential. As evidence of Harlow's conspiratorial activity respondent relies heavily on a series of conversations in which Harlow discussed Fitzgerald's dismissal with Air Force Secretary Robert Seamans.[2] The other evidence most supportive of Fitzgerald's claims consists of a recorded conversation in which the President later voiced a tentative recollection that Harlow was "all for canning" Fitzgerald.[3]

345

Disputing Fitzgerald's contentions, Harlow argues that exhaustive discovery has adduced no direct evidence of his involvement [457 U.S. 800, 804] in any wrongful activity.[4] He avers that Secretary Seamans advised him that considerations of efficiency required Fitzgerald's removal by a reduction in force, despite anticipated adverse congressional reaction. Harlow asserts he had no reason to believe that a conspiracy existed. He contends that he took all his actions in good faith.[5]

Petitioner Butterfield also is alleged to have entered the conspiracy not later than May 1969. Employed as Deputy Assistant to the President and Deputy Chief of Staff to H. R. Haldeman,[6] Butterfield circulated a White House memorandum in that month in which he claimed to have learned that Fitzgerald planned to "blow the whistle" on some "shoddy purchasing practices" by exposing these practices to public view.[7] Fitzgerald characterizes this memorandum as evidence [457 U.S. 800, 805] that Butterfield had commenced efforts to secure Fitzgerald's retaliatory dismissal. As evidence that Butterfield participated in the conspiracy to conceal his unlawful discharge and prevent his reemployment, Fitzgerald cites communications between Butterfield and Haldeman in December 1969 and January 1970. After the President had promised at a press conference to inquire into Fitzgerald's dismissal, Haldeman solicited Butterfield's recommendations. In a subsequent memorandum emphasizing the importance of "loyalty," Butterfield counseled against offering Fitzgerald another job in the administration at that time.[8]

For his part, Butterfield denies that he was involved in any decision concerning Fitzgerald's employment status until Haldeman sought his advice in December 1969—more than a month after Fitzgerald's termination had been scheduled and announced publicly by the Air Force. Butterfield states that he never communicated his views about Fitzgerald to any official of the Defense Department. He argues generally that nearly eight years of discovery have failed to turn up any evidence that he caused injury to Fitzgerald.[9]

Together with their codefendant Richard Nixon, petitioners Harlow and Butterfield moved for summary judgment on February 12, 1980. In denying the motion the District Court upheld the legal sufficiency of Fitzgerald's *Bivens* (*Bivens v. Six Unknown Fed. Narcotics Agents*, 403 U.S. 388 (1971)) claim under the First Amendment and his "inferred" statutory causes of action under 5 U.S.C. § 7211 (1976 ed., Supp. IV) and 18 U.S.C. § 1505.[10] The court [457 U.S. 800, 806] found that genuine issues of disputed fact remained for resolution at trial. It also ruled that petitioners were not entitled to absolute immunity. App. to Pet. for Cert. 1a-3a.

Independently of former President Nixon, petitioners invoked the collateral order doctrine and appealed the denial of their immunity defense to the Court of Appeals for the District of Columbia Circuit. The Court of Appeals dismissed the appeal without opinion. *Id.*, at 11a-

12a. Never having determined the immunity available to the senior aides and advisers of the President of the United States, we granted certiorari. 452 U.S. 959 (1981).[11]

II

As we reiterated today in *Nixon v. Fitzgerald, ante,* p. 731, our decisions consistently have held that government officials are entitled to some form of immunity from suits for damages. As recognized at common law, public officers require this protection to shield them from undue interference with their duties and from potentially disabling threats of liability. [457 U.S. 800, 807]

Our decisions have recognized immunity defenses of two kinds. For officials whose special functions or constitutional status requires complete protection from suit, we have recognized the defense of "absolute immunity." The absolute immunity of legislators, in their legislative functions, see, *e.g., Eastland v. United States Servicemen's Fund,* 421 U.S. 491 (1975), and of judges, in their judicial functions, see, *e.g., Stump v. Sparkman,* 435 U.S. 349 (1978), now is well settled. Our decisions also have extended absolute immunity to certain officials of the Executive Branch. These include prosecutors and similar officials, see *Butz v. Economou,* 438 U.S. 478, 508-512 (1978), executive officers engaged in adjudicative functions, *id.,* at 513-517, and the President of the United States, see *Nixon v. Fitzgerald, ante,* p. 731.

For executive officials in general, however, our cases make plain that qualified immunity represents the norm. In *Scheuer v. Rhodes,* 416 U.S. 232 (1974), we acknowledged that high officials require greater protection than those with less complex discretionary responsibilities. Nonetheless, we held that a governor and his aides could receive the requisite protection from qualified or good-faith immunity. *Id.,* at 247-248. In *Butz v. Economou, supra,* we extended the approach of Scheuer to high federal officials of the Executive Branch. Discussing in detail the considerations that also had underlain our decision in *Scheuer,* we explained that the recognition of a qualified immunity defense for high executives reflected an attempt to balance competing values: not only the importance of a damages remedy to protect the rights of citizens, 438 U.S., at 504-505, but also "the need to protect officials who are required to exercise their discretion and the related public interest in encouraging the vigorous exercise of official authority." *Id.,* at 506. Without discounting the adverse consequences of denying high officials an absolute immunity from private lawsuits alleging constitutional violations—consequences found sufficient in *Spalding v. Vilas,* 161 U.S. 483 (1896), and *Barr v. Matteo,* 360 U.S. 564 [457 U.S. 800, 808] (1959), to warrant extension to such officials of absolute immunity from suits at common law—we emphasized our expectation that insubstantial suits need not proceed to trial:

"Insubstantial lawsuits can be quickly terminated by federal courts alert to the possibilities of artful pleading. Unless the complaint states a compensable claim for relief . . . , it should not survive a motion to dismiss. Moreover, the Court recognized in Scheuer that damages suits concerning constitutional violations need not proceed to trial, but can be terminated on a properly supported motion for summary judgment based on the defense of immunity. . . . In responding to such a motion, plaintiffs may not play dog in the manger; and firm application of the Federal Rules of Civil Procedure will ensure that federal officials are not harassed by frivolous lawsuits." 438 U.S., at 507 -508 (citations omitted).

Butz continued to acknowledge that the special functions of some officials might require absolute immunity. But the Court held that "federal officials who seek absolute exemption from personal liability for unconstitutional conduct must bear the burden of showing that public policy requires an exemption of that scope." *Id.*, at 506. This we reaffirmed today in *Nixon v. Fitzgerald, ante,* at 747.

III

A

Petitioners argue that they are entitled to a blanket protection of absolute immunity as an incident of their offices as Presidential aides. In deciding this claim we do not write on an empty page. In *Butz v. Economou, supra,* the Secretary of Agriculture—a Cabinet official directly accountable to the President—asserted a defense of absolute official immunity from suit for civil damages. We rejected his claim. In so doing we did not question the power or the importance of the Secretary's office. Nor did we doubt the importance to the [457 U.S. 800, 809] President of loyal and efficient subordinates in executing his duties of office. Yet we found these factors, alone, to be insufficient to justify absolute immunity. "[T]he greater power of [high] officials," we reasoned, "affords a greater potential for a regime of lawless conduct." 438 U.S., at 506. Damages actions against high officials were therefore "an important means of vindicating constitutional guarantees." *Ibid.* Moreover, we concluded that it would be "untenable to draw a distinction for purposes of immunity law between suits brought against state officials under [42 U.S.C.] § 1983 and suits brought directly under the Constitution against federal officials." *Id.*, at 504.

Having decided in *Butz* that Members of the Cabinet ordinarily enjoy only qualified immunity from suit, we conclude today that it would be equally untenable to hold absolute immunity an incident of the office of every Presidential subordinate based in the White House. Members of the Cabinet are direct subordinates of the President, frequently with greater responsibilities, both to the President and to the Nation, than White House staff. The considerations that supported our decision in *Butz* apply with equal force to this case. It is no disparagement of the offices held by petitioners to hold that Presidential aides, like Members of the Cabinet, generally are entitled only to a qualified immunity.

B

In disputing the controlling authority of *Butz*, petitioners rely on the principles developed in *Gravel v. United States*, 408 U.S. 606 (1972).[12] In *Gravel* we endorsed the view that "it is literally impossible . . . for Members of Congress to perform [457 U.S. 800, 810] their legislative tasks without the help of aides and assistants" and that "the day-to-day work of such aides is so critical to the Members' performance that they must be treated as the latter's alter egos . . . ." *Id.*, at 616-617. Having done so, we held the Speech and Debate Clause derivatively applicable to the "legislative acts" of a Senator's aide that would have been privileged if performed by the Senator himself. *Id.*, at 621-622.

Petitioners contend that the rationale of *Gravel* mandates a similar "derivative" immunity for the chief aides of the President of the United States. Emphasizing that the President must delegate a large measure of authority to execute the duties of his office, they argue that recognition of derivative absolute immunity is made essential by all the considerations that support absolute immunity for the President himself.

Petitioners' argument is not without force. Ultimately, however, it sweeps too far. If the President's aides are derivatively immune because they are essential to the functioning of the Presidency, so should the Members of the Cabinet—Presidential subordinates some of whose essential roles are acknowledged by the Constitution itself[13]—be absolutely immune. Yet we implicitly rejected such derivative immunity in *Butz*.[14] Moreover, in general our cases have followed a "functional" approach to immunity law. We have recognized [457 U.S. 800, 811] that the judicial, prosecutorial, and legislative functions require absolute immunity. But this protection has extended no further than its justification would warrant. In *Gravel*, for example, we emphasized that Senators and their aides were absolutely immune only when performing "acts legislative in nature," and not when taking other acts even "in their official capacity." 408 U.S., at 625. See *Hutchinson v. Proxmire*, 443 U.S. 111, 125-133 (1979). Our cases involving judges[15] and prosecutors[16] have followed a similar line. The undifferentiated extension of absolute "derivative" immunity to the President's aides therefore could not be reconciled with the "functional" approach that has characterized the immunity decisions of this Court, indeed including *Gravel* itself.[17]

C

Petitioners also assert an entitlement to immunity based on the "special functions" of White House aides. This form [457 U.S. 800, 812] of argument accords with the analytical approach of our cases. For aides entrusted with discretionary authority in such sensitive areas as national security or foreign policy, absolute immunity might well be justified to protect the unhesitating performance of functions vital to the national interest.[18] But a "special functions" rationale does not warrant a blanket recognition of absolute immunity for all Presidential aides in the performance of all their duties. This conclusion too follows from our decision in *Butz*, which establishes that an executive official's claim to absolute immunity must be justified by reference to the public interest in the special functions of his office, not the mere fact of high station.[19]

Butz also identifies the location of the burden of proof. The burden of justifying absolute immunity rests on the official asserting the claim. 438 U.S., at 506. We have not of course had occasion to identify how a Presidential aide might carry this burden. But the general requisites are familiar in our cases. In order to establish entitlement to absolute immunity [457 U.S. 800, 813] a Presidential aide first must show that the responsibilities of his office embraced a function so sensitive as to require a total shield from liability.[20] He then must demonstrate that he was discharging the protected function when performing the act for which liability is asserted.[21]

Applying these standards to the claims advanced by petitioners Harlow and Butterfield, we cannot conclude on the record before us that either has shown that "public policy requires [for any of the functions of his office] an exemption of [absolute] scope." *Butz*, 438 U.S., at 506. Nor, assuming that petitioners did have functions for which absolute immunity would be warranted, could we now conclude that the acts charged in this lawsuit—if taken at all—would lie within the protected area. We do not, however, foreclose the possibility that petitioners, on remand, could satisfy the standards properly applicable to their claims.

IV

Even if they cannot establish that their official functions require absolute immunity, petitioners assert that public policy at least mandates an application of the qualified immunity standard that would permit the defeat of insubstantial claims without resort to trial. We agree.

A

The resolution of immunity questions inherently requires a balance between the evils inevitable in any available alternative. [457 U.S. 800, 814] In situations of abuse of office, an action for damages may offer the only realistic avenue for vindication of constitutional guarantees. *Butz v. Economou, supra*, at 506; see *Bivens v. Six Unknown Fed. Narcotics Agents*, 403 U.S., at 410 ("For people in *Bivens'* shoes, it is damages or nothing"). It is this recognition that has required the denial of absolute immunity to most public officers. At the same time, however, it cannot be disputed seriously that claims frequently run against the innocent as well as the guilty—at a cost not only to the defendant officials, but to society as a whole.[22] These social costs include the expenses of litigation, the diversion of official energy from pressing public issues, and the deterrence of able citizens from acceptance of public office. Finally, there is the danger that fear of being sued will "dampen the ardor of all but the most resolute, or the most irresponsible [public officials], in the unflinching discharge of their duties." *Gregoire v. Biddle*, 177 F.2d 579, 581 (CA2 1949), cert. denied, 339 U.S. 949 (1950).

In identifying qualified immunity as the best attainable accommodation of competing values, in *Butz, supra,* at 507-508, as in *Scheuer,* 416 U.S., at 245-248, we relied on the assumption that this standard would permit "[i]nsubstantial lawsuits [to] be quickly terminated." 438 U.S., at 507-508; see *Hanrahan v. Hampton,* 446 U.S. 754, 765 (1980) (POWELL, J., concurring in part and dissenting in part).[23] Yet petitioners advance persuasive arguments that the dismissal of insubstantial lawsuits without trial—a factor presupposed in the balance of competing interests struck by [457 U.S. 800, 815] our prior cases—requires an adjustment of the "good faith" standard established by our decisions.

B

Qualified or "good faith" immunity is an affirmative defense that must be pleaded by a defendant official. *Gomez v. Toledo,* 446 U.S. 635 (1980).[24] Decisions of this Court have established that the "good faith" defense has both an "objective" and a "subjective" aspect. The objective element involves a presumptive knowledge of and respect for "basic, unquestioned constitutional rights." *Wood v. Strickland,* 420 U.S. 308, 322 (1975). The subjective component refers to "permissible intentions." *Ibid.* Characteristically the Court has defined these elements by identifying the circumstances in which qualified immunity would not be available. Referring both to the objective and subjective elements, we have held that qualified immunity would be defeated if an official *"knew or reasonably should have known* that the action he took within his sphere of official responsibility would violate the constitutional rights of the [plaintiff], or if he took the action *with the malicious intention* to cause a deprivation of constitutional rights or other injury . . . ." *Ibid.* (emphasis added).[25]

The subjective element of the good-faith defense frequently has proved incompatible with our admonition in *Butz* [457 U.S. 800, 816] that insubstantial claims should not proceed to trial. Rule 56 of the Federal Rules of Civil Procedure provides that disputed questions of fact ordinarily may not be decided on motions for summary judgment.[26] And an official's subjective good faith has been considered to be a question of fact that some courts have regarded as inherently requiring resolution by a jury.[27]

In the context of *Butz*' attempted balancing of competing values, it now is clear that substantial costs attend the litigation of the subjective good faith of government officials. Not only are there the general costs of subjecting officials to the risks of trial—distraction of officials from their governmental duties, inhibition of discretionary action, and deterrence of able people from public service. There are special costs to "subjective" inquiries of this kind. Immunity generally is available only to officials performing discretionary functions. In contrast with the thought processes accompanying "ministerial" tasks, the judgments surrounding discretionary action almost inevitably are influenced by the decision maker's experiences, values, and emotions. These variables explain in part why questions of subjective intent so rarely can be decided by summary judgment. Yet they also frame a background [457 U.S. 800, 817] in which there often is no clear end to the relevant evidence. Judicial inquiry into subjective motivation therefore may entail broad-ranging discovery and the deposing of numerous persons, including an official's professional colleagues.[28] Inquiries of this kind can be peculiarly disruptive of effective government.[29]

Consistently with the balance at which we aimed in *Butz*, we conclude today that bare allegations of malice should not suffice to subject government officials either to the costs of [457 U.S. 800, 818] trial or to the burdens of broad-reaching discovery. We therefore hold that government officials performing discretionary functions, generally are shielded from liability for civil damages insofar as their conduct does not violate clearly established statutory or constitutional rights of which a reasonable person would have known. See *Procunier v. Navarette*, 434 U.S. 555, 565 (1978); *Wood v. Strickland*, 420 U.S., at 322.[30]

Reliance on the objective reasonableness of an official's conduct, as measured by reference to clearly established law,[31] should avoid excessive disruption of government and permit the resolution of many insubstantial claims on summary judgment. On summary judgment, the judge appropriately may determine, not only the currently applicable law, but whether that law was clearly established at the time an action occurred.[32] If the law at that time was not clearly established, an official could not reasonably be expected to anticipate subsequent legal developments, nor could he fairly be said to "know" that the law forbade conduct not previously identified as unlawful. Until this threshold immunity question is resolved, discovery should not be allowed. If the law was clearly established, the immunity defense ordinarily [457 U.S. 800, 819] should fail, since a reasonably competent public official should know the law governing his conduct. Nevertheless, if the official pleading the defense claims extraordinary circumstances and can prove that he neither knew nor should have known of the relevant legal standard, the defense should be sustained. But again, the defense would turn primarily on objective factors.

By defining the limits of qualified immunity essentially in objective terms, we provide no license to lawless conduct. The public interest in deterrence of unlawful conduct and in compensation of victims remains protected by a test that focuses on the objective legal reasonableness of an official's acts. Where an official could be expected to know that certain conduct would violate statutory or constitutional rights, he should be made to hesitate; and a person who suffers injury caused by such conduct may have a cause of action.[33] But where an official's duties legitimately require action in which clearly established rights are not implicated, the public interest may be better served by action taken "with independence and without fear of consequences." *Pierson v. Ray*, 386 U.S. 547, 554 (1967).[34]

C

In this case petitioners have asked us to hold that the respondent's pretrial showings were insufficient to survive their motion for summary judgment.[35] We think it appropriate, [457 U.S. 800, 820] however, to remand the case to the District Court for its reconsideration of this issue in light of this opinion.[36] The trial court is more familiar with the record so far developed and also is better situated to make any such further findings as may be necessary.

V

The judgment of the Court of Appeals is vacated, and the case is remanded for further action consistent with this opinion.

So ordered.

Footnotes

[1] Harlow held this position from the beginning of the Nixon administration on January 20, 1969, through November 4, 1969. On the latter date he was designated as Counselor to the President, a position accorded Cabinet status. He served in that capacity until December 9, 1970, when he returned to private life. Harlow later resumed the duties of Counselor for [457 U.S. 800, 803] the period from July 1, 1973, through April 14, 1974. Respondent appears to allege that Harlow continued in a conspiracy against him throughout the various changes of official assignment.

[2] The record reveals that Secretary Seamans called Harlow in May 1969 to inquire about likely congressional reaction to a draft reorganization plan that would cause Fitzgerald's dismissal. According to Seamans' testimony, "[w]e [the Air Force] didn't ask [Harlow] to pass judgment on the action itself. We just asked him what the impact would be in the relationship with the Congress." App. 153a, 164a-165a (deposition of Robert Seamans). Through an aide Harlow responded that "this was a very sensitive item on the Hill and that it would be [his] recommendation that [the Air Force] not proceed to make such a change at that time." *Id.*, at 152a. But the Air Force persisted. Seamans spoke to Harlow on at least one subse-

quent occasion during the spring of 1969. The record also establishes that Secretary Seamans called Harlow on November 4, 1969, shortly after the public announcement of Fitzgerald's impending dismissal, and again in December 1969. See *id.*, at 186a.

[3] See *id.*, at 284a (transcript of a recorded conversation between Richard Nixon and Ronald Ziegler, February 26, 1973). In a conversation with the President on January 31, 1973, John Ehrlichman also recalled that Harlow had discussed the Fitzgerald case with the President. See *id.*, at 218a-221a (transcript of recorded conversation between Richard Nixon and John Ehrlichman, January 31, 1973). In the same conversation the President himself asserted that he had spoken to Harlow about the Fitzgerald matter, see *id.*, at 218a, but the parties continue to dispute whether Mr. Nixon—at the most relevant moments in the discussion—was confusing Fitzgerald's case with that of another dismissed employee. The President explicitly stated at one point that he previously had been confused. See *id.*, at 220a.

[4] See Defendants Memorandum of Points and Authorities in Support of Their Motion for Summary Judgment in Civ. No. 74-178 (DC), p. 7 (Feb. 12, 1980).

[5] In support of his version of events Harlow relies particularly on the deposition testimony of Air Force Secretary Seamans, who stated that he regarded abolition of Fitzgerald's position as necessary "to improve the efficiency" of the Financial Management Office of the Air Force and that he never received any White House instruction regarding the Fitzgerald case. App. 159a-160a. Harlow also disputes the probative value of Richard Nixon's recorded remark that Harlow had supported Fitzgerald's firing. Harlow emphasizes the tentativeness of the President's statement. To the President's query whether Harlow was "all for canning [Fitzgerald], wasn't he?", White House Press Secretary Ronald Ziegler in fact gave a negative reply: "No, I think Bryce may have been the other way." *Id.*, at 284a. The President did not respond to Ziegler's comment.

[6] The record establishes that Butterfield worked from an office immediately adjacent to the oval office. He had almost daily contact with the President until March 1973, when he left the White House to become Administrator of the Federal Aviation Administration.

[7] *Id.*, at 274a. Butterfield reported that this information had been referred to the Federal Bureau of Investigation. In the memorandum Butterfield reported that he had received the information "by word of several mouths, but allegedly from a senior AFL-CIO official originally . . . . Evidently, Fitzgerald attended a recent meeting of the National Democratic Coalition and, while there, revealed his intentions to a labor representative who, fortunately for us, was unsympathetic." *Ibid.*

[8] *Id.*, at 99a-100a, 180a-181a. This memorandum, quoted in *Nixon v. Fitzgerald, ante,* at 735-736, was not sent to the Defense Department.

[9] See Memorandum in Support of Summary Judgment, *supra,* at 26. The history of Fitzgerald's litigation is recounted in *Nixon v. Fitzgerald, ante,* p. 731. Butterfield was named as a defendant in the initial civil action filed by Fitzgerald in 1974. Harlow was named for the first time in respondent's second amended complaint of July 5, 1978.

[10] The first of these statutes, 5 U.S.C. § 7211 (1976 ed., Supp. IV), provides generally that "[t]he right of employees . . . to . . . furnish information [457 U.S. 800, 806] to either House of Congress, or to a committee or Member thereof, may not be interfered with or denied." The second, 18 U.S.C. § 1505, is a criminal statute making it a crime to obstruct congressional testimony. Neither expressly creates a private right to sue for damages. Petitioners argue that the District Court erred in finding that a private cause of action could be inferred under either statute, and that "special factors" present in the context of the federal employer-employee relationship preclude the recognition of respondent's *Bivens* action under the First Amendment. The legal sufficiency of respondent's asserted causes of action is not, how-

ever, a question that we view as properly presented for our decision in the present posture of this case. See n. 36, *infra.*

[11] As in *Nixon v. Fitzgerald, ante*, p. 731, our jurisdiction has been challenged on the basis that the District Court's order denying petitioners' claim of absolute immunity was not an appealable final order and that the Court of Appeals' dismissal of petitioners' appeal establishes that this case was never "in" the Court of Appeals within the meaning of 28 U.S.C. § 1254. As the discussion in Nixon establishes our jurisdiction in this case as well, we need not consider those challenges in this opinion.

[12] Petitioners also claim support from other cases that have followed Gravel in holding that congressional employees are derivatively entitled to the legislative immunity provided to United States Senators and Representatives under the Speech and Debate Clause. See *Eastland v. United States Servicemen's Fund*, 421 U.S. 491 (1975); *Doe v. McMillan*, 412 U.S. 306 (1973).

[13] See U.S. Const., Art. II, 2 ("The President . . . may require the Opinion, in writing, of the principal Officer in each of the executive Departments, upon any Subject relating to the Duties of their respective Offices . . .").

[14] THE CHIEF JUSTICE, *post*, at 828, argues that senior Presidential aides work "more intimately with the President on a daily basis than does a Cabinet officer," and that Butz therefore is not controlling. In recent years, however, such men as Henry Kissinger and James Schlesinger have served in both Presidential advisory and Cabinet positions. Kissinger held both posts simultaneously. In our view it is impossible to generalize about the role of "offices" in an individual President's administration without reference to the functions that particular officeholders are assigned by the President. *Butz v. Economou* cannot be distinguished on this basis.

[15] See, *e.g.*, *Supreme Court of Virginia v. Consumers Union of United States*, 446 U.S. 719, 731 -737 (1980); *Stump v. Sparkman*, 435 U.S. 349, 362 (1978).

[16] In *Imbler v. Pachtman*, 424 U.S. 409, 430 -431 (1976), this Court reserved the question whether absolute immunity would extend to "those aspects of the prosecutor's responsibility that cast him in the role of an administrator or investigative officer." Since that time the Courts of Appeals generally have ruled that prosecutors do not enjoy absolute immunity for acts taken in those capacities. See, e. g., *Mancini v. Lester*, 630 F.2d 990, 992 (CA3 1980); *Forsyth v. Kleindienst*, 599 F.2d 1203, 1213-1214 (CA3 1979). This Court at least implicitly has drawn the same distinction in extending absolute immunity to executive officials when they are engaged in quasi-prosecutorial functions. See *Butz v. Economou*, 438 U.S., at 515 -517.

[17] Our decision today in *Nixon v. Fitzgerald, ante*, p. 731, in no way abrogates this general rule. As we explained in that opinion, the recognition of absolute immunity for all of a President's acts in office derives in principal part from factors unique to his constitutional responsibilities and station. Suits against other officials—including Presidential aides—generally do not invoke separation-of-powers considerations to the same extent as suits against the President himself.

[18] Cf. *United States v. Nixon*, 418 U.S. 683, 710-711 (1974) ("[C]ourts have traditionally shown the utmost deference to Presidential responsibilities" for foreign policy and military affairs, and claims of privilege in this area would receive a higher degree of deference than invocations of "a President's generalized interest in confidentiality"); *Katz v. United States*, 389 U.S. 347, 364 (1967) (WHITE, J., concurring) ("We should not require the warrant procedure and the magistrate's judgment if the President of the United States *or his chief legal officer, the Attorney General*, has considered the requirements of national security and authorized electronic surveillance as reasonable") (emphasis added).

[19] *Gravel v. United States*, 408 U.S. 606 (1972), points to a similar conclusion. We fairly may assume that some aides are assigned to act as Presidential "alter egos," *id.*, at 616-617, in the exercise of functions for which absolute immunity is "essential for the conduct of the public business," *Butz, supra*, at 507. Cf. *Gravel, supra*,

at 620 (derivative immunity extends only to acts within the "central role" of the Speech and Debate Clause in permitting free legislative speech and debate). By analogy to Gravel, a derivative claim to Presidential immunity would be strongest in such "central" Presidential domains as foreign policy and national security, in which the President could not discharge his singularly vital mandate without delegating functions nearly as sensitive as his own.

[20] Here as elsewhere the relevant judicial inquiries would encompass considerations of public policy, the importance of which should be confirmed either by reference to the common law or, more likely, our constitutional heritage and structure. See *Nixon v. Fitzgerald, ante,* at 747-748.

[21] The need for such an inquiry is implicit in *Butz v. Economou, supra,* at 508-517; see *Imbler v. Pachtman, supra,* at 430-431. Cases involving immunity under the Speech and Debate Clause have inquired explicitly into whether particular acts and activities qualified for the protection of the Clause. See, *e.g., Hutchinson v. Proxmire,* 443 U.S. 111 (1979); *Doe v. McMillan,* 412 U.S. 306 (1973); *Gravel v. United States, supra.*

[22] See generally Schuck, Suing Our Servants: The Court, Congress, and the Liability of Public Officials for Damages, 1980 S. Ct. Rev. 281, 324-327.

[23] The importance of this consideration hardly needs emphasis. This Court has noted the risk imposed upon political officials who must defend their actions and motives before a jury. See *Lake Country Estates, Inc. v. Tahoe Regional Planning Agency,* 440 U.S. 391, 405 (1979); *Tenney v. Brandhove,* 341 U.S. 367, 377 -378 (1951). As the Court observed in *Tenney:* "In times of political passion, dishonest or vindictive motives are readily attributed . . . and as readily believed." *Id.,* at 378.

[24] Although Gomez presented the question in the context of an action under 42 U.S.C. § 1983, the Court's analysis indicates that "immunity" must also be pleaded as a defense in actions under the Constitution and laws of the United States. See 446 U.S., at 640. *Gomez* did not decide which party bore the burden of proof on the issue of good faith. *Id.,* at 642 (REHNQUIST, J., concurring).

[25] In *Wood* the Court explicitly limited its holding to the circumstances in which a school board member, "in the specific context of school discipline," 420 U.S., at 322, would be stripped of claimed immunity in an action under § 1983. Subsequent cases, however, have quoted the *Wood* formulation as a general statement of the qualified immunity standard. See, *e.g., Procunier v. Navarette,* 434 U.S. 555, 562-563, 566 (1978), quoted in *Baker v. McCollan,* 443 U.S. 137, 139 (1979).

[26] Rule 56(c) states that summary judgment "shall be rendered forthwith if the pleadings, depositions, answers to interrogatories, and admissions on file, together with the affidavits, if any, show that there is no genuine issue as to any material fact and that the moving party is entitled to a judgment as a matter of law." In determining whether summary judgment is proper, a court ordinarily must look at the record in the light most favorable to the party opposing the motion, drawing all inferences most favorable to that party. *E.g., Poller v. Columbia Broadcasting System, Inc.,* 368 U.S. 464, 473 (1962).

[27] *E.g., Landrum v. Moats,* 576 F.2d 1320, 1329 (CA8 1978); *Duchesne v. Sugarman,* 566 F.2d 817, 832-833 (CA2 1977); cf. *Hutchinson v. Proxmire,* 443 U.S., at 120, n. 9 (questioning whether the existence of "actual malice," as an issue of fact, may properly be decided on summary judgment in a suit alleging libel of a public figure).

[28] In suits against a President's closest aides, discovery of this kind frequently could implicate separation-of-powers concerns. As the Court recognized in *United States v. Nixon,* 418 U.S., at 708:

> "A President and those who assist him must be free to explore alternatives in the process of shaping policies and making decisions and to do so in a way many would be unwilling to express except privately. These

are the considerations justifying a presumptive privilege for Presidential communications. The privilege is fundamental to the operation of Government and inextricably rooted in the separation of powers under the Constitution."

[29] As Judge Gesell observed in his concurring opinion in *Halperin v. Kissinger*, 196 U.S. App. D.C. 285, 307, 606 F.2d 1192, 1214 (1979), aff'd in pertinent part by an equally divided Court, 452 U.S. 713 (1981):

"We should not close our eyes to the fact that with increasing frequency in this jurisdiction and throughout the country plaintiffs are filing suits seeking damage awards against high government officials in their personal capacities based on alleged constitutional torts. Each such suit almost invariably results in these officials and their colleagues being subjected to extensive discovery into traditionally protected areas, such as their deliberations preparatory to the formulation of government policy and their intimate thought processes and communications at the presidential and cabinet levels. Such discover [sic] is wide-ranging, time-consuming, and not without considerable cost to the officials involved. It is not difficult for ingenious plaintiff's counsel to create a material issue of fact on some element of the immunity defense where subtle questions of constitutional law and a decisionmaker's mental processes are involved. A sentence from a casual document or a difference in recollection with regard to a particular policy conversation held long ago would usually, under the normal summary judgment standards, be sufficient [to force a trial]. . . . The effect of this development upon the willingness of individuals to serve their country is obvious."

[30] This case involves no issue concerning the elements of the immunity available to state officials sued for constitutional violations under 42 U.S.C. § 1983. We have found previously, however, that it would be "untenable to draw a distinction for purposes of immunity law between suits brought against state officials under § 1983 and suits brought directly under the Constitution against federal officials." *Butz v. Economou*, 438 U.S., at 504.
Our decision in no way diminishes the absolute immunity currently available to officials whose functions have been held to require a protection of this scope.

[31] This case involves no claim that Congress has expressed its intent to impose "no fault" tort liability on high federal officials for violations of particular statutes or the Constitution.

[32] As in *Procunier v. Navarette*, 434 U.S., at 565, we need not define here the circumstances under which "the state of the law" should be "evaluated by reference to the opinions of this Court, of the Courts of Appeals, or of the local District Court."

[33] Cf. *Procunier v. Navarette, supra*, at 565, quoting *Wood v. Strickland*, 420 U.S., at 322 ("Because they could not reasonably have been expected to be aware of a constitutional right that had not yet been declared, petitioners did not act with such disregard for the established law that their conduct 'cannot reasonably be characterized as being in good faith'").

[34] We emphasize that our decision applies only to suits for civil damages arising from actions within the scope of an official's duties and in "objective" good faith. We express no view as to the conditions in which injunctive or declaratory relief might be available.

[35] In *Butz*, we admonished that "insubstantial" suits against high public officials should not be allowed to proceed to trial. 438 U.S., at 507. See *Schuck, supra* n. 22, at 324-327. We reiterate this admonition. Insubstantial [457 U.S. 800, 820] lawsuits undermine the effectiveness of government as contemplated by our consti-

tutional structure, and "firm application of the Federal Rules of Civil Procedure" is fully warranted in such cases. 438 U.S., at 508.

[36] Petitioners also have urged us, prior to the remand, to rule on the legal sufficiency of respondent's "implied" causes of action under 5 U.S.C. § 7211 (1976 ed., Supp. IV) and 18 U.S.C. § 1505 and his *Bivens* claim under the First Amendment. We do not view petitioners' argument on the statutory question as insubstantial. Cf. *Merrill Lynch, Pierce, Fenner & Smith, Inc. v. Curran,* 456 U.S. 353, 377-378 (1982) (controlling question in implication of statutory causes of action is whether Congress affirmatively intended to create a damages remedy); *Middlesex County Sewerage Auth. v. National Sea Clammers Assn.,* 453 U.S. 1 (1981) (same); *Texas Industries, Inc. v. Radcliff Materials, Inc.,* 451 U.S. 630, 638 -639 (1981) (same). Nor is the *Bivens* question. Cf. *Bush v. Lucas,* 647 F.2d 573, 576 (CA5 1981) (holding that the "unique relationship between the Federal Government and its civil service employees is a special consideration which counsels hesitation in inferring a Bivens remedy"). As in *Nixon v. Fitzgerald, ante,* p. 731, however, we took jurisdiction of the case only to resolve the immunity question under the collateral order doctrine. We therefore think it appropriate to leave these questions for fuller consideration by the District Court and, if necessary, by the Court of Appeals.

Briscoe v. LaHue
460 U.S. 325 (1983)

Argued November 9, 1982
Decided March 7, 1983
JUSTICE STEVENS delivered the opinion of the Court.

This case presents a question of statutory construction: whether 42
U.S.C. § 1983 (1976 ed., Supp. V) authorizes a convicted person to
assert a claim for damages against a police officer for giving perjured
testimony at his criminal trial. The Court of Appeals for the Seventh
Circuit held that witnesses are absolutely immune from damages liability based on their testimony, and rejected the petitioners' contention
that government officials who testify about the performance of their
official duties may be held liable under § 1983 even if other witnesses
may not. We agree with that conclusion.

The Court of Appeals heard argument in three separate cases raising the absolute immunity issue and decided them in a single opinion.
Two of these cases are before us on a writ of certiorari. Petitioner
Briscoe was convicted in state court of burglarizing a house trailer. He
then filed a § 1983 complaint against respondent LaHue, a member of
the Bloomington, Indiana, police force, alleging that LaHue had violated
his constitutional right to due process by committing perjury in the
criminal proceedings leading to his conviction.[1] [460 U.S. 325, 327]
LaHue had testified that in his opinion Briscoe was one of no more than
50 to 100 people in Bloomington whose prints would match a partial
thumbprint on a piece of glass found at the scene of the crime. According to Briscoe, the testimony was false because the Federal Bureau of
Investigation and the state police considered the partial print too
incomplete to be of value, and without the print there was no evidence

identifying him as the burglar. He sought $100,000 in damages. The District Court granted LaHue's motion for summary judgment on four separate grounds: (1) the facts alleged in the complaint did not suggest that LaHue had testified falsely; (2) allegations of perjury alone are insufficient to state a constitutional claim; (3) LaHue had not testified "under color of law"; and (4) Briscoe's claim was collaterally estopped by his criminal conviction.

Petitioners Vickers and Ballard were jointly tried and convicted of sexual assault in state court. They subsequently brought a civil action under § 1983 against respondent Hunley, a member of the Cedar Lake, Indiana, police force, alleging that he had deprived them of their constitutional rights to due process and a fair trial. They alleged that, by giving false testimony suggesting that they had been able to harmonize their stories before making exculpatory statements to police, he had prejudicially diminished the credibility of those statements. Each plaintiff sought $150,000 in compensatory and $50,000 in punitive damages. The Federal Magistrate granted a motion to dismiss the complaint on alternative grounds: (1) Hunley had not testified "under color of law"; (2) he was entitled to absolute witness immunity; and (3) petitioners had failed to state a claim under § 1983 because they did not allege that the prosecutor had knowingly used false testimony. The District Court affirmed the dismissal on the first ground. Both cases were appealed to the United States Court of Appeals for the Seventh Circuit.[2] [460 U.S. 325, 328]

Although other issues were argued in the Court of Appeals, its holding in both cases was predicated squarely on the ground that, in litigation brought under 42 U.S.C. § 1983 (1976 ed., Supp. V), all witnesses—police officers as well as lay witnesses—are absolutely immune from civil liability based on their testimony in judicial proceedings. 663 F.2d 713 (1981).[3] Because of the importance of the immunity question, which has given rise to divergent conclusions in the Courts of Appeals,[4] we granted certiorari. 455 U.S. 1016 (1982).[5] [460 U.S. 325, 329]

Before confronting the precise question that this case presents— whether § 1983 creates a damages remedy against police officers for their testimony as witnesses—we begin by considering the potential liability of lay witnesses on the one hand, and of judges and prosecutors who perform integral functions in judicial proceedings on the other hand. The unavailability of a damages remedy against both of these categories sheds considerable light on petitioners' claim that Congress intended police officer witnesses to be treated differently.

I

There are two reasons why § 1983 does not allow recovery of damages against a private party for testimony in a judicial proceeding. First,

§ 1983 does not create a remedy for all conduct that may result in violation of "rights, privileges, or immunities secured by the Constitution and laws." Its reach is limited to actions taken "under color of any statute, ordinance, regulation, custom, or usage, of any State or Territory . . . ."[6] It is beyond question that, when a private [460 U.S. 325, 330] party gives testimony in open court in a criminal trial, that act is not performed "under color of law."[7]

Second, since 1951, when this Court decided *Tenney v. Brandhove*, 341 U.S. 367, it has been settled that the all-encompassing language of § 1983, referring to "[e]very person" who, under color of law, deprives another of federal constitutional or statutory rights, is not to be taken literally.[8]

> "It is by now well settled that the tort liability created by § 1983 cannot be understood in a historical vacuum. . . . One important assumption underlying the Court's decisions in this area is that members of the 42d Congress were familiar with common-law principles, including defenses previously recognized in ordinary tort litigation, and that they likely intended these common-law principles to obtain, absent specific provisions to the contrary." *City of Newport v. Fact Concerts*, Inc., 453 U.S. 247, 258 (1981).

See *Pierson v. Ray*, 386 U.S. 547, 554 (1967).

The immunity of parties and witnesses from subsequent damages liability for their testimony in judicial proceedings[9] [460 U.S. 325, 331] was well established in English common law. *Cutler v. Dixon*, 4 Co. Rep. 14b, 76 Eng. Rep. 886 (Q. B. 1585); *Anfield v. Feverhill*, 2 Bulst. 269, 80 Eng. Rep. 1113 (K. B. 1614); *Henderson v. Broomhead*, 4 H. & N. 569, 578, 157 Eng. Rep. 964, 968 (Ex. 1859);[10] see *Dawkins v. Lord Rokeby*, 4 F. & F. 806, 833-834, 176 Eng. Rep. 800, 812 (C. P. 1866). Some American decisions required a showing that the witness' allegedly defamatory statements were relevant to the judicial proceeding, but once this threshold showing had been made, the witness had an absolute privilege.[11] The [460 U.S. 325, 332] plaintiff could not recover even if the witness knew the statements were false and made them with malice.[12]

In the words of one 19th-century court, in damages suits against witnesses, "the claims of the individual must yield to [460 U.S. 325, 333] the dictates of public policy, which requires that the paths which lead to the ascertainment of truth should be left as free and unobstructed as possible." *Calkins v. Sumner*, 13 Wis. 193, 197 (1860). A witness' apprehension of subsequent damages liability might induce two forms of self-censorship. First, witnesses might be reluctant to come forward to testify. See *Henderson v. Broomhead, supra*, at 578-579, 157 Eng. Rep., at 968. And once a witness is on the stand, his testimony might be distorted by the fear of subsequent liability. See *Barnes v. McCrate*, 32 Me. 442, 446-447 (1851). Even within the constraints of the witness' oath there may be various ways to give an account or to state an opinion. These alternatives may be more or less detailed and may differ in emphasis and certainty. A witness who knows that he might be forced to defend a subsequent lawsuit, and perhaps to pay damages, might be inclined to shade his testimony in favor of the potential plaintiff, to magnify uncertainties, and thus to deprive the finder of fact of candid, objective, and undistorted evidence. See Veeder, Absolute Immunity in Defamation: Judicial Proceedings, 9 Colum. L. Rev. 463, 470 (1909).[13] But the truth finding process is better [460 U.S. 325, 334] served if the witness' testimony is submitted to "the crucible of the judicial process so that the fact finder may consider it, after cross-examination, together with the other evidence in the case to determine where the truth lies." *Imbler v. Pachtman*, 424 U.S. 409, 440 (1976) (WHITE, J., concurring in judgment).[14]

At least with respect to private witnesses, it is clear that § 1983 did not abrogate the absolute immunity existing at common law, and petitioners do not contend otherwise. Like the immunity for legislators at issue in *Tenney v. Brandhove*, the common law's protection for witnesses is "a tradition so well grounded in history and reason" that we cannot believe that Congress impinged on it "by covert inclusion in the general language before us." 341 U.S., at 376.

II

The Court has already addressed the question whether § 1983 permits damages recoveries from judges, prosecutors, and other persons acting "under color of law" who perform official functions in the judicial process. Again, we have found that, in light of common-law immunity principles, § 1983 did not impose liability on these officials. We have held that state judges are absolutely immune from liability for their judicial acts, *Pierson v. Ray*, 386 U.S. 547 (1967); *Stump v. Sparkman*, 435 U.S. 349 (1978), and that state prosecutors have absolute immunity from liability for their actions in initiating prosecutions, *Imbler v. Pachtman, supra.*

The central focus of our analysis has been the nature of the judicial proceeding itself. Thus, in his opinion concurring in the judgment in *Imbler v. Pachtman, supra*, JUSTICE WHITE explained that the absolute immunity of public prosecutors was "based on the policy of protecting the judicial process." [460 U.S. 325, 335] 424 U.S., at 439. He explained that this protection extended equally to other participants, including counsel and witnesses.

> "The reasons for this rule are also substantial. It is precisely the function of a judicial proceeding to determine where the truth lies. The ability of courts, under carefully developed procedures, to separate truth from falsity, and the importance of accurately resolving factual disputes in criminal (and civil) cases are such that those involved in judicial proceedings should be 'given every encouragement to make a full disclosure of all pertinent information within their knowledge.'" *Ibid.*

The common law's protection for judges and prosecutors formed part of a "cluster of immunities protecting the various participants in judge-supervised trials," which stemmed "from the characteristics of the judicial process." *Butz v. Economou*, 438 U.S. 478, 512 (1978); cf. *King v. Skinner, Lofft* 54, 56, 98 Eng. Rep. 529 (K. B. 1772) ("[N]either party, witness, counsel, jury, or judge can be put to answer, civilly or criminally, for words spoken in office"). The common law recognized that

> "controversies sufficiently intense to erupt in litigation are not easily capped by a judicial decree. The loser in one forum will frequently seek another . . . . Absolute immunity is thus necessary to assure that judges, advocates, and witnesses can perform their respective functions without harassment or intimidation." *Butz, supra,* at 512.

In short, the common law provided absolute immunity from subsequent damages liability for all persons—governmental or otherwise—who were integral parts of the judicial process. It is equally clear that § 1983 does not authorize a damages claim against private witnesses on the one hand, or against judges or prosecutors in the performance of their respective duties on the other. When a police officer appears as a witness, he may reasonably be viewed as acting like any [460 U.S. 325, 336] other witness sworn to tell the truth—in which event he can make a strong claim to witness immunity;[15] alternatively, he may be regarded as an official performing a critical role in the judicial process, in which event he may seek the benefit afforded to other governmental participants in the same proceeding. Nothing in the language of the statute suggests that such a witness belongs in a narrow, special category lacking protection against damages suits. We must ask, however, whether anything in the legislative history of § 1983 points to a different conclusion.

III

Petitioners point to a number of references throughout the debates on the 1871 Act to widespread perjury by Ku Klux Klan witnesses in state criminal trials.[16] They urge that, because perjury was one of the specific evils with which Congress was concerned, recognizing an absolute immunity for witnesses would conflict with congressional intent. We find this argument unpersuasive. The Act consisted of several sections establishing different remedies for disorder and violence in the Southern States.[17] The legislative history and statutory language indicate that Congress intended perjury [460 U.S. 325, 337] leading to unjust acquittals of Klan conspirators to be prohibited by § 2, the civil and criminal conspiracy section of the statute, now codified in relevant part at 42 U.S.C. § 1985(3) (1976 ed., Supp. V) and 18 U.S.C. § 241. But the language of § 1—now codified as § 1983—differs from that of § 2 in essential respects, and we find no evidence that Congress intended to abrogate the traditional common-law witness immunity in § 1983 actions.

The Ku Klux Act, 17 Stat. 13, was enacted on April 20, 1871, less than a month after President Grant sent a dramatic message to Congress describing the breakdown of law and order in the Southern States. Cong. Globe, 42d Cong., 1st Sess., 236, 244 (1871). During the debates, supporters of the bill repeatedly described the reign of terror imposed by the Klan upon black citizens and their white sympathizers in the Southern States. Hours of oratory were devoted to the details of Klan outrages—arson, robbery, whippings, shootings, murders, and other forms of violence and intimidation—often committed in disguise and under cover of night. These acts of lawlessness went unpunished, legislators asserted, because Klan members and sympathizers controlled or influenced the administration of state criminal justice. In particular, it was alleged that Klan members were obligated, by virtue of membership in the organization, to protect fellow members who were charged with criminal activity. They had a duty to offer themselves for service on grand and petit juries, and to violate their jurors' oaths by refusing to indict or to convict regardless of the strength of the evidence. They also were bound to appear as witnesses, and again to violate their oaths by committing perjury, if necessary, to exculpate their Klan colleagues.[18] Perjury was thus one of the [460 U.S. 325, 338] means by which the Klan prevented state courts from gaining convictions of Klan members for crimes against blacks and Republicans.

It is clear from the legislative debates that, in the view of the Act's sponsors, the victims of Klan outrages were deprived of "equal protection of the laws" if the perpetrators systematically went unpunished.[19] Proponents of the measure repeatedly argued that, given the ineffectiveness of state law enforcement and the individual's federal right to "equal protection of the laws," an independent federal remedy was necessary and Congress had the power to provide it.[20] See *Monroe v. Pape*, 365 U.S. 167, 174 (1961).

Section 2 was designed specifically to provide criminal and civil remedies in federal court for the conspiratorial activities of the Klan. Indeed the provision singles out those who "go in disguise upon the public highway." Earlier versions of the section enumerated precisely the activities that had been attributed to the Klan—murder, manslaughter, mayhem, robbery, assault and battery, perjury, subornation of perjury, criminal obstruction of legal process or resistance of officers [460 U.S. 325, 339] in discharge of official duty, arson, or larceny. Cong. Globe, *supra*, at 317. The more general language in the final version of § 2 was also intended to apply to the abuses that had been described repeatedly in congressional debate.[21] Part of the provision is particularly well tailored to reach conspiracies to commit perjury in order to prevent punishment of fellow Klansmen. It provides penalties whenever two or more persons shall "conspire together . . . for the purpose of preventing or hindering the constituted authorities of any State from giving or securing to all persons within such State the equal protection of the laws, or shall conspire together for the purpose of in any manner impeding, hindering, obstructing, or defeating the due course of justice in any State or Territory, with intent to deny to any citizen of the United States the due and equal protection of the laws . . . ."[22]

This evidence does not, however, tend to show that Congress intended to abrogate witness immunity in civil actions under § 1, which applied to wrongs committed "under color of . . . law." The bill's proponents were exclusively concerned with perjury resulting in unjust acquittals—perjury likely to be committed by private parties acting in furtherance of a conspiracy—and not with perjury committed "under color of [460 U.S. 325, 340] law" that might lead to unjust convictions. In hundreds of pages of debate there is no reference to the type of alleged constitutional deprivation at issue in this case: perjury by a government official leading to an unjust conviction. Indeed, the legislative history is virtually silent even with regard to perjury by private persons leading to convictions of innocent defendants.[23] There is a simple enough reason for this lacuna: the Klan had other, more direct, means of dealing with its victims. A "reign of terrorism and bloodshed" did not require the formal processes of law; at most, drumhead tribunals were convened at dead of night.[24] Even when the organization's intended victims had been taken into custody and charged with crimes, the evidence before Congress suggested that the Klan resorted to vigilante justice rather than courtroom perjury.[25]

In summary, the legislative history supports criminal punishment under § 2 for a witness who conspired to give perjured testimony favorable to a defendant, with the effect of preventing effective enforcement of the laws, and liability in a civil suit against the perjured witness by the defendant's victim. But these are not the issues before us today. We are asked to extrapolate from pro-defendant perjury to pro-prosecution perjury, and if willing to make that step, we are further invited to apply legislative history relating to § 2—a section specifically directed toward private conspiracies—to § 1—a section designed to provide remedies for abuses under [460 U.S. 325, 341] color of law. We decline the invitation. The debates of the 42d Congress do not support petitioners' contention that Congress intended to provide a § 1 damages remedy against police officers or any other witnesses.[26]

IV

Petitioners, finally, urge that we should carve out an exception to the general rule of immunity in cases of alleged perjury by police officer witnesses.[27] They assert that the reasons supporting common-law immunity—the need to [460 U.S. 325, 342] avoid intimidation and self-censorship—apply with diminished force to police officers. Policemen often have a duty to testify about the products of their investigations, and they have a professional interest in obtaining convictions, which would assertedly counterbalance any tendency to shade testimony in favor of potentially vindictive defendants. In addition, they are subject to § 1983 lawsuits for the performance of their other duties, as to which they have only qualified immunity, and their defense is generally undertaken by their governmental employers. Further, petitioners urge that perjured testimony by police officers is likely to be more damaging to constitutional rights than such testimony by ordinary citizens, because the policeman in uniform carries special credibility in the eyes of jurors. And, in the case of police officers, who cooperate regularly with prosecutors in the enforcement of criminal law, prosecution for perjury is alleged to be so unlikely that it is not an effective substitute for civil damages.

These contentions have some force. But our cases clearly indicate that immunity analysis rests on functional categories, not on the status of the defendant.[28] A police officer on the witness stand performs the same functions as any other witness; he is subject to compulsory process, takes an oath, responds to questions on direct examination and cross-examination, and may be prosecuted subsequently for perjury.

Moreover, to the extent that traditional reasons for witness immunity are less applicable to governmental witnesses, [460 U.S. 325, 343] other considerations of public policy support absolute immunity more emphatically for such persons than for ordinary witnesses. Subjecting government officials, such as police officers, to damages liability under § 1983 for their testimony might undermine not only their contribution to the judicial process but also the effective performance of their other public duties.

Section 1983 lawsuits against police officer witnesses, like lawsuits against prosecutors, "could be expected with some frequency." Cf. *Imbler v. Pachtman*, 424 U.S., at 425. Police officers testify in scores of cases every year, and defendants often will transform resentment at being convicted into allegations of perjury by the State's official witnesses. As the files in this case show, even the processing of a complaint that is dismissed before trial consumes a considerable amount of time and resources.[29]

This category of § 1983 litigation might well impose significant burdens on the judicial system and on law enforcement resources. As this Court noted when it recognized absolute immunity for prosecutors in Imbler, if the defendant official "could be made to answer in court each time [a disgruntled defendant] charged him with wrongdoing, his energy and attention [460 U.S. 325, 344] would be diverted from the pressing duty of enforcing the criminal law." 424 U.S., at 425. To some degree the individual's burden might be alleviated by the government's provision of counsel, but a case that goes to trial always imposes significant emotional and other costs on every party litigant.

It is not sufficient to assert that the burdens on defendants and the courts could be alleviated by limiting the cause of action to those former criminal defendants who have already vindicated themselves in another forum, either on appeal or by collateral attack. We rejected a similar contention in Imbler. Petitioner contended that "his suit should be allowed, even if others would not be, because the District Court's issuance of the writ of habeas corpus shows that his suit has substance." *Id.*, at 428, n. 27. We declined to carve out such an exception to prosecutorial immunity, noting that petitioner's success in a collateral proceeding did not necessarily establish the merits of his civil rights action. Moreover, we noted that "using the habeas proceeding as a 'door-opener' for a subsequent civil rights action would create the risk of injecting extraneous concerns into that proceeding." *Ibid.* We emphasized that, in determining whether to grant postconviction relief, the tribunal should focus solely on whether there was a fair trial under law. "This focus should not be blurred by even the subconscious knowledge that a post-trial decision in favor of the accused might result in the prosecutor's being called upon to respond in damages for his error or mistaken judgment." *Id.*, at 427. The same danger exists in the case of potential liability for police officer witnesses.[30] [460 U.S. 325, 345]

There is, of course, the possibility that, despite the truth finding safeguards of the judicial process, some defendants might indeed be unjustly convicted on the basis of knowingly false testimony by police officers.[31] The absolute immunity for prosecutors recognized in Imbler bars one possible avenue of redress for such defendants. Similarly, in this case, the absolute witness immunity bars another possible path to recovery for these defendants. But we have recognized, again and again, that in some situations, the alternative of limiting the official's immunity would disserve the broader public interest. As Judge Learned Hand wrote years ago:

> "As is so often the case, the answer must be found in a balance between the evils inevitable in either alternative. In this instance it has been thought in the end better to leave unredressed the wrongs done by dishonest officers than to subject those who try to do their duty to the constant dread of retaliation." *Gregoire v. Biddle*, 177 F.2d 579, 581 (CA2 1949), cert. denied, 339 U.S. 949 (1950).[32]

In short, the rationale of our prior absolute immunity cases governs the disposition of this case. In 1871, common-law immunity for witnesses was well settled. The principles set forth in *Pierson v. Ray* to protect judges and in *Imbler v. Pachtman* to protect prosecutors also apply to witnesses, who perform a somewhat different function in the trial process but whose participation in bringing the litigation to a [460 U.S. 325, 346] just—or possibly unjust—conclusion is equally indispensable.

The decision of the Court of Appeals is affirmed.

It is so ordered.

Footnotes

[1] The Court has held that the prosecutor's knowing use of perjured testimony violates due process, but has not held that the false testimony of a police officer in itself violates constitutional rights. See *United States v. Agurs*, 427 U.S. 97, 103, and nn. 8, 9 (1976) (citing cases).

[2] At the time of the Court of Appeals' decision, petitioner Briscoe's conviction had been set aside by the Indiana Court of Appeals on the ground that the evidence was insufficient to prove Briscoe's guilt beyond a reasonable [460 U.S. 325, 328] doubt. The opinion did not question the veracity of LaHue's testimony, but found that the State's evidence, including testimony that Briscoe was one of 50 to 100 persons who might have robbed the trailer, did not meet the State's burden of proof. *Briscoe v. State*, 180 Ind. App. 450, 460, 388 N. E. 2d 638, 644 (1979). Petitioners Vickers and Ballard were still serving their sentences when the Court of Appeals affirmed the dismissal of their complaint.

[3] On review of pretrial orders dismissing petitioners' complaints, the Court of Appeals assumed that the complaints' factual allegations of perjury were true. It also assumed that petitioners had alleged a constitutional violation—that they had been deprived of their liberty without due process of law by respondents' perjury in the judicial proceedings that resulted in their convictions. Because we granted certiorari to review the Court of Appeals' holding, we make the same assumptions for purposes of deciding this case, without implying that they are valid. In light of its resolution of the immunity question the Court of Appeals did not determine whether the respondents had acted "under color of law," though it suggested that it might have answered in the affirmative. 663 F.2d, at 721, n. 4.

[4] A rule of absolute witness immunity has been adopted by the majority of Courts of Appeals. *Brawer v. Horowitz*, 535 F.2d 830, 836-837 (CA3 1976) (lay witness in federal court; *Bivens* action); *Burke v. Miller*, 580 F.2d 108 (CA4 1978) (state medical examiner; § 1983 action), cert. denied, 440 U.S. 930 (1979); *Charles v. Wade*, 665 F.2d 661 (CA5 1982) (police officer victim; § 1983 suit), cert. pending, No. 81-1881; *Myers v. Bull*, 599 F.2d 863, 866 (CA8) (police officer witness; § 1983 suit), cert. denied, 444 U.S. 901 (1979); *Blevins v. Ford*, 572 F.2d 1336 (CA9 1978) (private witnesses and former Assistant U.S. Attorney; action under § 1983 and the Fifth Amendment). But see *Briggs v. Goodwin*, 186 U.S. App. D.C. 179, 569 F.2d 10 (1977) (dicta rejecting absolute immunity for government [460 U.S. 325, 329] official witness; *Bivens* action), cert. denied, 437 U.S. 904 (1978); *Hilliard v. Williams*, 516 F.2d 1344, 1350 (CA6 1975) (rejecting absolute immunity for agent of state bureau of investigation; § 1983 action), cert. denied sub nom. *Clark v. Hilliard*, 423 U.S. 1066 (1976).

[5] The petition for writ of certiorari presents the following question: "Whether a police officer who commits perjury during a state court criminal trial should be granted absolute immunity from civil liability under 42 U.S.C. § 1983." Pet. for Cert. i. The petition does not raise the question of immunity for testimony at pretrial proceedings such as probable-cause hearings, nor does petitioners' brief discuss whether the same immunity considerations that apply to trial testimony also apply to testimony at probable-cause hearings. We therefore do not decide whether respondent LaHue is entitled to absolute immunity for allegedly false testimony at two probable-cause hearings regarding petitioner Briscoe.

[6] Thus, even though the defective performance of defense counsel may cause the trial process to deprive an accused person of his liberty in an unconstitutional manner, *Cuyler v. Sullivan*, 446 U.S. 335, 342-345 (1980), the lawyer who may be responsible for the unconstitutional state action [460 U.S. 325, 330] does not himself act under color of state law within the meaning of § 1983. *Polk County v. Dodson*, 454 U.S. 312 (1981). This conclusion is compelled by the character of the

office performed by defense counsel. See *id.*, at 317-319; *Ferri v. Ackerman*, 444 U.S. 193, 204 (1979). It is equally clear that the office of the lay witness who merely discharges his duty to testify truthfully is not performed under color of law within the meaning of § 1983.

[7] It is conceivable, however, that nongovernmental witnesses could act "under color of law" by conspiring with the prosecutor or other state officials. See *Dennis v. Sparks*, 449 U.S. 24, 27 -29 (1980); *Adickes v. S. H. Kress & Co.*, 398 U.S. 144, 152 (1970). It is therefore necessary to go beyond the "color of law" analysis to consider whether private witnesses may ever be held liable for damages under § 1983.

[8] Nor is this the only piece of 19th-century legislation in which the word "every" may not be given a literal reading. See *National Society of Professional Engineers v. United States*, 435 U.S. 679, 687-688 (1978).

[9] The availability of a common-law action for false accusations of crime, see *post*, at 350-351, is inapposite because petitioners present only the [460 U.S. 325, 331] question of § 1983 liability for false testimony during a state-court criminal trial. See n. 5, *supra*.

[10] "We have therefore a large collection of cases where from time to time parties have attempted to get damages in cases like the present, but in no one instance has the action ever been held to be maintainable. If for centuries many persons have attempted to get a remedy for injuries like the present, and there is an entire absence of authority that such remedy exists, it shews the unanimous opinion of those who have held the place which we do now, that such an action is not maintainable." *Henderson v. Broomhead*, 4 H. & N., at 578, 157 Eng. Rep., at 968.

[11] See generally M. Newell, Law of Defamation, Libel and Slander 425, 450-459 (1890); J. Townshend, A Treatise on the Wrongs Called Slander and Libel 353-354 (2d ed. 1872). See, *e.g.*, *Lawson v. Hicks*, 38 Ala. 279, 285-288 (1862); *Myers v. Hodges*, 53 Fla. 197, 208-210, 44 So. 357, 361 (1907); *Smith v. Howard*, 28 Iowa 51, 56-57 (1869); *Gardemal v. McWilliams*, 43 La. Ann. 454, 457-458, 9 So. 106, 108 (1891); *Burke v. Ryan*, 36 La. Ann. 951, 951-952 (1884); *McLaughlin v. Cowley*, 127 Mass. 316, 319-320 (1879); *Barnes v. McCrate*, 32 Me. 442, 446-447 (1851); *Cooper v. Phipps*, 24 Ore. 357, 363-364, 33 P. 985, 986-987 (1893); *Shadden v. McElwee*, 86 Tenn. 146, 149-154, 5 S. W. 602, 603-605 (1887); *Cooley v. Galyon*, 109 Tenn. 1, 13-14, 70 S. W. 607, 610 (1902); cf. *Hoar v. Wood*, 44 Mass. 193, 197-198 (1841) (statements by counsel); *Marsh v. Ellsworth*, 50 N. Y. 309, 312-313 (1872) (same). Other courts appear to have taken a position closer to the English rule, which did not require any showing of pertinency or materiality. See, *e.g.*, *Chambliss v. Blau*, 127 Ala. 86, 89-90, 28 So. 602, 603 (1899); cf. *Calkins v. Sumner*, 13 Wis. 193, 197-198 (1860) (in absence of objection and ruling by court, lack of pertinency of responses to questions does not remove immunity, because witnesses are not in a position to know what statements are pertinent to the case).

Although some cases used the words "good faith," see, *e.g.*, *White v. Carroll*, 42 N. Y. 161, 166 (1870); *Shadden v. McElwee, supra*, at 149-150, [460 U.S. 325, 332] 5 S. W., at 603, good faith was established as a matter of law if the statements were pertinent and material to the judicial proceeding and given in response to questions. Indeed, even if the testimony was not pertinent, the plaintiff had the burden of proving bad faith. The testimony by respondents in this case would have received absolute protection at common law, because it was directly relevant to the criminal charges against petitioners. If the testimony had not been relevant, it is unlikely that petitioners would have stated a claim that their constitutional rights had been violated. Therefore, for purposes of § 1983 analysis, there is no material difference between the English rule and the American rule.

[12] JUSTICE MARSHALL's dissent relies heavily on an opinion rendered by this Court, *White v. Nicholls*, 3 How. 266, 286-288 (1845). The Court's discussion of privileged statements in judicial proceedings was purely dictum. The plaintiff sought dam-

ages for defendants' allegedly defamatory assertions in a petition to the President of the United States requesting the plaintiff's removal from office as a customs collector, a statement entitled at most to a qualified privilege. *White v. Nicholls* cannot be considered authoritative. In 1909 a leading commentator stated:

> "[T]he demands of public policy on which the rule [of absolute immunity] is based are so controlling that there is only one considered case in the English or American reports in which the existence of the general doctrine of absolute immunity under the common law has ever been questioned. Strangely enough this isolated instance was a decision of the Supreme Court of the United States, in the course of which Mr. Justice Daniel, speaking for the court, denied both the rule and its policy; but this expression of opinion was obiter, since the case in issue was one of qualified immunity." Veeder, Absolute Immunity in Defamation: Judicial Proceedings, 9 Colum. L. Rev. 463, 465-466 (footnotes omitted).

In 1860, a New York court asserted that "the reasoning of Judge Daniel's opinion, and the propositions which he deduces where he goes beyond the case in hand, are clearly unsustained by principle or authority." *Perkins v. Mitchell*, 31 Barb. 461, 468 (N. Y. Sup. Ct.). In 1878, the West Virginia Supreme Court severely criticized *White v. Nicholls*, stating: "We have reviewed all the authorities, cited by Justice Daniel, and have seen, that none of them are in conflict with the position, that express malice may be shielded by its being expressed in judicial proceedings in certain forms. . . . And the review of the American authorities will show, that the overwhelming weight of authority is opposed to Justice Daniel's idea, that [460 U.S. 325, 333] there is no case, in which an action of slander or libel will not lie for libelous matter, spoken or written in the course of regular judicial proceedings. . . . The authorities, both English and American, fully establish the position, that there is a class of absolutely privileged communications . . . ." *Johnson v. Brown*, 13 W. Va. 71, 128-129. See also *McGehee v. Insurance Co. of North America*, 112 F. 853 (CA5 1902) (declining to follow *White v. Nicholls*); *Shelfer v. Gooding*, 47 N.C. 175, 181-182 (1855) (suggesting that Justice Daniel miscited *Hodgson v. Scarlett*, 1 Barn. & Ald. 232, 106 Eng. Rep. 86 (K. B. 1818)). In short, *White v. Nicholls* was not even a reliable statement of the common law; still less was it "the most salient feature in the landscape of the common law at the time Congress acted" in 1871.

[13] In addition, some courts expressed concern that, in the absence of a privilege, honest witnesses might erroneously be subjected to liability because they would have difficulty proving the truth of their statements. This result seemed inappropriate in light of the witness' duty to testify. *E.g., Calkins v. Sumner*, 13 Wis., at 198; *Barnes v. McCrate*, 32 Me., at 446-447; *Chambliss v. Blau*, 127 Ala., at 89, 28 So., at 603.

[14] Cf. *Marsh v. Ellsworth*, 50 N. Y., at 312 (importance of placing all relevant evidence before court and jury "to enable them to arrive at the truth"); *Hoar v. Wood*, 44 Mass., at 197 (stressing impartiality of judge as sufficient antidote to inaccuracies and exaggerations by adversaries).

[15] The common-law immunity that protected witnesses as well as other participants in the judicial process drew no distinction between public officials and private citizens. See Veeder, *supra* n. 12, at 468-469. The general purposes underlying witness immunity at common law applied equally to official and private witnesses. Both types of witness took the stand and testified under oath in response to the questions of counsel. Both might be deterred by the prospect of subsequent, vexatious litigation.

[16] Brief for Petitioners 19-20, citing 1 B. Schwartz, Statutory History of the United States: Civil Rights 599-606, 625 (1970).

[17] In addition to § 1, codified as § 1983, and § 2, discussed in text *infra*, the Act permitted the President to use armed force in response to insurrection and

domestic violence (3), authorized the suspension of habeas corpus if the President deemed it necessary (4), required grand and petit jurors to take a test oath (5), and provided a civil penalty against persons who knew of and failed to prevent § 2 violations. 17 Stat. 13.

[18] Supporters of the bill repeatedly quoted the testimony before an investigating committee of two former Klan members, who described a Klan oath binding its members to commit perjury. Cong. Globe, 42d Cong., 1st Sess., 152, 158, 173, 201, 320-321, 322, 340, 437, 439, 443-444, 457, 458, 503, 516, 518, 653, 654, 687 (1871).

[19] See *id.*, at 322 (remarks of Rep. Stoughton); 334 (remarks of Rep. Hoar); 375 (remarks of Rep. Lowe); 428 (remarks of Rep. Beatty); 458, 459 (remarks of Rep. Coburn); 481-482 (remarks of Rep. Wilson); 486 (remarks of Rep. Cook); 501 (remarks of Sen. Frelinghuysen); 506 (remarks of Sen. Pratt); 608 (remarks of Sen. Pool); 697 (remarks of Sen. Edmunds).

[20] As Representative Coburn stated:

> "The United States courts are further above mere local influence than the county courts; their judges can act with more independence, cannot be put under terror, as local judges can; their sympathies are not so nearly identified with those of the vicinage; the jurors are taken from the State, and not the neighborhood; they will be able to rise above prejudices and bad passions or terror more easily. The marshal, clothed with more power than the sheriff, can make arrests with certainty, and, with the aid of the General Government, can seize offenders in spite of any banded and combined resistance such as may be expected." *Id.*, at 460.

See *id.*, at 334 (remarks of Rep. Hoar); 374 (remarks of Rep. Lowe); 428 (remarks of Rep. Beatty); 459-460 (remarks of Rep. Coburn); 486 (remarks of Rep. Cook); 501 (remarks of Sen. Frelinghuysen); 514 (remarks of Rep. Poland).

[21] Compare *id.*, at 317 (original version introduced by Rep. Shellabarger) with *id.*, at 477-478 (more general language in amended version); see *id.*, at 567, 702 (Senate amendment adding language punishing conspiracy for obstructing the due course of justice).

[22] It is noteworthy that the imposition of criminal liability on persons for conspiracy to give false evidence was not in derogation of the common law as it existed in 1871. Witnesses were traditionally subject to a prosecution for perjury committed in the course of their evidence, "or for conspiracy in case of a combination of two or more to give false evidence." *Newell, supra* n. 11, at 450, 44. The offense of perjury had been shaped in English law during the 16th and 17th centuries by Parliament, the Court of Star Chamber, and common-law judges. 4 W. Holdsworth, A History of English Law 515-519 (1924); S. Milsom, Historical Foundations of the Common Law 418 (2d ed. 1981).

[23] In several hundred pages of small triple-columned print, only one Senator—not a member of the Committee that reported the bill—referred to the possibility that perjury was being used to convict the innocent. See Cong. Globe, 42d Cong., 1st Sess., 653 (1871) (remarks of Sen. Osborn). His comments were made in connection with a proposal to retain a test oath for grand and petit jurors.

[24] The debates describe nocturnal Klan meetings passing decrees condemning political enemies. See *id.*, at 157, 209, 320, 321, 504.

[25] For references to lynch mobs attacking suspects held in custody, see *id.*, at 156, 157, 166, 200, 321, 444, 446, 447.

[26] The legislative history of the Civil Rights Act of 1866, discussed at length by JUSTICE MARSHALL's dissent, simply does not speak to the question whether Congress intended witnesses—private parties or public officials—to be civilly liable for false testimony resulting in an unjust criminal conviction. It makes clear that judges and other "state officials integral to the judicial process" are subject to

criminal liability for violating the constitutional rights of individuals. But we have never questioned that proposition, and we do not do so now.

Moreover, witnesses enjoyed no common-law immunity from criminal prosecution for perjury. See n. 22, *supra.* Therefore the criminal provisions of the 1866 Act and its successors apply to official witnesses. See n. 32, *infra.* But the 1866 legislative history, to the extent that it sheds any light on the meaning of the 1871 Act, does not support civil liability for such witnesses, because it does not show the requisite congressional intent to override the clearly established common-law immunity of witnesses from civil liability. With respect to witnesses, the legislative history of the 1866 Act is simply silent, and we are unwilling to assume that, whenever legislators referred to "state judicial officials" or to "the judicial power of the State," they were describing witnesses as well as judges, sheriffs, and marshals.

Moreover, our decisions recognizing absolute immunity for judges and prosecutors from civil liability under the 1871 Act implicitly reject the position that the legislative history of the 1866 Act defines the scope of immunity for purposes of the 1871 Act. See *Pierson v. Ray,* 386 U.S. 547 (1967); *Imbler v. Pachtman,* 424 U.S. 409 (1976).

[27] The contours of the proposed exception are not clear. Similar considerations would presumably apply to other government officials and experts, including coroners, medical examiners, psychiatric experts, and social workers.

[28] See *Butz v. Economou,* 438 U.S. 478, 513 -514 (1978) (administrative law judges enjoy absolute judicial immunity even though they are in the Executive Branch); *Imbler v. Pachtman, supra,* at 430-431 (reserving the question whether a prosecutor, who is absolutely immune for decisions to initiate a prosecution or put witnesses on the stand, has similar immunity for administrative or investigative tasks); cf. *Hampton v. City of Chicago,* 484 F.2d 602, 608 (CA7 1973) (prosecutor's immunity ceases when he acts in a capacity other than his quasi-judicial role), cert. denied, 415 U.S. 917 (1974).

[29] Moreover, lawsuits alleging perjury on the stand in violation of the defendant's due process rights often raise material questions of fact, inappropriate for disposition at the summary judgment stage. The plaintiff's complaint puts in issue the falsity and materiality of the allegedly perjured statements, and the defendant witness' knowledge and state of mind at the time he testified. Sometimes collateral-estoppel principles will permit dismissal at the pretrial stage. But if the truth of the allegedly perjured statement was not necessarily decided in the previous criminal verdict, if there is newly discovered evidence of falsity, or if the defendant concedes that the testimony was inaccurate, the central issue will be the defendant's state of mind. Summary judgment is usually not feasible under these circumstances. C. Wright, Law of Federal Courts 493 (3d ed. 1976). If summary judgment is denied, the case must proceed to trial and must traverse much of the same ground as the original criminal trial.

[30] We are not writing on a clean slate, and it is not for us to craft a new rule designed to enable trial judges to dismiss meritless claims before trial but to allow recovery in cases of demonstrated injustice, when an innocent plaintiff has already obtained postconviction relief. The States remain free to grant relief in such cases and, of course, Congress has the power to fashion an appropriate remedy if it perceives the need for one.

[31] There is no reason to believe, however, that this risk is any greater than, or indeed as great as, the risk of an unjust conviction resulting from a misidentification or other unintentional mistake. There is no federal damages remedy for such innocent persons, or for those who are acquitted after undergoing the burdens of a criminal trial.

[32] Finally, in those cases in which the judicial process fails, the public is not powerless to punish misconduct. Like prosecutors and judges, official witnesses may be punished criminally for willful deprivations of constitutional rights under 18 U.S.C. § 242.

Malley v. Briggs
475 U.S. 335 (1986)

Argued November 13, 1985
Decided March 5, 1986
JUSTICE WHITE delivered the opinion of the Court.

This case presents the question of the degree of immunity accorded a defendant police officer in a damages action under 42 U.S.C. § 1983 when it is alleged that the officer caused the plaintiffs to be unconstitutionally arrested by presenting a judge with a complaint and a supporting affidavit which failed to establish probable cause.

I

In December 1980, the Rhode Island State Police were conducting a court-authorized wiretap on the telephone of one Paul Driscoll, an acquaintance of respondents' daughter. On December 20, the police intercepted a call to Driscoll from an unknown individual who identified himself as "Dr. Shogun." The police log sheet summarizes the call as follows: "General conversation re. a party they went to last night . . . caller says I can't believe I was token [sic] in front of Jimmy Briggs—caller states he passed it to Louisa . . . Paul says Nancy was sitting in his lap rolling her thing." App. 78.

Petitioner Edward Malley (hereafter petitioner) was the Rhode Island state trooper in charge of the investigation of Driscoll. After reviewing the log sheet for December 20, petitioner decided that the call from "Dr. Shogun" was incriminating, because in drug parlance "toking" means smoking marihuana and "rolling her thing" refers to rolling a marihuana [475 U.S. 335, 338] cigarette. Petitioner also concluded that another call monitored the same day showed that the party

373

discussed by Driscoll and "Dr. Shogun" took place at respondents' house. On the basis of these two calls, petitioner drew up felony complaints charging that respondents and Paul Driscoll "did unlawfully conspire to violate the uniform controlled substance act of the State of Rhode Island by having [marihuana] in their possession . . . ." *Id.*, at 74. These complaints were presented to a State District Court Judge in February 1981, after the wiretap of Driscoll's phone had been terminated. Accompanying the complaints were unsigned warrants for each respondent's arrest, and supporting affidavits describing the two intercepted calls and petitioner's interpretation of them. The judge signed warrants for the arrest of respondents and 20 other individuals charged by petitioner as a result of information gathered through the wiretap.

Respondents were arrested at their home shortly before six o'clock on the morning of March 19, 1981. They were taken to a police station, booked, held for several hours, arraigned, and released. Local and statewide newspapers published the fact that respondents, who are prominent members of their community, had been arrested and charged with drug possession. The charges against respondents were subsequently dropped when the grand jury to which the case was presented did not return an indictment.

Respondents brought an action under 42 U.S.C. § 1983 in the United States District Court for the District of Rhode Island charging, inter alia, that petitioner, in applying for warrants for their arrest, violated their rights under the Fourth and Fourteenth Amendments. The case was tried to a jury, and at the close of respondents' evidence, petitioner moved for and was granted a directed verdict.[1] The District [475 U.S. 335, 339] Court's primary justification for directing a verdict was that the act of the judge in issuing the arrest warrants for respondents broke the causal chain between petitioner's filing of a complaint and respondents' arrest. The court also stated that an officer who believes that the facts stated in his affidavit are true and who submits them to a neutral magistrate may thereby be entitled to immunity under the "objective reasonableness" standard of *Harlow v. Fitzgerald*, 457 U.S. 800 (1982).

The United States Court of Appeals for the First Circuit reversed, holding that an officer who seeks an arrest warrant by submitting a complaint and supporting affidavit to a judge is not entitled to immunity unless the officer has an objectively reasonable basis for believing that the facts alleged in his affidavit are sufficient to establish probable cause. 748 F.2d 715 (1984). We granted certiorari in order to review the First Circuit's application of the "objective reasonableness" standard in this context. 471 U.S. 1124 (1985). We affirm.

II

Petitioner urges reversal on two grounds: first, that in this context, he is absolutely immune from liability for damages; second, that he is at least entitled to qualified immunity in this case. We reject both propositions and address first the absolute immunity issue.

A

Our general approach to questions of immunity under § 1983 is by now well established. Although the statute on its face admits of no immunities, we have read it "in harmony with general principles of tort immunities and defenses rather than in derogation of them." *Imbler v. Pachtman*, 424 U.S. 409, 418 (1976). Our initial inquiry is whether an official claiming immunity under § 1983 can point to a [475 U.S. 335, 340] common-law counterpart to the privilege he asserts. *Tower v. Glover*, 467 U.S. 914 (1984). If "an official was accorded immunity from tort actions at common law when the Civil Rights Act was enacted in 1871, the Court next considers whether § 1983's history or purposes nonetheless counsel against recognizing the same immunity in § 1983 actions." *Id.*, at 920. Thus, while we look to the common law for guidance, we do not assume that Congress intended to incorporate every common-law immunity into § 1983 in unaltered form.

Our cases also make plain that "[f]or executive officers in general, . . . qualified immunity represents the norm." *Harlow, supra*, at 807.[2] Like federal officers, state officers who "seek absolute exemption from personal liability for unconstitutional conduct must bear the burden of showing that public policy requires an exemption of that scope." *Butz v. Economou*, 438 U.S. 478, 506 (1978).

B

Although we have previously held that police officers sued under § 1983 for false arrest are qualifiedly immune, *Pierson v. Ray*, 386 U.S. 547, 557 (1967), petitioner urges that he should be absolutely immune because his function in seeking an arrest warrant was similar to that of a complaining witness. The difficulty with this submission is that complaining witnesses were not absolutely immune at common law. In 1871, the generally accepted rule was that one who procured the issuance of an arrest warrant by submitting a complaint could be held liable if the complaint was made maliciously and [475 U.S. 335, 341] without probable cause.[3] Given malice and the lack of probable cause, the complainant enjoyed no immunity. The common law thus affords no support for petitioner.

Nor are we moved by petitioner's argument that policy considerations require absolute immunity for the officer applying for a warrant. As the qualified immunity defense has evolved, it provides ample protection to all but the plainly incompetent or those who knowingly violate the law. At common law, in cases where probable cause to arrest was lacking, a complaining witness' immunity turned on the issue of malice, which was a jury question.[4] Under the *Harlow* standard, on the other hand, an allegation of malice is not sufficient to defeat immunity if the defendant acted in an objectively reasonable manner. The *Harlow* standard is specifically designed to "avoid excessive disruption of government and permit the resolution of many insubstantial claims on summary judgment," and we believe it sufficiently serves this goal. Defendants will not be immune if, on an objective basis, it is obvious that no reasonably competent officer would have concluded that a warrant should issue; but if officers of reasonable competence could disagree on this issue, immunity should be recognized.

C

As an alternative ground for claiming absolute immunity, petitioner draws an analogy between an officer requesting a warrant and a prosecutor who asks a grand jury to indict a suspect. Like the prosecutor, petitioner argues, the officer must exercise a discretionary judgment based on the evidence [475 U.S. 335, 342] before him, and like the prosecutor, the officer may not exercise his best judgment if the threat of retaliatory lawsuits hangs over him. Thus, petitioner urges us to read § 1983 as giving the officer the same absolute immunity enjoyed by the prosecutor. Cf. *Imbler v. Pachtman*, 424 U.S. 409 (1976).

We reemphasize that our role is to interpret the intent of Congress in enacting § 1983, not to make a freewheeling policy choice, and that we are guided in interpreting Congress' intent by the common-law tradition. In *Imbler, supra*, we concluded that at common law "[t]he general rule was, and is, that a prosecutor is absolutely immune from suit for malicious prosecution." *Id.*, at 437. We do not find a comparable tradition of absolute immunity for one whose complaint causes a warrant to issue. See n. 3, *supra*. While this observation may seem unresponsive to petitioner's policy argument, it is, we believe, an important guide to interpreting § 1983. Since the statute on its face does not provide for any immunities, we would be going far to read into it an absolute immunity for conduct which was only accorded qualified immunity in 1871.

Even were we to overlook the fact that petitioner is inviting us to expand what was a qualified immunity at common law into an absolute immunity, we would find his analogy between himself and a prosecutor untenable. We have interpreted § 1983 to give absolute immunity to functions "intimately associated with the *judicial* phase of the criminal process," *Imbler, supra*, at 430 (emphasis added), not from an exaggerated esteem for those who perform these functions, and certainly not from a desire to shield abuses of office, but because any lesser degree of immunity could impair the judicial process itself. *Briscoe v. LaHue*, 460 U.S. 325, 334-335 (1983). We intend no disrespect to the officer applying for a warrant by observing that his action, while a vital part of the administration of criminal justice, is further removed from the judicial phase of criminal proceedings than [475 U.S. 335, 343] the act of a prosecutor in seeking an indictment. Furthermore, petitioner's analogy, while it has some force, does not take account of the fact that the prosecutor's act in seeking an indictment is but the first step in the process of seeking a conviction. Exposing the prosecutor to liability for the initial phase of his prosecutorial work could interfere with his exercise of independent judgment at every phase of his work, since the prosecutor might come to see later decisions in terms of their effect on his potential liability. Thus, we shield the prosecutor seeking an indictment because any lesser immunity could impair the performance of a central actor in the judicial process.[5]

In the case of the officer applying for a warrant, it is our judgment that the judicial process will on the whole benefit from a rule of qualified rather than absolute immunity. We do not believe that the Harlow standard, which gives ample room for mistaken judgments, will frequently deter an officer from submitting an affidavit when probable cause to make an arrest is present. True, an officer who knows that objectively unreasonable decisions will be actionable may be motivated to reflect, before submitting a request for a warrant, upon whether he has a reasonable basis for believing that his affidavit establishes probable cause. But such reflection is desirable, because it reduces the likelihood that the officer's request for a warrant will be premature. Premature requests for warrants are at best a waste of judicial resources; at worst, they lead to premature arrests, which may injure the [475 U.S. 335, 344] innocent or, by giving the basis for a suppression motion, benefit the guilty.

Furthermore, it would be incongruous to test police behavior by the "objective reasonableness" standard in a suppression hearing, see *United States v. Leon*, 468 U.S. 897 (1984), while exempting police conduct in applying for an arrest or search warrant from any scrutiny whatsoever in a § 1983 damages action.[6] While we believe the exclusionary rule serves a necessary purpose, it obviously does so at a considerable cost to society as a whole, because it excludes evidence probative of guilt. On the other hand, a damages remedy for an arrest following an objectively unreasonable request for a warrant imposes a cost directly on the officer responsible for the unreasonable request, without the side effect of hampering a criminal prosecution. Also, in the case of the § 1983 action, the likelihood is obviously greater than at the suppression hearing that the remedy is benefiting the victim of police misconduct one would think most deserving of a remedy—the person who in fact has done no wrong, and has been arrested for no reason, or a bad reason. See *Owen v. City of Independence*, 445 U.S. 622, 653 (1980).

Accordingly, we hold that the same standard of objective reasonableness that we applied in the context of a suppression hearing in

Leon, supra, defines the qualified immunity accorded an officer whose request for a warrant allegedly caused an unconstitutional arrest.[7] Only where the warrant [475 U.S. 335, 345] application is so lacking in indicia of probable cause as to render official belief in its existence unreasonable, *Leon, supra,* at 923, will the shield of immunity be lost.

III

We also reject petitioner's argument that if an officer is entitled to only qualified immunity in cases like this, he is nevertheless shielded from damages liability because the act of applying for a warrant is *per se* objectively reasonable, provided that the officer believes that the facts alleged in his affidavit are true. Petitioner insists that he is entitled to rely on the judgment of a judicial officer in finding that probable cause exists and hence issuing the warrant. This view of objective reasonableness is at odds with our development of that concept in Harlow and Leon. In Leon, we stated that "our good-faith inquiry is confined to the objectively ascertainable question whether a reasonably well-trained officer would have known that the search was illegal despite the magistrate's authorization." 468 U.S., at 922, n. 23. The analogous question in this case is whether a reasonably well-trained officer in petitioner's position would have known that his affidavit failed to establish probable cause and that he should not have applied for the warrant.[8] If such was the case, the officer's application for a warrant was not objectively reasonable, because it created the unnecessary danger of an unlawful arrest. It is true that in an ideal system an unreasonable request for a warrant would be harmless, because no judge would approve it. But ours is not an ideal system, and it is possible that a magistrate, working under [475 U.S. 335, 346] docket pressures, will fail to perform as a magistrate should. We find it reasonable to require the officer applying for the warrant to minimize this danger by exercising reasonable professional judgment.[9]

The judgment of the Court of Appeals is affirmed, and the case is remanded for further proceedings consistent with this opinion.

It is so ordered.

Footnotes

[1] Respondents' complaint also named the State of Rhode Island as a defendant. At the close of respondents' evidence, Rhode Island moved for and was granted a directed verdict on Eleventh Amendment grounds. [475 U.S. 335, 339] Respondents have not contested the propriety of the directed verdict for the State.

[2] *Harlow* was a suit against federal, not state, officials, but as we stated in deciding the case, it is "'untenable to draw a distinction for purposes of immunity law between suits brought against state officials under § 1983 and suits brought directly under the Constitution against federal officials.'" 457 U.S., at 818, n. 30 (quoting *Butz v. Economou,* 438 U.S. 478, 504 (1978)).

[3] See, *e.g.*, *Dinsman v. Wilkes*, 12 How. 390, 402 (1852); *Randall v. Henry*, 5 Stew. & P. 367, 378 (Ala. 1834); *Bell v. Keepers*, 37 Kan. 64, 14 P. 542 (1887); *Finn v. Frink*, 84 Me. 261, 24 A. 851 (1892); 4 W. Wait, Actions and Defenses 352-356 (1878). The same rule applied in the case of search warrants. See, *e.g.*, *Barker v. Stetson*, 73 Mass. 53, 54 (1856); *Carey v. Sheets*, 67 Ind. 375, 378-379 (1879).

[4] See 4 *Wait, supra*, at 345 ("Whether malice is proved or not is a question of fact for the jury").

[5] The organized bar's development and enforcement of professional standards for prosecutors also lessen the danger that absolute immunity will become a shield for prosecutorial misconduct. As we observed in Imbler, "a prosecutor stands perhaps unique, among officials whose acts could deprive persons of constitutional rights, in his amenability to professional discipline by an association of his peers." 424 U.S., at 429 (footnote omitted). The absence of a comparably well-developed and pervasive mechanism for controlling police misconduct weighs against allowing absolute immunity for the officer.

[6] Although the case before us only concerns a damages action for an officer's part in obtaining an allegedly unconstitutional arrest warrant, the distinction between a search warrant and an arrest warrant would not make a difference in the degree of immunity accorded the officer who applied for the warrant.

[7] Petitioner has not pressed the argument that in a case like this the officer should not be liable because the judge's decision to issue the warrant breaks the causal chain between the application for the warrant and the improvident arrest. It should be clear, however, that the District Court's "no causation" rationale in this case is inconsistent with our interpretation of [475 U.S. 335, 345] 1983. As we stated in *Monroe v. Pape*, 365 U.S. 167, 187 (1961), § 1983 "should be read against the background of tort liability that makes a man responsible for the natural consequences of his actions." Since the common law recognized the causal link between the submission of a complaint and an ensuing arrest, we read § 1983 as recognizing the same causal link.

[8] The question is not presented to us, nor do we decide, whether petitioner's conduct in this case was in fact objectively reasonable. That issue must be resolved on remand.

[9] Notwithstanding petitioner's protestations, the rule we adopt in no way "requires the police officer to assume a role even more skilled ... than the magistrate." Brief for Petitioners 33. It is a sound presumption that "the magistrate is more qualified than the police officer to make a probable cause determination," *ibid.*, and it goes without saying that where a magistrate acts mistakenly in issuing a warrant but within the range of professional competence of a magistrate, the officer who requested the warrant cannot be held liable. But it is different if no officer of reasonable competence would have requested the warrant, *i.e.*, his request is outside the range of the professional competence expected of an officer. If the magistrate issues the warrant in such a case, his action is not just a reasonable mistake, but an unacceptable error indicating gross incompetence or neglect of duty. The officer then cannot excuse his own default by pointing to the greater incompetence of the magistrate.

Anderson v. Creighton
483 U.S. 635 (1987)

Argued February 23, 1987
Decided June 25, 1987
JUSTICE SCALIA delivered the opinion of the Court.

The question presented is whether a federal law enforcement officer who participates in a search that violates the Fourth Amendment may be held personally liable for money [483 U.S. 635, 637] damages if a reasonable officer could have believed that the search comported with the Fourth Amendment.

I

Petitioner Russell Anderson is an agent of the Federal Bureau of Investigation. On November 11, 1983, Anderson and other state and federal law enforcement officers conducted a warrantless search of the home of respondents, the Creighton family. The search was conducted because Anderson believed that Vadaain Dixon, a man suspected of a bank robbery committed earlier that day, might be found there. He was not.

    The Creightons later filed suit against Anderson in a Minnesota state court, asserting among other things a claim for money damages under the Fourth Amendment, see *Bivens v. Six Unknown Fed. Narcotics Agents*, 403 U.S. 388 (1971).[1] After removing the suit to Federal District Court, Anderson filed a motion to dismiss or for summary judgment, arguing that the Bivens claim was barred by Anderson's qualified immunity from civil damages liability. See *Harlow v. Fitzgerald*, 457 U.S. 800 (1982). Before any discovery took place, the District Court granted summary judgment on the ground that the search was lawful, holding that the undisputed facts revealed that Anderson had had probable cause to search the Creighton's home and that his failure to obtain a warrant was justified by the presence of exigent circumstances. App. to Pet. for Cert. 23a-25a.

The Creightons appealed to the Court of Appeals for the Eighth Circuit, which reversed. *Creighton v. St. Paul*, 766 F.2d 1269 (1985). The Court of Appeals held that the issue of the lawfulness of the search could not properly be decided on summary judgment, because unresolved factual disputes [483 U.S. 635, 638] made it impossible to determine as a matter of law that the warrantless search had been supported by probable cause and exigent circumstances. *Id.*, at 1272-1276. The Court of Appeals also held that Anderson was not entitled to summary judgment on qualified immunity grounds, since the right Anderson was alleged to have violated—the right of persons to be protected from warrantless searches of their home unless the searching officers have probable cause and there are exigent circumstances—was clearly established. *Ibid.*

Anderson filed a petition for certiorari, arguing that the Court of Appeals erred by refusing to consider his argument that he was entitled to summary judgment on qualified immunity grounds if he could establish as a matter of law that a reasonable officer could have believed the search to be lawful. We granted the petition, 478 U.S. 1003 (1986), to consider that important question.

II

When government officials abuse their offices, "action[s] for damages may offer the only realistic avenue for vindication of constitutional guarantees." *Harlow v. Fitzgerald*, 457 U.S., at 814. On the other hand, permitting damages suits against government officials can entail substantial social costs, including the risk that fear of personal monetary liability and harassing litigation will unduly inhibit officials in the discharge of their duties. *Ibid.* Our cases have accommodated these conflicting concerns by generally providing government officials performing discretionary functions with a qualified immunity, shielding them from civil damages liability as long as their actions could reasonably have been thought consistent with the rights they are alleged to have violated. See, *e.g., Malley v. Briggs*, 475 U.S. 335, 341 (1986) (qualified immunity protects "all but the plainly incompetent or those who knowingly violate the law"); *id.*, at 344-345 (police officers applying for warrants are immune if a [483 U.S. 635, 639] reasonable officer could have believed that there was probable cause to support the application); *Mitchell v. Forsyth*, 472 U.S. 511, 528 (1985) (officials are immune unless "the law clearly proscribed the actions" they took); *Davis v. Scherer*, 468 U.S. 183, 191 (1984); *id.*, at 198 (BRENNAN, J., concurring in part and dissenting in part); *Harlow v. Fitzgerald, supra*, at 819. Cf., *e.g.*, *Procunier v. Navarette*, 434 U.S. 555, 562 (1978). Somewhat more concretely, whether an official protected by qualified immunity may be held personally liable for an allegedly unlawful official action generally turns on the "objective legal reasonableness" of the action, *Harlow*, 457 U.S., at 819, assessed in light of the legal rules that were "clearly established" at the time it was taken, *id.*, at 818.

The operation of this standard, however, depends substantially upon the level of generality at which the relevant "legal rule" is to be identified. For example, the right to due process of law is quite clearly established by the Due Process Clause, and thus there is a sense in which any action that violates that Clause (no matter how unclear it may be that the particular action is a violation) violates a clearly established right. Much the same could be said of any other constitutional or statutory violation. But if the test of "clearly established law" were to be applied at this level of generality, it would bear no relationship to the "objective legal reasonableness" that is the touchstone of *Harlow*. Plaintiffs would be able to convert the rule of qualified immunity that our cases plainly establish into a rule of virtually unqualified liability simply by alleging violation of extremely abstract rights. *Harlow* would be transformed from a guarantee of immunity into a rule of pleading. Such an approach, in sum, would destroy "the balance that our cases strike between the interests in vindication of citizens' constitutional rights and in public officials' effective performance of their duties," by making it impossible for officials "reasonably [to] anticipate when their conduct may give rise to liability for damages." *Davis*, [483 U.S. 635, 640] *supra* at 195.[2] It should not be surprising, therefore, that our cases establish that the right the official is alleged to have violated must have been "clearly established" in a more particularized, and hence more relevant, sense: The contours of the right must be sufficiently clear that a reasonable official would understand that what he is doing violates that right. This is not to say that an official action is protected by qualified immunity unless the very action in question has previously been held unlawful, see *Mitchell, supra*, at 535, n. 12; but it is to say that in the light of pre-existing law the unlawfulness must be apparent. See, *e.g., Malley, supra*, at 344-345; *Mitchell, supra*, at 528; *Davis, supra*, at 191, 195.

Anderson contends that the Court of Appeals misapplied these principles. We agree. The Court of Appeals' brief discussion of qualified immunity consisted of little more than an assertion that a general right Anderson was alleged to have violated—the right to be free from warrantless searches of one's home unless the searching officers have probable cause and there are exigent circumstances—was clearly established. The Court of Appeals specifically refused to consider the argument that it was not clearly established that the circumstances with which Anderson was confronted did [483 U.S. 635, 641] not constitute probable cause and exigent circumstances. The previous discussion should make clear that this refusal was erroneous. It simply does not follow immediately from the conclusion that it was firmly established that warrantless searches not supported by probable cause and exigent circumstances violate the Fourth Amendment that Anderson's search was objectively legally unreasonable. We have recognized that it is inevitable that law enforcement officials will in some cases reasonably but mistakenly conclude that probable cause is present, and we have indicated that in such cases those officials—like other officials who act in ways they reasonably believe to be lawful—should not be held personally liable. See *Malley, supra*, at 344-345. The same is true of their conclusions regarding exigent circumstances.

It follows from what we have said that the determination whether it was objectively legally reasonable to conclude that a given search was supported by probable cause or exigent circumstances will often require examination of the information possessed by the searching officials. But contrary to the Creightons' assertion, this does not reintroduce into qualified immunity analysis the inquiry into officials' subjective intent that *Harlow* sought to minimize. See *Harlow*, 457 U.S., at 815-820. The relevant question in this case, for example, is the objective (albeit fact-specific) question whether a reasonable officer could have believed Anderson's warrantless search to be lawful, in light of clearly established law and the information the searching officers possessed. Anderson's subjective beliefs about the search are irrelevant.

The principles of qualified immunity that we reaffirm today require that Anderson be permitted to argue that he is entitled to summary judgment on the ground that, in light of the clearly established principles governing warrantless searches, he could, as a matter of law, reasonably have believed that the search of the Creightons' home was lawful.[3] [483 U.S. 635, 642]

III

In addition to relying on the reasoning of the Court of Appeals, the Creightons advance three alternative grounds for affirmance. All of these take the same form, *i.e.*, that even if Anderson is entitled to qualified immunity under the usual principles of qualified immunity law we have just described, an exception should be made to those principles in the circumstances of this case. We note at the outset the heavy burden this argument must sustain to be successful. We have emphasized that the doctrine of qualified immunity reflects a balance that has been struck "across the board," *Harlow, supra*, at 821 (BRENNAN, J., concurring). See also *Malley*, 475 U.S., at 340 ("'For executive officers in general, . . . qualified immunity represents the norm'" (quoting *Harlow, supra*, at 807)).[4] Although we have in narrow circumstances provided officials with an absolute immunity, see, [483 U.S. 635, 643] *e.g., Nixon v. Fitzgerald*, 457 U.S. 731 (1982), we have been unwilling to complicate qualified immunity analysis by making the scope or extent of immunity turn on the precise nature of various officials' duties or the precise character of the particular rights alleged to have been violated. An immunity that has as many variants as there are modes of official action and types of rights would not give conscientious officials that assurance of protection that it is the object of the doctrine to provide. With that observation in mind, we turn to the particular arguments advanced by the Creightons.

First, and most broadly, the Creightons argue that it is inappropriate to give officials alleged to have violated the Fourth Amendment— and thus necessarily to have unreasonably searched or seized—the protection of a qualified immunity intended only to protect reasonable official action. It is not possible, that is, to say that one "reasonably" acted unreasonably. The short answer to this argument is that it is foreclosed by the fact that we have previously extended qualified immunity to officials who were alleged to have violated the Fourth Amendment. See *Malley, supra* (police officers alleged to have caused an unconstitutional arrest); *Mitchell v. Forsyth*, 472 U.S. 511 (1985) (officials alleged to have conducted warrantless wiretaps). Even if that were not so, however, we would still find the argument unpersuasive. Its surface appeal is attributable to the circumstance that the Fourth Amendment's guarantees have been expressed in terms of "unreasonable" searches and seizures. Had an equally serviceable term, such as "undue" searches and seizures been employed, what might be termed the "reasonably unreasonable" argument against application of *Harlow* to the Fourth Amendment would not be available—just as it would be available against application of *Harlow* to the Fifth Amendment if the term "reasonable process of law" had been employed there. The fact is that, regardless of the terminology used, the precise content of most of the Constitution's [483 U.S. 635, 644] civil-liberties guarantees rests upon an assessment of what accommodation between governmental need and individual freedom is reasonable, so that the Creightons' objection, if it has any substance, applies to the application of Harlow generally. We have frequently observed, and our many cases on the point amply demonstrate, the difficulty of determining whether particular searches or seizures comport with the Fourth Amendment. See, *e.g.*, *Malley, supra*, at 341. Law enforcement officers whose judgments in making these difficult determinations are objectively legally reasonable should no more be held personally liable in damages than should officials making analogous determinations in other areas of law.

For the same reasons, we also reject the Creightons' narrower suggestion that we overrule *Mitchell, supra* (extending qualified immunity to officials who conducted warrantless wiretaps), by holding that qualified immunity may never be extended to officials who conduct unlawful warrantless searches.

Finally, we reject the Creightons' narrowest and most procrustean proposal: that no immunity should be provided to police officers who conduct unlawful warrantless searches of innocent third parties' homes in search of fugitives. They rest this proposal on the assertion that officers conducting such searches were strictly liable at English common law if the fugitive was not present. See, *e.g.*, *Entick v. Carrington*, 19 How. St. Tr. 1029, 95 Eng. Rep. 807 (K. B. 1765). Although it is true that we have observed that our determinations as to the scope of official immunity are made in the light of the "common-law tradition,"[5] *Malley, supra,* at 342, [483 U.S. 635, 645] we have never suggested that the precise contours of official immunity can and should be slavishly derived from the often arcane rules of the common law. That notion is plainly contradicted by *Harlow*, where the Court completely reformulated qualified immunity along principles not at all embodied in the common law, replacing the inquiry into subjective malice so frequently required at common law with an objective inquiry into the legal reasonableness of the official action. See *Harlow*, 457 U.S., at 815-820. As we noted before, Harlow clearly expressed the understanding that the general principle of qualified immunity it established would be applied "across the board."

The approach suggested by the Creightons would introduce into qualified immunity analysis a complexity rivaling that which we found sufficiently daunting to deter us from tailoring the doctrine to the nature of officials' duties or of the rights allegedly violated. See *supra*, at 642-643. Just in the field of unlawful arrests, for example, a cursory examination of the Restatement (Second) of Torts (1965) suggests that special exceptions from the general rule of qualified immunity would have to be made for arrests pursuant to a warrant but outside the jurisdiction of the issuing authority, 122, 129(a), arrests after the warrant had lapsed, 122, 130(a), and arrests without a warrant, 121. Both the complexity and the unsuitability of this approach are betrayed by the fact that the Creightons' proposal itself does not actually apply the musty rule that is purportedly its justification but instead suggests an exception to qualified immunity for all fugitive searches of third parties' dwellings, and not merely (as the English rule appears to have provided) for all unsuccessful fugitive searches of third parties' dwellings. Moreover, from the sources cited by the Creightons it appears to have been a corollary of the English rule that where the search was successful, no civil action would lie, whether or not probable cause for the search existed. That also is (quite prudently [483 U.S. 635, 646] but quite illogically) not urged upon us in the Creightons' selective use of the common law.

The general rule of qualified immunity is intended to provide government officials with the ability "reasonably [to] anticipate when their conduct may give rise to liability for damages." *Davis*, 468 U.S., at 195. Where that rule is applicable, officials can know that they will not be

held personally liable as long as their actions are reasonable in light of
current American law. That security would be utterly defeated if officials were unable to determine whether they were protected by the rule
without entangling themselves in the vagaries of the English and American common law. We are unwilling to Balkanize the rule of qualified
immunity by carving exceptions at the level of detail the Creightons
propose. We therefore decline to make an exception to the general rule
of qualified immunity for cases involving allegedly unlawful warrantless searches of innocent third parties' homes in search of fugitives.

For the reasons stated, we vacate the judgment of the Court of
Appeals and remand the case for further proceedings consistent with
this opinion.[6]

It is so ordered.

Footnotes

[1] The Creightons also named other defendants and advanced various other claims
against both Anderson and the other defendants. Only the *Bivens* claim against
Anderson remains at issue in this case, however.

[2] The dissent, which seemingly would adopt this approach, seeks to avoid the
unqualified liability that would follow by advancing the suggestion that officials
generally (though not law enforcement officials, see *post*, at 654, 661-662, and
officials accused of violating the Fourth Amendment, see *post*, at 659-667) be permitted to raise a defense of reasonable good faith, which apparently could be
asserted and proved only at trial. See *post*, at 653. But even when so modified (and
even for the fortunate officials to whom the modification applies) the approach
would totally abandon the concern—which was the driving force behind *Harlow's*
substantial reformulation of qualified-immunity principles—that "insubstantial
claims" against government officials be resolved prior to discovery and on summary judgment if possible. *Harlow*, 457 U.S., at 818-819. A passably clever plaintiff would always be able to identify an abstract clearly established right that the
defendant could be alleged to have violated, and the good-faith defense envisioned by the dissent would be available only at trial.

[3] The Creightons argue that the qualified immunity doctrine need not be expanded
to apply to the circumstances of this case, because the Federal [483 U.S. 635, 642]
Government and various state governments have established programs through
which they reimburse officials for expenses and liability incurred in suits challenging actions they have taken in their official capacities. Because our holding today
does not extend official qualified immunity beyond the bounds articulated in Harlow and our subsequent cases, an argument as to why we should not do so is beside
the point. Moreover, even assuming that conscientious officials care only about
their personal liability and not the liability of the government they serve, the Creightons do not and could not reasonably contend that the programs to which they refer
make reimbursement sufficiently certain and generally available to justify reconsideration of the balance struck in *Harlow* and subsequent cases. See 28 CFR 50.15(c)
(1987) (permitting reimbursement of Department of Justice employees when the
Attorney General finds reimbursement appropriate); 5 F. Harper, F. James, & O.
Gray, Law of Torts 29.9, n. 20 (2d ed. 1986) (listing various state programs).

[4] These decisions demonstrate the emptiness of the dissent's assertion that
"[t]oday this Court makes the fundamental error of simply assuming that Harlow

immunity is just as appropriate for federal law enforcement officers . . . as it is for high government officials." *Post*, at 654 (footnote omitted). Just last Term the Court unanimously held that state and federal law enforcement officers were protected by the qualified immunity described in *Harlow*. *Malley v. Briggs*, 475 U.S. 335 (1986). We see no reason to overrule that holding.

[5] Of course, it is the American rather than the English common-law tradition that is relevant, cf. *Malley, supra*, at 340-342; and the American rule appears to have been considerably less draconian than the English. See Restatement (Second) of Torts 204, 206 (1965) (officers with an arrest warrant are privileged to enter a third party's house to effect arrest if they reasonably believe the fugitive to be there).

[6] Noting that no discovery has yet taken place, the Creightons renew their argument that, whatever the appropriate qualified immunity standard, some discovery would be required before Anderson's summary judgment motion could be granted. We think the matter somewhat more complicated. One of the purposes of the Harlow qualified immunity standard is to protect public officials from the "broad-ranging discovery" that can be "peculiarly disruptive of effective government." 457 U.S., at 817 (footnote omitted). For this reason, we have emphasized that qualified immunity questions should be resolved at the earliest possible stage of a litigation. *Id.*, at 818. See also *Mitchell v. Forsyth*, 472 U.S. 511, 526 (1986). Thus, on remand, it should first be determined whether the actions the Creightons allege Anderson to have taken are actions that a reasonable officer could have believed lawful. If they are, then Anderson is entitled to dismissal prior to discovery. Cf. *ibid*. If they are not, and if the actions Anderson claims he took are different from those the Creightons allege (and are actions that a reasonable officer could have believed lawful), [483 U.S. 635, 647] then discovery may be necessary before Anderson's motion for summary judgment on qualified immunity grounds can be resolved. Of course, any such discovery should be tailored specifically to the question of Anderson's qualified immunity. [483 U.S. 635, 647]

Hunter v. Bryant
502 U.S. 224 (1991)

Decided December 16, 1991
PER CURIAM.

On May 3, 1985, respondent James V. Bryant delivered two photocopies of a handwritten letter to two administrative [502 U.S. 224, 225] offices at the University of Southern California. The rambling letter referred to a plot to assassinate President Ronald Reagan by "Mr. Image," who was described as "Communist white men within the National Council of Churches." The letter stated that "Mr. Image wants to murder President Reagan on his up and coming trip to Germany," that "Mr. Image had conspired with a large number of U.S. officials in the plot to murder President Reagan" and others, and that "Mr. Image (NCC) still plans on murdering the President on his trip to Germany in May, 1985." See *Bryant v. United States Treasury Department, Secret Service*, 903 F.2d 717, 724-727 (CA9 1990) (Bryant's letter). President Reagan was traveling in Germany at the time.

A campus police sergeant telephoned the Secret Service, and agent Brian Hunter responded to the call. After reading the letter, agent Hunter interviewed University employees. One identified James Bryant as the man who had delivered the letter, and reported that Bryant had "told her '[h]e should have been assassinated in Bonn.'" Another employee said that the man who delivered the letter made statements about "'bloody coups'" and "'assassination,'" and said something about "'across the throat'" while moving his hand horizontally across his throat to simulate a cutting action. *Id.*, at 718-719.

Hunter and another Secret Service agent, Jeffrey Jordan, then visited a local address that appeared on the letter. Bryant came to the door

388

and gave the agents permission to enter. He admitted writing and delivering the letter, but refused to identify "'Mr. Image'" and answered questions about "'Mr. Image'" in a rambling fashion. Bryant gave Hunter permission to search the apartment, and the agent found the original of the letter. While the search was underway, Jordan continued questioning Bryant, who refused to answer questions about his feelings toward the President or to state whether he intended to harm the President. *Id.*, at 719. [502 U.S. 224, 226]

Hunter and Jordan arrested Bryant for making threats against the President, in violation of 18 U.S.C. § 871(a).[1] Bryant was arraigned and held without bond until May 17, 1985, when the criminal complaint was dismissed on the Government's motion.

Bryant subsequently sued agents Hunter and Jordan, the United States Department of the Treasury, and the Director of the Secret Service, seeking recovery under the Federal Tort Claims Act and alleging that the agents had violated his rights under the Fourth, Fifth, Sixth, and Fourteenth Amendments. See *Bivens v. Six Unknown Fed. Narcotics Agents*, 403 U.S. 388 (1971). The District Court dismissed all defendants other than agents Hunter and Jordan and all causes of action other than Bryant's Fourth Amendment claims for arrest without probable cause and without a warrant. The court denied the agents' motion for summary judgment on qualified immunity grounds.

On appeal, a Ninth Circuit panel held that the agents were entitled to qualified immunity for arresting Bryant without a warrant because, at that time, the warrant requirement was not clearly established for situations in which the arrestee had consented to the agents' entry into a residence. 903 F.2d, at 723-724.

However, the panel divided on the question of whether the agents were entitled to immunity on the claim that they had [502 U.S. 224, 227] arrested Bryant without probable cause. The majority concluded that the agents had failed to sustain the burden of establishing qualified immunity because their reason for arresting Bryant—their belief that the "'Mr. Image'" plotting to kill the President in Bryant's letter could be a pseudonym for Bryant—was not the most reasonable reading of Bryant's letter:

> Even accepting the "alter ego" theory that by warning what Mr. Image was going to do, Mr. Bryant was in fact communicating what he himself planned to do, the letter, read in its entirety, does not appear to make a threat against the President. Most of the letter does not even talk about President Reagan. *A more reasonable interpretation of the letter might be that Bryant was trying to convince people of the danger Mr. Image and the conspiracy posed, rather than that Bryant was speaking through Mr. Image. Id.*, at 722 (emphasis added).

Our cases establish that qualified immunity shields agents Hunter and Jordan from suit for damages if "a reasonable officer could have believed [Bryant's arrest] to be lawful, in light of clearly established law and the information the [arresting] officers possessed." *Anderson v. Creighton*, 483 U.S. 635, 641 (1987). Even law enforcement officials who "reasonably but mistakenly conclude that probable cause is present" are entitled to immunity. *Ibid.* Moreover, because "[t]he entitlement is an immunity from suit, rather than a mere defense to liability," *Mitchell v. Forsyth*, 472 U.S. 511, 526 (1985), we repeatedly have stressed the importance of resolving immunity questions at the earliest possible stage in litigation. See *Harlow v. Fitzgerald*, 457 U.S. 800, 818 (1982); *Davis v. Scherer*, 468 U.S. 183, 195 (1984); *Mitchell, supra*, at 526; *Malley v. Briggs*, 475 U.S. 335, 341 (1986); *Anderson, supra*, at 646, n. 6.

The decision of the Ninth Circuit ignores the import of these decisions. The Court of Appeals' confusion is evident [502 U.S. 224, 228] from its statement that "[w]hether a reasonable officer could have believed he had probable cause is a question for the trier of fact, and summary judgment . . . based on lack of probable cause is proper only if there is only one reasonable conclusion a jury could reach." 903 F.2d, at 721. This statement of law is wrong for two reasons. First, it routinely places the question of immunity in the hands of the jury. Immunity ordinarily should be decided by the court long before trial. See *Mitchell, supra*, at 527-529. Second, the court should ask whether the agents acted reasonably under settled law in the circumstances, not whether another reasonable, or more reasonable, interpretation of the events can be constructed five years after the fact.

Under settled law, Secret Service Agents Hunter and Jordan are entitled to immunity if a reasonable officer could have believed that probable cause existed to arrest Bryant. Probable cause existed if, "at the moment the arrest was made . . ., the facts and circumstances within their knowledge and of which they had reasonably trustworthy information were sufficient to warrant a prudent man in believing" that Bryant had violated 18 U.S.C. § 871. *Beck v. Ohio*, 379 U.S. 89, 91 (1964).

When Agents Hunter and Jordan arrested Bryant, they possessed trustworthy information that Bryant had written a letter containing references to an assassination scheme directed against the President, that Bryant was cognizant of the President's whereabouts, that Bryant had made an oral statement that "'[h]e should have been assassinated in Bonn,'" 903 F.2d, at 719, and that Bryant refused to answer questions about whether he intended to harm the President. On the basis of this information, a Magistrate ordered Bryant to be held without bond.

These undisputed facts establish that the Secret Service agents are entitled to qualified immunity. Even if we assumed, *arguendo*, that they (*and* the magistrate) erred in concluding that probable cause existed to arrest Bryant, the [502 U.S. 224, 229] agents nevertheless would be entitled to qualified immunity because their decision was reasonable, even if mistaken. *Anderson, supra*, at 641.

The qualified immunity standard "gives ample room for mistaken judgments" by protecting "all but the plainly incompetent or those who knowingly violate the law." *Malley, supra,* at 343, 341. This accommodation for reasonable error exists because "officials should not err always on the side of caution" because they fear being sued. Davis, *supra,* at 196. Our national experience has taught that this principle is nowhere more important than when the specter of Presidential assassination is raised.

The petition for a writ of certiorari is granted, the judgment of the Court of Appeals is reversed, and the case is remanded for further proceedings consistent with this opinion.

It is so ordered.

Footnote

[1] Title 18 U.S.C. § 871(a) provides:

> "Whoever knowingly and willfully deposits for conveyance in the mail or for a delivery from any post office or by any letter carrier any letter, paper, writing, print, missive, or document containing any threat to take the life of, to kidnap, or to inflict bodily harm upon the President of the United States, the President-elect, the Vice President or other officer next in the order of succession to the office of President of the United States, or the Vice President-elect, or knowingly and willfully otherwise makes any such threat against the President, President-elect, Vice President or other officer next in the order of succession to the office of President, or Vice President-elect, shall be fined not more than $1,000 or imprisoned not more than five years, or both."

Rochelle Brosseau v. Kenneth J. Haugen
543 U. S. ___ (2004)

Decided December 13, 2004
Per Curiam.

Officer Rochelle Brosseau, a member of the Puyallup, Washington, Police Department, shot Kenneth Haugen in the back as he attempted to flee from law enforcement authorities in his vehicle. Haugen subsequently filed this action in the United States District Court for the Western District of Washington pursuant to Rev. Stat. §1979, 42 U. S. C. §1983. He alleged that the shot fired by Brosseau constituted excessive force and violated his federal constitutional rights.[1] The District Court granted summary judgment to Brosseau after finding she was entitled to qualified immunity. The Court of Appeals for the Ninth Circuit reversed. 339 F. 3d 857 (2003). Following the two-step process set out in *Saucier v. Katz*, 533 U. S. 194 (2001), the Court of Appeals found, first, that Brosseau had violated Haugen's Fourth Amendment right to be free from excessive force and, second, that the right violated was clearly established and thus Brosseau was not entitled to qualified immunity. Brosseau then petitioned for writ of certiorari, requesting that we review both of the Court of Appeals' determinations. We grant the petition on the second, qualified immunity question and reverse.

The material facts, construed in a light most favorable to Haugen, are as follows.[2] On the day before the fracas, Glen Tamburello went to the police station and reported to Brosseau that Haugen, a former crime partner of his, had stolen tools from his shop. Brosseau later learned that there was a felony no-bail warrant out for Haugen's arrest

392

on drug and other offenses. The next morning, Haugen was spray-painting his Jeep Cherokee in his mother's driveway. Tamburello learned of Haugen's whereabouts, and he and cohort Matt Atwood drove a pickup truck to Haugen's mother's house to pay Haugen a visit. A fight ensued, which was witnessed by a neighbor who called 911.

Brosseau heard a report that the men were fighting in Haugen's mother's yard and responded. When she arrived, Tamburello and Atwood were attempting to get Haugen into Tamburello's pickup. Brosseau's arrival created a distraction, which provided Haugen the opportunity to get away. Haugen ran through his mother's yard and hid in the neighborhood. Brosseau requested assistance, and, shortly thereafter, two officers arrived with a K-9 to help track Haugen down. During the search, which lasted about 30 to 45 minutes, officers instructed Tamburello and Atwood to remain in Tamburello's pickup. They instructed Deanna Nocera, Haugen's girlfriend who was also present with her 3-year-old daughter, to remain in her small car with her daughter. Tamburello's pickup was parked in the street in front of the driveway; Nocera's small car was parked in the driveway in front of and facing the Jeep; and the Jeep was in the driveway facing Nocera's car and angled somewhat to the left. The Jeep was parked about 4 feet away from Nocera's car and 20 to 30 feet away from Tamburello's pickup.

An officer radioed from down the street that a neighbor had seen a man in her backyard. Brosseau ran in that direction, and Haugen appeared. He ran past the front of his mother's house and then turned and ran into the driveway. With Brosseau still in pursuit, he jumped into the driver's side of the Jeep and closed and locked the door. Brosseau believed that he was running to the Jeep to retrieve a weapon.

Brosseau arrived at the Jeep, pointed her gun at Haugen, and ordered him to get out of the vehicle. Haugen ignored her command and continued to look for the keys so he could get the Jeep started. Brosseau repeated her commands and hit the driver's side window several times with her handgun, which failed to deter Haugen. On the third or fourth try, the window shattered. Brosseau unsuccessfully attempted to grab the keys and struck Haugen on the head with the barrel and butt of her gun. Haugen, still undeterred, succeeded in starting the Jeep. As the Jeep started or shortly after it began to move, Brosseau jumped back and to the left. She fired one shot through the rear driver's side window at a forward angle, hitting Haugen in the back. She later explained that she shot Haugen because she was "'fearful for the other officers on foot who [she] believed were in the immediate area, [and] for the occupied vehicles in [Haugen's] path and for any other citizens who might be in the area.'" 339 F. 3d, at 865.

Despite being hit, Haugen, in his words, "'st[ood] on the gas'"; navigated the "'small, tight space'" to avoid the other vehicles; swerved across the neighbor's lawn; and continued down the street. *Id.*, at 882.

After about a half block, Haugen realized that he had been shot and brought the Jeep to a halt. He suffered a collapsed lung and was air-lifted to a hospital. He survived the shooting and subsequently pleaded guilty to the felony of "eluding." Wash. Rev. Code §46.61.024 (1994). By so pleading, he admitted that he drove his Jeep in a manner indicating "a wanton or wilful disregard for the lives . . . of others." *Ibid.* He sub-sequently brought this §1983 action against Brosseau.

* * *

When confronted with a claim of qualified immunity, a court must ask first the following question: "Taken in the light most favorable to the party asserting the injury, do the facts alleged show the officer's con-duct violated a constitutional right?" *Saucier v. Katz*, 533 U. S., at 201. As the Court of Appeals recognized, the constitutional question in this case is governed by the principles enunciated in *Tennessee v. Garner*, 471 U. S. 1 (1985), and *Graham v. Connor*, 490 U. S. 386 (1989). These cases establish that claims of excessive force are to be judged under the Fourth Amendment's "'objective reasonableness'" standard. *Id.*, at 388. Specifically with regard to deadly force, we explained in *Garner* that it is unreasonable for an officer to "seize an unarmed, nondanger-ous suspect by shooting him dead." 471 U. S., at 11. But "[w]here the officer has probable cause to believe that the suspect poses a threat of serious physical harm, either to the officer or to others, it is not consti-tutionally unreasonable to prevent escape by using deadly force." *Ibid.*

We express no view as to the correctness of the Court of Appeals' decision on the constitutional question itself. We believe that, however that question is decided, the Court of Appeals was wrong on the issue of qualified immunity.[3]

Qualified immunity shields an officer from suit when she makes a decision that, even if constitutionally deficient, reasonably misappre-hends the law governing the circumstances she confronted. *Saucier v. Katz*, 533 U. S., at 206 (qualified immunity operates "to protect officers from the sometimes 'hazy border between excessive and acceptable force'"). Because the focus is on whether the officer had fair notice that her conduct was unlawful, reasonableness is judged against the back-drop of the law at the time of the conduct. If the law at that time did not clearly establish that the officer's conduct would violate the Con-stitution, the officer should not be subject to liability or, indeed, even the burdens of litigation.

It is important to emphasize that this inquiry "must be under-taken in light of the specific context of the case, not as a broad general proposition." *Id.*, at 201. As we previously said in this very context:

> "[T]here is no doubt that *Graham v. Connor, supra,* clearly estab-lishes the general proposition that use of force is contrary to the Fourth Amendment if it is excessive under objective standards of

reasonableness. Yet that is not enough. Rather, we emphasized in *Anderson [v. Creighton,]* 'that the right the official is alleged to have violated must have been "clearly established" in a more particularized, and hence more relevant, sense: The contours of the right must be sufficiently clear that a reasonable official would understand that what he is doing violates that right.' 483 U. S. [635,] 640 [(1987)]. The relevant, dispositive inquiry in determining whether a right is clearly established is whether it would be clear to a reasonable officer that his conduct was unlawful in the situation he confronted." *Id.*, at 201–202.

The Court of Appeals acknowledged this statement of law, but then proceeded to find fair warning in the general tests set out in *Graham* and *Garner*. 339 F. 3d, at 873–874. In so doing, it was mistaken. *Graham* and *Garner*, following the lead of the Fourth Amendment's text, are cast at a high level of generality. See *Graham v. Connor, supra*, at 396 ("'[T]he test of reasonableness under the Fourth Amendment is not capable of precise definition or mechanical application'"). Of course, in an obvious case, these standards can "clearly establish" the answer, even without a body of relevant case law. See *Hope v. Pelzer*, 536 U. S. 730, 738 (2002) (noting in a case where the Eighth Amendment violation was "obvious" that there need not be a materially similar case for the right to be clearly established). See also *Pace v. Capobianco*, 283 F. 3d 1275, 1283 (CA11 2002) (explaining in a Fourth Amendment case involving an officer shooting a fleeing suspect in a vehicle that, "when we look at decisions such as *Garner* and *Graham*, we see some tests to guide us in determining the law in many different kinds of circumstances; but we do not see the kind of clear law (clear answers) that would apply" to the situation at hand). The present case is far from the obvious one where *Graham* and *Garner* alone offer a basis for decision.

We therefore turn to ask whether, at the time of Brosseau's actions, it was "'"clearly established"'" in this more "'particularized'" sense that she was violating Haugen's Fourth Amendment right. *Saucier v. Katz*, 533 U. S., at 202. The parties point us to only a handful of cases relevant to the "situation [Brosseau] confronted": whether to shoot a disturbed felon, set on avoiding capture through vehicular flight, when persons in the immediate area are at risk from that flight.[4] *Ibid.* Specifically, Brosseau points us to *Cole v. Bone*, 993 F. 2d 1328 (CA8 1993), and *Smith v. Freland*, 954 F. 2d 343 (CA6 1992).

In these cases, the courts found no Fourth Amendment violation when an officer shot a fleeing suspect who presented a risk to others. *Cole v. Bone, supra*, at 1333 (holding the officer "had probable cause to believe that the truck posed an imminent threat of serious physical harm to innocent motorists as well as to the officers themselves"); *Smith v. Freland*, 954 F. 2d, at 347 (noting "a car can be a deadly weapon" and holding the officer's decision to stop the car from possibly injuring others was reasonable). *Smith* is closer to this case. There, the officer and suspect engaged in a car chase, which appeared to be at an end when the officer cornered the suspect at the back of a dead-end residential street. The suspect, however, freed his car and began speeding down the street. At this point, the officer fired a shot, which killed the suspect. The court held the officer's decision was reasonable and thus did not violate the Fourth Amendment. It noted that the suspect, like Haugen here, "had proven he would do almost anything to avoid capture" and that he posed a major threat to, among others, the officers at the end of the street. *Ibid.*

Haugen points us to *Estate of Starks v. Enyart*, 5 F. 3d 230 (CA7 1993), where the court found summary judgment inappropriate on a Fourth Amendment claim involving a fleeing suspect. There, the court concluded that the threat created by the fleeing suspect's failure to brake when an officer suddenly stepped in front of his just-started car was not a sufficiently grave threat to justify the use of deadly force. *Id.*, at 234.

These three cases taken together undoubtedly show that this area is one in which the result depends very much on the facts of each case. None of them squarely governs the case here; they do suggest that Brosseau's actions fell in the "'hazy border between excessive and acceptable force.'" *Saucier v. Katz, supra,* at 206. The cases by no means "clearly establish" that Brosseau's conduct violated the Fourth Amendment.

The judgment of the United States Court of Appeals for the Ninth Circuit is therefore reversed, and the case is remanded for further proceedings consistent with this opinion.

It is so ordered.

Footnotes

[1] Haugen also asserted pendent state-law claims and claims against the city and police department. These claims are not presently before us.

[2] Because this case arises in the posture of a motion for summary judgment, we are required to view all facts and draw all reasonable inferences in favor of the nonmoving party, Haugen. See *Saucier v. Katz*, 533 U. S. 194, 201 (2001).

[3] We have no occasion in this case to reconsider our instruction in *Saucier v. Katz*, 533 U. S. 194, 201 (2001), that lower courts decide the constitutional question prior to deciding the qualified immunity question. We exercise our summary reversal procedure here simply to correct a clear misapprehension of the qualified immunity standard.

[4] The parties point us to a number of other cases in this vein that postdate the conduct in question, *i.e.*, Brosseau's February 21, 1999, shooting of Haugen. See *Cowan ex rel. Estate of Cooper v. Breen*, 352 F. 3d 756, 763 (CA2 2003); *Pace v. Capobianco*, 283 F. 3d 1275, 1281–1282 (CA11 2002); *Scott v. Clay County, Tennessee*, 205 F. 3d 867, 877 (CA6 2000); *McCaslin v. Wilkins*, 183 F. 3d 775, 77–779 (CA8 1999); *Abraham v. Raso*, 183 F. 3d 279, 288–296 (CA3 1999). These decisions, of course, could not have given fair notice to Brosseau and are of no use in the clearly established inquiry.

Discussion Questions

1. What purposes are served by granting governmental actors immunity from liability? What are the different forms of immunity?

2. Who is entitled to the various forms of immunity? Is immunity based on the positions governmental actors hold or the activities and responsibilities they are assigned?

3. What is the balance the Court seeks to achieve when developing the law on immunity? Who benefits from granting police immunity for constitutional violations? Who is hurt?

4. How do official and personal capacity distinctions affect immunity?

5. What are the "objective" and "subjective" factors the Court considers in making decisions about granting immunity? Do these factors conflict with the Court's position on culpability in other aspects of Section 1983 litigation?

6. What is the standard the Court uses to determine if a police officer is to be granted qualified immunity?

7. What are the reasons behind granting witness absolute immunity? Is there a standard for determining witness immunity? What are the potential consequence of this form of immunity?

8. What is the relationship between probable cause and qualified immunity? Do probable cause and immunity constructions change based on different types of police action?

9. If an individual police officer is granted qualified immunity for a constitutional violation, can the municipality be held liable for the same violation?

10. Is there a difference between a good-faith defense and qualified immunity?

APPENDIX

Selected Amendments to
the Constitution of the United States

Amendment I

Congress shall make no law respecting an establishment of religion, or prohibiting the free exercise thereof; or abridging the freedom of speech, or of the press; or the right of the people peaceably to assemble, and to petition the Government for a redress of grievances.

Amendment IV

The right of the people to be secure in their persons, houses, papers, and effects, against unreasonable searches and seizures, shall not be violated, and no Warrants shall issue, but upon probable cause, supported by Oath or affirmation, and particularly describing the place to be searched, and the persons or things to be seized.

Amendment V

No person shall be held to answer for a capital, or otherwise infamous crime, unless on a presentment or indictment of a Grand Jury, except in cases arising in the land or naval forces, or in the Militia, when in actual service in time of War or public danger; nor shall any person be subject for the same offence to be twice put in jeopardy of life or limb; nor shall be compelled in any criminal case to be a witness against himself, nor be deprived of life, liberty, or property, without due process of law; nor shall private property be taken for public use, without just compensation.

Amendment VI

In all criminal prosecutions, the accused shall enjoy the right to a speedy and public trial, by an impartial jury of the State and district wherein the crime shall have been committed, which district shall have been previously ascertained by law, and to be informed of the nature and cause of the accusation; to be confronted with the witnesses against him; to have compulsory process for obtaining witnesses in his favor, and to have the Assistance of Counsel for his defence.

Amendment VIII

Excessive bail shall not be required, nor excessive fines imposed, nor cruel and unusual punishments inflicted.

Amendment XI

The Judicial power of the United States shall not be construed to extend to any suit in law or equity, commenced or prosecuted against one on the United States by Citizens of another State, or by Citizens or Subjects of any Foreign State.

Amendment XIV

Section. 1. All persons born or naturalized in the United States and subject to the jurisdiction thereof, are citizens of the United States and of the State wherein they reside. No State shall make or enforce any law which shall abridge the privileges or immunities of citizens of the United States; nor shall any State deprive any person of life, liberty, or property, without due process of law; nor deny to any person within its jurisdiction the equal protection of the laws.

Section. 5. The Congress shall have power to enforce, by appropriate legislation, the provisions of this article.

Selected Federal Statutes

Conspiracy against Rights 18 U.S.C. § 241

If two or more persons conspire to injure, oppress, threaten, or intimidate any person in any State, Territory, Commonwealth, Possession, or District in the free exercise or enjoyment of any right or privilege secured to him by the Constitution or laws of the United States, or because of his having so exercised the same; or

If two or more persons go in disguise on the highway, or on the premises of another, with intent to prevent or hinder his free exercise or enjoyment of any right or privilege so secured -

They shall be fined under this title or imprisoned not more than ten years, or both; and if death results from the acts committed in violation of this section or if such acts include kidnapping or an attempt to kidnap, aggravated sexual abuse or an attempt to commit aggravated sexual abuse, or an attempt to kill, they shall be fined under this title or imprisoned for any term of years or for life, or both, or may be sentenced to death.

Obstruction of Proceedings before Departments, Agencies, and Committees 18 U.S.C. § 1505

Whoever, with intent to avoid, evade, prevent, or obstruct compliance, in whole or in part, with any civil investigative demand duly and properly made under the Antitrust Civil Process Act, willfully withholds, misrepresents, removes from any place, conceals, covers up, destroys, mutilates, alters, or by other means falsifies any documentary material, answers to written interrogatories, or oral testimony, which is the subject of such demand; or attempts to do so or solicits another to do so; or

Whoever corruptly, or by threats or force, or by any threatening letter or communication influences, obstructs, or impedes or endeavors to influence, obstruct, or impede the due and proper administration of the law under which any pending proceeding is being had before any department or agency of the United States, or the due and proper exercise of the power of inquiry under which any inquiry or investigation is being had by either House, or any committee of either House or any joint committee of the Congress—Shall be fined under this title or imprisoned not more than five years, or both.

Trial of Right of Property; Burden of Proof 25 U.S.C. § 194

In all trials about the right of property in which an Indian may be a party on one side, and a white person on the other, the burden of proof shall rest upon the white person, whenever the Indian shall make out a presumption of title in himself from the fact of previous possession or ownership.

Civil Rights and Elective Franchise 28 U.S.C. § 1343

(a) The district courts shall have original jurisdiction of any civil action authorized by law to be commenced by any person:

(1) To recover damages for injury to his person or property, or because of the deprivation of any right or privilege of a citizen of the United States, by any act done in furtherance of any conspiracy mentioned in section 1985 of Title 42;

(2) To recover damages from any person who fails to prevent or to aid in preventing any wrongs mentioned in section 1985 of Title 42 which he had knowledge were about to occur and power to prevent;

(3) To redress the deprivation, under color of any State law, statute, ordinance, regulation, custom or usage, of any right, privilege or immunity secured by the Constitution of the United States or by any Act of Congress providing for equal rights of citizens or of all persons within the jurisdiction of the United States;

(4) To recover damages or to secure equitable or other relief under any Act of Congress providing for the protection of civil rights, including the right to vote.

(b) For purposes of this section -

(1) the District of Columbia shall be considered to be a State; and

(2) any Act of Congress applicable exclusively to the District of Columbia shall be considered to be a statute of the District of Columbia.

Intervention by United States or a State; Constitutional Question 28 U.S.C. § 2403

(a) In any action, suit or proceeding in a court of the United States to which the United States or any agency, officer or employee thereof is not a party, wherein the constitutionality of any Act of Congress affecting the public interest is drawn in question, the court shall certify such fact to the Attorney General, and shall permit the United States to intervene for presentation of evidence, if evidence is otherwise admissible in the case, and for argument on the question of constitutionality. The United States shall, subject to the applicable provisions of law, have all the rights of a party and be subject to all liabilities of a party as to court costs to the extent necessary for a proper presentation of the facts and law relating to the question of constitutionality.

b) In any action, suit, or proceeding in a court of the United States to which a State or any agency, officer, or employee thereof is not a party, wherein the constitutionality of any statute of that State affecting the public interest is drawn in question, the court shall certify such fact to the attorney general of the State, and shall permit the State to intervene for presentation of evidence, if evidence is otherwise admissible in the case, and for argument on the question of constitutionality. The State shall, subject to the applicable provisions of law, have all the rights of a party and be subject to all liabilities of a party as to court costs to the extent necessary for a proper presentation of the facts and law relating to the question of constitutionality.

Civil Action for Deprivation of Rights 42 U.S.C. § 1983

Every person who, under color of any statute, ordinance, regulation, custom, or usage, of any State or Territory or the District of Columbia, subjects, or causes to be subjected, any citizen of the United States or other person within the jurisdiction thereof to the deprivation of any rights, privileges, or immunities secured by the Constitution and laws, shall be liable to the party injured in an action at law, suit in equity, or other proper proceeding for redress, except that in any action brought against a judicial officer for an act or omission taken in such officer's judicial capacity, injunctive relief shall not be granted unless a declaratory decree was violated or declaratory relief was unavailable. For the purposes of this section, any Act of Congress applicable exclusively to the District of Columbia shall be considered to be a statute of the District of Columbia.

Conspiracy to Interfere with Civil Rights 42 U.S.C. § 1985

(1) Preventing officer from performing duties

If two or more persons in any State or Territory conspire to prevent, by force, intimidation, or threat, any person from accepting or holding any office, trust, or place of confidence under the United States, or from discharging any duties thereof; or to induce by like means any officer of the United States to leave any State, district, or place, where his duties as an officer are required to be performed, or to injure him in his person or property on account of his lawful discharge of the duties of his office, or while engaged in the lawful discharge thereof, or to injure his property so as to molest, interrupt, hinder, or impede him in the discharge of his official duties;

(2) Obstructing justice; intimidating party, witness, or juror

If two or more persons in any State or Territory conspire to deter, by force, intimidation, or threat, any party or witness in any court of the United States from attending such court, or from testifying to any matter pending therein, freely, fully, and truthfully, or to injure such party or witness in his person or property on account of his having so attended or testified, or to influence the verdict, presentment, or indictment of any grand or petit juror in any such court, or to injure such juror in his person or property on account of any verdict, presentment, or indictment lawfully assented to by him, or of his being or having been such juror; or if two or more persons conspire for the purpose of impeding, hindering, obstructing, or defeating, in any manner, the due course of justice in any State or Territory, with intent to deny to any citizen the equal protection of the laws, or to injure him or his property for lawfully enforcing, or attempting to enforce, the right of any person, or class of persons, to the equal protection of the laws;

(3) Depriving persons of rights or privileges

If two or more persons in any State or Territory conspire or go in disguise on the highway or on the premises of another, for the purpose of depriving, either directly or indirectly, any person or class of persons of the equal protection of the laws, or of equal privileges and immunities under the laws; or for the purpose of preventing or hindering the constituted authorities of any State or Territory from giving or securing to all persons within such State or Territory the equal protection of the laws; or if two or more persons conspire to prevent by force, intimidation, or threat, any citizen who is lawfully entitled to vote, from giving his support or advocacy in a legal manner, toward or in favor of the election of any lawfully qualified person as an elector for President or Vice President, or as a Member of Congress of the United States; or to injure any citizen in person or property on account of such support or advocacy; in any case of conspiracy set forth in this section, if one or more persons engaged therein do, or cause to be done, any act in furtherance of the object of such conspiracy, whereby another is injured in his person or property, or deprived of having and exercising any right or privilege of a citizen of the United States, the party so injured or deprived may have an action for the recovery of damages occasioned by such injury or deprivation, against any one or more of the conspirators.

Action for Neglect to Prevent 42 U.S.C. § 1986

Every person who, having knowledge that any of the wrongs conspired to be done, and mentioned in section 1985 of this title, are about to be committed, and having power to prevent or aid in preventing the commission of the same,

dants in the action; and if the death of any party be caused by any such wrongful act and neglect, the legal representatives of the deceased shall have such
action therefor, and may recover not exceeding $5,000 damages therein, for the
benefit of the widow of the deceased, if there be one, and if there be no widow,
then for the benefit of the next of kin of the deceased. But no action under the
provisions of this section shall be sustained which is not commenced within
one year after the cause of action has accrued.

Proceedings in Vindication of Civil Rights 42 U.S.C. § 1988

(a) Applicability of statutory and common law

The jurisdiction in civil and criminal matters conferred on the district
courts by the provisions of titles 13, 24, and 70 of the Revised Statutes for the
protection of all persons in the United States in their civil rights, and for their
vindication, shall be exercised and enforced in conformity with the laws of the
United States, so far as such laws are suitable to carry the same into effect; but
in all cases where they are not adapted to the object, or are deficient in the provisions necessary to furnish suitable remedies and punish offenses against law,
the common law, as modified and changed by the constitution and statutes of
the State wherein the court having jurisdiction of such civil or criminal cause is
held, so far as the same is not inconsistent with the Constitution and laws of
the United States, shall be extended to and govern the said courts in the trial
and disposition of the cause, and, if it is of a criminal nature, in the infliction
of punishment on the party found guilty.

(b) Attorney's fees

In any action or proceeding to enforce a provision of sections 1981,
1981a, 1982, 1983, 1985, and 1986 of this title, title IX of Public Law 92-318 (20
U.S.C. 1681 et seq.), the Religious Freedom Restoration Act of 1993 (42 U.S.C.
2000bb et seq.), title VI of the Civil Rights Act of 1964 (42 U.S.C. 2000d et seq.),
or section 13981 of this title, (FOOTNOTE 1) the court, in its discretion, may
allow the prevailing party, other than the United States, a reasonable attorney's
fee as part of the costs, except that in any action brought against a judicial
officer for an act or omission taken in such officer's judicial capacity such
officer shall not be held liable for any costs, including attorney's fees, unless
such action was clearly in excess of such officer's jurisdiction.

Revisions to Rules of the
Supreme Court of the United States

Adopted March 14, 2005
Effective May 2, 2005

The Clerk's Comments that accompany the revisions to the Rules are not part of the Rules. They are furnished solely to assist readers in understanding the revisions.

Current Rule 13.3

The time to file a petition for a writ of certiorari runs from the date of entry of the judgment or order sought to be reviewed, and not from the issuance date of the mandate (or its equivalent under local practice). But if a petition for rehearing is timely filed in the lower court by any party, the time to file the petition for a writ of certiorari for all parties (whether or not they requested rehearing or joined in the petition for rehearing) runs from the date of the denial of the petition for rehearing or, if the petition for rehearing is granted, the subsequent entry of judgment.

Revised Rule 13.3

The time to file a petition for a writ of certiorari runs from the date of entry of the judgment or order sought to be reviewed, and not from the issuance date of the mandate (or its equivalent under local practice). But if a petition for rehearing is timely filed in the lower court by any party, **or if the lower court appropriately entertains an untimely petition for rehearing or** *sua sponte* **considers rehearing,** the time to file the petition for a writ of certiorari for all parties (whether or not they requested rehearing or joined in the petition for rehearing) runs from the date of the denial of rehearing or, if rehearing is granted, the subsequent entry of judgment.

[CLERK'S COMMENT: THE PROPOSED RULE COMPORTS WITH THE COURT'S OPINION IN *HIBBS V. WINN*, 542 U. S. ___ (2004).]

Rule 19. Procedure on a Certified Question

1. A United States court of appeals may certify to this Court a question or proposition of law on which it seeks instruction for the proper decision of a case. The certificate shall contain a statement of the nature of the case and the facts on which the question or proposition of law arises. Only questions or propositions of law may be certified, and they shall be stated separately and with precision. The certificate shall be prepared as required by Rule 33.2 and shall be signed by the clerk of the court of appeals.

2. When a question is certified by a United States court of appeals, this Court, on its own motion or that of a party, may consider and decide the entire matter in controversy. See 28 U.S.C. § 1254(2).

Current Rule 47

The term "state court," when used in these Rules, includes the District of Columbia Court of Appeals and the Supreme Court of the Commonwealth of Puerto Rico. See 28 U.S.C. §§ 1257 and 1258. References in these Rules to the common law and statutes of a State include the common law and statutes of the District of Columbia and of the Commonwealth of Puerto Rico.

Revised Rule 47

The term "state court," when used in these Rules, includes the District of Columbia Court of Appeals, the Supreme Court of the Commonwealth of Puerto Rico, **the courts of the Northern Mariana Islands, and the local courts of Guam.** References in these Rules to the statutes of a State include the statutes of the District of Columbia, the Commonwealth of Puerto Rico, **the Commonwealth of the Northern Mariana Islands, and the Territory of Guam.**

[CLERK'S COMMENT: FEDERAL LAW CHANGES HAVE ALTERED THE RELATIONSHIP BETWEEN THE SUPREME COURT OF THE UNITED STATES AND THE COURTS OF GUAM AND THE NORTHERN MARIANA ISLANDS. THE SUPREME COURT OF THE UNITED STATES NOW EXERCISES CERTIORARI JURISDICTION OVER THE COURTS OF GUAM AND THE NORTHERN MARIANA ISLANDS. MINOR EDITORIAL CHANGES WERE ALSO MADE TO THE RULE.]

Members of the Supreme Court of the United States

Name	State App't From	Appointed by President	Judicial Oath Taken	Date Service Terminated
Chief Justices				
Jay, John	NY	Washington	(a) Oct. 19, 1789	June 29, 1795
Rutledge, John	SC	Washington	Aug. 12, 1795	Dec. 15, 1795
Ellsworth, Oliver	CT	Washington	Mar. 8, 1796	Dec. 15, 1800
Marshall, John	VA	Adams, John	Feb. 4, 1801	July 6, 1835
Taney, Roger Brooke	MD	Jackson	Mar. 28, 1836	Oct. 12, 1864
Chase, Salmon Portland	OH	Lincoln	Dec, 15, 1864	May 7, 1873
Waite, Morrison Remick	OH	Grant	Mar. 4, 1874	Mar. 23, 1888
Fuller, Melville Weston	IL	Cleveland	Oct. 8, 1888	July 4, 1910
White, Edward Douglass	LA	Taft	Dec. 19, 1910	May 19, 1921
Taft, William Howard	CT	Harding	July 11, 1921	Feb. 3, 1930
Hughes, Charles Evans	NY	Hoover	Feb. 24, 1930	June 30, 1941
Stone, Harlan Fiske	NY	Roosevelt, F.	July 3, 1941	April 22, 1946
Vinson, Fred Moore	KY	Truman	June 24, 1946	Sept. 8, 1953
Warren, Earl	CA	Eisenhower	Oct. 5, 1953	June 23, 1969
Burger, Warren Earl	VA	Nixon	June 23, 1969	Sept. 26, 1986
Rehnquist, William H.	VA	Reagan	Sept. 26, 1986	Sept. 3, 2005
Roberts, John G., Jr.	MD	Bush, G. W.	Sept. 29, 2005	
Associate Justices				
Rutledge, John	SC	Washington	(a) Feb. 15, 1790	Mar. 5, 1791
Cushing, William	MA	Washington	(c) Feb. 2, 1790	Sept. 13, 1810
Wilson, James	PA	Washington	(b) Oct. 5, 1789	Aug. 21, 1798
Blair, John	VA	Washington	(c) Feb. 2, 1790	Oct. 25, 1795
Iredell, James	NC	Washington	(b) May 12, 1790	Oct. 20, 1799
Johnson, Thomas	MD	Washington	(a) Aug. 6, 1792	Jan. 16, 1793
Paterson, William	NJ	Washington	(a) Mar. 11, 1793	Sept. 9, 1806
Chase, Samuel	MD	Washington	Feb. 4, 1796	June 19, 1811
Washington, Bushrod	VA	Adams, John	(c) Feb. 4, 1799	Nov. 26, 1829
Moore, Alfred	NC	Adams, John	(a) April 21, 1800	Jan. 26, 1804
Johnson, William	SC	Jefferson	May 7, 1804	Aug. 4, 1834
Livingston, Henry Brockholst	NY	Jefferson	Jan. 20, 1807	Mar. 18, 1823
Todd, Thomas	KY	Jefferson	(a) May 4, 1807	Feb. 7, 1826
Duvall, Gabriel	MD	Madison	(a) Nov. 23, 1811	Jan. 14, 1835
Story, Joseph	MA	Madison	(c) Feb. 3, 1812	Sept. 10, 1845
Thompson, Smith	NY	Monroe	(b) Sept. 1, 1823	Dec. 18, 1843
Trimble, Robert	KY	Adams, J. Q.	(a) June 16, 1826	Aug. 25, 1828
McLean, John	OH	Jackson	(c) Jan. 11, 1830	April 4, 1861
Baldwin, Henry	PA	Jackson	Jan. 18, 1830	April 21, 1844
Wayne, James Moore	GA	Jackson	Jan. 14, 1835	July 5, 1867
Barbour, Philip Pendleton	VA	Jackson	May 12, 1836	Feb. 25, 1841
Catron, John	TN	Van Buren	May 1, 1837	May 30, 1865
McKinley, John	AL	Van Buren	(c) Jan. 9, 1838	July 19, 1852
Daniel, Peter Vivian	VA	Van Buren	(c) Jan. 10, 1842	May 31, 1860
Nelson, Samuel	NY	Tyler	Feb. 27, 1845	Nov. 28, 1872
Woodbury, Levi	NH	Polk	(b) Sept. 23, 1845	Sept. 4, 1851

Name	State App't From	Appointed by President	Judicial Oath Taken	Date Service Terminated
Grier, Robert Cooper	PA	Polk	Aug. 10, 1846	Jan. 31, 1870
Curtis, Benjamin Robbins	MA	Fillmore	(b) Oct. 10, 1851	Sept. 30, 1857
Campbell, John Archibald	AL	Pierce	(c) April 11, 1853	April 30, 1861
Clifford, Nathan	ME	Buchanan	Jan. 21, 1858	July 25, 1881
Swayne, Noah Haynes	OH	Lincoln	Jan. 27, 1862	Jan. 24, 1881
Miller, Samuel Freeman	IA	Lincoln	July 21, 1862	Oct. 13, 1890
Davis, David	IL	Lincoln	Dec. 10, 1862	Mar. 4, 1877
Field, Stephen Johnson	CA	Lincoln	May 20, 1863	Dec. 1, 1897
Strong, William	PA	Grant	Mar. 14, 1870	Dec. 14, 1880
Bradley, Joseph P.	NJ	Grant	Mar. 23, 1870	Jan. 22, 1892
Hunt, Ward	NY	Grant	Jan. 9, 1873	Jan. 27, 1882
Harlan, John Marshall	KY	Hayes	Dec. 10 1877	Oct. 14, 1911
Woods, William Burnham	GA	Hayes	Jan. 5, 1881	May 14, 1887
Matthews, Stanley	OH	Garfield	May 17, 1881	Mar. 22, 1889
Gray, Horace	MA	Arthur	Jan. 9, 1882	Sept. 15, 1902
Blatchford, Samuel	NY	Arthur	April 3, 1882	July 7, 1893
Lamar, Lucius Quintus C.	MS	Cleveland	Jan. 18, 1888	Jan. 23, 1893
Brewer, David Josiah	KS	Harrison	Jan. 6, 1890	Mar. 28, 1910
Brown, Henry Billings	MI	Harrison	Jan. 5, 1891	May 28, 1906
Shiras, George, Jr.	PA	Harrison	Oct. 10, 1892	Feb. 23, 1903
Jackson, Howell Edmunds	TN	Harrison	Mar. 4, 1893	Aug. 8, 1895
White, Edward Douglass	LA	Cleveland	Mar. 12, 1894	Dec. 18, 1910*
Peckham, Rufus Wheeler	NY	Cleveland	Jan. 6, 1896	Oct. 24, 1909
McKenna, Joseph	CA	McKinley	Jan. 26, 1898	Jan. 5, 1925
Holmes, Oliver Wendell	MA	Roosevelt, T.	Dec. 8, 1902	Jan. 12, 1932
Day, William Rufus	OH	Roosevelt, T.	Mar. 2, 1903	Nov. 13, 1922
Moody, William Henry	MA	Roosevelt, T.	Dec. 17, 1906	Nov. 20, 1910
Lurton, Horace Harmon	TN	Taft	Jan. 3, 1910	July 12, 1914
Hughes, Charles Evans	NY	Taft	Oct. 10, 1910	June 10, 1916
Van Devanter, Willis	WY	Taft	Jan. 3, 1911	June 2, 1937
Lamar, Joseph Rucker	GA	Taft	Jan. 3, 1911	Jan. 2, 1916
Pitney, Mahlon	NJ	Taft	Mar. 18, 1912	Dec. 31, 1922
McReynolds, James Clark	TN	Wilson	Oct. 12, 1914	Jan. 31, 1941
Brandeis, Louis Dembitz	MA	Wilson	June 5,1916	Feb. 13, 1939
Clarke, John Hessin	OH	Wilson	Oct. 9, 1916	Sept. 18, 1922
Sutherland, George	UT	Harding	Oct. 2, 1922	Jan. 17, 1938
Butler, Pierce	MN	Harding	Jan. 2, 1923	Nov. 16, 1939
Sanford, Edward Terry	TN	Harding	Feb. 19, 1923	Mar. 8, 1930
Stone, Harlan Fiske	NY	Coolidge	Mar. 2, 1925	July 2, 1941*
Roberts, Owen Josephus	PA	Hoover	June 2, 1930	July 31, 1945
Cardozo, Benjamin Nathan	NY	Hoover	Mar. 14, 1932	July 9, 1938
Black, Hugo Lafayette	AL	Roosevelt, F.	Aug. 19, 1937	Sept. 17, 1971
Reed, Stanley Forman	KY	Roosevelt, F.	Jan. 31, 1938	Feb. 25, 1957
Frankfurter, Felix	MA	Roosevelt, F.	Jan. 30, 1939	Aug. 28, 1962
Douglas, William Orville	CT	Roosevelt, F.	April 17, 1939	Nov. 12, 1975
Murphy, Frank	MI	Roosevelt, F.	Feb. 5, 1940	July 19, 1949
Byrnes, James Francis	SC	Roosevelt, F.	July 8, 1941	Oct. 3, 1942
Jackson, Robert Houghwout	NY	Roosevelt, F.	July 11, 1941	Oct. 9, 1954

Name	State App't From	Appointed by President	Judicial Oath Taken	Date Service Terminated
Rutledge, Wiley Blount	IA	Roosevelt, F.	Feb. 15, 1943	Sept. 10, 1949
Burton, Harold Hitz	OH	Truman	Oct. 1, 1945	Oct. 13, 1958
Clark, Tom Campbell	TX	Truman	Aug. 24, 1949	June 12, 1967
Minton, Sherman	IN	Truman	Oct. 12, 1949	Oct. 15, 1956
Harlan, John Marshall	NY	Eisenhower	Mar. 28, 1955	Sept. 23, 1971
Brennan, William J., Jr.	NJ	Eisenhower	Oct. 16, 1956	July 20, 1990
Whittaker, Charles Evans	MO	Eisenhower	Mar. 25, 1957	Mar. 31, 1962
Stewart, Potter	OH	Eisenhower	Oct. 14, 1958	July 3, 1981
White, Byron Raymond	CO	Kennedy	April 16, 1962	June 28, 1993
Goldberg, Arthur Joseph	IL	Kennedy	Oct. 1, 1962	July 25, 1965
Fortas, Abe	TN	Johnson, L.	Oct. 4, 1965	May 14, 1969
Marshall, Thurgood	NY	Johnson, L.	Oct. 2, 1967	Oct. 1, 1991
Blackmun, Harry A.	MN	Nixon	June 9, 1970	Aug. 3, 1994
Powell, Lewis F., Jr.	VA	Nixon	Jan. 7, 1972	June 26, 1987
Rehnquist, William H.	AZ	Nixon	Jan. 7, 1972	Sept. 25, 1986*
Stevens, John Paul	IL	Ford	Dec. 19, 1975	
O' Connor, Sandra Day	AZ	Reagan	Sept. 25, 1981	Jan. 31, 2006
Scalia, Antonin	VA	Reagan	Sept. 26, 1986	
Kennedy, Anthony M.	CA	Reagan	Feb. 18, 1988	
Souter, David H.	NH	Bush, George	Oct. 9, 1990	
Thomas, Clarence	GA	Bush, George	Oct. 23, 1991	
Ginsburg, Ruth Bader	NY	Clinton	Aug. 10, 1993	
Breyer, Stephen G.	MA	Clinton	Aug. 3, 1994	
Roberts, John G., Jr.	MD	Bush, G. W.	Sept. 29, 2005	
Alito, Samuel A., Jr.	NJ	Bush, G. W.	Jan. 31, 2006	

Notes: The acceptance of the appointment and commission by the appointee, as evidenced by the taking of the prescribed oaths, is here implied; otherwise the individual is not carried on this list of the Members of the Court. Examples: Robert Hanson Harrison is not carried, as a letter from President Washington of February 9, 1790 states Harrison declined to serve. Neither is Edwin M. Stanton who died before he could take the necessary steps toward becoming a Member of the Court. Chief Justice Rutledge is included because he took his oaths, presided over the August Term of 1795, and his name appears on two opinions of the Court for that Term.

The date a Member of the Court took his/her Judicial oath (the Judiciary Act provided "That the Justices of the Supreme Court, and the district judges, before they proceed to execute the duties of their respective offices, shall take the following oath . . .") is here used as the date of the beginning of his/her service, for until that oath is taken he/she is not vested with the prerogatives of the office. The dates given in this column are for the oaths taken following the receipt of the commissions. Dates without small-letter references are taken from the Minutes of the Court or from the original oath which are in the Curator's collection. The small letter (a) denotes the date is from the Minutes of some other court; (b) from some other unquestionable authority; (c) from authority that is questionable, and better authority would be appreciated.

*Elevated.

(The foregoing was taken from a booklet prepared by the Supreme Court of the United States and published with funding from the Supreme Court Historical Society.)

Glossary of Legal Terms

Affidavit A written statement of facts confirmed by the oath of the party making it, before a notary or officer having authority to administer oaths.

Affirmed In the practice of the appellate courts, the decree or order is declared valid and will stand as rendered in the lower court.

Allegation The assertion or declaration of a party to an action made in a pleading that states what the party expects to prove.

Amicus curiae A friend of the court; a nonparty who interposes, with the permission of the court, and volunteers information on some matter before the court.

Answer The formal written statement by a defendant responding to a civil complaint and setting forth the grounds for defense.

Appeal A request made after a trial, asking another court (usually the court of appeals) to decide whether the trial was conducted properly. To make such a request is "to appeal" or "to take an appeal." One who appeals is called the appellant.

Appearance The formal proceeding by which a defendant submits to the jurisdiction of the court.

Appellant The party appealing a decision or judgment to a higher Court.

Appellate jurisdiction The appellate court has the right to review and revise the lower court decision.

411

Appellate court   A court having jurisdiction to hear appeals and to review a trial court's procedure.

Appellee   The party against whom an appeal is taken.

Arrest of judgment   Postponing the effect of a judgment already entered.

Assumption of risk   A doctrine under which a person may not recover for an injury received when he/she has voluntarily exposed him/herself to a known danger.

Brief   Submitted by the lawyer for each side in a case, a written statement that explains to the judges why they should decide the case or a particular part of a case in favor of that lawyer's client.

Burden of proof   The duty to establish a claim or allegation by admissible evidence. This is usually the duty of the plaintiff in a civil case and always is the duty of the state in a criminal case.

Caption   The heading or introductory clause of papers connected with a case in court, which shows the names of the parties, name of the court, docket number of the case, etc.

Case law   The law as laid down in cases that have been decided in the decisions of the courts.

Cause of action   A claim in law sufficient to justify a legal right to sue.

Certification   Generally used to refer to the process of transferring a minor's case from the Juvenile Court to the adult court for trial. Usually reserved for capital or first-degree felonies or for chronic offenders.

Charge to the jury   The judge's instructions to the jury concerning the law that applies to the facts of the case on trial.

Civil case   A lawsuit brought to enforce, redress, or protect private rights or to gain payment for a wrong done to a person or party by another person or party. In general, all types of actions other than criminal proceedings.

Common law   The legal system that originated in England and is now in use in the United States; it is based on judicial decisions rather than legislative action.

Comparative negligence   The degree to which a person contributed to his/her own injury, damage, or death; usually measured in terms of percentage. Contributory negligence is the failure to exercise care by a plaintiff, which contributed to the plaintiff's injury.

Complaint   A written statement by the plaintiff stating the wrongs allegedly committed by the defendant.

Concurrent jurisdiction   The jurisdiction of two or more courts, each authorized to deal with the same subject matter.

Costs   An allowance for expenses in prosecuting or defending a suit. Ordinarily this does not include attorney fees.

Counterclaim   A claim presented by a defendant in a civil proceeding in opposition to the claim of a plaintiff.

Damages   Money that a court orders paid to a party (usually the plaintiff) who has suffered a loss by another party who caused the loss (usually the defendant).

De facto   In fact; in reality.

De jure   As a result of law; as a result of official action.

De novo   Anew, afresh; a "trial *de novo*" is a retrial.

Declaratory judgment   One that declares the rights of the parties or expresses the opinion of the court on a question of law, without necessarily ordering anything to be done.

Decree   A decision or order of the court. A final decree is one which fully and finally disposes of the litigations; an interlocutory decree is a provisional or preliminary decree which is not final.

Default judgment   A judgment rendered because of the defendant's failure to answer or appear.

Defendant   In a civil suit, the person complained against; in a criminal case, the person accused of the crime.

Deposition   An oral statement made before an officer authorized by law to administer oaths. Such statements are often taken to examine potential witnesses, to obtain discovery, or to be used later in trial.

Directed verdict   An instruction by the judge to the jury to return a specific verdict.

Discovery   Lawyers' examination, before trial, of facts and documents in possession of the opponents to help the lawyers prepare for trial.

Dissent   A term commonly used to denote the disagreement of one or more judges of a court of appeals with the decision of the majority.

En banc   "In the bench" or "full bench." Refers to court sessions with the entire membership of a court participating rather than the usual quorum. U.S. courts of appeals usually sit in panels of three judges, but may expand to a larger number in certain cases. They are then said to be sitting *en banc*.

Et al.   An abbreviation of *et alii*, meaning "and others," ordinarily used in lieu of listing all names of persons involved in a proceeding.

Et seq.   An abbreviation for *et sequentes*, or *et sequentia*, "and the following," ordinarily used in referring to a section of statutes.

Ex parte   On one side only; by or for one party; done for, on behalf of, or on the application of, one party only. A judicial proceeding, order, injunction, etc., is said to be *ex parte* when it is taken or granted at the instance and for the benefit of one party only and without notice to, or contestation by, any person adversely interested.

Ex post facto   After the fact; an act of fact occurring after some previous act or fact, and relating thereto.

Harmless error   An error committed by a lower court during a trial, but not prejudicial to the rights of the party and for which the appellate court will not reverse the judgment.

Hearing *de novo*   A full new hearing.

Hypothetical question   A combination of facts and circumstances, assumed or proved, stated in such a form that an expert can express an opinion as evidence in a trial.

Immunity   Legal protection from liability. There are many categories of immunity in civil and criminal law. For example, sovereign immunity protects government agencies from civil liability and judicial immunity protects judges acting in their official capacities.

Instructions   Judge's explanation to the jury before it begins deliberations on the questions it must answer and the law governing the case.

Inter alia   Among other things.

Interrogatories   Written questions asked by one party of an opposing party, who must answer them in writing under oath; a discovery device in a lawsuit.

Issue of fact   Arises when a fact is maintained by one party and is controverted by the other in the pleadings.

Issue of law   Arises where evidence is undisputed and only one conclusion can be drawn therefrom.

Issue   (1) The disputed point in a disagreement between parties in a lawsuit. (2) To send out officially, as in to issue an order.

Judgment   The official decision of a court finally determining the respective rights and claims of the parties to a suit.

Jurisdiction   (1) The legal authority of a court to hear and decide a case. Concurrent jurisdiction exists when two courts have simultaneous responsibility for the same case. (2) The geographic area over which the court has authority to decide cases.

Lis pendens   A pending suit. Jurisdiction, power, or control that courts acquire over property in a suit pending action and until final judgment.

Locus delicti   The place of the offense.

Malicious prosecution   A meritless (civil or criminal) action instituted solely to harass the defendant. Such misuse of the judicial process may be the basis for a lawsuit.

Moot   A moot point is one that need not be decided, due to a change of circumstances.

Motion   A formal request presented to a court.

Negligence   Failure to exercise the care that an ordinarily prudent person would exercise in the same circumstances.

Nominal party   One who is joined as a party or defendant merely because the technical rules of pleading require his/her presence in the record.

Opinion   A judge's written explanation of a decision of the court or of a majority of judges. A dissenting opinion disagrees with the majority opinion because of the reasoning and/or the principles of law on which the decision is based. A concurring opinion agrees with the decision of the court but offers further comment.

Original jurisdiction   The court in which a matter must first be filed.

Panel   (1) In appellate cases, a group of judges (usually three) assigned to decide the case; (2) In the jury selection process, the group of potential jurors.

Parties   Plaintiffs and defendants (petitioners and respondents) to lawsuits, also known as appellants and appellees in appeals, and their lawyers.

Perjury   Lying while under oath.

Petitioner   One who files a petition with a court seeking action or relief. When a writ of certiorari is granted by the Supreme Court, the parties to the case are called petitioner and respondent in contrast to appellant and appellee.

Plaintiff   The person who files the complaint in a civil lawsuit.

Pleadings   Written statements of the positions of the parties in a civil case. In the federal courts, the principal pleadings are the complaint and the answer.

Precedent   A court decision in an earlier case with facts and law similar to a dispute currently before a court. Precedent will ordinarily govern the decision of a later similar case, unless a party can show that it was wrongly decided or that it differed in some significant way.

Prejudicial error   Synonymous with "reversible error"; an error that warrants the appellate court reversing the judgment before it.

Preponderance of evidence   The greater weight (in terms of quality not quantity) of evidence, or that evidence which is more believable and convincing.

Presumption of fact An inference as to the truth or falsity of any proposition of fact, drawn by a process of reasoning in the absence of actual certainty of its truth or falsity, or until such certainty can be ascertained.

Presumption of law A rule of law that Courts and judges shall draw a particular inference from a particular fact, or from particular evidence.

Prima facie Literally, "on its face." A fact presumed to be true unless disproved by some other evidence. In a criminal case, when the prosecution rests, the state's case is said to be *prima facie*, if the evidence so far introduced is sufficient to convict.

Pro se For oneself; in one's own behalf. One who does not retain a lawyer and appears for him/herself in court.

Probable cause A judicial finding that there exists reasonable grounds for belief that a person should be arrested or searched.

Procedure The rules for the conduct of a lawsuit; there are rules of civil, criminal, evidence, bankruptcy, and appellate procedure.

Proximate cause In a civil tort action such as a medical malpractice suit, the plaintiff must show that an act or omission of the defendant was a proximate cause of the plaintiff's injury or loss. In a criminal action, the state must prove beyond a reasonable doubt that the defendant's action was the direct cause of the crime.

Punitive damages Money awarded to an injured person over and above the measurable value of the injury to punish the person who caused the harm.

Record A written account of all the acts and proceedings in a lawsuit.

Remand When an appellate court sends a case back to a lower court for further proceedings.

Removal, order of An order by a court directing the transfer of a case to another court. For example, when a case is proper for jurisdiction in federal court, the federal court may remove the case from the state court in which it was originally filed.

Reply When a case is tried or argued in court, the argument of the plaintiff in answer to that of the defendant; a pleading in response to an answer.

Res ipsa loquitur Literally, "a thing that speaks for itself." In tort law, the doctrine that holds a defendant guilty of negligence without an actual showing that he or she was negligent. Its use is limited in theory to cases in which the cause of the plaintiff's injury was entirely under the control of the defendant, and the injury presumably could have been caused only by negligence.

Res judicata A rule of civil law that once a matter has been litigated and final judgment has been rendered by the trial court, the matter cannot be relitigated by the parties in the same court, or any other trial court. A court will use *res judicata* to deny reconsideration of a matter.

Respondeat superior Literally, "a superior (or master) must answer." The doctrine that holds that employers are responsible for the acts and omissions of their employees and agents, when done within the scope of the employees' duties.

Respondent (1) the person who is the subject of a petition, (2) the prevailing party in a court case against whom an appeal is taken.

Reverse When an appellate court sets aside the decision of a lower court because of an error. A reversal is often followed by a remand.

Sovereign immunity The doctrine that a government or governmental agency cannot be sued without consent.

Standing   A person's right to bring a lawsuit because he/she is directly affected by the issue raised.

Stare decisis   The doctrine that, when a court has once laid down a principle
of law applicable to a certain set of facts, it will adhere to that principle and
apply it to future cases where the facts are substantially the same. This is
a defining characteristic of the common law system followed in the U.S.,
Great Britain, and a few other nations.

Statute   A law passed by a legislature.

Statute of limitations   A law that sets the time limits during which parties
must take action to enforce their rights through litigation. In criminal cases, prosecution is barred if not brought within the statute of limitations.

Summary judgment   A decision made on the basis of statements and evidence
presented for the record without a trial. It is used when there is no dispute
as to the facts of the case, and one party is entitled to judgment as a matter
of law.

Tort   A civil wrong or breach of a duty to another person, as outlined by law.
A very common tort is negligent operation of a motor vehicle that results
in property damage and personal injury, such as an automobile accident.

Uphold   The decision of an appellate court not to reverse a lower court decision.

Venue   The geographical location in which a case is tried.

Verdict   The decision of a petit jury or a judge.

Willful   A "willful" act is one done intentionally, as distinguished from an act
done carelessly or inadvertently.

With prejudice   A dismissal "with prejudice" bars the right to bring or maintain another action on the same claim or cause.

Without prejudice   A dismissal "without prejudice" allows a new suit to be
brought on the same cause of action.

Writ of certiorari   A procedure requesting appellate review; it is discretionary.
If the writ is denied, the higher court refuses to hear the appeal and the
judgment in the lower court stands unchanged. If the writ is granted, the
higher court hears the appeal.